T0199215

LILLIAN HELLMAN

In the Presence of Audience:
The Self in Diaries and Fiction

LILLIAN HELLMAN

A Life with Foxes
and Scoundrels

DEBORAH MARTINSON

COUNTERPOINT

BERKELEY

For Barry Martinson

Copyright © 2005 by Deborah Martinson

All rights reserved. Printed in the United States of America.

Designed by Jeff Williams

Library of Congress Cataloging-in-Publication Data
Martinson, Deborah, 1946–
    Lillian Hellman : a life with foxes and scoundrels / Deborah Martinson.
        p. cm.
    Includes bibliographical references and index.

    ISBN 978-1-58243-723-1

1. Hellman, Lillian, 1906– 2. Dramatists, American—20th century—Biography.
I. Title.
    PS3515.E343Z773 2005
    812'.52—dc22
                        2005016616

COUNTERPOINT
2560 Ninth Street, Suite 318
Berkeley, CA 94710

www.counterpointpress.com

CONTENTS

PROLOGUE: THE STAKES

When the audience rose to its feet shouting "author, author" at the opening of *The Children's Hour*, young Lillian Hellman sat drunk at the back of the Maxine Elliott's Theatre. It was 1934, it was her first play, and she only woozily comprehended that she had made stage history.[1] She had come to this public test by the force of her personality, the help of a trusted and wild lover, and unfathomable luck. That night's performance was a proving ground for the woman she wanted to be: serious thinker, writer, playwright. At age twenty-nine, she had just begun to live her life, to direct her own waywardness, to create her own mythic character.

In the following years, Lillian Hellman wrote seven more original plays, four adaptations for the stage, at least eight screenplays, and four best-selling memoirs. In all of them, she enacted her own personal dramas—more gripping than those performed on the elegant Broadway stage. Craving a life she could live fully, aggressively, erotically, Hellman took center stage of her own drama.

What a life she had. Pugnacious from childhood, she fought for personal independence and professional integrity. She inflated her pride and ambition to avoid being trampled by the Broadway boys and the Hollywood heavies. In Hollywood where image is god, Lilly did fine. In New York, where brilliance matters most, she shone. In Washington, D.C., where politics is all, Lilly met mixed reviews. Her writing made her famous, but early on her "fortune's little funster" persona kept her in the headlines. She played it for all she was worth.[2] Hellman's demeanor was an art. She met reporters in silk lounging pajamas and narrow skirts designed to show her "great gams."[3] She posed, talking tough and seductively by turn, presenting her striking profile. She exuded an aura, blowing smoke to the ceiling from the ever-present cigarette.

During interviews, she used "a trick of dropping her voice and softening her facial expression after saying something that might be considered tough."[4] She became an early Hollywood celebrity in New York, but savvy New Yorkers demanded more hits on Broadway if she wanted to be considered more than a "girl" who could write. Washington watched her warily.

Fifty years after fame enveloped her, Hellman did not go gentle into that good night. Although she was blind, suffered repeated strokes, and experienced intermittent clarity and senility, alternating rage and humor, she fought to live. When she died in the summer of 1984, her death would seem to end the dramas, silence the memories, finish the woman. It did not, for me at least. When Hellman died, many were relieved, others saddened. Some celebrated, even cheered. I was in Europe and returned to California unaware that Lillian Hellman was dead.

The day after my return I read *Maybe*—Hellman's final memoir, the shrouded psychological drama of her life. I was puzzled and disturbed by the paradoxical quality of her not knowing, her desperate seeking—the sense of finality at this book's end. It made me edgy, and so I discussed her memoirs with someone I loved and knew I would soon lose to time, to distance, to new experience. I wanted this young "Dostoevsky sinner-saint" to know the importance of lifelong growing,[5] of not finishing relationships, of understanding Hellman's theory of relationship and memory: "pentimento."[6] I talked seriously about Hellman's work, fearing that for him the memory "strand," the "then and now" perceptions, the changing realities so central to Hellman and her writing would end as *Maybe* ended, with uncharacteristic finality.

Perhaps knowing my double agenda, this young man replied to my wandering analysis callously: "Too bad she's dead." Irritated by his lack of sensitivity, I refused to be convinced of her death. Then—in spite of supporting detail—I grew stubbornly obtuse.

In refusing to acknowledge her death, I was refusing to see an end to anything, to admit to any kind of death. Lillian Hellman's vitality, her perception of self, of life, politics, love, and memory—her distortions, her flaws—exemplified the human need to be imperfect and forever unfinished. That twilight in July, I decided she could not, would not, die. As Hellman once told Francis Ford Coppola, "I think you might consider that the dead do not always die for those who have respected them."[7] Hellman lives today through political controversy, through a canonical legacy for playwrights, through those who feel angry, appalled, and fascinated by the woman she was.

To write about Hellman, a woman with a monumental distrust of biographers, perhaps qualifies as chutzpah. Were she still living, she would probably prevent me from gathering the materials of her life. I can see her before me, frowning, hip cocked, bracelets jangling, cigarette atilt, phone—a weapon in the hands of Lillian Hellman—at the ready.

Saying she didn't like biographers is putting it mildly. She forbade her friends and anyone over whom she had influence to give interviews to William Wright, the man who had the temerity to begin her biography without her permission. His frustration and anger at being shut out is palpable in *Lillian Hellman: The Image, the Woman.*[8] Several writers wrote biographically of Hellman during her lifetime: Doris Falk, Katherine Lederer, Richard Moody, and Bernard Dick. But they critiqued her texts, not her life. She exercised editorial control over at least one of them—Lederer—by writing four pages of "corrections" to Lederer's draft but forbidding her to tell others she had in any way collaborated.[9] Hellman labored hard to explain her point of view to those who wanted to write about her, but heaven help them if they disagreed. Hellman could do battle, blasting word bullets in verbal barrages, threatening lawsuits, berating and belittling those who dared defy her. She cruelly controlled what she could.

Biographers who persevered saw her as contradictory. Like Scheherazade, she told stories to keep herself alive; nonetheless, she insisted that biography was a violation of privacy.[10] She who loved gossip and stories and dramas felt biography a "modern racket," a "gossip column." She only grudgingly admitted that there are serious biographers who are not "magazine hacks" pandering to public taste.[11] She, the master of biography by omission, insisted that biography be based on "fact," not just "some facts." A life with its passions comes "in a whole mesh, in a whole great football of mesh nets and hooks and eyes and scissors"; she didn't want it reduced.[12] She also insisted, however, that a biography must be short, focused, accurate—and of course only she could judge what was important.

An innovator of the literary autobiography, she nevertheless announced to one would-be writer that no one had the right "to use a real person and fictionalize any part of his life. In my terms that is immoral stuff. (And let us have no talk of Shakespeare)."[13] She reserved the "true" stories for herself, foiled attempts at information gathering, then announced that she was shocked by those who made mistakes. She refused to play the "bookkeeper" of her life, to document dates or check personal information, but she cut to size writers who missed a date or interpreted an event differently than she did.[14]

She also despised those who tried to write about her or her friends Dorothy Parker and Dashiell Hammett, for whom she held executrix power. She was especially prickly about Hammett, the renowned author of detective fiction with whom she lived on and off for nearly thirty years, the editor and inspiration for her writing. She reluctantly cooperated with and handily dismissed several would-be Hammett biographers; she gave respected author Diane Johnson permission to write about him but then sought to control her every sentence. When Otto Penzler dared write an entry about Dashiell Hammett for the *Encyclopedia of Mystery and Detection*, she responded, "You say you sent me the material as a courtesy. If that were true, you would have been pleased to have help from the only person on earth who has any true knowledge of Hammett."[15] Penzler was scalded by her "belligerent attitude and rudeness," which she called "natural upset at your inaccuracies." To this day Hellman's literary executors control so many aspects of his work and life that Hammett's daughter and granddaughter struggled to get materials.[16] Hellman wanted it that way.

She tenaciously hung on to Parker's literary texts to keep biographers at bay. Hellman snapped at one writer, "It seems to me of very little interest who was in Miss Parker's bed. The work is there and that's all, good or not good."[17] Yet she and Parker whooped it up to the end about who slept with whom and why. And Lillian Hellman's bed could tell enough stories of hoopla and intrigue to make a novel. Perhaps this is why Hellman sought to stifle this line of inquiry, sometimes brutally.

When a hapless biographer approached her about an interview concerning Tennessee Williams, she instantly dashed off a note to Williams telling of her refusal to talk without permission, her spreading the word to others, and detailing the errors the biographer had already made, even though she could no longer remember the man's name.[18] She punished those who violated her sense of events, finding "almost insane" their "unconscionable" errors.

In all this arrogant critique, she knew better. She confessed her own biographer's frailty, writing friend Louis Kronenberger that even after editing Anton Chekhov's letters and doing an "astounding amount of research" on Chekhov she was left with "large and mysterious gaps" about his life.[19] And she told Nora Ephron that she had come to like "biography and poetry and letters almost best."[20] She admitted that worrying about biographers is a "silly point, because what do you give a damn when you're dead. Any life can be made a mess of. Certainly mine can."[21] Most assuredly Hellman gave a damn; she said she would try to "leave as little as possible." Indeed, she destroyed much, but so much remains in the archives of others and in pockets of her own that her life arises from the tattered fragments.

Every biographer must recreate a character through information: thousands of pieces of paper, friends and enemies' memories, published memoirs, biographies and fictions. In her memoirs, Hellman sought to find the sense of her life through the porous and frail veil of memory, giving it shape and meaning. Her memoirs document an interior narrative, a psychological portrait of herself. And because she was a writer, she used literary techniques of craft and style to create that view. Inevitably, as memory makes its way to the page, it gains a life of its own—some would say it becomes fiction.

My task as a biographer is similar to that of the memoirist: to find the sense of a life. But my materials are different. I look at Hellman's words, plays, memoirs, stories, letters, calendars and diaries, bills and scribblings—the minutiae of a life lived. What have her other biographers said? What do her friends and enemies remember of her? Where is the woman in all of this? I take a stranger's view, seeking to find a woman in the details, looking for motivation, finding in contradiction the complexity of character. Inevitably, as her life is filtered through my mind and experience, as I seek to record the gist of a human being who actually lived and breathed, I put my own stamp on that life. Mine is an outsider's quest to know a woman, to write her life, to learn about the struggle of living from that life.

Without Lillian Hellman's assistance—or control—I persevere, thankful for the trust her executors gave me but frustrated at the limitations. After decades of research, I long to talk to her, to get her to explain ambiguous matters, to fill in the details of a life. I want to get the feel of her, know her in a way that only conversation can elicit. Yet in darker, more truthful moments, I thank the gods and goddesses she is unable to rise from the grave to chastise me for errors in judgment, interpretations she would call stupid, silly. Even Hellman admitted after writing *Pentimento* that there is a certain freedom in writing about the dead. But amid all the papers and quotes and date books and notes, Hellman won't quite die. She seems to raise her head, point her noble nose downward, thin her lips, demand retraction, revision, even if I am right. Especially if I am right.

Luckily, except in spectral moments, I am spared her ire. As a writer, I have ethics that come into play; and though I sense Hellman's presence and know her well, I don't think a biographer and her subject ever match exactly. In writing this biography, I had to give up my penchant for academic prose and theoretical lenses to get at the flesh-and-blood woman at the center. This project is doubly difficult because Hellman was as crafty as she was brilliant, as forgetful as she was creative, as despised as she was respected. Twirling her hair, drinking her whisky neat, blowing smoke my way, she would assess me, the would-be biographer, through narrowed eyes, her husky voice rasping, "Just who do you think you are? How dare you?"

Certainly Hellman would be suspicious of my California background. I am neither Jewish nor southern by birth, nor a New Yorker, except in spirit. I am most assuredly not a playwright but a writer, yes. And a dedicated teacher of writing—as was she. Professional, yes. Hellman despised the amateur. We have in common a great deal that helps me know Lillian Hellman. We share a determined insistence to live the way we want to live, though she was better at it, pushed harder, withstood punishment more brazenly. She laughed loudly, had an appetite for food and sex, liked smart people and smart talk. I admire her ability to know her own frailty, to ignore the untenable, to love—truly—many people in committed ways. Flying high in the intellectual ether (she far higher than I), we both come from families grounded in a puritan work ethic, the collars of our families only recently turned from blue to white. We both lived under the shadow of a beautiful southern mother and dealt with a wild, gambling, storytelling father. I understand Hellman's harangues, her baiting people to fury, because my father also used that technique to snap people out of comfortable stupors, to "stir the pot."[22]

Her hard look at cultural hypocrisy intrigues me, as does her blend of passion and anger. She struggled with the irreconcilable differences in the self—her love/hate relationships with money, with men in power, with women's rights. And she said out loud what many think but keep to themselves for reasons too numerous to list. She erred confidently. Worse, she couldn't see her own hypocrisy. But she didn't hide; she spoke out, took her lumps. She called it as she saw it, allowing that she was "a very difficult woman to handle . . . you're always difficult if you don't do what other people want."[23] She had guts.

I don't always like Lillian Hellman. She was often vengeful and mean-spirited. She undermined relationships for the pettiest of reasons. She could be haughtily arrogant, dismissive of others' pain. I feel the humiliation of those caught in the brutality of her words. I fear the rigidity and cruelty that came with her age and illness. She raised hell, hanging onto her dignity only by a thread. Years ago a friend, irritated by my intense interest in a woman writer he didn't know much about, read *Pentimento*. His defensive comment surprised and amused me: "You know she's not perfect." I laughed. No. Far from perfect, no more able to live absolutely to her own code than most of us. She could take criticism, expected it. She hated ass kissers. But those who found fault had to withstand the dragon's flames of retaliation. As she announced grandly to one critic, "It doesn't mean I'm right. It only means that I think I'm right."[24]

I regret that her kind of hard knowing and unyielding independence, her flagrant flaws and difficult character are currently under attack by neo-Puritans, cold postmoderns, and the righteous–whether religious, political, or intellectual. Before her death she told playwright Marsha Norman that she didn't want to go back to past "articles of faith," but wanted "other things to believe in."[25] She searched always, and when she found an idea to hold onto, she proclaimed it in booming clarity, only sometimes recanting in thoughtful whispers. She hated the self-righteous but knew them well; she was one of them, calling herself the Grand Inquisitor.[26]

But the quality of Hellman's work subverts her narrow personal intent: a solid screenplay writer sought after by Hollywood; a radical dramatist on Broadway who could "blow a stage to pieces"; an innovative prose writer of controversial memoirs. Her plays are culturally "on target," revived a half century from her writing of them.[27] Her memoirs, out of print for many years, have recently been republished. In writing, she could get her vision—often with brilliant clarity—on the page: "you write as you write, in your time, as you see your world."[28] And I write a new biography of Lillian Hellman.

Why? I think I've got a bead on her. I know her. After all these years, I don't have to wonder much about what Hellman herself would have thought. More to the point, this biography can do what others have not. Because of the passage of time, the changes in political climate, and the full support of Hellman's literary executors, I have unearthed entirely new personal, historical, and political accounts relating to Hellman's life. This book benefits from fresh material that ranges from recently released HUAC files to Moscow's accounts of American Communists. For the first time, intimates spoke freely about Hellman's politics and relationships. A more complete Lillian Hellman surfaces from the memories of people like friends Barbara Hersey and Warren Beatty, editor William Abrahams, psychoanalyst Milton Wexler. Such relationships held great importance to Hellman and assumed a mythic importance in the public eye. Interviews with acquaintances and those on the periphery offered an objectivity her friends and enemies didn't have: actor Walter Matthau, actress Kim Hunter, and Stanford professor Peter Stansky, for example. But nothing shaped Hellman's identity more than the context of her life, the where and when of her living. Talking to those who worked for her—such as Linda Lightner and her longtime secretary Rita Wade—moves the biographer into the reality of Hellman's life. This biography, then, tells the story of a writer whose life and landscape exhibit an indisputable American energy—different from many such stories but no less authentic.

Perhaps most important to those who know the controversies that still rage around her, in writing about Hellman I sought a rich truth born of exhaustive research and scholarly interest. Finding the truth of Hellman's "Uncle Willy," a character in *Pentimento*, for example, required extensive work in eight different archives in New Orleans and additional sweat at the Mormon Temple's Genealogical Study Center. In another instance, I spent months looking for corroboration or refutation of Hellman's "memories" of Spain, only to find it buried in Langston Hughes's papers. Determined to separate the rumor from the real, I write of Hellman as sometimes a truth teller of the highest order, sometimes a creative spinner of artful yarns, and occasionally the demon liar others assume she was. Hellman was neither a villain nor a hero but a writer and a woman far more complex, yet more human than other biographers found her. I strive to balance the famous and infamous legends about Lillian Hellman with the woman and the writer who lived as we do—day to day, buffeted by life's vagaries. The time of her life and the rhythm of her aging shaped and sculpted the material of this woman.

As a storyteller, I seek to understand the depth of her rage and the nature of her excellence, intuit the beauty and the muck of her actions, the romance and tediousness of her quest, the fear and the fire of her couplings. But I can only tell the story as I see it, through the facts of her life and through a critical look at her own retelling of it. There's no sense pretending that biography is objective, a mere compilation of facts and events. Carl Rollyson's *Lillian Hellman: Her Legend and Her Legacy* is rich with such details, but I don't find Hellman there amid the facts.[29] Joan Mellen's biography *Hammett and Hellman* displays the author's unabashed dislike of Hellman, a woman she envisions only in relation to a man.[30] I want to tell another story of Lillian Hellman, one that reflects her life through the thinking and understanding of another woman, another mind admittedly in a different time and place, looking back: at a woman who leaped into the political fray in a personal, intense way—fearless, electrifying "a mood of protest" in her time.[31]

Of course, Hellman told her own story better, more often, and more elaborately than anyone else before or since. The sheer diversity of her experiences in the movies, in the theater, in journalism, and in politics sparked her idea of assembling and rewriting many of her pieces for a memoir of sorts. *Unfinished Woman*, published in 1969 by Little, Brown, brought her instant acclaim and the National Book Award. It was less literary and more factual than her subsequent memoirs, and critics disputed little about the life Hellman reported. *Unfinished Woman* closes with its refusal to end.

Hellman was sixty-four years old at its publication, but she was far from bringing down the curtain on her life.

Pentimento: A Book of Portraits, which followed *Unfinished Woman*, moved from memoir to literature, whatever that might be to various people. The primacy of the imagination took hold of Hellman to make meaning, to explore the truth of an individual's interior nature. She sought to show the intersections of action and thought. Innovative in its form, *Pentimento* brought her literary recognition equal to what she received as a playwright. But when her third memoir, *Scoundrel Time*, was published in 1976, critics demanded that Hellman prove the veracity of both *Scoundrel Time* and *Pentimento* as history and autobiography, though neither was written as such. Garry Wills's "distorted" introduction to *Scoundrel Time* detailing the McCarthy era did not please Hellman, but it pleased her brooding political enemies even less. And her own retelling of the memory of this time and of her "heroism"—her disclaimers to the contrary—brought out the worst in her critics, avid for blood. Though she never backed down from her versions of the truth of her life, her last book *Maybe* explores the mind and its perversions of memory, its gloss of personal and national history. Distinctly Freudian, it permits a look into the mind's distortions of emotion, memory, and event, perhaps serving as a coda for the previous texts, an explanation of mind, as it were. Hellman's memoirs are as literary as they are controversial. Hellman often subordinated factual history and truth for another kind of knowing. Therefore, while I may suggest the truth behind a story, I have not used her memoirs as fact without corroborating documentation. Hellman felt no shame for living her life as she did, but she wanted the last word. No one gets that luxury.

Before she died, Hellman designated her friend and agent William Abrahams to write her authorized autobiography. Abrahams, busy with other projects, died before he could get the project started. She trusted only literary executors Peter Feibleman, William Abrahams, and Richard Poirier to guard what archives she didn't destroy. The executors have trusted me to use those materials and, to their credit, have not sought to exercise any control over my work. Given the controversy over the facts and details of her life, I have sought to check and document every detail.

Jo Marshall, Hammett's daughter, refers to biographers as "eaters of the dead," herself and myself included.[32] Through writing and reading about the dead, we find ourselves bloody and naked but once removed. We resurrect the shadow or outline of a human who lived and breathed and talked. Sometimes these shadows come to inhabit our minds and souls. Lillian

Hellman deeply inspired a wide array of writers: Marsha Norman, Wendy Wasserstein, Joan Didion, Nora Ephron, Judith Ortiz Cofer, myself. Hellman, who had no such intention, pushed others forward to tell life as they see it. Doubtlessly she would rage stormily about the truth or lies of our narratives, our own dramas. After years of getting into her skin, I can say that despite her willful stories and sometimes cruel lies Hellman told the truth as she knew it, deep truth, flawed truth—the truth of the paradox of our humanity. We are richer for her having lived.

This biography begins with the public assumptions surrounding Hellman's legend, which was shaped as much by the public perception of her as by her own machinations. The chapters that follow move from her birth to her death, exploring the why and the how of this woman, a gifted storyteller whose tales ensured her survival and, to some measure, our own. How she did it makes a great story.

PART ONE

THE GAME

1

UNLOVELY LEGEND

AT FIRST GLANCE, LILLIAN HELLMAN WAS UNLOVELY. CHAIN smoking and chic, she "looked like the Ancient Mariner in drag . . . formidable and wondrously-gnarled."[1] As she aged, her aggressive features softened and sagged, weathering into wise Tiresias perhaps—not Aphrodite. Nearly everyone appraised her looks: "she was NOT a good looking woman";[2] she "was no oil painting";[3] "she resembled George Washington";[4] she had the "big beaky face of a sea turtle."[5] Actor Walter Matthau insisted she was about as "seductive as a large bowl of oatmeal."[6] Many who knew her found her sensual and attractive, noting the vitality, intensity, and character in her face.[7] Actor Warren Beatty thought her "very attractive—you know . . . I don't know if you'd pick her out of a lineup but she was very beautiful to me at times."[8] Dashiell Hammett thought her elegant, a richly textured beauty; he instructed, "You are to have Luis Quintanilla paint you for me. I have spoken." Whatever the opinion, few failed to notice her, including the FBI, which described her in file 100–25858 1A6.

W, F 6/20/05 at New Orleans, La.
5'3" 105#—slim build
Brown-reddish hair (sometimes Blond)
Green, gray eyes
Hebrew aquiline nose

The FBI files included no fewer than ten physical descriptions of her and at least fifteen photos. Agents followed her intermittently for thirty years, less than enchanted by this diminutive fellow traveler—the term used for far left sympathizers of all stripes.

She inspired fear and awe in some, even though she was a petite woman. She showed off her good legs, lamented her "flat ass," and liked her formidable bosom, or "huge shelf" as Norman Mailer put it.[9] She knew well her physical shortcomings. When asked at age seventy-one to draw a self-portrait, she drew a caricature of a pretty young girl, annotating the picture with "blond curls, natural," and "deep blue eyes, natural."[10] Her caption read, "What I wanted to look like and don't." Hellman's success was rooted in knowing from the start that she wasn't "gonna make it on this image."[11]

There is no pretending her looks didn't matter. Always conscious of her appearance, as Hellman approached her seventies she crafted a larger-than-life image of herself. But the mythic Hellman was not just smoke and mirrors. This flesh and blood woman earned her legendary status through vigilance, a ready tongue, and a mixture of luck and nerve. She used what she had.

By age seventy, Hellman had a solid record of hard-won achievement as screenwriter, playwright, and political activist. Despite being blacklisted from writing scripts for Hollywood in 1948 and harassed by the House Un-American Activities committee in the early 1950s, she continued to write successfully for Broadway. She abandoned writing for the stage in 1963, however, after the crushing failure of *My Mother, My Father and Me*. For a time she retreated from the public eye, writing and teaching. Still bold and brassy, however, still a public name and face, she ranked seventy-eighth on Richard Posner's list of the twentieth century's top 100 public intellectuals.[12] With her record of substantial merit, she might have relaxed her efforts to pare and sculpt the public's perception of her. Not Hellman. She didn't want to get swept out of the public's mind. It's a long, long way back.[13]

She narrowly escaped obscurity, or so she thought. One morning in the mid-1960s, good friend and sometime lover Peter Feibleman found Hellman storming around her Vineyard Haven living room, clenching the *New York Times*. An article in it named Edward Albee, Arthur Miller, and Tennessee Williams as the three living great dramatists. She snapped, "*I'm* still alive. How dare they, how dare they forget about me! I can't stand to be forgotten. There are people who can take it. I can't take it. I'll have to get back on top."[14] She immediately began work on *An Unfinished Woman*, a memoir that hit the best-seller lists within weeks of its release. She followed it with an even greater hit, *Pentimento*. By 1976, when her third memoir, *Scoundrel*

Time, was released to explosive reviews, Hellman had made a new entrance into the public domain. She swore she wouldn't let herself be forgotten, and she hadn't.

As her comeback extended throughout the 1970s, Hellman asserted an aging woman's prerogative to shape the way others looked at her; not to obscure the woman she had become but to revel in lights and shadows of her own choosing. Even as age encroached, she loved to be photographed under her own direction. She asked Richard De Combray, writer and friend, to photograph her for the covers of *Scoundrel Time* and *Maybe*. For the *Scoundrel Time* pictures they walked from Hellman's Park Avenue apartment into Central Park, where De Combray took twelve shots of Hellman laughing and enjoying the session. "She loved to be noticed (even negatively), and this need outpaced any vanity she might have had about her self-acknowledged weather-beaten face."[15] The public recognition she achieved signaled success in her world, even though her writing, political battles, and friends meant more to her.

As relaxed as Hellman was for most photographs, she safeguarded the self-exposure, taking more care as she aged. Few women want their face and figure photographed on a bad day, even if the photo shoot promises legendary status. Hellman treated Berenice Abbott rudely, perhaps because the famous aging photographer took "straight" photography with no special filters or effects. Hellman failed to appear after inviting Abbott to take her photo. She strung her along for two days and then crowed, "I got her to come all the way down, to take my picture and then I hid out and she couldn't."[16] Hellman's behavior was patronizing and hard to forgive, even if understandable in a woman of "a certain age." Hellman more readily agreed to a sitting by Imogen Cunningham, a world renowned photographer of "anything that can be exposed to light."[17] But Cunningham was ninety years old when Hellman's aging face attracted her, and she could not make the trip from San Francisco.[18] It was a lost opportunity for two creative icons, one living for her art, the other loving to be its subject — under the right circumstances.

Those who publicly talked about Hellman's appearance or used it for their own purposes could expect either scathing verbiage or hoots of laughter. She haughtily corrected some interpreters. In May 1976, Miss Geisheker of the *Baltimore Sun* wrote an article portraying Hellman as "butch."[19] Incensed, Hellman fired off a letter of complaint to William Schmick Jr., the publisher. First noting that she never commented on "the literary opinions of a reviewer, nor do I do so now," she furiously disputed the writer's lengthy analysis of a Hellman photograph. "Thus I am in dress and in attitude

'butch,'" have an "air of sassy androgyny cultivated by Forties movie hero-
ines." The article went on to say that had Hellman ever been jailed for her
leftist activities in the 1950s, she would have been in "danger from tough
dykes." Hellman huffed, "It does not matter that the clear intimation that I
am a Lesbian happens to be a lie. It is low down stuff . . . in one sentence I
am masculine because I am wearing a suit, and in another sentence the suit
becomes a coat. (In the photograph I am, in fact, wearing a dress.)." She
wasn't about to let a snip of a reporter call her a dyke. Her talk might be
tough, but she cultivated a profound and never frivolous femininity. Even in
her seventies she had an erotic power and used it.

Taking a poke at Hellman's leftist politics and aging sexuality, political
jokester Dick Tuck superimposed an image of her head on a disco-dancing,
hip-thrusting figure in skin-tight jeans and four-inch heels. Far from screaming libel when it appeared in the *Washington Post*, Hellman howled with
laughter at the caption: "Mock advertisement for Lillian Hellman designer
Jeans."[20] Tuck used it in an issue of the *Great Wallpaper*, an occasional magazine. The clear satire showed Hellman as an aging political star and media
darling. Hellman approved its patent absurdity but probably asked for a royalty for its publication.

The class, money, and legendary status another media portrait gave her
was more to her liking: "What Becomes a Legend Most?"[21] The question
hung over the full-page portrait of the seventy-one-year-old Hellman in
Harper's Bazaar. Hellman posed for the Blackglama fur advertisement in
October 1976, swathed in black mink, cigarette poised. She gazed straight at
the camera, her thoughtful, aged, and wrinkled face framed by beautiful
hair—classic Hellman. A host of other legends posed for that ad over the
years, great beauties such as Marlene Dietrich, Joan Crawford, Judy Garland,
Faye Dunaway, and Sophia Loren.[22] Hellman and Rudolph Nureyev seemed
to be the odd men out. The prize for such exposure: the luxurious black
mink. She "wafted in a fur."[23] Hellman, however, chose a $5,000 credit on an
even more exclusive brown Swakara broadtail with a zip-on ankle-length theater piece, black being a little too harsh to frame the older face. Legendary
Hellman.[24]

Hellman could be bought, no news there; she loved what money could
buy and admitted it. But she named her own price, and the Blackglama ad
fit: self-promotion, money, fame. The Blackglama photo symbolized the
Hellman of modern memory. It defined the exhibitionist Hellman who created the "nonsense" of a "legend in her own time."[25] But the glamour of the
ad also displayed the aging woman exhibiting her dignity and public worth as

much for herself as for others. Few could resist such glamorous coverage and certainly not Hellman. The thinking, canny woman underneath that coat played all the angles. Former lover John Melby laughed about Hellman's selling of her image, saying he thought she had gone a "little too far." Hellman always went too far. Melby went on to say, however, "she knew exactly what she was doing: in exchange for the use of her picture she was conning the capitalist system out of a very expensive fur coat, period. And laughing about it."[26] Dashiell Hammett's daughter Jo Marshall thought that Hammett—the most significant man in Hellman's life for over thirty years—would have scoffed at Lillian's showmanship. But both Hellman and Hammett understood the role of the photo in a writer's legacy. Decades earlier when he was photographed for *Yank: The Army Weekly*, he wrote her, "Jesus, how us writers cram ourselves down the public's throat. Or do you want to make out that you're different?"[27] Hammett thought Hellman a "great and elegant woman," the image the Blackglama portrait conveyed.[28] The ad positioned Hellman where she wanted to be—among the legendary, the noted, the noticeable. Twenty-five years earlier Hammett had asked her, "Tell me, do you think obscurity is nice after one gets used to it?"[29] Hellman never bothered to find out.

Ever conscious of the presentation of self, Hellman loved splendid dresses, expensive shoes, exquisite hats. She used clothes to say "don't look past me, look at me."[30] And it worked. One young writer noted, "When I saw Hellman, standing in the middle of the gallery room, alone, with a smart hat on, and with a chic black veil covering half her face, I knew I'd babble . . . and did."[31] Hellman enjoyed the drama of fashion. Early in her career an *Esquire* article proclaimed, "Richard Maney, who has publicized all of her plays, will swear on a stack of libel suits that she once went fishing for tuna in an unmatchable ermine wrap."[32] Jo Hammett Marshall, however, always thought of Hellman as attractive and "always perfectly dressed for the occasion."[33]

Designer clothes were better as gifts or sale items. Jo Marshall remembered once admiring a "handsome camel hair coat" Hellman liked particularly because a "friend had gotten it for her wholesale." Hammett had Hellman buy herself one when he was in the army in 1944, writing her, "Buy an extravagant one so that when you tell people I gave it to you for Christmas they will say, "Ah, that Hammett. He certainly treats his women well. (I'm thinking primarily of debs and shopgirls; you may tell actresses that you won the coat in a crap game.)"[34] The antics great furs entailed pleased her. Actor Walter Matthau met Hellman for the first time by phone early one morning when she called his wife, Carol, to tell her she had "found a great fur coat at Filenes;. . . it was one of their things to go to Filenes in Boston to see if they could get a $20,000 coat for $6,000."[35] Matthau laughed at this penchant of Hellman's: "She loved elegant clothes . . . she kind of saw herself as the Catherine Deneuve of the literary set."

Once at a Leonard Bernstein party, Hellman could not find her mink coat as she was leaving. Whether she panicked or decided to take on the glitterati for the sheer drama of it is not clear. In any event, she left the Bernsteins' apartment in a huff, accusing Jacqueline Onassis of stealing her mink coat.[36] She insisted she saw Jackie wear it out of the party. Felicia Bernstein, a friend of both, called Hellman's literary agent Robbie Lantz, pleading, "What shall I do?" Lantz assured Mrs. Bernstein that the theft "seemed unlikely." A coat properly fitted for Hellman would not have worked for the taller and thinner Onassis. The next morning Hellman called the Bernsteins and said firmly, coolly, "Felicia, she didn't steal my mink coat. I never took my mink coat to your house." No apology. It would have destroyed her curtain line. At a party at John Marquand's, Hellman went over to a fur, felt it voluptuously, and then said, "Jackie's here." She knew by the coat.[37] Their coats, if not the women, had similarities.

The Glamorous Hellman

By the mid-1970s, Hellman was recognized the world over as a woman to be reckoned with. Her plays, literature, and politics had made her reputation. But it was her recognizable image that made her increasingly famous.

"She was a troglodyte, a dinosaur and then suddenly she is this glamorous figure."[38] By 1976 everyone suddenly wanted a piece of the action. The public renewed its interest in Hellman, Dashiell Hammett, Dorothy Parker, and other friends previously quieted by the red-baiting McCarthy era. As much by luck as good planning, Hellman's memoirs captured the public's recasting of the post–World War II era. Political activism was "in" and so was Lillian Hellman. The revivals of her 1930s and 1940s plays and her memoirs had a role. But Hollywood and its image-making machine was key. Hollywood took the newfound public curiosity for Hellman and Hammett and cashed in on it. So did Hellman, but money was not her only motive. She had worked for Hollywood in the 1930s and 1940s and she trusted Hollywood not at all. She was wary. She knew perfectly well that movie studios didn't just make photographic exposures. The film industry's celluloid strips had the power to remake a life for its own purpose, not the subject's. Still, she wanted in. Movies could make and destroy reputations, but the silver screen promised a kind of immortality. Deciding to use Hollywood rather than be used by it, she threw her lot in; she had a lot to gain. The comeback as much as the cash was powerful incentive. Hollywood's regard for Hammett's literary works, Hellman's memoirs, and the legendary lady herself should have pleased Hellman. Not so. Never easy, Lillian Hellman wanted life on her own terms. Her sense of herself, her version of the story of her life, her memory of loved ones was sacrosanct. She should have known better; absolute control of an image is impossible, especially in film.

Since early 1976 she had been staving off Francis Ford Coppola, who wanted to make a "fictional" Hammett movie based on Joe Gores's 1975 novel *Hammett*. Anytime a writer or filmmaker got too close to representing a private personal point of view about her friends, Hellman threatened a lawsuit. She was particularly protective toward those who had willed her legal and executor rights: Dashiell Hammett and Dorothy Parker. In Coppola she had to contend with a real power, and she knew it. Not that she backed off. The Coppola project galled her. She wrote him in January:

> There would be no sense repeating the reasons why I don't wish to see an inferior and false book made into a movie about Dashiell Hammett . . . It would seem to be true that given the choice between you and other movie producers one would prefer your most talented hands. But that is a choice I cannot make because I simply do not understand such choices.[39]

As Hammett biographer Richard Layman said, "Lillian Hellman was a controller. She . . . proceeded to shape his posthumous reputation with a lover's jealousy."[40] But now she was forced to depend on Hammett's daughters to guard Hammett's memory; she kept her antenna tuned and her advice at the ready. She tartly questioned Mary about an interview she had done for *City* magazine. Mary lied about the circumstances of the interview, and Hellman was incensed. With the Coppola project looming, she wanted Jo to control Mary, an alcoholic and notorious troublemaker. Jo agreed to try. Then Hellman went further, trying to force arguments of her choosing onto Marshall and her lawyer.

Marshall resisted Hellman's instructions and did fine. She chose to argue that her mother, Mrs. Josephine Hammett, "contrary to the representations in the novel, is very much alive . . . any notoriety with respect to her husband and their relationship would surely be detrimental to her health and well being."[41] This argument made Hellman livid. In her eyes the ex-Mrs. Hammett had no rights. Hellman had posed as the Widow Hammett for so long that the sudden resurrection of an old rival left her fuming. Hellman went along with Marshall's argument, but she and Jo only succeeded in put-ting off the inevitable. Coppola produced *Hammett* in 1983.

Hellman's control over her own story was put to the test in 1976, when she agreed to a Twentieth Century Fox production of *Julia*, the most straightfor-ward and plot-centered chapter in *Pentimento*.[42] She had flatly refused to work again for Hollywood after writing the screenplay for Sam Spiegel's *The Chase* in 1961. Now she refused to write the script for *Julia*. But she re-spected director Fred Zinneman and screenwriter Alvin Sargeant and agreed to the film. Already beleaguered by controversies over the truth or lies of her memoirs, she had to know that a film version of a memoir, with all of its cin-ematic artifice, would only add to the nasty brew of hostility and accusation. But she could not resist the big California dollars and her story writ large on the screen.

She also wanted her story of Hammett to supersede the inevitable—and coming—film about him. Coppola's film would exclude her; it was fiction and took place in 1928, before she and Hammett met in 1930. Her *Julia* put Hellman and Hammett as a couple firmly into the public realm. So, when she agreed to the producer's terms, she permitted the story of herself, a child-hood friend she calls Julia, and Hammett as a background player, to go forward. Jason Robards would play Hammett. While he lacked the craggy, waterfront toughness that underpinned Hammett's good looks, Robards was a nearly irresistible enticement. Nevertheless, she and Zinneman fought bat-tles fierce and hot. She vigilantly critiqued the least details in the film, from hairstyles to automobiles, her paranoia erupting as her sight and memory waned. The last struggle concerned her previewing the film. She sensed that Zinneman was chary of letting her see the film and she may have been right. Zinneman's frustration and the depth of the controversy erupted in his draft of a letter to Hellman in 1977.

Zinneman accused her of "clinging to the delusion" that he didn't want her to see the film, arguing that he gave her myriad opportunities that she did not accept. "There was always some reason why you couldn't make it. You couldn't travel from Cape Cod to New York because of your health, but at the same time you could manage to be somewhere else, Mount Holyoke, or Washington or Egypt. Finally you insisted on our bringing the film to your doorstep in Martha's Vineyard. This is where I give up."[43]

Oddly enough, once she saw the film, Hellman liked it. But at every turn in the mid–1970s she courted controversy over her version of truth compared to others. It's not surprising, then, that another feud of her own making involved Jane Fonda, who played Lillian Hellman in *Julia,* opposite Vanessa Redgrave. Fonda found the role an important change from the clichés of Hollywood. The characters intrigued her; the friendship between the two women was "not neurotic or sexually aberrant and it's about two friends . . . interested in each other's growth."[44] Liking the idea of two radical 1970s women playing two radical 1930s women, Fonda wanted the part so much that she said she came cheap at $250,000.

Fonda should have known that playing a difficult woman, still very much alive, would be hellish. To begin with, Hellman did not have the power to choose the cast but she wanted it, particularly with regard to the actress who would play this younger version of herself. Hellman had been eager to get Barbara Streisand, a nearly mythic woman with unconventional looks and feminine power.[45] Hellman liked the way Streisand smoked and her Jewishness. Although "every actress who was ambulatory" went after the roles, Streisand was not to be had for the film.[46] Since Hellman had no choice, she reluctantly agreed Fonda would do fine. While Hellman knew Jane Fonda was no pushover, she wondered if the young woman had the necessary similarity and substance to play the Lillian Hellman of the film.

When Fonda signed on for the role, she met Hellman at her house on Martha's Vineyard. When she arrived, Hellman was "battening down" for a hurricane that ultimately missed the Vineyard; Fonda thought her tough and sexy but hadn't expected her "bad temper and irritability."[47] The two women liked each other, and for a time all went well.

Fonda made the mistake of doing interviews, fairly typical fare about the film. The interviewers gleaned from Fonda that she thought Hellman a "homely woman" but seductive in a way that Fonda felt she couldn't act out.[48] She felt better able to act out the irritable Hellman, which she did for the film. What Fonda saw as truth, even flattery, Hellman thought blasphemous. Fonda told Dan Rather that Hellman "has a way of sitting, lounging in chairs, and the skirt kind of comes up above the knee and you see that she wears very expensive silk and satin underwear. And. . . she would sit with a regal quality about her, like Nefertiti." Hellman managed to keep quiet, but a series of new interviews ended the silence. Fonda's comments in *Newsweek* ripped it for Hellman. Repeating her comments about Hellman's sensuality, she said Hellman "moves as if she were Marilyn Monroe. . . She sits with her legs apart with her satin underwear partly showing."[49]

Hellman fired off a letter, defending herself and then taking a nasty swipe at Fonda and women's liberation:

Maybe the least interesting things about your second attack on me, this time in *Newsweek* is its lack of truth. One, because for many years I have had back trouble from a fall, I never lounge in a chair. I always find a straight chair in any room. Two, I have never had expensive underwear since a spree in Paris when I was very young: the underwear you did not see comes from the Vineyard Haven Dry Goods Store, Vineyard Haven, Mass. And runs in price from $2.95 to $3.95. . . What is interesting to me is why you wished to make me into a kind of other-generation whorish woman and yourself into an ascetic. But it is more than interesting, it is plain shocking, that women's liberation leads so many of you into cliché's rather than into thought: thinking might bring you loyalty, not to me, to whom you owe none, but to the idea that maybe you do not know the truth about all women and should examine what you say before it is in print. This way it is just plain nasty. Lillian.

Honor bound correction: the night you saw me at Sue Mengers I was reluctantly sitting on a soft couch. I wore pantyhose and a $10.95 petticoat. Make the most of it.[50]

Fonda, clearly chagrined, wrote back, trying to make amends. The formally typed letter and spiky shape of Hellman's signature contrasted with Fonda's loopy writing complete with circles instead of dots over the i's. Hellman had been stung by a beautiful young woman. Fonda had been whiplashed by an older woman accustomed to controversy:

Dear Lillian,
What I said about you during the *Newsweek* interview was said with love and meant to be complimentary so I was stunned when I read your letter. . . I was quoted out of context and cut in a way that made my meaning ambiguous.

Fonda goes on to explain her *60 Minutes* interview:

I said that one of the most appealing and unexpected things about you is your sensual presence. Your legend, your writing, being an intellectual, doesn't prepare one for the femininity and accessibility.
I certainly did not intend to paint myself as an ascetic. I wish I was more of an actress to have captured the totality of what I experienced with you. My stupidity was in not anticipating how easy it is for such a discussion to be twisted out of shape.[51]

Hellman, still cranky and irritable, could not resist upbraiding Fonda one more time. She responded with a more reasonable but condescending letter implying that Fonda might be jealous of her and telling her "to watch it."[52] Then she wrote, "I was very very careful to say nothing about you and me because the falling out of women offends me and always has, in my old fashioned woman's-personal-liberation-way. Too bad, all of it. You are too old to be naive about gossip and the press."

Fonda graciously folded, writing, "I am thinking of you with concern, fondness, and respect. Warmly, Jane."[53] It is little wonder Jane Fonda was nominated for the Best Actress Award for her portrayal of Lillian Hellman in *Julia* in 1977.

A more amicable meeting of the two women became spectacle when the Academy decided to honor Hellman in a backward fashion, asking her to present an Academy Award for Best Documentary Film. They chose Hellman as an icon representative of fighting the blacklist. Her appearance caused a sensation in a town used to the spectacular. When Fonda walked to the microphone with Hellman, they were met with thunderous applause. But Hellman didn't totter onstage just to read the winner's name. She used the platform to have her say:

> I was once upon a time a respectable member of this community. Respectable didn't necessarily mean more than I took a daily bath when I was sober, didn't spit except when I meant to, and mispronounced a few words of fancy French. Then suddenly, even before Senator Joseph McCarthy reached for that rusty poisoned axe, many others and I were no longer acceptable to the owners of this industry. Possibly they were men who had been too busy to define personal honor or national honor. Possibly. But certainly they confronted the wild charges of Joe McCarthy with the force and courage of a bowl of mashed potatoes. I have no regrets for that period. Maybe you never do when you survive, but I have a mischievous pleasure in being restored to respectability, understanding full well that a younger generation who asked me here tonight meant more by that invitation than my name or my history. I thank them for that because I never thought that would happen. And to make them and myself feel better I hope the rest of my life will not be too respectable.[54]

When she finished, Hollywood's elite leapt to their feet to deliver a noisy and "protracted standing ovation before a television audience of fifty million Americans."[55] The pleasure of the event overwhelmed her, though she knew too well it would be followed by backlash. But criticism beat oblivion.

William F. Buckley Jr. entitled his column immediately following Hellman's Academy appearance "Night of the Cuckoo."[56] He attacked her for the sins of Stalin and for her radicalism during the 1930s and 1940s, and attacked Hollywood's making a splendid spectacle of her. Those who equated anti-McCarthy with pro-communism could not understand Hollywood's outrage at the House Un-American Activities Committee and its collaborators who had blacklisted Hollywood's own. Nor could they understand the honor bestowed on Hellman, a diminutive woman whose voice rasped with cigarettes and fiery assurance and whose face sagged and jutted with an ancient wisdom they did not admit she had. The cover of the *National Review* featured Hellman's Blackglama photo over which Buckley had superimposed "Scoundrel Time & Who Is the Ugliest of Them All?"[57] The cover and the article denounced Hellman in a personal and sexually demeaning way. The Blackglama ad had come full circle. Buckley used Hellman's looks to bash her, a woman nearly seventy-two years old who had never been a beauty. Still, the Academy Awards recognition must have been worth it. She had recovered fame and infamy both.

Norman Podhoretz, editor of *Commentary*, remembered "shaking my head in wonder when she made an appearance" at the Academy Awards.[58]

The applause was swelled by a new crop of literary intellectuals who, like me, had been seduced by the pleasures of her company and the glamour and the glitz surrounding her, but who, unlike me, never saw anything wrong with their political views, either in the past or present. To them all her sins, even assuming that she had ever committed any worth mentioning, had been wiped clean for all time by her sufferings at the hands of the McCarthyite inquisitors.

Many political foes preferred the frozen image of Hellman in mink to Hellman as media darling on national television. Hellman relished both. Her scrupulous attention to defending her presence in the public eye kept her inventive, creative. Certainly her meddling expositions made her difficult, but that was part of her power. No one was immune to her cunning one-upmanship.

Hellman could not bear to be upstaged, even by Elizabeth Taylor. In casting Austin Pendleton's 1981 Lincoln Center revival of *The Little Foxes*, Hellman followed Mike Nichols's advice and cast the fifty-year-old Taylor as Regina, the central vixen and villain. Hellman had never approved of any actress playing Regina—not Tallulah Bankhead, not Anne Bancroft, not Betty

Davis, certainly not Elizabeth Taylor. But Nichols thought she had what it took, and Hellman respected Nichols. She also knew Taylor was big box office. By all accounts, Taylor is the consummate professional; she works hard, follows direction, and is a team player onstage. She is also one of the nicest actresses. In production of *The Little Foxes*, Taylor had "grace and humor and was extraordinarily thoughtful to the rest of the cast, the understudies, everyone . . . they all adored her."[59] As Austin Pendleton tells it, "Everyone trusted her on stage and she was one of the easiest people to direct that I have ever directed, so it was not like putting your head in the mouth of a lioness at all. With Lillian, it was." Hellman could be fierce, but Taylor's image had the glamour and the presence to render an audience awestruck.

Hellman and Taylor got along well and had only one blowout during production—with Hellman doing the erupting. The dispute flared up at a dinner with the cast at McMullen's in New York. Hellman had eagerly suggested she sit in on rehearsals. The cast blanched. Hellman had a reputation for disrupting rehearsals and insisting on her own directions. Taylor, speaking for the cast, replied, "Oh you don't want to come to a rehearsal hall and see any of it Lillian, you won't see the work, it's not like seeing it in the set. . . why don't you wait until it opens?"[60] Hellman, waspish about a writer's dominance in stage production, felt mortally wounded, thinking Taylor was usurping her rights. As Pendleton told it, Hellman loudly and rudely upbraided Taylor: "I should be allowed to come to a rehearsal of my own play, when it's about to go into previews, for Broadway, and who is Elizabeth Taylor, or anyone else, to tell me they don't want me there?" The press gleefully reported the exchange.

Hellman let the feud go; she knew better than to tangle with Taylor's reputation. Hellman may have apologized, as she often did when her rages got the better of her. She liked Taylor. Still, Hellman whined and complained to friend Maureen Stapleton about Taylor's performance. Stapleton defended Taylor. "Elizabeth was damn good in *The Little Foxes*, and got better and better. Lillian would be polite but she had this thing about Regina's part, and we got in big fights about Elizabeth because I loved her and no matter how good she got in it, Lillian wasn't satisfied."[61] She competed with Taylor for top billing.

Hellman managed to pull off an impossible coup, given her age and diminutive physical stature.

> The opening night of Elizabeth Taylor in *The Little Foxes* in Los Angeles was a great event. Miss Hellman was present in the house and it was already a celebrated production and Elizabeth had rightly made a great

personal success in it; and there was Elizabeth Taylor in person, appearing in this famous part in what had become her home town. After the curtain calls the audience insisted on a last call for Elizabeth Taylor to step forward so the house could welcome her; whereupon on the left of the stage, the broken, ill, frail—really very very sick Lillian Hellman appeared. And walked under her own steam, which was not easy for her.[62]

But Hellman knew what to do to steal the evening from her star and did it successfully. She could "upstage God."[63]

2

THE CURVE AND THE EDGE

The Curve: New Orleans

NEW ORLEANS, JUNE 20, 1905: LILLIAN FLORENCE HELLMAN, the first and only child of Julia Newhouse Hellman and Max Bernard Hellman, is born into genteel poverty in the magnolia-scented Garden District of New Orleans. Located between the ostentatious grandeur of St. Charles Avenue and the bleak but busy Tchoupitoulas industrial section, her home at 1718 Prytania Street inspired a whimsical, creative reality, surrounded as it was by streets named for all nine Greek muses.[1]

Both the Hellmans and the Newhouses had come to New Orleans in the 1850s and stayed. They were German Jews who assimilated easily to southern culture, like most Jews who immigrated to the South in the 1840s.[2] But both families ran high to colorful relations.

Max Hellman was born in New Orleans. After his parents died, he lived with his two adoring older sisters, Jenny and Hannah, in the boardinghouse they ran on Prytania.[3] His father, Bernard, had been a bookkeeper, and for a time Max worked for him. But Max found sales more attuned to his spirited, proud, and somewhat reckless character. His sisters were busy, funny, and generous, and when Max married they welcomed his wife Julia and later their baby Lillian into their home. Twenty-five when Lillian was born, Max got by on the generosity of his sisters, in addition to his friendliness and wit. He used his wife's dowry to buy the Hellman Shoe Company, a shoe store at 829 Canal Street, and made himself president.

In the boom-and-bust New Orleans economy, the Hellmans lived on the edge. Max's business acumen was suspect; he spent more time schmoozing than balancing the books, and in 1911 he lost his shoe store and Julia's dowry money. Family lore had it that Max's partner ran away with the cash. Publicly Lillian backed the partner story, but in her play *Toys in the Attic*, Julian — loosely patterned after Max — lost his "stake" because of poor choices. The riverboats tempted and Julian gambled — as did Max. Max, cavalier with money, lost his business but not his charm. He went on to become a successful traveling salesman.

Max Hellman took some getting used to, even for Lillian. Marred by excess, he seemed the essence of New Orleans masculinity: taking women to the bayous, gambling on the river, drinking in the French Quarter, consorting with racially mixed women. Max partook in disturbing rhythms more French than American. Lillian knew her father was a womanizer, discovering young a true rival for her father's attention, "Fizzy"[4] of the memoirs, probably the boarder listed as "Tessie" in the census.[5] Lillian Hellman hated the damaging power of jealousy, but she recognized that Max's wayward behavior, and later Dashiell Hammett's, Peter Feibleman's, and her own was a form of rebellion. "Cutting up is a form of belief, a negative expression of it, but belief."[6] As a child, Lillian unjustly blamed her gentle, vague mother for Max's profligacy.

Despite the shame of Max's business loss and her anger at Max's betrayal, Lillian forever adored "Pa," the first of many loved men. She thought him outrageous, amusing, and maddening. He thought the same of her. They knew each other's frailties but loved each other for their strong individualistic character and appeal. She trusted his honest if bantering raillery and loved his eccentricities.

Max visited the adult Lillian often, traveled with her, wrote letters, became part of the entourage of friends she entertained at Hardscrabble, her farm in upstate New York. During one Christmas holiday, Lillian wrote in jest that she had established "courtmartialling" in the barn for those who entered her room while she was writing, warning that the trial "would not be a fair one." The violators? "Samuel Dashiell Hammett, former eccentric; Mr. Arthur Kober, former itinerant street singer . . . Miss Nora, former dog. Mr. Bernard Hellman, father, a most constant offender. His age has saved him. This sentimentality may not continue."[7] Continue it did, but not without real agony. As Max aged, Lillian bore responsibility for his health. His rages and his eventual senility made caring for him a heart-wrenching duty. It exhausted her, but she did all she could to be a good daughter. She did not know that her own aging would follow Max's pattern, the intermittent paranoia causing herself and others much distress. The cycle of love and loss that characterized her life began early.

Julia Newhouse Hellman, Lillian's mother, came from a powerful alliance between the Marx and Newhouse families, who landed originally in Demopolis, Alabama, where they set up successful businesses, moved to Cincinnati when the opportunities did, and then introduced branches of the family business to New Orleans. While the Hellmans were quintessential southerners, the Marxes established financial networks in the South and the North, ultimately working with the Jewish bankers of New York to amass great wealth. They maintained ties to the many Jewish merchants who opened major emporiums on Canal Street such as Godchaux Department Store. Flora Marx, possibly Lillian's great-great aunt, married Leopold Godchaux in 1883. Regina Marx of New Orleans married Adolph Frankel in 1885, furthering ties with wealthy New Orleans Jews.[8] Hellman's play *The Little Foxes* portrayed a calculating, vengeful Regina, a woman Hellman readily admitted she named after a relative. Marx women, Lillian Hellman included, could indeed be imperious, certainly adding grit to the typical southern conception of women.

Hellman's mother Julia, however, hid her strength in eccentricity and fine manners. A southern belle, Julia was pretty, soft-spoken, "a beauty inside out," small, dainty, with a finished yet sincere charm.[9] First educated at the prestigious Marengo Academy of Alabama, Julia and her younger sister, Florence, arrived in New Orleans to attend Sophie Newcomb College's special bridge program at Tulane.[10] Uptown in the Garden District, the women's college focused on academic programs and economic independence for "self-willed, and exacting, but not self-reliant" southern women.[11] Julia's mother and Lillian's grandmother, Sophie Marx Newhouse, insisted her daughters attend. She didn't think they had backbone. Julia's father, who had little backbone himself, apparently had little say in the matter.

Julia dropped out after her first year and fell hard and forever for Max Hellman. Against the wishes of her domineering mother and the threat of being cut out of the will, Julia married Max. Of Sophie's children—Gilbert, Florence, Miriam, and Julia—only Julia had the courage to marry while Sophie lived. Although outraged that Julia chose a husband who was "beneath her," Sophie backed off and gave Julia a large dowry so Max would prosper.

In young Lillian's mind, Julia had a feminine prestige that clashed with her own. Hellman was a southern woman of a different type: unprosperous, gangly and bold featured, mouthy. She put Julia in a separate category to hold in contempt, knowing her mother's insider status depended on a frail scaffolding: family money, beauty, and marriage to a man she loved but was never sure of. Lillian would never be—by inclination or ability—the proper lady her mother wanted her to be. Although Lillian aspired to be a ballet dancer when she was very young, as she grew older she knew that would never happen, and why. Hellman showed off and made trouble, choosing bravura: smart, bold, earthy, noisy with laughter. Nice southern ladies got a lot of lip from Lillian Hellman.

Beautiful, ineffectual southern women in Hellman's dramas and memoirs portray her disparaging view of her lovely, passive southern mother. Lillian could not bear the pretend charm of southern femininity, and she mocked it. She once told a reporter, "You weren't considered a lady unless you had a headache and were resting."[12]

Young Lillian, caught up in competing with her mother, did not see Julia's problems: "a worldly husband, a difficult child, unloving sisters and a mother of formidable coldness had made deep marks on my mother by the time I was old enough to understand her eccentric nature."[13] Hellman's recognition came too late. Julia died of bowel cancer when Hellman was thirty. It took years for Hellman to admire Julia's capacity for love, her absolute loyalty, "inloveness" to Max, and her ability to live as she wanted under difficult circumstances.[14]

Sophie's stern, dour nature seeped into the walls of both the Hellman's seedy boardinghouse and later their relentlessly middle-class New York apartment. The year before Lillian was born, Sophie had leased a house near her daughter at 40 Rosa Park, complete with security guards, to oversee her daughter's life and officiate at the family businesses.[15] Wherever the Hellmans lived throughout Lillian's childhood, the entire Newhouse-Marx clan lived in nouveau riche splendor a few blocks from the Hellmans, scarcely hiding their contempt.

Sophie never let her daughter Julia or her granddaughter Lillian forget how far Julia's fortunes had plummeted since becoming a Hellman. A splendid house at 2408 Magazine, where Julia and her sister Florence once lived, now served as Sophie's reminder of Julia's "fall."[16] The Magazine Street house had "elaborate interior woodwork," huge sliding doors of stained oak, and mantles adorned with tile work. The Hellman sisters' boardinghouse on Prytania had utility but little charm. Julia didn't seem to mind the two family's differing lifestyles, but Lillian did. She was only too aware of having one foot in the damp puddle of genteel poverty and the other in the muck of profligate wealth. Hellman's Grandmother Sophie, vice president of the banking consortium known as the Marx Company, listed her job as "capitalist" in the 1900 census and ran the family like a corporation. Sophie, a classic battle-ax, subjugated nearly everyone except her brother Jake. Grandfather Leonard, merchant and liquor dealer, died before Lillian's birth. She never was able to imagine any man having the bursts of enthusiasm required to sire her mother and the Newhouse aunts and uncles.

"Given to breaking the spirit of people for the pleasure of the exercise," as Hellman called the behavior, they derived money from various sources: wholesale liquor, banking, and the United Fruit Company's exploitation of Honduras and Guatemala.[17] Hellman later patterned her play *The Little Foxes* after them, making Hellman's attitude clear: they fed off anyone, white or black, for their profits. But she found they were "high spirited" even if "they laughed too much over their own vigor and fancy money deals."[18]

For her first five years, Lillian was watched over by a black nurse Hellman called Sophronia Mason in her memoirs, provided by her mother's family money. This remarkable woman, Hellman's one "most certain love," was perhaps the Sophronia McMahon listed in New Orleans's 1910 census. Sophronia molded Lillian "to last for good," a forced legacy black women gave to white children in the South. Under Sophronia's guidance Lillian confronted her character: brash, nosy, impetuous—a show-off. An early portrait of Lillian and Sophronia delineates their sharp contrasts. "If you look at that picture . . . there's that little Lillian: broad, tough, chin jutting, powerful, determined, eyes flashing, and alongside of her is this absolutely beautiful Sophronia . . . that black nurse of hers was just so elegant, so beautiful, so intelligent looking; she was everything . . . right then and there Lillian decided that she was going to invent herself . . . standing there making up her mind to become some kind of inventor of things."[19]

As the portrait shows, a southern girl's display value was particularly important. With Julia's money and Sophronia's care Lillian measured up admirably for a few years. Photographs of Lillian show her as a cute little girl with distinct facial expressions, fluffy hair, and fashionable garb—starched organza dresses, nautical chic, or trendy coatdresses. Such starched, itchy dresses could only be borne by the stoic or well behaved, since air-conditioning and pesticides to make life easier in "the climate" did not exist.[20] Posing for photographs center stage may have had its enchantments, but living as display was dull. Doubtless even as an infant Lillian wasn't dull. At her third birthday party Lillian created a brouhaha because she played with a cat, mussed her dress, and in snotty shyness refused any overtures from her guests. She built rebellion into her character as an anti-dote to boredom and loneliness.

An only child due to a "dangerously botched" birth, Lillian soaked up at-tributes of others to feel vitally connected to life.[21] Her early roots tangled deep in New Orleans cultures—comfortable "downtown" or "uptown," as "part nigger," as "white," as Jew, Hellman relished complexity. Her father bantered, "Where do we start your training as the first Jewish nun on Prytania Street?"[22]

Even as a child Lillian felt ambivalent about the South, breathing deeply of its culture but wary of its racial politics. The Hellmans lived like "New Orleanians," not connected to the Eastern European religious Jews living in and around Dryades Street. Hellman's fraternal grandparents, Bernard and Babette Koshland Hellman, were both buried at Ahavas Sholem on Frenchman Street in New Orleans, and her aunts at Hebrew Rest.[23] Despite their burial sites, in most respects, little distinguished their traditions from those of their Catholic and Protestant neighbors. The oral historian for the Hellmans, Aunt Hannah, favored stories about humorous family eccentrici-ties, not religious heritage. The family's peculiar "Dinner in Remembrance of" celebrated the anniversary of a person's death by having a dinner, telling stories, and lifting their glasses to that individual. This ritual may have been a vastly changed Jewish tradition of sitting shivah, but if so, Hellman didn't know it, recalling in *Eating Together* that it was more like a version of the Irish wake with champagne toasts and good food.

When she first felt the brunt of anti-Semitism, she was shocked. She loved the Mardi Gras celebrations, but one year she suddenly refused to take part. She had discovered that the krewes, as the parade organizations are called, particularly Rex and Comus, excluded Jews from formalized New Orleans rituals. Since the first parade in 1872 "the circumcised have never had an-other chance to earn that kind of glory."[24] She took offense at the exclusion and never forgot it. Years later she chastised Kitty Hart for going to Mardi Gras: "They don't have Jews."[25]

Folk wisdom had it that everyone knew their "place" in the deep class di-visions of New Orleans, but Hellman didn't like rigidity of any sort. "Buglin' Sam"[26] Dekemel sold sugar-coated hot waffles for pennies in a horse-drawn wagon along Canal Street, and she wanted to be a part of his life as much as of those "betters" in the "uptown" department stores like Godchaux, Goldrings, and Krauss Company.[27] Lillian gravitated toward the generous warmth and lack of social pretense she found in many black people. Her presence sometimes made problems for Sophronia, who had to tread softly in racially divided New Orleans. Steadfast, strict, and savvy about the ways of the world, Sophronia influenced Lillian during those formative first five years. Hellman forever raged against racial divides. She knew the people of New Orleans and they were her.

Sophronia left when the family's means were reduced, and who had charge of Lillian after that never seemed settled. She made the most of such confusion. The family's laissez-faire attitude and chaotic living conditions gave her opportunity; that's all she ever needed for nosiness. Hellman never let an opportunity for adventure get away. She relished the fecund turmoil in the boardinghouse. From the typical two-story open gallery of her house she watched a steady stream of people coming and going, cleaning and cooking or talking and eating, moving up and down the unpaved streets. The detached outdoor toilets meant that no one was safe from her scrutiny.[28] Even the man who performed weekly maintenance on the streetlights excited her interest.[29] She observed it all and eventually became part of the street's movement.

Born curious, Lillian wandered about on foot or took the streetcar. She had to cross either Euterpe or Polymnia, streets named for the muses of lyric and sacred poetry. Drawing creative inspiration, she'd meander uptown, separated from the decadent French Quarter only by a small island called neutral ground. Lillian walked everywhere she could: the German merchant at the wharves, the "wop" section around Enrico's, the roofless picture show on the corner of Carrollton Avenue.[30] Just blocks away, riverboats brought ragtime and the laughter of gamblers from the Mississippi. The streets and waterways of the French and American quarters, drifting and blending into the Irish section, provided a backdrop of syncopated living.

Music and drama accompanied most of Lillian's activities in New Orleans. Tagging along with her aunts meant "making market,"[31] lunching at Tujague's, eating and drinking with the "afternoon crowd of locals" in the "Old World air," going to the Little Theater, movies, opera.[32] The French Opera House produced Ibsen's A Doll's House and Carmen when Lillian was six. She discovered the deep drama of women performing independent, passionate lives.[33] And in this city especially, drama wasn't confined to the theaters. Lillian browsed in grocery stores, restaurants, bars, churches, anywhere she could get in. Once in a secondhand bookshop, two rats jumped her, making her "rat crazy."[34] But nothing stopped her. The Irish Channel featured St. Mary's Market and numerous pubs. The American Poydras Market featured "rows of colored women waiting to be employed to wash or scrub."[35] A "negro section" in "Backertown" supplied service workers, entertainers, domestics. The Jewish merchant trade was located on Dryades Street for the religious and Canal Street for the wealthy. Lillian didn't miss a thing, relishing the exuberance of shady practices everywhere in New Orleans. The French Quarter particularly drew her as it vibrated with music and something beyond understanding. Jazz joined Caribbean drumming. Outdoor concerts, a legacy from slave sales, throbbed in what is now Louis Armstrong Park. The Quarter enticed customers with rich coffees and oyster loaf, along with alcohol, jazz, and sex. "Nice little girls weren't allowed to go down there. It was taboo."[36] Of course, Lillian's interests didn't include being a "nice little girl." The child Lillian was as outlandish, noisy, and high-spirited as the French Quarter. As a friend would later say, "Ten minutes with Lillian and Joan of Arc would have recanted."[37]

Although she admired the flamboyant, she valued most the hard work, decency, and laughter of her Hellman aunts. They were tolerant, good-humored, and opinionated. The Hellman aunts adored their brother, protected his wife, and loved his daughter fiercely. They had dignity and they had fun. If the aunts occasionally tried to protect Lillian from something smutty, saying *schweigen vor dem Kind*, they also pronounced uncensored, witty judgments about the outrageous antics of others.[38] The wry drollery of the Hellmans made bearable what could not be changed. The Hellmans, Lillian included, had raucous, ready laughs, inviting others in, making life joyful. Even later critics like author Rosemary Mahoney, who found the old woman Lillian a frightening termagant, admitted that "her laugh, a crashing water wheeze . . . was the embodiment of mirth and was itself entertaining."[39]

The only grandchild, Lillian was called "Baby" for years. She took the high humor of the Hellmans as her own and learned firsthand the evil comedy of the Marxes. She received lots of attention from both families, but little respect or affection from Julia's side. The two sides of her family constituted a wrenching disparity in manners, money, and morality. She could not ignore the Marx legacy: their wealth and power, their abuse of others, their arrogance, and their efforts to control. Lillian saw herself in them more than she ever cared to admit.

Southern Family Lust and Greed

The Newhouse-Marx companies made millions cashing in on the New Orleans cotton and fruit monopolies. These high rollers could buy anything and did—a wife, a mistress, a job, political influence. The *Times-Picayune* and the *States-Item* thinly disguised these machinations as news. Public spectacle played out privately in myriad ways within Lillian's family. Her Grandmother Hellman's younger sister Bethe Koshland came from Germany for an arranged marriage with "Styrie Bowman," a probable alias of one of fruit entrepreneur Jake Weinberger's many sons, connected by marriage to the Marx family.[40] Bethe was to "clean up" Styrie's activities in exchange for her immigration.[41] In the decadence of New Orleans, Styrie disappeared and Bethe allied herself with another wealthy New Orleans class—the mob.

Hellman's domestic dramas included the famous and infamous.

She hated the snobbery of her mother's family, but the intrigue and excess that accompanied money fascinated her. An ex-slave of her rich relatives told Lillian what she had already learned: "You got a hard road to go. . . Part what you born from is good, part a mess of shit."[42] Lillian knew firsthand who did what to whom and how she fit in, on both sides of the family. Hellman's aunts and uncles provided plenty of drama up close.

Julia brought Lillian into the family whirlpool of money, power, and violence. Julia, perplexed about what to do with a child in general and Lillian in particular, took her wherever she went "calling" but then forgot her. Lillian fashioned her own agenda, wandering through the houses of her wealthy family along St. Charles Avenue, where Uncle Charlie and Aunt Rosa Marx Weinberger lived; Uncle Charlie's brother Jake Weinberger lived nearby, as did his son-in-law Samuel Zemurray in his palatial home at 2 Audubon Place.[43] Uncles Charlie, Jake, and Sam brought the scandalous politics of the violent United Fruit Company to the already wealthy, corrupt Marx family. Lillian, in and out of the Weinberger and Zemurray houses in New Orleans, found their stories irresistible.[44] Servants and family gossiped about the company's imperial raids, her aunt's addictions to morphine and illicit sex with the black chauffeur. The scandalous whispers elated young Lillian, who even as a child had affection and awe for those uncles and their daring.

In response to the sordid politics of New Orleans and the United Fruit Company's corrupt dealings, Hellman later wrote *Another Part of the Forest* and *The Little Foxes*. In these plays Hellman focused on the semiautobiographical "Hubbards." Their infamous business practices allude without subtlety to Zemurray, who formed the Hubbard-Zemurray Steamship Company with his first partner, Ashbel Hubbard.[45] As critical as she was of her characters' greed, she cherished their glitter and their menace as "one would cherish a nest of particularly vicious diamond-back rattlesnakes."[46] They were family.

Because half of her family possessed great wealth and the other half struggled to make a living, money ran like a "firebrand" through Lillian's life.[47]

She reflected, "By fourteen my heart was with the poor except on the days when it was with those who ground them under."[48] She bitterly noted that her Hellman aunts locked the kitchen in fear of boarders' wasting food while her mother's family bragged about getting Washington to send "a man-of-war and two diplomatic agents" to maintain their interests on Central America's Mosquito Coast.[49] While her Hellman aunts made her special foods to "splurge," the Newhouse-Marxes gave ceremonial gifts to Julia and Lillian so they could keep up appearances: handmade dresses fashioned by New Orleans nuns, imported silk sashes. These proper clothes did not suit the life Hellman found in New Orleans.

Lillian grew up an earthy, funny, disruptive child—a southern Jewish girl rebel. The French Quarter offered nosy children sexual information and voyeuristic stimulation. A curious, headstrong Lillian longed to know what whores did beyond Bourbon Street in Storyville, "to stick around to see how things like that worked."[50] A man shook his "thing"[51] at her in the French Quarter, scaring her, but in a mansion on St. Charles Avenue a cousin shook his "thingy" at her too.[52] These glimpses appalled her, but once aware of sex's potential for perversity, she also learned the pleasures of forbidden sensuality. Lillian, playing at the Poydras orphanage near her house, thrilled when the orphan Pancho whispered to her, "Yo te amo." This early endearment set up in her "forever after both sympathy and irritability with the first sexual stirrings of little girls, so masked, so complex, so foolish as compared with the sex of little boys."[53]

Desire was strong in Hellman from early adolescence. "I know that I watched every movement that Carl Bowman, Jr. made as he dove off the pier, or pitched in the baseball game . . . and one night I was wracked with gagging, the emotion was so great, as he put his arm around me."[54] Sometimes wrenching, sex was a source of matchless sensation. New Orleans thrives on the forbidden, and so did Lillian. Mindful of Grandmother Sophie's attraction to her brother Jake's wit and worldliness, as well as the Hellman aunts' unconditional and fawning love for Max, the playwright Hellman later fictionalized emotionally incestuous relationships in her dramas, particularly *Toys in the Attic*. Hellman also explored her earliest understanding of the heady mix of sex, romance, and violence in *Pentimento*; cousin Bethe's relationship with the mobster Arneggio translated into "Love I think."[55] Sex made a great story, but more to the point, it made her feel powerfully alive.

Hellman's adolescence found her drawn to "fine-looking, heavy men with blood in their faces and sound to their voices."[56] She responded powerfully to a rich uncle's sexual attraction. "Willy," as she called him in *Pentimento*, introduced her to ecstasy, sexual desire, and guilt and recrimination. In the memoir, to obscure Willy's actual identity, Hellman combined the characteristics of her three "banana company" uncles: Charlie and Jake Weinberger, and Samuel Zemurray. These men's histories verify the tales and rumors Lillian heard as a child, alluded to in *Pentimento*: killings and gunships and Hatchey Moore, Guy Machine-Gun Molony, Lee Christmas.

These uncles separately and together brought Lillian to recognize the miasma of money, power, and sex. Tracing the family tree makes Charlie Weinberger, "fruit merchant," most like Uncle Willy.[57] He took Julia's youngest sister, Aunt Rosa, from Demopolis to New Orleans in 1898. Julia and Lillian frequently visited them at their grand houses, first above St. Charles at 2113 Palmer Avenue, then at 702 St. Charles. Also, Willy and Charlie seem to share a similar character: welcoming, trapped by an unloving wife, nice to Lillian. But the portrait isn't exact. More exciting, famous, and infamous than Uncle Charlie was his older brother Jake Weinberger, the "parrot king," as well as his son-in-law Sam Zemurray—the "banana man."[58] All three men had the charisma and arrogance to take women they wanted; all had ties to Hellman's family.

Jake's power and sexuality best fits the "Willy" who nearly seduced Lillian as an adolescent, though ultimately it was more his discretion than hers that prevented it. Owner of Bluefields Steamship Company, Jake, an "affable southerner," gambled, spoke the dog Spanish of the tropics, and traveled "the banana towns of the Central American coast, trading for bananas, coconuts, parrots and macaws."[59] Involved for years in violent politics, in one instance he loaned a Nicaraguan rebel "a banana boat for ferrying arms and men up the Escondido River in preparation for a major rebel drive into the interior." The brother of Uncle Charlie, Jake thrilled Lillian at fourteen with his outrageous behavior and fame. He fixed elections, ran for office. His political cronies in New Orleans bragged at a court hearing that "in an earlier mayoralty contest . . . thirty-five armed men had been stationed at the St. Charles Hotel to ensure the election's outcome." Hellman felt the dark attraction of such men all too well. As Nick Crossman says in *Autumn Garden*, "Boys will be boys and in the South there's no age limit on boyishness."[60]

Sam Zemurray certainly figured in Lillian's life, something she kept under wraps; odd for Hellman, who courted the famous as well as the infamous. Zemurray's fame in New Orleans remains unequaled and undiminished to this day. More powerful than the Weinbergers, he distanced himself from the worst of the corruption, but elements of his story arise in "Willy" too. Newspapers of the 1920s report Zemurray's owning a yacht that "eluded the

US Secret Service, beat a pursuing U.S. gunboat in Honduras."[61] Though he "denied it a shade wistfully," Lillian remembered the story from her childhood. She counted him as family, but caution and hypocrisy never appealed to Lillian, and his success in United Fruit brought him a spurious respectability that her character "Willy" did not have. In the 1950s, Hellman wrote Zemurray asking him to grant an interview to a friend who needed a job. She apologized for writing her first letter to him "in all these years—and all these years means from birth to whatever it is I am now." She went on to say, "Many times, when I was in Boston, I wanted to telephone to you, but it always seemed intrusive . . . but through the years I have so often heard people speak of you, and always felt an irrational, distant in-law pleasure in what they said."[62] Hellman never approved of the United Fruit Company or Zemurray's and Weinberger's politics. Drawn to men with power, she could not ignore the depth of her feeling for both. Ironically, on Hellman's last trip to New Orleans in 1977 as an honored speaker, she and friends attended a dinner at the Tulane University president's mansion at 2 Audubon Place, Zemurray's mansion.[63] References to him and the house abound in her story of youth, curiosity, and passion.

In the wild, thick heat of southern nights, whoever he actually was, "Willy" awakened a sexual hunger in the adolescent Lillian. Maybe he only half sensed her attraction to him and did little to foster it beyond simple affection. But in reflection she called that first rush of romance and lust she felt "love," saying she felt "exalted" when he let her tag along as he drove deep into the bayous to fish and eat and consort with his mistress. She later established a sneering political superiority to counteract her attraction to him. But a young Lillian swooned in desire for an uncle who broke all the rules for sex, money, dominance. She couldn't have Willy, but she could become him if that meant taking what she wanted, violating conventions, risking. She wanted to take his sexual intensity for herself. Hellman always said that "New Orleans does odd things to people." Growing up there did odd things to Lillian too.[64] Though she lived much of the year in a different culture in New York, the mess of sexual feeling she found in New Orleans summers transcended rationality and fear. She developed a seductive heat that would later invite sexual and artistic pleasure, even as she learned the importance of the intellect.

Her New Orleans invitation to pleasure and sensation became transitory when her life changed. Her father's shoe business failed, and he changed jobs—from smooth southern business owner to fast-talking New York salesman. The year Lillian turned six her life vacillated between southern curve and northern edge. From that time until she turned sixteen, she spent half her year in the easy pulse of the South, the other half in the pounding intensity of the North. She somehow had to join the sensuality and heat of summers in New Orleans to the raw winters and intellectual rigor of New York. The life of the mind so important to New York culture offered her another dimension of eroticism. But the gut-wrenching cultural changes were not tidy. The shock of New York was intense, and she only slowly became a New Yorker.[65]

For a time, Max dragged Lillian and Julia with him on his business trips, "in so many southern towns and cities that forever now Memphis is merged with Macon and Macon with Yazoo City." Finally they arranged for Julia and Lillian to spend the school year in New York and flee to New Orleans for vacations. The two worlds of East and South could hardly have been more different. Spending the first few months in Manhattan at a 63rd and Broadway apartment, then moving to Mrs. Krisner's Boardinghouse on West 81st, then finally to their permanent Upper West Side apartment life at West 95th Street and Riverside Drive, the family finally settled in to New York City, when they weren't "South."[66] Instead of the physical freedom, humorous tolerance, and ambient sensuality of life in "uptown" New Orleans, Hellman's New York dictated a rigid, shabby middle-class existence of social confinement and impossible intellectual expectation.

Spending only six months or less in New York every year, she maintained the fiction that she was a southerner temporarily trapped in Yankee territory. In the preteen years, buffeted by change, Lillian began trying on the actions and roles that suited her time and place, wherever it was. If she appeared inconsistent, so much the better. Though she hated New York, her parents finally decided that she had to stay there for school. She adapted, at least until the end of the school year when she bolted for New Orleans. She reluctantly became a New Yorker.

The Edge: New York

The culture shock rocked Lillian and created intriguing complexities in this smart, sensual young woman. Deeply insecure, she never permitted herself to look "uncertain" and became increasingly mouthy, startling New Yorkers with her grand southern oratory style.[67] The comparatively blurred class divisions of New York should have offered Lilly some relief from her daily awareness of her family's teetering economic position. But the Hellmans moved too close to the Marx family's ostentatious apartments, and their West

Side neighborhood was drab compared to the Marxes' Upper East Side upper-class trappings. Although Julia Hellman seemed blissfully oblivious of the need to keep up middle-class appearances, their shabby apartment shamed Lillian. To add to her malaise, school became a nightmare.

It took some time and doing for this erotically inclined southern girl to become a New York intellectual. The slapdash nod to education she found in one of the John McDonogh schools in New Orleans did not prepare Lillian for the rigor of New York's neophyte teacher trainees at Hunter College's demonstration school.[68] School in both places bored her stiff, and she stepped up her rebellion. However, she found in both cities the wherewithal to establish avid intellectual habits of mind that smoothed her transition. Books and magazines introduced her to a world of drama she was hell-bent on entering. In New Orleans, the curving drive and huge oaks of the Prytania house provided a cover for the fig tree, a private hideaway for thinking and reading. She created an inviting personal space in the tree to hang her dress, eat her lunch, read, sleep, then resurface to cover her absence.[69]

New York schools kept closer account of her truancies, but she could still lose herself in the crowds to find a private place to read. Often she sullenly slammed the door of her room and plunged into the world of fiction and scandal sheet. She devoured everything from Dickens to Flaubert, "from a dreadful magazine called *Snappy Stories*, which I borrowed from the elevator man, straight through Balzac," straight through *Love Confessions* "borrowed from the janitor." During a family vacation at the Hawthorne Inn in Massachusetts when she was eight, she wrote *Queen*, a hint of plays to come.[70] The aggressive, reclusive Hellman turned on her creativity any way she could. Books saved her from both loneliness and the company of those she could not abide. She lived in books, and everything she read hovered in her brain, waiting for expression.

In the first quarter of the twentieth century it was rare for women to graduate, and fewer than 10 percent of the female population received high school diplomas. Hellman obviously needed school to funnel her energy and future, but she resisted her parents' emphasis on education. Her "silent angers weren't always so silent."[71] She halfheartedly moved from the Hunter schools to Wadleigh High School for gifted girls, a place she remembered as a "large, smelly, unpleasant dump," where she spent most of her time "looking up naughty words."[72] Gaining confidence, she found inventive friends, Lois Jacoby and Edith Connor among them. She was so unruly, though, that the school principal warned her friend Helen's mother that Lillian "was a bad influence on her daughter." Lillian's penchant for truancy, twenty-three absences in one school year, infuriated the principal and her mother. The girls gave lame excuses: they skipped when it was "too cold," "too hot," or just "not a good day."[73] Although lazy and impatient with school, Hellman had smarts. But she hated the watered down curriculum deemed fitting for the education of girls and insisted on her own interpretations of what she read.

She worked only when she wanted and how she wanted—just enough to avoid real trouble. Her lackluster grades were better than she deserved. Mathematics bored her for its rigidity and her low C showed it; her best grades were in English and grammar, although she rarely studied.[74] Later she said she wanted to forget her first writing gig as a high school columnist for the chatty "It Seems to Me, Jr." Ever conscious of her audience, she knew the school wanted fluff, not opinions. Her life as a dramatist picked up about the same time. The drama teacher directed her to play the part of a villain in *Mrs. Gorringe's Necklace*. The night of the performance, a door stuck as Lillian tried to make her exit so she remained onstage, sat on the sofa, and "fattened up her own part by a number of showy remarks."[75] Hellman's penchant for drama, scripted and unscripted, accelerated.

Hellman developed a hard edge, becoming blunt, bold, and brilliant, while retaining the lusciousness of southern character. But her curves never blunted the incisive thrust of her critical knife. She seduced and cut by turn. A brilliant infighter, an aggressive and nasty enemy, she was a force to be reckoned with. Street smart and abrasive, she skewered, not always cleanly and sometimes cruelly. From 1915 to 1925, Hellman became New York City: intellectual, harsh, impatient, demanding—on the move. Immigrants flooded the city to fill jobs in manufacturing and commerce. The rivers chiefly served commercial traffic, unlike the Mississippi in New Orleans that offered pleasure too. Life in the city felt hostile, not lushly forgiving. Lillian had begun to acclimate to a new life, a new self.

In New York she found an atmosphere where Jewish culture resonated, although she was not a practicing Jew. Judaic ribbons of connection lay slack on both sides of the family. Too Jewish in New Orleans, where "the population is so mixed that adding another element—the Jew—didn't create a fuss,"[76] and not Jewish enough in New York, a city housing 50 percent of all the Jews in the United States, Hellman felt a double sting.[77] She fit, uneasily, the most "un-Jewish of Jews," a "breed apart" from New York's distinct and active Jewish communities.[78] Hellman never understood what being a Jew meant exactly. But she always insisted vaguely "I know I would rather be a Jew than not be."

Lillian's mother, more needy southern woman than self-reliant Jew, attended all manner of churches. Hellman recalled spending Sundays in Baptist churches in New Orleans and any church or cathedral in New York where her mother felt comforted. She remembered once being so "moved by a sermon I didn't understand that I ran from the church crying to be good and never sinful, and fell down the steps and went on home screaming . . . comforted and discomforted by people of strong belief."[79] Ever an observer and never a participant, Hellman saw organized religion as more spectacle than instructive. It took her years to learn about real Jewish rituals, and they made her uncomfortable.

Hellman hated anti-Semitism, yet Jews often accused her of being a Jew basher. Playing Herman Halpern in Hellman's *My Mother, My Father and Me*, Walter Matthau complained, "'Lillian, you know your play is anti-Semitic.' She said, 'Oh, don't be foolish . . . you know I'm Jewish. . . . I know about them, I like to write about them.' He said, 'You don't know anything about Jews. You're from New Orleans or wherever, and if another Jew shows up you all hide. . . . Can't you write about non-Jews?' She said, 'No, I'm writing about people that I know.' I said, 'Yeah, but the Jews got enough trouble without you throwing in your bag of grick.'"[80]

Open and curious about many cultures, she took what she could from her own. Even as a young girl she worshiped individuality and shrugged off any label, insulting nearly everyone. If Jewish angst and a penchant for insult weren't enough, her entrance into full-blown New York citizenry coincided with her becoming a woman. Harder still for Lillian, since she had no sense of who she was or where she belonged, only a growing sense of what she wasn't—a sweet southern girl.

Part of Hellman's bad behavior had to do with her mother, of course. Julia irritated the New Yorker in Hellman. She felt her mother's naïveté debilitating, the pretend charm of southern femininity unbearable, and she mocked it. Lillan's complex feelings for her mother surfaced in her dramas. Birdie in *The Little Foxes* was weak and ineffectual, and told young Alexandra not to love her "because in twenty years you'll just be like me. . . And you'll trail after them, just like me, hoping they won't be so mean that day or say something to make you feel so bad."[81] Hellman's fears surface again through "Lily," the young wife in *Toys in the Attic*, who is too much like Julia to ignore. She cannot see the world as it is and her blindness and pretense hurt others. Hellman arrogantly dismissed such women, preferring street smarts to loveliness.

With Hellman's mother tied to values Hellman could not share and her father absent more often than not, the young Hellman found ways to subvert her parents' best intentions. If their rules displeased her sufficiently, she threw dramatic fits, storming out of the apartment, cutting school, speaking out. During World War I, she and friend Helen Schiff established a spy-catching network, following likely suspects and enlisting a gullible girl as stooge. Hellman played rough, twisting the girl's arm to to demand more imaginative spying. Hellman and Schiff took things too far and in one instance ratted on two likely looking anarchists to the police. Perhaps her lifelong hatred of tat- tletales began when the police discovered the "spies" were a professor of Greek at Hunter College and a second violinist from the Palace Theatre.[82] As a preteen, Hellman should have been cowed by her mistake. Instead, she saw the possibilities of a dramatic life.

She relished the pleasures of any performance in the theaters and picture shows of New York. Eugene O'Neill's *The Hairy Ape* and John Barrymore's depiction of *Hamlet* both triumphed dramatically in 1922, when Hellman was seventeen. She was profoundly moved by those two plays, and her love of theater took hold. She also became enthralled with picture shows. She avidly consumed anything shown on the silent screen in New York. Women usually avoided going to performances alone, but Hellman did so from a young age. She later bragged that she was one of the first to take films seriously. When *Robin Hood* starring Douglas Fairbanks Sr. premiered in 1922, a solitary girl crazy for excitement found it at the movies.

Not all her performance pleasures were new ones. Jazz, the sound of the decade, bridged her southern childhood to her New York adolescence. The music's curvaceous rhythms sliced politically. For once Hellman found her- self at home—in music. In 1921 *Shuffle Along*, written by Eubie Blake and Noble Sissle, became the first African American musical on Broadway, and early blues recordings by Louis Amstrong and Bessie Smith brought close the sound of her childhood. Since black New York blues artists played in Harlem, strictly forbidden at night for the young Lillian, she had to make do with white musicians for live performances. For her sixteenth birthday party, she chose a hotel roof where "king of jazz" Paul Whitman's band played; the same band premiered in George Gershwin's *Rhapsody in Blue* three years later. When public radio brought music to listeners in the 1920s, it became part of her daily life. Hellman loved to dance, and if ballet was now a dim dream, she found the backward bends of the tango "a gym dance trick, and it looked very ugly but it felt very nice."[83] Dancing drew on the rhythm and sen- suality of her New Orleans consciousness. A loner, restless and wild, Hellman found in New York the stimulus to move, to be someone. Life swirled around her and could be had for a price.

As New York's population doubled between 1900 and 1930 to nearly 7 million, so did the shrill call for financial success and intellectual achievement. Hellman's conflicts about wealth intensified as money became "one with God" to New Yorkers in the 1920s. A Model T cost $395, and though women rarely drove, as a teen Hellman wanted her own automobile, to drive streets still packed with carriages.[54] But she couldn't afford it. At seventeen she admitted to a disparity between her reality and her slowly evolving political ideals: "I am intensely bourgeoisie. How can I be socialistic without even yet having reached middle classdom?"[55]

During the Progressive Era (1879–1920), New Yorkers cried out for high culture and knowledge. The city's print revolution heralded a new age of information, and it all had an edge: everything from Margaret Sanger's *What Every Girl Should Know* about birth control to Edgar Rice Burroughs's *Tarzan and the Apes* to D. H. Lawrence's *Sons and Lovers*. Most people read two or three newspapers a day, working their way through the *New York Times*, *New York Tribune*, or *Daily Graphic*—dubbed by New Yorkers the "Daily Pornographic," since tabloid journalism was the order of the day. New Yorkers constituted a vast and diverse public readership. New magazines printed in nearly every tongue appeared daily. *Vanity Fair* and *Vogue* epitomized the sophisticated cachet of New York's avant-garde snobbishness until Harold Ross established a magazine for the "man about town," or those who wanted to be, and published the first issue of the *New Yorker* in 1925. This witty, intellectual milieu would become Lillian Hellman's.

New York was the place to be, and the rhythm of the city eventually stirred her to a faster pace, furthering an ambition as yet unformed. World War I had opened thousands of jobs to women as the boys were "over there." After the war, women maintained a small part in the artistic and theatrical arenas. New York opened up the possibilities of the creative life and as curious as Lillian was, she wouldn't be left out of the loop for long. At nineteen she told her father she would give up an irritating litany of fake prayer that she had mumbled for years in exchange for a leather coat and a feather fan. He made good on the trade. In retelling the story to friends, however, she called her fan a "feather boa," undoubtedly thinking of *Vanity Fair* writer Dorothy Parker, whose famous feather boa was called "the only boa that ever molted." Hellman admired the Algonquin Circle—up-and-coming writers, artists, musicians, producers. The circle's willingness to have fun and its poisonous wit inspired her, even though she hated its slick superiority. Hellman was serious in her revolt against the older generation but had no clue how to act. When relaxed, she joined nearly anyone in the mood for fun. In a "crisp mood," she was the "kind of girl who can take the tops off bottles with her teeth."[86]

After all, what else could she do? When an older friend left for college, she began to ponder her own future. "Lois left for college. A new life for her. What for me?" The college question had not yet been settled, and Lillian feared marriage was the only avenue, but even that seemed out of reach. She did not have the big blue eyes, blonde curls, tiny nose, and rosebud mouth she said she wanted. Instead she grew up with the commanding features of a prow head on a whaling ship.[87] What she called sex, the "physical life," seemed out of reach as long as it depended on beauty and the whims of the necessary male. She might do everything the boys could do, but she affirmed the feminine self in her desire for them.

While friend Margaret Harriman described her as "sort of cute" with reddish hair, an aquiline nose, and a level, humorous mouth, what girlfriends thought made little difference. Mothers forever reminded their daughters that they had to look the part if they were ever to be married—the only role envisioned for them. Hellman's mother was no exception, buying her clothes designed to impress. Hellman liked clothes, though she felt insecure about choosing them, sometimes making errors that embarrassed her. If she wore a "pretty dress from Paris" made of a gold-shot satin material with gold fringe at the hem,[88] she also chose "an expensive error in yellow organdie, threaded with black velvet ribbon tied in girlish bows at the throat and wrists."[89] She hid in the bathroom when she wore it, suddenly noting its absurdity. In the 1920s of Lillian's adolescence, women's skirts went up, girls wore lipstick and rolled stockings showed the knees, and parents worried about loosening morals. Marriage solved the family's problem about what to do with an outspoken, aberrant girl. Julia did all she could to encourage marriage, and her daughter did all she could to ready herself for it–but the objective seemed elusive, based on standards she didn't understand and couldn't meet. Fortunately Hellman grew up some before marriage presented itself as an option.

Hellman simply could not submit to the will of another, could not obey out of convenience. In high school she began smoking ferociously, tossing her cigarette whenever a mother or teacher appeared.[90] Smoking was a forbidden pleasure for girls, but cigarettes only cost a dime a pack, and a cheap way to stick it to an older generation who thought only men should smoke. Action and intrigue saved her from flat routine if not trouble. She hid "militant undercurrents" behind a mild facade, according to Harriman, who told raucous tales of Hellman flouting curfews, running away with seventy-five cents in her pocket, dating older boys, and wiggling out of trouble by telling her mother she had heart trouble. If Hellman feared risk taking, she feared compliance even more. She knew she needed to shape southern invitation and New York imperiousness to succeed. The women characters of her plays show the split. Regina, an inspired power monger, and Birdie, a ruined and passive "mummie" of *The Little Foxes*, both sprang from Hellman's imagination and past.

Wildly impatient with the slow march to adulthood and spurred on by the roaring twenties, Lillian spent her late teens in fits and starts, by turn ambitious and aimless, sappy and cynical, optimistic and pessimistic. She attracted and sabotaged by turn all that she wanted—money, men, fun, vocation—whooping it up emotionally. She wrote about some of it, changing names and dates to avoid lawsuits. In one instance, she was asked to agree to an interview for a Sam Adams sequel to Warner Fabian's potboiler novel *Flaming Youth*. What followed was Hellman's idea of a great time. She egged on her friends Marie-Louise and Alice to share in outrageous behavior—drinking, laughing, undoing the smug—which they did with alacrity. Lillian finally begged Marie-Louise to take off her clothes, get in the shower, pop out, and offer herself to Adams to show him flaming youth in the flesh.[91] Marie-Louise finally objected, but not before she and her friends proved that Prohibition's dry epoch of American history was the wettest ever. Whether moping about, scripting scenarios, or rescuing men from fire escapes (she records two such events in her memoirs), she dramatized her life as she lived it. She made use of shadows and lights and illuminations to shift the presentation when needed. "She could imitate and disappear for the moment, becoming a version of herself which served her but puzzled her friends."[92]

Never capable of moderation, Hellman knew what the traffic would bear and made the most of each opportunity. But not without struggle. In *The Lark* Hellman wrote a line for Joan of Arc: "Learn not to be brave when you are outnumbered . . . unless you can't retreat. Then you must fight because there is no other way." She felt suffocated in the conventional life but also knew that excess was dangerous for her. Still she couldn't live any other way. In her adolescence, she felt "outnumbered" by the forces that tried to control her.

Though few young women went to college, her family expected it. She squelched her mother's hope that she go to Sophie Newcomb in New Orleans. She had become a New Yorker by 1922 and suspected her mother only preferred her own alma mater so that Aunt Jenny and Aunt Hannah could watch her. Lillian preferred Smith, a perfect place away from home for brilliant, wild girls. The family compromised on Goucher, a relatively conservative small liberal arts college in Maryland. With the onset of her mother's cancer, Lilly meekly (for her) agreed to attend New York University's new Washington Square campus and live at home. She had dreamed of being a "brilliant college student," but she was a self-professed smart aleck and saw college only as a series of boring professors and "narrow unrelated courses." Her grades, not as "terrible" as she later said, certainly didn't foreshadow a theatrical future: two C's in history of the theater and a D in contemporary dramatic art. Disgusted with the university and herself, she dropped out after three years, deciding "not to compete" because she wasn't a "dazzling student."[93] Later she admitted she "was both opinionated and impressionable, cocksure and frightened to death" that her haughty aimlessness might kill any future she had.

The extent of Hellman's angst can be measured by what she did next. Her irritable impatience with her mother had not abated, but when she dropped out of NYU she agreed to travel with her mother through the Midwest and the South. Her mother's bouts of illness may have worried her, or there may have been hellish family scenes that needed repair. Hellman was given to dramatic scenes that ended with her slamming doors or shouting "shut up" as she ran from the apartment. Besides, Hellman loved travel. Although tempted to adopt a listless sophistication as she approached Cincinnati, she toured and visited relatives with a liveliness that surprised her mother.

Hellman was still a long way away from figuring out who she was or how she wanted to live. Her favorite shows of 1924 featured Joan of Arc in George Bernard Shaw's *St. Joan*, and adoring harem girls in Fairbanks's movie *The Thief of Bagdad*. In her late teens, she wasn't sure which held the greater attraction. In her fluctuating self-inventions, she needed friends who were strong and willing to hang on for the ride. She never lacked friends, though all of them fell out with her at one time or another. An only child, she believed in her paramount importance, and she had to find those who could hold their own with her. At times she'd drag others into great fun and mayhem. Other times she read and smoked alone at Lee Chumley's restaurant in Greenwich Village. Those confident enough to withstand her force field made a friend for life.

Auspiciously, on the midwestern trip she met Louis Kronenberger in Cincinnati, introduced by mutual friend Stan Simon. Kronenberger, who later became a noted critic and Ivy League professor of theater arts, was impressed by Hellman's letters and by the young woman herself. At nineteen, before either of them achieved anything much, they became steadfast friends. As a Hellman "appreciator," he felt a "kindred elegance or exuberance or irony," celebrating their "joyous revolt against pundits," sharing their contempt for the "new-new rich of café society who live in homes no longer; they live in stage sets."[94] He liked her zest and her wit. Stories speculating on the probability of an affair vary widely, but their mutual fondness was real. Later it was rumored that Hellman and Louis had been engaged, much to his mother's disapproval, but broke it off because neither had any money.[95] An engagement with Louis Kronenberger is unlikely, but she seriously dated his roommate Gerald Sykes. Hellman, wild as a teen, was not yet capable of juggling men so closely allied.

Even as a child, Hellman despised snobs, bullies, tattletales, and the pompous. She took them on and took the punishment if they responded in kind. Hellman never liked anyone she could bully, publicly denouncing her victim as "stooge," "prissy" "scoundrel ass," or "mingy little man." She ferreted out what went on behind the scenes and sharpened her wit to offend and endear by turn. Hellman developed a lifelong penchant for twisting verbal knives. Poking holes in nonsense was sport. She had nonsense of her own, but even at an early age, she liked herself.

3

STILL LIFE

Diaries, Publishers, Husbands

IF IT WERE NOT FOR HELLMAN'S ADOLESCENT DIARY, HER teens would be a complete fog for a biographer forced to depend on sporadic anecdotes in memoirs more literary than historical. The three-year diary she kept between 1922 and 1925 provides some illumination. A gift from admirer Milton Glick, the leather-bound diary contains a record of Hellman's adolescence. In inks of various colors, Hellman writes her life in her distinctive scrawl. As careful as Hellman was in writing plays or screenplays for others, her early diary, like most of her diaries, is haphazard. She paid little regard to exact dates or times, writing where it pleased her, leaving most pages blank. An October 1 entry, for example, covered 1922, 1923, and 1924, but recounted just one date with Howard Meyer. Hellman rarely clarified which year was which and never cared about the accuracy of dates.

But she did care about meaning. At seventeen she wrote a "Forward: 'I will not describe my childhood or the prenatal condition of my mother & then showing how childhood's innocent risks culminated in youth's corruptness. Then having a number of asterisks signifying some gentleman ruining me.'" But Hellman did not escape the feminine experience or the excesses of soap opera language, trite as they might be. For the first few months she wrote a diary only occasionally, when "blue." She wondered if she would turn out "mush" if she wrote when happy because the diary functioned chiefly as a record of romances and her early forays into sexual activity.

Men aroused Hellman and she certainly knew it herself by then. She wrote of her dissatisfaction with the young men in her life, Nat R. Thomas and Weaver, who didn't write or call as promised. In September 1922, Jerry V came into her life, and subsequently reflections on him make up nearly all the diary. Other biographers speculate that her early passion was for Gerald Sykes or Arthur Kober, but Jerry V was a college man she had known for some years, funny, manipulative, and seductive: "I have a vague premonition that I will only meet one Jerry, delicious bottle of pure vintage which, while in the midst of drinking, some 18th amendment snatched away." Risking words, Hellman didn't have the control over language or men that she did later.

Hellman's diary recorded more than girlish longings. It portrayed a co-cooned writer, Lillian Hellman, emerging. She discovered that the urge to write was somehow tied up with the romantic and erotic stories of her life. The despair of failing to live fully tied to the despair of a writer fretting about clumsy efforts to record her life. She tried hard to avoid the trite language, the compulsive recording of inanities. She wrote in her forward, "Because every-body begins by describing their surrounds—I shall try to refrain from doing so. . . . I shall say—I am a seeker of the truth. I arrive at conclusions then dis-card them." She knew then that her protean personality moved toward meaning but couldn't settle. Her next sentence is contradictory: "I am essen-tially artificial in my struggle for the truth. For instance, what is written here will probably be strangely influenced by the fact that at least I can imagine someone reading it."

Repeatedly in the diary she wrote under Jerry's influence or in response to his interest, "unconsciously influenced by the idea of his reading it." Since "that thought is Cheap," she resisted the connections of eroticism, audience, and creativity. She had just begun to explore the intersections and possibili-ties that can result in the tangle of achievement. She had succumbed, sexually and rhetorically, to the age-old prescriptions for young women, but she had also begun to look for something complex, different in writing. She began to bring the parts of herself together, the eroticism of New Orleans and the innovative energy of New York. The two cities had introduced her to the peoples of the world, fostered her self-inventions, and forged in her a creative bent as wayward as it was adamant. She "never liked any life where there was one group of people." The mix of ideas and feelings moved her too. She asked in her diary, "When some emotions are entirely new, but intermixed with old, experienced ones—how are they expressed?" A playwright and memoirist to be, a "born actress," Lillian knew that performance and inven-tion figured in her approach to life.[1]

In February 1923 she wrote, "Tonight Jerry told me I am like bellrates ma-ganesed–effervescing for a moment, stimulating for a moment and then gone leaving a nauseating effect." In its natural form, manganese lacks luster and is brittle but has great market value. Perhaps Jerry didn't know quite what he was talking about so he went on to tell her she was "composed of another chemical, radium." Startled by his scientific assessments, she chose to think them complimentary. In classic Hellman contradiction she responded, "I be-lieve I got dramatic, but quite eloquently & subtly so. It's very amusing how my mind runs to extreme." By April, the romance was rocky, but in a face-saving gesture she wrote, "I haven't quite gotten over the idea that any one should tire of me—somehow I can't understand it—he's probably lacking, not I—However, that last statement,—what a sublime egofest! "On his reap-pearance some months later, she marveled, "He seems to think I'm quite wonderful—My God! The number of people I've managed to fool. Perhaps I shall make a success of my life this way." Insecurity lurked in her word "fool," as she seemed to attract those as outspoken as she.[2] Hellman never could re-sist passion if she felt connection, even if she knew pain was inevitable. She had learned on the bayou in New Orleans that "the mixture of ecstasy as it clashed with criticism of myself and the man was to be repeated all my life."[3] She recognized both emotions early and decided she had to upset things in order to develop interest. After a painful breakup with Jerry she wrote, "One year, only one year, and here we are ready to take the same path, I ready to endure all the pain & hurt once more merely seeing it all quite clearly and yet ready to take a running jump."[4] Hellman could vamp as well or better than most young girls, and she vamped with zest. She never had to invent that. But she never relaxed and depended on her success with men for a life. Her diary recorded her reluctance to give herself over completely, even when she wanted to hang on: "The intensity was universal and I know that I can not arouse such emotion often."[5]

While she may have had some previous sexual experience, at least with foreplay—petting was "in" during the 1920s—Hellman recorded one event with the finest of pens, writing in the smallest possible hand. Only with a magnifying glass can it be read: "Up to 2 hours we laid on the couch and should have had children but for many reasons didn't. Then I being the more sensitive of the two had a strong mental relapse. Anyway, this sort of thing makes me rather weak and inclined to be dramatic. . . Yet I couldn't leave— we seemed to reach a certain stage and their erections recede whereas the woman because she never reaches as high a point recedes with only 1/10 as much speed." Jerry's lack of attention to Lilly's high point didn't diminish her desire. Apparently the affair lasted about a year, on and off. On Christmas Eve she wrote of being with Jerry, who "kept quite still" while Lilly "enjoyed the ride." One regret she had when they broke it off was that she had just begun to find her "way in the bedroom."

At a later date, Hellman recorded getting drunk with Howard Meyer and kissing "rather wildly." She profoundly disappointed herself because he had great appeal physically but "held no attraction for her mentally." She wryly recorded that she would "have to create another excuse." She liked him, but that was never enough for Hellman, who needed a kind of brilliance to excite her. In the most impassioned sentence of the diary she wrote, "Oh god—if I could only find a human being with both attractions—are other people more easily satisfied—and do we always make compromises with ourself?" These two questions haunted her for life.

Both Hellman's diary entries about Jerry and the "story" of Alex at the center of *Maybe: A Story* recorded love/hate relationships and her lifelong quest to understand the connections of love and sex to the mind and body. *Maybe*'s narrator, Lillian, tells the story of "Alex," the first young man she slept with. She remembers that she went to bed with him four times, and the last time he questioned her cleanliness, her "smell." She should have known better, but for years afterward she could not relinquish the fear of her own sexual odor. She flirted, she had casual affairs, she married, but she restrained an ardor born of New Orleans heat. Only years later did Lillian discover Alex's malice. An acquaintance, Sarah, told her that "Alex" had complained about Sarah's "high odor," telling her she should learn the Jewish art of ritual bathing. "Alex" may have been a fictional name for Jerry, or Jerry may have followed in Alex's wake. Both stories show that Hellman, when things went awry, turned bitterly critical of herself, then avenged herself on others. Her contempt could be as powerful as her lust.

Hellman was also troubled by another fact of life. Inevitably others judge.[6] From the beginning of her adolescence to the end of her mother's life, Hellman fretted that her mother worried about Lillian's sex life. She wrote in 1934, "It still remains a constant irritant to me that at twenty-nine I have to account to mama for the details of my life. . . I guess someday she is going to find out I'm not a virgin, and that's going to be the end of our beautiful friendship."[7] Hellman had long since lost her virginal state, and she could not understand anyone's fascination with repression.

And luck was with her. At nineteen she found a good job and a good man, and started the process of becoming the Lillian Hellman of fame and infamy. When Lillian returned to New York from the trip with her mother, she quickly moved into her adult life with fortune and élan. Not surprisingly, she became part of the bookish party scene. She had attended summer school at Columbia University in 1922 and 1923 and one night attended a party where she met Julian Messner, vice president and sales manager at Boni & Liveright, a publishing house that "made the sky glow," publishing the likes of Theodore Dreiser, Eugene O'Neill, Sherwood Anderson, and William Faulkner.[8] Lillian must have shown off for him successfully, because she landed a job at the publishing house that fit her perfectly: "a merger of culture and anarchy . . . which responded to the fun of things."[9]

First she was a clerk, but she couldn't file and wandered aimlessly; finally she was set up as a manuscript reader. Blurred class distinctions set off the editors and staff, with women serving as decorative and available sexual objects. Still, a sense of democratic opportunity permeated the offices, creating a community of young male and female literary potentials. Through fellow employees and their connections she met Bennett Cerf, Leon Shimkin, and Richard Simon, who went on to start Simon & Schuster, and Edward Weeks, an author who would edit the *Atlantic Monthly*. In the years to follow, she would work with all of them. Louis Kronenberger signed on to work there too.

Boni & Liveright was a magnet for the talented, or perhaps its peculiarity fostered talent. In a six-year span, Liveright published six Nobel Prize winners. Brilliance and a penchant for the antic glossed over the troubles of the firm and the world. "Although the doings at other parties could involve public endearments, stained and ripped garments, periodical passing out in public, disappearing couples, maudlin recitals, unmanageable guests, almost as much spilled liquor as swilled, and almost as many gate-crashers as guests, what alone might have set Liveright entertainment apart was the prominence of the guest list."[10] Through these parties and a little actual work, Hellman, a kind of gate-crasher, saw firsthand the rigors and chances of publishing and the importance of activist politics.

New York politics had a long history of scandal, and she had little faith in government's ability to find solutions to city problems. Tammany Hall rubbed elbows with the Teapot Dome corruption affair heating up in Washington, reaffirming her suspicions of corrupt goings-on in high places. With the end of Woodrow Wilson's presidency in 1921 and the succession of Warren Harding (who died in 1923) followed by Calvin Coolidge, conservative politics began to put the lid on political and social movements. Hellman saw Horace Liveright on the front line defending literature from censors, his chief opponent John Sumner, secretary of the Society for the Suppression of

Vice. In 1923 Liveright opposed Supreme Court Justice John Ford's bill to impose censorship on publishers.[11] The passion for ideas she saw in men such as Liveright gave Hellman impetus.

The excesses of Boni & Liveright made Hellman's spirit soar. The office was "a wacky joint in a brownstone house on 48th Street."[12] Liveright "waged war on stodginess. . . . tousled the proprieties . . . refused to trample on life."[13] She alternated between keeping a low profile and making nasty statements to undo the smug. She bragged, "A lady told me I shouldn't make fun of Mr. Vanderbilt and I found, it seems, a new way of telling her to go fuck herself."[14]

Politically and philosophically, Hellman had found people like her — talented and reckless, procrastinating and driven, political and flagrant. But she saw, too, the time wasted, liking the "efficiency cleanups" at the office best of all, when a seriousness of purpose matched her goals.[15] Hellman learned that working the system was important to getting writing published. Her life had shifted for the better.

Always of a political mind-set, Lillian thrilled to her coworkers' passionate talk about the politics and scandals of the mid-1920s. Their political intensity set an example she never abandoned. Equality and freedom became more than abstract words for her, and politics became something worth the effort. She had taken for granted the Suffrage Amendment of 1920 giving women the right to vote. She now determined to act out the equality given to her by law. Politics began to seem upfront and personal. In the mid-1920s racial injustice seemed rampant. When others showed their prejudice against blacks arriving from the South, she confronted their racism but persisted in calling the naysayers wops or kikes, inventing names when she wasn't sure of their category, in "joyous revolt against pundits."[16]

Several notorious cases horrified her. In the Rosewood massacre, three hundred whites marched into Rosewood, Florida, and killed at least eight African Americans. Though no stranger to racism, Hellman began to fear signs of organized hatred. With the Harlem Renaissance close at hand and publication of Jessie Fauset's novel *There Is Confusion*, Hellman felt that literature, drama, and film could influence what she was already calling the masses. And though she knew she wasn't really "socialistic," she despised those who wielded power or picked on the poor to fatten their own wallets.[17]

Torn between the thrill of the passes men made at Liveright and the pretend-monogamous impulses taught to girls from birth, Hellman found a young man she thought would do for the expected marriage: Arthur Kober, a "fine man, kind, generous." He worked as a theater press agent, and possibly

Lillian met him at a Liveright publishing party. Just beginning a successful life as a writer of stage and screen, he went on to write over thirty screenplays between 1930 and 1946, as well as two smash hits on Broadway: *Having a Wonderful Time* and *Wish You Were Here*. His *New Yorker* articles and stories collected in books spanned five decades. Kober's record shows he was far more than the "folk artist of the Bronx and the Catskills" William Wright described in his Hellman biography.

Hellman liked Kober enormously and felt he was talented and hard-working in a field she respected. Her parents loved him. He was marriage material. She became pregnant by him while she worked at Liveright but refused to marry until she had an illegal abortion. The news of her pregnancy and abortion spread like fire at Liveright and made her a curiosity—a woman who did not bad-mouth the father and would not marry because she was pregnant. Hellman was livid at their prurient interest but was responsible for the furor. She told editor Donald Friede that she "was desperate to find an abortionist" and then chose to recover on the deep, worn couches in the publication house offices. She got herself noticed, knowing their avid interest in gossip and intrigue. Although she felt the physical and spiritual damage from such an ordeal, her drama kept them from firing her. She used it to show them a Lillian of strength and courage, a different kind of girl from the simpering brokenhearted ones men expected. She liked drama when it served her. In retrospect she wrote, "I was rash, overdaring, certain only that any adventure was worth having, and increasingly muddled by the Puritan conscience that made me pay for the adventures."[18] Surely marriage would cure it all.

She consented to marry Kober months after the illegal abortion, which he paid for. Whether or not she really substituted an ugly gray chiffon for a pretty dress on their wedding day, December 31, 1925, doesn't matter; the drab dress she described in memoirs symbolized her feelings about marriage. She liked Arthur better than that, telling him he was "the nicest man alive and mama worships your very feet." But fondness and physical pleasure didn't reach deep enough to electrify her. She married a man she liked, enjoyed. But what next?

Kober was serious, smart, and funny, and he adored her. A press agent, that breed of writer "traditionally first to be blamed and last to be thanked," Kober did well.[19] From 1922 to just before he married Hellman, Kober wrote press releases for the Shubert brothers, owners and managers of a large theater empire on Broadway, gradually moving to a more independent position as press agent for entertainment moguls Edgar Selwyn and Sam Harris, whose melodrama *Broadway* had hit it big in 1925. Nevertheless, Kober struggled to find a better place in New York's theatrical scene. He joked to friend Sam Marx that he married Hellman so her father would put up money for Arthur's production of *Me*, Henry Meyer's melodrama.[20] A week before the Kobers married, the only play he ever produced closed after a few days, ending his dreams of a career in production. But his dreams of a happy marriage seemed to be fulfilled.

The Kobers shared a love of talk, an ear for dialects, excellent wit. He worked hard and was ambitious, striving for a happy, conventional life. Raised in poverty in the Bronx, he went to temple weekly as a teen, attended night school to supplement his high school diploma, and had many friends. He worried about getting places on time, recording in his diary his time of arrival when he didn't.[21] Everyone liked "Artie," who patterned his famous satiric character, Bella Gross, after himself. With such a nice man, Hellman thought that she would settle into conventional womanhood. As was the custom, she left work to become a full-time housewife.

Kober hoped for a loving, supportive wife at home and Hellman assumed the role. Sex was good. Kober's diary records her eagerness, which often outstripped his own; he worried about her enjoyment of oral sex, "going down sessions" that he found perverse. But he loved his wife passionately and was game, as his diaries attest. They played bridge with other couples, joined Max for poker at the Hoyle Club, and went to the theater and theatrical parties Kober's job made available. He liked his wife's fire, though the cold wash of her lows unnerved him. Hellman, striving to fit into the married woman mold, was more mellow than she ever would be again. At ease with each other, willing to work hard, and sharing a love of laughter, they fit together remarkably well. Together they saved money to support his hoped for theatrical productions, and she definitely did her part. Both she and Kober imagined a life of good sex, children, and traditions. They worked on it.

Life as Mrs. Kober quickly settled into a routine in 1926, and while her affection for her husband didn't waver, her restless spirit found little fulfillment in marriage. She spent the first year of marriage finding her way as a married woman. Marriage manuals of the time praised the "benefit" of a married woman's freedom to go about on her own. But Hellman had always taken personal freedom for granted, even if she hid some of her wayward adventures. Married, she felt bound to an ideal and unsuited to the life it demanded. She felt stuck and she had the blues.

Too smart and aware to think marriage would be unremitting bliss, its structure and effect nevertheless surprised her. She had, after all, reached the highest goal for a woman: she married a man who loved her and presumably had a future. While she made light of the social pressure to marry, saying it didn't much matter if a woman found a suitable man she liked, she assumed only a "pretend cool." Marriage meant success and security, and she knew it. She tried on the role immediately, taking up New Orleans cooking and researching Alabama's southern food that her mother loved. She told Arthur amusing stories of bridge parties and long afternoons with friends. She even took Russian and English literature courses from Columbia University, developing a passion for Dostoevsky, thinking of writing about Lewis Carroll and his *Alice in Wonderland* or writing a biography of Herman Melville and his harpoon and white whale; she found herself classically caught between youth and manhood in a convoluted young woman's way.[22] Then she became enthralled with Dante and his dramatic version of heaven, purgatory, and hell.[23] The clearly defined misery and ecstasy contrasted with her own life, favorably and not. She lived the life she thought appropriate for a smart, liberated wife.

Disenchanted, she felt passive, unwound, tamped down. Her personal life lacked drama, interest. She read avariciously, racing through Marcel Proust and D. H. Lawrence. She began to sneak bouts of writing short stories. She didn't need stealth with Arthur, who encouraged her. But she knew her writing didn't measure up, knew she was expected above all to support his writing, knew that something ate away at her spirit making her listless. She felt unable to focus on an idea long enough to get its bite. She wanted work, some kind of intensity in a life dulled by routine. She sensed the publishing house wouldn't rehire her; she had been a lackluster employee, and she could already see the signs of its decline. By day she began to go into the city from their suburban house on Long Island, hang around Arthur's work on 42nd Street talking to Herman Shumlin or Jed Harris, and then wander to the 48th Street Liveright offices to see her "old friend Louis Kronenberger" or lunch with Julian Messner.[24]

Arthur knew keeping his wife happy was not merely a matter of paying the bills and taking her to the marriage bed. His own career had taken off, and he began to parcel out some of his press agent writing to her. In a sense, she became Kober's "assistant, the angular girl with frizzy hair and a masculine face."[25] She met people who one day would be "greats," but like herself seemed to be marking time–Ira Gershwin, Dore Schary, Billy Rose, and John Huston. Other than that, she diddled. As press agent for *The Bunk of 1926*

Lillian should have fared better, since the district attorney's office banned the play and took it to court as "smut." But the scandal didn't help the play and it closed, leaving Hellman to look for more work. She read scripts for Harry Moses, identified by Hellman as the "underwear magnate," and Leo Bulgakov, who owned an acting company. Working for them, she spotted W. A. Drake's adaptation of Vicki Baum's *Grand Hotel*, which became a huge hit in 1930–1931, after making the producer's rounds. Ironically Kober got the original rights at Hellman's suggestion, but when he couldn't get Rouben Mamoulian to direct, he let the option lapse.

Herman Shumlin finally agreed to produce and direct it, after Moses softened him up with two hot toddies.[26] Thus began Shumlin's rise to fame as producer and director during a low period when he reeled from his failed partnership with old friend Jed Harris—now the wunderkind of the 1920s. Shumlin, a fiery, outspoken man whose life would later intersect with Lillian's on many levels, already owed her one. Neither of them knew it in 1926, when all of them were unknowns—Arthur Kober, Herman Shumlin, Lillian Hellman, and George Haight. Each understood the devastation of failure before finding the wonderful coincidence of their success. In 1926, no one seemed significant, least of all herself.

She plugged on. Kober encouraged her to send book reviews to the New York newspapers, even to the newly founded, elite *New Yorker*. The last six months of the Kobers' first year together saw Hellman have four book reviews published in the *New York Herald Tribune* books section. Arthur undoubtedly arranged the deal for the first review, but after that editor Irita Van Doren commissioned them for $4.70 a column.[27] Hellman mocked this early career as a published writer, saying she was known as the "Ronald Firbank reviewer," who wrote short reviews buried in the back about nothing of importance. Mrs. Kober nevertheless found *Our Doctors* to be "fictionalized Science for Lay Readers" and *Summer Bachelors* to be "light reading good of its kind." She wrote opinionated, tight, and tart reviews; she had begun to find her writing style. What she lacked was an ineffable desire, stirring her to live fully, to write from the gut.

Lillian Hellman set her sights on stirring and being stirred. She needed impetus and audience to captivate, but that was to come. She was halfway there, embodying both the curve of New Orleans and the edge of New York City, the outlines of a character. Now she had to make use of them. At this time she began her most important and enduring creation, the character she called "I." To get it right she had to call on her erotic creativity and her blistery intellectual aggression to invent an ever-flexible self.

Neurotic Ennui

In the spring of 1928, the *Paris Comet* asked Kober to come to Paris as acting editor for several months and assured him he could bring his wife. They jumped at the offer with heady excitement. The *New Yorker* for nostalgic Americans in Paris, the *Comet* needed experienced writers and editors. Presumably because of his work ethic and his publications in the newly minted *New Yorker*, the *Comet* asked Kober to sign on.[28] He also came cheap. With the likes of Ernest Hemingway, F. Scott Fitzgerald, and Gertrude Stein holding court with the expatriot literati in Paris, the couple prepared to leave New York. Hellman began packing. Methodically detailing packing lists, making a budget, listing the gifts she would buy for those left behind, boning up on her New Orleans French, Mrs. Kober made ready to board the ocean liner for Paris.[29] Later she remembered going on this "honeymoon" in 1927, but their passport issued in 1928 says differently.[30] By early April they were on their way. The Kobers had been married a little over two years, and more than Arthur's career hung in the balance.

They set up housekeeping in a small hotel on rue Jacob in the sixth ar-rondissement,[31] just a few blocks from Pont Neuf, the oldest of Parisian bridges, on the left bank of the Seine. The Palais du Luxembourg and its lovely park were a few blocks from their hotel. While Arthur worked, Hellman walked and looked up at the sights. Curious to gain a feel for the place, she left their damp apartment every chance she got. On Sundays, she made a picnic and they ate at Versailles.[32] Picture-perfect in many ways, Paris depressed her. She couldn't locate its meaning, but it seemed a metaphor for her own "still life," or *nature mortre* as the French call this kind of painting.

Wet, dark, and cold, Paris oppressed. Yet shimmering light and mists rose from the Seine, glimpsed through leafless trees. Paris felt haunted, imposing. Theatrically Old World, its large buildings were smudged gray, stained from years of industrial commerce. Always a glamorous city, with the Eiffel Tower rising magnificently for all to see, Paris seemed brazenly new too. The tower sported 250,000 colored bulbs spelling out Citroën visible up to forty kilome-ters on three sides from 1925 to 1936. The sophistication of Paris was matched by a smaller charm too. In the streets off boulevard St. Germaine, rue Jacob, and the streets neighboring it, the buildings surrounded cobblestone court-yards that turned colorful with small tree blossoms and bulbs once spring arrived. Hellman could see the beauty but couldn't feel it.

Along the winding cobblestone streets lived writers Hellman revered. Disenchanted with the political climate and commercial capitalism of the

United States, the Lost Generation had come to Paris to publish, establish an intellectual community, and wait out Prohibition. Janet Flanner, who wrote "Letter from Paris" for the *New Yorker* under the name of Genet, lived on rue Bonaparte, a stone's throw away from the Kobers' lodging, one of rue Jacob's small hotels and apartments. Flanner, writer Natalie Clifford Barney, and artist Romaine Brooks all served as hosts to Stein, Colette, Anaïs Nin, Claire Booth Luce, Pablo Picasso, Ernest Hemingway, Jean-Paul Sartre, James Joyce, and T. S. Eliot. Artist Stella Bowen, then living with Ford Madox Ford, remembers parties in the rue Jacob given by Miss Barney, where André Gide and Edmond Jaloux and Paul Valéry mixed with "exotic young American women who, rushing in where angels feared to tread, obtained an excellent response from *ces messieurs*."[33] Throughout her life, Hellman rushed in where angels feared to tread, but not in Paris, certainly not at Barney's parties. The Kobers lived among but outside the society of the famous.

Kober's job made him a peripheral part of this intriguing mix of people. The Kobers gathered nightly at the intersection of the boulevard du Montparnasse and the boulevard Raspail, going to Le Dome for coffee, sharing their days with other young artists and writers. Many must have felt as gawky and adolescent as Lillian did, but they may have had the wherewithal to better pretend. John Bright, a fellow writer Hellman later met in Hollywood, joked that he went to Paris "officially to meet [Havelock] Ellis and Anatole France and Ernest Hemingway," but "secretly to get laid."[34] Hellman's goal differed. She went to Paris to meet the literati, the writers fast changing her thinking, and to become one of them. Disappointed, the best she could do was "get laid." Most literary lights gave her barely a glance. Although some like Flanner went out of their way to encourage her and make her comfortable, Lillian Hellman Kober was an outsider looking in, a "bent pitch" in the words of New Orleans blues.

In 1928, at age twenty-three, she knew little about art and high culture. Paris seemed the center of the world to the young couple, the gathering place of talented artists and writers, the nerve center of the arts, the "happy meeting-place of all those questioning foreigners who had succeeded in throwing off the shackles and prejudices of their home towns and had not yet wearied of an aimless freedom."[35] Hellman, too young to let go of her bearings, did not feel free. The writers later reflected that café life was often dead boring. It flourished because lingering over a coffee delayed the return to freezing lodgings in bleak Parisian hotels and houses.

So she watched, waited, and improvised. Life in Paris shimmered on the surface, outdoors, for all to see and hear of life's brilliance, its turbulence, its sordidness. American prudery and privacy capitulated in favor of French *aire de alfresco*. Americans in Paris adapted the café, extolling the food, the arts, and their own antics for all to see and hear. As Hemingway put café life without a hint of irony, "the scum of Greenwich Village, New York, has been skimmed off and deposited in large ladle fulls."[36] But Hellman knew the Left Bank émigré writers had something going. Extraordinary books came out of Paris at this time: Hemingway's *The Sun Also Rises* and F. Scott Fitzgerald's *The Great Gatsby*. She heard art and literature in the talk and felt it in the air of the crowded Les Deux Magots and the Café de Flore next door. The antics and the excessive waste bothered her, a work ethic puritan, but the crazy antics made good gossip, and Hellman loved gossip. The Nobel Prize–winning writer Sinclair Lewis was told to shut up by a resident "serious" artist because he was "just a best-seller." The painter Pascin offered Hemingway one of his beautiful young models to "bang," though reportedly Ernest declined.[37] Hellman wavered between envy and disapproval. She wrote a friend that she had seen Malcolm Cowley in a restaurant and he looked "decayed." She never liked exiles.[38]

Except for Flanner, Hellman didn't like the women much either, but she noticed the women artists of Montparnasse had liberated themselves from the traditional grind of home and family. She wanted their seeming liberation yet felt bewildered about how to get it. The independent woman of France had a political edge, not just the suffragette and liberation politics of America but the politics of nation. Even Carl Dreyer's film *La Passion de Jeanne d'Arc* made a splash in magazines and newspapers while she was there. The Catholic Church had beatified Joan in 1909, and the archbishop of Paris threatened to initiate a boycott on the film when rumor had it that a scene showed Joan disgusted by priests taunting her with Communion. Joan, abandoned by king and church, had Europe in an uproar. The antifascist message in the film connected with Hellman's surfacing independence, but it would be years before her own fascination with Joan surfaced in her adaptation of *The Lark*. For now, she watched these women of France. The furor that surrounded them and their politics began to cast ominous shadows from something darker in the murky climate of Paris. Both stimulated and cowed by the forceful political climate, Hellman watched and wondered.

The French and the American ways of life mixed uneasily during this period. Hellman couldn't see villains clearly enough, but she saw her own weaknesses all too well. Always an avid newspaper reader, she poured over *Le Temps*, *Paris-Journal*, *L'Humanité*–all politically different. She found the future unstable: six French governments rose and fell between 1924 and 1927.

Anti-Semitism wafted through Europe's streets, and even a naive, inexperienced young woman from the States could hardly overlook the signs of fascism in Europe. Paradoxically, in Paris many artists felt Mussolini the answer to Italian dysfunction and Stalin the hope of the Russian people. Paul Valéry announced "a crisis of the mind" in Europe; Paul Tillich identified the "anxiety of meaninglessness." Bombastic expatriot Americans, rich White Russians, suspicious British—all pontificated on everything. The expats living in Paris masqueraded as politically engaged, but their motivation likely narrowed down to an excellent exchange rate of the dollar and the franc.[39] Art, personality, and economics mixed with a vague kind of politics that excluded hangers-on, which Hellman definitely was.

Hellman's crisis in Paris was a neurotic ennui. Restless and aimless, she cast about for a life she could live, an invention that would adjust to unfamiliar and uncomfortable surroundings. She didn't want to be lost or found in Paris; what she wanted was meaningful work. An experienced New Orleans infighter and a canny New Yorker negotiator, she knew enough to lie low when outgunned. She decided to keep her chin down until she figured out what she needed to be and how to be it. Paris and her travels through Europe became an experimental thinking ground for personal change. In the meantime, she felt wretched.

Hellman clearly fashioned her character Lillian in *Maybe* after the young woman she was in 1928, lost among all those unknowables. In the novel/memoir, Hellman tells the story of showering in Paris repeatedly in her effort to clean up her sexual smell and come to terms with her femininity, her strong sexuality. Her self-consciousness erupted in a Kober family drama. "What passed for her refusal" of sex with Arthur forced her to self-reflection, and she took her conventional, repressed sexuality on the road. She left him to travel to Lake Maggiore alone. Lillian had a one-night stand with an Englishman who, with his wife's collusion, preyed on women he thought rich. The sordid outcome of the liaison tarnished the beauty of Stresa on the lake. When the man and his wife spoke German to cover their disappointment in Hellman's lack of riches, she understood their conversation, having learned German through Aunt Jennie and Aunt Hannah's coded exchanges. But she grasped more than their con, discovering her distaste and disappointment in loveless, meaningless sex.[40] The casual bed made a bad proving ground for the young Mrs. Kober. Such shabbiness suited her less than the uneasy and glorified marriage bed. Though discerning the fictive from the real in *Maybe* is difficult, other sources verify the liaison, and a letter Hellman wrote a friend at the time verifies her confusion: "Things seem so unarranged for me, so terribly in need of clearing up and settling for good and all."[41] She had begun to search for a meaningful, deeply sexual response, somehow knowing her autonomy and her creativity depended on it.

Though Hellman hesitated to give any theory too much credence, from her early days in Paris until the end of her life, she understood herself and her world through a Freudian lens. She knew little of Freud at that time, just party talk about his 1920 volume *The Ego and the Id.* Freud's recently published *Inhibitions, Symptoms, and Anxiety* seemed more descriptive of Hellman's malaise. Paris, alive with romantic cynicism, dripped Freudian complexity. Twelve years later she would read Freud's *Civilizations and Its Discontents* and begin analysis with the famous Gregory Zilboorg, plumbing the depths of her psyche. In 1928, without therapy or any particular psychological insight, she turned to independent experience to give her meaning; but until she turned in on herself, she learned nothing. She simply didn't know what to do about alternately craving solitude and connection.

Despite her cavalier attitude toward convention, she longed to integrate love, sex, and marriage. She itched for intensity. Marriage offered much but not white-hot heat. Kober gave her a long leash and never brought her to "heel," as biographer Wright so inelegantly suggested she needed. But a leash is a leash. Certainly a husband's demands and pleadings did not solve Hellman's worries. She had read T. S. Eliot's "The Hollow Men" and she feared her world ending in the "whimper" far more than the "bang." She needed to find the courage to experiment, then face the disappointments or punishment.

Hellman decided to leave Paris. Tired of authors and artists whose success and maturity and pretend freedom reminded her of how much she had yet to learn, she left without Kober, who was caught up in the excitement of becoming a writer among the world's writing elite. She didn't like the feeling of being tied down, and she felt humiliated in a city that shrouded her color in its own design. Going home would give her a respite—time for solitude, time to write, time to find out if the life she had was enough. She needed to grow up. Later she reflected, "I usually wanted to get away from where I was. Just blindly. Instinctively."[42] She wrote from New York to a friend, "I'm glad you liked Paris and am sorry that I didn't. I loved Italy . . . When you get tired of dirt and warm weather go into Switzerland, look at the mountains and be bored stiff."[43] Kober wrote these friends too: "An odd state of events this: Lillian left for New York last week, bored with Paris and anxious to get to New York to do some work, I . . . found a job on the magazine. . . . And so it stands."[44]

Torn between duty to Arthur and insecurity about her status, she toyed with the idea of returning to Paris, writing friends that she would go back if they would put her up, promising to "clean, sweep, cook, sing, fornicate, and sew."[45] The humorous litany of promises corresponds precisely to her notion of marriage. And it didn't sound all that appealing. She would stay a world apart, though she wasn't sure the separation was a good thing. Kober seemed to ride out her desire to live on her own; he was adoring, committed in his own way, and she liked him. In summer 1928 as she returned to New York City, even with others in attendance, she missed Kober but not life with him. She learned in Paris that some girls just "turn out to be more lawless than some other girls."[46] She turned out to be one of them.

To add to her woes, back in New York she stayed with her parents on West 95th Street. At first grateful to be home, she soon found the arrangement galling. Her mother tried to coerce her into behaving like a beleaguered young married woman mourning her husband's long absence. Hellman would have none of it. For her mother's sake she practiced the art of dissembling, of telling good-girl lies to get out of the house. Max knew her too well to be fooled, but Julia loved Kober and her naïveté helped her believe what she wanted. Since Julia traveled with Max whenever he let her, she did not understand Hellman's solo return. Julia's history told her that husbands stray, and she worried on Hellman's behalf about Arthur's behavior. Julia wasn't far off track. During their seven years of marriage, Arthur never spent an entire year faithful to Hellman. In 1966 Arthur wrote a zany letter to Norman Podhoretz, editor of Commentary, of the "girls he has bedded" noting in a postscript, "Not to breathe a word to Lillian who poor, benighted girl has always considered me a devoted and faithful husband. And so I was—in my own fashion . . . don't publish any of this . . . one or two of the above mentioned enthralled ladies are still alive—though breathing hard."[47] His fidelity or lack of it missed the point. Hellman knew of Kober's devotion and brushed off his wanderings just as she did her mother's misgivings. Hellman, desperate to get away from husband and parents, found a small apartment on West 55 Street—a nowhere neighborhood but one she could call her own.

Partying and sexual experimentation left Hellman feeling dissatisfied; she had felt soiled by her affair with the Englishman in Italy. But she needed a jolt to resurrect her desire to work, to move forward, to feel alive. David Cort wasn't the answer to her malaise, but for a while he seemed like he might be. Cort, a young writer who later wrote for Time and became the foreign editor of Life magazine, met Hellman sometime after her return to New York. Both in their early twenties, they leaped into a relationship that made them feel in love.[48] Cort was a romantic man who presumably believed in love's tie to sex, though he later published an article including a quip that became famous: "Sex is the great amateur art."[49] On-again/off-again lovers for four years, both found self-worth in the other.

Still devoted to Kober in her wandering way, Hellman wanted desperately to make the marriage work. But not at the expense of her spirit. Cort revived her spirit and didn't ask much. Their eventual breakup devastated Cort, and he cared enough to hang on to her letters, passionately romantic and sexual, complete with Hellman's erotic drawings in the margins. Their letters to each other contained mutual interest and inspiration. In the 1970s he wanted to publish them because his relationship with Lillian was a high point of his life, "the classic love story of pre-Depression New York emancipated morality."[50] Hellman threatened to sue, and he withdrew his plan. In 1976, forty-five years after their breakup, Cort wrote Hellman that their relationship was the "worst thing that ever happened to me," causing a near breakdown and five years of psychoanalysis. Her take on it was that they had been "lost kids, maybe, bewildered, sometimes mean to each other, but not bad, and in love."[51] Why they broke so completely is a matter for speculation. Hellman fostered and nurtured friendships with her ex-lovers but not with Cort.[52]

If being in love with one man while loving another wasn't conventional, it felt real. Hellman's affair with Cort taught her something valuable, something that would keep her sane during her years with Dashiell Hammett. She could and did love men simultaneously, for who they were and what they did for her thinking, her creativity.

Conflicted about men, she increasingly focused on her ambition to be a writer. She hit the New York writing scene as hard as she could. In her film *The Searching Wind,* written ten years later, the character David tells Cassie "go ahead and cry, kid. You know that's the best part of Paris. Nobody's ever watching you." But Cassie's reply is pure young Hellman: "I don't want to cry. I want to work." If she learned anything in Paris, she learned from Flanner the value of work and that "women of talent have a harder boat to row."[53] Nothing would be given to her. She knew she had to develop whatever talent she might have, and selling it wouldn't be easy. Working out of a small room on the fifth floor of a building on West 42nd, she clung to the center of Manhattan and wrote. The *Paris Comet* under Kober's influence published a couple of her stories that reflected a glib emptiness. "I Call Her Mama Now," published in the *Comet* and later in the *American Spectator,* shows Hellman's flair for dialogue and language but little else. She could mock the intellectual world, her narrator liking "inhibited writers," but she had few ideas of her own. In her piece "Introspective Writing" for the same magazine, only the rashness of her character allowed her to so glibly discuss the writing process with the voice of someone in the know. To her friend Helen she wrote in self-mockery, "I've had a story accepted by some idiotic magazine and it was variously compared to Proust, Laura Jean Libby, Virginia Woolf and Alger."[54] To be a successful writer, she needed to think harder. She felt outranked and she was.

Hellman took the time to write in earnest, determined to outgrow the gaping girl she had been in Paris. Kober returned from his stint at the *Paris Comet* in early fall. The *Comet* had closed four months after his arrival. Back in New York, Kober maintained a consistent presence in the trendy, well-respected *New Yorker*, but that didn't help Hellman. He simply didn't have enough clout to get his wife published. He managed to get other magazines to publish a couple of her "lady-writer short stories" as she called them, "the kind where a lady lays down her fork and knows it's over."[55] But she aspired to the *New Yorker*. Perhaps because of Kober's popularity, the editors wrote unfailingly polite rejection letters, extraordinary in their diplomacy, amazingly fast in their response. About "Daughter Alice," K. S. Angell wrote, "The modern daughter and the sorrows she causes her mother has been pretty well-over-written we fear. A good deal of this is excellent yet somehow the whole didn't ring entirely true as conversation." The *New Yorker* editors' frustration with Hellman's writing persisted. In another rejection letter, Angell wrote, "It doesn't seem to be actual life to us and is a bit improbable on some points. I felt it particularly didn't stand up when the girl began blowing out the candles and talking about Alice Foote MacDougall's school of house furnishings. No matter how outspoken a girl is, I am pretty sure she wouldn't say that about a young man's mother in any case."

Apparently the *New Yorker* had little knowledge of what a young woman like Hellman might hear and say. But Angell encouraged her kindly: "We hope you will not be discouraged by these rejections because we feel sure you will hit it before long."[56] Hellman felt hurt and furious at her inability to find her way in fiction. She knew her stories weren't good, but girlish romantic fantasy was all she could come up with. In her failure, she directed her anger inward, despising herself for her perpetual adolescence. Still, she persisted in writing stories and sending them to the *New Yorker*, sometimes under her maiden name (what a phrase for Hellman) and her married name when "Arthur suggested" she send a piece. In some cases, she had Kober speak to the editors about something she was going to send. That didn't work either. She just couldn't get the right pitch.

In these turning point years, she experimented with writing, looked for a successful genre, and tried to contribute to the family finances. Though women did get hired for writing in the late 1920s, the jobs often entailed lackluster, underpaid, rote work that male writers sloughed off. After Kober returned to the States, Hellman took the odd jobs that spun off Arthur's rising star as writer and press agent. Busy again as a press agent, Kober worked for Marc Connelly's Pulitzer Prize–winning play, *The Green Pastures*. Thus Kober's cast-offs were only third rate, not bottom of the barrel, so her work had its attractions.

She became a play reader for Anne Nichols, who was trying to become a producer after her wildly successful and rather hokey *Abie's Irish Rose*. Hellman then worked for an "arty little group who didn't pay me after the second week" and "had a good time" for four months in Rochester, New York, working for Cukor-Kondolph, a theater stock company. For a while she threw off thoughts of becoming a writer, giving her time "to listen to a gangster who ran Rochester's underworld."[57] She also gambled every night for money to spend in Europe that summer of 1929. Hellman's tales of winning at poker may have been her version of fish stories, as by some accounts she never knew how many cards she had and had no card sense. What she had was luck, however, and that sometimes sufficed. She liked being accountable only to herself in where she went and who she saw. Paris had shown her she needed time away. Autonomy was better than security. She admits that during the late 1920s, like other "lady extremists," she began a "history of remarkable men, often difficult, sometimes even dangerous."[58] But she didn't so much want the men as to be one of the boys.

With her sharp mind and brash manner, her only salvation was finding like minds. Looking confident, feeling vulnerable, Hellman craved a way to join, become a part of a "set" where she could command respect, be somebody. She knew she could do better–with everything. Distancing herself from Arthur without leaving him, she planned to go to school in Bonn, Germany. She attended summer session there in 1929 and found a group of activists working toward the betterment of society. Bright, alert, and fun, she hung out with them until they asked her to formally join their group by swearing she didn't have any Jewish relatives. Hellman, shocked at the anti-Semitism, realized she had nearly stepped into a fascist group, precursors to Hitler Youth. Hellman, still aimless, did not listen well. She often heard what she wanted, dropping out when the talk got ponderous or theoretical, assuming the dull was also innocuous. She had bought into the bright-eyed activism of young Germans, partly because they were so unlike the bright, cynical U.S. intellectuals she had watched in Paris and New York. The automatic equality adopted by the girls in the group attracted her too.[59] Despite the passage of the Nineteenth Amendment to the Constitution giving suffrage to women in 1920, American culture still relegated women–particularly young women–to the service of men. Despite the Dorothy Parkers and the Janet Flanners, the intellectual set was decidedly masculine. Years later even her friend Moss Hart claimed that a woman experiences true womanhood only when she rejects a career for a man; Ernest Hemingway claimed that women were not important to a genuinely virile man.[60]

The face of fascist feminism had its points, but once she saw the underbelly of the group's agenda, she fled. She had been fooled and she was ashamed. She had too late caught the whiff of fascism, but she knew too well the odor of anti-Semitism. The incident brought her self-recognition as a Jew, something she had always known but chose to ignore. Like the Jews of New Orleans who flee the city during Mardi Gras and return later as if their place and dignity had returned in their absence, Hellman had denied the part heritage plays in American politics, in global politics. Now she faced the reality that anti-Semitism put everyone she knew at risk. For the first time, Hellman saw beyond the personal to the political facts of her being. She would never be the same. Her political consciousness was born of fear, of fury at herself for being so slow on the uptake, so slow to take action. She developed a political watchfulness and struck impetuously as soon as she caught the faintest scent of liberty loss, oppression, or fascism. Thus far she had watched and wandered, fled when the going got rocky, seen the gray darkness of her own spirit. She had done nothing but retreat.

She fled once more to New York City, relieved to be back home but fearful and depressed as well. In the face of international malice, nothing felt so depressing as her impotence made manifest by a good life with a nice husband and a mediocre, undemanding job. The Kobers' big, shabby house in Douglaston, Long Island, comforted Hellman, who read and wrote and went into Manhattan to lunch with friends, play cards, visit Kober at his office. Long Island suited her during this time, with its mix of rural isolation and urban proximity. Boredom sapped her strength.

Oddly enough, the Wall Street crash on October 24, 1929, revived her; the chilling sweep of the domestic politics and the scarcity of their own funds demanded she settle. She joined other Americans in finding ways to scrimp, even enjoying the challenge of reduced circumstances. She kept track of the smallest expenses, made budgets. Arthur had lost all the money they saved for his future career as a producer, but so be it. They could join the multitude of others having to start over. Having felt impending doom, for a time she felt the other shoe had dropped. She began to feel adult and competent, if not happy. But for the first time she became truly worried about her parents. Her mother was ill with what was later diagnosed as colon cancer, and Hellman began to feel the pressure of the only child whose parents' health begins to flag.

Her father was well, but he lost a great deal during the Depression. Money was always a sore point with him. He prided himself on making a good living for his family, sneering at Julia's family who handed out their surplus in dribs and drabs when it suited them. Max hadn't really needed them. He gambled, went to clubs, lived well according to his standards. Now, however, he had been cut adrift. An aging traveling salesman selling clothing and shoes had little money or earning potential in the early 1930s. Arthur Miller's Willy Loman could have been patterned on Max, perhaps the reason Hellman "let drop" to Miller that *Death of a Salesman* was "a good play," rare praise indeed.[61] The Newhouse-Marx family suffered very little; in fact as bankers they cashed in on the troubles of others. These circumstances broke Max's spirit, the essential pride of the southern man. He aged in his own eyes and in Hellman's too. But if 1930 was a bad year for everyone else Hellman knew, it brought good fortune and good money to Arthur.

PART TWO

THE CHASE

4

FROM STILL LIFE TO CELLULOID

Hᴇʟʟᴍᴀɴ, ᴀʟᴡᴀʏꜱ ᴀ ꜰᴀɴ ᴏꜰ ᴍᴏᴠɪᴇꜱ, ʟᴏᴠᴇᴅ ᴛʜᴇ ᴛᴀʟᴋɪᴇꜱ. The advent of *The Jazz Singer*, Hollywood's first talking movie, changed the Kobers' lives: sound movies came to mean work. Hollywood desperately needed plots and writers to script them, and producers looked to New York and its intellectuals. The moguls, ever entranced with faces on the screen, needed a talented few who could give words to pictures. No longer could scripts merely summarize action. Dialogue became the medium of the message, and producers needed writers to create it. Movie theaters across the nation embraced the new technology, and by 1930 all sixty of the leading film studios had completed the transition from silent movies to talkies. Noted for his perfect dialogue in short articles published by the *New Yorker*, Arthur Kober also had a reputation for delivering a product. Kober—and later Hellman—could write words for pictures, and write them well.

When Paramount knocked on the Kobers' Long Island door in 1930, they knew Arthur had to go to Hollywood. He had made a name for himself through his work for the Shuberts, but as the Depression began, the couple feared they could not stay afloat. When the Shubert Brothers laid Arthur off because of the economy, he was freed to go to Hollywood. Losing a job undermined his confidence all the same. Ira Gershwin, beginning his own stellar musical career with his brother George, wrote Arthur a poem to cheer him up: "Oh, Shubert Press Department, You didn't know what ART meant—/Or else you weren't sober—when firing Arthur Kober. Your loss, I might explain, is California's gain."[1] Arthur's Hollywood salary offer—$450 a week seemed a great deal to them both, considering most writers made under $50 a week.[2] Moving to California made economic sense, but Hellman didn't share his elation. She felt so stuck she couldn't move.[3]

When Arthur boarded the train to Hollywood, Hellman stayed put. Already in a marriage dotted by periodic absences, both parties strayed and tension strained their relationship. Arthur didn't like leaving without his wife, but Hellman had her parents to tend to, her small jobs, and she liked her house. She had spent the five years of their marriage watching and waiting to see who she was, what their marriage would be, how she would live her life. She still had no idea. By spring 1930, she desperately needed time alone. To do what, she couldn't imagine. She argued that Arthur might hate Hollywood and insist on coming home. Then where would they be? If successful, he would have years of guaranteed income—more in a month than most Americans made in a year. She would stay on Long Island or with friends in the city, and they would see how Hollywood suited him. But she promised she would write, she would budget, she would find work, she would visit his family. She made these promises and kept them.

Although Arthur was unhappy in Hollywood, he stayed, ultimately becoming very well connected, always busy, a major player in the Hollywood writing world. From 1930 to 1946 he worked on more than thirty films, writing comedies and detective stories such as *Army Wife* and *Recipe for Murder*. His films starred Carole Lombard, ZaZu Pitts, Jimmy Durante, Jack Benny, George Burns, Martha Raye, and others. By 1934 he and Howard Dietz had written the hit *Hollywood Party*, though the screen-credit system was so murky that Arthur Freed received initial credit.[4] Famed screenwriter Phillip Dunne called Kober the "perfect writer," and his hits would range from *Wintertime* to *Ginger*. In 1930, however, he knew he had only to try for success but was miserable alone. He urged Hellman to come west.

She demurred. Finally he insisted vociferously enough that she knew she had to pack up and follow him. To do otherwise meant divorce, and she wasn't yet ready for that. Though fond of her husband, supportive, and loving, she knew she could not be monogamous. She found extramarital sex to her liking, but the other men she chose scared her or bored her or both. Only in writing and reading did she find solace. She seemed to watch life from the large end of a telescope. However vigilant she had been, a meaningful life had eluded her. She might as well go to Hollywood. "I fooled and fiddled with excuses until the day when I did go, knowing even then, I think, that I would not stay."[5] Without interest or passion, she boarded the Twentieth Century Limited for Southern California. At least she would be with Arthur.

She hated Hollywood from the beginning. Steep Canyons cut through raw hills, pretty in the winter and spring but brown and wild much of the year, a fitting site for the B westerns Hollywood churned out at an alarming rate: *The Gunless Bad Man, Daze of the West, Hard Fists*. The enormous fifty-foot-high Hollywoodland sign on Mount Lee dominated the Hollywood Hills. Hundreds of new buildings, each in a different architectural style, had sprouted up in the previous decade, giving the land and the city the feel of a movie set. Exotic movie palaces dotted the few blocks of Hollywood Boulevard, including Grauman's Egyptian Theatre and Grauman's Chinese Theatre, both built with ornate murals, carved columns, and rare artifacts. The architecture seemed to rise without grounding, without history, and the historical and cultural poverty incensed her. She recalled, "I first saw Hollywood at the end of the big period, the cutup boys and girls, the comic Spanish houses. Spanish shawls coming from the balconies." The efforts of the next generation to throw away the "throne chairs" and "tone down or tonie up" the Hollywood esthetic made her even more hostile.[6]

Hollywood Boulevard's magnificent Temple Israel, conceived at Fox Studios and founded in 1926, seemed to Hellman part and parcel of this culture of illusion. She was bewildered by "the attempt, running side by side with the new life, to stand by the old roots: Jewish mama stories and Jewish mamas proudly imported from the East; French cooks and stuffed derma; and one studio executive who lived in a colonial mansion with a mezuzah encased in pickled pine."[7] She couldn't ground herself in this Jewish culture that wasn't Jewish or anything else she could identify. Hellman felt uneasy about what Laura Perelman called "the Jewish situation in Hollywood," where Jews ran scared and Jewish executives "break chairs because their wives had used the wrong fork."[8] In this so-called promised land, Hellman found no intimacy of friends or family, no gathering places for fellow misplaced New Yorkers, nothing congenial. A lousy frame for living.

Though Jews largely ran Hollywood, the industry courted an "American" audience. In business, the producers mimicked the previous century's robber barons like Rockefeller and Carnegie, but an anti-Semitic America saw them more akin to foreign money merchants. Because American consciousness often equated Hollywood with some kind of "foreign" influence, those in power did all they could to establish a town and industry completely "American," whatever that was or is. Jewish but hardly a cabal, Hollywood moguls rallied to present American values of democracy and heartland Christianity.[9]

By the time Hellman arrived in Hollywood to join her husband, a new Hollywood tradition had begun—the Christmas parade. Hellman was no stranger to American Christmas celebrations, but she'd never seen anything like two reindeer pulling a sleigh on wheels carrying Santa Claus and actress Jeanette Loff, accompanied by a color guard, drum and bugle corps, and American Legion marchers. Southern California's good weather did not compensate for the fake furor of a cornflake snowstorm shot into the street by an airplane propeller mounted on a truck. The elaborate spectacle of lamp-posts draped in cotton batting and heavy glass icicles, as well as cactus adorned with colored lights, reflected the Hollywood culture of this one-industry town.[10] To Hellman, Hollywood was flimflam farce, from the 750-pound metal Christmas trees lining its boulevards to DeLongre Park's newly installed tribute to Valentino, a four-foot bronze nude male perched on a green marble world. Even the eccentricities of New Orleans had not pre-pared her for Hollywood.

While Kober made money, pots of it by Depression standards, he was tight and hopeless about houses. When Hellman arrived in Hollywood, they lived in a small, gritty apartment on Sunset Boulevard. The address was a good one for aspiring artists and writers, but the living space was tiny by California stan-dards, with only a Murphy bed to separate the living from the sleeping.[11] It was like New York City apartments in this respect, but it had none of the posi-tives that made living in the confined quarters of New York possible—no charged energy, few restaurants, and even fewer of the open, crowded cul-tural possibilities that existed on every Manhattan street corner. Even in the 1930s, Los Angeles—or Hollywood as Hellman called the whole southland— was spread out. It extended from Culver City to Pasadena to Burbank. As Hellman lamented, "there was a time when you didn't say I am going to Los Angeles—you said I am going to Hollywood and only when you got there did you realize that the city of Los Angeles is a long drive."[12] Hellman felt isolated in what she later called "a foggy edge-world of people who had come for rea-sons they had long ago forgotten." She lived in the worst of both worlds: friends, acquaintances, and activities scattered throughout Southern California; husband and wife wedged into a tiny space after hours.

Nothing kills romance faster than sharing a small space with a partner who sulks and pines. Hellman did both, and she drank to while away the hours. "My excuse for drinking—if I needed one—was that it made life eas-ier, made the evenings less dull and life less dull. Writers drank, intellectuals drank, in Hollywood everyone drank."[13] Clearly not above experimenting, Hellman tried pot but it made her sleepy, not high. She vacillated between reclusiveness and extroverted outlandishness. Arthur went to work and hoped for change.

On the face of it, the Kobers made a smart move in relocating to the Garden of Allah Hotel. A collection of buildings including a dark, seedy bar (which Hellman was never averse to), a restaurant, and small cottages that looked liked sets, each architecturally different, made up this infamous Hollywood hotel. Built in the California Spanish adobe style, the grounds came complete with palms and pools. The actress Alla Nazimova built the hotel on Sunset Boulevard and opened it in 1921 with an eighteen-hour party complete with troubadours, an enormous pool, and a lavish feast. By 1930 Nazimova had lost the hotel due to the Depression, but it continued to draw the famous and the rich: Errol Flynn, F. Scott Fitzgerald, and Sheilah Graham. Future Hellman friends Robert Benchley and Dorothy Parker lived there for a time, and future enemy Tallulah Bankhead took a plunge in the pool, nude. The hotel housed many up-and-coming Hollywood people, was the center of many parties and gatherings, and cut through the isolation of Hellman's life. Arthur's fellow screenwriters from New York, once they gained enough influence, also lived in Allah's cottages.

The silly name of this classy outback for eastern writers enamored of palms should have warned Arthur. When he had first stayed there previously, a woman's sleepy voice awakened him from a sound sleep: "Would you get me a drink of water, dear?" He stumbled to the bathroom to get one before realizing that he was alone; he had been duped by notoriously thin walls. Someone else's wife wanted water.[14] Hellman loved the story, if not the reality. Even the chamber of commerce acknowledged that "the garden witnessed robbery, murder, drunkenness, despair, divorce, marriage, orgies, pranks, fights, suicides, frustration, and hope."[15] Hellman sneered at this kind of half-baked pretense, though she loved movies with vulgar themes and antics. Presumably she had participated in a goodly share. In 1930 the Garden of Allah had a certain cachet, but it only exacerbated the couple's differences.

Finally she found a house she could live in, although it clung to the Hollywood hills right under the Hollywoodland sign. A long, low country French–style bungalow on Beachwood Drive in Hollywood, remarkable for its charm, it featured French doors off the back, enormous stone steps climbing the hillside to the street above, and surrounding hills ablaze with light or dark at different times of the day. At first, the house gave her a sense of home, of comfort, space, and privacy. But its small-paned windows looked out on the spreading oaks and California sycamores outside, giving it a dark, dank character. As her unhappiness grew, so did her new home's ugliness. They hired an ex-actress who cooked bad dinners and worried about going bald. She gave the twenty-four-year-old Hellman her first chilly fear of middle age. Hellman, without work or friends, alternated between bouts of "reading in a leather chair" during the day and drinking hard at night. The memory of her first year in California never left her. She felt cold in Los Angeles. She found the sun didn't shine on everyone; certainly it didn't shine on her.[16] "Torpor had touched down."[17]

Not that their life had no allure. She very much liked the movies, particularly westerns—any "shoot 'em up." She liked imaginative people, liked making up stories and having fun. Always social, she and Arthur drove to Tijuana, Mexico, or went to the beach with the Perelmans, to the tennis courts with the Gershwins, or to the Coconut Grove. She exchanged stories with Nathanael West, as they tried to top each another with the antics they observed in this western enclave. When her parents came to visit, the Kobers showed them the town. But mostly "the days and the months went clipclop along," as she played cards with the wives of Arthur's friends, read, or drank.[18]

The Kober marriage was in trouble. A split was just a matter of time and both knew it. Arthur's devotion to her and her fondness for him wasn't enough to sustain her but made her pause until she found the pluck she needed. They had financial security, no children, good sex. But she longed for security and liberty, a no-holds-barred intimacy. The romance of love and sex and adventure together gave meaning to life. As much as she liked him, even loved him, Hellman lacked the spirit of adventure with her husband, and it mattered.

Hellman wanted to direct her own life. Married, she felt too conscripted. Arthur wanted more fidelity to the spirit of the marriage, if not absolute faithfulness. Her spirit demanded autonomy and she didn't want to check in with others. Rebellious women like Hellman dreamed "not of male anatomy, but of male autonomy."[19] Hellman began to think she "was better with no formalities. . . . I would stay longer if I felt free to go any day."[20]

Kober did all he could to keep the two of them married, though others thought she was more trouble than she was worth. Ironically, she gave him much of what he wanted in a wife. She interested him, always. Hellman was the least boring person he knew. She had other qualities less obvious than her flamboyance. Kober was "probably the first to appreciate her great common sense and capacity for shouldering burdens, and certainly the last to want to give them up entirely."[21] But she was wayward, and Kober's friends urged him to leave her, to "take a firm hand."[22] He could not do that, and he knew it wouldn't work anyway. Hellman, for all her flaws, reassured Kober of his worth, and he needed reassurance.

Arthur's ambition and insecurity dogged him, and as much as he needed his wife, he liked other women too. His friend Jean Cohen Friedlander wrote him: "I don't see why you are so anxious to have anyone at Paramount read your work. What for, for Pete's sake? They pay you every week? Good hard cash? So what more do you want? . . . In the meantime, see that you save much so . . . you can support me in the style to which my movie training has accustomed me. Free use of your body is not to be sneezed at but freer use of your cash is what intrigues me more. Get me?" Clearly she teased him, flirtatiously testing his availability and the depth of the Kober marital waters: "My love to Lillian—even though she comes between you and me, I can't help liking that gal; and my great passion to you."[23] Kober might turn to other women for sex or even emotional support. But he wanted Lillian—a happy, fulfilled, loving Lillian. Hollywood was rough on many marriages, and it ended theirs: "the affinity between the passionate and the passive" was finally coming apart.[24]

Arthur, desperate to revive Hellman to the land of living, fell back on his habit of finding her work to alleviate her boredom and restlessness. Lillian working was far better than a brooding wife alternating between books and the bottle to make it through the day. Arthur begged Sam Marx: "Lillian is bored in California. She's going to leave me if something isn't done. She's a very talented reader." Despite Marx and Hellman's past relationship in New York, marred by mutual dislike and insult, Marx agreed to try her out.[25] She passed the synopsis test with higher marks than any other job seeker and he hired her. Hellman thought Marx a "Jewish Cossack" and he thought her a "Parlor Pink from a very luxurious parlor."[26] Neither proved far from wrong in their assessments, though Marx discovered something he didn't expect: she was responsible. Very. That goes a long way in the entertainment industry. When she began her work on movies in the early 1930s, Hellman had a long way to go, both personally and professionally. But she had begun to breathe life into the still numbness of her spirit.

She had bided her time, and she now composed an animated self quite different from the sullen tentative wife who had arrived in California. Crossing the train station's Bridge of Sighs in Pasadena, she had sunk to a new low— no house, no family, no friends, nothing to do but live with a husband.[27] Now she had work. Work—hard work—always transformed her. As she wrote to journalist Lucius Beebe, "The place isn't as bad if you're working there. Of course, it's unbearable to any civilized person as a mere visitor, but with something to do it's no worse than being in jail and working all day in the jute mill. It keeps your mind off things."[28]

Watching the antics of the city and the movie industry from the inside, Hellman snapped out of her semiconscious state. She felt unthreatened by the madcap lunacy of Hollywood. Away from New York and New Orleans, she saw the possibility of reinventing herself. Once Hellman got the sense of Hollywood, its bizarre contradictions of art and schmaltz, its antic seriousness, she determined to act when and how she wished. She could not do it any other way.

Paris had overwhelmed her; its ancient history and culture reminded her of her own insignificance and inadequacy. In contrast, Hollywood looked like it had been set up overnight, ready to be abandoned tomorrow, a "surrounding dream of old movie sets piled next to one another, early Rome at right angles to the painted roses of a girlie musical, at the left of a London street, side by side with a giant, empty whaling ship."[29] The Vine Street Theater became CBS Playhouse Theater for radio in the mid-1930s, the Hollywood Playhouse became the El Capitan, which became the Hollywood Palace. Hollywood was on the hustle. Radio pronounced the mercurial unpredictability of the city and its people with local news taking precedent over national syndicates, and gossip columnist Louella Parsons broadcasting from the Hollywood Hotel.[30]

Hellman saw Hollywood as facade, peopled by actors out for the big break and the big buck. As screenwriter Anita Loos reflected, "To place in the limelight a great number of people who ordinarily would be chambermaids and chauffeurs, give them unlimited power and instant wealth is bound to produce a lively and diverting result."[31] Hellman could do lively. And in Hollywood, no one had to stay himself. Quick change artists were in demand. Mae West, former Kansas City runaway, became the "blond bombshell" of *Hells Angels* the year Hellman arrived. Sickly Brooklyn boy Irving Thalberg became the "boy wonder" of Hollywood, vice president of MGM by the time he was twenty-five, even marrying glamorous Norma Shearer, a woman whose face Hellman found "unclouded by thought."[32] Greta Garbo—whom Hellman thought the most beautiful woman in the world—successfully moved from the mystery of mute beauty in the silents to fame in talkies by huskily muttering, "Gimme a whisky, ginger ale on the side . . . and don't be stingy, baby!"[33] Hellman had a husky voice and liked whisky; Garbo fueled her fantasy. Feeling the excited rush of a first writing job, she thought nothing could hold her back. Opportunity was all she needed.

Twenty-five years old, in a city whose industry was about the same age, she didn't take people seriously enough to fear them.

Hollywood gave her a slickness that didn't become her. Determined to become a main attraction, she tried too hard, came off too hard, lost her sensitivity. Rumor had it that she approached men with a blunt "let's fuck," but she was actually more seductive than crass—though she did have her moments.[34] Possibly the story comes from the mean-spirited gossip Hollywood thrives on. More likely is the story of her smoking a cigar and talking sexual exploits with the girls, when the men and women "separated" after a dinner party in classic boy-talk, girl-talk fashion. Confused and contradictory, her boozy madcap adventures often pleased her. But she sometimes unwound too far from propriety for her own comfort, not to mention her husband's. She tried out a new life with fewer restraints than those she'd wrestled with for the past five years. She turned from the dull, plodding Lillian Kober to the loud party girl Lillian Hellman that Hollywood seemed to like. She finally stopped watching everyone else and struck out on her own.

Arthur's getting her a job as script reader and summarizer for Marx was just the beginning. With no experience, she determined to write screenplays. A start. The job permitted her to match wits with the best of the writers, producers, and directors. She despised writing MGM's summaries, hated equally the producer's devaluation of summary writers. But the experience taught her to write screenplays—unlike F. Scott Fitzgerald and William Faulkner, who never had to do film scutwork and never did much in film. Hellman's early experiences as a reader taught her the structure of the work. Even boss Sam Marx admitted that her synopses were beautiful. Arthur greeted happily the signs of her changing confidence and independence. He may have hoped for a more conventional wife, but Hollywood didn't require one. At least she had come alive again. The writing transformed her view of what to do in Hollywood. She had found her West Coast 1930s groove, never smooth but always intense.

Hellman learned more than screen writing in MGM's summary shop; to Marx's chagrin, she learned a lot about activist politics too. Sensitive about oppression and now working as the lowest of the low, Hellman began to seek justice for writers at all levels, not easy in an industry that "reeked of caste."[35] Writers provided a service, like maids or caterers. Of course, only thoughtful, sensitive reading and pithy straightforward writing would do—and lots of it. But summary writers could expect unskilled pay for skilled labor. While she found writing summaries a snap, she couldn't believe what little value the studios put on the writers or the scripts they read. As fellow writer Sid

Perelman said, "Hollywood is a dreary industrial town controlled by hood-lums of enormous wealth, the ethical sense of a pack of jackals and taste so degraded that it befouled everything it touched."[36] In a studio hierarchy, a scriptwriter stands "somewhere just below the publicists but above the hair-dresser."[37] A mere reader ranked lower than either, and the powers that be let them know it. As Hellman put it, "Twelve men and two women sat in a large room in a rickety building on stilts," with earthquakes sending the building "atilt." She hated the lack of respect and salary of her early work writing sum-maries at $50 a week "if you could read two languages. You were paid sixty dollars if you could read three. And you sat, you had no office of your own. You sat with about 15–18 people in a large room. And you were required to read, unless you came across something very remarkable, two and three manuscripts a day. This is slave labor, real slave labor. And it takes you an hour to drive home at night."[38]

Hellman could never resist stirring the pot and once she began causing problems with her "organizing," Marx fired her. In getting canned, she had good company. Lester Cole, a famous screenwriter and leftist, had a desk right across from Hellman's. He lasted only two weeks. She lasted almost a year. Hellman never forgot the summary writers who persevered under the worst of conditions: the learned Austrian, the former English lady writer, and a respected editor hiding from an ex-wife.[39] She never admitted seeing studio executives as anything other than "preposterous little men."

A labor dispute was what Hellman needed in those early Hollywood days to revitalize a self threatening to disintegrate. How like Hellman to turn her personal angst into a macrocosmic political issue, hoping to stick it to flashy Hollywood moguls whose obscene wealth mocked a depressed America. She found she wasn't alone in her disgust; a horde of Hollywood leftists, many of them writers, protested disparate economic conditions. She got caught up in "the single forceful alliance" of "liberals, radicals, intellectuals and the edu-cated middle class" who took Hollywood politics seriously. Marx tagged Hellman correctly in saying (at least of her early days), "To her, every cause was good, there were no bad ones. Just the fact it was a cause made it worthy of support."[40] As scattered as she was, her heart was with labor.

She needed focus, but she maintained a political integrity of sorts, forging an ironic distance from the greed and the hype, even as she became part of it. These early ineffectual labor actions led to eventual power in the Screen Writers Guild and lifelong activism in the labor movement. Though Hellman was not a laborer in the traditional sense, her labor action of 1930 came from a writer's pride. In those golden years of Hollywood "women were treated like disposable Kleenex,"[41] with summary writers the most disposable of all. It mortified her to have to walk through the commissary and be recognized by men who felt they had to half rise to acknowledge Kober's wife. Hellman's early political stirrings prolonged her marriage for a few months. Kober soon became only a support, a backdrop to Hellman's reinvigorated life.

Another man was what it took to break the stale shell of the Kober marriage. By the time Dashiell Hammett walked into Hellman's life in November 1930, he had a dizzying appetite for booze and women. He had also an individuality which proved a nearly impenetrable fortress. She fell and fell hard, knowing the risk was great but knowing too that his demands on her weren't conventional ones. He moved her sexually but, more importantly, something of him reached to the center of her and stirred her creatively. It was not Hammett the man but who *she* was under Hammett's gaze and influence that became the mythic center of her life.

Waterfront Rough and Hollywood Smooth

Hellman met Hammett in Hollywood's classic Musso and Frank Grill. Lee Gershwin remembered the meeting taking place at the Roosevelt Hotel, while Bing Crosby sang;[42] Helen Asbury remembered it taking place at a party on Vine Street;[43] Hammett's biographer Richard Layman reports their meeting at a party given by Daryl Zanuck, place not named. But Hellman's memory of the meeting differed, perhaps joining feeling and symbol above fact. The Musso and Frank Grill, established in 1919 on Hollywood Boulevard, is unpretentious, serving hearty grilled food in a men's club atmosphere. Worn leather plush seats and high-backed booths ensured some privacy, but open aisles allowed observation of patrons coming and going. Musso's warm lights and comfortable, clubby shenanigans suited Hellman better than restaurants more glamorous, more Hollywood. Food counted for Hellman. She complained for years about the food in Hollywood. "Nobody in this town likes food—except for fancy drek like Beef Wellington or Baked Alaska."[44] But Musso's plain, rich fare gave her pleasure. Musso and Franks suited the Hellman and Hammett they were to become: part legend, part down home.

Perhaps the aura of stability and comfort led her to approach the tall, handsome but slightly rumpled man who was almost as good at demeanor as she. Hammett at thirty-six intrigued the twenty-five-year-old Hellman. Hellman (whose age waxed and waned to her will) wanted to impress him, so she said she was two years older than she was, later saying she didn't want to hurt his feelings. Hammett was gloriously handsome. Hellman was "Jewish and little and lively and tough as nails," as Hammett biographer Diane Johnson put it.[45] Hellman's energy enlivened and she had an edgy brilliance. Hammett could handle tough.

Standard fare Hellman was not. That night, or one shortly afterward, they sat in a car in Musso's parking lot, talking late. She'd read Dostoevsky, knew her Tolstoy and her Kierkegaard and her Nietzsche. Hammett liked smart women almost as much as he loved books. The words and the intimacy immediately took hold and held—whatever else would happen to them and their lives together. They fell in love unaccountably, unexpectedly. In Hellman's romantic view of truth, love existed and always would for Dashiell Hammett. At seventeen she had written in her diary, "Oh God—if I could only find a human being with both attractions," physical and mental. Hammett certainly had both. She could and would love others, but her feelings for him stayed strong.

Hammett shied away from serious discussions of love but zestfully told he loved her in letters signed "With love of the lewdest sort," "Jesus, do I love you," or "I love you v.m."[46] He could only manage love words in writing, but that did not mean he didn't feel an extraordinary bond. He just never trusted the emotional response words brought, especially the "ovelay" word, another corny code word he used with her. Sex was sport for Hammett, only incidentally connected to love. Hellman hoped that sex and love would merge. Later she could—and did—separate sex and love when she had to. For now, he drew her, urgently. He mattered to everything she was to become. Surprising everyone including himself, Hellman mattered to Hammett. Hellman rather cynically oversimplified their meeting: "Remember? You were getting over a four-day drunk and I was getting over a four-year marriage."[47] The ties were strange but strong.

In 1930 both wrote for film, but Hammett's success and fame was light years away from Hellman's invisibility. Hammett was in the spotlight, reveling in drunkenness, parties, sexy women who hovered everywhere. Hellman acted out on the edge, drinking too much at home, hanging out with Arthur and his friends, playing at partying. Hollywood, a small town in 1930, had marked class divisions, which only the beautiful or the rich easily crossed. Hellman was neither, Hammett was both. An affair wasn't far from the realm of possibility; Hammett had hundreds of women. A lasting relationship seemed out of the realm of possibility. But their intimacy revealed points of contact. Both had begun to careen out of control, skidding on excess in the same bars, clubs, and restaurants. Both needed more than the boredom of Hollywood's wild nights. She had wit and bite, took risks, and came alive when he was with her.

When Hellman met Dash, the flavor of the city changed for her. It sparkled and so did she, as they danced at the Montmartre Café on the second floor of the Toberman Building, as they drank daily at the Brown Derby, where stars gathered and their fans flocked for glimpses. As part of Hammett's life, Hellman moved from shadow to glitter.

Dashiell Hammett was as hot as a man can get in Hollywood, certainly hotter than any other writer. He was becoming well known for detective stories published in pulp magazines like the *Black Mask*; he also wrote and published the occasional verse. The year before Hellman met him he had sold the rights to *Red Harvest* to Paramount, which released the movie version, *Roadhouse Nights*. Hammett learned that writing novels paid double, screenplays only once. Not caring much about money, he nevertheless loved to spend it. In 1930, he had just published two novels featuring the Continental Op: *The Dain Curse* and *Red Harvest*. They gave shape to the first believable detective in American fiction. *The Maltese Falcon*, published in 1930, featured Sam Spade and was adapted three times for film; in the 1941 John Huston version Humphrey Bogart made Spade an American icon. Even with his success, Hammett did not see himself as a screen-writing hack. And even though he was a hot property, he didn't let Hollywood buy him.

The year Hellman met Hammett, he had just finished his favorite novel, *The Glass Key*, dedicated to his girlfriend Nell Martin, a beautiful, brainy actress-entertainer. Published in 1931, the novel featured Ned Beaumont, tall, thin, tubercular gambler and drinker, a partial self-portrait. Foreshadowing their separation, Martin dedicated her novel *Lovers Should Marry* to Hammett. Hellman put an end to whatever plans Martin had for Hammett, though Hammett and Martin stayed friends. Hellman, always a fierce negotiator—in love and money—encouraged Hammett to hold out when David O. Selznick originally offered him $400 a week to write the script for *The Glass Key*. Selznick raised the ante, writing, "Hammett is unspoiled as to money, but on the other hand anxious not to tie himself up with a long-term contract . . . his vogue is on the rise."[48] Hammett had just completed *City Streets* for Paramount Pictures. Released in 1931, it was a great success with Sylvia Sydney and Gary Cooper. Hammett made over $100,000 that year with the rest of the nation deep in the depression.

Hammett spent money as fast as he made it. He loaned money to anyone just for the asking. He bought Hellman and the other women in his entourage gifts galore. For Hellman he chose jewelry, especially jeweled pins and rings with large stones. He added beautiful clothes and exquisite hats. As much as he spent, he nevertheless liked Hellman's commonsense attitude about money and presents: "of a brooch, a pearl set in black metal, she asked, 'Did it cost more than $500?' And he said, 'Yes, but not as much as $600.' He put her down as the $500 type."[49] She loved nice things but wasn't greedy, nor inordinately impressed with riches. He mocked her thrift. Money didn't mean much to Hammett, though later not having any would.

Hellman's early days with Hammett in Hollywood were heady indeed; the couple somehow fit and knew it. He more than liked her, committing to her in a way wholly his own. She was simply overwhelmed. Neither was ready for a conventional relationship. They nevertheless made an alliance of lovers, though Hammett made clear that monogamy would never be his game. They fought in public because they both drank too much. Hellman's first real publicity came from gossip columns, and it wasn't of the good sort. Hammett laughed at the Louella Parsons columns and entertained Hellman with tales of the rich, famous, and flashy. His black chauffeur, Jones, took them to Hammett's favorite hangouts, the Trocadero and the Brown Derby, where Hellman was surrounded by his well-wishers and hangers-on. She laughed raucously at their foibles and those of others. They had a similar sense of life being as absurd as it was serious. They loved sharing crazy anecdotes and examples of language mangling. She wrote, "Hammett phoned me one night from Jean Harlow's house to tell me that she had rung the bell for the butler and said, 'Open the window, James, and leave in a tiny air.'"[50] He wrote her of "the radio announcer at the Stanford-California game who said into my ear personally: 'We'll now go down to the field microphone and see if we can pick up some of the cheers and innuendo from the stands.'"[51] Their wits matched.

Though born in Maryland, Hammett reminded Hellman of the stylish, dignified, roguish men of her childhood in New Orleans. Hammett had a rough-hewn sexuality ready to take more than it gave, glossed by good looks and classic manners. Gossip columnist Dorothy Kilgallen described him as "a fiction writer's version of a hard-boiled Dream Prince."[52] He had style, something Miss Hellman from New Orleans knew all about. If Hellman draped herself in soft wool trimmed with a touch of fur and wore her small brimmed hat at an angle, Hammett outdid her: "Hammett knew, and knew he knew, what to wear and eat and drink. He noticed that silk socks did not go with tweeds, that tweeds were classy, he noticed what expensive women wore and what the other ones wore."[53] She early sensed the importance of style but feared its emptiness. Hammett showed her style that went beyond clothing to the construction of creativity.

Hammett's style did not entirely hide the sexy, ex-detective roughneck. His talk was straight, sometimes crude. When Hellman reported André Gide's admiration, Hammett said, "I wish that fag would take me out of his mouth."[54] When Hammett drank, he became a hard man: insulting, whoring, abusing. He consorted with the "foggy edge-world of people who had come to Hollywood for reasons they had long ago forgotten . . . there were still traces of the days when most of them had wanted to act or write or paint, but those days passed into years of drinking and doing or grubbing." Hellman saw these people "only through a crack in the door." At first envying them for their free spirits, she grew repelled by what they'd become. She called Sis—one of the whores Hammett flaunted—a drug-induced loser. When sober, Hammett sharply turned away from that wild world, and Hellman never became more than a "tight, tense sightseer."[55] Unlike Hammett, Hellman couldn't go in and out of this underworld. She recognized how close she had come to becoming one of those lost ones with faded purpose and no creative urges left.

Hammett gave her plenty of urge. A shocking man, careless, brutally honest—this she could deal with. A violence underneath the sophistication kept her "in line" but not paralyzed. Unlike many women in abusive relationships, she held on to her selfhood. At one party Hammett punched Hellman and knocked her down as they argued. Her humiliation surfaced in her blazing retort: "You don't know the half of it. I can't bear even to be touched!"[56] The truth of Hammett's drunken cruelty occasionally showed on Hellman's bruised face. She always feared that side of Hammett, but his violence seemed mindlessly directed, an impersonal fury fueled by alcohol. Yet his deep-seated authority grounded Hellman, and she put up with its nastiness. Most importantly, she could leave and often did. He did not control her. He didn't seem to care if she left, and his apologies, oblique as they were, focused on his shame of drinking. His violence erupted in the boozing, destructive periods of their first ten years—their "loose fat" years. Those wild years ended when Hellman went into analysis and quit drinking. Forever after Hellman remarked about what a mild-mannered person Hammett was when sober, though on the subject of his drinking she always despaired and nagged until finally—years later—he quit too.

Dark nights in Hollywood have always hidden alcoholic rage and wife battering. The city's version of masculinity grew from a brutal frontier sense of man and woman. Hellman remembered an ex-star "who showed her knife

cuts on her body put there the night before by a very religious movie director."⁵⁷ Audiences cheered when James Cagney's character, Tom, in *Public
Enemy* pushed a grapefruit in the face of beautiful Kitty (Mae Clarke), degrading her. As Hedda Hopper said, "Hollywood was always a heartbreak
town." ⁵⁸ Women were expendable commodities. As for Hellman, she could
go or stay, behave or misbehave; he might lash out, but she could face it.
Hammett's extremes felt real and broke through her stiff spirit.

Both were married, but that seemed beside the point. When Hammett
met Hellman, he'd been married for ten years and had many women, from
Peggy O'Toole, his typist and a longtime friend he named a race horse after
in *The Glass Key*, to Hollywood actresses and whores he dismissed completely
from his mind. He had bouts of gonorrhea and a destructive impulse to
booze. He would go on the wagon for days or weeks at a time and work on his
writing. He earned and spent more money in a month than some people
earned in a decade. He told his wife nothing. He lived exactly as he wanted
to live. Whatever real intimacy Hammett had with his wife had evaporated
years before; he had moved out by 1927 and in 1929 traveled to New York for
an extended stay with girlfriend Nell Martin.

Kober, confused and distraught, was caught in the maelstrom, hating the
publicity, feeling the cuckold. His diary records his doubt, his misery, his
flings with other women, and even the time Jose came to Arthur for reassurance that this affair would not last. Both Jose and Kober were fooling
themselves.

Hellman also may have been fooling herself about Hammett's marriage.
As Hellman told it after his (and Jose's) death, he had behaved gallantly,
marrying Jose Dolan, an army nurse and good Catholic girl he had a short
affair with, who later became pregnant by another man. Hellman's story was
that he couldn't bear Jose's humiliation in having a child out of wedlock
and, having little regard for marriage in the first place, offered her his name.
They altered their marriage date from July 1921 to December 1920 to spare
Jose and the child the scandal. Hammett's family disputes the story, pointing
to a letter found recently that shows Hammett's words of love to Jose after a
night together—nine months to the date before Mary's birth.⁵⁹ Jose's shame,
inconsistent behavior, and ambiguous letters don't settle the issue, but
Hammett raised Mary as his own, if "raised" is the word for his sporadic attention and inconsistent economic support. Still, for twenty years, whether
broke or flush, Hammett sent enough money that Jose did not have to work
outside the home. She must have been an excellent money manager, since
the money she received varied from excessive to scant. Jose was too cowed

and needy to seek legal redress when Hammett's fluctuating fortunes left the family bereft.

Parenting meant occasionally picking up his daughters, showering them with presents, and letting them hang around with him and his buddies, sometimes forgetting to take them home. Later his money, letters, and affection appeared with greater consistency. He felt fond of his family and dedicated his 1930 hit *The Maltese Falcon* to Jose. Finances permitting, he was extravagantly generous to Mary and her younger sister, Josephine. He showed up now and again at his wife's rentals in Glendale, Burbank, Hollywood, and Santa Monica; the addresses shifted as the money did. For his entire life he saw the family, coming laden with gifts and money for Jose and their two daughters.

At twenty-five, Hellman had few maternal instincts and Hammett's family intruded. Hellman put up with Hammett's family with gritted teeth, pretending some affection to the children but impatient for his attention. In those early days, Josephine remembers Hellman as high-strung and irritable. Hellman may have felt her position as precarious as that of the Hammett family. Hammett's sense of responsibility was entirely selfish. He gave what he wanted to, when he could but seemed not to understand the need for constancy. Hammett, "as American as a sawed-off shot-gun . . . a good, hell-bent, cold-hearted writer"[60] could also be a "wild-eyed son of a bitch."[61] He had few illusions about himself or the future. But Hellman, despite fighting her own "entrapments," had not lost her illusions; she had faith in a future only she could see.

Hellman's great attraction to Hammett was that he could tell her anything. While she might violently disagree, it didn't rock her but made her—and him—think hard. Though Hammett was taciturn when sober and outrageous when drunk, Hellman sensed what he wouldn't reveal. She trusted her instincts about what she felt for him. His prematurely white hair, dissolute life, and lawless sexuality drew her inexorably. Importantly for Hellman, she didn't think she could hurt Hammett, a relief. She knew she hurt Kober. She couldn't measure up to his sweetness and kindness and she didn't want to. But she felt unworthy in comparison. Kober, with his Bronx, depressive, self-deprecating humor, deserved better than she could give. Only years later could Kober admit even to himself that Hellman had been "thoughtless, restless, and idle."[62] His passive goodness stifled her. But she knew, always, where she stood with Hammett, a man as "bad" as she. They shared a connected spirit, a gross generalization Dash would chide Hellman for, but one she nevertheless believed in. Each saw something of the self in the other, some deep sense of shared energy. Hellman and Hammett had real conversation. Erotic stuff, that.

Hellman's flagrant public involvement with Hammett did not break up the Kober marriage immediately. They could not get the divorce without first crushing each other, killing the spirit of their original union with sharp words and acts of betrayal. It took Hellman and Kober even longer than most, given Arthur's devotion and passivity, Hellman's guilt and indecision, and Hammett's womanizing. Hellman did nothing to disguise her shifted attention. Kober's friends were appalled. While Hellman sometimes wowed her Hollywood colleagues with her brilliance and her wit, for the most part they liked Arthur Kober more. No one liked Lillian hurting Arthur. The Gershwins, for example, loved Kober, and Lee Gershwin had much to say about Hellman's wild behavior during this time, none of it flattering and none of it friendly. Hellman's actions frayed the thin fabric of friendship the two women had shared. When Lee told Hellman to be kind to Arthur because he "was such a sweet man," Hellman snapped, "I don't want a sweet man." She complained about Arthur's alcohol-induced maudlin fits, knowing her behavior made his depression worse.

Though clearly smitten with Hammett, she wasn't ready to relinquish Arthur just yet. According to Diane Johnson, "It was difficult being around Hammett sometimes. The fun was frenetic and drunken; it could wear thin." So could his girlfriends, chief among them Nell Martin, whom he held onto for a year or so after he met Hellman. As Hammett flippantly wrote, "Love was real love, and sleeping around was 'whoring.'" He simply didn't factor his sexual exploits into their relationship. Hellman understood, came to terms with it, agreed, sort of. But that recognition did little to slacken the tension. Hellman took her relationship with Hammett very seriously, though his reputation, her fear, and her middle-class need for security kept her vacillating between going back to Kober or forward with Hammett. In the name of sociability and perhaps sophistication, Hammett, Hellman, and Kober often went together to parties, bars, and restaurants. No one fooled anyone. Only Hammett appeared not to mind, possibly because his maniacal drinking overwhelmed every other aspect of his social life. Hellman clung to the idea of romance and the idea of marriage, but neither man fit both. She even kept David Cort on a string, perhaps needing an admirer in the face of her own self-rebuke. Staying with Kober is what she should do; what she wanted for certain was Hammett.

A time came, however, when Hellman could not bring herself to drive one more time from the pseudo-Greek temple at MGM to the small French-style house in Hollywood. Going home paralyzed her, not the traffic. Running into Hammett with his "chance, casual ladies from time to time" made her sick. Her own actions as well as his violated her spirit and offended her up-bringing. She had to get out. The time to leave Kober and Hammett and Hollywood had arrived. As Hellman left for New York, she told Arthur she needed time to think and get herself straight. She told Hammett something different, saying she needed time to break with Kober. The Kober separation was permanent. All three knew it, but only Hammett pushed it. Hellman fled Hollywood in March 1931.

The two men, left in Hollywood and rather shocked by it, jockeyed for the first place position while faking friendship. They went to boxing matches to-gether while slyly insulting each other in letters to Hellman. Hammett mocked Kober as a good boy, telling Hellman that Arthur had stopped in and "left just a few minutes ago for an early bed so he could rise early."[63] On an-other occasion Hammett sneered at Arthur, Laura, and Sid Perelman for being inseparable. "They see more pictures and like fewer of them than any trio I know, though if you ask me how many trios I know I'll have to fall back on Jesus, Mary and Joseph."[64] For his part Kober felt intensely uncomfortable in the trio of himself, Hammett, and Hellman. She had unsettled both of them, not knowing when or if she'd be back; no one else did either. As Hellman noted later, "I think it was a relief to a lot of people on the West Coast when I went east."[65]

A relief it might have been, but both Hammett and Kober let her know im-mediately they didn't much like it. Two days after she left Hammett sent her a poem, the beginning of "a thousand-stanza verse" that satirically mocked them both:

> *In San Francisco, Elfinstone*
> *Fell in with a red-haired slut*
> *Whose eyes were bright as the devil's own*
> *With green-eyed greed, whose jaw was cut*
> *Wolfishly. Her body was lean and tough as a whip,*
> *With little of breast and little of hip,*
> *And her voice was thin and hard as her lip,*
> *And her lip was hard as a bone.*

If Hammett sneered, Kober wrung his hands and blamed himself for the two of them becoming so "emotionally upset, so terribly distraught."[66] Hellman bruised both men as she tried to survive emotionally.

Hellman never cut off relationships neatly. She muddied separations with vague promises characterized by impossible hopes. For a time, New York was just a more familiar version of hell than Hollywood had been. Still out of sync and now out of work, she merely bought time. She had breathed the fabricated air of fantasy on the West Coast and found only the cold, thin air of confusion on the East Coast. Lush excess gave way to barren sterility. She felt displaced, and it would be over a year before she admitted that she wasn't coming back, that she had opted for another life entirely. Analyzing her marriage from a distance, she used letters to buy time. She wrote painfully about her last failed attempt to get pregnant by Arthur. Perhaps she felt a baby would calm her restlessness, center her life. She certainly wouldn't be the first woman to feel that way. From New York she detailed her agony about starting her period, "lousy & unjust & a symbol of punishment," crying "like hell for two solid hours." "I always thought I was a super-creator of babies. Maybe it is better this way." Her failure to conceive made divorce certain, though she wrote, "It alters no promises I made you & I hope you understand that." The stresses of the separation surfaced cryptically and outwardly: "If you are still entertaining the idea of a divorce, now is your time to get it on record."

In other letters she rather defensively responded to Kober's complaint of "lack of information" and reminded him that she wrote more news than he did, then related the "news," lackluster pap filled with much activity. Though she treated Arthur abysmally, she cared about him deeply. In another letter she wrote, "I dreamed about you last night; you had four children and were leading them all by the hand down Fifth Avenue. I dream about you a good deal. I don't know what we should do about each other Artie, or whether we should do anything, but I think about you too much. I'm a thinker type." Torn as she was about leaving him—and the conventionality and stability he represented—she knew she wouldn't go back. But as long as great distance separated Hellman from both Kober and Hammett, she could sustain her illusion of being both married and not married.[67]

Still drinking too much but at least not trying to match Hammett highball for highball, she called and wrote Hammett in deep night. Hammett loved it but mocked her: "Angel, it was nice of you to phone me, even if you did have to get plastered to do it."[68] She felt his pull even 3,000 miles away. In the light of day she tried becoming Lillian Kober again, smoking madly in friends' stuffy apartments, writing stories the New Yorker would never publish, lunching, relying on the couple's old friends to make her feel real. She wrote Kober "please write more often & please love me," knowing as she said it that while she loved him, barring a vast change in circumstances, she could not stay married to him. Hitting her mid-twenties, she didn't know if life had just begun or stopped cold.

Hellman determined to fit into the free and antic New York drama scene that she and Kober had come to know. She surrounded herself with friends to escape the inevitable decisions of her own life. And what friends she had! She had dinner with the Ira Gershwins, talked with Chester Erskine, already famous for his *Harlem Review*, spent the weekend with the Shumlins, Herman presumably with wife Rose in tow.[69] She told Kober that Howard Lindsay took her to the *New Yorkers*, a musical comedy/revue featuring Cole Porter music. The lyrics of some of the songs—"Say It with Gin," "I'm Getting Myself Ready for You"—described Hellman's life in 1931 in New York, but songs meant for the revue and unused would have said it better: "You've Got to Be Hard-Boiled," "I'm Haunted by You," and "You're Too Far Away." In any event Hellman thought the revue had "swell stuff but Durante hardly belongs on a large stage." Russell Crouse squired her about, and she saw a great deal of Louis Kronenberger, who took her to *As You Desire Me* and *Three's a Crowd*, a particularly apt play for Lillian at this time. Both Kober and Hammett disapproved.

To provide cover—whether for herself or Kober is unclear—she peopled her schedule with many men and just enough women to give the appearance of a crowd. Kober could keep his eye on Hammett in Hollywood, but Louis Kronenberger became a sore point between the Kobers. Hellman made certain Kober knew their exact schedule of dates but grumbled to Kober about how irritating Kronenberger was, deflecting his interest, providing cover. The two had begun collaborating on *Dear Queen*, a never-produced play marked by high antics and great wit but not much dramatic potential. She carefully let Arthur know she wasn't sleeping with Louis, though she may have been. "Mr. Kronenberger and I—this letter was interrupted by his arrival—have just had a session. The kind of session where the results are two headaches, a lot of screaming, apologies, and no results." Nothing like an old friend and lover to give comfort.

Hammett didn't like Lillian and Louis together either. He began a tap dance or two of his own, increasing the pressure on Hellman to return to him in Hollywood. He told her over and over in letters that he loved her, though humor often accompanied it: "The emptiness I thought was hunger for chow mein turned out to be for you, so maybe a cup of tea"[70] or "I, as the saying goes, miss you terribly."[71] Flagrantly unfaithful to anyone, bedding starlets and secretaries, strangers and friends, Hammett nevertheless pleaded his case passionately. Against all odds, he committed himself to her, even as his eye wandered and his prick, as he said it, never ceased its quest for women, rather "ladies." He coerced cruelly: "So you're not coming home, eh? I suppose it doesn't make any difference if I have to go on practically masturbating."[72] He threatened her covertly with his womanizing. "I daresay my absence from the Brown Derby, coinciding with your departure, has started a crop of fresh and juicy rumors. I'll see they don't die from want of feeding."[73] His innuendo— no doubt true and no doubt understood clearly by Hellman—did little to force a commitment. Hellman stayed away.

Hellman was old-fashioned at heart, though valiantly acting the sophisticate, the wild woman, the unabashed bohemian. She felt threatened by Hammett's dissolute abandon, his out of control spending and drinking. That he loved her scared her to death. Hammett's detailed accounts of his treatment for his periodic bouts of venereal disease did little to entice her into his arms either. His confessions of lost days and nights to drink in spring 1931 didn't send her running for the train. After seven days sober, Hammett pleaded, "When are you coming home?"[74] She ignored it.

So why hold on? Hammett thrilled her. Hammett was brash, complex, and open to a wildness in her spirit. He interested her. Clashing emotions, intensity, and tension always drew her. Quoting Catullus in an early diary, Hellman wrote, "I hate you & I love you, which is more closely allied to me I cannot say. All I do know is the misery of the one is overshadowed by the perversity of the other." Hammett fit her pattern for passion profoundly. His fame drew her, but it wasn't what held her. They both knew she grounded him in some way, even as he flamboyantly flouted her efforts. He had found a strong and wayward girl who liked "Pushkin *and* fishing."[75] For Hellman, no good girl pretending was needed. Bad boys attract good girls, but bad girls like them too. And there was no doubt that Hammett was a bad boy, none at all.

Albert Hackett, another Hollywood screenwriter and good friend, recalled, "Remember the time there was this hooker in [Hammett's] bathroom, a call girl altogether nude up there—it was a practical joke against Sid Perelman. . . . And Sid went to the bathroom and gee, he was gone a long time, and then Laura Perelman and whoever went up there and caught them flagrante delicto. That was a story. It ended with Laura going off to San Francisco with Hammett. I remember that, they were gone for days and there was hell to pay all around."[76]

So much hell that fifty years later when Diane Johnson wrote Hammett's biography under Hellman's rather heavy-handed direction, Hellman gave her a letter Laura wrote to Hammett with the inscription: "Diane—This letter must not be used until we've set the ground rules." Apparently the ground rules forbade Johnson's use of it. The letter, however, showed the human side of Hollywood wild nights. Laura wrote of her anxiety in writing the letter, but went on, "I am very anxious to know how you feel, whether everything is alright with the studio, whether you and Lil have smoothed it out. Will you write and ease my mind a little. Even though our binge had painful results for everyone including Pep, even though I have been wild-eyed with remorse, I must tell you these last twenty-three days was the only reason I was able to keep my sanity all through the mess. . . . in desperately trying to square myself I had to tell a few lies which probably made a lot of trouble for you with Lil. Although it will be painful to do it, I would be glad to see her and do anything you say about it if you want me to." Laura tried to make it right with Hellman and continued her affection for Hammett. Gerald Howard of Viking Penguin said he had it on good authority that Perelman "wrote at least one letter— doubtless a dilly—to Hellman on the subject of that Hammett–Laura Perelman fling. Such a letter, if it exists today, would have to be handled with at least as much care as we accord nuclear wastes."[77] Biographers of the Perelmans and Hammett and Hellman do not agree on when these madcap antics took place, and the whirlwind travel between cities and coasts during the early 1930s make exact movements difficult to follow.

Whether Hammett was in San Francisco with Laura Perelman or with Lillian Hellman in New York for a quick two weeks in the spring of 1931, the pressure was clearly on. Hammett expected to join Hellman in some state of permanence in New York as soon as he could escape his movie duties and get himself on the wagon. By June 1931, he hadn't "had a drink for a week" and was "doping out a picture story for Gloria Swanson."[78] In early August, repulsed by Hollywood and its girlies, Hammett telegrammed Alfred Knopf, "Want to return to New York next week but am in terrific financial difficulty stop can you deposit twenty five hundred dollars to my account."[79] Hammett was broke but not for long.

He was awash in book royalties, movie money, and a deal to close in November. Edward Choate was to dramatize *The Glass Key* through the American Play Company, giving Hammett a hefty royalty. Thus, despite Hellman's shadow play, in October 1931 he left his Ivar Street apartment off Hollywood Boulevard and boarded the Santa Fe for the East.

When a friend wrote Kober, "Don't let Hollywood ruin your marriage, or perhaps your marriage is already ruined?" the question was rhetorical.[80] Hollywood wasn't the problem: the Kober marriage could not survive Hellman's feelings for Hammett.

Hammett's arrival pushed Hellman to make a decision. She found she loved him passionately enough to defy her parents and live with him. Determined to go her own way, she was still too young to do it without worrying—about Kober, divorce, her mother's approval, the anger of Aunt Hannah and Aunt Jenny. Hellman would not give him up, even if it made them both unfaithful wretches. His sexual promiscuity drove her crazy with jealousy, but by then she knew he could not, would not, be faithful. He seemed to demand fidelity from her, however. Hammett prodded and teased her, suspecting her of "the loosest sort of conduct . . . Just a she-Hammett."[81] A "she-Hammett" she wasn't. She wanted more from sex than unfettered pleasure, but she never wholly yielded to Hammett's attempts to make her faithful, either. While he flagrantly disregarded any attempt at fidelity, Hellman promised him she would "try." But she knew her bargain with him gave her just grounds to live her life as freely as he did his.

For a young woman who admitted that her generation might be sexually liberated but had "a deep uneasiness about sex, too," Hammett's lack of inhibition freed her to unleash her own eroticism. "You have to pay a very large price for freedom, and if you were willing to pay for it, then maybe you'd get it, and maybe you wouldn't. It's cost a fair amount to get it, I think, and I've lost a good deal along the way. But—But you play out your own nature."[82] In Hellman, the erotic spurred creativity that came deep from within. For a long time Hammett stimulated that creativity. Though she would love other men, find other lives outside the one with Hammett, he reached far into her being, kindling her attention, setting her alight forever. Hellman wanted Hammett, but more than the man himself—with all his fame and support—she wanted to sustain the feeling about herself that he gave her. He stirred her creativity, dredged her power from the nonsense and antics and churning of her personality. Most importantly, Hammett inspired her to write, gave practical advice, and edited and honed first attempts. His commitment to writing taught her the value of being faithful to an idea if nothing else. Desperate to become something other than a hanger-on, keen to impress the man who gave rise to thoughts and books and art, Lillian Hellman was on her way to becoming Lillian Hellman.

The Loose Fat Years

Once he arrived in New York City to stay, Hellman felt powerless to resist what she had wanted all along. What Hellman called the "loose fat years" with Hammett began, years marked by drink, partying, and domestic brawling, followed by depression, guilt, politics, and work—efforts to stay sober, to stay sane. Hellman could not see future success or the legend she would become. She joined Hammett in a new kind of limbo that nearly ruined them both.

Though he officially stayed at the Hotel Elysee, he often stayed with Hellman at the Lombardy Hotel. The Depression had largely ended the practice of living in luxury hotels, but midrange hotels still housed many permanent residents taking advantage of full services and lower rates. Hammett never managed his money and never knew how much he had to spend, and Hellman's decisions about living space were always better than his. They began their lifelong practice of living together only part of the time, even when the romance was at its most stable.

Now with Hellman in Manhattan, Hammett still could not settle. He attended boxing matches, drank, night-clubbed with Hellman, and tried to write *The Thin Man*, his last detective novel. Unfixed, abandoned in behavior, he became clinically depressed and used alcohol to drown himself. He wrote Hellman a poem. "Statement. Too many have lived / As we live / for our lives to be / Proof of our living. / Too many have died / As we die / For their deaths to be / Proof of our dying." Though he includes the "we" in his despair, Hellman did not share Hammett's dark depressions. Optimistic and scrappy, though prone to rage and dramatics, Hellman never saw the appeal of suicide or self-immolation. She knew Hammett was debt ridden and disgusted with himself over what he had previously written and his current failure to write consistently. But at twenty-six years of age, she did not understand how deep that black swath of self-disgust cut into Hammett. She saw him flush with possibilities, saw his drinking as destructive but part of the scene.

During this period Hammett hooked up with William Faulkner, another man stunned by fame.[83] They both drank themselves into near oblivion. On a daily basis, in hotel living rooms and every pub and restaurant they could find—from Tony's to 21—they told each other stories and discussed the books they both read avidly. Hellman, "Miss Lillian" as Faulkner called her, was once again an onlooker, sometimes drunk herself, often slumped in a chair or couch outside the action. The near-mythic culmination of Hammett and Faulkner's drunken antics came when they talked respected editor Bennett Cerf into getting them an invitation to their publisher's party, the same Alfred Knopf who had forwarded Hammett money to come to New York. Both drunk and disheveled in tweeds, they arrived at the black-tie dinner and were warmly greeted by the surprised Knopfs. Faulkner and Hammett, in the near paralysis of the eager-to-behave drunk, bore up through dinner, but as soon it was over Hammett passed out cold on the living room floor. The game was up. Faulkner mightily tried to yank Hammett to his feet so they could escape, but in drunken horror, he buckled and fell on Hammett.[84] Hammett and Faulkner's behavior may have been an act of contempt against the Knopfs, but more likely it marked each man's self-contempt. As outlandish as the two men were, Faulkner remembered the time with Hammett in New York "as one of the best in his life."[85] Hammett's alcoholism got worse. Why he drank is no mystery; he was addicted to it and alternately desperate to drink himself to death and desperate to sober up and write. Though Alcoholics Anonymous had chapters in the 1930s, few saw "hard drinking" as a disease. Hammett's alcoholism took more and more of his energy, whether giving into it or fighting it. Hammett was swept up in excess, remorse, and self-disgust.

Hellman hadn't left husband and boredom and misery in Hollywood to be an offshoot to a depressed, drunken lover in New York. As a center-stage only child, Hellman took care of herself first even as she too easily adapted to Hammett's reckless disregard. Hellman was swept up in the life of drinking and partying and excess. And undoubtedly some of the life with Hammett seemed worth it. The greats of the period drank in the same clubs and bars on both coasts, adding to the mythical lore of the era—Hemingway, Faulkner, O'Hara, Fitzgerald, Hammett. Hellman belonged. Drinking at Tony's one night, James Thurber threw a glass of whisky at her, beginning a melee that ended when Hammett pushed Thurber, who "heaved" a glass at him, missing but hitting a waiter.[86] Drama, even drunken drama, had its moments.

Hellman liked the madcap life, but she felt a tension born of puritan principles—work, loyalty, and holding oneself to a personal code—at odds with her current behavior. Restless, skittish, and never one to keep her opinions to herself, Hellman stayed with Hammett but stalled the divorce and looked elsewhere for entertainment. Alcohol, crazy living conditions, thwarted ambition, sexual infidelity, and jealousy dogged both Hammett and Hellman during these transitional years. Their early flagrant affairs with others came from the bizarre antics of the entertainment and literary scene in Manhattan and Hollywood. But their turning to others held an element of pathos, too, at least for Hellman. Hammett retaliated when Hellman loved or used others. Hellman felt the fierce jab of jealousy at Hammett's flagrant proclivities to the end of his life.

She had learned to play with men, to get even in order to subsume her jealousy of Hammett's many infidelities. He was partial to black and Asian whores and other men's wives. She was fond of old boyfriends like Kronenberger and Russell Crouse, both coming into their own as literary and theatrical men of influence, Kronenberger as critic, Crouse as the cowriter and coproducer of Broadway comedies like *Anything Goes* and *Life with Father*. Hammett hypocritically chided her, "If I weren't broke I'd go up to Moriarity's and probably find you there playing bagatelle with Buck Crouse."[87] Though Hellman attracted bright men, a middle-class morality hid in all her extravagance, and she was by turns wayward and faux nice girl.

In December 1931, Hellman and Kober finally admitted they would divorce, though Hellman convinced Kober it was his idea. Both lied to everyone about the real reasons for their divorce, calling it mutual necessity. They told Hellman's parents together, hugging each other to show their "passionate" and continuing fondness. Hellman's mother hated Dashiell Hammett, not least because he drank and spent money and provided her daughter no safety. Lillian and Arthur spared Arthur's mother, who loved Hellman, any details of her relationship with Hammett. It was years before "no-fault" divorce, and Hellman had to bring charges of cruelty against Arthur. She collapsed in laughter at the ridiculous necessity of lying in court. She knew firsthand where the fault lay. The split did not go as smoothly as they said; inevitably they had bitter quarrels, and it was painful for Kober, who hated her at times. Kober's diary lays out his misery in excruciating detail. "I brood a great deal what with Lil constantly on my mind now."[88] Hellman felt released.

Hellman tried to hide Hammett from her aunts. She knew they would disapprove of a married man winning her away from Kober, a wonderful man everyone liked. When she left for New Orleans to see them, she left Hammett behind, telling him not to write her there.

Hammett knew that Hellman's trip south marked a time of reflection and decision for her. She had to confront her upbringing and take him into her life permanently or abandon him. Hammett, awash as he was in women and drink, was jealous, intent on winning her for his own, wooed her hard. He wrote her silly, loving letters for her to pick up at train stops along the way. The day after she left he wrote, "A bed without Lily ain't no bed. . . The missing of you is terrific." In another sent the same day, he mocked his financial straits and his drunken infidelity. "I'm living here on Lenox Avenue with a woman named Magda Klemfuss . . . and while I'm at it. I don't believe there's any General Pershing Street in New Orleans or anywhere else."[89] He wrote her two or three telegrams a day and positively gushed. He worked to seduce her with wit, let her know she belonged north with him: "Watch out for strangers on those late trains. Them fellers are likely to take you for a Yankee and not respect you. Maybe you'd better use your accent—and be taken for Anna May Wong. All New York mourns your absence." [90] He felt his position with her was precarious.

In 1932, he deserved to be dumped. His drinking, womanizing, and battering began to have legal consequences. Elise De Viane, a Hollywood starlet, sued Hammett and won a $2,500 judgment for having been "bruised and battered in resisting the fervid love makings of Dashiell Hammett." [91] Hammett didn't deny it, writing matter-of-factly about the financial arrangements for payment, $300 a week for nine weeks, "stuck for it so I suppose there's no use bellyaching." [92] On another occasion Hammett asked Albert Hackett to send money to a woman "in trouble." When he arranged payment, Hackett warned him it might be a scam. Hammett replied, "Ask her to describe the chandelier." [93] He had to pay cash for his crass disregard for women, sporadically ignored his children, ran from Hollywood commitments, and ducked promises for *The Thin Man*. Hammett's patina had begun to tarnish and he knew it. Only Hellman made any sense to him.

Hammett's strong feelings for Hellman, perhaps his hopes for something different for himself, for them, can be seen in *Woman in the Dark: A Novel of Dangerous Romance*, which he published in *Liberty* magazine the following year. The detective Brazil tells Luisa, "I suppose I've just been waiting for something to turn up, something I could take as a sign which way I was to go. Well, what turned up was you. That's good enough." [94] His almost fatalistic sense of their ongoing importance to each other appears again and again in following years, Hammett writing Hellman of a song he could not forget, "You Are My Destiny."

Hellman took her trip and confronted her aunts with her decision to live with Hammett. Conventional enough to want commitment from him, she hated losing face. "I know that you will not approve of my living with a man I am not married to, but that's the way it's going to be." Aunt Jenny replied, "How do you know the difference between fear and approve?" [95] Hellman knew they feared for her and she feared for herself. "I was frightened of being hit, frightened of the humiliation, frightened of the superiority." [96] Hammett's draw was strong and she returned to him, signed divorce papers, and settled into a life of chaos at the Sutton Club Hotel, 330 East 56th Street. Hammett, who was broke, wore everything he owned and ducked out of the elegant Pierre Hotel without paying his bill. He asked Hellman to join him and they both headed to the Sutton, where writer Nathanael "Pep" West managed the hotel—badly.

Up to Good and No Good

Hammett and Hellman's time at the Sutton was by turns crazy and creative. The Sutton was a dormitory of sorts, a last refuge for writers. It had no lobby, and some rooms always remained vacant. A number of writers from Edmund Wilson to Erskine Caldwell stayed there from time to time. Some called the hotel "run-down and peopled by suicides . . . tennis bums and prostitutes." Others saw it as "an artist colony . . . where even the elevator man was writing a play."[97] The Hammett-Hellman duo got three rooms, the "Royal Suite," they ironically called it, though Hellman remembered it as the "Diplomat Suite" in a "fleabag hotel."[98] The Great Depression had forced a bank holiday, closing the banks in March 1933, and no one, least of all the profligate Hammett, had much cash. The Sutton allowed them to charge their meals, and Hellman recalled that "we had to eat there most of the time because we didn't have enough money to eat anyplace else. It was awful food, almost spoiled. I think Pep brought it extra cheap. But it was the Depression and I couldn't get a job."[99] Somehow the desperate straits or the Sutton's seedy atmosphere worked for Hammett. He locked himself in a room for days, writing feverishly, abjuring food and drink and Hellman to get this famous novel written.

Hammett didn't give his all to *The Thin Man*, finished in 1933, and he knew it; the writing and rewriting bored him.[100] The plot is tricky, the characters dissolute, the world murky, shallow. He portrayed a happily married couple who defied the insipid bliss offered by popular fiction. Nick and Nora lived a life in Manhattan of dazzling parties, sophisticated friends, excessive drinking, affectionate bantering. So contrary was the book to social mores, that the December 1933 serialization of *The Thin Man* in *Redbook* cut out much of the drinking, any reference to Nora's being drunk, Nora's smart mouth, and Nick's infidelity. Both *Redbook* and the 1972 Vintage edition cut the infamous line, "Tell me something, Nick. Tell me the truth: when you were wrestling with Mimi, didn't you have an erection?" Nick's reply, "Oh, a little," and Nora's laughing rejoinder, "If you aren't a disgusting old lecher," were cut as well. Detection rests on intelligence and understanding human frailty, as did their marriage. In the novel, Nick must solve a crime and cut through the fabric of illusion. Nora entertains him, makes him laugh, listens to him, and loves him even as she naively fails to see the rot at the center.

Fatigued, leading a life he didn't admire with a woman he did, Hammett wrote this novel for money, and indeed from 1933 to 1950 he earned nearly a million dollars from it and its many spin-offs,[101] including a Hearst syndicated serialization of it to promote *Secret Agent X9*, a comic strip with a story line by Hammett and drawings by Alex Raymond.[102] He dedicated *The Thin Man* to Hellman—heady homage for a twenty-eight-year-old woman.

Hellman often remarked that it was a great day when Hammett told her he modeled Nora Charles after her, only to add he modeled all the women characters after her, including liars, vixens, and murderous Mimi.[103] Traveling to Hollywood to make the numerous adaptations of *The Thin Man*, Hammett telegraphed Hellman, "SO FAR SO GOOD ONLY AM AMISSING OF YOU PLENTY LOVE = NICKY. His novel gave Hellman a public legitimacy outside of marriage, Hammett telling the *New York Evening Journal* in summer 1934 that Nora "is real."[104] The radio, film, and television *Thin Man* marriage was sexy, sensual, and funny, with Nick and Nora played by William Powell and Myrna Loy for film and Peter Lawford and Phyllis Kirk for TV. But an edgier relationship is portrayed in the novel, reflecting Hellman and Hammett's life: holed up in a posh hotel gone seedy; Hammett driven by writing demons he drank to drown; Hellman perched precariously on a ledge between stagnation and spiraling surplus. Both used booze and wit to act the parts of Nick and Nora Charles, and then some.

Hellman was not one to pine away in the lobby waiting for Hammett to finish the novel. Restless, she and Pep got up to all manner of mischief. They read people's mail. Hellman, "crazy about other people's lives," found her old boardinghouse curiosity resurfacing. Bored and unemployed, she began a halfhearted affair with Nathanael West, who was engaged to the beautiful Alice Shepard. Hellman certainly wasn't in love with him or jealous of Shepard's beauty, but she had motives. Hellman had let the brooding "wounded bird,"[105] Laura Perelman, off the hook for the Dash affair, and instead blamed Sid Perelman, who told her about it.[106] Never a woman to forgive, Hellman didn't speak to Sid for a year. Now she had an opportunity to insert the needle into Laura, who many felt adored her brother Pep West a bit too much. Variously described as "a gentle soft-spoken man with a taste for Brooks Brothers clothes" or an aristocratic Czechoslovakian prince, Pep had too much restless waiting time of his own, and his halfhearted attraction to Hellman gave way to afternoon sex and then innuendo.[107] His attachment to Shepard already waning, he used the Hellman peccadillo to break the engagement. To make matters even stranger, West's independent mother, Ana Weinstein, had a wild fantasy that her son would marry the independent Hellman.[108] Neither West nor Hellman bought into that scenario. West's sex play with Hellman was fun, but not for long. Their short-lived bedding was a steamy brew of intrigue that fizzled. Hellman spent more time swimming in the hotel pool than loving.

The Sutton drew an incestuous crowd with a penchant for high antics. In November 1932, Laura and Lillian, both suffering from unemployment and ennui, drove to Bucks County, Pennsylvania, with West, borrowing a convertible for part of the trip. After viewing a farm the Perelmans were thinking of buying, West gave them a wild ride back to New Jersey. Laura wrote, "He goes so fast and it's bad on the curving country road." But the real adventure began when Hellman took the wheel to Manhattan. As Laura recalled, "I lit a cigarette and put another one against it for Lillian. A spark flew in her lap and then the telephone pole came at us very slowly and I closed my eyes when the crash came and I heard the glass breaking. *Jesus Christ.* Don't step on the wires, they might be live wires."[109] Neither was hurt, but Laura and Lillian were live wires when out and about, and sparks flew around these antic, smoking women. Laura was sick of everyone and the next day wrote, "I would love not to see Pep, Perel, Lillian and Mother. I would love Gurky," her schnauzer.[110] Unfortunately for Laura, the whole group often went to Bucks County together. Hellman remembered hunting trips as a "fuzzy snapshot," since the group was usually drunk. "My memory of those hunting trips is of trying to be the last to climb the fence, with the other guns in front of me, just in case."[111]

A wild ride, birdshot, and whisky weren't enough of a life for Hellman, who badgered the *New Yorker* to publish her stories. Oddly, given her jealous nature, the center of Hellman's early malaise with Hammett centered not on his women but on her need to make her own living. Even when Hammett was flush with money, she didn't like a life without her own accomplishment. She liked writing for money, despite her complaints about the writing slave shop at MGM. Living off Hammett's uneven income made her feel edgy, wary. She continued to submit articles to the *New Yorker*, which replied with kind rejections: "Dear Lillian: These [stories] are both good, as I've told you, but not practical for The New Yorker. We are such a rational little magazine."[112] She tried improving the stories and published two of them in the *American Spectator.* But she knew they stank and in despair drank the nights away, with or without Hammett. "I drank more than I wrote and so I couldn't remember very well what I had written the day before."[113]

Reality didn't help. The country was mired in the Depression; her relationship with Hammett was fraught with difficulty—no marriage, no fidelity, no financial security. Nick and Nora Charles's marriage bordered on the scandalous in the 1930s; Hammett and Hellman just lived in sin. Hellman knew it and hated it, her smart talk about her generation's laissez-faire sex just that—smart talk. At twenty-eight, she needed work.

In these rather desperate straits, Hammett accomplished two miracles: he finished *The Thin Man* and coerced, cajoled, and mentored Hellman into working hard on her writing, urging her to try drama. Hammett gave her a plot and started her along a path she later recommended for all novice writers: find something concrete and make it your own.[114] With *The Thin Man* bringing in cash and Hammett setting Hellman to work, the Hammett–Hellman duo took up residence in the opulent Hotel Elysee. Glamour returned. Hammett's money funded the couple's rising fortunes, buying them time and opportunity.

Hellman swallowed whole all he gave her, maybe making more of their relationship than he did, but maybe not. Hammett wrote a happy ending for the first time, with Brazil and Luise in *Woman in the Dark*. Raymond Chandler noted that the "happy ending seems a bit forced, as if Hammett, in order to bring Brazil and Luise together after all, might have bent his hard-eyed gaze away for a moment." Tired of the detective genre and tired of himself as writer, Hammett bent his gaze on Hellman's work. As Diane Johnson reflected, "He couldn't be James Joyce and he couldn't be content with being this recently-of-the-working-class hack writer—as he saw it . . . And so he was stymied."[115] Through success and failure, he continued to try to write something of significance, leaving half-written novels: *My Brother Felix* (which became *Toward Z*), *There Was a Young Man*, *The Valley Sheep Are Fatter*, and *Tulip*.[116] Hammett's passions shifted to politics, intellectual inquiry, and breaking free from a dissolute life that both tempted and repulsed him. As Hellman later wrote, "Good as it is, productivity is not the only proof of a serious life . . . he was without envy of good writers and was tender about all writers, probably because he remembered his own early struggles."[117]

No writer has been as vilified as Hellman for reaping the benefit of a willing mentor. Many Hammett fans blame her for the "coincidence" of their relationship and the cessation of Hammett's writing. Anti-Hellman animus paints the young Hellman as "ugly . . . a succubus who drained Hammett of his talent and his testosterone."[118] But teaching Hellman—and others—to put their talents to work gave him the satisfaction all great teachers have.[119] Hammett saw in Hellman a brilliant potential.

Reading scripts in Hollywood had prepared Hellman for a sense of dramatic movement. The child voyeur of New Orleans found any taboo exciting; the unconscious motivations and assumed guilts of others played out in her family, in herself. Hellman friend and psychologist Milton Wexler defined her as "a psychologist who could look at the evil, wicked underbelly of humanity; she was extraordinary."[120] She knew too that although purveyors of evil and injustice might be mindless or petty, the devastating results on others could be monumental. She had a writer's mind. As mentor and critic, "cool teacher" Hammett ignited the creative spirit of a brilliant woman, recognizing her raw talent, forcing her to draw on her experience as a screenwriter, ultimately giving her what she needed to excel: a plot.[121] Hammett's granddaughter tells it: "When Hellman and amorous writing partner Louis Kronenberger were unable to complete a satiric drama [*Dear Queen*] and threatened to go away together to work on it, Hammett responded by giving her his idea for dramatizing a true crime story by William Roughead called "Closed Doors: or the Grand Drumsheugh Case" about a girls' school in Edinburgh forced to close in 1810 because its owners were rumored to be lesbians."[122] Hammett urged her to take the bare outline of circumstance and make it her own. Whether to deflect her jealousy or out of frustration for her inability to write an adequate story from her own limited experience, he taught her structure. He always said, "Lock me in a room with a set of encyclopedias, and I'll come up with a plot," exactly Hellman's weakness.[123]

Never thwarted by shocking subjects—and lesbianism shocked most 1933 audiences—Hellman submerged herself in writing the play, though she later reflected, "How the pages got there, in their form, in their order, is more of a mystery than reason would hope for."[124] Hammett forced those pages out of her. "He felt that you didn't lie about writing and anybody who couldn't take hard words was about to be shrugged off, anyway."[125] Hammett's presence and her feeling for him made the mystery of creation manifest for her, and she wrote *The Children's Hour*. That she hated him at times, left him often, and loved others with great passion is beyond dispute.

The young Hellman began *The Children's Hour* in the grimy back offices of the Sutton, at first belting back gin as she wrote, later shifting to gallons of dark coffee and a hundred cigarettes a day as she became serious and dedicated. With the move to the Elysee, the couple critiqued her work in the newly opened Monkey Bar, "built to resemble a nightclub in a Joan Crawford movie." Hammett's attention to Hellman and her writing changed her by her own admission from a young loser trying to "sell her sense of humor"[126] to a self-respecting writer. After a day of writing, cigarette aloft, martini poised to drink, Hellman reveled in newfound self-respect. Hammett drinking alongside of her, proud of their work together, showed her off.

Finally the couple took the play down to Florida where Hellman "tore it up seven or eight times," then finished it in May 1934.[127] Auspiciously, she had also taken a job with Herman Shumlin, the young ambitious director. She was rising from the ashes.

"I'm not at all sure I would have written without Hammett,"[128] Hellman later said. She forever after praised his talent and assistance in her writing career. Critics sometimes imply that Hammett wrote Hellman's plays. But the assessment made by Hammett's granddaughter Julie Rivett is far more accurate. She acknowledged that the following plays were Hellman's alone, but thinks Hammett's detailed editing of *The Children's Hour* made him a cowriter. Rivett feels Hellman never gave Hammett enough public credit for his work on that first play. But Hammett clearly saw it as her play. Since Hammett made Hellman write every word—even as he suggested strategy and demanded rewrites and changed dialogue here and there—she bore the responsibility for it. Hammett's strategy meant going over each line, each word of the draft with "a relentless drive for the least words possible and the right word." As Jean Potter, another young writer he helped, commented, "He seldom changed anything himself, but asked questions, forcing the writer to look, to make appropriate changes."[129] Because Hammett gave Hellman his ideas, time, and editorial supervision, she elevated him to mythical status. He propelled her creativity and then taught her how to shape it, discipline it. She called him "teacher," "mentor," and "critic" in her memoirs and in interviews long after his death.

As much as he later frustrated, indeed infuriated, her, she never lost sight of his importance in her life. In the 1950s, she wrote her secretary, "Call Dash and tell him . . . that I have his snapshot on the fireplace and that I think he's a fairly nice old boy who has a grandchild growing up to be a Goddamned actress and that if he hadn't been such a ham, holding onto that cane for the picture of *The Thin Man*, it would never have happened."[130] Whether "it" was the horror of having an actress granddaughter or something else isn't clear. The letter, however, implies the attraction, love, connection, fame, and flamboyant charisma of the man who was Hammett. He gave Lillian Hellman the gift of becoming a writer, and Hellman was indebted to Hammett erotically, creatively. Hellman's audience was Hammett. Always.

Hellman and Hammett worked together on the drafts, with Hellman writing them in the morning and Hammett editing them at night.[131] At least one friend insisted Hammett typed the six new drafts he demanded. More likely, Hellman, struggling for a rough equality, typed each new draft on the typewriter her still pining ex-husband sent her as a gift.[132] It takes an experienced writer to understand the rhythms of the creative process. Hellman did not know about those rhythms as she turned out clever dialogue in stories not quite good enough. With Hammett, she typed a draft and then he read it and advised as she took notes. Then she cut and cut and cut until stark, clear drama came from the characters. She learned to write the hard way: draft after draft after draft. Once he had given the "okay" for the play, he entrusted *The Children's Hour* to her, never seeking to influence its production, never seeing credit. Her dedication of the play reads "For D. Hammett with thanks." As mentor, Hammett was first-rate.

Electrifying Broadway

"The cunning little coaxer" who manipulated, threw tantrums, and lied about her teachers' lesbianism for malicious fun in *The Children's Hour* seemed very like Lillian Hellman to her detractors. If Hammett assisted with plot, Hellman found her characters' central motivation and psychology in her own experience and nature. As she said of this first play, "I reached back into my own childhood and found the day I finished *Mlle. De Maupin*; the day I faked a heart attack; the day I saw an arm get twisted."[133] The tantrum-throwing "Mary" gave the play life; Mary stirred up the action, bated the principles. Writing and producing this play for Broadway resurrected the Hellman "I." She developed a fierce independence, stage-managing her own life with surprising successes and predictable failures. She always had a sub-plot simmering, however, ready to take over when the main action faltered.

Hellman set about getting the play produced the minute Hammett pronounced it ready. Almost as quickly she began an affair with its director, Herman Shumlin. No more suited to monogamy than Hammett or Hellman, Shumlin was a "comer from the word go."[134] He became one of the most powerful directors in Broadway history, producing *The Grand Hotel*, *The Male Animal*, *The Corn Is Green*, *Inherit the Wind*, and *The Deputy*. His name is foremost attached to the electrifying Hellman productions he directed for Broadway: *The Children's Hour*, *Days to Come*, *The Little Foxes*, *Watch on the Rhine*, and *The Searching Wind*. Shumlin and Hellman made a great match, theatrically—and had she loved him as he did her—perhaps romantically.

Born in 1898 to a Russian Jewish father and Ukrainian mother, Shumlin inherited his father's passion for politics and his mother's "lively, aggressive . . . joi de vivre . . . intoxication with the theatre."[135] Young Shumlin became enthralled by melodramas. When he saw Johnston Forbes-Robinson's *Hamlet*, he determined to have a life in the theater. He met "the wunderkind of the 20s," Jed Harris, later one of the most successful director/producers on Broadway, and got his big break. Harris, breaking into Broadway via a press agent job, invited Shumlin to work on a theatrical weekly, the *New York Clipper*. Shumlin said he learned by osmosis and followed Harris to *Billboard*, the oldest theatrical journal in New York. As a press agent, Shumlin screened seven hundred films, which he remembered as "one big blur." But that experience gave him a keen eye for successful plots. Thus Shumlin, Harris, and Kober got their start in theater as press agents, "a nobler breed then."[136] All were trying to break into producing, When Harris struck it rich on Broadway with *Love 'Em and Leave 'Em*, his arrogance drove Shumlin wild. As Edward Choate, who once worked in the office, said, "Harris was a god. He was young, rich, creative and had a knack for stirring up trouble."[137] Shumlin split with Harris after a fistfight and Kober went to Hollywood; the men didn't see each other for years.

All three ultimately became Hellman's lovers—each one favored for different reasons, in varying intensities. She found literate, successful men irresistible. Of the three, Shumlin was the least handsome but the most dynamic; he mattered to her for the rest of her life, just as Kober did. Shumlin, a striking figure who shaved his head daily and wore a short mustache, offered the attractive, but hardly beautiful, young Hellman more than good looks. Shumlin offered passion and a focused volatility; he interacted close-up.

When Hellman took *The Children's Hour* to Shumlin, "a tireless searcher for promising scripts,"[138] she had been working for him as a script reader at $15 a week.[139] They worked out of the same 42nd Street office where, young and newly wed, she had assisted Kober eight years earlier. Now Hellman told Shumlin she was writing a play with a story line concerning lies and lesbians; he told her to take up another line of work. Finally Ira Gershwin joined forces with Hellman to get Shumlin to read Hellman's script on a rainy day in Manhattan. According to Gershwin's wife Lee, they sat in Shumlin's office while he read the script, with Gershwin pushing Shumlin and calming Hellman until Shumlin agreed to produce it.[140] Shumlin said, "I was all a-tremble, it was so good. When I finished the second act, I was afraid to go on, for fear it couldn't last. As soon as I was through reading, I immediately agreed to produce it. Who wouldn't?"[141]

Shumlin knew the lesbian topic would cause censorship problems, but he had guts and courage too. Against Schumlin's advice, Hellman took the title *The Children's Hour* from Longfellow's 1860 poem of the same name, the sweetness of the poem ominous in the play's context: "They climb up into my turret / O'er the arms and back of my chair; / If I try to escape, they surround me; / They seem to be everywhere." Shumlin fretted that audiences would misjudge and buy tickets for a children's play, not the "indecent" show banned in Boston for nearly thirty years.[142] He wanted the play despite his fears. Shumlin's preoccupation with social and political themes would become his trademark, and Hellman shared his commitment to confront audiences.[143]

Despite the forceful bravado of Hellman's play and production, her first smash hit depended as much on Hammett and Shumlin as it did on her. Shumlin immediately began staging *The Children's Hour*. With his job as editor done, Hammett took off for Hollywood to write adaptations, flying high on liquor and women. In October he wrote Hellman several letters, in one telling her that he and Mrs. Joel Sayre "did a little town-roaming until nearly five this A.M."[144] But he also wrote, "I miss you awfully honey—it would be so thoroughly nice being back here if you were only along. I hope the rehearsals are going smoothly and I hope you are being a good girl."[145]

The rehearsals did go smoothly, but Hellman wasn't being a good girl. For ten years, from 1934 to 1944, Hellman and Shumlin established a personal and professional pattern that lasted through five plays and a movie. Shumlin shared her plays, her politics, and her bed. Their dramatic collaboration and complex relationship was marked by anger, tension, romance, and political passion. The two of them broke up after many years, many battles, and many ugly money issues shattered their alliance.[146] But they had a long run. Yelling and screaming and fighting over every detail of the plays aroused them. Shumlin, commanding, with a razor-sharp intelligence and wit,[147] was capable of great gentleness and had an "easy kind of common sense" that appealed to Hellman.[148] "Poor Rose Shumlin" the first of Shumlin's three wives, was no match for the intellectual and theatrical sparks the two generated.[149] Hellman loved Shumlin's masterful vigor, his booming voice ringing out for all to hear. Yet he could be caustic and he had a low boiling point. Hellman's temper sizzled as she demanded attention to every one of her rehearsal notes. The *New York Times* reported that "the strapping producer-director and the slim red-blond playwright were seen together very frequently, and generally in animated conversation."[150] Shumlin reflected, "I wouldn't call it a peaceful, calm relationship."[151] According to actor Tony Randall, Shumlin had, like Hellman, "a huge and overwhelming intellect coupled with a frightening articulateness and a psychotic inability to be wrong about anything . . . naively unaware that he is like this, seeming to like everybody, even those he yells at."[152]

Full of mischief, Shumlin and Hellman had fun. They also made great theater together. Shumlin respected writers because he thought the script "the soul of the theatre."[153] Hellman insisted on being at the very center of production. She admitted she was "not good at casting," while Shumlin's expertise was widely known.[154] Whether he trusted her judgment or couldn't shake her loose, casting involved both of them. It took five long months to find the cast for *The Children's Hour*.

A problem arose over choosing a child actress to play the nasty, scheming Mary Tilford, who lied about the teachers' lesbianism, blackmailed a fellow student to act as witness, and manipulated every adult she knew. Hellman wrote her (and understood her, having been a rebellious, manipulative little girl who faked pains) as full of "I want, I want" and demanding center stage. But Mary turned from obnoxious to plain nasty, no dream part for an actress, especially since the "children" of the play had to be eighteen because Shumlin insisted the subject matter was "unfit" for children. Finally they hired Florence McGee as Mary because she had the "necessary acidity" for the role.[155] In one scene, Mary had to twist the arm of Peggy, played by Eugenia Rawls. McGee recalled that she twisted and twisted Rawl's arm, with Shumlin giving instructions for more and more violence. Noting that McGee caused Rawls real pain, Hellman finally said, "Herman, you're hurting her," to which he replied "no, no, no. She's just acting."[156]

Critics applauded McGee's performance, with one remarking, "She is so good that one wants to strangle her."[157]

Shumlin's bossing made more than one young actress cringe. As Rawls began her character Peggy's recitation of Shakespeare's *Merchant of Venice*, she tried to sound like the famous actress Ellen Terry. Shumlin stopped her cold. "What do you think are doing? Who do you think you are?" She said, "Ellen Terry." Shumlin nearly shouted. "Eugenia, you are playing the role of a thirteen-year-old girl. Forget elocution. Read it in a sing-song fashion . . . you are bored with Mrs. Mortimer's elocution class!" Presumably no one was bored at Shumlin's rehearsals.

Casting and directing woes didn't stop with the actresses hired to play children. Hellman and Shumlin had trouble finding actresses who would play "a lesbian," even if the original charge of lesbianism was a lie and the feelings were repressed in Martha Dobie. So many stars rejected the role that Hellman enlisted ex-husband Arthur Kober to scour Hollywood for likely candidates. He wasn't successful but he caused another ruckus. Kober wrote that Margaret Sullavan, just starting her career in Hollywood, would think about it, but she would have Jed Harris (with whom she was having an affair) read it first. Shumlin's blood boiled. He wrote Kober in October, a month before the show was to open. "Sullavan out as I will not tolerate a madman's perception." A day before opening rehearsals the cast was still incomplete.[158] Finally interviewing two actresses Hellman and Shumlin had seen in a "bad" summer play, they found their "matched set": Katherine Emery played Karen, and Ann Revere played Martha—a closet lesbian even to herself.[159]

They chose Maxine Elliott's Theatre because it was way off on 39th Street and scheduled to be torn down. It came cheap but turned out perfect for its intimacy, its "sumptuous old ivory, brown velvet and gold appointments" and sweeping staircases, a fitting backdrop to the girls school set.[160] The success of *The Children's Hour* gave the theater new life, though the risqué play could have been its ruin.

The Children's Hour needed Shumlin's firm direction, as the controversial plot weighed on the cast and had to be handled adroitly. No prude (he had a personal collection of nude paintings), Shumlin, as director, nevertheless worried about the censors and the play's reception. Fearful of being shut down, Shumlin insisted on following every regulation "to the letter," including the fire regulations forbidding smoking backstage. This put considerable strain on two chain-smokers: himself and the playwright, who attended all the rehearsals.

When rehearsals finally began, Shumlin established himself as boss, sitting at a table with the actors and actresses grouped around him as they read their parts. As actor/producer Phillip Schopper noted, "His firmness and conviction was almost cravenly welcome by the cast . . . he had a very understated brilliance, not flashy, not concerned with his own image of 'the great director.' He had a clear vision of what was needed."[161]

Tension grew between a director who suffered from migraines and an untried playwright with her own ideas. Hellman vigilantly noted every aspect of the play's performance, taking notes, critiquing everything from "sound over the air system," to the cadence of an actor's lines, to Miss Revere's short, fuzzy hair, which she thought was "un-teacherlike."[162] She expected directors to listen and do her bidding. Later directors groaned when they saw Hellman coming, and when she directed her own plays, she made actors and actresses weep with frustration. Shumlin listened, however, and attended to every detail, never cutting her out of the loop but not losing his own sense of the play. Shumlin finessed her complaints when necessary, but his word was law.

He was "dictatorial in his quest for orderliness."[163] He insisted on every detail according to his own vision. The people in the audience know how a man drinks a cup of coffee, how a woman lights a cigarette, and how a mother speaks to a child. He insisted actors attend to the audience's sense of reality; each aspect of the set had to work. In another of Shumlin's productions, Gary

Blake wrote that he "went so far as to have Ethel Barrymore's derriere measured for a Windsor chair."[164] Hellman wrote Shumlin, joking about his exacting measurements and his obsession with "sight lines" for the audience:

Herman dear
This poem which you cut off
Is cut off as one would cut off
An arm
A leg
An organ
$1/2$ dimension

For all the fights and the fun, the two revered the theater. Hellman never forgot that Shumlin produced a play by an unknown, and she always admired his penetrating talent. Shumlin respected Hellman's insight and demanded dramatic perfection, expecting success. He said, "If it's done right, 1000 playgoers will sit there silently. If you make a mistake the silence breaks, and 400 of them will cough or rustle their programs."[165] No one coughed at *The Children's Hour*.

When the play opened on November 20, 1934, the audience gave standing ovations, calling "author, author." The thrill of success was palpable—everyone knew it was a hit. The stunning success of the play's opening caused Shumlin, excited and tactless, to embrace Revere and Emery and say, "Thank God we HAD to take you." The actresses, "on top of the acting heap," had no objection.[166] Shumlin had taken Hellman's direction and help but didn't complain in public.

The telegrams poured in for Hellman: from Pep West, "It is really a swell play darling a really swell play"; from "Manfred the press agent" (Louis Kronenberger), "Lillith the lithe Lillith the lovely Lillith the Mazeltov"; from her aunts, her friends, and her Newhouse relatives—typical in its emphasis—"May your opening be crowned with success and financial glory" signed Mr. and Mrs. Louis J. Jink and Julia Newhouse; from the rising star Moss Hart: "To tell you how thrilled I was with the play and I wish I were in your boots today."[167]

The play electrified Broadway. Reviews, which break—or make—a production on its first night, praised Hellman for her "stinging tragedy."[168] Her work won praise for its venomous portrayal of a liar and the horrible potential of a lie to ruin lives. Brooks Atkinson of the *New York Times* proclaimed that *The Children's Hour* "until the final scene is one of the most straightforward driving dramas of the season, distinguished chiefly for its characterization of little Mary." From Walter Winchell to Robert Benchley, critics elevated her from a novice to a lauded playwright "perched high on the pedestal."[169] Some critics complained about the play's end, or its "too many endings,"[170] but they uniformly praised both Hellman and Shumlin for "an outstanding event in American footlights history."[171] Nothing mattered more than that to Hellman, not even the unprecedented 691-performance run.

But gasps of moral outrage could be heard from the start. Shumlin called *The Children's Hour* "a highly dangerous drama," "provoking alike to authorities and moralists."[172] He fought hard to put it in theaters from Boston to Chicago to London, where it was banned—in Boston for nearly thirty years. Hellman and Shumlin fought the battle together and passionately. As a reporter in New York exclaimed, "With the censors in Boston out to behead her play, Miss Hellman does little or no weeping. She tosses her head and feels combative."[173] Shumlin even offered to pay to move the production to Boston to show Mayor Frederick Mansfield its worth and moral underpinnings. Mansfield roundly refused, commenting that *The Children's Hour* (which he had not read or seen) was "unfit," "the portrayal of a moral pervert or a sex degenerate."[174] Shumlin was irate, saying "I–I–I, then stopped," rendered speechless.[175] A fierce advocate for playwrights in general and Hellman in particular, he sometimes lost a battle but usually made it noisy and protracted.

The Children's Hour should have won the Pulitzer Prize in 1934. When it did not, the New York Drama Critics Circle Award was created. The Pulitzer Prize committee had dismissed *The Children's Hour* as inappropriate subject matter for an award and then lied about it. The Pulitzer jurors at first said that they had dismissed *The Children's Hour* because "the last act was bad" but later admitted they had not considered the smash hit at all because of the "undue affection in a girls' school."[176] They gave the award to Zoe Akins's adaptation of Edith Wharton's *The Old Maid*, which ran for only 305 performances. Critics and fans alike screamed foul. The drama critics, in their outrage at the Pulitzer's stodgy, safer choice, instituted the Drama Critics Circle Award, now Broadway's most prestigious award to a dramatist. It is presented each May by critics from all New York City newspapers, magazines, and wire services, except the *New York Times*. Too late for Hellman and *The Children's Hour*, the first award, in 1935, went to Maxwell Anderson's *Winterset*. In 1947, the Tony Awards were created to give drama awards in seven categories. Hellman went on to win both awards, but not for her 1934 play. Still, her success and influence were astonishing for a young playwright.

All the attention overwhelmed Hellman. Drink dominated, and it wasn't a solace. She had turned to booze to distance herself from a world she said her parents "didn't know," but she didn't know it either. She felt overwhelmed in the world of the theater and in her relationships with Hammett and Shumlin. They were exciting and made her feel alive, but they threatened her sense of self.

At this her finest hour, Hammett was nowhere to be seen. He felt happy for her but he was in Hollywood—profligately drunk and bedding someone. In *Pentimento*, Hellman said she called him a couple of days after *The Children's Hour* opening at 3:00 A.M. Hollywood time, only to have the phone answered by a woman Hammett said was his secretary. But he didn't have a secretary, and the jealous, enraged Hellman flew to California to destroy the soda fountain at his rented mansion in Pacific Palisades. Hellman critics dispute her recounting of events as lies, but something extraordinary occurred between them after *The Children's Hour* opened.

A letter to Hellman from Hammett six days following the opening night shows the Hellman drama off-stage. He wrote, "Darling, Here is the thingamagigger and I love you very much please. I haven't a single bit of news beyond what I told you over the phone except that I still love you very much please and would ask that you might find it possible to return my affections if it so happens you could do it without too much trouble . . . and I love you very much. . . . And I love you very much . . . Now—still loving you very much—I'm off for another crack at the thin man sequel. . . . I love you very much, Dash."[177] Hammett did have a secretary in Hollywood, Mildred Lewis, someone "Hellman never chose to remember,"[178] according to Diane Johnson. But Hellman could have talked to one of a hundred women in Hammett's bed at 3:00 A.M. on any given night. In the drunken blur of *Children's Hour* success, she hardly knew the time of day or the day of the week. She did fly to Hammett in the weeks following *The Children's Hour* opening. As to whether she actually destroyed a soda fountain at 325 Bel Aire Road, Hellman told Nora Ephron years later, "Well, he deserved that."[179]

Hellman told bitter stories of putting up with Hammett's women and her violent anger at finding a woman in his house: "This was not the first time Hammett had brought ladies home, not having any intention of their staying—unless, of course, I was away, when he had moved two in for a week."[180] She wanted to rip and render his life on the West Coast. She had worked as much for him as herself on the play. She hurt. She had not scripted his aloof disregard.

Young, overwhelmed, drinking too much when Hammett wouldn't sleep with her or wasn't there, she coped with her loneliness and anger by sleeping with Arthur Kober or Shumlin. Kober could not stay away and provided comfort and fun in the interludes his diary called "hits on the wing." The Shumlin affair, begun in the heightened tension that quivers in a theater, continued to flourish. Shumlin, sure of the play and sure of her, shared her basic insecurity about continued success, but he was ready to continue their work together without second-guessing theatrical success or their relationship. A month after the opening he wrote, "Dear, sweet, gorgeous, lovely, darling Lillian," followed by a letter showing his eagerness to talk to her: "it was a happy minute talking to you—I felt you so close to me."[181] He reveled in the rare air of success; she still felt like a gawking onlooker, but not for long.

Hollywood Star on the Rise

The success of *The Children's Hour* on the New York stage made her a hot commodity in Hollywood. "The twenty-nine-year-old playwright was praised and courted, and Sam Goldwyn wooed her back to Hollywood at $2,500 a week. A star on the rise." [182] Coming back to Hollywood famous in 1935 was an intoxicating rush. She told a reporter, "The most interesting part of my trip to Hollywood is that I'm going back to take a job at just thirty times what the movies paid me the last time I worked for them."[183] She wanted to *earn* the fabulous sums of money she made in Hollywood, and she did. Money wielded its power over her, but she was ever aware of Dorothy Parker's dictum: "The money you make in Hollywood is congealed *snow*—it melts before it hits the ground."[184] She wouldn't sell her soul for something that ephemeral.

Better than the money was that she was no longer a "summary girl" but a writer of picture shows. Though she didn't acknowledge it, reading scripts and writing summaries at MGM had taught her what words and images must do together. MGM readers saw 20,000 pieces of literature a year, and Hellman had read her fair share. She had always been "genuinely interested in movies . . . genuinely did my best."[185] She used her talent and did not feel degraded by film work. "When I first went to Hollywood, I heard talk from writers about whoring. But you are not tempted to whore unless you want to whore."[186] Even those contemptuous of the "colony" of writers from the East Coast knew that Hellman (and Arthur Miller too) took writing scripts seriously and had integrity

as writers. When Hellman signed a contract, she turned her talent to those celluloid strips.

Hellman didn't rest on her newfound dramatic fame but got right to work
adapting Lowell Brentano's book *The Melody Lingers On*. For eight years,
Hellman would be the major writer on Samuel Goldwyn's staff; she was "one
of the boys," and every film she wrote was a hit.

Hellman rarely said a good word about Hollywood, but she had fun there.
And not just because of Kober and Hammett. Hollywood catered to eccentrics,
had electric energy, and drew a remarkable crowd of citizens, all eager to work,
play, change their lives. She was one of them, whether she admitted it or not.
She caught the feeling, joined conclaves for lunch and marathon talk at
Lucey's across from Paramount Studios. Hellman's refusal to see herself as an
alternate "category" to the mixture of fraternity row and old boys' network of
Hollywood culture fueled her success and her rage. Hollywood made an apt
setting for Hellman's need for high adventure. As she said, "it still stands as the
most preposterous civilization of all time."[187] California nights invited action
year round, with lush hideaways in the hills only minutes from nightclubs and
pleasure domes. Adventures were everywhere.

This time around, she had not only a great reputation but also big connections. Hammett was "the great American mystery writer," whose fame was
already legendary in Hollwyood. Arthur Kober was a man of many connections; his list of friends and supporters reads like an article in *Variety*, from
Humphrey Bogart to John O'Hara. Just beginning a successful life as a writer
of stage and screen, he would write over thirty screen plays between 1930 and
1946, and later two smash hits on Broadway: *Having a Wonderful Time* and
Wish You Were Here. His *New Yorker* articles and stories collected in books
spanned five decades. Kober's record shows he was far more than the "folk
artist of the Bronx and the Catskills" that biographer William Wright depicted. He had serious clout in Hollywood and New York.

Hellman knew everyone, or so it seemed. Her huge laugh and great
humor made her friends. Her letters are replete with references to the Ira
Gershwins, the Collier Youngs, Sam and Frances Goldwyn, Bette Davis,
Freddie Kohlmar, and Charlie Chaplin, whom she describes as "a crazy man,
but warm and rather nice and interesting." She and director Willy Wyler
began what they both called a lifelong "platonic love affair."[188] She gave him
unsolicited advice on his love life, telling him early on to beware of actress
Margaret Sullavan, advice he hated but should have followed. Later Wyler's
wife, Talli (Margaret Tallichet Wyler), and film producer Hannah Weinstein
became intimate friends of Hellman's for life. Hellman loved the rush of re-

lationships wherever she went, and Hollywood drew nearly everyone she knew at one time or another.

In 1935, despite Hellman's rising fame in the East, Hammett still paved the way to many of Hellman's contacts. Alice Toklas, for example, thought that Gertrude Stein might want to see Dashiell Hammett and asked a friend to invite him to dinner. He got the invitation on April 1 and thought it an April Fool's joke. But when assured of its authenticity, he asked to bring "someone."[189] When they got there, no one noticed Hellman. She later repaid Stein's snub by telling the story of Chaplin's spilling coffee all over an "exquisite tablecloth," with Stein's only response being, 'Don't worry, none of it got on me.'"[190] As Hellman said later, "Two greater egos, Miss Stein's and Mr. Chaplin's, have seldom faced each other across the dinner table."[191] Dorothy Parker, now writing scripts in Hollywood, was an ego and wit more in tune with Hellman. She sustained Hellman for "many good days and years," though they had vast differences in outlook.

Hellman had first met Parker three years before at a party in New York. Parker had made a fool of herself by bowing and kissing Hammett's hand. In Hollywood in 1935, the two were drawn to each other by their shared penchant for high antics and wit as well as radical, if vague, political affinity. They had story contests, each one trying to outdo the other with true stories of the zany. Dottie told droll tales, making Hellman hoot with laughter. One such story involved Parker's ubiquitous long, gray knitting, which once caught fire at a boring, cigarette-flinging script conference. Gossip and story served as antidotes to what both of them came to see as the deadly dull process of writing for Hollywood. They thought each other uproariously funny. After one party that Parker and her husband Alan Campbell threw in their North Canon Drive house, Parker declared that her "hangover was impressive enough to be referred to as "we."[192] Hellman loved her wit. They also shared an interest in affairs of the heart, though no two women could be more different in their choice of men or their response to men. In her memoirs, Hellman wrote of Parker looking up from her book to tell her, "The man said he didn't want to see her again. That night she tried to climb into the transom of his hotel room and got stuck at the hips. I've never got stuck at the hips, Lillian, and I want you to remember that."[193] Hellman wrote this memory as if Parker referred to the book's characters, but both knew the man was Robert Benchley, and the stuck-at-the-hips woman "the wife of a well-known banker." The two women shared that peculiar intimacy between women that disregards commonality in favor of the pleasure of being oneself. And of course no two more outspoken women existed.

Hellman's sharp nature and biting wit didn't always endear her to others. She loved exploding people's vanity. She wrote that one night she got "slightly tight" with a couple she called Bubby (short for Bubbles) and Hornblow. "Hornblow leaned across to Bubby and said: 'I can't see you in this light, but I can feel the vibrations.' He wasn't joking because he glared at me when I screamed with laughter."[194] Hellman reveled in the slurred high comedy of Hollywood social life. With eyes and ears tuned to the absurd, she mocked nearly everyone: Jack Warner wearing a colonel's uniform "which turned out to be kosher" at a party during the war; Ben Hecht's assertion that he would work for Goldwyn only if supplied a "beautiful Goldwyn dancing girl in a beaded evening dress as a receptionist outside his office."[195] As much as she loved outlandish gossip, Hellman didn't like being the subject of witty tales, or at least those told by those she didn't know well. In the late 1940s, she asked writer and producer Harry Kurnitz to go for a ride in her "newly imported German folk-waggen." He turned her down, saying, "I've been in bigger women than this."[196] Kurnitz irritated her and she bitched about him to Sam Goldwyn, of all people. Kurnitz's tactless jest could not hope to compare to what both she and Goldwyn dished out.

Sam Goldwyn was Hellman's Hollywood boss for nearly every film she made, and Goldwyn had "more fights than any other man in Hollywood." "You always knew where you stood with Goldwyn—nowhere," or so said F. Scott Fitzgerald. Goldwyn was stubborn, persistent, and wily; his success depended on it. "He was a titan with an empty skull," Billy Wilder said of Goldwyn in retrospect, "not confused by anything he read, which he didn't." But he had an "instinct for better things."[197] Originally Goldwyn didn't have the money to attract the expensive beauties, the actress faces that guaranteed independent studio success. So he decided to substitute quality pictures for starlets and courted the best writers, relatively cheap labor. Goldwyn had high hopes and recruited inexorably. He was never stopped by a simple no. He pressed and cajoled and threatened. One time Paul Jerrico wanted to take a Goldwyn job but had made a verbal commitment to another filmmaker. Goldwyn wanted Jerrico too, and Jerrico recalled, "This is a true Goldwynism . . . He said, 'do the decent thing. Take this job and don't even tell him.'"[198] Indeed, Goldwyn's relentless nature paid off. By the late 1930s, his Formosa Avenue studio housed great writers like Elmer Rice, George Hecht, Robert Sherwood, and Frances Marion, along with Hellman, who became the star of his stable. Goldwyn bragged, "Just classy writers, Goldwyn's got just classy writers."[199]

Hellman went to Goldwyn after the Broadway success of *The Children's Hour.* Herman Shumlin convinced Goldwyn to hire her to write *The Dark Angel*, a film she called "an old silly, directed by Sidney Franklin." Hellman "didn't care much about the seduction of Hollywood fame" but liked coming back to write for real and for a man she respected more than Sam Marx.

Those who knew both Goldwyn and Hellman waited for their volcanic wills to erupt. Inevitably two exhibitionist egos like theirs would melt down. Even after he struggled to sign her on to *The Dark Angel*, Goldwyn tested her. Goldwyn's way to solve any problem was to "bluster, telephone, flatter, bully and phone back." Hellman, working on *The Dark Angel* in 1935 and flush from her success in New York, couldn't stand "breaking the back" of a story, the endless hashing out of scripts and production notes. She took a night plane back to New York. As soon as Goldwyn could reach her, he promised that if she flew back instantly she'd be allowed to go into a room by herself and begin writing. She promised him she'd think about it, which she didn't, and left for Europe. Her willingness to say no to Goldwyn enhanced her worth and reputation; she was an "unattainable woman as desirable as such women are, in another context, for men who like them that way."[200] Hammett explained Hellman's success with Goldwyn: "When Sam doesn't look at you, you cease to exist. Lillian solves that by just not looking at *him*."[201] When Hellman did say yes to writing a Goldwyn script, she delivered high-quality goods. She understood when Goldwyn assigned British playwright Mordaunt Sharp to watch over her as she wrote *The Dark Angel*, however, and didn't make a fuss. It would have taken too much energy. Hellman and Sharp share the film's credits, but she insisted she wrote 90 percent of it and critics agree.

Goldwyn had adapted *The Dark Angel* from a Guy Bolton play years earlier, and Marion Davies had rewritten it as a silent film in the "weepie" genre: Kitty, the girl left behind, loves the soldier Trent, who appears as a dark angel in her dream. When he doesn't return from the war, she assumes him dead. Trent returns later, blinded from battle, to find she loves another; he releases Kitty from her old vow of fidelity. To Hellman such stuff was nonsense. She wanted fewer tears and more real relationships, making the three protagonists childhood friends and "fashioning two sets of cousins . . . to exploit the ironic potential of a plot abounding in chance encounters."[202] As silly as the resulting plot is, critics sat up and took notice of the clearly defined plot sequences and interlocking themes. The script attracted an outstanding cast: Fredric March, Merle Oberon, and Herbert Marshall. The Hollywood press, which adulated stars over all others, nevertheless lauded Hellman for her "highly literate" screenplay.

Hellman knew well the tussles with the Motion Picture Production Code. In late 1921, the Roscoe "Fatty" Arbuckle scandal had confirmed public suspicions about an immoral, repugnant Hollywood culture. A young actress, Virginia Rappe, was found nearly dead in Arbuckle's San Francisco hotel room on Labor Day, and she died several days later of advanced peritonitis and a burst bladder. Even though Arbuckle was exonerated in the courts, the moviegoing public was disgusted by 1920s debauchery and demanded that thousands of theater owners serve "middle America" by adopting a less permissive attitude. The public outcry against Hollywood licentiousness alerted Congress, which introduced over one hundred censorship bills in 1921 alone. Hollywood producers saw the censors looming and began a ritual bowing to political necessity. On April 18, 1922, the producers appointed as their regulator Will H. Hays, the "czar of all rushes," as the censorious president of the Motion Picture Producers and Distributors of America.[203] His first fiat was to request that producers and distributors cancel all bookings and showings of Arbuckle films. Fatty had been blacklisted—the first but not the last victim of Hollywood censorship.

Hays, charged "to negotiate, so to speak, with an insistent public opinion," ruled with a heavy hand, demanding Christian principles with himself presiding as judge. By the time Hellman returned to Hollywood, Joe L. Breen, hired by Hays Public Relations, was the actual hatchet man. Breen, a strict Catholic, was hardly a neutral choice. "Throughout the early 30s, he railed against the Jews. . . . He blamed evil films and Hollywood's dissolute lifestyle on the 'lousy Jews,' 'the scum of the scum of the earth.'"[204] Breen hated capitalistic, communistic Jews—no matter the incongruity. With thinly disguised anti-Semitism, several Protestant churches joined the Catholic Legion of Decency to demand that Hollywood self-censor. Leaflets proclaimed, "Boycott the Movies! Hollywood is the Sodom and Gomorrah where International Jewry controls Vice-Dope-Gambling where young gentile girls are raped by Jewish Producers, Casting Directors who go unpunished." After the censors thrashed Jews, they turned on screenwriters. Hellman, of course, was both. Hays and Breen argued that Jewish executives could "keep the screen from offensiveness" by controlling pagan screenwriters who promoted "all the filth of the pictures."[205]

Jewish, decidedly leftist, outrageous, and outspoken, Hellman did remarkably well with the Code, beginning with negotiations about *The Dark Angel*. Breen sent a telegram to Geoffrey Shurlock refusing to distribute *The Dark*

Angel as written. The telegram doesn't clearly state whether the implicit sexuality in the romance or the class differences of the characters most violated the censors' sensibilities: "*The Dark Angel* is basically in violation production code and impossible from standpoint political censorship stop Unless basic story is chnged." Hellman had been around Hollywood long enough to know the futility of butting heads with the Hays office, so she changed the script to comply. She took out all sexual innuendo between the two leads, "particulary with regard to the episode in the English Hotel."[206] Hellman's first film received two Oscar nominations: Merle Oberon for best actress and Richard Day for art direction. Goldwyn liked working with Hellman because she wasn't intimidated by him, and she wrote as well as anyone in Hollywood. By his lights, better than any.

Encouraged by the success of *The Dark Angel*, Goldwyn paid $40,000 for the screen rights to Hellman's play, *The Children's Hour*, even though Will Hays immediately informed him that the name and content had to be changed to meet Hays Code regulations forbidding "low forms of sex," not to mention "sex perversion or any inference of it."[207] According to one apocryphal story, when Goldwyn was denied permission to use the play's title for the film version because the main characters were presumed to be lesbians, he replied, "We'll make them Americans." Goldwyn, habitually riding roughshod over objections, stubbornly refused to believe he couldn't make any film he wanted. In this, Goldwyn and Hellman agreed.

Hellman was still smarting from difficulties she had working with *Dark Angel* director Sidney Franklin. She found him indecisive and too ready to listen to anyone who had an opinion; he thought her rude. So when she agreed to write the film version of her play, she suggested director William Wyler to Goldwyn: "I'd seen *Counselor-at-Law*. . . . I'd met Wyler and liked him. We had fun." Goldwyn tried to persuade her to find a more experienced director, but Hellman demanded Wyler. Goldwyn later described Wyler as the most brilliant director in the business; Bette Davis described him as a "handsomely homely dynamo."[208] For now, both Hellman and Wyler were unknown commodities, trying to make a name for themselves in the most fickle of industries. Wyler took a risk in undertaking to direct a film version whose subject matter was beyond the pale of Hollywood sensibilities. Wyler thought, "What the hell . . . how is the man going to do this? . . . So I met Hellman, who I was very impressed with, and she explained to me that the story was not about lesbianism."[209] Hellman always insisted the story was about the power of a lie to ruin lives, and that functioned as central to a reworking of the film's plot to portray "innocence in an evil world, the world of childhood, the world of lies, brutality, complete inhumanity."[210] As powerful and cinematic a story as it was, the film took some doing.

Like Goldwyn, Hellman and Wyler had "picture sense." All boldly opinionated, they fought to make intelligent, arresting movies. But this heady brew of producer, director, and writer could have been disastrous, ending Hellman's career just as she got started. *These Three*, the title of this early film version of *The Children's Hour*, seems particularly well suited for these three huge egos. Yet somehow their differences meshed in that interest, and except for a few spectacular ruckuses, Goldwyn approved their work. He complained to all who would listen that Wyler took "thirty-six takes and prints one and six," and Wyler complained Goldwyn never changed his mind "until he saw you burst every blood vessel in your head."[211] Perfectionists at their craft, Hellman was articulate where Wyler was not. Hellman mastered dialogue above all, while Wyler demanded action at the center of cinematic drama. Wyler found Hellman opinionated, relentless, intrusive, "not easy in any respect."[212] Hellman believed in his artistry and made him believe it too.

Somehow Wyler's talent tempered Hellman's problem with possessive ownership of her work. She drove him as much as he drove himself. If she used the whip of her tongue a little too often, well, he was a "sadistic son of a bitch" while directing, according to actress Sylvia Sidney.[213] Wyler's domineering directing, Hellman's vigilance over the script, and Goldwyn's interference (he seldom left his people alone) met a different kind of ego in the actors and actresses. When Merle O'Brien, who played Karen, panicked because Bonita Granville's part of the child Mary dominated, she begged leading man Joel McCrea to go to Goldwyn to complain. Exasperated, Goldwyn replied, "I'm having more trouble with you stars than Mussolini is with Utopia."[214] The intrigue continued. Goldwyn had promised he wouldn't tell McCrea that Wyler had wanted Leslie Howard as the lead, but he did and McCrea showed his resentment. Everyone was off center during the making of this film, but no one complained about the results. *These Three* was "a stunning piece of mise-en-scène, stylistic and expressive, all in the form."[215]

These Three brought Hellman, Wyler, and Goldwyn newfound Hollywood triumph. Even with two great successes writing for him, Hellman realized the halcyon days with Goldwyn must be numbered. She wrote Kober, "Goldwyn continues so nice to me, that I am sure he has found out that I am his illegitimate child by Hilda Wilinchowski in Minsk."[216] She mockingly signed the letter "mimete, everybody's dream girl." Goldwyn's dream girl she wasn't, but he admired her talent, and he was determined in his fashion to squeeze every drop of her ability to his own ends. Gossip columnist Louella Parsons noted that "Sam regards the brilliant playwright as his own particular property" and described his rage when he thought some other producer tempted her to write for his studio: "Goldwyn hit the ceiling! He raved. He ranted." He was vigilant about protecting "his" Hellman from other producers.

Goldwyn kept strict accountings of how much employees contributed and how many pictures and projects they had to write under the contract. Getting writers to work beyond strict contractual terms was one of Goldwyn's specialties. He had Hellman write "treatments" for films yet unmade or yet to be adapted from silent films. On one occasion he had Hellman write a seven-page treatment for *Graustark*, an adaptation of Schenck's 1925 silent film based on George Barr McCutcheon's 1901 best-seller. Originally starring Norma Talmadge and adapted for the screen by Frances Marion, a "talky" version written by Hellman seemed a sure thing to Goldwyn. In theory, it looked perfect for Hellman: three lovers tangled in the politics of a fictional country, Graustark. The original script combined love, democracy, and social evil in a melodramatic mix of courtly and military characters.[217] In the treatment, Hellman rid the plot of its saccharine quality and turned it to a thriller, but not a good one. Hellman admitted that her halfhearted script was terrible, which resulted from Goldwyn's manipulating her. Goldwyn never made the film and never gave Hellman credit against her contract for her work. Nevertheless, much later Goldwyn told agent H. N. Swanson that in Hellman's fifteen years of working with him, she had acted "in a very fine manner toward him" even though he "wasn't an easy man to get along with."[218] But he told his wife to tell her to "go to hell" the last time she called.[219] Hellman wasn't easy either; they screamed at each other, loudly declared their opposing principles. Despite all the thwarting and balking, they kept at it for a long time. They had movies to make and the work mattered to them both.

With *The Children's Hour* still running on Broadway to unprecedented acclaim and *These Three* a resounding film success, Hellman, ironically, spun out of control. Electrified by success, she became part of a network of famous writers on the West Coast. Back on the East Coast, she and Shumlin filed a lawsuit against Boston over its censorship of *The Children's Hour*. Wearing a sassy, expensive suit and a hat draped over one eye, in New York she was thrust into the limelight as a scandalous playwright who wrote a dirty play. With all that acclaim and recognition, it is no surprise that tumult and "the most rambunctious drinking period" of her life followed. She reflected, "I was naive enough to think that the great fuss made over me meant that people where interested in me. . . . I was as sick of other people's drinking as I was of my own. I couldn't afford the emotions."[220] Forces conspired against her, both internal and external: runaway drinking, alternately loving and revenging herself on Hammett, the need to write, the thrill of political ferment.

High on success one minute and disbelieving in the next, she didn't quite know what she should be doing. Success separated herself from herself and others. Only a few years before gossip columnists had sneered at Hellman as an immoral, illicit groupie of the married Dashiell Hammett. Not everyone was as generous in forgiving and admiring her newfound success as ex-husband Kober, who wrote, "Now you're solidly on your own two feet, very much an individual and very much in the position to confound those awful malicious people who have gossiped and sneered."[221] The current toast of Broadway, she soaked up the praise but didn't quite believe it when suddenly Hollywood courted her too.

In 1935 Hellman began *Days to Come* but could not finish it until June 1936. Life had taken a fast but dark turn: long train trips or frightening plane rides between the coasts; the differing demands of Broadway and Hollywood; one lover awash in excess and other lovers vying for attention. Hellman and Hammett fought in both Hollywood and New York over money, over his whores and whose money paid for them, over her claim on him and his on her. She hated herself and she hated him. Shumlin, Kober, and Hammett often squired Hellman around Hollywood, all too cozy and congenial for Hellman who wanted a romance more than a ménage à quatre. In disarray, she put off writing for the theater. She later understood that she should have gotten to work immediately after she finished *The Children's Hour*: "You cannot be happy unless you are working on something new, something fresh, something that grows under your hands."[222] But she let personalities and Hollywood antics dictate. Rather than collapse under the weight of fame and unresolved relationships, Hellman did what she always did under stress: she found a new man.

She met Ralph Ingersoll in June, as she once again fled from Hollywood to New York. When their plane was forced to stop overnight in Albuquerque, they had a drink and fell into an immediate intimacy that sustained a long relationship of mutual interest, shifting from passion to friendship over the years. He thought her "very handsome, ugly but handsome," admiring her beautiful clothes, her blond hair, and her top-heavy but slim figure. She thought him masculine, good-looking, and smart, a perfect combination. He felt a "violent physical attraction"[223] and said that Hellman made him feel intensely alive and "knew how to make love, and how to receive it."[224]

Hellman, driven by a desire for action and admiration, needed Ingersoll. He added a new dimension to Hellman's life. Former managing editor of the *New Yorker*, he had just started managing *Fortune* magazine. Brilliant and ambitious, Ingersoll was married to Tommy (Mary Elizabeth) Carden, whose tuberculosis, he said, drove him into the arms of Hellman. Clearly he was open to change; he ultimately divorced Tommy and married three more times.[225] And Ingersoll, the man who had developed and written Talk of the Town in her favorite magazine, the *New Yorker*, was a coup indeed. As usual, she chose an interesting, complicated, unavailable man over easier fare. Ingersoll kept her interest, kept pleasure alive, and introduced her to a higher level of national politics than she had previously known.

Divorced from Kober, estranged from Hammett, and lacking a play to present Shumlin, Hellman was still young enough at thirty to look for a lasting romantic relationship. Whether she still hoped a man could fulfill her romantic ideals of marriage and family or was looking for love to escape the disappointment of Hammett's limits, she was excited by Ingersoll's interest. Hellman added Ingersoll to her list of valued lovers with whom she had long-standing, if sporadic, affairs: Kober, Shumlin, and Hammett. "Juggling oranges" Hammett called it.

A year after they met, Ingersoll would be "probably the most powerful journalist in New York."[226] He became an editor at *Time* and started an innovative leftist newspaper, *PM*. Hellman and her men—her father, Kober, Shumlin, Hammett—invested in *PM* during its heyday from 1940 to 1948. Hellman felt Ingersoll's power and intensity, admired his politics, loved his sexuality. Ingersoll added to the complications of her life. When Ingersoll joined Hellman in September on Tavern Island, eager to continue their romantic liaison, he found Hammett, Shumlin, and Kober there too. Hellman wisely blocked any entrance to her bedroom, remarking in a diary that for years she hoped for such a visit, but all of the men gathered together were too much for her. But in 1935 the Ingersoll romance flourished, and Hellman's creative juices flowed once again.

Muddled Drama

Even with Ingersoll and her newfound energy, Hellman had a difficult time starting a new play. Having denied the severity of her mother's illness for years, she didn't anticipate her death shortly after Thanksgiving from colon cancer. It crushed her. Home from Hollywood work on *These Three*, Hellman alternated between numbness and shock. Max fell apart, crying when anyone mentioned Julia. Family tension was high. Father and daughter fought over funeral details and left many decisions to Kober, who held them all together through the funeral. Kober and Julia had loved each other and were close, perhaps consoling each other over Lillian's affectionate disregard for them. Leaving Kober to sort out the will (Julia left him $10,000 in the family trust), Hellman characteristically fled family complications, taking the train to Hollywood and then traveling to Ohio to research the details of labor troubles in the manufacturing sector. Restless, she needed to escape emotions that tore at her and threatened to undermine the dizzying heights of her success. Labor unions she knew from her own Screen Writers Guild battles in Hollywood. Ingersoll's intellectual take on leftist politics made her interest keen. She would write a drama with labor turmoil as the center of the plot.

Even with the best of motivations, she wrote *Days to Come* in personal chaos, trying to give form to the personal and professional angst that beset her. She later saw her professional life as "out of bounds: the photographs, interviews, 'appearances,' party invitations are so swift and dazzling that you go into the second work with confidence you will never have again if you have any sense."[227] Dazzled at her professional self, she ignored the despair that attended every other aspect of her life. She may have begun *Days to Come* in Princeton, living with Hammett in one of his most dangerously profligate periods. He had come to Princeton from Lenox Hill Hospital, where he "recuperated"[228] from "suicidal despair," alcoholism, and venereal disease. He "attempted to drink himself well."[229] In Princeton, he threw money and booze at attendant students, and trashed the house; he had to pay the owner for repairs caused by the damage from "spilled beer and liquor and carelessly tossed cigarette stubs."[230] The tidy, organized Hellman loved him and hated his behavior. She despised their circumstances and fled to Hollywood when she could, leaving Hammett and Baby, one of the many large poodles they shared in their life together. He repulsed her, and she could not live with him. In response to a press inquiry about marrying Hammett, she said, "I've known Mr. Hammett for about five years and I guess he is my best friend. . . . But please don't think I'm going to get married. I don't want to get married to anyone."

She escaped by taking short trips—Tavern Island and Cuba with Ralph Ingersoll, reveling in their intimacy and battle of wits. When she returned she bought her first apartment, at 14 East 75th Street in New York City. She had the money, the independence, and the need to live alone. Even with the new apartment, she felt adrift, mourning her divorce but not

Kober, mourning her mother's death, mourning the loss of Hammett as mentor. She probably considered marrying Ingersoll; he was ready if not quite unattached. But Hammett still mattered too much emotionally. And she may have had another abortion. Lee Gershwin, gleefully ready to denigrate Hellman, reported that Hellman had seven abortions in the time she knew her. Gershwin, known to embellish, likely exaggerated, or Hellman did. Hellman relished needling the smug. Whatever the exact circumstances, in 1935 and 1936 Hellman alternated between high expectations and too many lows. Hellman recalled, "I was serious or semi-serious about another man and Hammett knew it. Neither of us ever talked about it until I told Dash that I had decided not to marry the man. . . . to which he replied: I would never have allowed that. Never."[231] She laughed at the time, but Hammett did stand in the way of her marrying another man, then and later. Work usually helped her ignore the frenzy around her; now it took time.

Her writing was not going well, and she turned her vexation on both Broadway and Hollywood—Shumlin and Goldwyn in particular. She wrote Kober of her malaise, detailing her irritation at Shumlin for signing a manager's contract during Dramatist Guild negotiations. She had fought for a play's "ownership being entirely vested in the writer. . . . I begged, argued, screamed with Herman not to sign the manager's contract. But it did no good." Goldwyn had gone "bats" about the production-room screenings of These Three. She found it all "very screwy."[232] She tried joining the party scene in Hollywood and the theatrical scene in New York, only to be disgusted. As she told Kober, "I saw two acts of S. N. Behrman's play, and gave up the ghost, pretending to be very ill and faint. I've seen two acts of almost every hit in town. The Sherwood play[233] had a "few good things," but she hated the audience as "the most disgusting in-the-know group of people I ever sat with . . . when Lunt does six dance steps, easily learned by a bright child of three, they have a fit.[234]

Hellman's real problem was she couldn't write her own play. "The truth is I'm scared of plotting, that the few things I've ever done well, were plots laid out for me beforehand. I'm getting panic stricken about the short time left. (It takes up all my waking hours being panic stricken, and that's probably why I don't work.)"[235] She felt like a fraud, unsure of her own worthiness in the light of her success. Finally, in the summer of 1936, she again flew to Havana—this time alone—to finish the play in relative peace. She tried to adapt Hammett's careful method of plotting but added subplots to show life's complexity. She finally finished it.

Hellman's anxiety was palpable. Although she had driven a hard bargain with Shumlin about advertising the play, demanding her name appear anytime his did, she wasn't sure the ideas she had tried worked. She told an interviewer the day before the play's opening, "You may have a clearly defined point of view and something, as we say with a titter, vital on your mind when you sit down to those nice new pencils and that nice fresh copy paper. But when you get all through. . . where are those fine ideas?"[236]

Her subject was a labor strike, focusing on the wrenching divisions between labor and owner. In the mid-1930s, little could be as topical. In 1932 unemployment reached 13 million people, and FDR's election divided America. Labor tensions threatened to erupt in every state, with strikes and threats of strikes in the General Motors plant in Michigan, the steel workers in Atlanta, the auto workers' strike at Bendix in South Bend, Indiana, and the rubber workers strike at the Firestone plant in Akron, Ohio. Hellman's play put a labor strike in Callum, Ohio. The plot was a natural, staging a distinctly partisan bias for the strikers. Hellman focused on the many personal consequences of calling in a band of homicidal strike breakers. When she searched for a title, the irreligious Hellman turned to the Bible. Her early notes show she pondered Isaiah (1:21): "How is the faithful city become a harlot! It was full of judgement; righteousness lodged in it; but now murderers."[237] She rejected *Faithful City* as title, but it fit her mood—self-righteous, unfocused anger. Hellman's play confronted the underside of the American dream. She wanted to dramatize personal and political conflicts and create a wholeness of vision. She couldn't control it.

Without Hammett and his "paring knife," Hellman tried for too much. "It's a story of innocent people on both sides who are drawn into a conflict and events far beyond their comprehension. It's the saga of a man who started something he cannot stop."[238] Many of the lines of Julie Rodman, unfaithful wife, sound like the confused, rudderless Hellman. Julie to an old lover: "I've hoped for a very long time that everybody or anybody would mean something. *(Smiles)* Things start as hopes and end up as habits."[239] Whatever hopes Hellman had for her lovers, each became a lifelong friend, possibly a habit. Her political hopes seemed more sure of success. In 1936, *Days to Come* foreshadowed decades of hope and despair on Broadway.

The play's beginning had seemed so auspicious. Hammett told her he liked it "very much." Shumlin eagerly directed and produced it. Broadway papers buzzed with the forthcoming Hellman "hit." She gladly played the role of a dazzling young success, greeting reporters sipping pale sherry, dressed in "a gray dress . . . with a black silk scarf crisscrossed in front like a soldier's and secured with a crystal clasp," petting "a sort of buffalo-robe color French poodle . . . stenciled in curious arabesques and clipped like an old box hedge." Newspapers heralded the play as Hellman's second coming.

But not all was well. Though Hammett had helped her in the initial planning, he was depressed and drinking heavily. In no condition physically or mentally to do much of anything, he gave lip-service approval. Without him forcing her to rewrite and revise, she didn't hone the dialogue or focus the action as she should have. She lost her nerve on the cuts. She felt scattered: her dedication to Max and Julia Hellman indicated Hellman's sadness of having come to love her mother "too late."[240] Shumlin staged the play at the Vanderbilt on West 48th Street, a small theater that from 1930 to 1936 had two hits and a "chain of flops." Only Langston Hughes's 1935 *Mulatto* and Leonard Sillman's 1936 edition of *New Faces* broke the dismal record.

Days to Come is a fascinating read with believable characters and relationships, undercurrents of feeling leading to violence engendered by politics. The dialogue is funny at times, edgy, and very smart. More novelistic than dramatic, *Days to Come* didn't work on stage. Too late, Kober saw a rehearsal and tried to intervene. Hellman saw possibility, rather than reality, until the curtain went up. Cruelly, William Randolph Hearst trooped out of the theater in the middle of the second act, he and his guests talking loudly and rudely in case anyone missed their exit, signaling his dismissal of the play, and of her.[241] Hearst alone wouldn't have been enough to damage her, however. She wouldn't expect Hearst, with his right-wing politics, to favor a play with labor strife as its subject and adultery as its subtext, despite his well-known affair with Marion Davies. But Hellman saw firsthand in *Days to Come* that what worked on the page did not always work in the theater, where the damage is immediate and excruciating. On opening night, the audience awaits, and a play that doesn't work creates an airless atmosphere. Hellman knew it had failed minutes after the curtain rose.

"*Days to Come* was botched, including my botching. Botched. . . . It was an absolute horror of a failure. I mean the curtain wasn't up ten minutes and catastrophe set in. I vomited in the back aisle. I did. I had to go home and change my clothes. I was drunk."[242] Hellman and her guests gathered at Ingersoll's Fifth Avenue "castle" for an opening night gala "in a state of shock." The reviews confirmed their fears. The *Post* called it a "dull, incredible, muddled drama . . . several bad plays which refuse to have much of anything to do with one another."[243] The *New York Times* assessment was more thoughtful: a "bitter play, shot through with hatred and written with considerable heat" but "elusive," "plagued . . . with . . . plot and counterplot," with some parts appearing to be "analysis of female neuroticism."

Hellman, on hearing the reviews "bristled, then launched into a vivid counterattack" and asked Hammett for support, reminding him that he had liked it. "Hammett rose to his feet, reached for his cape, swirled it over his shoulder and replied: 'I did indeed. But I saw it tonight at the Vanderbilt and I've changed my mind.'"[244] Hellman recalled feeling an unspecified guilt. In this one play she let Hammett, Shumlin, and Ingersoll down. She agonized. "The failure of a second work is, I think, more damaging to a writer than failure ever will be again."[245] When *Days to Come* flopped, Hellman watched her hopes collapse. For her, the play had meant a chance to dramatize the political complexity of the era, not just an attempt to achieve a second Broadway success. She feared she had failed at both.

But the political tension of the 1930s, along with her excellent reputation in Hollywood, brought her more opportunities to combine creativity and politics. Her life changed in profound ways—for good and ill. Shortly after the failure of *Days to Come*, she agreed to collaborate with Ernest Hemingway and Archibald MacLeish on Joris Ivens's documentary *The Spanish Earth*. She had a reputation on both coasts for her tough, graphic grasp of the "temper and trouble of our time."[246] As an unabashed partisan of the Republicans in Spain, Hellman signed on to cowrite the script and coproduce *The Spanish Earth*. The documentary was privately funded and filmed to earn money and generate support for wresting Spain from Franco's forces, especially for Americans fighting on behalf of the rebels, the beleaguered Abraham Lincoln Brigade. The group took on the the *Spanish Earth* project at a time when the only traditional films about the conflict were Paramount's *The Last Train from Madrid*, which took no political stand and made no thematic statement, and United Artists' *Blockade* depicting "synthetic" war.[247] Ivens signed Hellman not only because of her commitment to the cause but also because of her work.

Though the young Hellman was seldom sick, pneumonia kept her from working on the script with Hemingway. The illness, possibly related to problems with Hammett and a subsequent abortion, came at a most inopportune time. Hemingway thus wrote his own narration, and for the sake of the film, this was beneficial. The prickly Ernest cowriting with the controlling Hellman . . . well, the mind boggles. Talent she had in another arena made her valuable for the project. A year earlier she had begun to learn the ropes of production when she became "a kind of producer" for *These Three*, to reap some benefits that writers usually did not receive.[248] Her concern for detail, her control, and her cinematic vision made her most suited for production.

If women writers were legion in Hollywood, though few of Hellman's caliber, a woman producer was unheard of. Even the idea of her coproducing *The Spanish Earth* shocked many old-line producers. But Ivens, a Dutch director, and others, including Herman Shumlin, knew they needed her skill and political fearlessness. She took to the task with her remarkable brand of energy. She immersed herself in everything, from fund-raising to helping arrange the June and July showings at Carnegie Hall in New York City and at Fredric March and Florence Eldridge March's home in California. Her talent helped make this film "the most powerful and moving documentary ever screened."[249]

President and Mrs. Roosevelt invited Hemingway and Ivens to the White House to preview the film shortly before it went to Hollywood. (It wouldn't be long before Hellman had her own invitation for a different production.) *The Spanish Earth* established her place in national leftist politics and among the expatriot literati, those who had rendered her invisible in Paris nearly ten years previous. Hellman thought cinema, like dramatic opera and Broadway, had potential to change experience, not just mime it. Forever after she performed political work à la big shot, à la Hollywood.

Dead End (1937), Hellman's third screenplay, gave her a chance to write a film with a political edge and recover from the failure of *Days to Come*. The film, an adaptation of Sidney Kingsley's play of the same name, depicts the slums of New York. *Dead End* shows vividly the devastating toll poverty takes on the poor, particularly children. Under Hellman's control and Wyler's direction, the Sidney Kingsley characters shifted from "philosopher heroes" to activists. And to satisfy Hollywood, Hellman changed the seedy lead character of Kingsley's play to the appealing idealist Dave (played by Joel McCrea), who wanted to tear down the slums and build housing for the poor. His love interest Drina (Sylvia Sidney) became an angelic union marcher. Baby Face Martin (Humphrey Bogart) is the epitome of evil. He turns the Dead End Kids to a life of crime in the disease-ridden streets. Goldwyn considered *Dead End* his contribution to the "social gangster films" of the era.

The play had been a great success on Broadway, but editorials pronounced Hellman's film as "the finest social drama of which the screen has record . . . dumbfounding the arty boys."[250] *Dead End* was nominated for four Academy Awards, including Best Picture of 1937. One of the best features of the film was Hellman's dialogue for Baby Face Martin. Hellman wrote speech with an ear toward realism. Bogie captivated Hollywood and got the boost his career needed, with lines like, "I'm glad I ain't like you saps. Starving for what? Peanuts?"[251] Columnist Louella Parsons wrote, "There isn't an actor in town who wouldn't do nip-ups for the *Dead End* role, a choice bit of acting in the play."[252] The part was meaty, the lines perfect for Bogart's roguery.

Not everyone shared Hellman's street smarts or her politics. As rigidly as she held her views, however, she compromised with those who sought to undo her themes. The Hays Production Code not only excised sex and violence but demanded escapism at the expense of honesty, themes, politics, or messages. She rode the edge in this respect. Hellman began the movie with a printed prologue, "Every street in New York ends in a river," while Wyler directed Greg Toland's camera in an unbroken crane shot, tracking terrace dwellers to slum children. The film's beginning frames the stark contrasts between affluent urban dwellers intent on river views and those in the culture of poverty, squeezed on the docks of New York City's East River. The whole movie had moxie. It bore her stamp of outrage at those with wealth and power who oppress others. It also shows an unbending hatred of stool pigeons. One of the Dead End Kids pities "the guy who snitched." Tommy (played by Billy Halop) leaves, "But I ain't going 'til I catch the guy who snitched." He drew a knife diagonally across his own cheek—the mark of the squealer.[253] Inevitably the Code office wrote cautionary "tonedowns" for the film to pass muster. For example, Hellman had to excise a scene showing cockroaches, and the office instructed her to deemphasize the contrast between the rich and the poor.[254] Goldwyn agreed with the code.

Wyler, who shared Hellman's political and cinematic sensitivities, also struggled with Goldwyn, who could not leave the script or the set alone. Goldwyn would arrive daily on the set, insisting on newer curtains for the tenements, picking up the trash from the streets, and demanding clean trash cans. Each day to shoot the film, Wyler had to haul the trash out and create poverty once again on the waterfront streets of 1930s New York. Goldwyn prowled the set, picking up the trash and yelling, "This set is filthy, clean it up, clean it up."[255] On one occasion, Goldwyn fired Wyler over the state of the set.[256] Hellman refused to work without Wyler, and as he customarily did after a tantrum, Goldwyn recanted. Sylvia Sidney swore that the film almost ended her career, calling Wyler "a sadistic son of a bitch." The tension was nearly unbearable at times.

Sam Jaffe pointed out part of the difficulty: "Goldwyn had class with a capital K, dressed well . . . was very difficult, difficult . . . you had to do it his way."[257] Hellman could do it Goldwyn's way to a point and could turn him around to her way when necessary. She had watched the producers in Hollywood from the outside and from the inner circle. Goldwyn offered the best in a strange world. Hellman called him a "man of great power" who "would rise to an inexplicable pitch of panic anger when he was crossed or disappointed, and could then decline within minutes to the whispered, pained moral talk of a loony clergyman whimpering that God had betrayed him."[258] She knew he could be a terror and called herself his "oldest living employee" after making three movies, noting the rate of attrition after a Goldwyn rant.

Hellman said she and Wyler had to become friends because "we were the only two people in the Goldwyn asylum who weren't completely loony."[259] Sometimes Hellman took part in the craziness, but sometimes it was too much even for her. After years of pining for a musical revue, for example, Goldwyn finally decided to hire every talent he could and produce it. He gathered George Gershwin to write the music, Vera Zorina to dance ballet, and George Balanchine to do the choreography. He lacked a screenplay, so he called Hellman to his office. When she got there, "It was pure Alice in Wonderland." She walked in to find all the talents gathered and silent, tense. Goldwyn turned to her and asked, "What are you doing here?" She reminded him he had invited her. "Well, as long as you're here, why don't you write 'The Goldwyn Follies'?" She refused. He bullied, then cajoled: "You'll learn very nice, very quick. You'll write a great musical." She said she didn't want to learn. Then he offered a bribe: "You'll get a raise . . . you'll like the Gershwins." When Balanchine got his back up about being left out, Goldwyn said, "And it is wonderful to have a genius," pointing to Balanchine. The other talents stiffened. Goldwyn recovered: "I mean a bunch of geniuses, but all this modern music . . . it's so old-fashioned." Swallowing their laughter— even Hellman—the group broke up into smaller conversations. Gershwin told Hellman about a meeting the others had with Goldwyn the previous day at Goldwyn's house. Goldwyn descended the stairs in a bathrobe and said, "Hold on fellas, I'll be right there. And then we'll get into a cuddle." Too much for Hellman's sense of decorum, she "exploded with laughter, prompting Goldwyn to dismiss everybody from the room. "You call yourselves geniuses? . . . I call you dumbbells!" Hellman liked Goldwyn, but she saw film as a potential art form and could not be a party to his "Follies."[260]

Hellman loved lunacy, too, but off the set, not on. The whole industry relished practical jokes, betting pools, gossip, and madcap adventures. Prone to playing while working at the studios, Hellman began one of her favorite adventures with writer and producer George Haight, just for fun.

She had found nine unique matchboxes in Cuba. She and Haight arranged for the publicity department to put director Henry Potter's picture on the boxes. "He did look like the cleanest of juveniles," and indeed was the respectable grandson of a bishop. Hoping to spice up Potter's image, Haight and Hellman stamped "twenty-seven condoms with the words 'Compliments of Henry C. Potter.'" They planned to roll them like miniature rigatoni, pack them three to a box, and distribute them at Potter's cocktail party. The project turned into days of hard labor. "The carefully carved stamps broke the condoms . . . after a time our drugstore ran out of condoms and one of the lasting minutes my eyes will hold is the picture of one of the owners as he stared at George on his last request for twelve boxes."[261] With considerable revision of the stamp and the rolling changed to stacking, they packed twenty-seven perfectly stamped condoms in the boxes for cocktail party distribution.

On another occasion, Haight and Hellman took on the great Goldwyn himself. When Hellman observed Goldwyn taking a short taxi ride at the same time each day, she got Haight to tail him. They discovered that Goldwyn had a yen for Vera Zorina, a Balanchine ballet dancer, and each day he zipped to her address to catch a glimpse of her return from the studio. Apparently the detectives were as indiscreet as Goldwyn, and everyone found out about the adventure.[262] An ironic outcome of this escapade was that Frances Goldwyn began to suspect her husband of many peccadilloes long after he had slowed down his casting couch ritual. Frances added Hellman to her private list of Sam's women.

Hellman liked Sam but not in the "sex way," swearing, "I never wanted to sleep with Sam, and he didn't want sex from me. All he ever wanted was another good script."[263] Goldwyn could be as single-minded as Hellman. He wanted "sure-fire stuff" and from Hellman that meant a script. But his demands had the intensity of a sexual relationship. Every time Sam approached Hellman about a film, they would "fight like hell" about the financial settlements, over the phone, face-to-face, through secretaries, through the mail.

Goldwyn demanded absolute loyalty, tying up his "star," director, and writer in contracts he manipulated to his own purposes. He also wanted the credit for the success. Goldwyn was unwilling to acknowledge the efforts of the writer and the director, insisting the myth of the "Goldwyn touch" was his alone. After Wyler read Johnston's *The Great Goldwyn* years later, he snapped, "Tell me, which pictures have 'the Goldwyn touch' that I didn't direct?"[264] And that Hellman didn't write? But both Wyler and Hellman understood Goldwyn, his ego, his insecurity, and his quirks. In matters big and small, they all demanded "credit" for what they did, which sometimes overlapped. But a breach between Goldwyn and Hellman seemed inevitable; he was management, she labor.

Political Fury

By 1937, if Hellman couldn't quite sing Bessie Smith's "Poor Man Blues," she plainly saw Hollywood's glittering economic discrepancies. No one who worked starved in Hollywood; the whole studio system paid enormously well compared to other industries. Its riches nevertheless highlighted class hierarchies. The Depression had spotlighted the growing divide between the haves and have-nots. Labor, increasingly controlled by profit-hungry corporations, too often had too little, even in Hollywood. "At $1.3 million, Louis B. Mayer was the highest-paid employee in the country, earning 'more salary in 1937 than all members of the United States Senate combined.'"[265] Hollywood affluence gave birth to a paradoxical leftist activism, at least in those not reaping the millions in production. Hellman, who never forgot a slight, remembered red-eyed readers and writers housed in shacks next to palatial production offices like Irving Thalberg's office, called the "iron lung" by those working for him. As Hellman became part of the Hollywood scene, the labor movements of Hollywood workers became more important to her than Goldwyn or any other producer currying her favor.

Beginning as a writers club of sorts in 1920, the Screen Writers Guild emerged after the first organized stirrings of writers' unionism in 1933. Ten writers, among them Donald Ogden Stewart, Charles Brackett, Phillip Dunne, and Dorothy Parker, met at the Roosevelt Hotel in Hollywood to begin the process of seeking protection for writers under the U.S. labor codes. This organized movement's response to changes in national law under Franklin Delano Roosevelt was a far cry from Hellman's high-handed complaining about the underhanded torture of employees when she worked as a script summarizer at MGM. Hellman, still having no screen credits and out of Hollywood at this time, jumped in wholeheartedly the minute she returned in 1935. Friends Dashiell Hammett, Sid Perelman, Frances Goodrich, and Albert Hackett joined the founders and were fiercely active, with Laura Perelman on the executive board and her brother Pep West an active member. Ogden Nash joined them, and the group hung out together socially. Their political alliances seemed natural, "not only because we liked each other, but because we were in what was called 'the same salary bracket.'" The Hacketts noted that MGM had 155 writers, on and off. "We had a wonderful table there in the commissary. Just think of the people who were there! Stromberg used to call us 'his stable.' But then in the center of the room there were the big writers that had the die in the cage and would toss it to see who paid the bill. Those were the big boys . . . the ones who wanted to break the Guild: Patterson McNutt, James Kevin McGuinness, John Lee Mahin, Howard Emmett Rogers. It was especially galling to see 'The Four Horsemen' taking studio time to break the Guild when Guild members were forbidden to do so."[266] The Hacketts remembered being so busy with writing and guild business that "we had to bring a flashlight into our garden to see how the vegetables were doing."[267]

The guild fought above all for respect. And in Hollywood respect means credit and a decent wage. Mention, or "credits," meant more work, a career in the making. The industry, desperate for good writers and scripts, nevertheless tried to squelch individual recognition as well as standardized regulations. When writers wrote films but got no screen credit, Hellman and other guild members sought remedy. In the 1930s and into the 1940s most writers never got a credit and never made enough to live on. Peter Feibleman noted a joke that circulated which said it rough: "What does a Polish starlet do to get ahead? Fucks writers."[268] If a writer wrote parts of a film, or even most of it, someone with more pull with the producers might get all the credit, irrespective of contribution. *The Westerner* is a Hellman script in large part, for example, though she went uncredited for it. The early work she did on *The Melody Lingers On* is also uncredited. Even writers of whole scripts typically earned nothing from the film's profits. Writers earned good wages only by getting new contracts. Thus a writer getting screen credits was seen as a key provision for fair labor practices. The fierce fight for credits was not a struggle to control film subjects but to have some say over what their work became and to be paid fairly. Hollywood made the distinction early on: playwrights sell a product and screenwriters serve a studio.[269]

Producers, little more than con men in Hellman's eyes, were reminiscent of her Uncle Jake and Grandmother Sophie, making deals and profits by someone else's labor and at their cost. The enormous studio profits, generated by great scripts, seemed the height of injustice. The political pot boiled over on studio lots when the Academy proposed a sliding scale of pay cuts. Hellman felt ready to tackle important issues. Money equalled self-worth. Even if she got big bucks out of Goldwyn for her adaptations, she knew she was more exception than rule. By the time she finished *Dead End*, she had become a known labor activist in Hollywood.

The new Screen Writers Guild was a huge step up from the earlier Authors League. Countering the pressure of high-profile producers, they roamed the lots talking to young screenwriters. Hellman recruited writers or readers who were afraid to join the guild because of the political fallout and also served in executive positions on the labor boards.[270] As the respected Miss Hellman, she made a lasting impression producers could scarcely ignore. Maurice Rapf remembers meeting all the "marvelous writers" because of the battle between the Screen Playwrights and the Screen Writers Guild. "I had just become a junior writer, thanks to nepotism, at MGM. And then, the first thing that happened to me was that Hellman came into my converted broom-closet office and asked me to join the Guild. It was most extraordinary—the formidable playwright—unbeautiful, wearing one of her extraordinary hats and chain-smoking."[271]

The producers knew that the guild meant business, and they alternated between threats and sweet talk to bring members in line. On one occasion the producers sent Sam Goldwyn into an executive meeting of the SWG. Seeing Hellman and Dorothy Parker there, he enthusiastically blurted, "I think I'm gonna have to hire only women writers from now on." Then he noticed Alan Campbell, Parker's husband and collaborator. He backpedaled, "Of course Dottie if anybody like you wants to bring her husband along that's okay." In those days, producers "wanted their writers in quantity" and cheap.[272] Hellman used her name and power to thwart such policies. As Hellman said years later, she wasn't afraid because "my temptations are not swimming pools and cars. . . . If they are, then I think it's dangerous for the writer."[273] Producer greed got her back up. Hellman's pink political heart was with labor.

As tension escalated between writers and producers in 1935, boycotting and blacklisting began in earnest. Dudley Nichols boycotted the Academy Awards dinner, refusing to accept his Oscar for his 1935 film *The Informer* and resigning from the academy rather than "turn my back on nearly a 1,000 writers of the Writers Guild."[274] Embarrassed by Nichols's move, the Academy still didn't want to chip away at production profits, though MGM, for example, averaged $9 million per year between 1934 and 1940.[275] Furious about the publicity over Nichols's move and the change in guild politics, the producers were scared to death that writers' demands would rob them of absolute control. In a huge showdown, Louis B. Meyer and Jack Warner formed the Screen Playwrights to break the union, draining the membership down to less than half of the original five or six hundred members.[276] Additionally, producers blacklisted the early guild activists, not for the last time. A grinning Warner admitted to the blacklist but laughed that no one could prove it since there was really no list—they did it by phone.

Producers loathed giving writers more than the minimum and turned to dirty tricks to ensure their political impotence. Dangerous, frightening, fraught with risk, guild activity put early writers' careers on the line. As guild activity escalated, producers frothed out accusations of communist control, unprofessionalism, disloyalty, anti-Americanism. They kept the blacklist meticulously. The writers took their case to the National Labor Relations Board, and, as writer John Bright said, "Oh god! We almost—we were saved by the Wagner Act[277] and the NLRB's ruling that the producers had conspired to carry out a plan of interference."[278] Guild elation and celebration followed, along with a lot of hard work to set up a labor election.

Following the NLRB decision, Hammett gave a party at the Beverly Wilshire in a "big suite that had been occupied by the President of Mexico, or some shah, something like that . . . everybody was coming up there and ordering a drink . . . getting them to join the SWG. After trying to get a big writer at MGM to join, poor Hellman came out of the room and said, 'Well, if I get Talbot Jennings to join this thing, somebody's got to pay for the abortion.' Dorothy Parker in another room lost patience with writer Everett Freeman who said creative writers shouldn't join unions—the producer's line. Parker seethed: 'That sonofabitch, telling me that he's a creative writer! If he's a creative writer, I'm Marie of Rumania.'"[279] In 1935 and 1936, guild politics and writing scripts filled Hellman's life.

Personal and Political Ties

Caught up in the excitement of guild business and renewed political interest in *The Spanish Earth*, Hellman let her personal life spiral increasingly out of control in 1937. Reeling from the public failure of *Days to Come* and Hammett's dismissal of the play, she drank, fought, hated, and loved in equal measure. Ingersoll was in New York City, and she was "playing very domestic" in Hollywood with Hammett.[280] Temporarily on the wagon, Hammett seemed for a while to have got his life together—and she loved the renewed stability. The two went to dinner with friends and worked hard unionizing writers. Then he got her pregnant. This time she vacillated between hopes that she and Hammett could become parents to a more realistic assessment of their untenable life together.[281] She thought Hammett would be a wonderful father and dreamily fantasized that he would divorce his wife.

Reality hit hard. She came home to their fabulous Beverly Wilshire suite with flowers to celebrate their happiness to find Hammett in bed with one of his Hollywood "ladies."[282] She knew he would not change. Hellman never relished the role of martyr. Lack of freedom suffocated her and she fought against it. Secure about her choice, she decided on abortion. Years later she said in an interview that "anti-abortion law is a very irreligious law to me. It's forcing on people that which they cannot properly cherish and understand."[283] As sure as she was, it made for a lousy year, personally.

In mid-August, with *Dead End* getting rave reviews and *The Spanish Earth* finished, Hellman found herself fed up with Hollywood politics in general and Hammett in particular. She traveled to Europe with Dorothy Parker, whom she loved, and Parker's husband, Alan Campbell, whom she could barely abide. She had been invited to Moscow for a theater festival, though she wasn't yet famous enough to warrant the VIP treatment later invitations brought. Now she used Moscow's interest as an excuse to travel, also intending to get the abortion in Europe. Where she never said.

She set off blithely to play in Paris and attend theater in Russia. Hellman loved traveling and would go anywhere. Hammett never left the States and teased her about this trip, saying she only pretended she wanted to go to Moscow to see the theater. He told her she would never betray anyone, "unless somebody offered you a free subway ride to Jersey City and then we'd all be in danger."[284] He knew Hellman had other agendas, and indeed he was right. In addition to getting away from him, she needed the stimulation and change that travel delivered, no matter the difficulties. She knew intellectually that tensions in Europe threatened to tear it apart. Nazis had banned Jews from professional occupations, forced people of color to be sterilized, and expelled most Jewish students from German universities. Hitler boasted that the Third Reich would last a thousand years. Most of this the press reported, though many on the right denied it, calling it Russian propaganda. Less clear was the extent of Stalin's purges, which the left excused as justice to traitors of the revolution. Hellman's travel into these political hells as tourist and visiting writer—Paris to Moscow via Berlin and Warsaw, from there to Prague and possibly Helsinki then back to Paris—showed a headstrong, naive willfulness to travel in defiance of current events. Aimless when she left for Paris, she told reporters she would be gone "two to five months."[285] She planned to ramble, but the fascist face of much she saw gave her pause. A later trip to Spain triggered her commitment to international politics.

The strictly autobiographical narrative of this trip in *Unfinished Woman* shows her leaving Paris for Moscow. She recalled "changing trains in Berlin.

I had been warned that I might have trouble in Berlin—I had a four or five hour wait and a change of railroad stations—and a young Russian consular officer met me at the station. There was no trouble or I didn't think so, until the second train was nearing Warsaw." She looked for her trunk, found it gone, and was told she would get it in Moscow because "the Nazis were not barbarians, a mistake had been made, my name was German." The trunk arrived two weeks later, "the insides had been slashed to pieces, every book had been torn apart, every bottle had been emptied."[286] That sabotage set the stage for Hellman's later story "Julia," a chapter in *Pentimento* that documented Hellman's personal induction to antifascism, even as she recorded Julia's heroism, not her own.

Ever the playwright, Hellman wrote "Julia" as a journey narrative, illustrating the escalating dangers of commitment and her own fearful growth in acting forthrightly. Hellman cloaked Julia's identity, at once dramatizing and disguising her political importance in Hellman's own vacillating political growth. The story of Julia is a compilation of events that may have happened between 1934 and 1937. Thus the portrait of Julia cannot be read as straight autobiography. The story tells of Hellman's induction into international politics and the necessary commitment she feared she could never live up to.

In Hellman's portrait of political dedication, Julia, a beautiful and wealthy school friend, was a hero in prewar Europe, a committed antifascist socialist in Vienna. She studied with Freud and joined the Austrian underground. In Hellman's story, Julia asked her to bring $50,000 of Julia's money undercover to her in Berlin when Hellman traveled to Europe in 1937. Hellman played little more than a passive bit part for Julia's selfless drama.[287] Julia's courage and loss were at the center of the story, along with Hellman's admiration for her. In early drafts Hellman called this central character Helen Bormer, then Frieda Bormer, finally Julia. Even in the finished version of the portrait, lawyers demanded that Hellman delete any remaining identifiers, noting that "truth is not an absolute defense in an action for libel where 'actual malice' is involved."[288] Whoever this friend was, she put a personal face on the risks of resistance.

Her death, perhaps in 1934 during the Vienna riots, perhaps later, compelled Hellman to risk her pleasant life and join others to thwart the violence raging in the world during the 1930s and 1940s.[289] Julia, whoever she was and whenever she died, influenced Hellman's actions as she went through Germany to Moscow in 1937. Hellman certainly could have taken money to give the resistance; if not to Julia then to another friend. Hellman's method of tangling together several stories into one drama in this case was done for political and legal ends. Without taking the bow herself, she tried to show, through another woman's actions, what she aspired to, what she thought noble.[290] She conveyed her truth in shattered fragments—embellishments she called them—to the core reality.[291]

Hellman's truth in the "Julia" portrait was a political one as she depicted late 1930s Europe, its victims and its heroes. After Hellman published "Julia," she received many letters from those who believed their lives paralleled the people and events in the chapter. Each letter writer wondered if Hellman had referred to his or her life. Each begged her for more information, some desperate to find an identity that the war had eradicated. Ellen Adam's birth mirrored that of Julia's lost baby; playwright Michael Dyne reported meeting an American in Vienna, a "radical agitator who threw vast sums of money around in order to stir up opposition . . . a gallant, embattled woman" who seemed to be Julia; Muriel Gardner, "Code Name Mary," an avid antifascist who worked the underground, wondered if Hellman had stolen her life story for Julia.[292] When asked if Gardner was her model for Julia, Hellman insisted that Gardner might be someone's Julia, but not her Julia. Hints of this woman's identity come through in the Hellman archives. Francis Ross wrote Hellman from Europe; Hellman dreamed of Peggy Williams and her daughter, Judy. Never one to cry much, Hellman wept on three occasions related to her friend Julia: when a friend asked Hellman about her, when Hellman read "Julia" in a public forum, and years later when Marilyn Berger interviewed Hellman for television.[293] Away from Hollywood and Hammett and Ingersoll, the woman she called Julia urged Hellman to make a life of serious political pursuit.

Before her trip to Europe, Hellman had politicized on the margins. Working on *The Spanish Earth*, she had already embraced the cause of Spain, the most perilous place of all in 1937. But it wasn't until she met Jim Lardner in Paris that she seriously considered traveling there. Lardner was a journalist who later joined the International Brigades and was killed.[294] A dinner in Paris with communist Otto Katz, "a kind of press chief" for Spain's Republicans, further motivated her to risk Spain's violence, even though Hammett wanted her back in the States. As a respected playwright and intellectual public figure, Hellman decided to join other writers like Martha Gellhorn, Ernest Hemingway, and Dorothy Parker, who supported the international brigades and used their fame and writing talent to make Spain's plight more visible in the United States. The *New Republic* agreed to publish a few Hellman pieces (which later became "A Day in Spain") after she returned. Thus in October 1937 she traveled to Spain to support the Spanish Republicans. She reflected, "I had strong convictions about the Spanish war, about Fascism-Nazism, strong enough to push just below the surface my fear of the danger of war."[295] Julia, Katz, and Lardner gave her the strength she would need in Madrid.

"Madrid in 1937 was the most dangerous foxhole in the world," but Lillian Hellman stepped into that danger willingly.[296] Hellman's accounts of her time in Spain only obliquely portray her real jeopardy. In writing about her month there, she chose a reflective, nearly stream of conscious exploration of war's daily toll on everyday people—the humiliating deprivations, the hunger. She wrote, "Most people coming out of a war feel lost and resentful. What has been a minute-to-minute confrontation with yourself, your struggle with what courage you have against discomfort, at the least, and death at the other end, ties you to the people you have known in the war and makes, for a time, all others seem alien and frivolous."[297]

Memoirs about Spain—Hellman's and others—create confusion about the reality of life in the chaos of violent events and Hellman's part in those events. In her accounts, she bragged only that Hemingway told her that she had "*cojones*, after all." She supposedly told him, "Go to hell with what you think." Her response sounds like false bluster, given her real respect for him. Journalist Martha Gellhorn, Hemingway's woman at the time, disputed nearly everything Hellman said about her trip to Spain. Gellhorn's dated record did not match Hellman's, though Hellman admitted her own notorious inaccuracy about dates. More to the point, Gellhorn didn't like the way Hellman depicted their evening together. Mocking Hellman's abbreviated version of those memories, Gellhorn snorted, "Does such modest silence, such a waste of truly dramatic details sound like our Miss H?" Apparently Gellhorn knew little of Hellman's odd mix of bragging bravado and respectful silence. The sacrifice and heroism of the soldiers in the brigades awed the American writers who came to Spain. Hellman was not alone in her courage. She knew it and chose reticence; she understood they all risked their lives.

Despite her efforts to credit the courage of others, critics have always found Hellman too ready to trumpet her own heroism. When it came to personal peril, Hellman most often let her actions speak, keeping silent about her most shining hours or waiting many years to publicly acknowledge them. She blurted out small victories or took cheap shots at others, but at the time of danger, the real fear that lay under her own courage made her reluctant to burnish the public record. Dead serious about political matters, Hellman learned from Julia and Spain that "the filthy indignity of destruction . . . is the real immorality."[298] In her writings about war, Hellman trumpeted the honor she owed committed fighters. She could join the battle, but paralyzing fear limited her. Political impotence fatigued her as much as sleeplessness, hunger, and tension. In writing about Spain in *Unfinished Woman*, Hellman's focus was on the people she met. Depicting herself as dizzy with hunger like other Spaniards and sharing anchovies with hungry journalists, she exposed the daily loss and war's ironies. By giving expensive shoes to a woman who admired them, she ironically mocks her own affluence when compared to the sweep of the Spaniards' loss. It took her years to find effective political strategies and even longer to find a way to write of their complexity. Hellman's mixture of exhibitionism and reticence created her political mystery, but it would be a mistake to undervalue her dedication.

A more intrepid "Miss Hellman" is remembered by Langston Hughes, who was in Madrid the night in October when she broadcast to America from Madrid Radio:

A shell tore half the cornice off the front of the building from which she was talking. At the Alianza a few blocks away, we heard it strike like a million great fire crackers exploding simultaneously in one spot—a quick, dry, loud BANG! Of a terrific power. But Miss Hellman kept right on talking. Her broadcast was already twenty-four hours late because the night before Madrid had experienced an even bigger shelling. Then more than a hundred projectiles crashed into the city, so Miss Hellman could not leave her hotel to go to the radio station. The following evening in her talk she said of the bombardment the night before: 'You are quiet when a shelling comes because the bravery of these people who have seen so much, and will see so much more, reaches you and makes you quiet. And maybe you get quiet because you, too, are angry; you can't believe in a world which allows foreign dictators to wreck a city by carefully picking the poorest and the most crowded part of that city, where houses are flimsiest and the children play most, then shell it and shell it with monotonous regularity. You would think the human heart would turn and make them stop.'[299]

Hellman knew she could do nothing.

Hellman witnessed a fierce war and knew it would be lost to fascists. She saw war in Spain as the first battle of a coming world war, the world confronting the evil of fascism and Nazism. Hellman supported the communists there because they supported the Republican Army. Of all the world powers, only the Soviet Union stepped in to stop the fascist alliance. But she saw atrocities on all sides, discovered a complexity in the Russians' violent presence that troubled her. The Republican Army was no match for the firepower of Franco, Hitler, Mussolini, and Salazar of Portugal. Hellman met the American communist Steve Nelson, a Lincoln Brigade war hero, in Valencia as he recuperated from wounds and was assigned to escort prominent Americans.[300] They talked and she liked him enormously, but could give him little encouragement. She had discovered the bleak reality of Spain in the face of American apathy. Nelson later wrote to her, but the FBI intercepted the letter and she never received it.[301] When Spain's government, soldiers like Nelson, and Spaniards themselves asked Hellman and others like her to "explain, write, plead that the United States and France must send arms immediately," she could only despair. "God in Heaven, who do they think I am, any of us?"[302]

Out of her mourning and loss came a political rage that lasted for years. She spent most of October 1937 in Spain and then left for France, then England. At a dinner where a silly Englishman worried more about her rudeness to his even sillier wife than the horror she had just seen, she fled, breaking her ankle. As Hellman wrote of her recovery, "Nothing of course, begins at the time you think it did but for many years I have thought of those days in the lonely London hotel room as the root-time of my turn toward the radical movements of the late thirties."[303] She was thirty-two with a wild-eyed idealism: "The story of the foreigners who came to fight for what was the Spanish Republic is a noble story and one of its most noble parts was written in blood and courage by the Abraham Lincoln Brigade. When you saw steelworkers and teachers and cab-drivers and seamen and college boys fighting as these men fought in Spain, you felt fine about being an American."

But she had seen the ugly side of war and came home to the United States to begin a notable antifascist activism. In a fund-raising letter she wrote, "It is impertinent of me to plead for men who have given eyes and legs and feet; their history pleads for them."[304] For a time, the communist help for the Republicans in Spain and the party's emphasis on labor led Hellman to believe she could support communists ideologically. As George Orwell said, "In essence it was a class war. If it had been won, the cause of the common people everywhere would have been strengthened."[305] All over America, concerned progressives and liberals looked beyond their own country to a world that seemed to be collapsing under the fascist onslaught. As one veteran of the Abraham Lincoln Brigade put it, "We felt in going to Spain we were continuing the fight that started on the picket line, a worldwide fight for decent living conditions and human justice."[306] Many on the left, including Hellman, thought, "We're going to bring about a better world, whether it is here . . . or whether it is over there with the people in Spain."[307] Deeply committed to antifascism, politics was no longer a sideline for Hellman. She had integrated political belief into her very being. She identified herself as a radical fighting for moral equity.

Private and Public Change

When Hellman returned to the United States, she determined to take more concerted action, to stop letting the wind blow her where it might. She had been grounded in others' pain and was committed to work harder to alleviate it. But first she had to regain her personal equilibrium. In Spain she had received a telegram that Hammett had finally gotten a divorce: "Have Divorce and Flu Stop Remaining Here Until Twentieth Much Love Dash."[308] He had previously avoided divorce because he honored his wife Jose's Catholicism and stoic nature even if he didn't honor his vows.[309] Hellman had thrown a fit, seemingly to no avail. Now the divorce suited them both: Hammett got Hellman off his back; Hellman got the myth of Hammett's marital freedom. (A friend told Jose Hammett that "it was one of those Mexican mail-order jobs . . . probably invalid."[310] And it was. After Hammett's death, Jose applied for—and got—Hammett's veteran's benefits.) But as always in the Hellman–Hammett relationship, periods of tranquility and commitment were followed by periods of destruction and waste.

As 1938 dawned, Hammett and Hellman were seemingly on the way to permanent separation. Hammett had stayed sober for six months, working in Hollywood on various *Thin Man* projects while Hellman worked in New York. Staying in the Beverly Wilshire Hotel's Royal Siamese Suite, "which he liked because of its awful decor and corny name," Hammett turned inward, reclusive, depressed. He started drinking again in May, substituting bourbon for food. Friend and fellow screenwriter Albert Hackett recalled that Hellman had called his wife, Frances, asking her to go see Hammett. She herself had tried to get Hammett back to New York when it became clear he was thin, ill, and broke. He refused. In desperation over Hammett's "deplorable" state, Hellman got Hammett to agree to follow the advice of the emminently sensible and cheerful Frances Hackett. When the Hacketts arrived at the hotel, the manager tried to extract payment from them for Hammett's expenses. Hackett was ready to agree; they had often tried to give Hammett money so he would eat. Now they found him at six feet two, weighing "about a hundred and twenty-seven pounds . . . you could practically see through him."[311] Hammett had slurred, "You can't give me money, I live flamboyantly." Hammett's bill was $8,000, a colossal amount in 1938. It included a $1,300 bill for liquor bought in Hollywood pharmacies.[312]

Somehow the bill was paid and the Hacketts put Hammett on a plane to New York, where Hellman met him at the airport and took him first to the hospital and later home with her. Distraught at his condition but relieved he was back with her, she was nevertheless irate. Hammett's condition and presence imposed an emotional and physical burden. But she stuck to their commitment, as loose and challenging and horrifying as it was at times. She respected him, not least because of the political integrity he held onto when he let everything and everybody else down.

Many writers like Hammett found that heightened political engagement overwhelmed their urge to write novels, plays, stories. The money they made writing Hollywood scripts could fund radical causes; in too many cases, their own writing diminished. True for those such as Samuel Ornitz, John Howard Lawson, Albert Maltz, Dorothy Parker, and Hammett, it was not true of Hellman. She made both political and creative use of her political commitments.

And Hammett helped her do it. She supported leftist causes out of an "intense interest in personal rights and freedom."[313] People-centered, she enjoyed political action but "was not really on top of it." Theoretical politics bored her. She liked action. NLRB secretary Nate Witt remembered Dashiell Hammett as "astute" but not Hellman, whose politics were born of emotion, not doctrine.[314]

Since her return from Spain, Hellman's political work had become increasingly loud, public, angry, and strident—with victory for the screenwriters, with fierce fighting for the antifascists. When the National Labor Relations Board finally held an election between guild and playwrights organizations in early August 1938, the Screen Writers won handily, 267–57, despite threats and inducements to writers from the producers. Political excess on both sides characterized Hollywood, and tempers exploded. Fox vice president Darryl Zanuck took SWG and political activism as a personal affront; he screamed in fury when he saw pickets: "If those guys set up a picket line and try to shut down my studio, I'll mount a machine gun on the roof and mow them down."[315] On the left, Donald Ogden Stewart, an activist and SWG ally of Hellman's, converted completely to left-wing causes and became an open communist. Humorist Robert Benchley told the story of one evening finding Stewart at a rich man's dinner party in Hollywood, waving his caviar-piled cracker and glass of champagne and telling anyone who would listen, "Comes the Revolution, none of you will have any of this . . . join us while you can, because we are going to take this away from you." Hellman never went that far. Still, without abandoning her American labor work, Hellman's gaze turned increasingly international. She developed a new firebrand activism, focusing on the international scene. Although she had been politically active in Hollywood and New York, her political apprenticeship in Spain made changes in her life.

Hellman took to a more public political podium. In drama her politics wore the mask of art, but now she exposed her radicalism by speaking out for the Republican government in Spain, then working tirelessly for Spanish refugees. Labeled a strident political battle-ax, Hellman became a believer in a fierce antifascism as personal as it was public.[316] She joined and cosponsored every appropriate organization she could find: Hollywood Anti-Nazi League, Medical Bureau and North American Committee to Aid Spanish Democracy, Joint Anti-Fascist Refugee Committee, National Committee for People's Rights, Spanish Refugee Relief Campaign. With cosponsors James Cagney, Carl Sandburg, and Langston Hughes, she raised funds for the Friends of the Veterans of the Abraham Lincoln Brigade. She attended refugee luncheons honoring Dorothy Parker, sponsored a New Year's Eve ball for the benefit of political refugees from Nazi terror. She gave $150 contributions everywhere, signed a myriad of petitions such as the Friends of Spanish Democracy's appeal to President Roosevelt.[317] She became so well known for her work on Spain that Walter Winchell asked Hellman to do a feature article on the Spanish Civil War for the Hearst newspapers. Hearst, furious, wrote him, "You are engaged to do a Broadway column. Any political columns written in my paper will be American in spirit. Not alien. They will be democratic in character, not communist or fascist. Furthermore, Walter, you are not a little boy, although you are acting like one."[318] Hearst ordered his editors to watch Winchell; he had shown too much interest in leftist causes.

Hellman did not always make informed decisions, but she adamantly believed in practicing her "inherited rights." Since her trip to Spain, she was far more canny and more suspicious of conventional political regimes and parties. She keenly watched political power brokers for hypocrisy, dangerous decisions, Bill of Rights infringements. She felt it her duty to speak or act or write against it. To do otherwise was dangerous. Of course, she wasn't alone, just bicoastal. Nearly all writers were antifascist liberals and Hellman was high-profile left, contributing to the ongoing confusion as to whether she was red.

The Communist party wasn't illegal, and Stalinist Russian reality shrouded itself in a fog of Soviet propaganda. In both Manhattan and

Hollywood, the Communist Party was barely distinguishable in policy and activities from the noncommunist left, "a conscious coalition of liberal and radical political opinions."[319] Few at that time saw the Communist Party as incompatible with democracy. Humanitarian impulses drove many creative people to the party. So did fear—of another depression, of impending war, of fascist control. They would learn that for all their ideals, "dissenters pay a price."[320] The antifascists' alliance with communists in Spain against Franco would not be forgiven by Cold War politicos; participation in Spain got them labeled subversive and communist in FBI director J. Edgar Hoover's files. A few years later, all Americans joined in the antifascist fight, but Hellman was decidedly premature.

The years from 1937 to 1940 were the most politically radical of Hellman's life. Still, in those Popular Front years, even the American Communist Party dropped its revolutionary agenda in a practical move to include greater diversity in progressive politics. Hellman attended Marxist meetings with Hammett and openly joined all manner of causes later labeled communist "with little thought as to the serious step I was taking." In joining those small Marxist study groups of intellectuals, "she presumed that during that brief period that constituted membership, but that was her only connection with the Party."[321] Busy in her own related causes, Hellman's CP membership, if it can be called that, was associative rather than active. She followed in Parker and Hammett's communist wake for a bit, then began to backslide a year after she joined. The FBI cited an informant reporting Hellman's attendance at the 1938 Communist Party convention, but Hoover found no evidence to back her participation. Those active in party politics never considered her a member, nor did she ever consider herself a committed communist.[322] When later forced to defend her political past before Congress, she told her lawyer, Joseph Rauh, "I was a most inactive Communist Party member. I attended very few Communist Party meetings in Hollywood in 1938–9 and an equally small number in New York in 1939–40. I stopped attending meetings or taking part in Communist Party activities in the latter part of 1940 and severed all connections with the Party."[323] She drifted off to form alliances with other progressives. Rigid CP politics did not correspond to her beliefs, but she was loath to deny those early ideological beginnings.

It seems hard to believe that the Communist Party recruited between 50,000 and 75,000 American members, just when news of Stalin's purges emblazoned every newspaper's front page.[324] Hellman, along with countless others, swallowed the CP line. Hellman signed a manifesto in defense of Stalin and joined 150 progressives in signing The Moscow Trials: A

Statement by American Progressives. "The text of the statement makes clear that the signers' pro-Soviet attitude was conditioned by Soviet resistance to Hitler, by Soviet attempts to improve the living conditions of Russians, and by Soviet efforts to strengthen the League of Nations as a force for peace. Lillian's signature on this document is neither surprising nor damning."[325] The "demonstration trials," as Stalinists called them, appeared to many outsiders legitimate consequences of treason and Trotsky's efforts to retake power from Stalinists.[326] Stalin seemed the Russian premier of choice, since Trotsky actively promoted worldwide revolution while Stalin preferred domestic stability first. The trials seemed far away and the consequences of someone else's political upheaval. "Even the *New York Times* seemed to accept the verdicts."[327]

Propaganda machines in Europe, the Soviet Union, and the United States spewed out so much conflicting news that people could rationalize any position, blaming media bias. John Bright admitted he had been "taken a little bit in by the party press," and others like Hellman admitted thinking the anti-Stalin press was Nazi propaganda.[328] Some of it was, but years later she paused in the middle of a room to tell her goddaughter Catherine Kober: "I can't believe I was so naive about the Moscow Trials."[329] Utterly committed to antifascism, Hellman still lacked political sophistication. Her development as a writer and political thinker came in the 1940s with increased exposure on Broadway and in Washington.

Hellman never said what caused her to break away from Communist Party politics. Her friends were communists, near communists, or progressives in various shades of red or pink. But Hellman suffered disaffection with party politics and its dogmatism. Even when Hammett's position remained solid, she never followed his political track. Herman Shumlin and Ralph Ingersoll, admired lovers and mentors, were leftists, both loud and articulate in stating their belief in democracy. She would have listened to all three men and made her own judgments. Any efforts to control Hellman drove her away. Hellman's political gestalt was echoed in the first issue of *PM*, as editor Ingersoll laid out the paper's political philosophy. "*PM:* is against people who push other people around; belongs to no political party; is absolutely free and uncensored; is anti-Poll Tax, anti-Fascist, and supported Roosevelt."[330] The inconsistencies seem hers, as well.

As long as the communists fought the Nazis, Hellman refused to cut whatever flimsy ties she had to the CP. Then on August 24, 1939, Stalin announced a nonaggression pact with Hitler and made plans to carve up Poland. Hellman had to face facts she couldn't stomach. "In the wake of such stunning news, many on the left quickly muzzled their Communist exhortations. But Hellman would abide none of this; she could not respect what she considered an illicit union."[331] Confusion reigned as Hollywood renamed the Hollywood Anti-Nazi League as American Peace Mobilization. The party scrambled to find excuses to explain away Stalin's alliance with Hitler. Thousands resigned the party in fury. Many, with some justification, thought Stalin just bought time, knowing the Nazis would attack the Soviet Union sooner or later. Hellman had this to say: "While I believed that the Soviet Union's disillusionment with Munich in 1938 afforded some justification for the Nazi-Soviet Pact of 1939, I wholly disagreed with the position of the Communist Party in its glorification of Nazism."[332]

To counter the CP stance, she started her antifascist play *Watch on the Rhine* the same day.[333] In the strength of her anger, Hellman honored antifascists and mocked those comfortable at home in the United States as dangerous to others. "It didn't endear her to her leftist friends and fellow travelers. Her heresy did not sit well" in such left-wing and Party publications as the *New Masses* and the *Daily Worker*."[334] Washington had as many concerns about her as the left—and she began to doubt both. But she had made the national scene, no doubt about it. She finally threw her lot in with the New Dealers, supporting homegrown politics that seemed to care about labor, race, and the arts.

In New York, she set about leading seminars, giving keynote speeches, heading up antifascist refugee dinners and fund-raisers. Hellman's zest in championing the underdog made for a weird mix of causes. No theoretical thread bound her to causes, but emotional ties to her struggling middle-class past did. As vice president of the League of Women Shoppers, for example, Hellman's goal was to investigate working conditions in stores and factories and press "for better wages and working conditions."[335] Women's labor conditions mattered to her, and she chaired the Sponsors Committee of the Fifth Annual Stenographers Ball. She said, "I feel that the thousands of stenographers and office workers who are members of this union deserve the support of every progressive and liberal person in this country."[336]

Dressed in expensive suits or fancy chiffon and taffeta gowns, she headed organizations, sponsored dinners and balls, and donated money to dozens of organizations. East Coast politics called for an intellectual, hierarchal approach, and she played her politics on stages, at lecterns, or standing at the head of a table. Sticking her neck out, she did not know how vicious the national fight against antifascists would become.

In October 1941 she and Hemingway cohosted a dinner forum on Europe Today to raise money for Spanish Civil War refugees and other victims of the Nazis. Isolation and neutrality were still the politics of the period, so she was elated when Governor Lehman of New York accepted an invitation to act as cosponsor. Then Lehman sent her a Western Union refusal when someone told him that some of the organizations listed on their letter of invitation "have long been connected with communist activities." He went on to say he supported victims of "Nazi persecution and oppression" but did "not in the slightest degree endorse the organizations under whose auspices the dinner is to be given." She shot back a telegram of her own saying she didn't know and didn't ask the politics of committee members, "but I will vouch for the decent and humane aims of this dinner and I will vouch for the distribution of the proceeds . . . every cent of them." He adamantly refused to go. Newspapers got wind of Lehman's pullout and the Hemingway-Hellman fury and widely published the fight.

Hellman wanted the last word, so she wrote him in November reviewing their differences and denying his accusation that they had formed "something called a new united front for the Communist party." She enclosed an itemized list of every cent made and expended to "the unfortunate victims of Nazi persecution." She went on, "I am sure it will make you sad and as ashamed as it did me to know that, of the seven resignations out of 147 sponsors, five were Jews. Of all the peoples in the world, I think, we should be the last to hold back help, on any grounds, from those who fought for us." Whether chagrined or politically insistent on making his point, he replied a week later, thanking her for the financial report. Then he backpedaled a bit ("he had other engagements"), remarked on his own "practical demonstration" of sympathy, and then told her she should have done the work with an independent sponsoring committee rather than with "organizations with whose political views many of us disagree." His political rhetoric is not convincing, but in his final paragraph he foreshadowed the Cold War: his distrust of American communists who "take orders from a foreign power" and their weak anti-Nazi stance when the Soviet Union vacillated politically.[337] Although Europe Today made the most money and received the best newspaper coverage of any cause she advocated, Lehman's stance and his politician's logic should have warned Hellman of political jeopardy.

There would be consequences, punishment. She didn't know yet that the pejorative label "premature antifascist" would stigmatize her. Nor did she care. Hellman called the term "one of the comedy terms of all time."[338] Right-wing politicians from J. Edgar Hoover to Eugene McCarthy labeled all who dared join the fight against fascism before the government did in the 1940s. They certainly fingered Hellman; her fame, her energy, her vitriol made her a target. Hellman became a political force. Often oblique and metaphoric in her memoir writing, she sketched her political self in bold, clear lines, exhibiting the tangle of politics in a personal and public life.

5

FAME AND FOXES

HELLMAN FIRST THOUGHT OF DOING ANOTHER PLAY COMING out of Spain. She didn't know what spurred her creatively; she "only thought about the play to keep from thinking about the plane ride and to keep from admitting to myself that in a few hours I would be having a fine dinner in Toulouse. I would be so hungry that I would forget about my friends in Spain who would not eat so much that night or the next one."[1] She had been afraid to write another play and used politics to avoid it, but she had not lost touch with Broadway drama or Hollywood cinema. She was thrilled by ex-husband Arthur Kober's own Broadway hit, *Having a Wonderful Time*, which opened in February 1937 to a successful yearlong run. No doubt she invested in it. Hellman saw Kober's play as written in a unique voice, his background in the Bronx moving the themes and the humor. Embarrassed by *Days to Come*, she knew that she would have to write a drama that tapped into her own vision of the world from her own background.

From that premise, she began the six two-inch-thick notebooks of research that gave factual reality to those southern voices from her past. She said she tripped into "a giant tangled time-jungle" of her family history.[2] Then she drew from herself, "the half-remembered, half-observed, the half-understood which you need so much as you begin to write."[3]

Hellman did not invent the carnivorous, sly, comic-evil Hubbards as much as expose them.[4] Her script tells the story of the Hubbard family of Alabama, ready to sell out anyone, including their own kin and what is left of their souls, to gain wealth and standing. Through their antics she traced

143

the excesses of capitalists who crush their own history and the "little people" around them, including family and friends. Hellman created a world "populated by killers and victims, by eaters and the eaten, by foxes and geese."[5] These characters, not their politics, carried the plays and drew on her family connections to the United Fruit Company, notorious for its entrepreneurial interference in the politics and economies of banana republics.

The Little Foxes and its 1946 prequel *Another Part of the Forest* focused on the Hubbard family drama and community exploitation. In *Foxes* the year is 1900, the place a small Alabama town. By manipulation and hard ways, the Hubbards have become prosperous. Now they need northern capital to finance a cotton mill. Family manipulation, theft, extortion, and blackmail ensue. Ben Hubbard, heavy-handed and corrupt, tells his sister Regina, "The world is open. Open for people like you and me. Ready for us, waiting for us. After all, this is just the beginning." The Newhouse-Marx family history and Hellman's knowledge of the South created an atmosphere as universal and steamily southern as Tennessee Williams's later plays. The Hubbards speak her particular southern language: witty, sly, charming, and malicious. Yet Hellman insisted her foxes live everywhere, telling a New Orleans audience years later, "I simply happened to write about the South because I knew the people and I knew the place . . . but I didn't mean it to be just for the South."[6] In the world of business without ethics "these fictional turn of the century robber barons bear an all too close resemblance" to greedy "fine gentleman" of any time and place.[7]

In early drafts she made Regina's abysmal treatment of her husband Horace more in keeping with her own extended family history, as she moves him first to an attic, then to slave quarters.[8] Hellman originally wrote in a scene plucked from family legend: Regina rode a horse in circles outside the house as Horace died without his medicine.[9] Retelling some of this family history for *Pentimento*, Hellman reflected, "All that seemed fine for the play. But it wasn't; life had been too big, too muddled for writing." So she whittled it down to the more believable act of Regina withholding Horace's medicine as he struggles and dies of a heart attack. What the audience sees is brutality under the patina of soft southern accents and gruff, appealing humor. The irony sizzles beneath.

Money and power, or the desire for it, dominated Hellman's Hubbards. Oscar ravages the land and his wife, Birdie. Ben, shrewd and cunning, controls the family business. Sister Regina manipulates and schemes and gets the upper hand over them all, as she disregards her own family in blatant self-interest and exploitation. Tallulah Bankhead later wrote of the character she brought to life, "Regina Giddens was a rapacious bitch, cruel and callous. Etched in acid by Miss Hellman."[10] So sinful, so flamboyant was Regina that Marc Blitzstein wrote *Regina*, an opera adapted from *The Little Foxes* and produced on Broadway in 1949. Hellman praised it as "the most original of American operas and the most daring."[11] The complexity of the human spirit, the tragedy and comedy of all motivations and actions was Hellman's dramatic subject.

A popular story circulated that after *Foxes* opened, Hellman and her father, Max, stood at the back of the theater. "Miss Hellman leaned over and whispered into the ear of a mutual friend, 'ask papa if he recognizes any of us.'" Years later when an interviewer commented, "Your family is incredible," Hellman replied, "Everybody's family is incredible."[12] Hellman objected to attempts to find exact correspondences that make the play personal rather than universal, though her Uncle Samuel Zemurray's first partner was named Ashbell Hubbard, and Regina Marx was part of Hellman's family tree. After she unearthed her family and set them in motion, she went to her own experts for advice. Kober read her first act and encouraged her; Kronenberger gave her his views from the critical side of the stage. She dedicated the play "For Arthur Kober and Louis Kronenberger Who Have Been My Good Friends." Shumlin played his part too, as his powerful production made magic on the stage. Most important of all was Hammett, who paid her back for rescuing him in Hollywood by recovering sobriety long enough to help her do what he could no longer do himself—write a hit.

Hellman maintained that of all her plays, *The Little Foxes* owed most to Hammett. The two had stayed together because their bonds were strong, their ties complicated. They understood each other. Hammett's flagrancy gave her freedom; his rigid codes required her own. But one of the strongest aspects of their relationship was their work together on a play. Hammett loved Hellman despite all the shenanigans and gave her plays more than his editorial talent. He gave himself, knowing she gave everything too. Her plays became *their* center and she always credited him for his part, an odd symbiosis. He joked, "You're practically breaking my heart with letters about the play. I think we're going to have to make a rule that you're not to tackle any work when I'm not around to spur, quiet, goad, pacify, and tease you."[13] Work gave Hammett a reason to sober up temporarily. He demanded and got from her a disciplined work ethic he could no longer stomach. Whether or not he knew he was finished as a writer, he dogmatically refused to let her fail. He saw her wicked, funny wit as a creative force. She had talent. Hammett thought Hellman worth it.

Hammett could have made a name for himself as an editor. In his usual fashion he urged her through the drafts, pointing out characters, scenes, and lines that didn't work—sometimes telling her why, sometimes not—just telling her to fix it: "Get line right."[14] At this stage, he would write questions or remarks on the draft, or Hellman would listen and take notes. He liked talking it out while she took notes. He teased her, "If I haven't got you mixed up with somebody else, you have nice wrists but do not get much out of written instructions, having a tendency to go into action long before you've read as far as the first comma."[15] She honored his opinion and gave him credit for his suggestions, labeling them from the start or putting them on long yellow or white lined sheets. "Horace-Regina scene too long" or "Birdie's scene went too far."

After Hellman straightened out the larger issues, Hammett exactingly attended to specifics: choosing another word, sometimes making the lines less southern but more terse, dramatic—"going to be" instead of "g'wan be." He badgered her and coerced her. She recalled, "I'd done the ninth draft of *The Little Foxes* and I finished it and left it in a briefcase in front of his door . . . and he said 'well, you're on your way. Now start all over again.'"[16] She often told the story of bringing a draft of *The Little Foxes* to Hammett who said, "Things are going pretty well if you will just cut out the liberal blackamoor chit-chat."[17] That she left in a bit of it in the characters of Addie and Cal gives credence to his complaint. He wasn't always right, but he mostly was. He simply would not give up on her and would not let her rest. Throwing the seventh draft in her face, Hammett threatened, "If you're going to write like Rodgers and Hart go live with someone else!"[18] He insisted she become a serious thinker and writer, forcing her to square off, to confront the woman she was becoming. *The Little Foxes* was proof of that.

To stage the vibrant *Foxes*, Hellman again turned to Shumlin. His intensity was exactly right. At forty-one he reentered the thirty-four-year-old Hellman's daily life with great energy, pleased to produce and direct *The Little Foxes* at the National, his lucky theater.[19] With its early-Renaissance-style carvings and gold embellishments in warm Italian walnut, the theater's interior provided a backdrop for southern Old World ambience; its yellow bulbs lighting the gilt ornaments warmed the room—perfect for the cold, steely nastiness masked by southern charm played out within.[20] Howard Bay's gorgeous sets worked with the theater's mood, making him Hellman's favorite set designer.

Shumlin's chief production coup was casting Tallulah Bankhead as Regina, one of America's "most cunning female villains."[21] Hellman had originally picked Ina Clare, who refused, and then Judith Anderson, who dismissed the script as disgusting.[22] But Bankhead epitomized Regina, though Hellman never could say it aloud. She rather snobbishly said later that she and Shumlin "were both very nervous about Tallulah . . . her reputation by that time was rather scarlet," though Hellman herself had been painted by that same red brush.[23] In exasperation over Shumlin's insistence, Hellman asked Dorothy Parker why "people thought Tallulah was witty. Dottie said, wide-eyed, 'Do they dear? *People?*'"[24] Shumlin ignored Hellman's skepticism—and Parker's—and looked only at the potential performance. Bankhead as Regina was "one of the most electrifying performances in American Theatre history."[25] Bankhead, delighted by her wild reputation ("I'm pure as the driven slush"), drew on her sins and flagrancies to fit the character.[26] Despite later exciting performances by actresses such as Bette Davis, Elizabeth Taylor, and Stockard Channing, Bankhead was the ultimate Regina. The actress called Regina "the best role I ever had in the theater."[27]

In the original production, Bankhead dominated the action onstage with her superb performance, as well as the action offstage. Drema Paige said she was hired secretly to learn the part of Regina Giddons in case Bankhead bolted. During one of Bankhead's temper tantrums, Paige apparently got her chance, for just one act. "During rehearsals Tallulah was very demanding and was being a total bitch to everyone except the director, Herman Shumlin, who she was sleeping with. She threatened to walk out several times. After they opened and Herman wasn't around to calm her down anymore, things got worse. . . . Tallulah blows up at something or other, announces she has had it with the play, storms out of the theatre and disappears . . . I was *magnificent!* Unfortunately, Bankhead came back just in time to hear the applause for the first act. After an 'argument' that lasted for half an hour and sent two of the stage hands to the hospital with concussion and broken bones, Tallulah went on to finish the play."[28] Bankhead was certainly "a tramp, in the elegant sense."[29]

Hellman knew she would have difficulty with Bankhead and did. Dorothy Parker had predicated as much: "Lilly does things the hard way. Why didn't she have sense enough to get Harpo Marx instead of Tallulah?"[30] Both Bankhead and Hellman wanted absolute control of the stage and both were known for demanding attention. But Hellman's complaints about Bankhead weren't entirely without merit. The gorgeous Tallulah had all the makings of a petulant diva. Hellman's rehearsal notes reported that "Bankhead cuts in on important lines."[31] Hellman admitted years later that

Bankhead was wildly successful, though she usually tempered the praise with criticism of later performances, examples of her petulance, or "uneven" attention given to her part. As in so many of the Hellman-Bankhead stories, truth blurs into speculation. Hellman wrote stories about Bankhead's crude sexuality, her cocaine use, her outlandish drinking. A friend of Hellman's speculated, "You might ask yourself what Lillian felt about Tallulah Bankhead and why; wasn't there a man in here somewhere?"[32] That man would have been Shumlin. He loved women and if Paige was right, he had an affair with Bankhead. Hellman would have hated it. During a rocky opening in Baltimore, Bankhead drew great praise while a drunken Hellman threatened to leave the company, extreme even for her. Bankhead's biographer Lee Israel has a different take on the women's rivalry. "Hellman knew that Tallulah Bankhead, in spite of her self-presentation, was not very smart or sophisticated politically. And Tallulah knew that Hellman, for all her brilliance, was not a pretty woman. And each knew what the other knew. I'd say the situation between them was Damoclean."[33]

Bankhead's flamboyance of a flavor different than her own inflamed Hellman, who gave way to the extremes in her character she later regretted. "I drank as much as Miss Bankhead and while a mint julep made her temper flashing and often attractive, it often fixed me in a kind of gloom whose quiet was broken by sudden swings of anger, more unpleasant I guess because they were preceded by soft politeness."[34] Press reports recorded the two women's every fight—and there were many—from the way Bankhead played Regina to hosting benefit performances: for Spanish Civil War refugees (the cast turned that down) or a Finnish war benefit (Hellman and Shumlin turned that down).[35] Exaggerations abounded. Writer and critic Joseph Wood Krutch sixty years later reported that he and critic George Jean Nathan had shared a cab with Hellman and Bankhead. "Bankhead said: 'That's the last time I act in one of your god-damned plays.' Miss Hellman responded by slamming her purse against the actress's jaw. . . . I decided that no self-respecting Gila monster would have behaved in that manner."[36] Whether or not this report or the story that Bankhead slapped Hellman in the face before the entire *Little Foxes* company is true, Bankhead and Hellman were, as Hellman later wrote "indeed, a pair."[37]

Tantrums, fights, two professional women both seeing themselves as "center stage, the principal actress" with the "right to be outrageous," it took Shumlin's authoritative, demanding presence to get *The Little Foxes* staged.[38] Hellman took rehearsal notes daily, expecting Shumlin to make adjustments. When Regina's daughter Alexandra is to show excitement, Hellman notes on the script, "no jump, please. She is not a gazelle."[39] Hellman micromanaged. Still, Shumlin staged the play with his customary command and it ran flawlessly to audiences riveted by what newspapers hailed as the play's "anguishing tension,"[40] which left them "squirming."[41] Shumlin never let up, demanding consistent performances from all the actors and, as the play began its long run, managing every detail, even adjusting ticket prices nightly depending on demand.[42] For this smash hit, he didn't have to do much. Audiences still love it.

The Little Foxes opened to packed crowds and rave reviews on February 15, 1939. *Time* magazine hailed it as "the season's most tense and biting drama," and the all-important *New York Times* hailed it as vivid theater, with Bankhead giving the finest performance of her career. However, some critics complained that it was too melodramatic or "a sinister play about sinister people."[43] The play originally ran for 410 performances, and it has become an American classic, playing to full houses at each revival. *Foxes* productions draw critical esteem and complaint each time, depending on the expertise of the director: Mike Nichols's 1967 Lincoln Center revival, Austin Pendleton's 1980 revival, and Jack O'Brien's 1997 revival. Much also depends on the actress who plays Regina and the politics of the time it plays. Even with all these variables, Hellman's script still draws fire and acclaim, a play that according to Patricia Collinge, who played the original Birdie, "was a play so perfect that nothing could be imposed."[44]

Hellman loved *The Little Foxes* best of all her plays. Mike Nichols had to bar her from rehearsals because she wouldn't, or couldn't, let him direct without constant commentary. Austin Pendleton tells a story of her second-guessing him in every scene and loudly berating him in front of the company. He didn't have the will or the clout of Nichols or the cruelty to send an elderly, ailing Hellman from the theater. On opening night, however, they clashed openly:

> Between acts two and three she started in " —and that last scene of act two was terrible!" I thought, something snapped in me, we argued about every single scene in this play, and now she's gonna start in on this one? The one scene that I thought she liked? The whole audience was out in the lobby — and I began kicking the wall of the Martin Beck Theatre, and yelling: "This is — This is the worst fucking night of my life!" And she pounded her cane on the floor of the lobby of the Martin Beck, and yelled, "Every night I see this play is the worst fucking night of my life." This can't have been reassuring for the audience, but they went back in for the third act anyway.

Production difficulties aside, *The Little Foxes* took Hellman "smack-dab before the portals of immortality."[45] The Pulitzer didn't reward her nor the Drama Critics' Circle, though she gathered six votes of twelve and split the committee, forcing a tie. She began to be leery about such prizes. When *Oklahoma!* opened in 1943, she wrote Kober, "It should get the Critics prize, being far better than the pretentious shit that will get it."[46] If prizes didn't matter, success did, and reinstatement in the rarefied world of Broadway. She asked her literary executors to guard *The Little Foxes* production after her death, to "be careful" with it.[47] Its success came to mean hers. It proved her worth as the most "relentless" of female playwrights—a "species far more deadly than the male."[48]

The Little Foxes tantalized Sam Goldwyn from the minute he heard of its success as a Broadway play in New York. Goldwyn snapped up the rights to it, despite his story editor Edwin Knopf's warning that the story was "too caustic." Rumor had it that Goldwyn blew up: "I don't care what it costs, I want it!"[49] And he got it. Then he asked Hellman to adjust the script for a more conventional audience. Hellman's screenplay begins simply. Following the credits, the words on the screen appear: "Little foxes have lived in all times, in all places. This family happened to live in the Deep South in 1900." The flamboyant, comic-evil Hubbards of the theater became flatter, more universally human for the film. Hellman invented for the film version a predictable romantic relationship for Alexandra and created outside scenes to give the setting an openness it lacked in the theater. Goldwyn loved it. William Wyler directed, making use of Greg Toland's camera work once again. Goldwyn insisted on Meredith Willson as film composer for music, adding another cinematic dimension. The whole crew was poised to go. Then in his fashion, Goldwyn changed his mind and asked Hellman to give less love and more bite to the script. She told him she'd "written over a dozen versions" and was "through with it." She suggested Arthur Kober, Dorothy Parker, and Alan Campbell do the future rewrites.[50]

Making the film proved almost as intriguing as the screenplay's plot, which pits wit against a backdrop of wickedness. Politics in 1940 gave Goldwyn a new set of troubles. He began to worry that the picture might be seen as a "communist play." Dorothy Parker was on the set when he made the comment and told Hellman she fixed it for her by saying, "Oh, Mr. Goldwyn, I don't think that could be true. The play takes place in 1900 and the Communist Manifesto was written in 1848. That makes no sense at all." "Wonderful," he replied, "I'll tell everybody that."[51] As a tale of greed, *The Little Foxes* might be anticapitalist, but its critique has more to do with fire and brimstone evil than it does any particular political philosophy. The Hubbards, for whom Hellman had a "graveyard affection," are much too human for pure politics. But such subtlety was lost on Goldwyn.

The principles of production also engaged in backbiting. Wyler "was starting to squirm under the producer's thumb" and told whoever would listen that "the theme of exploiting cheap labor in *The Little Foxes* interested him so much because it was the story of Sam Goldwyn."[52] For his part, Goldwyn felt outraged at Kober, Parker, and Campbell's "boondoggling." He thought they were pretending to work on the script at his expense. So he ordered his latest story editor, Niven Busch Jr., to fire them. Busch, the "polished Princetonian," began with Parker, saying, "I'd rather cut my heart out than tell you what I'm about to tell you." He should have known better. Parker cut him off. "Let me stop you. If you act on your first suggestion, no one will care less than I."[53] Hollywood critic Bernard Dick suspects that the writers only wrote lines for the character of David Hewlitt, Alexandra's beau.[54] Hellman, who despised Alan Campbell, indicated that any rewriting came only from Kober and Parker. In this maelstrom, she wrote Kober about his screen credits for the film. Addressing him "Dearest Baby" and signing it with "much, much love" the letter is all about getting credit for "polishing" the script. She told Goldwyn she wanted each to have a separate "credit" card. "This, said Mr. Goldwyn, lying, he could not do because the titles were already scored and it would cost him $3,000 to put in an extra." She finally agreed to put all of them on her "credit" card even though it "means compromising with my own contract which I have always made a great point of not doing with Goldwyn." She'd rather pay for a new card if "only a couple of hundred dollars." She insisted Kober got credit, "and if it means dragging in Mr. Campbell at the same time, then let us admit he's got us by the balls and give up."[55] In contrast to this version, Parker's biographer Marion Meade says Campbell was essential, giving the others discipline to get the job done.

Apparently this behind-the-scenes intrigue was nothing new to any of them. Busch got in on the action, telling Goldwyn he thought Hellman's screenplay a "big, scrawly script" that he wanted to cut. "I cut the shit out of it. Goldwyn loved the cuts—they saved him lots of money. . . . but Wyler's 'giving me this snarlish Hungarian look.'"[56] Hellman and Wyler had to take the changes and actually made good use of them, a testament to Busch's expertise and Hellman's horrific schedule. Hellman tended to micromanage each detail, but in 1941 she was busy elsewhere. Between the preproduction of a new play in New York, struggling with Hammett, and increased political involvement for both of them, she trusted *The Little Foxes* film to go smoothly without her, if everyone would just follow the script.

As might be expected, Bette Davis as Regina Hubbard presented the biggest challenge for Wyler. In a classic case of he said, she said, Davis and Wyler each blamed the other for Davis's performance being too close to Tallulah Bankhead's Broadway portrayal. Davis had seen Bankhead's performance and could not break away from Regina's unmitigated evil. But Davis went on to add a flat, nasty twist to Regina's character that drove Wyler crazy. She played Regina as a monstrous bitch, not a woman of many sides, sexy and devious, and funny and evil. When Davis showed up on the set made up in white "to make her look older," Wyler snapped. "It makes you look like a clown. Take it off!" She got nasty, and his "scathing tongue" drove her off the set; she disappeared to Laguna Beach and did not come back for sixteen days. Wyler had to film around her and finally asked Hellman to write her a letter to "help exorcize Bankhead's ghost from her performance." Hellman wrote, "I am bewildered that you are having so much trouble with Regina. . . . I never meant Regina to be a violent woman or a fiery woman. . . . You will be better as Regina than Bankhead ever could have been: better by looks, by instinct, by understanding." Davis returned to the set, probably more for the $385,000 salary than Hellman's pleas. But Wyler never worked with her again, much to her regret.[57]

In absolute contrast to Bette Davis was Teresa Wright, making her movie debut by playing Alexandra. Wright must have heard stories of Hollywood excess and the antics surrounding this particular film because her contract was a corker. It forbade Goldwyn to film her in a bathing suit, running along the beach, posing in shorts, playing with dogs, digging in gardens, whipping up a meal. In short, Goldwyn had to use Wright as a fully formed character, not a stereotypic woman "attired in firecrackers and holding skyrockets for the Fourth of July; looking insinuatingly at a turkey for Thanksgiving; wearing a bunny cap with long ears for Easter; twinkling on prop snow in a skiing outfit while a fan blows her scarf."[58] Hellman must have whooped with delight at Wright's demands. Goldwyn agreed to Wright's restrictions but he was never to be deterred in his style or in what he wanted. At one filming he suggested that Wright was too stiff and recommended, "Teresa, let your breasts flow in the breeze."[59] Apparently Teresa loosened up sufficiently to be nominated for a supporting actress Oscar.

The film was foolproof, as much as anything made in Hollywood could be. The Hays office harped more than ever about language and behavior: "We suggest changing the line 'Like a preacher' to avoid the possibility of giving offense to the ministry. . . . Birdie will not be shown offensively drunk, and that any drinking, or display of liquor will be kept down to the absolute minimum."[60] But even the censors couldn't break the script's hold. In the heart attack scene where Herbert Marshall as Horace Giddens must stagger up the stairs, the trio had to adapt to Herbert Marshall's wooden leg: "a trade secret." Toland's solution to put him "out of focus" gave even more power to the climax.[61] Even Russian film great Sergei Eisenstein loved the film, playing it over and over at private parties. He wrote Hellman to say that Wyler deserved "motion picture fame for the rest of his life."[62] He marveled over Wyler's genius in directing Oscar and Leo's "shaving scene," which established the shared, crass understanding of father and son. The American audience agreed, and critics acclaimed it as "a whole new course of motion-picture making."[63] During its filming, Hellman remained remarkably calm in the Hollywood hoopla and ultimately agreed with critics who felt that Wyler's adaptation of the film gave it its greatness. *The Little Foxes* was nominated for nine Oscars: best picture, director, screenplay, actress (Bette Davis), and two for best supporting actress (Patricia Collinge and Teresa Wright)—the most Goldwyn had ever received for a single production. But there were no winners. Up against *Citizen Kane* and *The Maltese Falcon*, the runaway winner in 1941 was *How Green Was My Valley*.

Twenty years later, when they were all "getting older," as Goldwyn put it, Hellman, Arthur Kober, and the Wylers were invited to the Goldwyns' for dinner. When Bette Davis's name came up, Goldwyn said, "I had her in a very good picture I made, *The Three Little Foxes*." Hellman was not amused. Not only had Sam never once gotten the title right, but apparently he didn't remember that she had written it. She snapped, "Oh, really Sam? Well, I wrote the play and I wrote the movie." Covering, he said, "Of course you did. Who said you didn't write it? It was a great picture." Turning to Wyler, Goldwyn asked, "Did you ever see it?" Wyler replied, "I directed it." Goldwyn, a little truculent by then, said, "Who said you didn't direct it?"[64] The miracle is that such good films came from such an odd mix of people.

The Little Foxes made Hellman one of the most successful playwrights and screenwriters in the 1940s and the most famous woman playwright in the world. As Hammett's daughter Jo admitted, "My father was a great storyteller, but Lillian was even better."[65] Hellman—with Hammett's help—came of age, became a woman, became a star. As the theatrical saying goes, Failure is painful and success is intoxicating. With 410 performances, *The Little Foxes* blew up her world, for the better this time.

With *Foxes* selling out box offices on two coasts, Hellman held court at the luxurious Plaza Hotel, borrowing its grace and glamour for herself. Admiring reporters flocked to her rooms, gushing about her elegant legs, her blonde hair, her hospitality, and her "retinue of friends, the main train-bearers being Dashiell Hammett, Ralph Ingersoll, Shumlin, Kronenberger, and ex-husband Arthur Kober."[66] She greeted one reporter in an apricot negligee while accepting Shumlin's calls from Havana, dismissively telling a press eager for gossip that she had become very fond of Tallulah Bankhead. To say that, she must have had more than the mere "spot of brandy" the press reported.[67] One reporter gushed, "Miss Hellman likes people, she likes an occasional drink, a game of poker, a whirl at chem-de-fer. She is, in brief, merry rather than morbid." For this man she cagily admitted her flaws, seducing and winning his acclaim. The media broadcast her fame nationally, pushing her to the forefront of national attention. Hellman and Shumlin served as "guest armchair detectives" in "Napoleon's Razor" during a broadcast of Ellery Queen's nationally syndicated radio show. [68] Hellman's husky bravura voice and quick wit sped through the radio waves. Hellman knew how to play to an audience of one or twelve hundred or ten million.

Drama wasn't always limited to a theater stage, and her characters weren't always fictional. Hellman berated the critics for missing the dark comedy of human betrayals and corruption. The characters might have represented the sinners in capitalism, but her relationship with them was intimate. She saw greed, waste, aristocratic posturing, and political shenanigans in her present life as well as her past. She relished anecdotes that proved her cynical yet comic view of the world. In a letter to Kober, for example, she detailed an outlandish drunken party she had been to, and closed by remarking that Dick Maney was drunk and "spilled things and said it was just like Versailles and Dotty, God bless her, told the younger Benchley he was a Fascist bastard."[69]

Later she called this period following her second Broadway hit the most destructive and drunken time of her life. She did well for the public, faked it, but fell into a "wasteful ridiculous depression."[70] Two weeks after *Foxes* opened, Hellman fled to Cuba, where she couldn't hear reporters clamoring or critics praising or read about Hammett who was drunk once again in Hollywood while she was drunk in New York. She began short-lived affairs to match Hammett's recklessness, to prove her sexuality. In her choice of men she verified her attraction to the brilliant: Kenneth Crawford, the Washington bureau chief of *PM*, and St. Clair McKelway, also a *PM* editor. Wealthy, acquisitive, the darling of the intellectual set, she should have reveled in her moment of success. Quite the reverse, she later wrote, "I was

blind drunk during the whole experience . . . and I thought, 'there's something the matter with this lady. Something's very wrong with a woman with
the biggest hit on Broadway, and this miserable and this drunk and I better do
something about it.'"[71]

Hellman feared the fierce kind of mindless drinking that ruined lives.
After *Foxes*, she narrowly escaped the destructive alcoholism of Hammett and
Dorothy Parker. She became impatient with the tedious and ugly task of dealing with drunks, though she insisted Hammett was a "stylish drunk."[72] But she
stayed with Hammett as much as she did and loved Dorothy Parker for as
long as she did because of her staying power and the boozy atmosphere of her
childhood. As Diane Johnson wrote, "Like other people who became adults
during Prohibition, and like Hammett himself, she thought of drinking and
alcoholism as romantic, even chic."[73] *The Little Foxes* and all the subsequent
gigs made Hellman enough money to change her life. She consulted famed
psychiatrist Gregory Zilboorg, and with Hammett she bought Hardscrabble
Farm in Westchester County as a retreat. She soon quit drinking—a near abstinence that she says lasted six years. She was never to return to the drunken
excesses of the 1930s. In her latter years she drank too much by some standards, but not by hers. She ordered her "drinks like a swinger: 'A bullshot,
please, lots of vodka and very little consume.'"[74] But she didn't have to drink,
and that is what counted.

Hardscrabble Farm

Psychoanalysts notoriously fail at treating alcoholics, but Hellman credited
Zilboorg for changing her. As she told it, one day he said, "You will either
stop drinking or not come back here on Monday morning. I can't analyze
you this way. You're an alcoholic." She denied it. He asked her if she drank
before parties, not just during, and she said, "Oh, yes!" That settled it for him.
Zilboorg said, "In my definition you are, and we can't. . . . I can't go on this
way. I'd just be taking your money and wasting my time." She said, "Ok. I'll
try."[75] Zilboorg is an odd figure in Hellman's life. A short, dark Russian Jewish
immigrant, a veteran of the Red Army and a Catholic convert, he earned
great fame for his treatment. Nearly all of Hellman's friends ultimately saw
him professionally: Kober, Ingersoll, George Gershwin, and Shumlin. They
all saw him and his wife, Peg, socially too.

Terribly expensive ($75 an hour in 1940), Freudian, and Catholic, he told
her to get married and have a couple of children to cure what ailed her. His
analysis nevertheless worked for her.[76] Even Hammett, who scoffed at much,

remarked, "Also it's nice that you're feeling so well about the analysis—a feeling that you've earned by staying with it like a little major, and I guess maybe the eminent Doctor Z deserves some credit for his part in it."[77] Hellman's letters and calendars record the ongoing solace of Zilboorg, whom she calls "Gregory."

Wife Peg reportedly said that he hoped to cure Hellman of her "chronic lying" and "anti-Semitism" too.[78] Conflicted about her Jewishness, Hellman never considered herself anti-Semitic (though after meeting a particularly unpleasant Jewish writer she joked to Kober that "If you were not a Jew, I would be anti-Semitic").[79] As a Jew, she was sensitive about such accusations and hotly denied them. Certainly in the 1940s Hellman still tempered her language, if not her politics. Peg Zilboorg's accusation that Hellman was a liar also seems problematic. Her husband's other patients might have thought so and certainly Hellman must have come up in those therapy sessions. But the forthright and bold Hellman more often told the truth in doses too candid for comfort. Curing Hellman of lying would not have been part of the therapy if Hellman set the agenda. Apparently doctor-patient confidentiality or conflict of interest wasn't an issue for any of them in these relatively early days of therapy.

Hellman didn't always follow Zilboorg's advice, which was often contradictory: leave Hammett, marry, stay with Hammett through the hard time. But after Zilboorg's death and years of psychoanalysis with George Gero, Hellman wistfully wished Zilboorg were still there to consult. "Wanting some other way to live, is proof enough of deserving it. Having it is hard work, but not having it is sheer hell."[80] Zilboorg made a difference.

Hellman could afford therapy and, just as important, a retreat and lifestyle change. She committed to Hardscrabble Farm in Pleasantville, New York, 130 acres and an hour and a half drive from New York City.[81] Pleasantville was as rural and calm as Manhattan was urban and full of energy. Conservative, Pleasantville nevertheless was part of an old American history that appealed to Hellman.[82] She loved the revolutionary past of her white clapboard home, from the slate roof to the old eighteenth-century remains of a fireplace at St. John's rectory, to the cave in the cemetery where runaway slaves were hidden. Pleasantville's Choate House, now part of Pace University's extension, "once served as a private asylum for cerebral nonconformists."[83] She and Hammett felt right at home.

Half of the property was fields and meadows, and half woodlands, with bridle paths, stables, and poultry houses sharing the property with finished guest houses and caretakers' houses, as well as a beautiful main house. What clinched it for Hellman, who swam and fished her entire life, was the "spring-fed eight-acre lake, with three islands, running to a depth of nine feet."[84] A farm it would be—not a rich lady's estate—so Hardscrabble Farm it became, meaning "earning a bare subsistence, as on the land."[85]

The farm saved Hellman as much as Zilboorg did. It gave her an escape, albeit not a permanent one, from the life of fame and fortune and sly foxes in the theater world. Hammett "had a permanent room at Hardscrabble Farm, which she purchased in her name . . . but which was a joint investment between them, and they entertained friends—and often lovers—independently there. They recommitted themselves to each other in a relationship as strong as marriage but with a different set of vows. Their lives took separate paths, which intersected at intervals. What they shared was a home base."[86]

Stability, the hard work of writing, and the harder physical work of farming saved Hellman from spinning out of control. She was at her best in the country.[87] She remodeled, painted, landscaped, furnished, and decorated a home. She built herself a separate suite of rooms complete with study and library; Hammett took over the old master suite. Apart but together, they needed space.

Hellman reveled in the work, finding solace and pleasure in reviving misued land, hunting, trapping turtles, and fishing. She sold "an enormous amount of eggs,"[88] took the chickens, ducks, and geese to market.[89] She tilled vegetable beds to make a working farm, though Hammett insisted she planted them inefficiently. She told a reporter, "I am regarded as a nuisance in spring by everyone. I put out seeds on Monday and, as one friend says, on Wednesday if plants haven't come up I go out and reseed the whole plot."[90] The ever frugal Hellman, who valued expertise above all, "wrote the U.S. Department of agriculture for their free planting instructions and advice."[91] As she said, "I had energy in those days. Yes, I wrote a great deal. I would get up about six o'clock in the morning, make some coffee, and then go over and help the farmer milk the cows or clean the barn, come back about eight, eat breakfast, and then to work for two or three hours. After lunch I would go back and help with the vegetable garden, or whatever the season called for, for another three or four hours. Then a nap."[92] She stayed home at night, went to bed about 10:00, and got up early, "the Bohemian life not up my alley."[93]

She reestablished a rhythm in her life, broken only by wild trips to New York City in her big Cadillac, bringing home crates of Peking ducks, food for the ponies, including a brown and white pony named Herman after Shumlin.[94] She worried that such comfort made her fat, though her small frame never seemed to bulge, despite her lifelong zest for eating everything from peach cobbler to calf's liver on a bed of buttered apples.[95] She had appetite, confessing that once in New Orleans she had eaten five meals in a day. She never gained an ounce, or so it seemed. But at Hardscrabble she admitted, "I am on a diet, one I made up. It has taken me six weeks to lose five lbs."[96] The diet could not have lasted long. A letter to Kober noted a different diet called "the chocolate cake diet."[97] Not that Hardscrabble's healthy dose of nature and good living didn't have its downside. Many letters mention poison ivy, "itching," and a failed experiment in cooking skunk cabbage. Hunters poached on the rural estate, so much so that Hellman filed a complaint to the Mount Pleasant town council.[98] Nevertheless, friends told her that such living improved her disposition, soothed sharpish nerves.

Rotating her sports clothes at Hardscrabble with the silks and minks of Manhattan, Hellman took years to learn what a farm entails, but she was an eager learner, willing to work with the hired farmer and do the dirty work. A dog lover, she raised standard poodles, her bed full of "three panting dogs" when a man wasn't there to provide a different kind of affection.[99] She introduced a favorite, Flora, a brown French poodle, to all manner of pedigreed studs, only to have her "make friends with a half-breed dog down the road named Yippee."[100] Perhaps because she had curtailed her drinking, she reported being mystified by one of her three cows acting peculiarly in the vicinity of her apple orchard. Two vets summoned explained the cow had been eating fermenting apples and was "thoroughly drunk and was suffering sort of a bovine hangover."[101] This rural drunken craziness she could tolerate.

Hardscrabble made work in New York and Hollywood tolerable as well. After a trip to Hollywood and a long, difficult trip back on the train with flooding toilets and missed connections, she wrote to Kober from Hardscrabble, "It is very, very beautiful. All suddenly beautiful, the way it is when you haven't seen it for a long time. It's a particularly lush year and I caught the dogwood and the lilacs and the wood violets before they were gone. If all this doesn't sound like a bad English poet I'll hang myself on Goldwyn's grave."[102] Though a southerner who said she never liked the northern winter, she loved the gentle, hushed beauty of snow, the ice where she and Hammett skated, the comfort and warmth of the five fireplaces in her house. She wrote five plays there, sometimes in solitude, sometimes with people surrounding her.

As a writer she needed quiet and time. But she was gregarious and also needed people. With the clamoring people and hectic schedules of New York City when she had a play on, she relished Hardscrabble's peace. She made the farm a house full of friends who stayed for days or even weeks. "Yes, I was running a boardinghouse. It wasn't entertaining people, it was just an old boardinghouse. People came and stayed."[103] Her hard maple floors were perfect for dancing, which she loved, and the "old-fashioned bar decorated with antiques" obviously had a place in her hospitality.[104] She liked it that way, and for the most part, so did Hammett, who opted out when he wanted. They read, swam, ice-skated, played cards, cooked, and argued. In spite of the relaxed and often zany atmosphere at the farm, she worked well there, as did a number of her guests.

Hellman's men came to visit: Kober, Shumlin, Kronenberger, her father Max. Zilboorg and his wife Peg came. Henry Sigerist, a famous medical historian whom Hellman revered, came, recalling the "very refined dinner with excellent wines and conversation like fireworks."[105] They brought wives and girlfriends at their pleasure, though sometimes Hellman had to fake enjoying their visit. Kronenberger's wife Emmy gave Hellman dyspepsia for years, who complained later to friends, "Madame is still a trial—snippy and smugger as the years go by."[106]

But women figured importantly in Hellman's life too, pretty or homely, of varying wealth and status. Usually critical of the wives of men she thought of as hers, Hellman loved Margaret Frohnknecht, called Maggie, the only woman Hellman ever welcomed into Kober's life. Hellman served as matron of honor in their wedding in 1941 and subsequently became the godmother of the Kobers' only child, Catherine. The many letters between Kober and Maggie and Hellman and Hammett testify to the strength of their affection, with Hellman traipsing through apartments to find the Kobers housing when they were in New York, each of them involved with buying the other birthday presents—towels, flower holders, lawn chairs, bathrobes, loaning Hammett $20 here, $50 there, giving advice to one another. Maggie, for example, instructed Kober to tell Shumlin that "Lil is the only girl for him and he will never be happy with any one else or at least not as happy as with her."[107] If Maggie minded Arthur's continuing close friendship with Hellman, she kept it to herself and seemed to enjoy the fun of it. Hellman once signed a letter to Maggie, "My love to you, our husband, and child. Lilly"[108]

Dorothy Parker came often, although Hellman could not stomach Alan Campbell, her husband. She once wrote, "Dottie Parker called up crying to read me a caddish cablegram from the fairy-shit to whom she is married."[109] The two women played off each other's wit and bonded in laughter. Hannah Weinstein became a fast and firm friend complete with cookoffs and laughter and daily telephone calls for more than forty years.[110] Tally Wyler, William

Wyler's wife, became a friend for life and their travels together and correspondence showed their fun and enjoyment of each other. Hellman drew on the character of friend Ruthie Field, wife of Marshall Field, for writing "the upper-class lady" in her plays. Ruthie, warm, tolerant of Hellman's "occasional tantrums," loved her enough to make Hellman godmother to daughter Fiona. Hellman especially loved Edmund Wilson's wife Elena "when we were both middle-aged . . . but then somehow after Edmund's death, [1972] we lost each other."[111] Fond of poet Muriel Rukeyser, she urged her to visit, to bring her work. Friendly, outgoing people stimulated Hellman. And they were drawn to her "immense vitality, her humor, the strength of a nature for whom the dead were still alive and old scores were never settled—qualities which have indeed their reverse side of rancor and controversy, yet add up to an embodiment of human spirit which is strangely bracing if you are not its object or victim."[112] She welcomed them to Hardscrabble, roomy enough to give her the solitude she needed when she needed it, the excitement of a gathering at other times.

Children were welcome, especially Cathy Kober and the Weinstein children, Paula also a Hellman godchild. Though Hellman liked the idea of children more than the children themselves, Hammett was particularly fond of children, calling Paula "Hank" because of her middle name "Henry."[113] Toto and Hamilton Basso came with their son Keith, who received Hammett's beautiful crossbow because the child wanted it more.[114]

How Hellman wrote on a working farm with an open door atmosphere is a question answered in part by the warning posted on her study door during a holiday with visitors:

This Room is Used for Work
Do Not Enter Without Knocking
After You Knock, Wait for an Answer
If you get no Answer, go Away and
Don't Come Back
This means Everybody
This Means You
This Means Night or Day

Kober wrote his daughter Cathy of one outlandish weekend that began at Hardscrabble and moved to George Kaufman's country house in Pennsylvania: "Dotty and Lil went to town on the Kaufman's cooking," the "dreck" they would get after traveling sixty miles from Westchester. Once there, George "confided to me that he hadn't been speaking to Dotty in years because she insulted him." Then the "ladies" critiqued Lillian's birthday guests from the weekend before: "Mrs. Averill Harriman's feathers were completely plucked and her skin along with them, Mr. Jimmy Sheehan got a thorough roasting, J. Raymond Walsh, the news commentator, was praised but it was revealed that he is a fairy, und so *vieder*." After the Kaufman's cooking fiasco, "the week-end consisted mostly of gin rummy playing, I regret to say." He especially regretted that Hellman was his partner and she played badly, and he had promised their joint therapist "Zil" that he wouldn't gamble. "In that circle you play cribbage furiously, or croquet furiously, or gossip furiously, but the calm and gracious method of exchanging thoughts, ideas and opinions—oh, no." Then there was the drama of hiding Parker's scathing review of Kaufman and Hart's "nasty little play, 'The Man Who Came to Dinner.'" Written for the *Chicago Sun's Book Week*, it had just arrived in the *Times*. After all sorts of antics, Hellman and Parker agreed to bury the section in "Dotty's suitcase . . . Lillian told me later that Kaufman picked up the *Times* and said, 'My favorite part is missing'—and when she looked at him with fearful eyes, he added, 'the real estate section.' Lillian said she found herself saying 'It's probably up in Dotty's room, locked in her suitcase.' Well, it was all very tense and very dramatic."[115] Maybe so, but they had fun.

Hammett thrived at Hardscrabble, with long periods of sobriety, able to join or escape the Hellman entourage as it pleased him. He wrote his daughter Mary in 1941, "I'm doing this in a boat in the middle of the lake with forsythia to the right of me, dogwood to the left, a couple of pintail ducks swimming at a safe distance ahead of me and bass refusing to bite all around me."[116] Most at peace in the boathouse that held his guns and fishing gear, the very private Hammett loved the lake's beauty and solitude. His daughters Jo and Mary came for visits, staying in one of the guest houses. His daughter later wrote, "There was a stone barn, a guesthouse where Mary and I stayed and another for the farmer who took care of the livestock and put in a couple of crops of alfalfa and corn each year."[117] Hammett could invite girlfriends to the farm too, even if he had to endure a bout of sulking from Hellman. If Hammett and Hellman had made "a Faustian bargain," it worked for both.[118]

With a full-time farmer, two spring and summer farm helpers, two maids and a cook, Hellman and Hammett managed well. She left Hammett's rooms in their customary mess, but the rest of the house was carefully maintained. Hellman, never one to trust others to do their job without supervision, kept a sharp and managerial eye on the help. She demanded new linens every day, a place for everything. Tidy and organized, she needed control over her life and over her surroundings, which were rich and lush in earthy greens, reds, browns. Hammett's daughter provides insight into Hellman's housekeeping: "The house was roomy, comfortable and, like everything Lillian put her hand to, in flawless taste. She had brought her maid, cook, and driver up from the city. Lillian had definite guidelines for hiring servants. No elderly, she told me. They were too crabby. And no Jewish. They always wanted to give you advice. She seemed happiest with blacks."[119] Nothing of this is surprising given Hellman's background, even the fact that she kept an "eagle eye on the staff" and did much entertaining. She set a beautiful theatrical stage, even in the country.

In Pleasantville she had space and quiet to write. But as a dramatist, when Broadway called she came. She stayed at her old apartment on 56th Street, then the Plaza, even Arthur Kober's apartment on 63rd Street. After a stint in the old Henry Clews house at 5 East 82nd, in 1944 she moved to the elegant townhouse, a "smaller mansion"[120] at 63 East 82nd Street, where she would live her New York City life for the next twenty-six years. After leaving the Plaza for more permanent city luxury, she vented to the press: "To hell with domesticity and living at home. Anybody's a fool who doesn't live in a hotel, and me—I'm going right back to the Plaza where everything comes up in silver service elaborate enough for royalty and with an illusion of the great fire in Chicago created by the lamps under the chafing dishes." Her tirade was for the benefit of the press, who reported "she was cross in a restrained kind of way."[121] It was pure public relations: Hellman liked the outlandish statement, enjoyed needling the easily shocked. A gossip columnist reported in 1941 that when Hellman was hospitalized for removal of a swallowed bone, she had a tube inserted in her throat. She sent words to her friends: "At last, I'm speechless."[122]

Fighting the Writers' Wars

Though she missed New York City and Broadway when she flew west, she made the most of her California stays. But she never bought a house there, staying with friends or in posh hotels like the Beverly Wilshire. In the early 1940s while making the movie version of *The Little Foxes*, she reveled in the victory of the Screenwriters Guild, made possible by Franklin Delano Roosevelt's election and his pro-labor administration which (temporarily at least) put the producers at a disadvantage. Phillip Dunne, Don Stewart, Charles Brackett and Hellman made up the negotiating committee. Finally the fun could begin. "Sam the good," as Hellman dubbed Goldwyn at this time, had his troubles with Hellman, but they were only marginally about Guild politics. She infuriated him, but their skirmishes related to control of an individual script and control of her outrageous sense of humor conducted in scenarios carried out on company time. The antics Goldwyn objected to had to do with Hellman's getting in her digs about producers' abuse of writers.

She and Reeves Espy, a Goldwyn executive Hellman referred to in jest as "a disappointed former con man from Seattle," must have had quite a flirtation. Hellman only liked creative play with men who stirred her. Apparently amused and interested in each other as well as politics, they did some fancy false detective work. They played at trying to identify a writer on the payroll named "Estabrook," who "might not even exist." She and Espy skulked around the lot looking for anyone "who looked like a writer, God should forbid."

Certainly they both knew Howard Estabrook was a successful screenwriter who won an Academy Award for *Cimarron* in 1931. But the Hellman-Espy "espionage" came to represent the questions at the center of the Screenwriters Guild: What is a writer, and what presence does a writer have in film? If a writer is missing from his office, does that mean he is not writing? Is he or she a threat to the industry? In a series of clever and insulting false memos, Hellman and Espy sparred over this paradox. Hellman wrote that the missing writer must be a danger to the whole system: "Save Goldwyn. Save Austria. This is a pure example of Fascist terror and deception. Save United Artists!" Espy decided Hellman's point of view resulted from "something elementary such as sex frustration" and should be studied by someone who "diagnoses with the naked eye; by stealthy observation," noting in a postscript that "Hellman says she is a writer. Encourage her."[123] This kind of play—a mixture of sexual and political innuendo—was Hellman's forte.

In other studios, more pressing but less personal concerns increasingly came between management and writers. The producers got nastier. Noting the "unstable situation" and for once in a position to wield some power, the Guild asked for a writer's minimum wage. Other producers felt relieved at the minimal request, but not Harry Warner. He "got up and turned to his men and swearing, screaming said, "Is that all they want? That's all they want . . . Those dirty communist sons of bitches . . . they want to take my goddamn studio, my brothers built this studio . . . they want to take my goddamn studio. I came from Europe . . . my father was a butcher. . . you dirty commies." The other producers dragged Warner out, then came back and agreed to the Guild's proposal.[124] Warner was raging out of control. He certainly wasn't worried the agreement would hurt his studio. This same year, the major producers turned out over 350 movies, which earned over a billion dollars a year in the United States alone. Their union-busting fury erupted alongside huge profit-making industries just like those owned by the Rockefellers, the Carnegies, and the Fords.

Many writers in Hollywood had long distrusted wealth, fostering a guilty and sometimes hypocritical activism in honor of "the little man" as FDR called America's citizenry. Hellman's firebrand economics—not new then or now—made sense to her. She liked money but was disgusted by the outlandish display of wealth in Hollywood: "there is something odd about people vying with each other for better bathrooms."[125] She and thousands of others in Hollywood thought the industry's huge profits should be spread more evenly among those who helped earn them. It forever galled her that studios controlled the sacred ground of a writer's words. Even after writer's wars and the so-called victories, the 1942 Guild contract contained a clause that keeps writers in check to this day: "The studio, hereinafter referred to as the author . . ." This phrase asserts studio ownership of the intellectual property created by the screenwriter. Hellman never gave up the fight.[126]

Hellman's politicking for Hollywood writers provided her with a political and personal network. In Hollywood, Hellman vented energy and anger as part of a group working to oppose "intolerable injustice" in their workplace.[127] In those days, screenwriters banded together, gathering at Musso and Franks or the writers' table at Rose's bookstore during the day, and the Clover Club and Trocadero at night. Sober or smashed, writers felt demeaned by Jack Warner's characterization of them as "schmucks with Underwoods."[128] While Hollywood writers supported the talent of writers emigrating from New York, they were wary of "Broadway carpetbaggers" who arrived "proclaiming theatre to be a higher calling and movies a degrading pit stop." Even the Hacketts, one of the most successful screenwriting teams in Hollywood, felt the tension: "If playwrights immeasurably enhanced the standard of motion pictures by their contributions, they also by and large scurried back to NY to mount their next productions, leaving the full time mop-up Hollywood screen writers feeling understandably tenuous."[129] Hellman spent as much time away from Hollywood as possible, and she rarely had to do the scut work of other writers. She demanded big money and screen credit and got both. The successful union organizers worked for the less successful, who reminded them of the insecure, dismal place they had so recently vacated.

Hellman never forgot her own pale beginnings, writing summaries in the back lot of MGM's ostentatious fake-marble facade in Culver City. She had concocted a philosophy that honored individual talent and collective effort too, and she stuck to this equation even after she had made it big on Broadway. Other writers respected her. Hellman delivered the goods when asked to write a script and worked hard at it. In those slick strips of celluloid and in the politics of the industry, she had found meaning.

Even amid the victory of Guild recognition, trouble was on the way for leftist screenwriters, and Hellman would find herself caught up in it. Donald Ogden Stewart, a prolific communist screenwriter (*The Philadelphia Story*) wrote Hellman at this time, praising *The Little Foxes* script but really asking for help with the Screenwriters Guild. It was increasingly being attacked by Washington.[130] The newly formed House Committee on Un-American Activities, under the chairmanship of Texas congressman Martin Dies, again raised the specter of red Hollywood treason. California legislators like Sam Yorty and Senator Tenney "overnight . . . joined the ranks of the witch-hunters" leading them in "dubious battle" against the movie industry.[131] The escalation of misinformation and suspicion began with the 1940 investigations of Phillip Dunne, screenwriter, and three actors: Fredric March, James Cagney, and Humphrey Bogart. Though their definite antifascist leanings made them fair game for a committee out to undermine FDR any way it could, the committee could not prove the actors bore any taint of communism. But the furor made good press. Movie stars and their ilk were high-visibility targets for political darts. Hellman, as leftist as any, wasn't yet big enough.

Increasingly Hellman joined left-wing causes allied with the industry. She and Herman Shumlin once again collaborated with Joris Ivens, with whom they had worked on *The Spanish Earth*. This time they formed a production company, History Today, Inc., to promote the film *The Four Hundred Million*, which documented Chinese heroism against Japanese aggression.[132] In Hellman's eyes, the imperial slaughter in Spain and China made the Communist Party's "ultimate aims . . . humanitarian and idealistic."[133] Hollywood was still a year away from seeing Japan as an enemy; Hellman was premature in this regard too. She, along with thousands of others, joined the Hollywood Anti-Nazi League, in itself not communist but with a significant red membership, largely because it was "a true attempt to develop an organized front against fascism. . . with a goal to generate active propaganda against Nazism."[134] Dorothy Parker, who formed the league with Oscar Hammerstein II, probably asked her to join. As the left got stronger and more organized, so did the right.

The newly formed Motion Picture Alliance for the Preservation of American Ideals fought to keep leftist messages out of films, a backlash of sorts against the New Deal and FDR's social and political leftism. Headed by John Wayne, Walt Disney, Ward Bond, Clark Gable, and John Ford, this group ripped the industry in half. The anti-Roosevelt Alliance supported America's supposedly neutral position with regard to Germany and Italy. Russia and leftist labor were the enemy, not Germany and fascism.

In Hollywood, each side of the political spectrum feared the other's political influence. The left disparaged the (ostensibly politically neutral) slick and glossy fare that could be sold easily to fascist nations to earn the studios vast profits. The Motion Picture Alliance and the more general conservative right suspected that leftist writers might slip progressive politics into the movies, despite the Hays committee. Thus leftist writers were vulnerable to accusation, no matter what film they worked on. Yet even writers who later admitted to being communists covered over any political wrinkle in their scripts at the producer's request. John Howard Lawson, for example, wrote the screenplay *Blockade*, the first serious Hollywood movie to address the Spanish Civil War. At the request of the producers, they changed it into a generic antiwar movie. The studios feared cancellations from abroad and domestic opposition and pickets from the Knights of Columbus and other Catholic opposition, which happened anyway.[135]

Most producers settled for fluff and wanted writers to churn it out. "Instead of writing furious films about silver-shirted Nazis parading in the streets of New York, or about Trotskyites, Townsendites, Socialists, New Dealers, and the toiling masses, they were asked to come up with 'screwball comedies' and escapist entertainment, usually set in high society and dealing with millionaires and chambermaids, smart-aleck cab drivers and nouveaux riches." A right-wing faction kept the lid on anti-Nazi films, either out of political alliance or economic reliance on the overseas market. In the three years before Pearl Harbor, Hollywood made over a thousand films, only fifty anti-Nazi in theme, and none pro-communist. Hollywood movies could hardly be more tame. Writers and actors found themselves butting heads with the Alliance, a powerful enemy that now had support from HUAC. Citing the Anti-Nazi League as unnecessary and anti-American, HUAC cranked up the anti-Soviet Hollywood investigations. No one could stay neutral, not that Hellman was that way inclined. She publicly called California "the home of Fascism . . . considerable nationalism . . . virulent anti-Semitic organization."[136] She mocked Hollywood producers as "Caspar Milquetoasts" and Dorothy Parker referred to all antileft factions uniformly as "shits." Billy Wilder, trying to be reasonable, called the right "red-baiters" or "social fascists" later reflecting that it was an "unreal historical period in which to live."[137] Writer John Bright reported that J. Edgar Hoover showed up and told producers to focus on projects that attacked the Soviet Union: "that's the enemy."[138]

Hellman had nearly always supported the Soviet Union in international politics. She believed socialism the answer to unemployment, war, and racial discrimination. Of course Hammett mentored her, and his political rule was "be in favor of what's good for the workers and against what isn't. Follow that, and . . . you'll at least be able to hold your head up when you look yourself in the mirror."[139] Always a fighter for the underdog, Hellman agreed. Along with most other leftists, she naively believed that Soviet communism worked toward a better world. As screenwriter Bernard Gordon remembered, "What about Stalin? What we knew then, what we knew for certain, was that he was heading the most ferocious, bloody, and heroic fight against Hitler."[140] In response to the Moscow trials of the Trotskyite-Bukharanite traitors, Hellman, Nathanael West, John Garfield, Ring Lardner Jr., Dorothy Parker, and many others signed an open letter of support for Stalin published in the *New York Times*. They were wrong about Stalin's oppression, but he held the best hope of stopping the Nazis.

Hellman knew the power of the spotlight, but she didn't always know the facts. Few did. As Judith Crist wrote in her influential study of the films of World War II, "The tragedies abroad brought twists and turns at home with strange fellows sharing beds when pacifist socialists found themselves with the isolationist America First and the internationalists saw the Moscow-manipulated League Against War and Fascism become the League for Peace and Democracy during the Nazi-Soviet pact. But then in no time the schoolgirls knitting for Bundles for Britain were extending their needles to Russian War Relief."[141] The lines had split between those favoring antifascist intervention into a world about to explode in war or appeasing Hitler. In New York, Hellman's interventionist politics fit better, but the events of the 1940s tattered political alliances on both coasts.

The Little Foxes and *Watch on the Rhine* came during Hellman's most radical years, each in its own way dramatizing the evil men do to others in the name of greed. Personal evil in *The Little Foxes* turns to the sin of omission and political apathy in *Watch on the Rhine*. As she was writing *Rhine*, she began to develop a political philosophy that could not find comfort in American Communist party ideology.

Ahead of the Curve

In 1939 and 1940, when she wrote *Watch on the Rhine*, Hellman chose a public stance against the Communist Party line in the United States. The party
had asked members to support the Soviet-Germany nonaggression pact
signed by Stalin and Hitler on August 23, 1939. Many leftists and communists
immediately reversed course to support the Soviet Union and joined the
nonaggression isolationists to lobby for peace. Not Hellman. She compiled
notebook upon notebook on fascism in Europe, and that research, along with
the actual writing of *Watch on the Rhine*, solidified her views on fighting fascism, irrespective of any political party.[142] Hellman's drafts show her changing
attitudes, from fellow traveler lassitude to forthright deviation. Begun in 1939,
early drafts show her equating socialism with antifascism—hardly radical
thinking in the late 1930s. Subsequent drafts, however, move the entire action
to capitalist America. Undecided about whether her hero should be a communist or socialist, she ultimately portrayed him as a leftist devoted to
bettering the world—Hellman's political philosophy in a nutshell.

Hellman needed no prodding from Hammett or anyone else to write
Watch on the Rhine. She felt certain "the hurricane was somewhere off the
coast and death around the corner."[143] She wanted to dramatize the political
"wound in the heart" begun during the Spanish Civil War.[144] She made several attempts to combine labor themes with antifascist themes. She thought
of using Zola's *Germinal* as a model, then the more international themes of
Henry James's *Europeans*, because "Europe had come to America and had
come to do us no good but the greatest possible harm."[145] In the original draft
of *Watch on the Rhine* she set the scene in Ohio, the center of America, but
the shadow of failure cast by *Days to Come* hung over that setting. She made
"digests of twenty-five books, political argument, memoirs, recent German
history" to find the core of her political malaise.[146] She finally set the play in
Washington, D.C., where power resides. Next came the creation of characters, complacent Americans easily fooled by appearances. A titled couple
from Europe who move into an American home keep changing faces and
roles: from the naive to the villainous, charming fascists. She outlined and
planned and shifted characters and plot, but once she began writing, it "was
the only play I have ever written that came out in one piece, as if I had seen
a landscape and never altered the trees or the season or their colors."[147]

Her drama takes place in the nation's capital, in a lovely home furnished
by wealth and family taste over the years; it has "space, simplicity, style."[148] It's
a home shaped by the comfort of time-honored routines, where everyone,

from Fanny Farrelly, the widow of an important judge, to Joseph, "a tall middle-aged Negro butler," knows his or her place and class and function. Into this comfortable American tableau come the visiting aristocrats, Marthe and Teck, her fascist aristocrat husband. Slick and smooth, more decadent than vicious, the two nevertheless lead others into the wake of Nazism.[149] Sarah comes home after twenty years with her three children and Kurt, her antifascist husband. This combination of characters brings politically volatile Europe into the Farrellys' life. When Teck discovers that Kurt is the leader of an anti-Nazi underground and tries to blackmail him, the Farrelly family is forced to confront world politics in their home. *Watch on the Rhine* is as much about Hellman's family as *The Little Foxes* was. Hellman's lifelong complaint about her mother's apathy comes through in Fanny, the aging upper-class mother who can only be wrenched from her nice, hospitable ways by the immediacy of violence.

Here Hellman used the domestic as a metaphor for the international. She characterized national policy in individual characters, emphasizing the personal responsibility of each American in shaping the government. "What it contrasts are two ways of life—ours with its unawakened innocence and Europe's with its tragic necessities."[150] Hellman never doubted that the enemy to American democracy was Nazi Germany. In the play, after a first draft giving communists credit for their antifascist commitment, she defined the antifascists as broadly as possible to effectively combat the Nazis—and Stalin's pact with Hitler. When Kurt, the antifascist son-in-law, succinctly justifies his intention to continue antifascist work in Europe, Hellman was at her most persuasive politically. Typical Hellman devices like spying, subterfuge, blackmail, and threats expose the vicious ideology that has invaded the Farrelly household. The edgy, polite cuts of conversation, the mounting tension just below the surface move the audience, forcing their interpretation and commitment to dramatic justice, at least.

On opening night, April 1, 1941, *Watch on the Rhine* gave its first performance to "unanimous huzzahs."[151] "The curtain calls were so thunderous and repeated . . . that the house lights had to be flooded three times."[152] That acclaim would be repeated in the 378 performances that followed. Tartly humorous and "jubilantly bitter," *Watch* played at that "great barn," the Martin Beck Theatre, in the center of Broadway's theatrical district at 45th and 8th.[153] The same month it opened, it won the Drama Critics Circle Award.

A photo shows Hellman and Herman Shumlin, who again produced and directed, during intermission of the play's premier performance. Hellman is in large hat and tightly fitted plaid jacket over pleated skirt. Shumlin wears a suit, starched shirt, and snappy bow tie. Both hold cigarettes, their faces show-ing great pleasure in the show and each other. Hellman reported later that after the first act she was convinced it had failed, and Shumlin ordered her to "get out and stay out."[154] Broadway critics praised Shumlin for the quick pac-ing of a play with much dialogue, and for staging a gruesomely realistic fight between Teck and Kurt. When Kurt killed Teck at the end as the only means to everyone's survival, most New Yorkers accepted the necessity of bloodshed in the circumstances. The play had wit and grace, but it was tough.

The Hellman-Shumlin skirmishes this time out were minor. Characteristically unsure about titles, she called it number 5, even into re-hearsals. Shumlin finally forced the issue by threatening to stop rehearsals until she picked one. [155] He got a "case of the vapors" when she titled it *Die Wacht am Rhein*, the name for a traditional German song. Shumlin, his eye ever on audience attendance (he stood in the lobby of opening night hissing at those who were late),[156] feared that a title in German would mean that "people who couldn't speak German would be afraid of asking for seats."[157]

Absent were the usual fights about casting. Everyone wanted a part this time because the characters were likable Americans. The exception was Teck, whose dirty politics were covered over by polish and sophistication, ad-mirably played by George Coulouris. Lucile Watson played Fanny and "gloried in the sure-fire delights of one of Miss Hellman's salary and officious great ladies."[158] Mady Christians starred as Sarah. "But for making it all as vivid as life itself, credit must go to Paul Lukas . . . he lives Kurt Mueller."[159] Lukas, a Hungarian actor, troubled Hellman, who considered him nearly as fascist as her character Teck. Shumlin demanded him, however, and he proved himself worth every worry.

Hellman agreed Lukas did a fabulous job, but he just didn't measure up to the man she fashioned Kurt Mueller after: the antifascist fighter and passion-ate patriot Otto Katz, born Otto Simon, later renamed Andre Simone. A journalist of international renown, Katz served as the propaganda minister of the Spanish Republican Government, though Hellman first met him in Paris. A communist, he served various causes, both political and theatrical. He was "charming, intense, and intellectual in a way many communists were not—for fear of not adhering to the party line."[160] Hellman was taken with his commitment to antifascism and his charisma. That combination in men never failed to leave a lasting imprint. Hellman wrote of a dinner she had with him in Paris when a beautiful ex-lover of his, a "German movie star," came to speak with him. (Hellman doesn't reveal Marlene Dietrich's name in *Unfinished Woman*.)[161] Katz's fame, attractiveness, and charismatic politics influenced her greatly. In writing *Watch*, Hellman channeled Katz into Kurt Mueller, and in subsequent drafts he becomes nearly unrecognizable, except for his passionate political force. Hellman, never patient with actors, wanted the real thing, not Lukas. The cannier Shumlin knew that only what appeared real mattered. He prevailed.

The timing of Hellman's *Watch on the Rhine* demonstrates her personal confrontation with the fascists and their Soviet allies. Hellman took the complex political world of 1939–1941 and showed it in stark, unmistakable terms, much to her political critics' surprise. When Hitler attacked Stalin on June 22, 1941, Hellman's play had already showed publicly her present anti-Soviet stance. Communists turned on her for the play. Alvah Bessie, screenwriter and reviewer for *New Masses*, criticized her "antifascist message," saying it needed to be "redefined in socialist terms," [162] and the critic for the *Daily Worker* insisted her "political issues need explanation."[163] But her leftism was so well established in some circles that screenwriter Allen Rivkin found traction in a story he circulated that "Lilly Hellman walked in dressed all in white. She was somewhere between ecstatic and furious, and I don't know if she was kidding or serious, but she said, 'The Motherland has been attacked.'"[164] Hellman denied it vehemently, though complimented its teller for the 'nice touch' of the white dress. The political establishment didn't like the play much either, thinking Hellman exaggerated the Nazi menace. Even *Newsweek* called the play "eloquent propaganda."[165]

Nine months after *Watch on the Rhine* opened, Americans everywhere got word that the Japanese had bombed Pearl Harbor. As Hollywood critic Bernard Dick reported, "On December 8, *The New York Times*, as expected, ran an editorial calling for a declaration of war: President Roosevelt did not have to be told what to do. At 12:33 p.m. he did precisely that, declaring December 7, 1941 'a day which will live in infamy.' That same day, The Greenwich Village Savoyards canceled its final performances of Gilbert and Sullivan's *The Mikado*. Lillian Hellman was right. We had been shaken out of the magnolias."[166] And as Fanny says at the play's close, "Tomorrow will be a hard day."[167]

Following Pearl Harbor, President Roosevelt invited Hellman and the entire production company to give a "kind of command performance" before the president in Washington to benefit the Infantile Paralysis Fund "on a Sunday night, early in 1942." FDR was most interested in *when* she wrote *Watch on the Rhine*: "When I told him I started it a year and a half before the war, he shook his head and said in that case he didn't understand why Morris Ernst had told him that I was so opposed to the war that I had paid for the

'Communist' war-protestors who kept a continuous picket line around the White House before Germany attacked the Soviet Union. I said I didn't know Mr. Ernst's reasons for that nonsense story, but Ernst's family had been in business with my Alabama family long ago and that wasn't a good mark on any man. Mr. Roosevelt laughed and said he'd enjoy passing that message on to Mr. Ernst."[168] Indeed, Mr. Ernst, the civil rights lawyer and Roosevelt's personal envoy in World War II, also reported that false story to the FBI, which Hoover duly noted.[169]

This performance—both of the play and the playwright—may have given FDR the germ of an idea to send Hellman to Russia on a goodwill cultural mission in 1944. Clearly leftist, Hellman nevertheless made her own way politically, seldom daunted by naysayers, communist critics, or Washington lawyers. But she was a patriot too, and along with countless others, the call to arms after Pearl Harbor changed Hellman's life, although she would understand the full extent of that change only years later.

The bombing of Pearl Harbor had an instant effect on Hollywood, Hellman's role there, and her eventual political ostracism. Every national priority shifted after the Japanese bombed Pearl Harbor and the United States waged open war on the Axis. Hollywood joined in enthusiastically, making anti-Nazi movies, contributing money, entertaining soldiers on leave, promoting bond efforts. Actresses, including Marlene Dietrich, Betty Grable, Dorothy Lamour, and Lana Turner, posed for pinup posters. The early enthusiasm and war movies "had a celluloid crackle that was a pleasant unreality, a slick-step away" from the fear, the death and the politics of the War itself.[170]

Hollywood turned itself into a military camp in a day, diverting one hundred studio trucks and drivers to transport army troops and equipment, prop rifles, machine guns, revolvers—anything to fortify undersupplied posts along the West Coast. And with rationing, the Roman feasts, as Hellman called them, disappeared. With shelves empty, those coming into Hollywood from New York depended on its citizens for food. Apparently some in the city gave more than others. Hellman wrote from Goldwyn studios: "The food situation is bad and must be awful for the poor in L.A. Eggs, butter and cream, meat and canned goods are almost impossible to buy. My rich friends sent none: a new secretary, the research dep't, a grip who used to work at the studio, and an unknown fan, brought little bags of butter and a few eggs and coffee and I was very touched by it, and warmed."[171] Hammett's faith in the laborer seemed borne out in countless small ways.

It became increasingly clear that war was serious business, even in the movie industry. When Carole Lombard's plane crashed coming from an Indianapolis bond rally, shock waves reverberated throughout the industry. Her husband, Clark Gable, enlisted immediately; of the 240,000 persons employed in the production, distribution, and exhibition of motion pictures, over 40,000 served in the armed forces, including 48 executives and 230 screenwriters.[172] Those who didn't enlist did what they could. For Hellman, that meant writing for the effort. In 1942 the Office of War Information became the government's central contact with the film industry, urging writers and producers to make movies to assist the war efforts: shorts, documentaries, and feature films. No other industry gave so freely to the war effort.

The film industry, more politically controlled than controlling, responded quickly to the changed political climate. One studio hastily shelved a planned musical called *Pearl Harbor Pearl*; Goldwyn agreed to yank *The Real Glory* from further distribution because it "made our new allies villains."[173] Producers searched frantically to adjust to a prowar thrust not permitted in films a week earlier. The studios immediately complied with government requests for change. As film critic Judith Crist wrote, "The issues were clear-cut; we wanted no tonings. And we got none . . . what the hell, the German and Italian and Japanese markets were gone, so why not make the nasties as nasty as the public stomach (and production code) would allow?"[174] Lowell Mellett, chief of the Bureau of Motion Pictures of the Office of War Information, recognized that government needed to stay out of films. But he also knew that Hollywood producers were superpatriots, first-generation immigrants proud of their success and their new country.

Hellman's patriotism, her work ethic, and a liberalism that Hollywood could take only on its own shaky and vacillating moral terms are demonstrated in two important film adaptations of her Broadway hits: *Watch on the Rhine* (1943) and *The Searching Wind* (1946). She had originally written *Watch on the Rhine* to indict Americans with "drifting good will" and passive, apathetic politics—the Americans Hollywood seemed intent on pacifying.[175] Now Hollywood was echoing her outrage. Pearl Harbor validated the play's politics, and Warner Bros.' East Coast story editor recommended the play for production. Hal Wallis, the executive producer of Warner Bros., snapped up the film rights. Hellman wanted to write the film adaptation, but she couldn't simply switch from Goldwyn's studios to Warner's. Before agreeing to sell the film rights to Warners, she insisted Hammett write the adaptation and Shumlin direct. Hal Wallis, in charge of production, agreed. She got Hammett to write the script from her play, promising to add scenes and dialogue, and polish. She not only wanted to give him meaningful work, but she trusted his understanding of her and the political edge of the film. Hammett adapted it for Hellman, receiving a phenomenal salary of $30,000 plus 15 percent of the gross.[176] Clearly Hellman, sharp and demanding in business, negotiated the deal. But Hammett had burned many bridges in Hollywood by not carrying through on promises, oral and contractual. Only after director Shumlin and Hellman guaranteed a "timely delivery" did Hal Wallis agree to the deal.

A better writing team than Hellman and Hammett didn't exist in Hollywood. Because of the changed political atmosphere and the war, Hammett and Hellman had to turn a drawing room political play about an approaching menace into a timely, forceful drama, something the studio could sell. The film downplayed Kurt's adamantly leftist leanings to make his politics general, more geared toward the general betterment of mankind. In so doing she (but presumably not Hammett) again drew fire from the communist press, which thought she'd sold out left-wing politics.[177] Hammett's opening scene focused on an embassy in Mexico, a brilliant cinematic move, showing the political intrigue at play in the world.[178] Hellman praised his integration of character and politics. Then she took the sharp paring knife he had taught her to use and excised long, intellectual speeches that were anathema to cinema. She tweaked some scenes and changed dialogue as they had agreed. The film's script thus shows a definite blend of Hammett and Hellman. He adeptly worked on straightforward plot, and Hellman honed the speech. Hammett, writing from New York, sent Wallis a telegram in April, 1942: "IF I DON"T BREAK A LEG WILL FINISH SCRIPT THIS WEEK."[179] Ten days later he sent another saying simply: "DONE." As written by the Hellman–Hammett team, the *Watch on the Rhine* is not sentimental fare designed to leap "into the hearts of audiences; it does into their minds."[180]

After Hammett did his part, his focus shifted—this time to serving his country, not women. Hellman went back to Pleasantville, where she worked on a new screenplay and new Broadway drama. Hammett improbably went to boot camp. Hellman had always trusted Hammett's assessments of actors and actresses and had counted on his help in casting. But now with both of them gone, she had to cede casting decisions to others. This worried Hellman, since she saw her characters as flesh and blood and took casting seriously.

Thus Shumlin—whom she had recommended as director—chose the cast of *Watch on the Rhine* without her. Hellman knew Shumlin would pick a first-rate cast. But there were glitches, and she berated him in letters for not telling her what was what, who was who. Even though she trusted Shumlin, giving up control rankled her. To add to the turmoil, Shumlin kept asking Goldwyn's advice, though Wallis was the producer. Shumlin didn't quite play by the rules—and of course neither did Goldwyn. Goldwyn had Hellman under contract but not Hammett, who held the Wallis contract for writing the screenplay. And Goldwyn being Goldwyn, he meddled. He saw his help on *Watch* as a way to keep Hellman on task writing for *him*. Hellman made a huge fuss, however, when Wallis and Shumlin, following Goldwyn's advice, arranged to hire Paul Lukas to play Kurt. Shumlin had doubts; he didn't think Lukas would play well on screen, or so he said.[181] But Goldwyn had decided Lukas was "the real thing" and he somehow prevailed. They were stuck, but in this instance Goldwyn was right: Lukas wowed film audiences. When Bette Davis agreed to play Kurt's wife, Sarah, Hellman felt of two minds—knowing Davis's fame would serve them well but knowing too that she'd have to change the relatively minor character to fit Davis's larger-than-life presence. She made the changes but it hardly mattered. Davis would have taken over in any case, turning Sarah's "commitment" to "saintliness," much to Hellman's disgust.[182] Hellman, never a fan of any saint but Joan of Arc, couldn't get Shumlin to control Davis's performance. He tried, but Davis did what she wanted. Davis wasn't all trial, however. Though she remained the star, she generously offered to give Lukas top billing, which the studio had to refuse. Davis, after all, had the name recognition. George Koulouris and Lucille Watson skillfully adapted their stage performances of Teck and Fanny, and Geraldine Fitzgerald and Donald Wood did well in their supporting roles. Hellman wanted a good film, and she got it.

On this film, Hammett's contributions enhanced Hellman and Shumlin's work together, which was always as politically relevant as it was popular. Hellman, in high gear, imagined she could juggle all her relationships and commitments. Hammett performed admirably. But Hellman had more problems with Shumlin than she expected with his directing the film. He had, after all, directed the play. But his high-maintenance personality got in the way. Hellman could handle only so many crazy characters at once and she had overextended herself on many Goldwyn projects. She didn't have the time or energy to hold Shumlin's hand.

Shumlin thought he knew producers and thought Hollywood a simple extension of Broadway. He saw a chance to work in Hollywood on a Hellman film, even with Wallis instead of Goldwyn, as a new career in the making. Both George Haight and Hellman had warned him that Hollywood was considerably different than Broadway. Hellman particularly warned him never to "give Goldwyn any options."[183] Shumlin only half-believed his two friends. But Hollywood business methods varied considerably from Broadway's, and this bewildered Shumlin. Before he even got to the studios, he found his name on the standard "available" list every agent sent out to producers and studio executives. Shumlin erupted in outrage.[184] His agent reassured him that they were not "peddling him." He saw being "listed" as beneath his "dignity and prestige." He wrote Columbia Pictures, trying to understand why he couldn't work "only on pictures that I wanted to do."[185] But more to the point, it turned out that he didn't direct films as well as he did plays.

Haight tried to tell him that, waxing eloquently on Shumlin's still camera use in *Watch on the Rhine* but noting pointedly the strengths of a moving camera and differing methods of "camera direction."[186] Shumlin was neither Alfred Hitchcock nor Willie Wyler. But for a time he thought he was. This city wasn't just East Coast meltdown; it had a cultural glaze of its own. Hellman could work it; Shumlin could not.

With Shumlin out of sorts and Hammett done, Hellman battled a lack of time. She had so many projects in the works she felt overwhelmed, flying back and forth from New York to get everything done. She kept her promise to revise and polish Hammett's script, but it wore her down. From the Beverly Hills Hotel she wrote her ex-husband, "I am so tired of writing at the end of the day . . . I've worked hard and fast. I find cutting and editing to be worse of a nuisance than writing."[187] She felt relieved when worried screenwriters Frances and Albert Hackett trimmed twenty minutes off *Watch on the Rhine* for an air force showing; she approved the Hacketts' editing, lopping off another three minutes herself.[188] As usual, though, she wanted things done her way. But it was wartime, and she didn't always get it. She knew the reasons behind the decision, but she bemoaned the government's wartime financial restriction on the sets (no more than $5,000 total). For once, Hellman objected adamantly to the Hays office tampering with the script.

The Hays office required that Kurt be killed as punishment for killing Teck, a fascist. All crimes, their reasoning went, must be punished in film, no matter how sympathetic the perpetrator. In "the old days" in Hollywood no matter how ridiculous or unintelligent the suggestions for censoring were, Hellman had bowed to Joseph Breen's Hays office requests. Not this time. She wrote him saying she found their demand "deeply shocking."[189] In wartime, with soldiers and civilians dying daily, Breen's rules seemed ludicrous. Hellman further insisted the love affair between David and Marthe survive as written; after all, according to Hellman, Marthe's marriage to "a Nazi and a villain" made an affair with David a moral choice. Hellman's rhetorical explosion, her threat to Wallis to gather material and write an exposé on "Hays office censorship," and her insistence that Breen acknowledge wartime standards, prevailed. Breen finally approved the script, though it is never quite certain that Kurt will die, only that he probably won't see his family again. The difficult personalities and conditions involved in the collaboration damaged Hellman's relationship with Shumlin and ultimately with Hollywood too.

Hammett received an Oscar nomination for best screenplay, *Watch on the Rhine*, which was a box office smash. It enhanced both Shumlin and Hellman's reputations, but ironically most critics in Hollywood seemed to forget Hammett's contribution, which was considerable. He wrote the entire screenplay. New York critics, however, praised Hammett and selected the film as the Best Film of the Year. Coming as it did in the middle of World War II, the film lacked the earlier stage play's revolutionary, prophetic appeal. But the film succinctly reinforced the reasons for engagement and indicted the American tendency to let international politics slide. Even David O. Selznick wrote Hellman about *Watch on the Rhine* to say that she "should be very proud of having written infinitely more effectively . . . something that says what ten thousand books and plays and editorials have tried to say."[190]

Thus Hellman's political, professional, and personal lives merged—only somewhat successfully—in wartime Hollywood. Hellman was big and getting bigger in a town where success or failure feeds on itself. Sylvia Thompson remembered Hellman at parties thrown by her mother Gloria Stuart and father Arthur Sheekman at the Garden of Allah in the early 1940s. These outlandish parties featured great food and lots of liquor, even during war rationing, and attracted Hollywood celebrities. While the "meritocracy was for men only" and even the brilliant Dorothy Parker and Ethel Butterworth only "zinged zingers at the end of the stories, forgoing a full performance. . . . The exception to the rule was Lillian Hellman. . . . She was so prestigious, the men deferred to her."[191] With all the food and liquor, Hellman probably charmed everyone too, before the work got too much and the mix of eccentrics began to take its toll. Only thirty-six, she loved what she did and felt energized by the oddities and ironies. She wrote Kober, "Did you know that when Irving Caesar changed his name from Isidore, his mother always called him Irvadore? I guess you knew it, but it made me feel better all week."[192]

She reveled in her involvement in this crazy city, but sometimes it was all too much. The writing jobs stacked up and she didn't have the time she usually had for the men in her life. Scripts took over.

Writing for the War

Work on two coasts exhausted her, but she looked forward to doing films with Sam Goldwyn. Maybe it was the combustion between her and Goldwyn that made those projects so rewarding. She had planned an extended American tour of *Watch on the Rhine*, when shortly after Pearl Harbor new Goldwyn projects began to consume her. She also agreed to write documentary narratives (such as *Soviet Medicine*) for the war effort.[193] Her frantic pace, and that of others in the industry, was set by the government's efforts to further certain causes: the enlistment of African American soldiers and the redefining of Russians as "our allies the Soviets."[194] Goldwyn received an indirect order from FDR through Harry Hopkins to assist in these politically charged projects. Suddenly military enlistment documentaries and pro-Russian films were hot items. The show, after all, must go on.

Negotiations about producing *Watch on the Rhine* began in late 1941 with Warner Bros., but Goldwyn's first request came in early spring 1942. He wanted Hellman and Wyler to work together on a documentary film the war department wanted, referred to as a Negro short. Both jumped at this chance to promote civil rights. Someone in government had recognized that Negro men might not see the necessity of enlisting in an army that was neither integrated nor necessarily fighting for the equality of all. But a film, they thought, might reinforce the necessity of the whole citizenry joining in a fight against fascism.[195] Hellman wrote the treatment for the short, and Wyler agreed to direct. But the studio's interest flagged, which made her livid, of course. On May 25, 1942, Wyler's official leave from the Army Air Force ended and he was out of the project, filming bombing missions over Europe instead. She ultimately wrote *The Negro Soldier* at director Stuart Heisler's request. Goldwyn then shuffled *The Negro Soldier* off to Hal Wallis, who shepherded it to "Colonel Warner," who urged another director, Vincent Sherman, to "rewrite it."[196]

Hellman's original script emphasized two young black men's dialogue on whether to join the war effort, their voices relating the bitterness and hope of blacks in America. Clearly a quickie done on the fly, the script had too much dialogue and the taint of propaganda, something Hellman usually hated. But it had power, pitting the black man's memory of southern lynching against the vision of white men working for the betterment of African Americans. Hellman ended the film with sloppy Hollywood sentimentality: Paul Robeson would sing with the Fisk choir in front of the Lincoln Memorial. Hellman instructed that "the camera work should be simple, and the scene enormously impressive."[197] On paper, juxtaposing black singers and Lincoln dramatizes America's history of racism; the producers feared the film would inflame white America. The producers trashed her ideas in favor of an upbeat review of the Negro soldier's historical participation in America's wars. Hellman thought the producers cowardly in their failure of will and morality. When it was finally released in February 1944, the film bore no resemblance to her script. Already working on two other films for the war effort, Hellman shrugged off her failure to get Goldwyn to make *The Negro Soldier*. It made her skeptical when she should have been wary. But she was on a roll, ignoring even Hammett's warnings to slow down and take stock.

Washington began to ask Hollywood for movies that ultimately caught Hollywood, and Hellman too, in a cynical game of pressure and politics. Beginning in 1941, Warner Brothers started filming *Mission to Moscow*, antired producer Jack Warner produced *The Song of Russia*, and Goldwyn asked Hellman to write what eventually became *The North Star*. Hellman finally had her chance to write an original political film. She and Wyler had wanted to do a documentary in winter 1941 on Russia's war against the Nazis, but their plans fell through. Goldwyn now proposed she write a "semidocumentary" about the Russian people, with Wyler directing. At presidential adviser Hopkins's specific request and Goldwyn's concurrence, both Hellman and Wyler went to see the Soviet ambassador Maxim Litvinov in February 1942. They wanted to get permission to fly to the Soviet Union and film the fighting. Stalin's foreign secretary Vyacheslav Molotov immediately approved the film. Goldwyn was set.

For all their commitment, they got off to a bad start. Their original plan was scrapped as too dangerous. Wyler knew he would soon enlist and wasn't sure when he would leave for the war. He asked that his salary be sent to his wife in monthly installments. Goldwyn blew up! He turned to both Wyler and Hellman, fuming. "You say you love America, you are patriots you tell everybody. . . . Now it turns out you want money from me, from me who am sacrificing a fortune for my government because I love my country."[198] When Wyler pugnaciously pointed out that the Russians were underwriting most of the film and that Goldwyn was making a profit, Hellman chimed in and called the whole discussion "nonsense." She sensed Goldwyn wanted only to "shave" their salaries rather than dispense with them. But such antics put a damper on the project. Wyler joined the army, leaving Hellman and Goldwyn to find another director. Lewis Milestone seemed the perfect choice. His *All Quiet on the Western Front* had proved him a first-rate director, and Hellman liked him. Known for his ability to clearly narrate a war film, he also was smart and artistically disciplined. Moreover, he had emi-grated from Kishinev, Bessarabia, in the Soviet Union and seemed to understand the character and lives of the people.

Hellman began to write *The North Star* in August 1942 and called it a "tough, tough job."[199] She complained she was "just no good at writing about people and places I don't know about." For Hellman, following a political line from afar was one thing, but it was quite another to depict the complexities of that philosophy in wartime. Hellman had been to Russia on "a grand touristy tour" in 1937, so she had a superficial feel of the culture. Working seven weeks with Goldwyn's research department, she gathered background, rereading Russian novels every night; "in that way, I found myself actually living in Russia."[200] She read a translation of *Pravda* for a month and a half to glean the Russian viewpoint on current events.[201] "I know about Russians now, in a thick research book, and maybe it will work."[202] When she finally wrote the screen-play, she had immersed herself in the country, its people and history. She took six months to write the script, twice as much time as she had planned on.[203] But her first absolutely original screenplay was clean and striking. Film might be recorded on bits of plastic, but by 1942, she had grown enough as a writer to put her vision into those frames with an intense seriousness.

Using actual German atrocities—forcing Russian children to supply blood transfusions for German soldiers—Hellman portrayed the tragic conse-quences of war on the humanity of the Russian people. The character of Claudia, played by Jane Withers, was a "fattish, lumpish little girl of about 14" who hates her nose and her straight hair. Her fate poignantly reminded the audience of the human tragedy of war: Claudia dies, bewildered by events. Marina, a young girl from the collective played by Anne Baxter, intones, "We will make this the last war; we will make a free world for all men . . . the earth belongs to the people . . . If we fight for it."[204] Hellman's political stripes show clearly in the film, though for once everyone thought her politics brilliant. Even American values booster Joe Breen thought it just fine. *The North Star* should have represented success on many levels for Hellman, but Hollywood wanted slick and she didn't.

As usual, she had "Goldwyn trouble." Always fierce competitors for con-trol, they clashed as never before. "Sam and I were love-birds until last week when I lost my temper over very little and have been losing it ever since. . . . He's gone insane about this picture with money flying in all directions and much indecisiveness flying with it."[205] Goldwyn, in a patriotic fervor, wanted spectacle, calling Hellman a "vandal" every time she cut. He insisted on adding music by Aaron Copeland with lyrics from Ira Gershwin. She resisted. Hellman did not see the film as a musical romp in a commune, "an extended opera boufee peopled by musical comedy characters."[206] An explosion on the sound stage roof caused an unplanned blaze that Lewis Milestone made part of the script's action, filming the bellowing fire that shrouded Hollywood for several hours. This kind of sham infuriated Hellman. She wanted substance. She abandoned the film while it was being made, contrary to her usual intrusions.

In Hellman's opinion, Goldwyn and Milestone ganged up on her and ruined her script; her relationship with Goldwyn was about to end. Outraged by Milestone's one hundred pages of suggested "basic" changes, she simply left Hollywood and refused any further negotiations, even when Goldwyn telegraphed her to come back and help with rewrites. He swore he would attend to her disagreements if she would only detail them. Her cryptic telegram in response shows the depth of her disgust and fury, but also her affection for the man. "I LOVE YOU TOO MUCH TO TELL YOU ABOUT IT IN A TELEGRAM."[207] When Goldwyn's wife, Frances, begged Hellman to come back to look at the script and fix some problems, Hellman relented and came to see a screening. The print broke in the middle of the preview. She flew up the aisle to the projectionist's booth screaming at Goldwyn, "You bastard! You can't even get a good projectionist!" Goldwyn shouted, "Don't you talk to me! I'll kill that god damned projectionist." When the screening proceeded, the fight got uglier. After forty minutes she began to cry, first to herself, then histrionically. "Shut up, shut up, shut up! How dare you cry!" Goldwyn yelled. Hellman lashed out, "Don't tell me when to cry; you've turned it into junk."

"My name is Samuel Goldwyn and I do not turn out junk! How dare you cry over my picture!" She told him to go fuck himself and screamed, "it's a piece of shit, you've allowed this fool to do anything he wanted—it's a piece of whole comedy shit."

Hellman returned to her hotel until Goldwyn's secretary called, begging her to come talk. When she arrived at his Laurel Lane house, Goldwyn shouted, "I hear you tell people that Teresa Wright was your discovery!" Hellman stood, flummoxed. When he demanded an answer she told him she never again would take orders from him. "Ever." Furious, Goldwyn ordered her to leave. She rigidly held her ground, and they had their final face-off. "I will not get out of this house until you have left the room."[208] He refused. Frances ran into the room to make peace, and Sam Goldwyn stormed up the stairs. After he left, Hellman walked out to her waiting taxi. She subsequently bought out her contract with Goldwyn for $30,000.

The film opened in early November 1943 to mayhem. William Randolf Hearst ordered his newspaper reviewers to pan the film as "Bolshevik propaganda."[209] However, a million and a half copies of the New York Daily Mirror had already hit the streets carrying critic Frank Quinn's early review praising the film. Furious, Hearst stopped the presses and demanded that Jack Lait do his bidding and rewrite the review for the remaining 300,000 papers.[210] In contrast, the New York Times praised the film: "This lyric and savage picture suggests in passionate terms the outrage committed on a peaceful people by the invading armies of Nazi Germany." The government used it too. The North Star made its way to army posts to anoint the Russians with ally status. Hammett wrote Hellman from the Aleutians that he was "agog" at its being scheduled for "our Post theater on 9 and 10 of January" 1944; he would try to get prints of it for his army training programs. Of course, at that point Hammett had only read the script and had praised the "documentary effect," saying it was "nice and warm and human and moving."[211] Everywhere else the film caused hoopla.

The filmmakers themselves added to the whirl of words surrounding The North Star. Shamed and furious at the changes made in "her" film, Hellman did not keep her opinions to herself: "I should have known that the combination of Lewis Milestone and the dominant Mr. Goldwyn would hoke it up to the ecstasy about the Russians which could only have been matched by the previous hatred."[212] Later Hellman published her original script to show only passing resemblance to the movie. Milestone reflected that in directing it he forgot the "reality" of war, probably because Goldwyn goaded him. "People want to be entertained, not educated after dark."[213] It wasn't long before Goldwyn sold off his rights to the film, for the first and only time. The toxic brew of personalities, competing political agendas, entertainment, and propaganda must have turned him off. Goldwyn remarked later, "When Stalin got depressed, he ran that picture."[214]

Others used the film to skewer Hellman's politics. Mary McCarthy called it "a tissue of falsehoods woven of every variety of untruth."[215] For once, Hellman agreed, at least partially. She never liked The North Star or her part in it; it wasn't an important film and it wasn't literature. It was "folksy peasants, pure of mind, body, and spirit [who] romp about like so many Kansas corn huskers in Eastern European drag."[216] A sad epilogue to the film was that a few years later during the Cold War, The North Star ran on late-night television under the title Armored Attack. It had been transformed into a muddled anti-Soviet film. No wonder the mention of it made her sick.

Yet with all the film's excesses, amid all the controversy, Hellman, Milestone, and Goldwyn kept their names on the credits and enjoyed its five Oscar nominations. Hellman wanted to bask in what little glory those Oscars might bring. *The North Star*, her one original screenplay among all her important translations for the screen, won her a 1943 Oscar nomination for best original screenplay, the same year as Dashiell Hammett's adaptation of her play *Watch on the Rhine* was nominated for best screenplay adaptation. Both lost to *Casablanca*.

Hellman's career in Hollywood was spectacular. The *New York Times* wrote, "Hollywood not infrequently cracks sharply the knuckles of its minions who talk back. But if it bullies the writers it turns rigid with respect for the box office, and here the angels above the wickets supported Miss Hellman from the very beginning."[217] Hellman, irate about *The North Star*, nevertheless valued her Hollywood work; she didn't know she had only five more years to write there. On the lookout for novels and plays to adapt, she tried to get Hal Wallis to let her write *The Seventh Cross*, a suggestion he passed up, one he surely regretted given producer Pandro Berman's tremendous success with Helen Deutsch's version of this Spencer Tracy classic.[218]

But she was soon to bear the consequences of her loyalty to FDR and Goldwyn, and to *The North Star*. The government's denial that it requested the film was just one of a number of betrayals that made Hellman and other writers, directors, actors, and producers vulnerable to anticommunist attack by the House Un-American Activities Committee. But first she had the nation's acclaim.

Hellman's pragmatism most often carried the day in her writing for the movies. Now as the intensity increased in the 1940s, Hellman's fatigue began to show. Writing Kober, she gave excuses for not writing him: "I'm lazy, I am sick of all writing when I've finished a day's labor on the picture, and I was in bed with the grippe, or half in bed and half working, which only fucked up the work and my health."[219] Her irritation with Hollywood and Goldwyn increasingly erupted: "The weather stinks, cold and damp in the mornings, and depressing. Goldwyn calls them the 'American Latin countries' and refers to the 'Army Emanual,' a Jewish version, I guess of Manual."[220] Unable to take Hollywood for long, Hellman flew cross-country when she could, rode the train when she couldn't, back and forth from New York to Hollywood, where the Office of War information and Sam Goldwyn both prevailed on her to keep writing.

Though part of her war effort was entertaining the president, Hellman did not rest on her laurels. She also joined the New York push to help, speaking in countless fund-raising appearances for relief organizations, playing madam chairman:[221] "Joint Antifascist Refugee Committee principal speaker, League of American Writers, Medical Aid to Russia, National Committee to Combat Anti-Semitism, Stars for Democracy, American Committee to Save Refugees, Artists' Front to Win the War."[222] Other notables joined these events as well. The Stage Door Canteen opened in March 1942 to provide food, entertainment, and interaction with celebrities from Broadway who volunteered their time to cook and wait on servicemen being sent out or returning. Three cities joined the effort, and by October 1945 when it closed, over 20 million people had been served and entertained by celebrities such as Walter Pidgeon, Jane Cowl, and Tallulah Bankhead. Some sold war bonds and many enlisted or tried to enlist, from Herman Shumlin to critic Brooks Atkinson.

Hellman had little time or energy for two personal blows that coincided with the war. Both were entirely unexpected. Hellman told Diane Johnson, Hammett's biographer, that one night in the early 1940s, Hellman was driving into New York City with Hammett. He was "disgusting drunk, pawing her and leering. . . . He suggested making love . . . Something borne of her deep exasperation, of her sense of his waste of his time, of his life, of the stupidity of all this, made her say no, she wouldn't sleep with him when he was like this. She had never said no before to any of his demands or sexual whims. Tonight, simply no. . . . He decided he would never make love to her again, and he never did, and never spoke of it."[223] They stayed together, lived together much of the time, but this part of their relationship was over, for better or worse. She still figured as the central woman in Hammett's life. That he still loved her is indisputable, inscribed in numerous letters: "I love you with the utmost extravagance."[224] Hammett, until the end of his life, demonstrated his love for Hellman in letters, perhaps to make up for his lack of passionate display face-to-face. Hellman and Hammett were a committed couple—just unconventional.

His enlistment in the army also knocked her out. On September 17, 1942, just after finishing the *Watch on the Rhine* script, Hammett walked into the Whitehall Street recruitment center and enlisted in the army. At forty-eight he was frail and had to have X rays to prove his tuberculosis had not returned. He wrote ex-wife Jose from Fort Monmouth, New Jersey, to say he was "back where I started twenty-four years ago—a private in the United States Army." He was being trained for combat, with a "fair chance of making it," though army regulations kept men over forty-five out of combat. He had planned his finances, got his army insurance set up to cover his daughters, and for the first time in a long time, he made specific long-range plans.[225] First stationed in

New Jersey, then Pennsylvania—in Camp Shenango, rumored to be a holding camp for "politically suspect soldiers"—he went in July 1943 to Fort Lewis, Washington, and then to Fort Randall, Alaska, then to Adak, Alaska, on the Aleutian Islands, where he published a camp newsletter. Hammett, true to his word, wrote often and wrote words of love: "I love a girl like you," "Mountains of love and many kisses." He wrote Hellman the detailed itinerary of each day, from making "as much of your bed as possible before five-forty" to drilling until six; "then to supper and to mail-call where you receive a note and some welcome money from a very nice girl's secretary . . . and you're a pretty tired old fellow who feels at least fifty-eight as you sit down to dash off a few lines to some sweet young thing on Eighty-Second street whose life is some bed of roses, eh, kid?"[226] He signed it "Love and thanks for the money. You're a cutie. Dash." Hammett loved the army, its regulations, its exhausting rituals, its clear sense of purpose. He thrived there, had all his teeth pulled out to meet dental hygiene requirements, got a good set of "plates," and even gained weight. He called his enlistment "the happiest day of my life."

Hellman threw a fit. "Lillian was stunned, appalled, he'd get killed, he was too frail, it was a silly stunt to escape from real-life problems."[227] Hammett's decision undoubtedly made Hellman's life easier. But sadder too.

With Hammett gone and her Hollywood work temporarily completed, Hellman went back to New York for most of 1943. At Hardscrabble, she raised vegetables and fruits and one reporter noticed her hands had "blisters from canning." Hammett wrote her, "You sound as if you're having a good time with the butchering, harvesting and other bits of husbandry."[228] For business, she drove her Cadillac back and forth from Hardscrabble to her new 82nd Street townhouse until gas restrictions put her on the Harlem line train into the city. She wore cotton stockings because of silk shortages.

Now in her mid-thirties, she had settled into a kind of maturity that wore better than her brittle youth. Reporters still could not resist describing her slim figure, her hair color (changing from blonde, to red, to "coppery-brown") and her beautiful and feminine clothing, including "not one pair of slacks."[229] But she also impressed them with her down-to-earth quality, with no pretentiousness, or "fanciness" as she called it.

She was determined to do all she could to stop fascism. As a woman, she couldn't do much, but as a writer, she could. She wrote bits and pieces for Hollywood and the Office of War Information, and she kept an eye on the film, Broadway, and London versions of *Watch on the Rhine*, which continued with great success. Finally she began another play steeped in the politics of the era. With *The Searching Wind* (1944), Hellman changed from knee-jerk radicalism to a more sophisticated critique of institutionalized politics. She kept her political passions but she got smarter. She used a personal failing to show a national one—the global consequences of national timidity. She wrote that she had a habit of "alternating from vagueness to rigid demands," and her cook once told her, "It takes a seaching wind to find the tree you sit in."[230]

No parlor drama, *The Searching Wind* was praised by the *New York Daily News* as a "strong and measured indictment of appeasers who eventually caused WWII . . . grimly and forcefully written."[231] The plot is tightly focused on three generations of a diplomatic family, the Hazans, so Hellman tried a less rigid, more innovative structure. She began in wartime Washington, D.C., then flashed back to Italy and the political dithering following Mussolini's march on Rome in 1922. In act 2 she moved to Berlin in 1923 and the mobs turning against the Jews, then to Paris in 1938 and finally back to the present. Hellman added a love triangle symbolizing lost chances, lost integrity. It worked, for the most part. Most critics agreed that it wasn't Hellman's best, wasn't as good as *Watch on the Rhine*, but was better than anything else of that spring's drama season. The searching wind that goes "right through to your backbone" showed Hellman had backbone, though as usual the chill was there too.[232]

Of all her plays, *The Searching Wind* required Hellman to go it alone. The dedication to Dorothy Parker honored her friendship, not her editing. Hammett sent general advice early on: "I hope the play is coming along better than if I was on hand to get into quarrels with you about it, and that therefore you are devoting to sheer writing those periods you used to take out for sulking because I was hampering your art or objecting to a glittering generality. . . . I still distrust everybody's advice but my own—to tell you about what you are writing.[233] Finally, less than a month before the play opened, he read it and offered a critique: "It doesn't seem to me that you make your point" though he admitted he was a little lost with the "light comedy" throughout. He was not entirely pleased with the flashbacks, and he worried that her best parts were historical and were "subordinated by the triangle." He found too much that the play didn't do: "The essential frivolity that fucked things up—and I take it that's the real point—isn't *shown*."[234] No one reading Hammett on Hellman can doubt that his advice was straight. His criticisms prefigured the critics, but she didn't have time to make the changes.

Hellman and Shumlin had at this time the longest collaboration on Broadway. No other producer or director had ever been offered a Hellman play. In interview after interview each praised the other, Hellman nearly always giving her highest compliment: "He knows what he's doing." But things had been rocky with them during this play, both personally and professionally. She had consulted Hammett, who wrote her a month before the show opened: "Dearest Lily, I'm sorry I can't help you on the Herman thing, honey, but I've never understood your relations with him. The professor's store of knowledge is—now the truth comes out—not limitless and that whole set-up has always been a closed book to me . . . I simply mean that I've never been able to understand what you and he—as a pair—were all about: you never made any recognizable pattern for me."[235]

Hellman was troubled about Shumlin as a lover, as a director and coproducer of the production company she and Shumlin were forming. Shumlin seemed rather "grim and taut" during rehearsals, suffered more than usual with his migraines, was impatient with the actors and actresses—quite different from how those in other productions characterized him. For the first time Hellman and Shumlin questioned each other's performance. He was irritated because she had put in too many unprofitable sets and characters.[236] For her part, she was clearly upset about the "casting of Cornelia Otis Skinner and Barbara O'Neil in the female roles," which rendered them nearly indistinguishable.[237] The Shumlin-Hellman collaboration didn't get it quite right this time—nothing unusual on Broadway. Restless, she worried, she fidgeted. Hellman didn't feel well, having taken a hard fall on her back in February, but her malaise was more emotional than physical.[238] When she began to market *The Searching Wind* to Hollywood producers, she discovered tax difficulties in forming the production company and began to wrangle with accountants. Nothing seemed right.

Opening on April 12, 1944, at the Fulton Theatre, it featured a top cast. Dudley Diggs, Montgomery Clift, Cornelia Otis Skinner, Barbara O'Neil, and Dennis King, drawn astutely in caricature by Hirschfeld, took up the entire above-the-fold page of the *New York Times* Sunday drama section.[239] Better than any advertisement, Hirschfeld and the *Times* illustrated just how important to Broadway a Hellman drama had become. As the playbill proudly proclaimed, "With *The Searching Wind* Miss Hellman violently dissents from those theorists who hold that in wartime theatre audiences will only patronize escapist pap. She feels that in time of crisis our theatre has a more dignified function than to cater to the amatory complexities of those who quail at the prospect of looking the truth in the teeth."[240] The *New York World-Telegram* critic enthused that she had reached "her full stature as a serious, thoughtful and original dramatist, a brilliant analyst of behavior and emotions, and a master craftsman, in *The Searching Wind*."[241] Shumlin got due praise for the play's "splendid quality, even giving force to one or two clumsy flashbacks."[242]

The play was panned for political and dramatic reasons. Communist Party publications—duly clipped and put in Hellman's FBI file—hedged. The *Daily Worker* praised her for attacking "fascism at its core" but faulted her for not going "quite far enough. . . . She is in there fighting, perhaps not with full courage, but better than almost anyone else at this time."[243] Other less political critics worried that the play lacked excitement, that its love theme got in the way of the political, that the women characters lacked individuality. Unlike her other plays, no one villain carried the weight of the wickedness of the world. All the characters seemed to cater to those in authority and shrug as they watched the slaughter of innocents. *The Searching Wind* is pure Hellman and validated her status as a playwright who could "wrench many a complacent, unthinking person from his orchestra chair—make him more aware of the real forces at work in today's world."[244] Praise for the play outweighed the panning, and it ran for 318 performances. Hammett celebrated when he heard she had a hit and wrote, "And let this be a lesson to you, my fine buxom cutie. You are a big girl now and you write your own plays the way you want them and you do not necessarily give a damn for the opinions of Tom, Dick, and Dashie."[245] The Drama Critics Circle did not give an award in 1944, but *The Searching Wind* won seven of twelve votes, one shy for the award. She had earned enduring fame as a dramatist, but the play had brought a personal crisis with Shumlin. Then she got an offer from the government that she could not refuse.

Overseas Duty

Harry Hopkins, adviser to President Roosevelt, had earlier arranged for Hellman to represent the United States by making a film in the Soviet Union to strengthen a cultural alliance with our newfound ally. Though the film deal fell through, he found a Moscow production of *The Little Foxes* a perfect excuse to send her. Stalin had dissolved the Comintern, which was to fulfill Lenin's cause of world revolution, in return for Allied support, but he felt FDR and Churchill had reneged on promises for a second front and supplies. Both Roosevelt and Churchill looked for ways to placate Stalin, and sending goodwill emissaries was part of the plan. So in August 1944, the government, "acting with faceless discretion," arranged for Hellman to go in the fall.[246] At first glance, Hellman might seem an unlikely peace offering to Stalin. She fit the bill admirably, however.

Hellman agreed to deny the government's involvement and to stick with the story that Russia invited her to visit as an American citizen. The Moscow theater production provided perfect cover. Few would have believed Hellman arranged the trip on her own, but it had to look apolitical. J. Edgar Hoover knew about the arrangement but was suspicious anyway. A later FBI memo gossiped that Hellman "had had an affair with Hopkins who was 'very pro-Russian, pro-Communist.'"[247] No evidence exists of such an affair, nor that Hopkins was pro-communist, but Hellman's flying to Russia fueled the rumor mill for years to come. Allied help was laudable, but later that ally would be deemed the enemy and the trip could—and would—be deemed treasonous. She was oblivious to this risk; she felt impotent while her best friends more actively entered the fray to fight fascists. Wyler, Shumlin, Hammett had all enlisted. While she mocked Hammett's desire "to be in the African landing force," she leaped at the chance when Washington gave her a mission nearly as dangerous.[248]

Hellman had excellent credentials as a cultural emissary to the Soviet Union: her well-known leftist sentiments; her friends in high places from the left, center, and right; her support from Ambassador Averill Harriman, who knew of her leftist sentiments as well as her patriotism and loyalty to the United States.[249] A wonderful conversationalist, brilliant and funny, Hellman was also gutsy enough to make a long flight on a Russian plane. VOKS, the Russian cultural exchange organization would invite her, but the government searched for a reason for her acceptance.

Thrilled at the opportunity, "a believer in the international politics of culture," Hellman immediately bought gray and blue canvas duffle bags, planned and packed, made her customary lists of necessities, gifts to buy, reminders.[250] She taped a short budget on the cover of the small notebook she would use as a diary and noted the need for laxatives, money, stamps, a bedroll, and books.[251] Above all, she arranged to publish her findings about Russia in time of war. The *New Yorker*, *Colliers*, and Moscow Theatre's enchantment with her plays gave her the cover she needed to go. Editor Harold Ross at the *New Yorker* waxed enthusiastic about her work but warned her, "All the dope is that the Russians won't give the writer any freedom, that the Russians won't talk to outsiders, and that all projects to get stories that Russians don't want got are futile."[252] More optimistic, *Colliers* agreed to publish several articles about the trip but insisted that two of the articles be posted from Moscow to heighten their authenticity.

This trip changed her life. She fell in love with a man and with the Russian people. Both these affairs were messy politically and in both she found joy and suffering.

Had she known about the intense FBI surveillance of her as she traveled from New York City to Los Angeles and then to Seattle and Fairbanks, she might have had some inkling about what was to come in the 1950s. The FBI tracked her every move from when she left on October 7, to her final departure to the Soviet Union on October 19, 1944. In retrospect their reports seem comical. Los Angeles agents noted among other myriad details that "On the evening of October 10, 1944, Special Agents [deleted] observed subject arriving at the Glendale station in a 1937 Cadillac . . . subject was accompanied by a man and a woman. The man was described as 40, 5'10", 180 pounds, black receding hair, dark eyes, glasses. The woman was described as 30, 5'5", 120 pounds, dark brown hair, dark eyes, attractive face. Subject was described as wearing a dark brown sheared beaver coat, a dark blue chalk striped suit and brown pumps. The chauffeur was observed to be carrying a leopard skin fur coat for subject and a number of books, the top one of which was observed to have the inscription "Russia." The man and woman both kissed the subject good-bye. The man was believed to be Arthur Kober, subject's former husband."[253]

The Seattle agents tracked her so assiduously that their report offers insights into how the thirty-nine-year-old Hellman spent her time. She shopped for clothes, made several phone calls, bought books—several mystery stories, including *Kent's Last Case*, and a pocket Bible. Both of these were twenty-five-cent editions. Dwight Spracher, of the Washington State Democratic Party Committee, ferried her about in his green Buick, and Jay C. Allen arranged for her to stay at the Washington Athletic Club. The FBI was particularly interested in Allen, a reporter and "noted lecturer" because he had been "sympathetic to Loyalist regime" in Spain. Hellman had her packages of books preapproved by the censor's office, but the FBI opened them anyway and searched her luggage. How they found what she carried in her purse is a mystery, but she had $92.00 cash, a cablegram inviting her to visit Russia, identification cards, passport, and visas to the Soviet Union, Egypt, and Iran. The bureau noted the preapproved censor's stamp just before listing the contents of the newly opened packages. Among them:

A book, "How to Say It in Russian"
Two small French dictionaries

One Kroll Map of Alaska
New York Driver's license issued to subject
10/7/44 issue of "Coliers" [sic] magazine. It is noted that this issue con-
    tained the article by Wendell Wilkie, "Citizens of Negro Blood"
One copy "The Little Oxford Dictionary" by George Ostler
One copy "The Kings English" by Fowler
One copy "The Searching Wind" by the subject
A power of attorney issued to Herman Shumlin dated Sept. 1944.

She traveled with bare-bones resources and as many winter coats as she
could pack. Shumlin would run things the three months she was gone.

The State Department memo to the American embassy in Moscow stated
that Hellman had "no connection with any of the government agencies and
is making this trip as a private individual." If the bureau believed that, it
would have been surprised by a letter from the British Information Service
noting that Hellman had been asked to go to Britain to make a film but "had
a prior commitment for the U.S. Government to go to Moscow" and would
work in Britain after her Moscow trip. More surprising still to those who suspected her of subversion, was the "intercept" of telephone conversations with
Colonel Kisilev of Ladd Field, Fairbanks, which expressed his irritation
about her appearance. He complained about the lack of winterizing on the
planes available, and "this writer, Lillian Hellman. She was showing me the
telegram of who had invited her. It was Poudovkin and Moskvin and other of
our artists. . . . Listen, next time I would like you to give me advance notice."
She had to wait several days to get clearance, with the thermometer in
Siberia plummeting.

Hellman had not prepared for the hardships she would endure on the un-
heated C-47, a converted DC3 that had two engines and a maximum speed
of 240 miles per hour. She flew from Fairbanks, Alaska, to several towns in
Siberia and finally to Moscow. Just before she left, she wrote Arthur and
Maggie Kober, "I may be scared, but no bomber trip could be much worse
than Los Angeles–Seattle train ride, with an interesting roach sharing my
room, food beyond belief and almost none of it, and dirt that you'd expect to
find on the Peasant Express from Bucharest."[254] She had no idea.

The four-day trip to Moscow via Siberia took fourteen days because, as
Hellman understood it, "the crew had been instructed to take no chances
with their guest." She shared the plane with a Russian soldier, Vanya (called
Kolya in *Unfinished Woman*), hitching a ride home. They taught each other
English and Russian to pass the time. Hellman called those two weeks the

"hardest time of my life, physically."[255] She had to sit on boxes, and the heating system went out on the second day. "When it got so cold we couldn't stand it any longer . . . One of us would go into the pilot's compartment, and the radio operator would move out." They flew on good days only, and during long stretches of bad weather, they found lodging in "log cabins on Siberian airfields." An Unfinished Woman records the trip in glorious detail, its wonderful moments and its privations. Her diary documents her story with greater immediacy and intimacy. She noted the "strange landscape—muddy sand and round hut-like houses that look like bee hives with rounded brick around them." She praised the "spotless rooms" and listed what she had to eat. "Fine meal: good cabbage soup, meat and potatoes, wine, sausage, good red caviar, etc." Some of the rooms were freezing and she slept "in woolen stockings, pants, girdle, & jersey top, two blankets & my fur coat."[256]

A constant refrain was what she called the "toilet business." "Outhouses in the cold of Siberia shouldn't be," and "the whisky bottle was ice-cold & the toilet—haunting me in some form everywhere—was like an ice box."[257] She needed a laxative, found Enco's Fruit Salts 7 didn't work, and the physical discomfort irritated her as no other privations did. This problem came to an end, ironically, when she twisted her "once-broken ankle in the ice ruts."[258]

Vanya escorted her to a doctor where Hellman bravely asked for a laxative as he fixed her ankle. After much collaboration between Vanya and the two nurses in charge, they gave Hellman "a small bag of salts in rough, large chunks." Vanya told her to dissolve them and "all would be excellence." Thinking they prescribed the salts as laxative, Hellman drank the brew meant for soaking the ankle. She confided in her diary, "Friday Vanya & I went to have my ankle strapped, which didn't need strapping, and they gave me a large dose of salts with results that I won't forget and neither will Krasnov." Besides solving the toilet business, the salts produced delirium, shakes, fever, sweats, and eventually pneumonia.

All's Fair in Love and War

In these unlikely circumstances, a new love affair was beginning—with the Russian people. They seemed cool and remote at first and she didn't know Russian, nor they English. But she was intrigued and inclined affectionately from the start when she spotted the engineer on the plane reading Anna Karenina. When she met her fellow passenger, she noted Vanya was "nervous & surprising and flirty." His English was very limited and she noted his penchant for saying, "I love Betty Grable & Dorothy Lamour" and "he announced he loves me, too . . . I do all right with these people." As she recorded daily, her interest in the Russian people and theirs in her increased. It was no surprise to her that "they tell me I am the first foreigner to stay here, and that it is the coldest place in the USSR. It's nine thirty and I am playing the phonograph they loaned me. Sadie Thompson." "The two maids—one a sixty looking black one . . . and the other the squarest girl I've ever seen—are as various & polite as the others. . . . They quite frankly stay to watch me dress or wash or look around. I am a little pleased with myself because they like & yesterday said so." The crew shared pictures of their wives and children and queried her about her life. She recorded the stories of all she talked to, respectfully, cheered by their warmth. As to Vanya, she found "flirty pants a real darling." He called her "Miss Hell."

Hellman's fame in Russia later gained her a mythic status, so much so that a man who had been twelve years old in 1944 told biographer Joan Mellen a story full of operatic drama. According to Yevgeny Yevtushenko, as soon as the plane landed at Stantsia Zima in Siberia, Hellman, "wrapped in a voluminous fur coat, and the pilot ran out into the snow, fell into each other's arms and engaged in passionate love making . . . oblivious to the presence of a twelve year old schoolboy wandering down the road who came upon them only to stand there watching transfixed."[259] The couple could not have been unaware of the other three men on the plane. Hellman made no mention of a relationship with the pilot in her diary, only of flirty Vanya, a constant presence: "He has dignity and balance." The alleged lovemaking would have been a near impossibility given the multiple layers of clothes she wore to stave off the cold: "ski pants, 2 sweaters and a blouse, long woolen underwear, which bulged in strange places, woolen stockings, socks, boots, an American army sheep lined coat with good hood, and a large shawl to keep the hood in place."[260] Thus the snow adventure was most likely high-spirited wrestling—quick and fully clothed. The average temperature in November is -54 degrees Fahrenheit.

Not until she reached Moscow on November 5 did she begin a more public cultural exchange. Sergei Eisenstein, the great Russian filmmaker, eased her way at a VOKS reception. VOKS booked her into the National Hotel and introduced her to the much livelier world of the Metropole Hotel, which she describes with great detail and wit in *Unfinished Woman*. She liked these cultural emissaries; they praised her dramatic abilities, talked about theater and stage, invited her to join them in Moscow's lively, rich cultural scene: *Ivan Grozny, Swan Lake, Don Quixote*. Her candid remarks at the rehearsals of *Watch on the Rhine* and *The Little Foxes* made them a little "uneasy" but they "found her candor refreshing."[261] Even in Moscow Hellman had her say, but her limited Russian language and her place as visiting playwright didn't give her the insider role she had in New York. She had to ignore the Russian stage excesses, such as those reported by a friend concerning the part of the dignified Fanny in Moscow's *Watch on the Rhine:* "She clowned . . . she whooped and she howled, she grinned and smirked, she danced, she tried to climb the wall, she draped herself against the bookcases . . . And the Russians loved it."[262] Outside Hellman's own cultural mileau, for the most part she let the productions be; she saw herself as more amused owner than controlling influence.

Eisenstein became a friend. They shared witticisms, film stories, intimacies of experience. After she left he cabled, "Why should I survive you never returning . . . stop the rests of my broken heart always a votre disposition Eisenstein."[263] She and Eisenstein flirted, talked theater and film, and enjoyed all manner of events: film, theater, their "almost daily cup of tea."[264] She respected his ability and they talked long hours about his many interests. His sweet character and wry humor captivated her. He did all he could to alleviate the strangeness of being a foreigner in 1944 Moscow. Eisenstein and Raya Orlova, her guide and translator for VOKS, gave generously of their friendship during the nearly five months Hellman spent on the cultural mission, three of them in Russia. Hellman returned the feelings of friendship, gratefully.

Raya, then twenty-six, had been schooled in the Institute of Philosophy, Literature, and History for at least seven years when she went to work for VOKS and was assigned a job with the department for Anglo-American countries in the theater section. The first person from the world outside the Soviet Union she "actually got to see was Lillian Hellman."[265] Except when Hellman was at her hotel or the American embassy, Orlova was with her, in Moscow, Leningrad, Kiev, the military front in Poland. They openly disagreed about Russian politics, but their time together made Hellman and Orlova friends for life. As Orlova said in her memoirs, "Our friendship has permeated my entire life."[266] With Raya, Hellman felt comfortable and at ease.

Life in the political and diplomatic community was grimmer. At first, Moscow's pressure and the diplomatic complaints brought her depression "in the same old way."[267] Russians were known for their secretiveness and she didn't speak Russian, though a cryptic note "Com. for Hammett" seems to be a reminder to find evidence of Communist Party practices to report to him. The diplomatic corps had grown gloomy with their isolation and the petty bureaucracy; the foreign journalists groused, frustrated at the censorship and the travel restrictions. Money was tight for everyone, and there was not much to buy. In addition, "Moscow winter weather is terrible and darkness comes depressingly early in the afternoon and moves into lovely nights."[268] Everyone complained. Hellman could hardly escape the sour mood.

Hellman was drawn into constant debates about the state of the world, but she didn't find her fellow debaters very astute. She found most career diplomats and state department officials at Spasso House, the U.S. embassy in Moscow, to be bores, the journalists pompous: "Mr. Lawrence of the *Times* is something. Ivy is the same, childish, vain & malicious with talk of anti-Semitism." She could barely abide the Russian party functionaries she met at cultural functions. When she and her translator Raya Orlova attended a state-sponsored peoples council of Lubin, Poland, for example, several political leaders spoke. Orlova remembered Hellman saying, "Raya, there was no Lenin among those people there, am I right?"[269] Understanding the political climate of a foreign nation did not come as easily to her as making friends. She hotly defended the Russians to the Americans and the Americans to the Russians.

The diplomatic community baited her and she reacted fiercely, exaggerating claims, zeroing in on faulty arguments. A friend noted, "On several occasions I heard her in arguments with Russian literary and artistic people strongly support anything American which cropped up in the conversation, even when it meant attacking something Russian I had previously heard her defend to us."[270] Hellman despised the smug and the facile in any culture. The *Soviet Arts Weekly* reported a "talk with Lillian Hellman" where she praised Russian writers, especially Chekhov, but admitted having only a passing knowledge of Russian literature, and that in translation. Then she went on to praise *Yank* magazine, written by soldiers for soldiers, which produced many talented young writers. She acknowledged American literature's debt to Russian writers but also said, "I think that in the last fifty years American literature outgrew all other literature." As for Americans, "We are all, I think, becoming newly aware of the good, sound principles which are so deeply rooted in our land and people."[271] For their part, the Russians lauded her admiration for them and her deeply rooted patriotism for the United States.

Though admiring Russia, Hellman knew she could never live in Moscow. She duly noted the information the guides gave her (she loved tour material); she stood in awe of St. Basil's, "one of the architectural freaks of the world . . . The cathedral rises to violate all rules, and maybe it reflects the nature of the people who move past it today as truly as it reflected the

sixteenth-century men who built it for Ivan the Terrible."[272] Hellman liked
risk, liked to violate the rules, and saw little space for that in the dreary political climate: too cold, too repressive. Isolating. Diary notes suggest her
disenchantment: "Moscow were the bad days! Parachutists, presenting
themselves as Soviet officials, telephone factories to close down, Stalin
speech that afternoon . . . Siberian army brought in . . . and sent by Metro
to the front. Eisenstein saying it was Stalin's nerves."[273]

When Stalin agreed to see her on February 2 or 3, she had already planned
her trip home and in truth did not want to see him.[274] She loved the stature
the invitation implied, but she had seen and heard enough. Possibly
Washington asked her to take a pass. Now that the Nazi threat had lessened,
both nations looked to the future with suspicion. Cultural emissaries were
one thing, but the appearance of support for Stalin was beyond the pale.[275]
Stalin's thick dark cloak of secrecy had dominated conversations in Spasso
House. Her close association with the diplomats made Hellman more canny
about Soviet politics, more ready to admit she knew little about Stalin's government. Hellman admired the intellectuals' "deep reverence and respect for
Stalin" but saw the repressive effect of Stalin's rule.[276] Her 1944 visit gave
Hellman her first inkling about Russian censorship and the difficulties facing
Russian writers. She knew the U.S. war propaganda machine, too, but she
saw a harsh difference in Russia. Though Hellman left Moscow giving Stalin
the benefit of the doubt, she had seen and heard enough to know she could
not live under such conditions. Still, she came home hitting the "red bashers" hard. She had seen so much devastation in war-torn Russia, she later told
reporters, that she couldn't imagine that Russia would ever plan another war,
insisting they wanted "to get on with the pursuit of peace."[277] War trumped
discussion of Stalin's purges in 1945, and presumably she still denied them—
to herself at least.

However much the Russian government disappointed—after all, she had
believed in the grand experiment—she loved the Russian people: their manners, their gentleness, their passion for music and literature, the great
sacrifices they made during the war. Her horror of war and her admiration
for Russian heart, courage, and friendship were solidified the first week in
December, when she visited Leningrad. As she told the *New York Tribune*
upon her return, "A million and one-half Russians are said to have starved
during the German siege of the winter of 1942." She reported, "In Leningrad
the damage was not done by shells but by starvation. The people there still
have a weak, dazed look."[278] Following Christmas in Moscow, Hellman traveled with Raya and a Russian major from the Ministry of Defense to the

front, just outside Warsaw. Neither woman suffered fools gladly and their leader in the excursion was definitely a fool. Hellman recorded in her diary, "We started for the front—with the idiot in what I think was a Jeep with what I think was a machine gun following us. There was a lot of shooting the previous night and some of it in front of the hotel with a machine gun. I wasn't nervous now, I don't know why not.[279] Raya agreed that the major was a "fool, boor, and coward."[280] He had put their lives in danger by letting a detachment of German submachine gunners penetrate the town and get to the hotel. As Raya put it, "During those moments that brought us close to death, I was with Lillian."[281]

A busy travel schedule, theater and political visits, and the antics at the Metropole Hotel entertained Hellman, but early in the visit the dizziness she put down to flu was diagnosed as pneumonia. The salts dosing and freezing plane had done its damage. Ambassador Harriman invited her to stay at the lovely Spaso House, the American embassy and Harriman's official residence in Moscow. The magnificent staircases, the chandeliers, the fan windows, and wide halls made an enchanting palace to have a love affair. It was there, amid war privation and architectural splendor, amid all the boring diplomatic and political chatter, that she found John Melby.

Melby was a career foreign service officer, one of three in the entire service at that time with a doctorate—his from the University of Chicago. Eight years younger than Hellman, he loved the arts, was an accomplished speaker and an excellent officer. Fluent in Latin languages, he spent most of his training and service in Venezuela, Ecuador, and Peru. When the service denied his request to serve in the military, he asked to be posted in Moscow. "The focus of the Western world was on the Soviet Union, where a nation most Westerners assumed was little more than one giant gulag was shattering Hitler's legions."[282] A fervent New Dealer, intellectually curious and determined to serve his country, Melby had spent over a year in Moscow's war information office when his duties brought Hellman and him together at Spaso House. They did not click. To her, Melby was a foreign service officer like Alex Hazen in *The Searching Wind*. She was "not interested in his reports of Murmansk, or the probable wheat crop, or of Russian generals dancing together." To him, Hellman "was just another big shot; he had barely heard of her."[283] Nearly two weeks later they met at an embassy Thanksgiving party. "It was love at second sight."[284] They both spent the best Christmas holidays of their lives together. Off and on for the rest of their lives they sent each other anniversary telegrams on December 10, the date of the first night they made love. Melby saw a Hellman as few ever did: soft, playful, generous, loving. Writing her, he recalled Christmas morning, 1944: "You came padding down the hall in those oversize pajamas and made a dive into bed. I think you really needed me that morning and I am glad that you came to me. We talked a while and had each other and slept as long as time seemed to permit and I said that unless I could wake up each morning with you I did not want anymore mornings."[285] She recalled Christmas Eve: "I would like to have it all back, and to know that tomorrow morning I would be crawling into bed with you."[286]

Melby fulfilled Hellman emotionally as no other man ever did; their relationship was the closest she ever came to the "real life" she said she wanted. Theirs was a relationship cemented by intense conversations and lovemaking. Those conversations changed Hellman's politics and, indeed, the way she dealt with the political world. His approach was rational, analytical, sophisticated, tempering her penchant to join any and all leftist causes. Melby didn't change her principles; he raised her consciousness. She wrote later of their time together: "Conversation of that period of 1945; a fever—such a fever almost physical."[287] Her passionate interest and fierce belief in the people ignited his interest and his heart. Robert Newman noted in his astute book *The Cold War Romance of Lillian Hellman and John Melby* that the two were compatible because they shared basic values about people and ideas, which made their bond deeper than mere physical passion.

Neither felt ready for such a passionate affair. Melby was married with two sons; his wife and he were separated by miles and by a coldness he couldn't understand. Hellman still valued her relationship with Hammett, though he was in the Aleutian Islands in the army. She and Hammett were friends, family, but not lovers. She and Shumlin saw each other twice a week, which she described as "nice." Now a brilliant man in the Department of State wanted her passionately. Hellman was "the rapture of his life."[288] She wrote, "You seem to me this minute all security, and pleasantness and warmth."[289] The "officer-gentleman" had captivated her; he deepened her insight into the global politics of the mid-twentieth century and he meshed well with her literary and artistic background.[290] In ordinary circumstances, they would have married, but circumstances weren't ordinary. His livelihood demanded that he bend to the State Department's will. He might have discarded that career had Hellman been more certain of her plans with regard to him. He loved her. Hellman was "a fine, lovely, saucy person. . . . also a lusty wench. . . . Thank God. My love for you is such that I would take it on any terms."[291] Still, he had to divorce. The world was at war and that war had to end before they could truly begin.

She loved him. But she was Lillian Hellman, and New York was her home. When she left Moscow she wrote in her 1945 diary: "I left Moscow on Thurs, Jan 18 . . . And John, quiet and staring at me. I don't remember the ride down, but I remember feeling sorry to go, hoping the plane wouldn't, and sorry about John. He is a nice man, a dignified man, and as I write this I feel more. It was good for me—but there were many times when I wasn't, many times when, as usual, I made the rebuff. He was so really kind to me and so really thoughtful . . . I am pleased by it and puzzled, too. I wish I could remember more of it. What was unreal I can remember—this time I think it was real, and I can't."[292] Emotion sometimes clouds the memory, dulling the pain and the senses. Hellman more than Melby was comfortable with separation and loose commitment, but she called it "unnatural" and she longed for him. The timing did not favor them.

In late 1944, seeing the danger and the privation of the front, Hellman came to respect the fighting men of the Red Army, who brought her to tears by their courage and sensitivity. When she came back to the States after five months of hard travel, she never lost a chance to remind Americans—who seemed intent on demonizing the Soviet Union—of the sacrifices those soldiers made in the fight against Nazi fascism. The fighting, the soldiers, the blooming friendship with Raya, made the trip to the front a heady experience—particularly since she was the first foreigner allowed to go. Surrounded by the soldiers' masculinity and the power of military hierarchy, Hellman was filled with elation and despair. "I said that I thought I was dining with more generals than any woman since Catherine the Great and they were over-delighted. We drank a great many toasts—to Pres. Roosevelt, to the Red Army . . . Russian men, almost all of them, have a very attractive quality: they are men who know they are men and like all such act with simplicity and tenderness . . . anxious to show me that war has not roughened them. I think every little girl, when she is about thirteen, has a dream of being grown up and going to the ball. A whole room of handsome gentlemen in uniform turn as one and move toward her to do her bidding for the rest of the evening. That dream never came true for me, and I never thought about it again until this dinner."[293] She found that despite the language difference, she could share the cold glass of vodka and the simplicity of experience and enjoyment.

With Raya beside her—a young woman she came to love—even a Russian front felt welcoming, perhaps more so because of the danger and tension. She relished participating in Russian culture, but even Raya knew she wasn't "one of us." Hellman told her, "I'll start listening to the victories of socialism after you've built the kind of toilets that don't make you want to retch at all the airports from Vladivostok to Moscow."[294] Even with her sharp-tongued critique, the Russians loved her. "Harriman thought hers was the most effective goodwill mission in his experience."[295]

Back in the United States, Hellman described Moscow as "Los Angeles without the sun or grass" but expressed her love for the Russian people and her amazement about the state support of writers and artists.[296] The FBI and the media eagerly investigated. The agents frantically sought evidence of her return, sending out alerts to all major cities; they wanted her detained so they could search her bags for anything she might have brought back from the Soviet Union.[297] They missed her when she flew into Baltimore. The media sought her avidly; too few Americans knew anything firsthand about Russia. Hellman talked to reporters from all the major dailies and was a guest on John Daly's *Report to the Nation*. Her opinions were outspoken. She told reporters that when Soviet officers asked her what the United States would do about fascism in Argentina, she queried, "What will Russia do about Franco?" Asked about communism, she said, "I wouldn't want to see Communism here. We're never going to have it. It is no problem with us. I see no signs of it here."[298] Hoover deleted these anti-red comments from the FBI summaries "that were passed out to right-wing columnists, congressional committees, and the Passport Office."[299] Less popular opinions she expressed with equal force. Commenting on an anti-Soviet book, she said, "It is not a question of whether we approve of the Soviet system. They like it and fight for it remarkably."[300] Always fond of blunt talk, she said what she meant.

For Harold Ross of the *New Yorker*, however, she disappointed. She had not "cracked the great Russian sphinx."[301] She wrote of human relationships, the Russian people, the soldiers, but nothing of hard data about the war. He wrote her that he didn't want "articles of opinion"; he wanted stories but she hadn't written one with facts. "What you've written is a very good little piece on your emotions and what you think about things . . . my attitude is the hell with the foreigners at the Metropole and their pals and so on. That's not Russia. What about the Russians?"[302] *Colliers* published "I Meet the Frontline Russians," which she later reworked for *Unfinished Woman*.

Hellman dumbfounded the editors of both *Colliers* and the *New Yorker* by her inability to keep dates and times straight, but *Colliers* accepted her stories of Russians and soldiers and relationships. The diplomats and the Russians in VOKS had treated her with affection and respect, later sending her witty postcards and "cute letters."[303] She reciprocated, sending books and gifts to Harriman and others she had met at Spasso House—"Brassieres size 24 Handkerchiefs and gloves to Pamela Churchill" or "dried apricots, dried prunes, chicken noodle soup to George Backer."[304] But personalities, not politics, dominated her time in the Soviet Union, and those relationships filled the pages of her articles. She wrote of asking one of her military escorts about her lodgings. "Do you think when I'm very old I could truthfully say that I slept in Marshal Zhukov's bed? Zeidner laughed and said, 'perhaps the Marshall would be honored in the years to come, but in the meantime where you sleep is a military secret.'"[305] Everyone agreed that she could write, but she was not a war correspondent. She was a political enigma.

With victory in sight in spring 1945, the anti-red critics came out swinging at Hellman and *Colliers*, which published the article along with one by communist journalist Ella Winter. Westbrook Pegler of the *Washington Times-Herald* was back to counting citations of fellow traveling indexed by the Dies Committee of HUAC. "Hellman has 42 citations in this index of the Dies Committee. . . . Of course this index contains the names of many individuals who are no more Communist than Mussolini is a Chinaman, so it doesn't follow that these two old babes are Commy or pro-Commy merely because they run such a high score." But Pegler thought *Colliers* should note that its writers were not "unbiased."[306] No reader could have missed Hellman's clear personal voice, "old babe" or not.

She returned to New York changed in some ways. She was softer, more reflective. About to turn forty, she tried to put together the pieces of her life. She felt guilty about Dash, who had not quit drinking—quite the reverse. She couldn't give up Hammett, but she couldn't count on him either. She had not slept with him for two years, but she wrote Melby that she was "devoted to Dash, deeply devoted."[307] Melby knew Hammett lived at Pleasantville for much of the year, and the two men met when Melby, back in the United States on assignment, visited as he often did from April to October 1945. Between visits, Hellman and Melby wrote nearly every day. One letter sharpens the image of the relationships between Hammett and Hellman and Melby. She wrote, "Last night Dash, who is here, got slightly tight and asked me with the greatest affection and good taste what I felt about you. I told him as honestly as I could. He said he had liked you and had thought we were very nice together, very 'decent,' was his word. I don't think in the many years of our relationship have I ever felt more warmly toward Dash than I have the last two months, and more sad that so much that is so wonderful, should be so neurotically handicapped in working or in living. He is a fine, fine guy made of honorable stuff, and I only hope to God he will live to fulfill himself."[308]

The intimacy between Hellman and Melby created a serious, thoughtful self that her public behavior sometimes belied. Hellman wrote Melby from the Roosevelt Hotel in New Orleans that she drove to the "very regional, very French influenced Louisiana. . . . It's too bad the South belongs to Southerners—its so really beautiful here . . . the fruit trees in bloom, the violets coming up, the magnolias starting and the ditches and canals choked with wild lilies." She had dinner of bitter coffee and doughnuts, but the dark streets made her uncomfortable, perhaps unsafe this first night of Carnival. "I came back fine—scared a couple of times by drunks. I am now cleaner and in bed and wanting you."[309]

Hellman's letters to Melby and his 588 saved pages of letters to her document a dynamic personal conversation and some shared political opinions. FBI and State Department worries to the contrary, their letters did not share secrets—just the electricity of two people involved with each other and their political world.[310] Melby's letters show a man deeply interested in politics who made a serious effort to understand national politics and climates. In keeping with his career in the State Department, he explored political philosophy and conflict. A reflective insider, he came closest to divulging state secrets in comments he made after the successful Yalta Conference between Stalin and Roosevelt: "The big show went wondrously, far better than anyone had dared to hope."[311] With no background, she had to intuit what that meant.

Often Melby lectured her on the historical and theoretical. In a heartfelt letter in May 1945 he wrote that the government wanted him to go to Chunking but only if he would follow the accepted Washington line that had made everybody already in China "misbehave" when they reported what they felt were the facts: "We must reinforce the case against the Soviets because that is the only possible answer. I must report according to the line, not according to what I believe. Sweetheart, suddenly I felt very sick and very cold inside. And then I became so angry I could not speak. Magazines like *Cosmopolitan* used to write articles about the Russians priming their boys that way. And there I was looking down the same barrel in the United States of America."[312] He used her as a sounding board for his thoughts. Her opinions held no political surprises. During the first two years of their separation, they mutually wondered and despaired at world events, and met often enough to rough out their political differences.

Hellman's letters tended to be general in politics, more specific in romance. In one letter written during a trip to New Orleans, Hellman mentioned meeting a friend, how nice it was to "see a semi-liberal" and their visit to two restored plantations, lovely, but "the people in the houses were just what you'd expect—maybe even bad literature tells the truth."[313] Closer to their mutual interest of Russia, she told of going "to a meeting of a lot of famous gents," scientists working on a penicillin memorial for Dr. Hugh Cabot in Russia. Hellman noted, "Mrs. Roosevelt is obviously very annoyed with the Russians." When Mrs. Roosevelt invited Hellman to lunch, Hellman thought she would go, "although I have never been comfortable with her and never sure, despite many points of admiration, that I liked her."[314] Hellman and Melby were both respected in high places, but politically Melby had the edge and she knew it. Hellman wrote in another instance, "It is my conviction that we are now entering a period of indifference to foreign affairs, and an occupation with domestic ones. That will be the problem: to keep away from the rich isolation of the boom of the twenties, while everybody cuts up with us while our heads are turned to buy diamonds."[315] With Melby's decision to go to China, Hellman became increasingly interested in the domestic scene she so derided in her letter. They grew apart gradually while retaining great affection for each other.

FDR's death on April 12, 1945, devastated her and further clarified the political divisions between Melby and Hellman. Harry Truman took office in Roosevelt's shadow but soon instituted policies that were anathema to Hellman's progressive pro-Russian politics. Truman's Fair Deal seemed far right of FDR's New Deal. His loyalty oath portended political oppression. Melby had doubts about Truman's policy but knew that in his position, he must follow it. He came to support the administration's secretary of state, General George Marshall, who "understands the Russians without illusions."[316] Hellman still had her illusions and viewed the plan with suspicion, further dividing the two politically.

Hellman fought Washington's Cold War as the only stumbling block to global harmony, particularly with the Soviets. Hellman blamed Truman and Churchill for "warmongering."[317] As early as November 1945 she participated with other Broadway heavyweights like Harold Clurman, Cheryl Crawford, and Aaron Copeland in the First Conference on American-Soviet Cultural Cooperation, which insisted the two superpowers cooperate. A leader in a newly formed group opposed to Truman's foreign policy, the Independent Citizens' Committee of the Arts, Sciences and Professions (ICCASP), she lobbied for U.S.-Soviet friendship, spoke at the Soviet consulate on International Women's Day, and joined a banquet to celebrate Harold Ickes's ICCASP chairmanship. By that time, Hoover saw such conferences as borderline treason. Worried politically and personally, Hellman wrote several depressed and worried letters to Hammett in Fort Richardson, Alaska, finishing his tour of duty. He replied, "My elderly statesman advice to you on the new President and international, as well as domestic affairs, is to wait and see before you start shivering."[318]

Hellman, a world renowned writer, loved Melby but knew life with him would mean giving up too much—following him to China and then his next post, wherever it was. Her career would be over. In *The Searching Wind* she had written of the lives of diplomats, the necessary compromises that came with the post, the unnecessary ones politics impelled. She could not live that life of domestic and political subordination, but some part of her wanted to take a chance on love. She would love John Melby, but she wouldn't change her life for him. She had become Lillian Hellman, playwright, public figure, glamorous advocate of leftist politics. It felt hollow.

Playing for High Stakes

When Hellman returned to the United States knowing she might have given up her last chance to live what she called a "normal life," she threw herself into the world she had chosen. In New York she finished her article for *Colliers*, was interviewed by reporters from nearly every daily newspaper, began a new play at Hardscrabble, which eventually became *Another Part of the Forest*, then took off for Hollywood to write the screenplay of *The Searching Wind*. Life seemed back on track, if not fulfilling. She threw herself into the project and a new play, perhaps this time hoping the frenzy of a bicoastal life would fill the void.

In 1946 Hellman was still "in" on the West Coast. Conservative Jack Warner had once shown great interest in *The Searching Wind*. But even as it garnered terrific reviews on the East Coast, he let her know he was no longer interested in having her adapt it for Hollywood.[319] *The Searching Wind* was thus produced by Hal Wallis Productions-Paramount Theater, with the newly formed Dashiell Pictures, Inc., owning the motion picture rights. Hellman owned 76 percent of Dashiell, with Herman Shumlin, Max Hellman, and Dashiell Hammett also owning shares.[320] This foray into pre-production rights brought the investors money and some control, but later big tax problems. Ever since she assisted in making *These Three* in Hollywood, Hellman had moved increasingly into production; her work with Joris Ivens had given her experience and a good reputation. She had begun to assist in the production of her own plays on Broadway, moving quietly and in a small way to a career as a producer. Production kept her in the theatrical world while she percolated another play and found the courage to try again. Crescent Productions, the Searching Wind Company, and Dashiell, Inc., all stock corporations, handled investments in movies and stage productions. On forming Dashiell, she wrote Hammett that the name might be a dubious honor. He replied that he was "flattered."[321] He trusted her, asking her to invest in productions as she saw fit.

Hellman had a keen eye for contractual detail, possible profit, and a business sense everybody trusted. Norman Mailer later recalled, "She was a wonderful mixture of naivety and acumen, and very very tough in negotiations."[322] In production she was on the phone for hours, wrote letters in her typical two-three finger typing; kept in touch—didn't let up. Shumlin, who courted lots of investors for his productions and always invested in his own productions, taught Hellman a thing or two about the production game, and he helped make her and her other men good money.[323] Investing in her friends' productions along with a cadre of men to support her endeavors— Hammett, Kober, Shumlin, Ingersoll, Max Hellman—she stayed the course. The letters of Kober, Hammett, Shumlin, her father and later Kermit Bloomgarden are replete with references to their mutual investments, borrowing from each other, paying each other back, splitting percentages, making money.

With her definite opinions on investment and production, Hellman had plans that didn't always jibe with her investors. She complained to Kober about an investment she made in a Kermit Bloomgarden production, saying she was "sick of these investments . . . done on the basis of loyalty.[324] Later she and Bloomgarden formed LH and KB Productions. Accountants advised that they "dissolve this corporation immediately" in order to report income from it to the IRS.[325] Hellman, along with Arthur Miller, Tennessee Williams, Clifford Odets, and Elia Kazan, came up with a "wild idea" for a corporation of playwrights: where each would be obliged to produce each play written by each of the authors" as well as others.[326] The company plan never reached fruition. Politics, life's travails, and the competition that makes Broadway fierce put an end to this company of supertalents. Nervy and smart, she began a minor career in production that made money but later caused tax difficulties. Production was risky for those without great wealth and a cadre of accountants.

The Searching Wind film was a high-stakes risk for Hellman, who "double-dipped" as writer and partial producer. When it was released in June 1946, she received a whopping $75,000 salary, irrespective of production profits, which were considerable.[327] A brilliant adaptation from stage to screen, it begins dramatically with FDR's voice broadcasting from Yalta in 1945: "Twenty-five years ago American fighting men looked to the statesmen of the world to finish the work of peace for which they fought and suffered. We failed them then. We cannot fail them again, and expect the world to survive." The film, which may now seem sentimental and overly patriotic, did well in postwar America. *The Hollywood Reporter* praised Wallis, Hellman, and director William Dieterle for its "power and beauty" and for its "intelligent truths" told with "superior forcefulness." It pulled "no punches . . . in indicting a section of typical American appeasers and timid politicians who might have avoided the disaster of a second World War."[328] Thus it foreshadowed the difficult time she sensed, unconsciously perhaps, hanging over her future.

The Hays office had once again exercised its control, asking her to omit "God in Heaven" as it was "not used quite reverently." Presumably referring to the characters Alex and Cassie, Joe Breen asked Hellman to eliminate Robert Young and Sylvia Sidney's "kissing and fondling."[329] As if taken from life, the character of Cassie complained when the editor, with his "fat blue pencil" excised much of the pointed commentary of her articles for the *Washington Bulletin*. Another reporter's response? "You'll have to learn that when you attack what [the editor] doesn't like, that's freedom of the press; when you attack what he does like, you're overthrowing the government." Obviously the scare was in the air, and Hellman had sniffed it out. It had been a long time in coming.

Drama and Directing

The Searching Wind had emphasized a generation's judgment errors that nearly ruined the world. Hellman's new play, *Another Part of the Forest*, used a different scene and plot to connect past and present. In *The Little Foxes* the Hubbards, with full malevolence, set out to trammel anyone in their way to personal profit. Ever the Freudian, Hellman decided to explore the previous generation of Hubbards to see what made them tick, what caused their comic disregard for each other, what made their offspring such nasty, grasping people. The new play's summary sounded wildly melodramatic but made terrific drama. The Hubbards of Bowden, Alabama, come from an earlier generation than the *Foxes* Hubbards. Patriarch Marcus's great wealth derived from illegal deals with the Federal army during the Civil War. His wife, Lavinia, ill equipped to deal with her avaricious, disloyal husband and their conniving, power-hungry brood, keeps the secret of their wealth hidden, but it drives her to the brink of insanity. Marcus feels contempt for all of them. What follows is straight out of soap opera, but also straight out of Hellman's past. Regina, as cold and nasty as she was in *Foxes* but younger and more passionate, wants to marry a man intent on preserving slavery in Brazil. Oscar is in love with a whore, Laurette Sincee—perhaps the most likable of the mangy lot. Ben, clever and funny and completely without scruples, outwits them all and blackmails his father into giving him absolute control of the family wealth. Hellman had done her customary research of the period—this time, the early nineteenth century—and filled notebooks with details as small as the kind of buttons women wore to the political headlines of the day. She knew her characters and she let them create the action. She knew the play was good and set about working on production issues.

Instead of going to Shumlin with the play, she decided to direct it herself, with Kermit Bloomgarden producing. Hellman had been at odds with Shumlin and struggling with the relationship ever since he directed *Watch on the Rhine* in Hollywood. Working together on *The Searching Wind* had not eased the strain, and when they formed their new production company, Dashiell, Inc., money differences further worsened their relationship. Besides, she thought directing looked easy, and as the writer, she had always wanted complete control of the stage. With the right stage manager, she thought she could write and direct the new play.

Kermit Bloomgarden, a man who spent ten years stage managing for Shumlin, "wise in the ways of Broadway," with "innate gentleness and good taste," became Hellman's most trusted and respected producer.[330] Beginning with a "brilliant cycle of Hellman plays," his productions subsequently won two Pulitzers, for Arthur Miller's *Death of a Salesman* and Frank Loesser's *The Most Happy Fella*; he was the first person in theater to receive the annual Humanitarian Award from B'rith Sholom. Bloomgarden looked like an accountant (which he had been) and was famous for his dour expression. He nevertheless did excellent work and had the winning eccentricities that Hellman valued in her friends. The cigar-chomping Bloomgarden "could do damage to a joke, and fractured all foreign words" but had a "bulldog tenacity" along with being a "fierce and avid gin player."[331] Known widely for his absentmindedness, the story goes that he and his wife, Ginny, had taken a taxi into the center of Manhattan when he alighted briefly to buy a newspaper and a cigar. Ginny watched helplessly as he stepped out of the store and hailed another cab: he had forgotten her.[332] Hellman delighted in such antics and valued also Bloomgarden's common sense and practical nature.

A devoted liberal who had many friends, including Arthur Kober, whom he fleeced at cards each week, Bloomgarden fit the bill. Married to a young actress (his first wife fell from a seventh floor window in 1942), he apparently felt no physical attraction to Hellman or she to him; they worked together long and well because of that.[333] She depended on him. Hellman needed his calming presence, and he put up with this difficult woman better than most.

When Hellman asked him to produce, he told a reporter, "To me, it's one of the high points of my life."[334] She let Bloomgarden call the production shots, but she always had an opinion. And he listened. Bloomgarden saw production as a collaboration and knew too that Hellman wasn't a collaborator. Bloomgarden surely felt that Hellman aggravated his stomach—he got two ulcers from learning to control his temper. Hellman had a penchant for calling him at dinner, something that drove his wife crazy, thinking Hellman rude and manipulative in doing so.[335] But he liked and respected her.

They pulled out all the stops when it came to casting. Their discovery of Patricia Neal was the coup de grâce. Hellman had gone on the road to find a suitable actress, dragging along her new producer. Acting in summer theater in Westport, Neal got two lucky breaks. Both Richard Rodgers and Lillian Hellman spotted her talent and wanted readings. Rodgers was at the point of signing Neal when Hellman's agent asked her to read for *Another Part of the Forest*. When Neal said she had another firm job offer and the agent would have to tell Hellman no, the "agent was aghast. I am *not* telling Miss Hellman no. You'll have to tell her yourself." Neal agreed to audition. Helen Horton, the stage manager, tried to get Neal in a better position for the audition, hissing and whispering advice before Neal went on to read as a young Regina Hubbard. Horton whispered, "Regina wouldn't do anything more underhanded than cut your throat." Neal got the job immediately. When she told Rodgers she had to decline his offer, "He was flabbergasted. But then so was I." Patricia Neal's career began in earnest with *Another Part of the Forest*, with one critic exclaiming, "As a young Regina, Patricia Neal is the handsomest and toughest snake-woman I ever saw."[336]

Tough she was, and tough she had to be. The entire production company from actors to stagehands had to withstand Hellman, an unstable and driven director who only knew about directing from watching others direct. She had a "good eye and ear for what was wrong" but moved the actresses and actors around like dead animals and never had, and never would have, any skill at all for "cajoling, flattering, inspiring and molding actors to the director's will."[337] Although she later admitted she didn't know anything about directing, she trusted so few directors she felt she had to do it. Shumlin clearly was on the outs. She complained that directors get caught up in one theme, which they drive home to audiences without subtlety or grace, spoiling the writer's intent. So Hellman, to the production company's dismay, directed *Another Part of the Forest* from start to finish. The script was too good for her to ruin, but the actors nearly walked out, from Percy Waram who played Marcus, to Leo Glenn who played Ben to Mildred Dunnock who played Lavinia. Ultimately though, these seasoned actors and actresses just stuck it out.

"As the Germans say, God knew everything and Lillian Hellman knew everything better," quipped friend Robbie Lantz.[338] When the company took *Another Part of the Forest* on the road to Chicago, Neal was onstage on opening night when she noticed Hellman "in the wings . . . her hand cupped to her mouth. 'Louder!' she whispered." This went on until Neal was speaking "at the top of my lungs." Nothing deterred Lillian. "Louder! Louder!" Hellman kept insisting. "I was so angry by the time the curtain came down, I could hardly contain myself. I stomped offstage to find her. 'Lillian,' I snapped. 'I heard you! Every time you said it. I heard you!' 'Well, then,' she growled, 'you should have nodded.'"[339] Jean Hagen, who played Laurette Sincee, Oscar's whore, commiserated: "You're not the only one with problems, Pat." Hellman was about to replace her until someone leaked the news to a gossip column. "Lillian was in a rage. 'Who the hell gave that out without my permission? Jean will not be replaced as long as I'm running the show. I'll rehearse her until she's great.'"[340] Hellman's need to control every detail, her iron hand and blunt tongue nearly undid the production company. She was no great director. But Neal at least understood her. "Instinctively, I . . . knew that when I got an angry swat, all I had to do was duck and wait it out. Being annoyed was her way of being Lillian Hellman."[341]

What annoyed Hellman most at this stage of her theatrical career was the critical harping on her writing "melodrama." Each critic had his own definition of what melodrama meant, from letting plot dictate character rather than the reverse, to over-the-top drama, to "melodrama is when you care what happens next."[342] Audiences never seem to mind the melodramatic play, but critics used it as a term of censure. Hellman's "melodrama" used too many devices like revenge, suicide, blackmail, coincidence, and secrets; critics charged that these devices overshadowed the characters.[343] With each new play she experimented, loosening or tightening plot, adding and subtracting subplots, moving the play forward or backward into history or myth.

In *Another Part of the Forest*, she intended to dramatize an Elizabethan excess (she took her title from stage direction in Shakespeare's *As You Like It* and *Titus Andronicus*). Original music by Marc Blitzstein heightened the antic nature of the characters and their actions. When Joseph Krutch complained in *The Nation* that *Another Part of the Forest* was "the story of four scoundrels, two half-wits, one insane woman, and a whore" he missed her intentional parody, carping that her unrelieved "depravity" began to sound funny—exactly what she intended. Indeed, the play combined the elements of classical comedy and chicanery with Hellman's quick, sly dialogue. When it opened November 20, 1946, at the Fulton Theatre, it was described by the *New York Daily Mirror* as "magnetic and lusty theatre."[344]

Reviews were evenly divided between those who blanched at the melodramatic plot and those who thrilled at her Elizabethan-by-way-of-Alabama innovations. Louis Kronenberger wrote in *PM* that he saw in the play "more than a little in common with those somber Elizabethan 'comedies' swarming with cheats and knaves and evildoers."[345] Brooks Atkinson from the *New York Times*, however, accused Hellman of taking the play "over the line into old fashioned melodrama . . . a witches' brew of blackmail, insanity, cruelty, theft, torture, insult, drunkenness, with a trace of incest thrown in for good measure and some chamber music in the background."[346] When the early reviews indicated the play might not be the resounding success she had hoped for, Bloomgarden took her aside to "tell her the bad news. Then she did something I'll never forget. She put her arms around me and said, 'I feel badly for you; I do not write for critics.' Then she calmly went back to being the grand hostess."[347] Although it ran for a respectable 182 performances, *Another Part of the Forest* did not finish out the season on Broadway, placing third after Arthur Miller's *All My Sons* and Eugene O'Neill's *The Iceman Cometh*.

The melodramatic label dogged her just as surely as the political playwright label. Misapprehensions of her dramas drove her relentlessly. Plenty of critics gave her high marks, and the great box office successes told her the public was willing to decide for themselves. But she reeled at criticism from Mary McCarthy: "Except in the neighborhood of Moss Hart and Lillian Hellman there is everywhere in the theatre this season a sense of restored dignity, of limitations accepted and formal conventions embraced." Blasted as too crafted, or too melodramatic, or too out of kilter and skewed, the play stood on its own merits. Critical complaint led Hellman to more experimental, innovative dramas, but it sometimes led her to error.

She felt the heat and vowed silently to answer the critics with a new kind of drama next time. But life intervened, and she didn't write another original play for five years, although she adapted a play in 1949. On the opening night of *Forest*, her father Max shifted his behavior in ways that had dismaying consequences for him and his daughter, who would exhibit similar traits in her own last years. Max had prided himself on his robust life: he courted women, had a permanent girlfriend, and played poker and chemin de fer with Hellman's friends on his frequent visits to Hardscrabble. He invested in the circle's plays and hobnobbed with Hammett at bars in the city. He seemed indefatigable. But during the scene when Ben Hubbard counted out his cash,

Max Hellman, sitting front and center in the audience, "followed suit, rustling through his bills and annoying those around him. When the curtain closed on Act I, as if to placate his neighbors, he stood up and announced: 'My daughter wrote this play. It gets better.'"[348] Her psychologist Gregory Zilboorg took the occasion of the postplay party to tell Hellman that her father suffered from senile dementia.

Hellman did what many adult children do and tried to find a perfect solution for Max. But he wasn't willing to go along with her plans to live with a visiting nurse, live at Hardscrabble, or go live once again with Jenny and Hannah. Every effort met criticism from his girlfriend Sally Morse or his sisters Hannah and Jenny. Hellman found no way to win this battle. When he collapsed six months later after several falls and similar incidents, Hellman forced his hospitalization. Clearly he was ill and unable to live on his own. Others weren't so sure. Max's senility was intermittent. Sometimes he was lucid, funny, absolutely himself. Then he became paranoid and hallucinated, with "the violence of his angers . . . worse than they ever were."[349] Hellman loved her father and wanted to do what was right. She didn't need second-guessing, which she got from nearly everyone. Her Aunt Hannah wrote to Edith Keanes, Hellman's secretary, "His condition, in my opinion, does not warrant him being so jailed. . . . Lillian no doubt is in Hollywood."[350] Frustrated, Hellman wrote, "I must point out again that while I know you do not mean it, there is something very cruel about my making these very large sacrifices and then to have both of you so unsympathetic about it."[351] She paid for his hospitalization, visited often, took care of complaints, and organized visits for others. When she visited or assisted in the hospital, she never knew which Max would greet her: the father she loved or an abusive man she hardly knew. Bitter that her aunts blamed her for poor care, she carried on. What else was there to do? Only after Hellman's aunts traveled to New York and saw Max's condition for themselves did they see the wisdom of her choices and apologize for their earlier suspicion. Hellman as daughter suffered the uncertainty of the care giver. When Max died of heart failure after an emergency operation for a strangulated hernia on August, 4, 1949, Hellman was devastated. She called Hammett in the city and the two buried Max together.

Detours

In the late 1940s she found life had changed, not always for the better. She had worked hard and acquitted herself admirably in her own eyes, both politically and creatively. She found fame, lasting fame. At forty-one she was inducted into the prestigious National Institute of Arts and Letters (later merged with the American Academy of Arts and Letters). Only the critically acclaimed and famous gain entry. Limited to 250 members, the institute honors artists, musicians, and writers, giving awards and even financial backing to those without funds. Until the end of her life she took an active part, joining a membership that included Mark Twain, William Dean Howells, and Henry James; as part of the academy, she rubbed elbows with Edward Hopper, Wallace Stevens, who was inducted the same year, William Faulkner, and soon Georgia O'Keefe and William Carlos Williams. Hellman had arrived. For the next several years members consulted her on everything from membership nominations and awards to seating plans at awards banquets. She and Carson McCullers nominated Carl Van Vechten for membership; she turned down one playwright and offered up Bertolt Brecht; she nominated poet Muriel Rukeyser for an award; she served on the grant committee. Best of all, she had the power to reward those she respected. Life should have been on track.

But it was not. Hammett continued to be miserable and wonderful by turn, giving hope and destroying it. He celebrated the end of the war with a drunken period so dissolute and incapacitating that crisis after crisis arose. She wanted nothing to do with him but at the same time felt responsible and helpless. They stayed together. A *New York Times* picture showed the two of them together at the 21 Club in Manhattan, dressed up, doing the town, but things weren't good.[352] When he was on a drunk, it didn't matter where he was, but he preferred drunken rampages in Greenwich Village. He alternated living in his studio apartment in Greenwich Village and drinking with staying at Hardscrabble and drinking. "He was charming, old-fashioned, and gentlemanly when he was sober. He was nasty, insulting, and sneering when he was drinking. As his drinking increased, so did his nasty streak."[353] Drunk or sober he continued his political commitments, always "sobering up by Thursday night" to teach mystery-story writing at the Marxist Jefferson School.[354] He didn't always give Hellman the same regard when he returned to Hardscrabble. He belittled her life. "Lillian was leading the life of a famous playwright . . . returning from town each week with he didn't know what 'grotesques.'"[355]

She didn't know what to do with him. Responsibilities she hadn't bargained on plagued her, and they had not been lovers for at least three years. Pat Neal noted that Hammett was "sometimes in a stupor" and praised Hellman's tender regard for him.[356] But Hellman's regard wore thin when he wound up in the hospital drunk and sick, only to resume drinking the day of release. He continued to chase women and had a particular soft spot for Neal, whom he "couldn't keep his eyes off."[357] Once at Hardscrabble he compared Neal's legs with Virginia Bloomgarden's and thought Ginny's better.[358] When Hellman appeared, he gruffly told her to get back to work. (Even with Neal as rival, Hellman admired and loved her and graciously brought a bottle of brandy to her dressing room at *Another Part of the Forest* the day she turned twenty-five.)[359] Hammett was hard to take and sometimes brought family—for good or ill—into the complicated mix of people at Hardscrabble.

When Hammett's daughters, Jo and Mary, had visited before the war, Hammett showered them with attention, taking them to see the film version of *The Little Foxes*, Ethel Merman in *Panama Hattie*, *Pal Joey*, even the Brooklyn Dodgers. During their time in the country, Hammett showed patience and understanding. Jo recalled that even Lillian, "the Boogie Man" of her childhood, was kind and generous during those prewar country visits.[360] But Mary's 1946 visit was a different story. She added to Hellman's worry about Hammett's alcoholism and fear that she had made the wrong choice in leaving Melby. Twenty-four-year-old Mary brought heartache to everyone. A sober Hammett and a sober Mary were bearable. But both were often drunk and abusive to everyone in their path. Jo recalled, "When Papa was sober he kept himself to himself. He was in control, impenetrable, private." Drunk he was profligate, "a kind of lashing-out desperation."[361] With only rare periods of sobriety himself, Hammett brought Mary home with him from Hollywood in hopes of getting her psychiatric treatment. Mary had deep psychological problems, exacerbated by alcoholism. Just what they were is not clear.

A beautiful girl, Mary started drinking early, quickly becoming an uncontrollable alcoholic. Then came the pills. According to Jo, Hammett tried to keep his drinking to a minimum when he was with them, but "Mary drank, and he drank with her. And he drank on his own."[362] Hellman stepped in with unwanted advice, telling Hammett he worsened Mary's condition. It was not well received. Hellman demanded he get his own apartment away from Mary, furious at the mutually destructive behavior. He did, but still spent much time with her. Mary was in and out of their lives until 1951, when she returned to Los Angeles for good. The thin veneer of her tolerance for Mary nearly worn off, Hellman could not, would not tolerate Hammett and his messy, unstable life. Falling down drunk, grabbing women, vomiting, unable to eat, Hammett spiraled toward total self-immolation. At Hellman's insistence, he visited Zilboorg, who sympathized with Hammett's irrational behavior.[363] He believed Hammett simply could not control it.

Hellman, despairing, visited Zilboorg a day later and told him she never wanted to see Hammett again. Zilboorg told her Hammett needed her and urged her to keep their ties. Hellman hated him drunk, but when he was sober he could win her every time. In the mid 1940s his sobriety was nearly nonexistent and her patience wore thin.

Her life bewildered her. By the late 1940s she had it all, had made good choices, or so she thought. But she was still restless, unsure. She missed John Melby, the one man to offer her a life of fidelity and stability. At Hardscrabble she missed him most: "We have many new ducks, and funny new geese, and the new calf has an arrowhead on its forehead. . . The seeds are up, and I've just picked the first radishes and gobbled them down like Salud does beef. . . The dogwood is going now, and all the trees are out, which means to me that Spring is over, whatever the date. It always goes so fast, and it always makes me so sad. I hope very much that we can see next spring together: I wanted so much to be with you in this one."[364] In her mind, they had not ended their affair; plans for a life together dwindled because of divergent paths, lack of time. She missed the everyday fun of being with a man like Melby. After buying clothes she wrote him, "I wish you would come home and see them. I intended to eat dinner with Dash tonight and then come straight home to work, but he got quite drunk and sad, and it is now late. . . . I don't know why I feel guilty but I do. He has been drinking a lot lately, and tonight I gave out with my monthly lecture, as worthless as the night I must have given it fifteen years ago. It is very sad for me to see him drink this way, with no work, and very little happiness in it."[365] Hammett still visited Hardscrabble, the farm was theirs after all, but a couple they were not.

Hellman avoided contact with Hammett by traveling or working on projects both political and creative. Thrilled by Norman Mailer's *The Naked and the Dead*, she began an adaptation that went nowhere. Mailer blamed his publishers in part. "They gave Lillian a tough time. Instead of being honored and overwhelmed that the famous Lillian Hellman wanted to do a play of *The Naked and the Dead*, they got her anger up, and as we all know, Lillian's anger was a sight to behold." Mailer and Hellman worked together for a bit, but she couldn't get a play from it. She did not know enough about the military to make it work. Mailer was protective of his novel, but she reminded him he knew nothing of plays. So they tried. They became friends, with sexual tension charging the relationship at times. Hellman liked Mailer. He was handsome, brazen, and brilliant. She liked men who could do things, manly men. When she attended a party at Mailer's flat where he had converted the plumbing, she quipped that she admired his handiwork more than his novel.

For his part: "She was not at all pretty or beautiful, but she was quite attractive, and there was a vitality, there was an intensity, there was a character in her face that made her—reasonably attractive."[366]

At Hardscrabble Hellman tried to seduce Mailer, showing him "a truly formidable bare breast" before being interrupted by Kober's arrival. Hammett was no help at all in this muddle of convoluted relationships. He made drunken sexual overtures to Mailer's sister while she was at Hardscrabble. In Manhattan he got Mailer drunk and left him stranded.[367] When Hellman finally admitted to Mailer that despite her respect for the novel, she could not adapt the *The Naked and the Dead*, he graciously agreed to waive the $10,000 rights fee. He had no hard feelings about the failed seduction attempt and tolerated Hammett's evident dislike. As he tells it, "We stayed friends. In fact, we finally became friends after that, because she realized that I didn't care so much about the play that I wasn't going to speak to her again and all that, and I in my turn felt that—I was now out from under, I didn't have to placate her, I didn't have to charm her, I didn't have to keep the powerful playwright—in a good mood or anything of that sort, and so we began to have a nice relation that went on for a while."[368] Wanting passion, Hellman settled for friendship and long-distance love in her personal life. Professionally she was on top of the world, but that would soon change.

Judas Goats and Blacklists

Hellman's time in Hollywood was almost up, but she didn't know it. The "panic of movie bosses" and her politics would eradicate her name from the producer's lists.[369] Though 1947 began as a terrific year for Hellman, riding the crest of high demand in Hollywood with *The Searching Wind* and *Another Part of the Forest* ripe for adaptation, it was a very bad Hollywood year overall. Hellman, as a tough-minded dramatist, was so deeply entrenched in Hollywood that from the end of 1946 to the beginning of 1948 a flood of film offers came to her: *Under Capricorn*, *Ballad and the Source*, *Raintree County*, *Bleak House*, and *About Lyddy Thomas*.[370] Hellman turned them all down, waiting for just the right movie. Goldwyn told literary agent H. N. Swanson to woo Hellman for *Earth and High Heaven* and *Secrets*, acknowledging that she might turn him down but ready to make amends for their break after *The North Star*.[371]

Hellman was offered a "great, great deal of money to write, direct, produce all three or any" for Columbia pictures. Money and control were always high on Hellman's list of goals, and this offer gave her control over her material and her time—rare indeed. But it could not have come at a worse time. Hollywood was about to enter an era when even the promise of professional freedom came with a catch.

The top Hollywood producers had just met the resurrected Washington red baiters to "appease them down."[372] Gossip columnist Hedda Hopper, always in the pocket of right-wing Republicans, blamed communist John Howard Lawson, the first president of the Screen Writers Guild, and his "gang" of presumed communists for Washington's scrutiny of Hollywood. She accused the reds of convincing "the stooge writers, directors, and stars who fell for what was called the 'progressive' line that they were serving humanity by turning out pictures dealing with 'real life'. . . throwing patriotic themes to the winds and focusing instead on bigotry, injustice, miscegenation, hunger, and corruption."[373] She thought Hellman's *The Searching Wind* a case in point. Hopper had little use for Hellman anyway, since Hellman had actually gone to Russia. The ring-wing Motion Picture Alliance for the Preservation of American Ideals was founded a few years earlier, but not until 1947 did the political climate change sufficiently for them to mount "a sharp revolt against a rising tide of Communism, Fascism, and kindred beliefs." Sam Wood and (undercover) William Randolph Hearst led this odd group of collaborators—Walt Disney, John Wayne, Robert Taylor, Gary Cooper, Adolphe Menjou, Charles Colburn, Ward Bond, and Hedda Hopper along with lesser lights. They intended to rise up against those who would wrest "the loyalty of the screen from the free America that gave it birth."[374]

Railing against those who had made pro-Russian movies, they ignored the past political climate, the alliance with Russia during the war, and the government's insistence that the studios make such films. Vehemently anti-FDR, the alliance succeeded in joining forces in May 1947 with the House Un-American Activities Committee. Until 1949, when he was imprisoned for kickbacks, J. Parnell Thomas led HUAC in its attack. John Rankin, previous head of HUAC, accused Hollywood movies of sending coded messages about German air raids to communists in Europe.[375] *Screen Actor* magazine found it "difficult to be serious about Mr. Rankin's latest ridiculous accusation against the motion picture industry." Ridiculous or not, the producers sold out. Politicians and studio heads "didn't trust writers—they thought they were dangerous people with ideas."[376]

The initial result of the Washington collusion with scared producers was a new clause in movie contracts, intended to suppress political activism in Hollywood or at least forestall activism the producers did not deem acceptable. Hellman said the clause was "a lulu," a form of the "old morals clause" asking the signer to write a note saying he or she wouldn't embarrass the studio. "This time it didn't mean drunkenness or fights or murder, it meant simply that my politics must not embarrass them" which she interpreted to mean "a straight demand that nothing you believed, or acted upon, or contributed to, or associated with could deviate from studio policy."[377] When she went to sign the contract of her dreams, her lawyer Charles Swartz warned her to look at it carefully but not make a fuss. She found the new inclusion and asked Columbia Pictures head and "legendary bully" Harry Cohn what the new "mishmash attachment" meant.[378] He rambled and dissembled. Finally she said, "You know, Harry, I live with Dashiell Hammett. I don't think he is going to stay in the attic and be taken out on a chain at night." Cohn told her she was just "looking for trouble." [379] She wanted the contract badly but didn't sign. The battle ground had been laid, the boundaries set, and as Norman Mailer said, "Hellman had a marvelous sense of when to go into battle: If she'd been a man she'd have been a great general. . . she knew the time to fight and the time when not to."[380] Now she geared up for the fight she knew would come.

By the fall of 1947, Hopper reported in her column that forty-one Hollywood witnesses had been summoned to Washington, and the *Hollywood Reporter* labeled nineteen of them "unfriendly."[381] The nineteen, many of them communists, nearly all of them writers, collectively decided to present a single defense based on the First Amendment. In solidarity, they hoped to show the HUAC hearing as "an outrage," a constitutional violation. Not all of the nineteen liked the strategies planned by the group and its lawyers; some suspected that the Communist party planned the strategy but hoped their group solidarity would prevail.[382] Strongly behind the Hollywood writers but not yet on the firing line, Hellman watched events closely.

Hellman lashed out immediately, writing "The Judas Goats" for *Screen Writer* on November 4. Sympathetic to the progressive causes that communists espoused, she firmly allied herself with the Screen Writers Guild, which HUAC determined to have unequivocal un-American sympathies. If the charges themselves weren't enough to ignite Hellman, she exploded at the unfairness of the committee, which did not permit "unfriendly" witnesses to read prepared statements. Some of the unfriendlies behaved as outrageously as the committee, but Hellman privileged words over the law's right to deny them. Words meant power, censure impotence.

Hellman, never one to ignore blatant injustice or stupidity, rushed to protest. She berated politicians for making "Congress into a honky tonk show; of listening to craven men lie and tattle, pushing each other in their efforts to lick the boots of the vilifiers; publicly trying to wreck the lives, not of strangers, mind you, but of men with whom they have worked and eaten and played, and made millions." If she saw her own Hollywood fortune going up in smoke, she didn't refer to it. As a writer she was constantly drafting and paring and choosing, but this time she let it fly rhetorically. She damned the "sickening, sickening, immoral and degraded week." Calling the congressional committee a circus, she pointedly analyzed the proceedings, blazing at politicians, hangers-on, and Hollywood power mongers: "Has it anything to do with Communism? Of course not. There has never been a single line or word of Communism in any American picture at any time. There has never or seldom been ideas of any kind."[383] The comic evil she articulated so well on stage and celluloid came alive in print. Lela Roger's assertion that in *Tender Comrade* Dalton Trumbo "sneaked in a line he made Ginger say— 'share and share alike, that's democracy'"[384] seemed so patently ridiculous that Hellman spewed. "One character only outdid the other. To me, even Mrs. Rogers, mother of the middle-aged queen, was put in the shade by the most blasphemous and irreligious remark I have ever heard in public, a producer's referring to God as a 'character' in one of his pictures."[385] Hellman, going for the righteous kill, certainly exaggerated her own virtuous sensibility to God in this article. Then it got personal.

Hellman viciously attacked those who ran the industry. Goldwyn's prewar softening of the message in *The Negro Soldier* seemed endemic of the injustice and weakness of Hollywood political morality. In 1939 Hellman tried to persuade Goldwyn to buy John Steinbeck's *The Grapes of Wrath* but he refused, put off by the "gloom and sordidness of the back ground and the people."[386] Such lack of courage infuriated her: "Naturally, men scared to make pictures about the American Negro, men who have only in the last year allowed the word Jew to be spoken in a picture, men who took more than ten years to make an antifascist picture, those are frightened men and you pick frightened men to frighten first, Judas goats; they'll lead the others, maybe, to the slaughter for you."[387]

While Goldwyn seems a likely target for her poisonous remarks, he probably was not . Congress did not call him to testify. He "was too much of a wild card. You never knew what was going to come out of his mouth."[388] Goldwyn was as outraged as Hellman. When he was denied the chance to give his statement before Congress, he published it in the press. Its thrust was as cutting as hers: "The most un-American activity which I have observed in connection with the hearings has been the activity of the Committee itself."[389] Given Goldwyn's production policies, Hellman might have guffawed at his assertion, "I resent and abhor censorship of thought." Nevertheless, she did not blame Goldwyn as she did others.

She knew Hollywood's feet of clay up close and knew they belonged to men in every studio. Others agreed with her and joined the public attack. Under the headline "Red Quiz Barnum Show," *Variety* attacked the committee as "under-the-belt punchers."[390] Insiders knew that while communists might write in Hollywood, the production codes mitigated any political subversion on the screen. After all, even Goldwyn's sentiment was, "If you want to send a message, use Western Union."[391] Real trouble was brewing. Hellman felt it but believed that American democracy would not punish innocents.

Accusing writers of subversive texts previously passed by strict censoring boards seemed to her grandstanding. HUAC deserved a nasty rejoinder. From her earliest film she had followed the code's strict guidelines. Thorough vetting of every film had given rise to every screenwriter's ire for years. When she agreed to write the screenplay for *Dead End*, for example, she knew her adaptation would require "much treatment for the pictures," to get it past what Breen called the political "censor boards."[392] She remedied with mere murmurings Breene's long lists of complaints, even the unexpected: "eliminate, wherever it occurs, the action of Spit actually expectorating"; change the word "sissy" to "softy." Though Goldwyn hired her to "clean up the play," she said later, "What he meant was 'to cut off its balls.'"[393] She did.

Hellman and all the other screenwriters in Hollywood knew who decided the ultimate content of movies, and it wasn't writers. Producers and the code watched everything. "Movies always belonged to one man—the director—and early movie makers like Griffith and Chaplin knew it. Then along came talking pictures. Words are something else again, and they frightened the boys who didn't know many, so they brought out good writers like Faulkner and Fitzgerald. But such people can't and don't take, or even understand, fiddling and mangling, and so they were lost or went away."[394] For a long time Hellman understood the fiddling and she stayed—for the money, certainly, but also for the fun of doing what she did well. A talented exhibitionist needs an audience.

While Hellman blasted those delivering the punishment and blacklisting, she denied to herself that she was at risk. What she overlooked was that her own films put her in the line of fire—not at the present time but certainly in the future. When the president of the Motion Picture Alliance was asked what films he thought had "sizable doses of communist propaganda" he listed nine, including *The Searching Wind*, *Watch on the Rhine*, and *The North*

Star.[395] Times had changed, and *The North Star* sealed her fate. Perhaps she had been fooled because the Hays office had relatively little to say about *The North Star*, asking only that they remove scenes showing blood transfusions and operating rooms. Hollywood needed films about "the necessity for American-Soviet friendship during a period in which both America and the Soviet Union were fighting Nazism."[396]

Consequently she thought HUAC's complaints about those war films could not be serious. Those writing such films considered it an act of patriotism. As Paul Jerrico said about *The Song of Russia*, written at Louis Mayer's request, "I felt it was a matter of real urgency, that I was making some real contribution to the war effort by working on that film." Vigilantly anticommunist, Mayer early berated Jerrico for the "commie" script. When Jerrico asked what was commie about it, Mayer said: "take out the word community. It's too much like Communism. I will not have a collective farm in my movie." Jerrico did as Mayer asked. HUAC now used the film in the hearings to show the "communist propaganda" that had infiltrated the screen. Jerrico recalled that "it became exhibit A of communist infiltration of Hollywood, along with a picture Hellman had written for Sam Goldwyn [*The North Star*] and *Mission to Moscow* made by Warner Bros. Those were the three A pictures, major pictures, that Hollywood had made under the Roosevelt administration's pressure." Jerrico assumed all of them were in trouble but knew the ax would fall on him. His friend and writing partner Richard Collins, "the first snitch, stoolie, squealer," turned cooperative witness before HUAC. As Jerrico tells it, Collins named Jerrico a "communist which I was" and a foreign agent "which I wasn't." When someone reported to Jerrico that Collins had issued a declaration of independence to distance himself from Jerrico and the other writers, Jerrico said, "Yes, he wanted to stand on his own two knees."[397] Friendships as well as lives collapsed under the weight of the HUAC hearings.

Arguably HUAC was not really interested in the films' communist content. After all, there was nothing more suspicious in the lot of them than *Mission to Moscow*'s plot— which, as Jerrico explained, "seemed to be an apology for the Moscow purge trials but turned out to have been made at the request of the President to improve relations with our Russian allies."[398] HUAC wanted to purge leftists in an influential sector and paint FDR as pink. If they could prove he encouraged communist propaganda, they thought they had him. The right, having taken a blow when the Nazis turned out to be an enemy, needed to regain footing after the war. Hellman, for one, believed that the committee's investigation was "tied heavily to the

Southern desire to keep Negro labor in its place." This bitter retort was in response to HUAC's discovery of communist-inspired heresy in a religious
black character in the *Negro Soldier*, for example. Hellman drew clear and
firm lines from HUAC's censorship to crackdowns on liberal politics of all
stripes.[399] "It is necessary to have worked in Hollywood to understand that it
is most certainly Communist propaganda to pretend that a black man could
be religious," she wrote.

Postwar labor actions in Hollywood caused friction, but the producers
punished writers for their poltics and/or unionism obliquely: vigilant oversight of film content by the Hays office; insisting writers cross picket lines
even if they worked from home and firing them if they refused. The Dies
committee, and California's Jack Tenney, used press releases to fix blame.
They offended many—taunting Jews for their gentile aliases and using
Hearst's newspapers to broadcast headlines with "bellicose bluster."[400] Since
Tenney's 1940 aborted attempt to brand March, Cagney, and Bogart as traitors, the political committees had been leery of punishing anybody
directly—they had settled on smearing groups. The rules had changed, and
so had the penalties.

The Cold War had begun, and the United States discovered anew Stalin's
plans for aggression. But Hollywood leftists, however misguided, constituted
no threat to the United States and HUAC knew it. The committee had a full
list of actual communists in Southern California; the naming of names exercise was little more than a purging ritual demanded of those too far to the
left.[401] What better examples, what better press, than to use the film industry
to wage a war against the Soviets, as well as labor, civil rights, and socialism.
Hollywood had been set up as a straw man for political reasons; any true danger to the country was not housed in studios.

Of course Hellman wasn't the only one in Hollywood driven to fury by the
HUAC hearings and the threat of harsh punishment. To defend the writers,
William Wyler, John Huston, and Phillip Dunne had formed the Committee
for the First Amendment at Ira Gershwin's house in Los Angeles. Their petition insisted on a commitment to free speech and assembly and the
individual's right "to keep his political beliefs to himself."[402] Five hundred
people signed it and several famous Hollywood faces delivered it to Congress:
Lauren Bacall, Humphrey Bogart, Danny Kaye, Gene Kelly, Jane Wyatt,
Sterling Hayden, and a few others.

The Committee for the First Amendment and others supporting the unfriendly witnesses, including Hellman, were stunned on November 25, when
the House of Representatives voted to cite a select group of scapegoats for

contempt: the famed Hollywood Ten. Committee member John Rankin from Mississippi defended the "Christian people of America" by reading a list of Hollywood "names" who presumably weren't Christian or American: "Danny Kaye, we found out his real name was David Daniel Kaminsky. . . One calls himself Edward G. Robinson. His real name is Emmanuel Goldenberg. Another one here calls himself Melvyn Douglas, whose real name is Melvyn Hesselberg."[403] Apparently HUAC believed Jews as dangerous as communists.

Following the HUAC hearings before Congress, the frightened producers made a devil's deal with HUAC in a meeting at the Waldorf-Astoria Hotel on November 24, 1947. Hoping the ritual sacrifice would satisfy the congressional committee, the heads of every studio demanded the heads of the Hollywood Ten: screenwriters Alvah Bessie, Lester Cole, John Howard Lawson, Dalton Trumbo, Ring Lardner Jr., Herbert Biberman, Adrian Scott, Samuel Ornitz, Albert Maltz, and director Edward Dmytryk. As Jerrico told it, producer Dore Schary of RKO brought the bad news to the Screen Writers Guild, trying to "sort of sell the blacklist of the Ten. Schary said in effect that if we would just give the producers these ten heads, no other heads would roll."[404] Their decision didn't reflect the producers' fear of writers "inculcating communist propaganda" in the film subliminally. They feared Hearst's conservative, reactionary press and the American Legion's anti-Semitic, anti-red agenda, which threatened nationwide movie boycotts. As Hellman put it, "The convictions of Hollywood. . . are made of boiled money."[405]

Throwing herself headlong into the line of fire and simmering with resentment, Hellman didn't consider Goldwyn's initial refusal to go along "a vote for freedom" but rather evidence of his habit of being "against any group decision."[406] She made distinctions among traitors and particularly hated Jack Warner, who named dozens of those he thought might be communists without even being asked by HUAC. Goldwyn finally had to go along with the other producers if he wished to go on producing, and his participation in the blacklist sickened Hellman. She became more than a little bitter but not toward Sam Goldwyn, who after all had told President Truman that HUAC chairman J. Parnell Thomas "is seeing this though pink colored glasses."[407] Thomas's pink glasses damaged Hollywood; the producers' response was the blacklist. No more than 10 percent of those blacklisted ever returned to careers in Hollywood.

Not everyone in Washington threw their weight behind HUAC, and the producers could have held tough against the committee. During the 1947 hearings, Harold Ickes, FDR's interior secretary, responded to the furor by telling the press, "They've gone to Hollywood and there discovered the great Red Plot. They have found dangerous radicals there, led by little Shirley Temple."[408] Critics responded furiously that "HUAC never accused the child star of being a Red, only that her managers were derelict in permitting Communist front groups to use her name in endorsements."[409] The Hollywood left, progressives, Democrats, and communists all moved in and out of social and political organizations in support of many leftist causes: FDR's political philosophy, economic changes to surmount the Depression, wartime alliances with Russia. These agendas made nearly all leftists fellow travelers, but hardly subversives.

The legality of the Communist party was not questioned until after World War II, nor affirmed until the McCarran Act of 1950. What Hellman knew for certain was that communist propaganda had not been "inserted" into American films. Even the wartime government-supported pro-Soviet films glittered as entertainment, not social dogma. She felt the charges laughable, the rights of man inalienable. She did not believe her own government would crush artists. But she and others felt the chill.

In November 1947 the congressional committee turned up the heat on Hollywood. The earlier hearings focused on participants' activities in the screen guilds, particularly the Screen Writers Guild, which until 1937 had been the most focused site of Hellman's activism. Since 60 percent of all those the committee called before it were writers, simply being a screen-writer was cause for worry. Additionally, Hellman, one of the most respected and well known writers in the business, never left anyone in doubt of her leftist leanings. She confronted the most complex, emotional topics of her era publicly and pointedly. Why the committee didn't call her earlier is a mystery. Perhaps she, like Goldwyn, was a wild card who couldn't be controlled and, unlike the Hollywood Ten, didn't have a long list of screen credits to sift through for suspect lines. The committee may have held a patronizing contempt for Hellman because she was a woman. They called Lucille Ball, for example, but allowed her to pass with garbled, meaningless testimony. But Hellman was no Lucy who could dissemble prettily. Hellman had more anger and less to lose. She was spoiling for a fight and didn't know she would lose it.

Ominously, Hollywood's organized opposition to the hearings fell apart. The Committee for the First Amendment collapsed before the outrageous actions of the unfriendly witnesses on the stand. Writer John Howard Lawson refused to answer questions and demanded to ask his own. Lawson then antagonized his questioners by saying, "I am not on trial here, Mr. Chairman.

This committee is on trial before the American people." Dalton Trumbo brought boxes of scripts and notes and demanded the committee find evidence of subversive content. Both he and Lawson were dragged from the witness stand by police, with Trumbo shouting, "This is the beginning of the American concentration camp." Ring Lardner Jr. was considered contemptuous (and was) when he was asked, "Are you now or have you ever been a member of the Communist Party?" and he replied, "I could answer it, but if I did, I would hate myself in the morning."[410] Bogart felt so stunned by events that he wrote an article for *Photoplay* saying he had been a "dupe" when he flew to Washington to support fellow actors and the Hollywood Ten. When William Wyler of the Screen Directors Guild, Ronald Reagan of the Screen Actors Guild, and three members of the Screen Writers Guild met on November 27, they tried to compromise, saying they wanted to protect the industry from government threats but didn't want to challenge the blacklisting of the Ten. Instead, they demanded assurances that the studios would not begin a more comprehensive blacklist.

Dore Schary met with this group in early December and promised there would be no blacklist. All three guilds waffled, not wanting to upset the producers but not wanting to support them either. They shut their eyes and hoped the producers and Congress would be happy with the ten sacrifices as evidence of industry "housecleaning." Theirs was a false hope: wholesale blacklisting began immediately. The producers, however, denied the reality of the punishment phase of this inquisition. Instead of openly shunning suspected communists, they would ask, "What have you done lately?" This question, repeated often enough, made the blacklist indefinite.[411] Once the producers could keep a writer at bay for an extended time, he or she had done "nothing" lately, and therefore hiring a different writer could be excused as merely hiring the most sought after.

Overtaking the unaware and edging out the politically incorrect, the lists controlled Hollywood production, though layers of secrecy masked their power. Actress Kim Hunter, probably best known for playing Stella opposite Marlon Brando in *Streetcar Named Desire*, says, "Suddenly the work dried up. . . My press agent desperately couldn't understand why I wasn't working and said, 'I don't know how political you are but I know you aren't Anti-American for Christsake." Hunter's press agent "got onto one of the vigilantes—the Motion Picture Industry Council—in California" who charged him $200 to tell him "what Hunter's problems are." Hunter suspects the "vigilantes" might have listed her because she was friends with Hellman. Both believed in civil rights and both signed lots of petitions. Hellman may

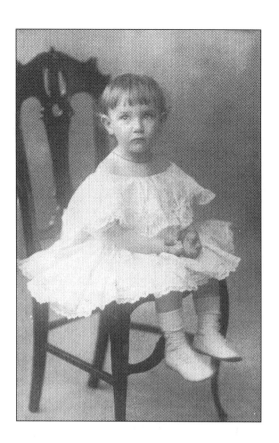

Even at age three Lillian Hellman's level gaze and hard-edged intelligence overpowered conventional femininity with its starched lace trappings.

(Courtesy of Times-Picayune*)*

Lillian, age fourteen, on her "religious truth kick, having sworn on the steps of St. Louis Cathedral, and then in front of Temple Beth Israel," never to lie "under threat of guillotine or torture."

(Courtesy of Lillian Hellman Estate)

Lillian Hellman Kober trapped in Hollywood and in marriage. She bemoaned that "Torpor had touched down."

(Courtesy of the Library of Congress and Lillian Hellman Estate)

Arthur Kober, Hellman's only husband. After their divorce in 1932, she dropped his name and began her journey to fame as a playwright; he became a first-rate satirist.

(Courtesy of Academy of Motion Picture Arts and Sciences)

The twenty-something Hellman loved her husband, Arthur Kober, but she wanted Dashiell Hammett. Desire prevailed.

(Courtesy of Lillian Hellman Estate)

Dashiell Hammett, "a fiction-writer's version of a hard-boiled Dream Prince."

(Dorothy Kilgallon quoted. Courtesy of the Library of Congress)

Hellman in the early 1930s. "A woman with military undercurrents . . . and genuinely feminine to a degree that borders engagingly on the whacky."

(Margaret Harriman quoted. Courtesy of the University of Southern California History Collection—Los Angeles Examiner Collection)

Lillian Hellman "stands where no female playwright has ever stood—smack-dab before the portals of immortality."

(Sidney Carroll, quoted in the New Yorker, 1942. Courtesy of the University of Southern California History Collection—Los Angeles Examiner Collection)

Ralph Ingersoll, one of the most brilliant men of his generation, began a love affair with Hellman in 1935; they shared passion and politics for many years.

(Copyright AP Wide World Photos, 2005)

Hellman's great friend Dorothy Parker, and Allan Campbell, the man Hellman called "the fairy-shit to whom she is married."

(Courtesy of Academy of Motion Picture Arts and Sciences)

Lillian Hellman, Tallulah Bankhead, and Herman Shumlin at an amicable script conference over *The Little Foxes* in 1939; both women claimed the right to be outrageous and were.

(Billy Rose Theatre Collection, New York Public Library)

Bette Davis played the magnificent "monstrous bitch" Regina in the film version of *The Little Foxes*.

(Courtesy of the Academy of Motion Picture Arts and Sciences)

Hellman with Herman Shumlin, producer and director of *Watch on the Rhine*. The newspapers reported that they "were seen together frequently, and generally in animated conversation."

(News clipping from the New York Times. Watch on the Rhine Collection, Harry Ransom Center for Humanities. Courtesy of Lillian Hellman Estate)

Lillian Hellman and Hal B. Wallace on his roof-top "office" in Hollywood in 1943, discussing the script of *Watch on the Rhine*.

(Courtesy of Motion Picture Arts and Sciences)

Hellman at forty: "Neither pale colors nor pale people appeal to her. . . . her spirit is bold to the point of violence."

(John Mason Brown quoted. Courtesy of Lillian Hellman Estate)

Dashiell Hammett, 1944, stationed in Adak of the mid-Aleutions. This image shows his multifaceted persona as Marxist, soldier, and patriot.

(Copyright Jo Hammett Marshall, 2005)

Irving Penn's photo of Hellman in 1947. Hellman said she wanted to be remembered as "a good writer." *(Courtesy of Lillian Hellman Estate)*

Hollywood producers together: Samuel Goldwyn, Joseph M. Schenck, Darryl F. Zanuck, Jack L. Warner, and Louis B. Mayer met at the Waldorf-Astoria Hotel on November 24, 1947, instituting Hollywood's infamous "blacklist."

(Courtesy of the University of Southern California History Collection— Los Angeles Examiner *Collection)*

Lillian Hellman served by maid at Hardscrabble in 1950. This image seems the essence of privileged conventionality. Both she and Hammett soon drew heavy fire for their radical politics.

(Courtesy of Lillian Hellman Estate)

Dashiell Hammett in 1950. "He believed in man's right to dignity and never in all the years did he play anybody's game but his own."

(Lillian Hellman quoted. Copyright Jo Hammett Marshall, 2005)

Joseph McCarthy and Roy Cohn were not Hellman's interrogators during her House Un-American Activities Committee hearing, but they controlled those who were. "McCarthy is a very inaccurate name for a shameless period."
(Lillian Hellman quoted. Copyright AP World Wide Photos, 2005)

Hellman and Alexander Korda in 1953. She loved water and boats. While she didn't love Korda, she appreciated his offer to hire her to write a film in Britain, saving her from insolvency and loss of pride after Hammett's jailing and her interrogation before Congress.

(Courtesy of Lillian Hellman Estate)

Hellman with Julie Christie in 1955. Christie won a Tony in 1956 for her portrayal of Joan of Arc in Hellman's adaptation of *The Lark*.

(Courtesy of Lillian Hellman estate)

Albert Hackett and Frances Goodrich, with George Stevens and Millie Perkins: writers, director, and star, respectively, of the film version of *The Diary of Anne Frank*. Hellman suggested that Hackett and Goodrich write the play and the film, prompting critics of the productions to charge Hellman with leading a Stalinist conspiracy to "de-Judaize and universalize the text." The play's production won the Pulitzer Prize in 1955.

(Courtesy of Ann Huntoon)

Dashiell Hammett, Lillian Hellman, Hammett's son-in-law Lloyd Marshall, and Hammett's grandchildren just months before Hammett's death.

(Copyright Jo Hammett Marshall, 2005)

The convoluted relationship between Blair Clark and Lillian Hellman proved Hellman's thesis that "No society has ever found the answer between men and women."

(Copyright AP World Wide Photos, 2005)

Lillian Hellman at seventy: "She never bored anyone—but she made some very mad!"

(Peter Feibleman quoted. Courtesy of Richard DeCombray)

Peter Feibleman, c. 1990: "Lillian's mind was the sexiest thing in the world."

(Courtesy of Peter Feibleman)

The only known photo of Lillian Hellman and John Melby, at a conference on the McCarthy Era in 1970, twenty-five years after their love affair. He called her the "great rapture of his life." She considered him "all security, and pleasantness and warmth."

(Copyright by Ilke Hartmann, 2005)

Hellman, with Lynda Palevsky in 1981, performs her role as a "cross between a world-famous courtesan and a grumpy little old lady."
(Peter Feibleman quoted. Courtesy of Max Palevsky)

Lillian Hellman loved playing poker with men. She is shown here with Hamilton Fish, Stanley Sheinbaum, Bill Kornhausser, Howard Smith, and Peter Feibleman.
(Courtesy of Max Palevsky)

Mary McCarthy called Hellman a liar on national television and Hellman sued. "How could we not understand that Lillian as a crusader had to destroy this meaningless wench?"

(Milton Wexler quoted. Copyright AP World Wide Photo, 2005)

Lillian Hellman in 1980. "Fellini said Lillian had the only real face in America."

(Annabel Davis-Goff quoted. Photo by Richard DeCombray, courtesy of Richard DeCombray)

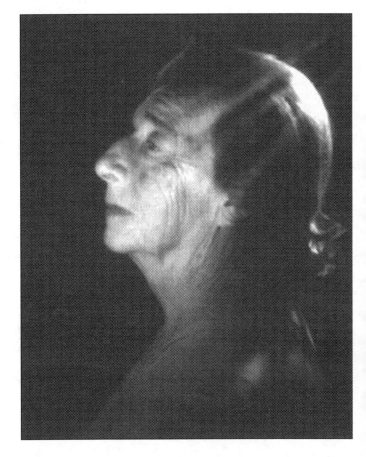

have been the one who asked her to help sponsor the 1949 World Peace Conference in New York, a favorite FBI source of fellow travelers, which Hunter was not, at least not in the overt sense Hellman was. Still, Hollywood graylisted her, which was as insidious as being blacklisted but unclear as to reasons or duration.

At least those on the blacklist knew why; those on the graylist wondered and floundered. Being graylisted meant "suddenly things quieted down," as agent Sam Jaffe recalled the unsettling experience.[412] When John Cromwell's work dried up after *Dead Reckoning* in 1947, Jaffe finally asked Roy Brewer, a Hollywood anticommunist, to investigate. "We checked him out. . . . He's not a communist. But he's very, very left-wing. . . . If he'll appear before the committee and admit that he made mistakes, we'll clear him." Cromwell balked: "I'm not going to get down on my knees to anybody. I'm not sorry for what I did. I'm going back to New York and I'll work in the theater."

Some writers escaped the repression by going to England, Mexico, or Italy. They often had to change the name of their films when they were released in the United States so that the American Legion would not shut them down. Others caught in the Red Scare just disappeared from the screen. "Their lives were pretty much ruined," Jaffe reflected. He himself lost half his business because of the lists. For a price, those "listed" could go to Eric Johnson, "the clearance man. . . the equivalent of a communist commissar with veto power" who could clear a suspect, but not until proper payment was made and proof of changed politics was furnished. Even then, the decision making was quixotic.

In 1948 the film version of *Another Part of the Forest* brought things to a head, though Hellman didn't write the screenplay. The play had been adapted for film by Vladimir Pozner and was released by United Motion Pictures in the spring. Fredric March played Marcus Hubbard, Ann Blythe played Regina, and Jean Hagen played the trashy whore Laurette Sincee. Though director Michael Gordon had once been a communist and Pozner was Russian, returning to Russia in 1950 to become a reporter, the adaptation stayed clear of leftist politics. An FBI informant wrote that the film, "written by Hellman," was one of several pictures that showed "the Communist technique to play up the weak spots of American life."[413] HUAC later brought in both Gordon and Hellman to testify but not about this movie, which became known for its "dynastic skulduggery," not leftist causes.

Hellman knew nothing of the controversy brewing over the film or her "blackened" name. In May, Hellman traveled to Hollywood for Warner Bros. to prepare a treatment for the screenplay of *A Streetcar Named Desire*, getting it ready to pass the Breen office of the Hays Code. Tennesee Williams would write the screenplay, but the producers wanted Hellman's experience to guide the story line. She saw Wyler, and he proposed they do another film together, this time Theodore Dreiser's *Sister Carrie*. She was elated. When he asked Paramount to hire her, he was told, presumably by President Barney Balaban, that she was on a "secret" list.[414] Her failure to sign a studio loyalty oath and her public disagreements with producer policy had made her unemployable. According to actress Kim Hunter, there was no need for Hellman to pay the $200.00 fee that industry vigilantes demanded to verify inclusion on the blacklist. Everybody knew it and she did too.[415] Every studio denied her work. A conspiracy of silence prevailed among producers, and for a time several people outside the loop had potential projects they wanted Hellman for, only to write later that they couldn't obtain the funding. Alan Grogan in the United Kingdom, for example, wrote to her in 1952 concerning a a film called *A Town Like Alice*: "Since dictating the above I have heard rumours relating to this frightening 'witch hunt' in America."[416] Grogan then asked if the witch hunt had something to do with Hollywood's failure to produce his project with Hellman on board. "Do you think?" Hellman thought yes.

She should have known that she would be blacklisted and eventually called before HUAC. Yet it never occurred to her. Her particular blend of naïveté and arrogance made her miss the signals. Hammett had known "that if you differ from society, no matter how many pieties they talk, they will punish you for disturbing them."[417] And punish Hellman they did. For all practical purposes, Hellman and Hollywood went kaput in 1948—as a relationship, a lifestyle, an industry, an income. Thirty years later in *Scoundrel Time*, Hellman told the story of her heartsick anger at Hollywood's turning on its own, at the industry's failure to face down a congressional committee. As in her 1947 "Judas Goats" article, she let the spit fly. Dalton Trumbo, a fellow screenwriter, one of the Ten and openly contemptuous toward the committee, forgave "friendly witnesses," noting that "the blacklist was a time of evil, and . . . no one on either side who survived it came through untouched by evil . . . it will do no good to search for villains or heroes or saints or devils because there were only victims." And when Hellman once told him that "forgiveness is God's job, not mine," Trumbo parried, "Well, so is vengeance, you know.[418] Not for Hellman. Vengeance was hers, but she waited a long time to exact it and paid a high price.

Though she was not ruined, Hellman's forced retreat from Hollywood cost her much. The exorbitant salaries she disparaged had nevertheless given her a lavish lifestyle, one affording her the farm in Westchester County, the money to travel, and the opportunity to write drama for Broadway.

She had invested her ego as well as her talent and her money in writing for stage, but she liked writing for film and missed its craziness and its possibility. "The movie business is big business. It's an enormous industry. I don't know that a writer approaches any serious work with that much money riding on it; the movie writer is still the low man on the totem pole. That hasn't changed."[419] Fellow screenwriter and friend to the Kobers, Sid Perelman echoed her disdain: "Hollywood is a dreary industrial town controlled by hoodlums of enormous wealth, the ethical sense of a pack of jackals, and taste so degraded that it befouled everything it touched."[420] Of course, writers like Perelman, his brother-in-law Nathanael West, Hammett, and Hellman loved the money Hollywood threw at them. It gave them the financial backing they needed to write what they wished in New York, to take artistic risks.

Though loath to admit it, they had depended too long on the power of its wealth. Hellman advised another writer, "Go and make the money and then go and write what you want but don't stay here because you'll spend it the way they do, and live the way they do, and buy a car the way they do; you'll live that life based on the income, which is based on making a lot of money."[421] Hellman also relied on the money, but she liked spending it elsewhere. She was lucky. Hollywood was not her life. "She discovered, like Ben Hecht, that the key to maintaining one's integrity as a writer while working in the movies was to spend as little time as possible in Southern California."[422] She got a kick out of writing for film because she saw herself as a writer, independent of the industry. Thus she survived even when it turned its back on her. But for fourteen years, from 1948 until 1961, when she and Wyler did a remake of *The Children's Hour*, Lillian Hellman was not welcome in Hollywood.

Men in High Places

Frustrated and not feeling up to writing a play or finding a man to love on either coast, Hellman showed signs of lonely despair. She didn't feel at home anywhere except Hardscrabble, and if Hammett was there, that was out of the question. Despite the parties, travel to Cuba and Cape Cod, the fame and the fortune, for the first time in years she felt at loose ends. One man recalled meeting Hellman "at Norman Mailer's east side cold water flat . . . she was so shy she couldn't meet the eyes of people introduced to her and sat silent in a corner all evening. Mailer, who saw everything before it happened, rescued her regularly with exquisite tact."[423] Her physical fatigue and problems with Hammett did not stop her headlong rush into postwar politics. She felt the threat of what Hammett dubbed the "thought-control" attacks of the Thomas-Rankin House Un-American Activities Committee.[424] Not cowed, she raised her political profile.

Nationally engaged, networking with high-level entertainers and government officials, Hellman became central to many of the friendship and progressive movements of the American left, usually in the arts and culture divisions: the Theatre Arts Committee or the Cultural Freedom Conference. Hammett's continued presence and activism prompted her own activity. Melby's thoughtful tutoring reminded her that it takes clout to make political changes. Hellman thus moved toward a newly formed national Progressive Citizens of America party. Formed initially as a pressure group, it leaders hoped to establish PCA outlets all over America as an alternative to the established parties.[425] Hammett joined her, both of them serving as vice chairmen. Once the party shifted its purpose to supporting Henry Wallace's third-party bid for the presidency, Hammett dropped out. Hellman stubbornly persevered, against her better political instincts and John Melby's advice.

Of all the men to come between Hellman and Hammett, Henry Wallace was the most unlikely. A convention delegate of the newly formed Progressive party, Hellman urged Wallace to run for president, despite her certain knowledge that he could not win in a race between Harry Truman and Thomas Dewey. She wanted a clear choice. Hellman reportedly met Republican Dewey at the convention. When he asked her if she would vote for him, she told him, "No, you're too reactionary." He scoffed, saying that someone that very morning had called him a "radical." She replied, "Who? Louis XIV?"[426] Wallace wasn't reactionary. He was, according to historian and author Arthur Schlesinger Jr., "editor, geneticist, economist, businessman, the best secretary of agriculture the country has ever had, a vice president of the United States during World War II, a third . . . party candidate for president at the start of the Cold War and . . . an incorrigibly naive politician and privately a mystic given to improbable spiritual quests."[427] Mailer, an early Progressive party member, recalled that Wallace offered a choice for those who "were bewildered because the Russians, after all, had been treated as the great heroic Soviet Army who had conquered so much of Nazism and suddenly in one year it all turned. And now we were dealing with godless materialism and—the Wallace campaign came out of that."[428] Hellman had seen firsthand the Russians' privation and courage in World War II and she did not understand the increasing bitter breach between the United States and the Soviet Union.

Hellman, an FDR Democrat, felt comfortable with Wallace's "genuine liberal spirit," even though she marveled at the oddities of his character. Swept along in his presidential campaign, she worked hard because their beliefs meshed; she ignored the "funny mixture" the Progressive party had become. American communists had similar goals to the progressives and infiltrated the Progressive party until only a "scholar of that period would be able to separate out who was a Communist, who was a fellow traveler, who was gulled by all of it."[429] The progressives—Wallace, Hellman, Ruth Field, Norman Mailer, and others—found to their chagrin that communists increasingly tried to shift policy. Hellman knew the communists didn't mind doing the grunt work of the campaign, though she along with other influential intellectuals and politicians balked at the increasing demands. She reasoned that communists had their own party and didn't need to interfere. The communists' dogma-driven presence annoyed her.

Late in the failing campaign Wallace asked Hellman if communists were important members of the PCA, and Hellman said they were. Six months earlier she had told Women for Wallace "the most repeated charge against the third party has been . . . that we are controlled by the Communist Party and that all of us are therefore communists. I do not have to tell you here today that is a lie. We are not controlled by the Communist Party and never will be."[430] The communists never controlled the PCA, but their demands gutted the party's influence. Hellman reported in *Scoundrel Time* that she told Wallace of the CP presence. When he later denied knowing anything about it, she said "there is a chance that so strange a nature had put aside our conversation at a time when it didn't suit him to hear. He was not a simple man."[431] Nor was she a simple woman.

The excitement of the campaign, the fun the committee had planning and partying, didn't mean activists agreed with everything the Progressive Party did or didn't do.[432] Hellman got caught up in the rush of national politics and the new set of people. She even decided to try a Wallace agricultural experiment at Hardscrabble. She tried to breed chickens that were both tasty and proficient at laying eggs. Wallace failed in this cross-breeding experiment, as did Hellman. But Hellman's efforts failed because she let her godchild Catherine Kober play in the chicken coop. The child, having an "excellent forgettery" as her father said, left the door open between red and black-footed chickens, ruining the experiment and exciting Hellman's considerable temper.[433] The resulting mess seems an apt metaphor for a campaign that started with great promise and ended in disarray and animosity. Mailer says of his and Hellman's participation: "We were writers, so we were enjoying ourselves as we groused. So the bubble burst, as it were, and the Wallace Campaign fell on its face."[434]

Hellman's Progressive party politics irritated Melby, and he noted that Wallace's professed policy, especially his articulation of it abroad, "leaves a bad taste in my mouth." Melby thought Wallace's traveling abroad and speaking against President Truman's foreign policy unseemly. Melby was also critical of Wallace's naïveté concerning communism.[435] Still in love with the Russian people, Hellman didn't want to hear Melby's increasing resistance to the policies of Stalin and the Soviet Union. But Melby was no pushover. He wrote her, "I do, in fact, think you are wrong about events and about a lot of people."[436] Her politics had matured, but she never bought into the government's anti-Soviet rationale, even with Melby's say-so. He knew foreign policy but got his cues from the government and trusted them. She had come to think the government might betray everything she believed. The Cold War separated more than nations.

Their breach was becoming personal as well as political. He and Hilda Hordern, China ambassador John Stuart's secretary, had begun seeing each other and would eventually marry. When Melby hinted that he was spending time with someone else, Hellman was devastated. She wrote and pleaded with him to keep options open to her.

With Melby creating distance, Hellman pinned her hopes on politics, not romance. Randall Pete Smith was a labor leftist of the National Maritime Union. Although adulated by the workers, his leftist politics got him fired. Besides campaigning for the Progressive party, he hired himself out to do odd jobs. Columbia professor and progressive Leo Huberman brought him to Martha's Vineyard to work for him and introduced him to the vacationing Hellman. She liked men who were bright but also labored with their hands, and his politics and military past in the Spanish Civil War earned her respect and friendship. He and Hellman started a low-maintenance affair while he cleared Huberman's property, but more than anything, he took Hellman fishing. "She used me more for that than for sex," Smith laughingly recalled.[437] He filled the void temporarily. She didn't love him, nor he her. She loved Melby, loved Hammett—enough love already. She wanted diversion and sex. As Smith recalled, "It was more absentminded than erotic. She was a little lonely, and I was a little lonely."[438]

Smith regretted his own aimlessness at the time, his need to bum handouts. But politics ruined him when the labor movement had "gone to hell. The left-wing had gone to hell."[439] He was more realistic than Hellman, who believed then that progressive politics had a chance to thwart the right-wing destruction of the left. Smith's experience in the new political order should have dismayed her. Hellman, on the inside track of a national political party, drawing attention from all parties, felt just hoity-toity enough to believe she could not be threatened by political chicanery. Smith admired her political independence and her ability to "pluck the thorn. She didn't look around. She didn't count to ten before she answered. She was spontaneous."[440] As time would prove, she could be crushed as badly as Smith.

Hellman continued to support the Progressive Party because of its peace and civil rights platform, but Wallace's leadership disappointed her, giving her "headaches and sick stomachs." Hammett advised her, "You'll simply have to stop playing around with that Iowa yogi and his fringe impracticals."[441] One of the fringe impracticals assigned to Hellman was Wallace's wife Ilo, who muttered all manner of odd, conflicting comments. On one occasion Ilo couldn't come up with Henry's ethnic heritage (which was Scotch-Irish). Hellman told her, "If Henry were dead, he'd turn over in his grave."[442] Henry wasn't yet dead politically, but he was close, and Hellman began looking around for more productive political and personal activities. She and Melby still wrote occasionally, but he coolly. Politicking with Wallace and fishing with Smith wasn't enough to quiet her political rage and personal need.

Thus when Yugoslavia's foreign minister, Srdja Prica, invited her in the fall of 1948 to go to Yugoslavia to interview Tito after his break with the Cominform, she leaped at the chance. She was to go on behalf of Yugoslavia's Committee of Culture and Science to see *The Little Foxes* premiere.[443] But the interview was the real coup, and she was expected to write an article on Tito as one of a series she had agreed to write for the *New York Star*. She took the opportunity of the journalist and managed to arrange unheard-of interviews with heads of state. She saw nothing but advantages in the trip.

Her diary and article reflect her travel, but also a familiar edginess and an unfamiliar neediness. Only three years after the war, she resented the Germans aboard her flight, outwardly warm and comradely. She ate breakfast in Shannon, Ireland, "ignoring four, foolish elderly ladies, one of whom looked like Hannah. Then I went to the bar and a nice intelligent seedy drunk came over & wanted to buy me a Grand Marnier. 'I'm crazy about you.'" Intelligent drunks she knew a lot about. In Amsterdam she took a "fine boat & went sight-seeing," noting the cleanliness, the "decently dressed" Dutch. She visited orphanages, listened to many talk about the death of Jews, longed for children she didn't have—and thought the depressed, war-torn cities much like Moscow. She disparaged the speed of traveling through these countries and then said, "I wouldn't want to stay alone anyway." "Alone" for

Hellman was a state of mind, not dependent on the number of parties she attended or people she saw. "Alone" was sometimes a relief, a grateful retreat into the self. But in 1947–1948, "alone" was lonely.

It is hardly surprising that she began an affair with Minister Srdja Prica soon after "the progressive American authoress"[444] arrived on a rainy Tuesday in early October. She had met Prica once before when her friend Leo Huberman brought him to Hardscrabble. He greeted her warmly and by Saturday she wrote cryptically: "Prica Marriage," a Hellman code for the new relationship. But she wasn't so confident. She wrote that Prica was different, "sharp and handsome and aggressive" with a European urbanity and charm that was a little cold.[445] A challenge, she invited and enjoyed his attention. "I am probably doing it all over again—but someday soon the need must be fulfilled—it is getting late." Sex wasn't the need. A dynamic relationship that mattered was. But even she knew that their fling was more fantasy than real, a feather in both their caps, fun, glamorous, a life embellishment.

For Hellman the mix of important political man and charming lover was irrestible. She thought him dignified and principled. She always felt she was a "prize sucker for heroic action."[446] Prica embodied heroism by his position and his political stance. Yugoslavia had bravely broken with the Soviet Union, though it remained communist. Prica was attracted by her fame and literary cachet; her politics didn't impress him. She told him she feared she was getting in too deep, meaning with him. He took it politically. He replied by telling her she was "a middle-class liberal and had not gone too deep into things." She admitted, "I pretended I meant it that way."[447] The affair mattered. They talked politics; they laughed together; they admired each other. This was a heady time in Hellman's life as she breathed the rarified air of international politics and men in high places.

Interviewing the famed Premier Tito unsettled her. His worldview differed from that of Vice Premier Zdenek Fierlinger of Czechoslavkia, whom she also interviewed. Their conflicting world perspectives treated her to socialist political rhetoric as clashing and self-serving as any uttered in Moscow and the United States. Fierlinger warned her, "I would like to tell my capitalist friends if they wish to maintain their way of life, they had better avoid war in Europe because they will wake up to find that the people in Europe won't fight for them."[448] Tito's attitude was far more critical of the Soviets, more conciliatory concerning the West. The headline of her Tito story read, "Sure of Strength, Foresees No War."[449] Although her byline implied an expertise she didn't have, she knew enough to slam American anticommunist critics: "Anyway, it seems to me more sensible and effective to understand something before you denounce it." She reported what she saw and her opinions about it, and her commentary infuriated Cold Warriors.

Catapulted into the national political arena by her trip to Eastern Europe and her place in the Wallace campaign, Hellman became a lightning rod for the division in Cold War public opinion. She advocated peace and friendship with the Soviets, and civil rights in the United States. In 1950 *Red Channels*, a right-wing publication, listed her along with other respected writers and thinkers as a "red." As writer Studs Terkel said, "If you were listed in that, you'd be dead. . . . People I love were in it—Arthur Miller, Zero Mostel, Lillian Hellman—but where was me? I felt like the blue-haired dowager who didn't make the social register." (He finally got his wish because he too had signed anti–Jim Crow and anti–poll tax petitions and attended "subversive meetings.")[450] Hellman paid no heed to warnings. In her world, if you weren't left, you weren't worth knowing.

The desperation in her affair with Prica, however, speaks to the despondent state of her relationships with Melby and Hammett. Melby was far away in China and stalled her when she suggested meeting. Hammett continued drunk and increasingly dissolute. In her early forties, she still longed for the romantic ideal, but one that would work with her whirlwind life and her fame, and with a sober Hammett ever in the background. She wanted the impossible.

Hammett was absent emotionally, but she could never wash her hands of him completely, though she tried. He spent long periods in town and she sent friends to check on him: Pete Smith, Ginny Bloomgarden, and Patricia Neal. She knew he adored these young women, but she was past jealousy at this point; she couldn't cope with seeing him drunk and couldn't bear his being alone. Hellman had welcomed Hammett's trip to Hollywood to see his daughter Jo's wedding in 1948. She liked Jo and gave her an antique blue and silver locket to wear on her wedding day. Jo felt wearing the necklace would be a betrayal of her mother, Jose Hammett, and wore pearls instead.[451] Hammett, sober, charming, and generous in Hollywood, came home to begin the last and worst drunk of his life. Hellman kept her distance, calling his Greenwich Village apartment occasionally, visiting seldom, relieved but a little hostile seeing Hammett under the watchful eye of Rose Evans, the black housekeeper and caretaker Hammett had hired. Evans was fiercely loyal to Hammett and not at all pleased with Hellman, whether attentive or absent. But Hellman was the one she called when Hammett's condition became grim.

As Hellman recalled, "I hadn't seen or spoken to Hammett for two months until the day when his cleaning lady called to say she thought I had better come down to his apartment. I said I wouldn't, and then I did."[452] Finding him unable to walk, shaking and shivering with the DTs, they took him first to Hellman's house on 82nd Street, then in the dark hours to Lenox hospital, where the doctor told him if he'd be dead in a few months if he didn't stop drinking. Hammett told the doctor he would stop drinking, and he did. Hellman wrote Maggie Kober, "I hope to God he stays on the wagon, but I am not sure I have much faith that he will."[453] But he did, cold turkey. Six years later, when she told him that she and his doctor doubted he would ever make it, he said, "But I gave my word."[454] Life changed for both Hammett and Hellman for the better. But they had lost much too. She had not written for the stage since 1946. A new play would unite them once again in shared purpose. Hammett's recovery renewed Hellman's creative spirit.

In Paris on the way home from Yugoslavia, she had gone to see one act of Emmanuel Robles's play *Montserrat*, at Norman Mailer's urging. She thought the political and moral dilemma at its center interesting and exemplifying moral and political courage. The play is set in Venezuela during the Spanish occupation of 1812, attended by political oppression and principled resistance. With Robles's support and a good translator she felt she could save herself months of research time and still write something original—what a good adapter does. She denied that she sought "to draw parallels with contemporary life in her free adaptation," but given her political penchant, it had to cross her mind.[455] But writing the play wasn't her top priority; progressive politics was. Thus distracted, she failed to do her customary historical and cultural research. She was pressed, evident in a series of letters she wrote friend Malcolm Cowley, a leftist and literary editor who had served in France in the military and spoke French fluently. She feared she was getting a late start on the adaptation because she hadn't seen a "complete translation" and asked for suggestions. Finally she wrote him, "I don't think I would ever have started *Montserrat* if I had known the amount of work."[456]

The plot is simple; Hellman used dialogue of conflict to reveal the themes. A young soldier, Montserrat, now sides with the liberation and knows where the revolutionary Bolivar and 6,000 soldiers are hiding. The monstrous Colonel Izquierdo and the Spanish occupiers insist he tell them and he refuses. The Spanish arrest six innocents off the street, and Izquierdo promises to shoot each citizen to squeeze the answer out of Montserrat. The young hero resists and ultimately saves Bolivar. The six citizens are taken out and shot—from a mother whose death may also mean the death of her two babies to a woodcarver who cries for his life. Silent and holding on to his principles, Montserrat is taken from jail and shot at play's end.

Hellman, still smarting from being called a melodramatic playwright, worked to change the pattern of presentation in *Montserrat*. She used a "Sartre thematic technique" that takes "a situation and then proceeds to question, cross-examine and probe, not the forces of reaction responsible for the situation, or the oppressors. . . but the 'revolutionists' themselves."[457] This technique worked for Hellman only minimally, as any subtlety was eclipsed by the over-the-top dramatic situation. She did not change the original play's structure of six innocents shot one at a time, and it made the action static, predictable, occasionally maudlin. She wasn't familiar with Venezuela, Spain, or the army and military life. It showed. Her biting humor still erupted in terse dialogue, but in stiff mimicry of Spanish phrases. She also used too many American rhythms and idioms, completely at odds with the Latin action and character of the play. The philosophical moral puzzle at the play's center could not hold the play together.

Unhappily, she decided once again to direct the play herself. Athough she acknowledged that she hadn't directed *Another Part of the Forest* well, she thought she learned from it. And she was determined to keep production costs down. Accompanying Hellman for interviews, Kermit Bloomgarden, who once again produced, "munched on a cigar, and made his only conversational contribution. 'She never wanted to be a director. I had to talk her into it.'"[458] He humored her. Hellman had the audacity to tell the reporter that "directing is no great feat," implying that it didn't take a "genius" if the play had good stage directions.[459] *Montserrat* proved her wrong.

When the play opened at the Fulton on October 29, 1949, reviewers all had something different to say about it. As startling and bold as Hellman's adaptation was, it drew little real praise: the *Commonweal* reviewer found the play absorbing and "gratitude is hereby tendered."[460] If "typical Hellman astringency" can be considered praise, the *New York Morning Telegraph*'s review was positive, but the poor direction was also noted. The *New York Herald Tribune* noted that Hellman was "fully eloquent in her translation and remarkably full of action in her staging" but chided her for repetition. The production showed its flaws: a "heavy, stilted play,"[461] "monotonous" action, "static bore,"[462] "frequently talky,"[463] "brutal melodrama."[464] Terrible casting—particularly of the two central figures, William Redfield as Montserrat and Emlyn Williams as Colonel Izquierda—sealed the play's fate. The *New York Times'* Brooks Atkinson, the ruling voice in New York drama, thought the writing barren, noting the carnage on stage and the "monotonous" direction. Audiences agreed. The "minor league drama" closed after sixty-five performances.[465]

Montserrat wasn't a failure, precisely (oddly enough Hellman won the Vernon Rice Award for direction), but the play was a big disappointment. Hellman knew the fault was mostly her own. She was down but not out. Hellman knew that she had what it takes as a playwright, but she discovered she could take no short cuts. It would be awhile before she wrote another adaptation for Broadway; another play of her own was what she wanted.

But before that could happen, she would have to be content with others adapting her work. Marc Blitzstein's *Regina*, an operatic adaptation of *The Little Foxes* for which she wrote the libretto, opened the same month to wild applause and rekindled her acclaim in New York. In Moscow, *Ladies and Gentleman* (the Russian title for *Another Part of the Forest*) opened to enthusiastic audiences, with the *New York Times* reporting a five-hour performance drawing twelve curtain calls.

Moscow's praise might have felt better had she not been aware of political rumblings about her from the right. She had been named as a Communist party line follower for the first time by the California State Senate Committee on Un-American Activities. National blame would follow.

PART THREE

THE SPOILS

6

POLITICS AND POWER

Middle-Age Chill:
Cold War Politics and The Autumn Garden

HAD SHE BEEN ABLE TO FOCUS ON MONTSERRAT RATHER than politics, the characteristic Hellman punch might have awakened her audiences to its themes. Instead, she focused her coiled energy on the 1949 Waldorf Conference for World Peace, sponsored by the National Council of the Arts, Sciences, and Professions. This group, as an arm of the Progressive Citizens of America, tried to revive the postwar peace movement after Henry Wallace's electoral defeat in 1948. The conference planners included Hellman and famous friends and colleagues who lent their names to peace; they all drew jeers and barbs from Cold War supporters nationwide. The country was deeply divided on the movement, some remembering the USSR's enormous contribution as an ally in World War II, others fearing Stalin's aggressive postwar politics. The media reported two thousand people inside the ballroom and two thousand protestors outside the hotel. Inside or out, controversy reigned.

The anti-Stalinist American left—Dwight Macdonald, Mary McCarthy, and Robert Lowell—accused the organizers of featuring Russian intellectuals who knew nothing of freedom and therefore could not lobby for peace. The "other left," the organizers and speakers, included such well-known names as scientists Harlow Shapley and Albert Einstein, composers Dmitri Shostakovich,

Frederick Shuman, and Leonard Bernstein, along with writers Norman Mailer, Arthur Miller, and Thomas Mann. They felt that peace talks had to proceed to avoid another war and to maintain friendship with the Soviets. No mere political skirmish, "the conference was significant . . . because it was one of the first occasions in which there was an all out attack on the group that sponsored it."[1] As an organizer and a participant, Hellman drew increased attention from anticommunists and the FBI.

Hellman and Russian composer Dmitri Shostakovich were photographed sitting and laughing together at a dinner table, and the picture brought virulent condemnation. American audiences who had never heard of her suddenly had a name and face to recognize as the enemy. She was guilty by association—Americans saw in black and white Lillian Hellman sitting next to a Red. Neither his standing as a composer nor hers as a playwright meant anything to an American public wrapped up in fear of Russian armies and ideas. In the eyes of the public, the composer was Russian, therefore Red. Her admiration for him made her Red, too. Hellman's talk at the peace conference gave the lie to this accusation: "Nowadays on the Right it is fashionable to pretend that only Russia is at fault. I am sorry to say that there are too many on the Left who pretend that only the United States is at fault. It no longer matters whose fault it is. It matters that this game be stopped. . . . He who has seen a war and plans another must be either a villain or a madman. This group of intellectuals can do no worse than statesmen."[2] She ended with a call for peace, asking both sides to listen.

The Waldorf Conference and its sweeping photo coverage thrust Hellman to the forefront of partisan politics. Other photos and condemnations followed. *Life* published head shots of more than fifty people under the headline "Dupes and Fellow Travelers Dress Up Communist Fronts." Hellman was in good company. The conference organizers included Dorothy Parker, editor George Seldes, and Charles Chaplin. More ominously, the coverage caused Hoover to step up the research he gave to HUAC and subsequently published an anticonference report listing Hellman as belonging to "thirty-one to forty" red-front organizations. As Hammett wrote his daughter Jo, "Lillian's . . . sulking a little because the newly published Congressional Committee on Un-American Activities pamphlet on the recent Peace Conference lists her in the group of sponsors who have been affiliated with 31–40 red-front organizations while I'm in the smaller and more elite 41–50 group."[3] Hammett joked, but he knew better than Hellman the danger of such exposure. Hellman captured the attention of her audience and then antagonized it. From the 1949 Waldorf Conference to the mid-

1950s, the Red Scare accelerated across the country, with the media adding to the hysteria. Headlines boldly accusing celebrities of treachery sold newspapers. Hellman tried to stand her ground under the onslaught and was more or less successful. Under conservative pressure, Little, Brown published a pamphlet, "a kind of apology" for its leftist authors, Hellman among them. Hellman jumped on a train to Boston to confront editor Arthur Thornhill. As D. Angus Cameron, a former editor at Little, Brown said, "If anybody was going to apologize for her or her work, she'd be the one to do it."[4] At another time she buckled under the pressure, reluctantly signing a loyalty oath required of Dramatists League members.[5] Nevertheless, the American Legion labeled Hellman one of 128 "Untouchables," a list of suspect notables.

Outwardly Hellman's life seemed to move forward as usual, with fits and starts, pleasure and trouble. She and Hammett reaffirmed their affection in countless ways. When he stopped drinking at the end of 1948, they were "garrulous together," as Hammett termed it. No longer lovers, they settled into life as family. They bred their poodles, Cirque, Meg, and Flora, and loved the puppies. At one time they had fifteen dogs in the country, which Hellman affirmed "is enough even for me."[6] They spent time together at Pleasantville and Martha's Vineyard, where they summered. Hammett grew "fat, sunburned, and contented."[7] They dined with Cary Grant, Pat Neal, Kermit and Virginia Bloomgarden, Henry and Ilo Wallace. Hammett got them a television, though Hellman could not work it until Hammett carefully jollied her into learning: "The chief things to remember are that you start off A, B, C, D in simple order, and that a little turning of a knob or ring usually goes a long way."[8] Domestic life had seldom been quieter. Though Hollywood had blacklisted Hellman and she could not get work, it inexplicably beckoned Hammett with offers of screenplays for *The Fat Man*, *Detective Story*, and a Hitchcock movie. The *Mirror*, a California newspaper, made a bid to syndicate the Spade series. But Hammett's failure to finish any of his projects made his blacklisted status moot. Then suddenly he lost his radio shows, which had brought him financial stability. As he put it, they went "all hubbabubba" in 1950.[9] Still, Hellman and Hammett felt stable if not secure.

Hellman's father died and Hammett's first grandchild was born, bringing death and new life to the couple. When Hammett's daughter Jo married Lloyd Marshall in the spring of 1948 and later had a child—Ann—both Hammett and Hellman embraced the role of grandparents. Hammett flew out to Hollywood to see her, lavishing attention and bearing "a Steiff kangaroo with a baby kangaroo in its pouch and a ton of expensive baby clothes."[10] A year later he went to Hollywood and returned to Hardscrabble with Ann, to the delight of Hellman, who also fell in love with the baby. They succumbed to the disease of grandparents everywhere, telling stories and showing pictures and expecting their friends to share their admiration for the baby.

Hellman farmed, fished, and entertained both simply and lavishly, and drove to Manhattan when duty called. She visited the dentist often; her teeth constantly troubled her. The sober Hammett slowly recovered his health. Both Hammett and Hellman scrutinized the physical and mental health of Hammett's daughter Mary and worried. They tried desperately to keep up the spirits of Maggie Kober, a beautiful, sensitive woman who had a wretched time of it with multiple sclerosis. Hellman and Maggie, without jealousy or animosity, wrote letters showing a shared affection for the man they called "their husband," Arthur Kober. In this rhythm of regenerated and declining life, filled with joy and worry, Hellman began a new play and watched over its production. Their lives mellowed in the rich colors of middle age, but they continued to be polygamous and political—nothing mellow about that.

On the way to writing her next play, she uncharacteristically took a creative detour to write a different kind of book. When old friend Louis Kronenberger asked Hellman to edit *The Letters of Anton Chekhov* and write an introduction, she agreed. The project emphasized life's progression as it moves from year to year and ultimately deepened her themes of value and loss. It also changed the shape of her next play. A beautiful, carefully edited book, *The Letters of Anton Chekhov* displayed the depth of Hellman's understanding of Chekhov, and the introduction reaffirmed her ability to write prose. It brought her the respect of the New York intellectual community, which tended to dismiss playwrights. Smart and academic, *Letters* brought in little income. And for the first time, because of the blacklist, money began to haunt both Hellman and Hammett. Working on the book, thinking of a new play, living more conventionally than she had in years, Hellman became reflective. The tranquil richness of life with Hammett cheered her, but their passion had vanished. She felt sad about all that had been lost or deferred or mediocre. She looked for meaning in her life and the lives of others, and wondered if she could capture these midlife years in drama.

She wanted to know what the accumulated years of a life meant. Her diary entry for New Year's Day 1950 says, "Childless women do not grow up. It becomes their custom to pretend they are like the young, and are the children of people their own age. In their own eyes they are closer to the children of their friends than are the friends."[11] She felt outside the lives of many of her friends. As the year progressed, she wondered whether she had ruined her last chance to have a normal life when she and John Melby went their own ways—both reluctantly. They had met again that year, just before Melby left for a tour of Indochina. She reflected on the relationship's change: "Conversation of that period of 1945; a fever—such a fever almost physical," but all diminished now.[12] Who she was and how she related to others was on her mind.

What kind of woman was she, had she become? In an entry in June she wrote, "Dash's book: How to tell a woman from a lady. Tickle her under the table. If she says "Please stop it," she is a lady; if she smiles, she is a lady; if she demands protection from another man she is not a lady. No lady would snitch."[13] She wondered how she fit his definition, always important to her identity. No one could doubt that she had lived fully: the beautifully clothed, chain-smoking, scotch-drinking Hellman could turn a theatrical company or a dinner party inside out with abrasive wit and a winning laugh. Yet she had not lived traditionally, and she was not content with conventional patter. Hellman had reached middle age.

Out of a well of reflective melancholy tinged with hope for a meaningful future came *The Autumn Garden*, the play both Hammett and Hellman said was her best. In writing the play, she turned into herself and and then out toward those who peopled her world. Hellman abandoned the villains and villainesses she was known for, along with the Ibsen-like well-made play, for something like Chekhov's drama: diffuse, driven more by character than plot. Writing without taking sides, detached from her characters, and looking for the truth in their lives, she sought to counter critical charges of her penchant for "melodrama" and plays "too well made." The inevitability of change coupled with the desperation to find value in the self came alive on the pages of the play, but not always on the stage. *Autumn Garden* was her personal test.

The text of the play centers around two huge portraits of Constance Tuckerman, painted by her first lover. One shows a young, vital woman and the other, painted years later, depicts the woman cheerless, washed out, and aging. Constance painfully sees the toll of years, though the later portrait is mean-spirited and inaccurate. These portraits set up Hellman's theme of reflection. The self, not another, must judge the effect of the years and changes. Hellman was enigmatic about whether she thought she had wasted or proven herself in her own life (she bore only a passing resemblance to the character of Constance). But Hellman said outright, "If you are inwardly a serious person . . . in the middle years it will pay off."[14] Those years had not served Constance well, but still she put too much faith in a lover's cruel depiction of her. Hellman called her play in progress "Five or Six Kinds of Love," and in it she sought meaning in life's actions and decisions.

Staying in a summer house along the Gulf of Mexico "about one hundred miles from New Orleans," the guests, Constance (the owner) and Sophie (Constance's refugee niece from Europe) work through a complex network of relationships and emotions, memory and accusation. Though Hellman's "shrewd wit" works through the dialogue, the residents are self-involved, desperate for change and new meaning, but clinging to memories of what once was.[15] Rose and Benjamin Griggs are poised for a divorce. Old Mrs. Ellis alternately worries and wields power over her daughter-in-law and grandson; Ellis's grandson Frederick is engaged to Sophie but adores a gay novelist. Edward Crossman—a Hammett-like character—drinks in isolation much of the time, with Constance realizing too late they could have had something meaningful between them. Into this dysfunctional mix comes Constance's ex-beau, Ned, eager to paint her again, followed by a watchful and jealous wife, Nina. Given the intricacies of the relationships, a soap opera drama could have ensued, but, as one critic pointed out, Hellman's "realism is to the essence of human existence, not to the representation of life. . . . The characters all belong on the set: each has a legitimate reason for being at the Tuckerman house at this particular moment in history; each is searching for the meaning of life, and for love. Some are weak, some a little stronger . . . this is not melodrama; these are people, not puppets."[16] Hellman's dry, trenchant wit combined laughter with pathos. The time of her life and her need to experiment dictated the new form.

Hellman had two astute editors suggesting changes—Arthur Kober and, as usual, Hammett. But in a change of pattern, Hellman was finishing the play as it went into production and didn't have time to make the structural changes Kober suggested. He worried about the lack of character focus and was unsettled by Ned's quasi-seduction scene with Sophie. In a detailed analysis, he apologetically but candidly suggested she revise.[17] Kober stressed the need for a strong character "with whom you emotionally identify yourself," though he admitted he hated to use "those foolish kinds of terms." He insisted she needed to change the third act—feeling the drama of Sophie's near-seduction forced and unbelievable. He suggested changes in tone so that "Sophie thus gets the money to go back to her country and away from— well, they're hardly little foxes for they're not as vicious or as violent: they're the little gophers in their own particular kind of destruction."[18] Hellman unwisely disregarded his suggestions. She felt the subtleties would work on stage as they did on paper, and thanks to Hammett, they almost did.

Hammett marked sluggish passages, insisting that "Mrs. Ellis must not want marriage—must be *Old Lady* Ellis," and he diagrammed the pace of the action to better move the performance. One scene he wrote completely. Twice Hellman tried to improve Griggs's definitive speech at the end of the play, but in rehearsal it never quite worked. Finally she turned to Hammett, who wrote it for her; it defined perfectly the theme of the play: "So at any given moment you're only the sum of your life up to then. There are no big moments you can reach unless you've a pile of smaller moments to stand on. That big big hour of decision, the turning point in your life, the someday you've counted on when you'd suddenly wipe out your past mistakes, do the work you'd never done, think the way you'd never thought, have what you'd never had—it just doesn't come suddenly. You've trained yourself for it while you waited—or you've let it all run past you and frittered yourself away."[19] Hammett sober was a practical, focused, and generous editor. Hellman gave Hammett 15 percent of her royalties for the rest of his life for his work. She dedicated the play simply, "For Dash," and praised him publicly: "Dashiell Hammett wrote those lines."

To everyone's relief she hired Harold Clurman to direct, abandoning her role as director. She could not direct it and had to find someone suitable. Her schism with Shumlin was too great to cross. Though she didn't think Harold Clurman was a director who counted, those being "Elia Kazan, Jed Harris, Herman Shumlin—and maybe one or two others," he was available and she took a chance.[20] She still insisted on being in charge—in fact, her interference was worse than ever.

Though she never stopped giving him advice on how to direct, Clurman—clearly a professional—soon learned how to handle Hellman. "She began giving me notes the second day or third day. . . . She'd take notes and she'd whisper most audibly at rehearsals. I said, 'Don't do that. It's disturbing me and it's disturbing the actors. They hear whispering going on when they've hardly begun working.' 'This is not a school,' she answered. . . . She was a very hard person to work with . . . She'd say, 'He is an utter shit.' And I'd say, 'Kent, in that moment will you please not plead but command' . . . She'd say . . . 'God, how stupid that person is! What an idiot!' And I would say, 'Colin, don't cry on that line.'"[21] She was relentless during rehearsal. She exasperated him so much that Clurman finally refused to review all her suggestions. She wept—out of rage or frustration or fear–which one isn't clear.[22] Although she praised Clurman for his diplomacy with actors, she feared for the play. He abandoned the symbolic double portraits without explanation. And worse, she saw the life go out of her play on stage and had no idea why or how it happened.[23]

The *Autumn Garden* opened Off-Broadway at the Locust Street Theatre and finally with little turnaround on Broadway at the Coronet on March 7,

1951. The reburbished Coronet (later named the Eugene O'Neill) was a glorious theater with an interior covered completely in gray silk, which designer Howard Bay used to create a "comfortable and colorless" set in keeping with the theme of midlife angst. Hellman and Clurman had collected a first-rate, uniformly praised cast starring Fredric March and Florence Eldridge. *Autumn Garden*, which one critic called Hellman's "ripest, juiciest, wisest play," should have been a smash.[24] With 101 performances—just one over the number that marks a hit—the box office disappointed. Nominated for the Drama Critics Circle Award, *Autumn Garden* lost to Sidney Kingsley's *Darkness at Noon*.

A Hellman play always divided critical audiences, but this time critics and reviewers were sharply at odds. They had come to expect a certain Hellman approach, and this play was not typical. Literary critics still find *The Autumn Garden* one of the best—if not *the* best—of her plays. Broadway's drama critics were conflicted. Brooks Atkinson of the *New York Times* couldn't decide what he thought of it. In the space of one review he called the play "scrupulous," the characters "truthful . . . written . . . out of knowledge and integrity," "Miss Hellman at the peak of her talents," the play "boneless and torpid."[25] She got much press, but the headlines warred: "*Autumn Garden* Is Rich and Mellow"[26]; "Miss Hellman Buries the Middle-Aged."[27] Hellman responded, "I don't want to be dull about this . . . I don't like cheerless plays. I don't feel cheerless about the world." Snapping the silver cigarette case given to her by the production company of *Watch on the Rhine*, Hellman lit one of her endless cigarettes, blew smoke, and said she stubbornly and politely refused to listen to critics. She didn't need critics' palaver to see the play had problems with the audience. Herman Shumlin believed that the worst thing any director had to contend with was that "forty percent of an audience is coughing and sneezing all the time . . . But not at a Hellman play."[28] *Autumn Garden* failed this test.

Autumn Garden lost the initial $75,000 investment and more. Since Hellman and Hammett both had financial woes, she watched the box-office receipts closely, recording each evening's take in a small brown book. *Autumn Garden*'s receipts barely covered the production costs. Hammett wrote Jose Hammett that "financially, this year's going to be a holy terror" and warned that it might continue in years to come. Hellman prevailed on Hammett to try to get both his and her taxes straight; she hired Stanley Isaacs to find accountants to straighten the mess out.[29] For the government, it would be too little too late.

Hellman later reflected, "Somewhere we both knew—the signs were already there, Joe McCarthy was over the land—that we had to make it good because it had to end."[30] *Autumn Garden* recorded those first niggling fears, the middle-aged chill, that there's no going back, no redoing the destiny you've built for yourself. Time and life are the villains. In some ways, *Autumn Garden* marked the pinnacle of Hellman's theatrical career. The play was original, had defied the perjorative "melodrama" label that critics threw at her to diminish her earlier achievements, and had excited universal comment if not praise. Following *Autumn Garden*, politics usurped her energy and hemmed her in. Political controversy, which had helped fuel her creativity, spun out of control. She became ensnared by national politics. Broadway did not see a Hellman play for three years; she wondered if she would ever write again as governmental forces beyond her power stepped in to take a punitive role in her life.

Scoundrels and the Darker Forces

More energized by political action than theatrical staging, Hellman's very soul was political.[31] She considered working for political justice the highest mark of integrity—one way to make a life meaningful, moment by moment. Whether in New Orleans, Hollywood, New York City, Pleasantville, or Martha's Vineyard, her home was the polis, the place where people gather to live in shared action for the citizenry. A public intellectual, she drew attention, demanded others see the world her way, and was caustically critical of political power. Phoning, writing, signing petitions, raising money, planning benefits, she lectured to power brokers and laborers by turn. She ate rubbery chicken at political luncheons all over Manhattan, Hollywood, Paris, Yugoslavia, Russia. As hostess, she invited diplomats, entertainers, labor organizers, and writers to her New York City apartment or her Westchester farm. The heady atmosphere of political vocation moved her as nothing—or no one—did.

Not surprisingly, the darker forces of governance watched her. Her political instincts had shown her the ways in which race activism related to labor, especially the labor of performers and writers—Screen Writers Guild, Drama League, Authors League of America, National Council of Arts and Sciences and Professions—all organizations the FBI suspected of having communist principles. Her work on labor, particularly the Screen Writers Guild, put her at risk because the FBI listed it as a communist-front organization. Her first encounter with the FBI was merely interesting, though it was up close and personal. In 1940 agents Harold Ranstad and Birch D. O'Neal met Hellman face-to-face when they were investigating Nathan Witt for a supposed National Labor Relations Act violation. The agents deposed her about guild activities involving Witt, but she could tell them very little, only that she had no contact with the National Labor Relations Board (NLRB) except in regard to Screen Writers Guild business. In that regard she had earlier been slated to testify before the NLRB but was never called. She admitted to the agents, "I was very interested in everything that was going on."[32] She felt no alarm at the visit, and not until the 1950s, if ever, did she realize the extent to which the government watched her.

FBI records released under the Freedom of Information Act show the Bureau began a file on her in June 1940, when Hellman was no longer even loosely allied with the Communist Party. They documented her writing an article for Ralph Ingersoll's leftist *PM*, which may have been the first "zine" to combine entertainment and politics without advertising. Hellman's article, headlined "The Little Men in Philadelphia," covered the Democratic Convention for the 1940 presidential race.[33] In it she voiced her disapproval of the political climate. People she interviewed seemed too frightened to speak about politics. Apparently her critique of a censoring city or party or secret police cut too close to the bone. Someone had asked taxi drivers "not to talk about politics, the war, or the state of the nation," and she found "at least three white men and two black men are too suspicious and too tired and too frightened to exercise their primary right of free and easy speech." Given her radical politics in the previous decade, this article seems small fare indeed. This "informational" file Hoover began before the war comprised a few articles she wrote for *PM*, a few petitions she had signed, and a check of her bank accounts.[34] Her visibility and influence galled Hoover, convinced as he was that she was a secret communist. The FBI considered Hellman potentially seditious. Rumors flew that "Lillian Hellman was being urged to enter the political showcase as an American Labor Party candidate."[35] Too rebellious to follow political discipline, she never felt tempted to run for office. Hellman, never secretive, began her political career working for labor in the highly visible Hollywood setting. She represented much that the right hated, but she was hardly subversive.

Calling Lillian Hellman a "key figure" in communist-inspired activism, J. Edgar Hoover ordered a more secret file on her in the late 1940s, with particular attention to her work for the Progressive Party. (Oddly, Hellman's lifelong relationship with Dashiell Hammett, an avowed Marxist—most probably a Communist Party member—didn't much interest the FBI, which took years to realize that Hammett wasn't merely a boarder or visitor in her residences. If anything, he is tarred by her brush and not the other way around. His file reads, "Lillian Hellman, playwright . . . has previously been reported to have befriended the subject.") Hoover put her on his custodial detention list, which consisted "of persons to be rounded up and imprisoned in concentration camps should the need arise."[36] When Hellman made the "list," he cautioned the agent in charge of the New York office, "You are reminded that this subject has a national reputation through her writings in which she has opposed Nazism and Fascism. Under no circumstances should it be known that the Bureau is conducting an investigation of her."[37] When Attorney General Francis Biddle ordered Hoover to get rid of his list because it was "impractical, unwise, dangerous, illegal and inherently unreliable," Hoover renamed it Security Index, or SI. Hellman made the SI, too.[38]

Hoover had his hands full investigating Nazi and American Bund agents as well as the Japanese threat. But he was relentless and accelerated information gathering on everyone who championed leftist causes that communists also promoted: civil rights, antifascism, labor movements, and critics of the FBI. Hellman certainly qualified.

Despite her southern upbringing, she got involved early—too early for the FBI—in the struggle for civil rights and racial equality. The FBI recorded her signature on a petition "in Defense of Civil Rights," and as early as 1939 she sat on the editorial council of *Equality* magazine, which the FBI found suspicious for its intent to bring about racial harmony. It labeled the publication a "Communist Party enterprise" because of its agenda. Hellman hosted a dinner for *Equality* at Hardscrabble, inviting Paul Robeson and Lucille Turner in hopes that Turner would sing at the party.[39] Hellman's willingness to "aid the cause of the Negro" was duly noted by the FBI. One Bureau memo described her as assisting "in the drawing up of the code of the Committee for Democratic Culture," which had racial equality as its goal. Several pages of her file reported her speaking at a Harlem meeting organized by Marshall Field to assist "Negro soldiers" and her talk at the New York Public Library, 135th Street Branch, Harlem.[40] The FBI was hostile to that topic of discussion, too: the Negro's stake in postwar America.

A passionate believer in equality of opportunity, Hellman sometimes offended those with more progressive views, as well as reactionaries. *People's Voice*, a Marxist publication, was less than enchanted with her answers to questions about the "Negro characters" in her plays: "Lillian Hellman Not Up on Minority Problems." She admitted that she didn't know northern middle-class blacks and wrote about those she knew—the southern working class. Her FBI file included a clipping of the article, as well as a *Daily Worker* review of *Little Foxes* that praised Hellman for creating "Negro characters" who were not "whining travesties" or "caricatured Aunt Jemimas."[41] They also noted that she headed up a group to discuss "Jim Crow illegality in the Armed Forces at the Citizens' Emergency Conference for Inter-racial Unity" sponsored by Hunter College.[42] Though her knowledge of the real racial divides in America was limited, she either stuck to what she knew or relied on the research of others. She joined writers Carl Carmer, Robert Littell, and Elmer Rice to encourage producers to air a continuing radio series promoting civil liberties for the American Civil Liberties Union.[43] Hellman's work on race relations was so well known that she was the principal speaker at an Ethical Culture forum during Negro History Week in 1946. That same year, to the FBI's consternation, she joined thirty-three playwrights, lyricists, and composers who refused to permit production of their work "unless doors are opened to Negro patrons."[44]

As galling as her work on race relations was, more important to the FBI was an informant's contention that Hellman had been assigned by the Communist Party to devote her activities to "smearing the FBI," but even Hoover could find no evidence.[45] Of course Hoover didn't need evidence to begin close scrutiny. In 1949 the FBI grew increasingly alarmed with Hellman when an anonymous tipster accused her of hosting a dinner for the Comintern spy and commie-on-the-run Gerhardt Eisler. Hellman did not know Eisler or his wife and never had dinner with them. The smear was enough for Hoover; the dinner that never was became key evidence of sedition in Hellman's file because Eisler was "hotter than a sheriff's pistol."[46]

Writing and politicking on two coasts, her name appeared everywhere on committee boards, petitions, and political lists. Until the day she died she remained a joiner of causes that furthered the status and economic security of the working class and writers. She enlisted in so many allied organizations that on at least one occasion she forgot about her membership. The National Council of American-Soviet Friendship insisted she needed to pay her dues but she refused, saying she was not a member. The organization sent her written confirmation and she apologized and resigned.[47] In 597 pages of her file, the FBI couldn't keep all her activities straight either, although it stepped up interest and surveillance as the Red Scare took hold.

Both Hammett and Hellman had by then become national political figures. She believed the American and Soviet governments were right for their own people. After seeing war-torn Russia and England, "peace among nations" became her mantra. Hoover considered the peace movement communist based, believing "every organization which stands for any sort of concerted effort to maintain peace in the world a transmission belt between the masses and the Communists."[48] International organizations were especially suspect, and Hellman and Hammett both belonged to many such organizations.

Hellman and Hammett publicly and visibly represented those organizations and showed interest in countries the United States now saw as enemies. The Yugoslavians and the Russians honored Hellman at their embassies. Ambassador Kosanovic of Russia even sent flowers to Hellman on Max Hellman's death. Hammett wrote public letters in support of *Soviet Russian Today* magazine, the Trenton Six in the Scottsboro frame-up, and the Civil Rights Congress (CRC). As New York State president of the CRC, Hammett said he worked "on behalf of Jews, Negroes, trade unionists, Communists, pseudo-Communists, suspected Communists, imaginary Communists and god knows who all the Trumans, Tom Clarks, Tom Deweys . . . and other so-and-sos of the sort choose to jump on."[49] She worked for world peace; he cynically predicted World War III. In April 1951 Hellman traveled eagerly to an international theater conference in Paris. Hammett turned down an invitation the next month to go to Paris for communist-inspired "doings about Intellectual Comfort vs. Conscience," noting in a letter to Maggie Kober that "Madame is a little bitter about my not thinking I'll go. Madame has a firm belief that one should go almost anywhere for almost any purpose if it's free."[50] He laughed, but the signs of real trouble had begun.

The Red Scare seemed like media hot air, unrelated to them but worrisome. Alger Hiss had been found guilty of espionage in January 1950, leading to Cold War polarization: those, like Hellman, who saw him as an innocent victim of anticommunist fervor versus those who saw him as evidence of Soviet subversion and infiltration across America. The Rosenberg trials further divided the country. The ambiguity of the cases in 1950 lit firestorms of suspicion on both sides. To add to these fears, McCarthy grabbed media attention early in 1950 with sweeping, inaccurate, and unspecific charges. "He sold fear and conspiracy pure and undiluted."[51] The State Department responded to his allegations of communists in the government by setting up the Tydings Committee, a foreign relations subcommittee that met from March to June 1950. McCarthy named as "subversives" Harlow Shapley and Frederick Schuman, with whom Hellman had worked in the ICCASP, Wallace campaign, and the Waldorf Conference. "She knew these two to be loyal American citizens: the fact that they could be publicly pilloried was cause for disquiet."[52] John Melby, too, sat up and took notice: Shapley had been his dissertation director, and any direct links were dangerous. National pressure lead the Author's League to ask Hellman to sign a "NonCommunist Union Officer" affidavit. She protested but signed in April 1950. When the Korean War broke out in late June of that year, with Soviet support of North Korea's aggression on the South, even the skeptics bought into McCarthy's rants. Ominously the passport office demanded that her requests for renewal be accompanied by explanatory letters and verifications from sponsors.

Trouble brewed where she couldn't see it, buried under government secrecy. The FBI had an official "mail cover" at Hardscrabble under which her mail was scrutinized.[53] Then the FBI found a diary of a woman [blanked out in FBI files] that said "lunch with Lillian Hellman." The FBI added "Soviet Writer" in parenthesis next to Hellman's name and put the accusation in Hellman's file.[54] In another file the FBI noted finding Hellman's name in an address book of a General Frankel. In 1950 the FBI received a postcard that said, "I happen to know of [Blanked out]. I think it is worthwhile investigating also Lillian Hellman of Chappaqua, NY." Noting that Hellman visited Dorothy Parker and was a good friend of Paul Robeson and that Dashiell Hammett received mail at her Hardscrabble address, they increased their interest.

When Louis Budenz, former communist, quasi-spy, and *Daily Worker* editor, named Hellman and four hundred others as concealed communists, the FBI took his testimony as truth.[55] It opened a new file on her in January 1951. "This time, what was 'alleged' or simply reported by an unnamed 'informant' became accepted as fact without qualification. The mere existence of such raw data in the file gave the material acceptability."[56]

When the FBI finally came out of hiding, it wasn't Hellman they were gunning for, however, but Hammett. His work in the Civil Rights Congress had unforeseen consequences. The congress, formed in part to provide defense and bond for leftists arrested for political crimes, provided bail for eleven communists indicted under the Smith Act of 1949. (Years later the Supreme Court ruled that the act could only apply to active espionage agents, but in 1951 it applied equally to those convicted of un-American activities.) Hammett, president of the CRC and head of the bail fund committee, had raised the bond money from hundreds of contributors for these eleven men. The men were convicted but released on bail. Then four of those indicted skipped bail and disappeared.

On July 4 an unnamed source told the FBI to look at Hardscrabble for the missing men. Duly noting that Hellman's house was suspiciously hidden from the road and surrounded by trees, the FBI set up road blocks and block-ades around the farm and arrived the next day—without a warrant—to search and interrogate. The FBI file noted that "Hellman denied knowing any of the fugitives and a search was made of her property with negative results." Hellman said she was "coldly polite," drove them around, and insisted they search every-where, even the attics.[57] She was furious and indignant. Hammett had joked to his daughter Jo two years earlier, "Red-baiting's kind of rife these days in these parts and it keeps space between floors and beds fairly well filled with otherwise intrepid characters."[58] Hammett wasn't much surprised by the visit, but Hellman's naive belief in the basic justice in the system took a heavy blow.

On July 9, 1951, Hammett appeared in court under subpoena to name the bail contributors. "There was no doubt about the seriousness of the situation. The prosecutor was U.S. District Attorney Irving Saypol, who had prosecuted the Rosenbergs."[59] To all questions Hammett cited the Fifth Amendment. Hellman begged him to admit he did not know the names of the contributors and had never seen them. His daughter Jo knew as well as Hellman that "his decision had been no decision at all." He "had lots of faults, God knows, buckets of faults, but ratting on people who trusted him with their money and names wasn't one of them."[60] Victor Rabinowitz defended the others named, but Hellman retained Charlie Haydon to represent Hammett and to appeal his contempt verdict.[61]

In the fear and flurry of Hammett's imprisonment, Hellman's actions seem less than exemplary. For a short time it seemed as if Hammett might be re-leased on $10,000 bail; Hammett's secretary, Muriel Alexander, posted it, but the court legally forbade her to do so unless she named the source "which she still refuses to do nearly fifty years later."[62] Controversy dogged the bail re-quirement for Hammett, who was indicted for refusing to name bail contributors. A rumor circulated that bail would be raised to $100,000. Before bail was revoked altogether, Hellman and Alexander frantically tried to raise the money. In Hellman's version, she pawned jewelry and got $17,000. She certainly had the jewelry to pawn; Hammett's gifts to her ran to expensive pins and bracelets. An anonymous source to the FBI reported that she "had sold her jewelry" for communists.[63] William Wyler ponied up $14,000 and fi-nally friends and fellow activists Leo and Sarah Huberman promised the entire amount by mortgaging their house.[64] Hellman loved Hammett. She paid for his lawyer, feared for his life, and found the means to get the huge cash outlay for his bail. But Hellman had a tight grip on her own finances when her security was at risk and preferred having others put up the money instead of mortgaging her own homes.

In any case, the court denied Hammett bail, and he was sent to jail for six months. The Treasury Department proudly "filed notice of an income tax lien for $100,629.03, announcing that it was the first such action taken against anyone involved in an investigation of subversive activity."[65] Hammett first went to the Federal House of Detention, then to prison at Ashland, Kentucky. Forbidden from sending or receiving messages from anyone but his family and his secretary, Hammett had to exclude Hellman from contact. Hellman fled, claiming that Hammett's lawyer slipped her a note that said, "Do not come into this courtroom. If you do, I will say I do not know you. Get out of 82nd Street and Pleasantville. Take one of the trips you love so much. You do not have to prove to me that you love me at this late date. DH."[66]

Critics assail this Hellman story. Hammett definitely used his lawyer and his daughter Jo to spirit notes to Hellman, Pat Neal, and Muriel Alexander, whom he could not reach directly by force of law.[67] The sentiments in the alleged note echo Hammett's letters to Hellman. But as Jo Marshall points out, "The whole thing sounded so much like Lillian and so unlike Papa that it would have been funny if you were in a laughing mood. Not one of Lillian's more credible creations."[68] Hellman obviously felt guilty but was determined to go. She was scared and needed the work a trip would bring.

In this anxious and dramatic climate, Hellman knew another passport renewal was iffy. On July 13 she wrote Mrs. Shipley of the passport office, "I have been hired by Hoche Productions of Paris to adapt for motion pictures Ibsen's play 'A Doll's House.' . . . I need to work and I need to earn the money. Most certainly I do not intend, and shall not, take part in any political activity of any kind . . . I am not a Communist. I am not a member of the Communist Party. In the past I have been a member of many left-wing organizations but, while I may have made many foolish decisions in my life, I have never done anything which could be called by any honest person, ugly or disloyal or unpatriotic."[69] The lengthy letter detailed her previous travel, cited former Ambassador Averill Harriman (who now was planning to run for president) and John Melby as references, and closed by saying she felt sad that such proof was needed, stressing her "absolute conviction that I have never been, nor could ever be, any part of any action that I considered disloyal to my country. The truth is that I am a rather old-fashioned patriot."[70] The letter worked; she got the passport. The letter would become a draft of another letter—this one to HUAC—that she wrote less than a year later when the strong arm of congressional oversight reached her. At this time, however, she simply left the country.

The unconventional Hellman flew to Europe, hoping to adapt a play. Hammett may have been, as daughter Jo surmised, "surprised and hurt. But not angry."[71] Hellman wrote Hammett often, sent letters in plain envelopes through her secretary, Sophie Lange, who gave them to Alexander to get to Hammett. She reminded Lange to call "from the outside always."[72] Suspicious about governmental surveillance—rightly so as it turned out—she worried and grew frantic when Haydon didn't report to her as he had promised about Hammett's well-being and whereabouts.[73] Her flight after Hammett's sentencing didn't sit well with her conscience, but telling a story that justified it assuaged her shame in the face of others; after a time she believed it herself.

Hammett's behavior also defied convention. He asked his daughter Jo to phone Pat Neal, give her his love, and "tell her sometimes I've found it awfully easy to be in love with her in jail." In the same paragraph, he asked his daughter to find out if Hellman was back from Europe.[74] Marshall felt squeamish: "It seemed disloyal or at least indiscreet. I thought of Lillian as my father's wife . . . he and Lillian had been together as long as I could remember. Under any other circumstances he would never have shown his feelings openly like this. That he did told me just how alone and isolated he felt."[75] Both Hammett and Hellman were beside themselves. Hellman wrote, "If anything ever went right once again, I think I'd drop dead from surprise."[76]

Hellman hated being out of control, and was: the FBI searching her farm, Hammett jailed and forbidden contact, Hardscrabble suddenly at real risk, the Red Scare virulent. She warned her secretary that her phone might be tapped; she worried about their association with others under government scrutiny, in one instance writing frantically to keep a former lover and communist away from them: "NO Pete Smith is not to go to Pleasantville at any time (I hope it hasn't happened?)"[77] His reputation could only harm hers and Hammett's.

In the Crosshairs

Deep suspicion surrounded Hellman; her life and the lives of those she loved seemed twisted in government vice grips. Soon what had been hidden was made public, and she found herself fighting for her reputation and her livelihood. In September 1951 Martin Berkeley, a sometime screenwriter and former communist, named 161 Hollywood communists, Hellman among them.[78] As Berkeley put it, "I vaguely recall Hellman having attended either a Marxist meeting or a new members' class in the Hollywood Section of the Communist Party in 1937; however, I can't be absolutely positive."[79] Despite his vague recollections, the FBI took the testimony as hard evidence. Ring

Lardner disputed Hellman's presence, and he was there.[80] But when Berkeley's testimony made its way to HUAC, it was taken as gospel. HUAC put Hellman in the crosshairs.

John Melby, too, received his first interrogatory—questions from the Senate State Department Security Office to those suspected of disloyalty. The first three questions the board asked "dealt with Lillian Hellman."[81] The government had begun its squeeze.

The first questions he was asked were about his sexual relationship with Hellman; only then came questions about the failed Chinese diplomacy resulting in a "lost China." A following interrogation led Melby to suspect Hellman's phone was tapped. In 1950 Hellman had seen Melby in Washington for the first time in nearly five years. They immediately connected, conversing animatedly. Hellman was pleased that Melby's career had taken off; she saw his promotion to foreign service officer class II as validation of her respect for him. In March he spent a weekend at Hardscrabble where they slept together, no real surprise given their affair and the strength of their affection. They knew a future together was impossible, but their feelings hadn't and wouldn't change. As Hellman said later, "The relationship at this point was neither one thing nor the other; it was neither over nor was it not over."[82] The following month he visited her at her home in New York City on his way from Illinois to Washington. Their bond remained strong, even as life and politics scattered their hopes. This reunion spoiled his political career, however, and led to increased FBI scrutiny of both of them.

Hammett's return to New York in December 1951 did little to comfort Hellman. The slim, consumptive man had lost over fifteen pounds and seemed deeply tired. She had pictured herself going to Ashland, Kentucky, to pick him up, but the rules about family and representation kept her from meeting him there. His attorney, Charlie Haydon, was unsure the prison would release him to her, so ultimately no one was there to get him. Fortunately prison officials gave him $50 to get home. He took a bus to catch a plane, and Hellman met him at LaGuardia. Somehow she imagined a happy homecoming with a restored Hammett. He came back a shadow of a man who refused to admit he had suffered. He rushed off the plane to a restroom to vomit. "Bad hamburger," he explained. She took him to 82nd Street and the meal she had prepared "on order for his release: oysters on the half shell, quail, and sweetbreads."[83] The excess of food, the energetic and anxious woman, and the luxurious apartment unsettled him. He needed time to find himself again; he left the following day for his own small Greenwich Village apartment. His dark view of humanity played out cinematically before him.

When Hammett returned from the Federal Correctional Institute in Ashland, Kentucky, he had "no means or earning potential."[84] The IRS had impounded all his income. The financial pinch of the past year became pressing. Even though Hellman, Herman Shumlin, and assorted accountants had been working on tax problems since *The Searching Wind* in 1947, the IRS now told her she had to pay $110,000 fully and immediately in back taxes. If things got any worse, Hardscrabble Farm might have to go, and Hellman had made provisional plans to sell it as early as August 1951.[85] She made great efforts to save it, however. She wrote her secretary, Sophie Lange, to arrange to have the road repaired, since there is "no such thing as 'in the light of selling the place.' I do not intend to sell it unless I can't help myself."[86] But the expense of maintaining the farm made it an improbable luxury as a second home. It required a huge outlay of money for labor. She had tried to make it a working farm so that she could use agricultural tax breaks to ensure its survival.

The IRS, however, ruled that Hardscrabble was a "gentleman's farm" and therefore excluded from exemption. Hellman appealed the IRS rulings, thinking they just might prevail. Hellman had not reckoned on the IRS's concerted malice, nor the legal bills both she and Hammett incurred. She needed large sums to pay back taxes. They both feared she, too, would be called before HUAC and would need lawyers. Hammett knew reality and made no move to block her intent to sell. Neither had a choice. In April they left Hardscrabble forever, with the sale finalized in July 1952. For thirteen years Hellman and Hammett had made Hardscrabble their main home, and having to sell it was depressing to Hellman and "a terrible blow to Hammett . . . it had been his refuge."[87]

Packing up a farm of that size was no mean feat, but in the final days before the move, Hammett remained in New York, writing his daughter that Hellman "suspects me of having taken to bed to avoid the unpleasantness of helping her move."[88] She wrote more tellingly, "We shouldn't say good-bye to this place together. It will make it bad for both of us."[89] The move was bad, and circumstances were about to get worse. They both knew Hellman would soon be under fire.

Hellman wrote movingly of the hundreds of deer that came down to the farm in the last week before they packed.[90] Hellman's lines signify more than a nature scene. They portray her loss, her attitude: "It was after six o'clock when the deer began to disappear, in small family groups, some heading for the main road and then flying back to the rock garden, some a new course into a large stand of pines, most of them going as they came, by the road to the lake. There were four last stragglers."[91] The deer went reluctantly, just as Hellman and Hammett, who mourned the loss of the farm. For the next six years Hammett lived in Katonah, New York, in a four-room cottage on the estate of friends Samuel and Helen Rosen. Hellman wrote a friend that the "income tax mess cleaned us out."[92]

"That was a tough spring, 1952."[93] Awaiting IRS judgments, in touch daily with accountants, Hellman forgot to watch her back. On February 21, 1952, an "over-respectable-looking black man, a Sunday deacon" rang at her 82nd Street house; she buzzed him up. He handed her a subpoena from the House Un-American Activities Committee requiring her appearance as a witness before a congressional subcommittee investigating subversive activities in the entertainment industry. She knew her appearance would also be a shaming ritual about her activist ties to the Screen Writers Guild and organizations suspected of being communist. And worse, she would be required to "name names" of others or be held in contempt. Typical for Hellman, she lashed out at the process server: "Smart to choose a black man for this job. You like it?"[94] The committee knew her racial politics of equality would not let her spurn a black man at her door, and Hellman knew they knew. She felt set up, angry at the process server and at herself for being manipulated by the slick and the powerful.

In times of trouble, Hellman often took a long time to rein herself in, to figure out how to think, what to do. An inevitable pattern set in: lash out angrily, fiddle aimlessly, sleep, and awake to decision. In this instance, she took a nap, slowed her heartbeat, pulled herself inward, gave herself time. She awoke "in a sweat of bewilderment" needing to act, as if a flurry of movement would absolve the fear, solve the problem of having to face HUAC, of resisting their lust for names, ever more names.[95] She picked up the phone and called frantically: Hammett, lawyer Stanley Isaacs, anyone who might help.

She ultimately called Abe Fortas in Washington, D.C. Hellman believed in going straight to the top. A world-renowned New Deal lawyer, Fortas later became a Supreme Court justice. (He was ultimately forced to resign because of financial irregularities.) In 1952 no one had more power and political savvy in defending HUAC witnesses than Fortas. He came to see her on 82nd Street, meeting her in her own milieu to better size her up. She passed muster. Because Owen Lattimer, an educator with the Institute of Public Relations charged with espionage and then perjury—both of which were eventually dismissed—had also hired him as defense before HUAC, Fortas felt he could not represent Hellman. He sent her on a "hunch" to Joseph Rauh.

Rauh was a savvy choice. He was founder and national chairman of the liberal Americans for Democratic Action, fiercely anticommunist and anti-McCarthy. His adamant belief in civil liberties had led him to defend many government employees in trouble over the Employees Loyalty Program. His credentials and steadfast principles could not fail to impress Hellman. And Fortas guessed that the time had come for a witness to "take a moral position," to testify about oneself but refuse to talk about any others. Both he and Rauh thought Hellman might try it. She stood fast to her beliefs and had a nearly pathological hatred of informers.

The two lawyers might have been canny enough to count on her flair for the dramatic and the Committee's tendency to discount women. Both the smart, sly Lucille Ball and Judy Holliday had fared well by acting so ditzy and confused the Committee dismissed them without demanding information about others. The Committee grew impatient with Holliday about her vague, off-beat answers: "Do you have any difficulty with your memory?" Holliday answered, "Now I'm getting one, but I didn't know then that I needed one."[96] Hellman could not, would not play the Ball/Holliday defense, however. Her public persona was as a rebellious, serious, often regal intellect. She would not dither. Fortas and Rauh had to proceed with caution; the HUAC committees were not shy about sending smart women to prison; the new release of HUAC files shows the Committee increasingly resorted to closed-door sessions to choose for public hearings those most likely to give the Committee good press releases.[97] The Committee, too, counted on Hellman for drama. They hoped her notoriety would make good press.

Together, Rauh and Hellman, both wrinkled, craggy, and outspoken, set her legal course. Hellman liked Rauh as a man and a lawyer, which saved them from the worst scrapes. Rauh was handsome, charismatic; they enjoyed each other, despite the ugly circumstances. Both were used to having the upper hand, so naturally they conflicted. Rauh told her that "if she wanted to escape indictment and trial and jail, the only safe way was to rely upon the self-incrimination clause of the Fifth Amendment."[98] She insisted on three stipulations: she did not want to go to jail, she didn't want to take the Fifth, she wouldn't tell about others. He told her, "Madam, that makes you a very difficult person." Rauh recalled, "It would be a rather complicated performance."[99] They wanted to try Fortas's hunch to tell all about herself and refuse any testimony about others. But they needed time to create a strategy and received a postponement from a March hearing to May 21. Rauh continued to insist she take the Fifth. She resisted but finally agreed if she could volunteer to talk about herself, not others. Rauh fretted about legal complications revolving around the Fifth Amendment: "If you tell about yourself, you have waived the privilege as to others." The answer didn't please her. He warned that any legal advice he gave her might be flawed because "in a case of this kind, political and public pressures often become strong enough to break down legal precedents."[100]

Legal ambiguity increased her stubbornness, as well as her anxiety. Their meetings didn't go well. He advised her that "the only completely safe (though distasteful) course of conduct before the House Committee would be to answer all questions put to you, including those concerning other persons . . . the next safest alternative would be to refuse to answer, on grounds of self-incrimination, any and all questions . . . And to refrain from issuing any public statement."[101] She opposed both. After much discussion, they chose to do the "limited Fifth" with a letter setting out willingness to tell all— without names. But he feared such a stance might not be "wise from a legal point of view." Hellman preferred to tell everything about herself and nothing about others in the hearing room, where it would be on the public record. But Rauh cautioned, "You would in all probability be cited for contempt if you adopted this position." Contempt meant a jail sentence. Hammett opposed the strategy. He thought she should plead the Fifth and called Hellman and Rauh's final decision "liberal shit." Fortras's partner called it "legal shit."[102]

Another heated battle concerned Hellman's communist past. She wanted to admit she had been a member for two years and cite 1940 as the year she quit. Rauh opposed her because she didn't seem to have formally joined the party and she didn't seem apologetic enough: "too cavalier on this subject." Unless she said she was wrong and gave lists of reasons as to why she was wrong, Rauh didn't think her confession had legal or public value: "Please don't take offense, but your statement is likely to be compared by unfriendly sources to a lady retiring from the Republican Party because she is tired of politics, although she still thinks Bob Taft is a dear, sweet thing."[103] He wanted her to make a strong pitch about her present commitment to anticommunism. Face set, she refused. She felt such an admission would validate the Committee's position. He then demanded she take out her early affiliation altogether. Hellman agreed to follow his script, his direction showing just how scared she was.[104]

He knew the law and she knew writing. Each wanted final say on the letter she wrote to the Committee. Drafts and counterdrafts flew through the mail and in office meetings; she paced and smoked as he edited.[105] The letter got written in tandem, his legalities uneasily wed to her distinctive style. Finally, on May 19, 1952, they delivered it to the Committee on the Hill.

Three hours later Hellman and Rauh got "a snotty reply," saying a congressional committee couldn't permit a witness to set the terms of her testimony.[106] It went on to say that many early communists didn't feel the Communist Party was a subversive organization, but that "the contributions made to the Communist Party as a whole by persons who were not themselves subversive made it possible for those members of the Communist Party who were and still are subversive to carry on their work." They reassured her, however, that anyone she named would "be afforded the opportunity of appearing before the Committee in accordance with the policy of the Committee."

She prepared herself legally and rhetorically. But how to do so psychologically? In great crises Hellman said she used a "roped control," not giving way to emotional displays or long talks and reflections with friends. Now, irrespective of lawyers, she had to go this alone. The previous weeks had not boosted her confidence. Hammett had yet another "little session with the Grand Jury" and was told he had to "ready" himself for a possible recall.[107] Then playwright Clifford Odets and director Elia "Gadg" Kazan succumbed to the pressure of the public, the committee, and their own future. Odets insisted he would not name names, insisted he would show them "the face of a radical man." Odets answered the Committee's questions belligerently, but he answered and named many old friends as former communists. Hellman called that "an unpleasant, mysterious ending to the story," guessing the ruin of a Hollywood career was too much for him.[108]

Kazan had not wanted to name names, telling Arthur Miller, Kermit Bloomgarden, and others he would not. He had willingly testified about himself in January and named a few names but not enough to satisfy the Committee. He was recalled in April and folded. The Committee accepted his prepared letter: "I have come to the conclusion that I did wrong to withhold these names before, because secrecy serves the Communists, and is exactly what they want."[109] He not only named names and explained himself in great detail in his mea culpa, he took out a full-page ad the following day in the *New York Times* explaining his rationale. Kazan became a "patriot" to the right, an ultimate "betrayer" to the left. The $500,000 contract he signed the day after he gave his names to the Committee sickened Hellman and hundreds of others like Kim Hunter who respected his talent but no longer respected him.[110] Hellman never forgave him, accusing him of selling out for money. Kazan later referred to her as a "coiled snake."[111]

Hellman had liked and esteemed the men who collapsed under pressure, and she never came to despise Odets as she did Kazan, perhaps because she once held Kazan in high esteem and thought him capable of great integrity. But he betrayed that. Now Hellman wondered: could she, would she, hold up?

As Holliday had said after she slipped through the net rather than challenge the Committee's rights, "You think you're going to be brave and noble. Then you walk in there and there are microphones, and all those senators looking at you."[112] Hellman wasn't used to this kind of stage. She could direct others but had watched herself spiral out of control when she least expected it. As carefully as they had scripted the HUAC hearing, everything could go wrong. She knew she would never be able to live with herself—or with Hammett—if she broke down under questioning. If she went to jail, she didn't know if she could live. In retrospect, neither of these scenarios was likely, but both felt real. Rauh's assistant, Daniel Pollitt, stood at the ready with Hellman's letter, mimeographed, waiting for the slightest legal opening to distribute it to the press. Rauh knew the law. Hellman just worked on not disgracing herself. She prepared herself as a playwright, a director, a woman.

All accounts emphasize her dignity and the care she took with her person. She wore a designer Balmain dress, tailored, brown-and-black checked silk. Her hat fit closely. Some reports say she wore white gloves, others that she twisted a white handkerchief in clasped hands. Some articles call her blonde hair gray. Some note her trim figure. Her formal rigidity and paradoxically soft femininity came through in her testimony.

She sat before the Committee at a witness table, separated from her lawyer, the press, and the crowd by a low wall.[113] Before her, arrayed against her on a slightly curved and elevated dais, sat her interrogators: seven stiff, correct lawyers in dark suits, their air of righteousness palpable. The Honorable John S. Wood, chairman, presided, but Frank S. Tavenner Jr., counsel, did the grilling. His questions seemed friendly for a time as he traced her career. Then he became frustrated and disbelieving when she couldn't remember the precise dates of her tenure in Hollywood. He turned sharper. She kept her focus. Tavenner stepped up the tension by quoting at length from accuser Martin Berkeley's testimony. It incensed her that she couldn't refute it. Tavenner demanded her response. Finally she said, "I would very much like to discuss this with you, Mr. Tavenner, and I would like at this point to refer you to my letter . . . I have worked very hard over this letter, and most seriously. I would like to ask you once again to reconsider what I have said in the letter."[114]

Tavenner paraphrased her, his first misstep: "In other words, you are asking the committee not to ask you any questions regarding the participation of other persons in the Communist Party activities." She kept her head: "I don't think I said that, Mr. Tavenner."

Hellman's testimony made history because Wood stepped in to further clarify: "In order to clarify the record, Mr. Counsel, at this point would it be wise to put into the record the correspondence that has been between the witness and me as chairman of the committee, pertaining to her letter." Tavenner agreed, putting Hellman's May 19 letter and the committee's reply into the record as exhibits 1–2. Rauh's assistant, Pollitt, began passing out copies of the prepared letter, "scurrying back" as quickly as he could to his "lawyer's seat" as the bailiff marched toward him.[115]

Tavenner looked around, exclaiming, "I notice the press is passing around copies. Are those copies being disseminated by you?" Rauh spoke up, "By me, Mr. Tavenner. I thought you had accepted them in the record and that was proper. I am sorry if I had done anything that was not proper."[116] Caught off guard, Tavenner replied, "Not at all. I was just interested to know whether you were prepared to do that before you came here." Rauh said he just wanted to be prepared, wouldn't have done it had it not been part of the record, and now thought it was proper.

Tavenner continued, "The letter by Miss Hellman reads as follows":

Dear Mr. Wood:

As you know, I am under subpoena to appear before your Committee on May 21, 1952.

I am most willing to answer all questions about myself. I have nothing to hide from your Committee and there is nothing in my life of which I am ashamed. I have been advised by counsel that under the Fifth Amendment I have a constitutional privilege to decline to answer any questions about my political opinions, activities, and associations, on the grounds of self-incrimination. I do not wish to claim this privilege. I am ready and willing to testify before the representatives of our Government as to my own opinions and my own actions, regardless of any risks or consequences to myself.

But I am advised by counsel that if I answer the Committee's questions about myself, I must also answer questions about other people and that if I refuse to do so, I can be cited for contempt. My counsel tells me that if I answer questions about myself, I will have waived my rights under the Fifth Amendment and could be forced legally to answer questions about others. This is very difficult for a layman to understand. But there is one principle that I do understand: I am not willing, now or in the future, to bring bad trouble to people who, in my past association with them were completely innocent of any talk or any action that was disloyal or subversive. I do not like subversion or disloyalty in any form, and if I had ever seen any, I would have considered it my duty to have reported it to the proper authorities. But to hurt innocent people whom I knew many years ago in order to save myself is, to me, inhuman and indecent and dishonorable. I cannot and will not cut my conscience to fit this year's fashions, even though I long ago came to the conclusion that I was not a political person and could have no comfortable place in any political group.

I was raised in an old-fashioned American tradition and there were certain homely things that were taught to me: to try to tell the truth, not to bear false witness, not to harm my neighbor, to be loyal to my country, and so on. In general, I respected these ideals of Christian honor and did as well with them as I knew how. It is my belief that you will agree with these simple rules of human decency and will not expect me to violate the good American tradition from which they spring. I would, therefore, like to come before you and speak of myself.

I am prepared to waive the privilege against self-incrimination and to tell you everything you wish to know about my views or actions if your Committee will agree to refrain from asking me to name other people. If the Committee is unwilling to give me this assurance, I will be forced to plead the privilege of the Fifth Amendment at the hearing.

A reply to this letter would be appreciated.

Sincerely yours, Lillian Hellman

By the time the Committee put its refusal on the record, the cat was out of the bag. Members asked her a few more questions, read more long passages from Berkeley's testimony, asked more questions. Hellman answered either "I refuse to answer on the ground that it might incriminate me" or "I must refuse to answer on the same grounds." Mr. Woods objected when she said "must refuse," irritably proclaiming, "You are still not under any compulsion." Hellman replied, "I am sorry. It is a way of talking, I suppose. It is rather hard to cure myself."

Rauh had told her she must not answer three leading questions together, or she would abrogate her lawful ability to take the Fifth. When she answered no twice in regard to previous Communist Party membership, she had to take the Fifth when asked if she had been a Communist Party member three years previously. Many newspapers took that to be an admission of Communist Party membership in 1949, which was not true. Finally Tavenner said that he didn't think that "pursuing the question further would be of any particular help to the committee." No one had further questions.[117] Chairman Wood's only comment was, "Why cite her for contempt? After all, she's a woman."[118]

HUAC's "big show," held in the Old House Office Building's ornate Caucus Room, as big as a basketball court with its two-hundred-foot ceilings, usually didn't shut down until five or six HUAC members provided statements and asked questions. They didn't want to disappoint the large crowds that gathered daily or their local newspapers. On this day it was over quickly, "almost in and out."[119] The Committee closed up shop at 11:37 A.M. and would not reconvene until the following morning.

Making certain Hellman vanished as the curtain over the proceedings swooped down, Rauh hustled Pollitt and Hellman into a getaway taxi. As Brooks Atkinson always said, "A good performance solves all problems in a naughty world."[120] What Hellman and Rauh did was "out-maneuver the House Committee on Un-American Activities through a media ploy."[121] She had to perform flawlessly because the consequences of failure were grim. Legally transcripted, exquisitely performed, Hellman's testimony made the front pages of the press and she made history.

On that morning in mid-May, Hellman made a moral choice. She took the Fifth to avoid contempt charges. She said later she wanted desperately to tell the Committee to go to hell but simply didn't have the nerve for it.[122] She prevailed at public relations, however, and set a courageous example for others. Rauh's office from that point on called this strategy the "Hellman defense." By agreeing to testify about herself—but not others—she had identified the rotten core of the HUAC mission. The Committee wanted ritual shamings, purgings; they staged "degradation ceremonies."[123] She chose a different drama. But they did rein her in for a time. Hellman did not write of HUAC or her part in it for twenty-six years. As blacklisted director Abraham Polonsky noted, "The best kind of censorship is self-censorship . . . that is the effect of Fear."[124] As a member of the press reported, Hellman went into "eclipse about the time Joseph McCarthy began catching Communists in every corner of the country."[125]

Though she maintained silence about her experience, others wrote a lot. She saved the hundreds of letters of thanks and congratulations and pleasure from all over America. From director and critic Harold Clurman: "wonderful, wonderful, wonderful—in feeling, effect, and diction. It strengthens the heart." From actress Anne Jackson: "I am sure you are enjoying the comfort, which is your reward, for keeping your head when all about you, etc." From Mr. Elliott Sullivan: "This is a word of thanks and appreciation from an actor who has been blacklisted out of the entertainment industry after serving it for 22 years." From Mr. and Mrs. Joseph Weinstein: "Good girl—good fashion—good luck. Love." From Mr. Hamilton Basso: "I think you are a nice lady. I like your honesty and your decency, but most of all I like you." From Hannah Weinstein, cable from London: "Excellent Reaction Here. You Were Wonderful." From Anita Alverez: "you are to many of us in the theatre not only a great author but a worthy human being of dignity & courage."

Hellman wrote a thank-you note to each letter. To Diana Trilling, who wrote congratulations: "Dear Diana, It could have been better, but so much had to be covered for so many legal reasons. I was glad I spoke to you the other day, and I will look forward to lunch." One critic conquered (if briefly) was Edna Ferber, noted author of *Showboat* and *Giant*. As Hellman wrote Rauh: "And Miss Edna Ferber, who is a very harsh lady, and none too liberal, told a friend of mine that she had disliked me as long as she had known me, but that I had finally done a good thing."[126] She wrote Melby about her amazement at her reception and the odd mix of congratulation: "A sampling is this: The Bellevue Nurses Assoc. composed, I am told of elderly Catholic ladies, commended me most highly; as did the stuffy luncheon of the American Jewish Congress, as . . . the young leader of Long Island society who told Ruthie Field to tell me she thought it had real 'chic.'"[127]

Of course, others were not so enchanted. A friend wrote her about Walter Winchell's column: "Incidentally, there was a vicious lie in Winchell's last Sunday *Mirror* column . . . it said something to the affect that your appearance on the stand revealed something everybody knew, i.e. That Dorothy Parker was a Communist. . . . I understand you named absolutely no names, and it seems to me Winchell's lying . . . a most vicious thing."[128] What Winchell, meant, however, was that Hellman was a "Fifth Amendment communist." At this moment in time, common wisdom was that anyone who took the Fifth was a communist; anyone who knew someone who took the Fifth—Dorothy Parker—was also a communist.

Battle lines had been drawn; the *New York Herald-Tribune* wrote, "Balky-Witness." The *New York Times*: "Lillian Hellman Balks House Unit: Says She Is Not Red Now, But Won't Disclose If She Was Lest It Hurt Others." Murray Kempton of the *New York Post* wrote with criticism and praise: "Lillian Hellman had been for years one of the ornaments of the pro-Communist milieu of New York and Hollywood." Then, "it is hardly relevant whether Lillian Hellman understands every crime of the Soviet Union yet. It is enough that she has reached into her conscience for an act based on something more than the material or the tactical . . . she has chosen to act like a lady."[129] Hellman had put a chink in HUAC's armor and acted decently.

She suspected more battles to come: "Some instinct tells me that I will now be got at in other ways and through other people. I am foolishly restless and frightened to be alone."[130] Indeed, her "victory" angered inquisitors of all stripes and intensified the desire of Hoover and others to "get her . . . her triumph over HUAC simply increased her visibility as a target."[131] The FBI filled her file with newspaper clippings describing her defiance before HUAC. Records show they increasingly watched her travel, opened her mail, and clipped reviews of her plays. Strangely, even the ACLU was poised to attack her position and Rauh feared their interference. For months, Rauh corresponded with ACLU members on the legality of her position. The ACLU executive committee, deeply divided on how to deal with questions regarding the congressional committees and inclined to duck difficult cases, feared the Committee's gaze would drift their way. They became legally cautious as to the legality of the Fifth. Rauh wrote, "For the ACLU to indicate that such a position is illegal and leaves one open for contempt proceedings is a most frightening prospect for one who has served the organization and who believes so strongly in its purposes."[132] Ultimately, through much legal analysis and citing of precedents, the ACLU gave her stance reluctant if grudging approval.[133]

Before she could feel relief or succumb to political paralysis, Hellman, ever orderly, took care of business. She would not allow herself space to celebrate being a "local heroine" or grieve what she'd lost until she had done all she could to help John Melby, whose political troubles with the State Department Loyalty Security Board seemed wrapped around her.[134] She volunteered to write, witness, or do anything she could to support his case. The board was chary of Hellman's assistance, afraid that as she testified for Melby, she might clear herself and then put the board at odds with the House Committee. They also thought she was a communist who played fast and loose with her past before the Committee. The relationship between Melby and Hellman seemed suspect.

Melby's own record "was without blemish," but given the security board's assumption that Hellman was a communist—and a lover of Melby's—he had little chance to set things right. Melby answered truthfully their questions about Hellman's politics, stating that neither he nor Harriman, ambassador to Russia during Hellman's stay in Moscow, "believed her to be a Communist at all—a fellow traveler in the days gone by, yes, but I never had reason to believe it was more than that."[135] The board kept after him, digging, seeming to know guilty material about Hellman but refusing to tell him its source or content. Melby could not see the board's evidence, had no access to FBI files, and thus could not make a rebuttal. He began to doubt Hellman because he had no way of knowing that the board's "evidence" was based on the hearsay and innuendo. At the end of his June hearing the board invited him "to participate in a typical degradation ceremony, which, if handled correctly," would clear him.[136] Asked at this hearing what his future intentions were in regard to Hellman, Melby replied, "I have no intention of seeing her and I see no reason or cause for it." Humiliating for Melby, who felt forever that Hellman had made a "man of him,"[137] his agreement wasn't enough for the board; it wasn't "categorical."[138]

In July Hellman and Melby met with Joe Rauh to sort out the pair's tangled legal problems. Rauh's concern rocketed for both of them: Hellman's politics were "the crux of the whole problem."[139] The board refused to let Melby, Hellman, Rauh, or other lawyers see the supposed evidence assembled against her. She was furious, knowing she had done nothing illegal, and knowing Melby's worth. The board pounded, questioned, noted inconsistent memories, condemned Hellman as a dangerous, devious, and conniving secret communist. When Hellman and Melby met in September, he asked her to testify for him before the Loyalty Security Board. Although risky for her, she agreed.

A letter to the board written before that testimony set out her position. She was "puzzled" that she had not been called to testify during earlier Melby hearings, adamant that she had done nothing "disloyal or subversive," and was surprised that Melby's record of accomplishment had anything to do with her at all. She hoped they "would feel free to ask me any question about my political activities, and I will answer in full truth."[140] Rauh, Hellman, and Melby met again after Christmas—always a time of sentiment and nostalgia for Melby and Hellman—to strategize. He took her to the airport after the last meeting, sealing his fate. The board affixed an exclamation point next to his admission that he drove her and underlined it in heavy black marker. Twisted thinking and guilt by association made for a sad, disheartening scandal of minute proportions. They made it monumental, nearly ruining Melby's life.

She testified before the board on February 5. They pounded her. She admitted having a "confused" relationship with Melby, which continued after his marriage in 1950, admitted to a poor memory for dates, muddled through their efforts to get her to contradict his earlier memories, but summarized by saying, "It has been a completely personal relationship of two people who once past being in love happen also to be very devoted to each other and very respectful of one another, and who I think in any other time besides our own would not be open to question of the complete innocence of and complete morality, if I may say so, of such people."[141] Hellman unintentionally damned Melby by that statement, which was underlined with marginal gasps from board members. Personal loyalty and bad lawyering in slippery political circumstances—where no evidence can be revealed and what evidence there is can't be disputed—brought it all to an end. Melby once said, "She knew how to make a man feel like a man."[142] Hellman once wrote, "Thanks is much too light a word for what you gave me."[143] Somehow their relationship got twisted into politics. This degradation ceremony didn't go well enough for the board, and it could not indict him. However, his career was over. He was first suspended and then dismissed from State Department duty because he had loved Lillian Hellman.

Interludes: Work, Play, Travel

When trouble struck, Hellman coped by working or fleeing or both. As Hellman fought political battles in Washington, Bloomgarden mounted her revival of *The Children's Hour*, which opened in December 1952. In the frigid atmosphere of a nation riveted by HUAC chronicles, the malicious, ruinous lie at the center of the play had particular relevance. A lack of funding meant that Hellman mounted a barebones production.

She would direct, with Bloomgarden producing. But after the initial showings, Hellman uncharacteristically felt "others" could handle the directing, namely, Del Hughes, the production stage manager. Hellman and Bloomgarden, of course, cast the play together. Hellman had remained friends with Patricia Neal after her 1946 performance in *Another Part of the Forest*, so she drafted her for the revival of *The Children's Hour* in 1952. Hellman and Bloomgarden asked Neal to read the Martha and Karen parts. Neal was so good that they told her she could choose the part she wanted. She chose Martha, with Kim Hunter playing Karen. Neal knew it would be rough with Hellman directing, but she could take it; she had been through it before in *Forest*. Hunter's inner calm and her openness to others stood her in good stead. But Hellman drove Robert Pastene, who played Karen's fiancé, into a nervous collapse.[144] Both Neal and Hunter felt helpless to stop Hellman's brutal direction. They watched her paralyze him and felt "his hatred of her for doing it."[145] Even with her clumsy, heavy-handed directing, Hellman's play drew critical and popular raves, and she was a hit, with 189 performances; she used the profits to payer lawyer bills. (She forever won Neal's friendship by introducing her to Roald Dahl, who became her husband. When Neal later had a stroke, Hellman went to her hospital bed and read to her.)

When times got rough, Hellman held fast to friends and grabbed fun where she could. But nothing gave her much pleasure. Girlfriends mattered more to Hellman now than the men, who all had troubles of their own.[146] When Maggie Kober finally succumbed to multiple sclerosis in May of the bleak year 1951, it wrenched Hellman's heart. Hannah Weinstein, Hellman's confidant, listened and kept her counsel on Hellman's griefs and joys through this particularly rough period.[147] More sad and aimless than gutsy, Hellman coasted during the immediate post-HUAC months, perhaps insecure about what the future would hold. When Arthur Miller's *The Crucible*, directed by the brash genius Jed Harris, and *The Children's Hour Revival* both played in Delaware, she and Harris reignited a half-baked interest in each other stemming from her earliest years with Kober. Now they pursued a short-term fling big on booze and laughter and little else. Arthur Miller told a story of Harris taking an "author's bow" after the first showing of *The Crucible*. Miller looked on stunned as Harris took his place onstage while "Lillian who had taken a fancy to Jed, was doubled over with her choking laughter and Bloomgarden, having learned the word from her, kept repeating, 'Shocking, shocking.'"[148] Hellman loved high jinx yet would never have tolerated such trespass on her own work. But she had known Harris for over twenty years, he had "legendary appeal to women," and being with him was escape—just fun and crazy.[149] Neither took it for more than that. Hellman had always liked Harris and he her, though he could be cruel; he told young theater critic Martin Gottfried that "I have to close my eyes to fuck her."[150] He passed the time during a bad period—the early 1950s.

As she waited for *The Children's Hour* production to settle and the Melby affair to resolve, she turned cautious politically, nervous enough to watch who she saw. She still valued personal friends, no matter their political difficulty. Dorothy Parker, though not called before HUAC "proper," had to testify at a Senate operations hearing. Hellman was stricken by Melby's downward spiral and her unintentional role. Hellman feared for them both but stayed loyal. She began to shy away from those she didn't know that well. She didn't want to add to her political troubles. She had always respected and liked actor and singer Paul Robeson, and the two had appeared together at countless civil rights and Progressive cause events. He had attended many dinners at Hardscrabble during the 1940s, and when Hellman invited the communist Robeson to attend the famed Biltmore dinner for exiled writers in

1941, she wrote, "It will make me feel much better to have you there, and it will make everybody else feel better too."[151] By 1952, with Robeson also under HUAC scrutiny, Hellman no longer thought he would make her feel better. Helen Rosen recalled that "Hellman upbraided her fiercely for having Paul as a fellow dinner guest, insisting his presence put them all in danger since the FBI was known to be following his movements."[152] Of course the FBI was also following her, though she didn't know it. She tried to stay loyal to those under attack, but inevitably fear eroded some relationships.

Between Hellman and Helen Rosen little love was lost, even though Hammett lived rent free in the Rosens' Katonah cabin. Each woman was eager to blame the other for Hammett's poor health and increasing reclusiveness. Rosen thought Hellman bossy and unwelcoming to Hammett. Hellman thought Rosen gossiped about Hammett's economic situation and wasn't careful enough politically, putting Hammett at greater risk. For his part, Hammett seemed to like Helen and worried about Hellman's low spirits more than his own problems. After her hearing, Hammett wrote Hellman, "I love you with the utmost extravagance."[153] Politics increased their worry for each other, but neither could change anything.

As Hellman had feared, HUAC and its many satellite committees decided to go another couple rounds with Hammett. Just after Hellman testified before HUAC, the attorney general of New York, Nathaniel L. Goldstein, filed a civil action against Hammett and other Civil Rights Congress bail-bond trustees and threatened criminal action. Then in 1953 McCarthy, under the guise of the Senate committee on government operations, began inquiries into the federal funds that bought books written by known communists for State Department libraries abroad. Hammett was subpoenaed to explain the presence of his books in those libraries. When questioned under oath, he said he did not believe communism should govern the United States unless most people wanted it. Then he was asked if he were fighting communism whether or not he would buy books by communist authors to be distributed throughout the world. Hammett answered, "If I were fighting Communism I don't think I would do it by giving people any books at all."[154] There was no futher action in this committee.

A few years later, a joint state legislative committee investigating funds and fund-raising in philanthropic communist-front organizations subpoenaed Hammett to testify. Under oath Hammett testified that "Communist to me is not a dirty word. When you're working for the advancement of mankind it never occurs to you if a guy's a Communist or not."[155] Hammett continued to teach at the Jefferson School and "meticulously to sign petitions, lend his name to causes, put up a couple dollars when he could."[156] He did not abandon leftist causes under attack. Hellman did not change her beliefs, but she dropped her political activism for nearly a decade. Events justified her caution.

Desperate with tension, she wanted out of Washington, out of New York, out of the United States. She felt she had done all she could for herself, for Hammett, and for Melby, and wanted to go to Europe to write a screenplay for Alexander Korda. She had a contract for a "shockingly" low salary but needed money and the work that always helped her straighten out in times of trouble.

But first the government required her to play a few more scenes in the drama of the political 1950s. Once again she sought a passport, with little hope. It was nearly unheard of for HUAC-unfriendly witnesses to receive one. To apply, the government required her to write yet another of her numerous letters to Mrs. Shipley. This one was a complete promise of political abdication: "I wish to repeat here our conversation of yesterday, and to do so under oath: I am not a member of the Communist Party and I have no affiliation with the Communist Party of any kind whatsoever. Any association that I did have in the past ended in the year 1940 and never from that day to this has it ever been resumed in any sense. In any case—although most certainly I do not wish to stand on technicalities—my association was of the most casual nature and never included anything more than the discussion of current events or books on philosophy and history." She went on to admit being "a member of many left-wing organizations, but I have never done anything that could be considered disloyal or subversive. Nor have I ever witnessed such acts or heard such talk from anybody else." What she would not do for the HUAC hearing, she did for Mrs. Shipley. She talked about the communist disapproval of her and of her play *Watch on the Rhine*. She went on, "However, I do not wish to use such attacks, either from the political right or the political left, in the rather shabby way I think they have been used by many people. Like most other people, I have made mistakes, but I feel guilty of nothing and I am secure in the belief that I have never done more than exercise my rights as an American citizen."[157] Shipley granted her request and Hellman left for Italy.

Arriving in Rome relieved, almost exultant, she said in a letter, "I am in love with Rome." In another, "I went to High Mass. I am still a Jew," and in another "I feel ever so much more cheerful and happily without plans." She met friends Sam and Frances Goldwyn, Joe and Bobbie Weinstein, and her old standby lover, Jed Harris. She wrote wittily of Harris's antics during a hospital stay for possible cancer that turned out to be a stomach ailment. Hellman posed as the concerned wife. She loved seeing him but was disgusted with herself for liking it so much. He probably was the "wrong man" who enticed her to break a vow of celibacy made when she and Hammett fell into political trouble. As she later told an interviewer, "I made some kind of idiot bargain that I would lead a very pure life if we were allowed to survive . . . doesn't sound like a grown woman, does it?[158] Regardless, the celibacy did not last for long.

The reality of work moved in quickly amid the relief, the social whirl, and the usual madness of putting a script together. Competing personalities pulled at the writer and the script Korda wanted her to adapt: Jessica Mitford's *The Blessing*. The whole project was ill conceived and salary trouble was exacerbated by the impending bankruptcy of Korda's company. The fancy hotels of the past were just a memory, though Hellman stayed in a "frightfully expensive hotel off the Via Ludovisi" before moving to a small, self-contained apartment. She watched her money carefully. She had money to spend but felt broke compared to past extravagance. "I am determined to live on my expense money and so I have learned to take buses which is an experience since, without a language or a sense of direction, anything is likely to happen, and does."[159]

She played the suffering survivor when she met up with artist Stephen Greene. They became friends and saw a great deal of each other. She admired him; at thirty-six he was already a prize-winning artist. They gossiped and she cooked for him. He later remarked about the myriad contradictions of her personality, her romantic, passionate nature that allowed her to have a series of lovers while never ceasing to care for Hammett. He admired her because she was "warm and compassionate and kind. But when it really came push to shove, she had demons at her all the time."[160] Hellman adored Greene but missed Hammett. She missed Melby. She missed her life. Greene insisted she was not alone, but loneliness haunted her. She felt scared and vulnerable even as she felt relief at her freedom and gratitude at the opportunity for work. Not sure who she was at this point, she concentrated on living day to day.

Trying to piece together her shattered identity, she wrote demanding letters in tones of haughty disregard or humble supplication to her secretary, Lois Fritsch: call Kober, call Dash, call Kermit. Call Hannah Weinstein. Send a cable, send a letter, send an explanation. Send a list of clothing. "Find references or innuendo about me in the *New Statesman* and send." "Where is the car? WHERE is the car?" She begged Fritsch to tell her why her affairs seemed inefficiently run, trying not to blame Fritsch but doing so all the same. She berated, cajoled, and sympathized to get more information.

Everyday troubles worried her. She learned that Flora, her beloved poodle, had died, and she admitted crying. She had "menstruated in an appalling amount for about nine or ten days—and appalling is the exact word: I ruined dresses, coats, and the steps of hotels." She feared she needed an operation and wanted Dr. Kilroe in New York. Hellman, out of New York, was out of control. "I don't think I have ever felt quite so cut off from the house or business."[161] Forty-eight years old, beginning the hormonal dysfunctions of middle age, Hellman wanted health and security. Although she ultimately took estrogen to relieve her menopausal symptoms, her health and security were at risk.

For the first time, Hellman had exiled herself, geographically and literally. It worked for a while; she had time to reflect, to settle herself, to breathe. But political fear lingered. "The last two years, and this period of recovery in Europe has given me a real hatred of trouble that does not have to be and malice that does not have to exist."[162] Fear and suspicion lurked in corners, making her frantic. She often advised Fritsch to make sure Hammett had money, to look in on him every couple days without him knowing Hellman asked her to, to give Hammett every address change, "but not on the phone." Every letter, no matter how witty, how filled with activity, also dropped the curtain on full disclosure: "Will you put this envelope in another & mail to Melby?" "I am sending a letter for John. Don't send it to the office. And the news is bad—he has been fired. It's just too sickening to think about."

She suspected her cables and letters were intercepted. She shied away from strangers. Hammett's court appearance had her "dodging reporters." "I have been a little nervous these last few days for reasons that you can guess. Remember . . . when we had a gentleman visitor from the TV business only we thought him somebody else?" She had more mystery visitors. She stopped using hotel phones. She sent Hannah Weinstein money, saying to her it was "for reasons which will be gone into only when I see you." She would have been considered paranoid if it hadn't all been real: CIA files indicate that the government was still keeping tabs.

She finally left Rome for Milan, Paris, England, and home. She wrote she was "very sad . . . to be leaving Rome. This is the first time in a good two years that I have felt the lifting of burdens, and I shall always love the city for giving it to me." In personal disarray when she arrived, Hellman had depended more than ever on her identity as a writer. As her mentor, Hammett wrote in his last unfinished novel, *Tulip:* "A writer writes for 'fame, fortune, and personal satisfaction' . . . that is and should be your goal. Anything less is kind of piddling."[163] Hellman never piddled. She needed to work to live, and it gave her focus in the face of loss. In Italy she was gainfully employed; she was writing. But as she explained, "I have always believed that my place was home and my duty was there, also."[164]

She went home to renew her life, to revitalize it without political involvement. Politics had been a life force, but for nearly a decade she avoided its snares. She concentrated on regaining a position of influence and interest on Broadway. Her success paid the tax man and his penalties, and she had enough left over to buy a small house on the beaches of Martha's Vineyard. She swam, she fished, she started love affairs. She wrote for the theater.

Stooping Fatally to Conquer

In 1955 Hellman broke her promise never to adapt again and brought to Broadway her version of Jean Anouilh's *The Lark*, the story of Joan of Arc. Daringly, Hellman presented Joan as "a crop-haired, sensible little warrior . . . less a press-agent symbol than an exalted gamin who understands the weaknesses of the men she inspires."[165] Hellman called her Joan "the first career girl," though *Theatre Arts* asserted, "This Joan is a man of action."[166]

Writing *The Lark*, "a crisp and shining new version of the Joan of Arc story," was not without travail; some of it was like the mix-ups she had with *Montserrat:* translation, cultural changes of perception, and personality clashes with various people—from John Simon, one of the student translators she tried to get on the cheap, to Jan van Loewen, Anouilh's agent-attorney, to Joseph Anthony, the relatively unknown young man Hellman chose to direct. She and Anthony had their predictable blowup. She alternately played haughty employer to hired hand and naughty older woman to naive younger man. The more insecure Hellman felt, the more she acted out. And insecurity was the order of the day, even in the theater.

Hellman hired Anthony for his talent and low fees. When she consistently second-guessed his directing, he called her bluff. She then retreated a bit but continued signaling her agreement or disagreement as she sat behind him at rehearsal. His threats to quit resulted in a tense impasse, which ironically was resolved when a difficult actor stopped rehearsal to say he didn't feel comfortable because he didn't have anything to do. Anthony, fed up, whispered, "Jerk off." Hellman "erupted in her now famous rusty-ratchet laugh," so amused that "she wet herself" and had to go to the ladies room. After that, they "got along fine."[167] Hellman sought to paralyze the weak but respected those who showed strength. As Hellman's Joan says, "I am not a witch. But I have a charm."[168]

Starring Julie Christie, *The Lark* won both raves and box-office receipts in its 229 performances at the venerable old Longacre Theatre on West 48th

Street, which held fourteen hundred playgoers in the illusion of intimacy.[169]
Audiences and critics alike greeted both the script and Julie Christie's acting with excitement, even awe. Christie's performance was "electrifying"
and "triumphant." She won "bravos" on her first night's performance and
won a Tony for best actress of the season. Christie even attended the after-
performance party at the Plaza, reluctantly, as she claimed she would "rather
submit to the water drip than attend any party, anywhere."[170] But Hellman
and producer Bloomgarden had prevailed on her goodwill, and the success
made her generous. Press agent Richard Maney was the "bearer of hot tid-
ings." Hellman won nearly universal though muted praise for a script that
managed to take Anouilh's solidly reasoned play and give it stage power.
Christie outshone everyone in the excellent production, including Boris
Karloff and Christopher Plummer, who both won Tony nominations for their
acting, as well as director Joseph Anthony, whom critics mostly ignored.
Once on stage, a production has a life of its own, and in this one it was
Christie who gave it that life.

A huge box-office and critical success, *The Lark* earned Hellman enough
money to buy a house on over three acres with a private beach at Martha's
Vineyard. The house had a separate apartment in a three-story turret that
seemed tailor-made for the ailing and increasingly reclusive Hammett, who
had a heart attack in 1955. Increasingly ill but hesitant to move in with
Hellman, he visited and then became what he called a "permanent guest" in
August 1958. Hellman's new summer house restored an optimism she
thought she had lost with her farm. She quickly made friends and enemies on
the island, becoming part of the community. In New York she worked, performing the spectacle of the great playwright. At Mill House, as she called it,
she tended a vegetable garden, wrote at her desk, swam in the morning, invited guests for cocktails, and cooked each evening. Theatrical even here, she
played out the softer version of Lillian Hellman, the great playwright.

With renewed confidence, Hellman felt high on possibility. Leonard
Bernstein had composed the musical backdrop for *The Lark*, and Hellman
thought it brilliant. So even before the play opened to raves, Bernstein and
Hellman had begun thinking about doing a show together. Hammett probably
greeted the project with less enthusiasm as he didn't have much use for
Bernstein, whom he called "a homo-exhibitionist."[171] The issue of who approached whom has never been settled, but as early as 1951 Bernstein wrote
friend Helen Coates, "I know nothing about working with Lillian H., but I
would of course love to. I think I'll write her."[172] Thus, two arrogant, demanding, and high-strung talents gave birth to *Candide*, "a score swaddled in a book

by Lillian Hellman which, though heavy-handed and humorless, served the music well," according to a *Daily News* reviewer.[173] *Candide* proved a catastrophe for Hellman. Too many talents and too much ego created havoc in this operatic adaptation of Voltaire's classic. Explosive, dazzling theater should have come out of Leonard Bernstein's remarkable musical talent, Hellman's dramatic sense, Richard Wilbur's lyric poetry, Dorothy Parker's wit, John Latouche's lyrics, and Jack Cole's choreography. It did not. The Bernstein/Hellman duo never agreed on what held the center of the drama: the action or the music? The dialogue or the lyrics? Peter Brooks of *Opera News* reported that "during heated bull sessions at Bernstein's and Hellman's hideaways on Martha's Vineyard, it soon became clear that Hellman was not a born collaborator, and catfights ensued."[174] A catfight takes at least two cats, and these cats were something else. Bernstein, who behind her back called Hellman "Uncle Lillian," did not appreciate the importance of a tight plot or dialogue that moved the play forward. For him, the play was a scaffold for music.

Starting out as a light, satirical musical in keeping with Voltaire's text, Bernstein's music soon "veered from light musicale to serious operetta."[175] Hellman, trying to follow his wavering lead, rewrote and amended and shifted and ended up with a script that some critics today insist is "unwieldy and unfunny"[176] or "tedious" and "pretentious."[177] Hellman's inherent wit and gift for dialogue seemed less an issue than Bernstein's switch to serious. They never decided on tone or a consistent vision; Hellman did not understand a play loosely woven around musical pieces. For two years and through fourteen rewrites the two battled. Poet Richard Wilbur, a friend of Hellman's, replaced LaTouche as lyricist, literature apparently winning over music in that round, but then Bernstein "toyed" with the lyrics and alienated Wilbur.

Candide became a production nightmare. Director Tyrone Guthrie wrote, "Hellman fought this battle with one hand tied behind her back. We had all agreed that when necessity demanded we would choose singers to do justice to the score, rather than actors who could handle the text. . . . Consequently, line after line, situation after situation, fell flat on its face. . . . Miss Hellman stooped fatally to conquer."[178] Conquer she did not. Guthrie could manage the actors but lost control of the production overall. Hellman shoved him out for a week and directed until he forced his return. Though bloodied by behind-the-scenes wrangling, Barbara Cook, who played Cunegonde, says Bernstein, Hellman, and Guthrie always appeared professional in public.[179] The façade came at a cost to all. Brooks, referring to Voltaire's ill-fated character, observed that "not even a cock-eyed optimist like Dr. Pangloss could have found a silver lining in this pre-opening storm cloud."[180]

When the operetta opened at the Martin Beck on December 1, 1956, it became clear that Bernstein had won the tug-of-war. The reviews were mixed but uniformly praised *Candide* as a "musical feast," with Bernstein's score "magnificent" and "exhilarating." Wilbur's wife, Charlee, wrote Hellman, "Most of the publicity I have seen of late comes by way of Lennie who spreads all over the American cultural scene like a skunky mulch."[181] Many reviews praised Hellman's attempt, but as one critic noted, Hellman's "precise talents do not lie in the vein of elegant vaudeville." The FBI included one review of *Candide* in its file: "Miss Hellman has taken good care that the real Voltaire, who at the risk of his life struck heavy blows at persecution and prejudice, shines through every scene of this stunning production."[182]

The Hellman script is clever, wry, sometimes subtle, and not the cloddy script some critics saw at opening. She received a Tony nomination for a script that is hilarious. A snippet shows the satiric tenor. One of the characters is "Lilybelle of Castile," a horse with the movable face that shoves the hapless Candide. Covering the curtain is an insert stating "Supplementing Faded Charms." All is written in high humor, consistent with Voltaire's satirical optimism. The dialogue is silly-satiric but fun: "Lady: bon soir, monsieur. You are bemused with wine?" Candide: "Oh, no, sir. I am bemused with weariness." Lady (angry): "I am not a sir. I am a madame."[183] But satire on the page did not transfer to the stage. *Candide* closed after seventy-three performances.

Years later Hellman wrote Bernstein a narrative entitled "The History of the Record." "The first book I did was a good book, I think. . . . For various reasons, some of them my fault, some of them your fault, some of them Guthrie's fault, the book was altered, cut and tailored . . . but no matter how much justice was on your side, you did not know enough about the theatre, you do not now, to do much more than flounder around trying to help us all and most of the time keeping us edgy about ourselves." She said the price she paid wasn't the failure of a production. "For two years after *Candide* I could do no decent work, was sick about myself, and only recovered when I figured out that it was not the failure that had worried me . . . but my panicked passivity about a business I knew more about than the rest of you."[184] She then quoted something Tyrone Guthrie said to Wilbur during the furor of production: "Lillian is almost always right, but Lennie is more charming."

When literary agent Robbie Lantz wrote her about the production's closing, she replied, "I think it is the saddest story I have ever known in the theater: a valuable property now ruined forever, and ruined out of vanity and ignorance. Maybe just as important, old friendships, Lennie's and mine, yours and mine, gone as if we were silly children, unable to control our lives. Disgusting waste, all of it."

Hellman didn't easily forgive Bernstein for what she saw as his usurpation of her show. But she loved his wife, Felicia, and after a time of swearing and public reprisal, she seemed to let it go. She was sick with disappointment and sick of Bernstein. Apparently he had charged the production company $25,000 for "supervising," which came out of their royalties. When the others challenged him, he said he didn't deal with "contracts or money." Wilbur protested but had no rights, and Hellman let it drop because "I was frightened of scandal for all of us, and that is the truth."

In 1971 when *Candide* played in Washington, she received an apology from Bernstein. Still irked, she replied that he apologized for the "wrong things." She expressed friendship to both Lennie and Felicia and closed the letter with a joke, asking him to call her so they could all meet in friendship: "I can't call you because my Mama told me boys had to call girls."[185] But Hellman ultimately exacted a small revenge. In 1978, twenty-one years after *Candide's* opening thud, Hellman was asked to speak on national TV to celebrate Leonard Bernstein's sixtieth birthday. Jo Hammett remembered, "When Lillian took the podium, beautifully dressed as always, she spoke eloquently for about five minutes—with not one word about Bernstein but a glowing and fond remembrance of his wife, who had recently died. It was perfectly Lillian—moving, apparently sincere, and, I have no doubt, it properly skewered the maestro."[186]

Trouble and Triumph

Hellman's troubles with *Candide* were both professional and personal. She felt diminished and frustrated by her work on the musical, and friendships among the all-star collaborators began to fray. One of the friendships she prized most was with Dorothy Parker. After *Candide*, Hellman began to worry about her. The two women loved to laugh together and they continued to enjoy each other's company, but Parker was drinking too much. After the years of Hammett's hard drinking, Hellman had lost her tolerance for drunks, and Parker increasingly lost herself in drink. "When they were together, Hellman tried to limit Parker to one drink, for purposes of relaxation. This might seem sensible to a nonalcoholic, but for Dorothy it amounted to abstinence. The self-denial, the torment of being unable to assuage her craving, was the same."[187] Hellman loved Parker sober but would settle for "tight."

Drunk she could not take. Hellman could never understand how Parker and Hammett gave themselves "bad-beatings for a great many years."[188] Parker put up with Hellman's bossiness and restrictions, but Hellman grew tired of Parker's game of "flattering people to their faces and then once they had left declaring, 'Did you ever meet such a shit?'" Patricia Neal heard Parker do exactly that to actor Percy Waram at the first-night party for *Forest*.[189] Hellman defended Parker, however, saying Dottie did it out of fright. Time with her had become "weari-some."[190] Hellman felt guilty about her impatience. She never lost touch and always wrote with affection, but began to put distance between them.

Hellman's sometime friend and rival playwright, Ruth Goetz, judged the Hellman/Parker friendship as unequal, saying that Parker admired Hellman, but Hellman was so "frantic for male company" that she "was never a good friend to a woman."[191] Hellman certainly loved men, if aggressively, and men flocked to her. But Hellman also liked women and she loved Dottie Parker. Troubles, her own and other people's, weighed her down.

In the mid-1950s the world of the theater and the world of politics exploded in a public controversy with Hellman at the center. Though some saw her as a hero for refusing to name names in the House Un-American Activities Committee, others saw her as a ball-busting Stalinist. Such animosity—both iron fisted and knife edged—can be seen in the senseless brouhaha launched by writer Meyer Levin over his failure to mount a Broadway production of *The Diary of Anne Frank*. He accused Anne Frank's father, Otto, producer Cheryl Crawford, producer Kermit Bloomgarden, and Hellman of stealing his chance to produce his own script. Levin's clamor for vindication was as odd as it was rancorous.

It began for Hellman when producer Cheryl Crawford, finding Levin's draft wanting, asked Hellman, along with others including Carson McCullers, to do the adaptation. Hellman turned her down, saying the diary was "a great historical work which will probably live forever, but I couldn't be more wrong as the adapter. If I did this it would run one night because it would be deeply depressing. You need someone who has a much lighter touch."[192] She suggested Frances Goodrich and Albert Hackett as adapters.

When the writing couple came up with a first draft, Bloomgarden asked Hellman to read it; both she and Bloomgarden gave it a thumbs-down: too light, few dramatic undercurrents, not enough fear of the Nazi threat to Jews, too little war context. The Hacketts wrote eight more drafts, asking Hellman to read only the sixth. Hellman gave "brilliant advice on construc-tion" but otherwise was uninvolved.[193] Director Garson Kanin is the man credited with having "immense" and pervasive influence on the production and tone of the Goodrich/Hackett play.[194] *The Diary of Anne Frank* opened to rave reviews at Broadway's Cort Theatre on October 5, 1955, and won the Pulitzer Prize for drama. As Hammett said, "Everybody is very happy about it—those that aren't jealous."[195]

By the time the play opened, Levin had sued, finally settling out of court in 1957. The agreement gave Levin $15,000 to renounce his claims and stop the ads, publications, and public rants about Broadway cheating him. He agreed. Discovering Hellman's involvement, however peripheral, he once again spiraled out of control. As David Goodrich put it, Levin insisted "he was the victim of a powerful conspiracy; a cabal of powerful, theater-world Jews of German descent . . . [who had] suppressed his play because he wasn't like them and because his play was 'too Jewish.'"[196] He insisted that Hellman was the leader of a Stalinist conspiracy and had somehow convinced everyone (including Otto Frank) to "de-Judaize and universalize the text." He attacked her in his memoirs and fiction, and to anyone who would listen. For the next fifty years the controversy raged as books and articles revisited his charges.[197] Hundreds of pages in the Bloomgarden archives chronicle the inflamed antics surrounding Levin's effort to discredit the production. One handwritten word atop the folder reads "crazy?"[198]

"Dramaturgical reasons, not ideological ones, led to any advice Hellman gave in opposition to Levin, if indeed she gave that advice," argued writer and political critic Victor Navasky.[199] She certainly did not expect political blame and upheaval on a theatrical matter peripheral to her own career. For twenty years Broadway's glittering lights had spotlighted her achievements. In the early days she rejoiced in the exposure, sharing the Plaza's breakfast herring and lamb chops with reporters as they ogled the young, unlovely but stunning playwright. Over the years, she had matured into a theatrical and political presence whose drama and charisma sucked the air out of any room she entered. Getting embroiled in petty theatrical blame games added to her disenchantment with the theater. Her newly resurrected political interests supplied plenty of crises, and after *Candide* and the Levin debacle, she stayed away from Broadway for a time.

Hollywood Flirtation

Disenchanted with Broadway and its politics, perhaps having forgotten the absurdity of Hollywood politics, she agreed to try writing for film again.

She had renounced the film industry in 1948, when the producers blacklisted her. But she always resisted giving up entirely on the people and places in her life and was not wholly surprised when Goldwyn called her out of the blue in 1958 or 1959 (Hellman remembered about 1960), after the blacklist began to lift: "My phone rang and Mr. Goldwyn's secretary said he had been trying to reach me for two days to ask if I wanted to write *Porgy and Bess*. After a long wait Mr. Goldwyn's voice said, "Hello Lillian, Hello. Nice of you to call me after all these years. How can I help you?"[200] But the deal fell through; Goldwyn had a myriad of troubles making *Porgy and Bess*, and at one point he had asked William Wyler to replace Rouben Mamoulian as director. Wyler may have suggested Hellman to adapt the script. In any event, Goldwyn hired Otto Preminger, and both Wyler and Hellman were out. But Goldwyn's move signaled the possibility that the changing political climate might improve Hellman's status in filmmaking. She was right, but the change was slower than she expected.

As the 1960s began, she began to hear from producers once again. Producer David O. Selznick had apparently written to offer her a contract for the script adaptation of F. Scott Fitzgerald's *Tender Is the Night*, and she eagerly agreed to sign. When Selznick found that Hellman's name was still on the blacklist, he went elsewhere. But he worried that he wasn't getting the expertise he needed, and he asked her to do a detailed critique of the script. He wrote to producer Henry Weinstein that he had asked Hellman to "give us detailed criticisms of our lines, criticisms we studied very carefully." Selznick was afraid that the script did not have what Fitzgerald had called "the sound of my generation."[201] After losing the contract for the full adaptation, Hellman charged Selznick a fat fee for her criticisms, enjoying the interplay of his need and fear. Selznick ultimately sold the production rights to Twentieth Century Fox. After twelve years many producers favored lifting the blacklist for quality films, but some did not have the nerve. No one wanted to be the first to violate the decade-long blacklist.

Hellman, burned earlier that year when Selznick reneged, was cautious. But she eagerly contemplated wading back into the Hollywood scene. Finally, in 1961 Wyler met Hellman in Rome to discuss the possibility of collaborating on a remake of *The Children's Hour*. At that time the Hays Code had relaxed a bit, and Wyler proposed they make the movie again, using the play's original lesbian motif—something they couldn't do in the earlier film called *These Three*. Hellman first turned him down, then said she'd think about it. She wrote Wyler that his daughter Cathy was "right and I was wrong. I have done a little research and without question very young ladies now know what Lesbianism is, although I hope they don't know the details."[202] Whatever "research" she did, given her lack of subtlety, certainly gives one pause, but Wyler had clearly piqued her interest. She went on to say that "we" will have to "take care of this" in the script. She had, however, promised Harvard University she would teach writing in the spring of 1961, and she would not go back on on her promise. She would "do the polish" for the script if someone else would do the initial writing. Given the sorry salary even the Ivy League could pay Hellman to teach writing, her adamant refusal shows her firm belief in following through on commitments, in keeping promises. She didn't mention it in her letter, but Dashiell Hammett was dying and she was taking care of him. She simply could not do the film justice and she knew it.

Not to be ignored, however, she later wrote "Dearest Willie" with suggestions for writers. As usual Hellman wanted the best—a woman who became one of the foremost American writers of the century: "I have had a wonderful idea, if the rumor that she is very sick is only a rumor. Her name is Flannery O'Connor."[203] O'Connor, a fellow southerner from Savannah, Georgia, had a style completely unlike Hellman's, but *Time* magazine called her writing "highly unladylike . . . a brutal irony, a slam-bang humor, and a style of writing as balefully direct as a death sentence."[204] She fit Hellman's requirements. But O'Connor was ill with lupis (she died only three years later), and Hellman and Wyler chose John Michael Hayes to adapt. Hayes had a history of writing controversial scripts and getting them approved: *Peyton Place, Butterfield 8*, and *The Rat Race*. Hellman toyed with setting the new production in England, insisting they consider "a wonderful young actor called Peter O'Toole for Cardin." She pondered whether the film would be effective if set in the 1880s. Her letter details her excitement in returning to film with a new Hellman project, but it wasn't quite hers this time. And as usual Hellman did not like Hayes's results; she spent only minimal time on the polish, having once again become wary about Hollywood and its promises. Though it had a star-studded cast with Audrey Hepburn and Shirley MacLaine playing Karen and Martha, the film got only so-so reviews, failing to "arouse the imagination." As film critic Bernard Dick sums up, "Hellman was her own best adapter . . . *The Children's Hour* will reveal its secrets only to its author; to others, it behaves like a silent oracle."[205] Wyler called it a flop. Hellman was neither ashamed nor proud of the film, merely tired of high hopes later dashed.

Back to Broadway: A Hit

The disappointments on Broadway and in Hollywood would have hurt Hellman more had she not been writing a new, original play that she thought good, reviving her self-respect and reigniting her pride in her career. The triumph of *Toys in the Attic* again raised Hellman to the glorified heights of the Broadway marquees, winning her a Drama Circle Award for best play and a Tony nomination for best play. Best of all, after opening in February 1960, it ran for an astonishing 556 performances at the Hudson Theatre. *Toys* was a shining and brilliant production.

In *Toys in the Attic* Hellman went back to a place and time she knew, New Orleans. The play is tightly plotted and intricately woven. Hammett gave her the theme of the play when he said, out of the blue, perhaps referring to himself, "There's this man. Other people, who say they love him, want him to make good, be rich. So he does it for them and finds they don't like him that way, so he fucks it up, and comes out worse than before. Think about it."[206] She did, but later told him she couldn't write about a man, so she focused on the women around him. She turned to her own family to make the drama, the parallels striking but not exact, exaggerated but not ludicrous. The psychological realism holds. Hellman reached deep into the family psyche, took herself out of it to write it, and dramatized a legacy of good and evil, strength and weakness, fantasy and reality.

The action rests on the Berniers family: two sisters, Carrie and Anna, an overly beloved and spoiled brother, Julian, and his fey wife, Lily. Albertine Prine, Lily's mother, provides the cynical counterpoint to the nearly incestuous plot. Prine's affair with an African American chauffeur stirs the erotic mix. Carrie and Anna's slavish devotion to their brother excludes all others and narrows their own lives. Julian's wife, Lily, adores him and refuses to acknowledge his cheating. The three women's loving excess poisons their sense of self. The violence of desire, spiritual and secular, works through the play. When Julian suddenly brings riches to the family, each character is set in motion, drawing parallels between lust and greed.

Hellman's ear for southern speech never left her and the dialogue is both luscious and laconic. One sister says to the other, "You lusted—and it showed." In an entirely different tongue, Lily, steeped in romance, speaks of her wedding day: "It was all days to me: Cold and hot days, fog and light, and I was on a high hill running down with the top of me, and flying with the left of me, and singing with the right of me—(softly) I was doing everything nice anybody had ever done nice."[207] Harold Clurman in his capacity as critic gave Hellman her due, saying the dialogue approached "nobility."[208] Hellman added just enough music to move the pacing and evoke New Orleans: Marc Blitzstein wrote "Bernier Day," and Hellman added lyrics to his "French Lessons in Songs." Though the success of her libretto in *Candide* may have prompted this move, the opera's failure had "haunted" her. Hellman wrote twenty-three drafts of *Toys* before she was satisfied.

At fifty-five, Hellman showed her dramatic maturity and stagecraft in every aspect of the play. Bloomgarden produced and Jason Robards played Julian. They both almost turned it down to do Saul Levitt's *The Andersonville Trial.* Bloomgarden cabled Hellman, "I told you not to assume anything stop after night of soul searching both Jason and I decided there are many andersonvilles but only one Lillian Hellman we'll stick with you.["209] Maureen Stapleton played Carrie, and Anne Revere played Anna. Both Robards and Stapleton were nominated for Tonys, and Revere won the Tony as best actress for her performance.

Arthur Penn directed and Howard Bay created a set that won him a Tony as well. The cast was first-rate—as usual in a Hellman production—but for the most part she let Penn deal with the actors. This was good news for her and the show. Hellman only chided Revere once, "affectionately," for saying something in an interview that Hellman thought undermined the play. Irene Worth played an excellent Albertine Prine. She was so much like Hellman's grandmother Sophie that Hellman feared her strength threatened to take over the play. Some rewriting and Worth's nuanced performance made it perfect. Professionals of the highest order made *Toys in the Attic* a classic.

Of course, even in a hands-off mode, Hellman didn't just write the script and give the director the go-ahead. Stapleton had been forewarned that Hellman was "cranky," but she loved her and could work with her; they became friends. Some of the other actors and actresses, however, could not handle the intensity. As Stapleton said, "They would wilt.["210] One night the two women had dinner together and were on their way back to the Hudson Theatre to discuss rehearsal. Stapleton told her, "Lillian, it was terrific . . . when you go back don't give the benefit of your wonderful opinion; just try not to destroy their feelings . . . just encourage them; don't give them the benefit of your brilliant brain. Just talk nice." Hellman agreed. They got back to the theater and Stapleton took a seat at the back as Hellman went down the aisle. "She's going in, and she gets halfway down and she turns around and screams, 'I can't do it, I can't do it! I can't make nice!' I said, 'oh God, God.'"[211] Stapleton also believed that Hellman was "involved" with Arthur Penn during production, which gave him some leverage over her. Hellman took care of the script and had fun with the production but held her breath until she heard the reviews.

Most critics proclaimed that Hellman's play was "brilliant," one adding that the "text operated like strokes of a surgical blade.["212] To be sure, some grumbled about "manipulated action." Harold Clurman, who had directed the bland *Autumn Garden*, complained that the "play is congested by irrelevantly melodramatic turns in plot, implausibilities and jags of lurid violence."[213] But it was oh-so-southern, oh-so-psychologically real. Even those who had reservations called it "head and shoulders above the level of the season."[214] Hellman's power had not receded, but she had shifted her focus from "greed to need as the root cause of human suffering."[215] If other critics were incensed by the Freudian influence, the sexual innuendo, the slick theme, it hardly mattered to Hellman. *Toys* was a critical and financial success. The box office held strong for months; when it began to wane, she cut her profits in half to keep the production going. Hellman recalled, "The money came at the right time."[216]

Hellman was grateful that Hammett, even though ailing, "lived long enough to have great pleasure from the play, and the last trip he ever made was to Boston for the opening."[217] Sick, angry, and hateful as the dying can be, Hammett, complete with tuxedo, saw the curtain rise on one of Hellman's greatest successes. But his response to the play was not the pure pleasure that Hellman implied. He railed at her, calling the play a "piece of shit!" He complained bitterly about myriad mistakes, scenes gone wrong, speeches that didn't work.[218] Whether Hellman understood his anger as part of his illness or had the wisdom to keep quiet, she said nothing. She knew Hammett had given her much in his life and knew the cost to them both. She knew the strength of the play and the costs of the obsessive love the play depicted. *Toys* rested on that knowledge. Hammett had demanded her excellence, had abhorred the second-rate. She had worked hard and long with great brilliance to prove her worth, first to Hammett and later to herself.

Toys in the Attic was Hellman's paean to Hammett. She used the play to show her grateful acknowledgment of his success with her. As playwright Marsha Norman understood, "Lillian Hellman appreciated that lots of times you used plays, used the writing of plays to have conversations that you would otherwise not be able to have."[219] Hammett held the place of mythic hero in Hellman's scheme of things; it wasn't that Hellman made Hammett mythic for the world to see. She felt she owed him. He had anchored her emotionally for the length of their relationship. However fraught with angst, Hellman had become a writer under his expert if brutal tutelage, producing a run on Broadway that lasted the length of their relationship. He had helped create the woman she had become—Lillian Hellman, playwright.

7

DEATH AND RESURRECTION

DASHIELL HAMMETT DIED OF LUNG CANCER ON JANUARY
10, 1961. He was sixty-seven years old, and he had lived on his own terms. In
spring 1960, his daughter Jo and her family had visited Martha's Vineyard. As Jo
said, "It was to be the last time I saw my father, and we all knew it . . . part of
him was already gone."[1] But he lived through the summer and winter, sometimes lucid and laughing, other times disoriented and angry. Hellman wrote
movingly of Hammett's death—her hope that he did not know he was dying of
lung cancer, and her admiration for his courage and dignity in his infirmity. On
New Year's Eve 1960, Hellman went out and came home just after midnight to
a panicked practical nurse who said Hammett was irrational. He refused all
help in a kind of "mysterious wariness," but he had to go to Lenox Hill Hospital
in Manhattan. Several days later the hospital called to say he had gone into a
coma. Hellman wrote, "As I ran across the room toward his bed there was a last
sign of life: his eyes opened in shocked surprise and he tried to raise his head.
He was never to think again and he died two days later."[2]

Dashiell Hammett's death left the fifty-five-year-old Hellman with the profound grief of a woman losing a man at the center of her emotional and
creative life. He had become family. No longer her lover, he had remained
mentor, companion, partner. Hammett shaped her integrity, her creativity,
her life. She wrote to please him, her primary audience—always. What had
made their life together and apart disappeared: his whores, their flagrant
spending, their shared friends, pleasures, political agreements and disagreements, conflicts—always a form of lovemaking for Hellman. Relief followed

death, then grieving, then denial, then romancing of the memory through the blurred lens of the past. Her portrayals of him—too hero-based, too romantic, too reductive—typified a wife's reflection of a husband now gone. Time and age softened the difficulties, covering over the dirty corners of wear. Hellman, the widow in everything but name, saw Hammett as a co-combatant fighting long and hard to make so strange and important a relationship work. The two had built their attachment, rich in complexity, in a thousand little details. His death was a blow.

Seeking to diminish Hellman but not Hammett, critics mocked Hellman's memories, citing as evidence their long absences from each other, the scantily clad bit players, their rigid individuality. Hellman and Hammett's dynamic, human connection challenged conventional assumptions about romance, love, familial bonds. In the stifling political and repressed sexual climate of postwar America, Hellman and Hammett seemed too weird to take seriously. The critique of their relationship was nothing new; it had begun in the 1930s with the Nick and Nora of Hammett's *The Thin Man*. He depicted the early days of romantic excitement, shared wit, enjoyment of the other, and publishers and filmmakers bowdlerized the heavy drinking, the hints of infidelity that complicated the fiction. Fifty years later, the 1999 made-for-television movie *Dash and Lilly* enacted the worst years of Hellman and Hammett's life together, pronouncing it and them excessive and dysfunctional. The Hammett and Hellman relationship both fascinated and threatened audiences. Gore Vidal quipped, "Has anyone ever seen them together?" Biographer Joan Mellen could not see beyond her affection for Hammett and dislike of Lillian to understand them as a couple. Yet Hammett's letters attest to their strong bond and the longevity of their relationship. In one he quoted a song: "You are what you are to me." In others, she was Lillian, Lishka, Lilishka, Lilly, Lillest, an essential and integral part of his life. On a Thanksgiving anniversary in 1943 he wrote her:

Yes, ma'am, it's thirteen years just about this day. And that's nice, that is, and I thank you, I do. They have been fine grand years and you are a fine grand woman and for all I know I must have been a fine grand man to have deserved them and you. And with such a start, think of, not only the next thirteen, but the next after that![3]

Hammett, or Dash, as Hellman called him, occupied the center of who she had become. Throughout their years of turmoil and trial, she wanted him to acknowledge in writing all they had meant to each other, though he had

written dozens of letters attesting to his devotion. Her feelings were more traditional than she wanted to believe; she needed reassurance. On their
Thanksgiving anniversary, three months before his death, Hellman wrote a
note to him and asked him to sign it:

> On this thirtieth anniversary of the beginning of everything, I wish to
> state:
> The love that started on that day was greater than all love anywhere,
> anytime, and all poetry cannot include it.
> I did not then know what treasure I had, could not, and thus occasion-
> ally violated the grandeur of this bond.
> For which I regret.
> But I give deep thanks for the glorious day, and thus the name
> "Thanks-giving."
> What but an unknown force could have give me, a sinner, this
> woman? Praise God.
> Signed.

Hammett laughed, as she meant him to, and signed the letter. But
Hammett provided a postscript: "If this seems incomplete it is probably because I couldn't think of anything else at the time."[4]

Of course, he often drove her to despair throughout the course of their
thirty-year relationship. Two wars, wasting venereal diseases, chronic lung diseases, and chronic alcoholism had destroyed him physically. The IRS, a jail
term, and his profligacy had ruined him financially and stripped him of his
political fire. Hellman had gone to his aid over the course of their long and
rocky relationship, reluctant and furious sometimes, enthusiastic and loving
at others. She had been his primary caretaker for five years in this last illness.
As had become their habit throughout the years, he lived either in her house
or close by, with the exception of his cabin at Katonah in his early sixties. If
other notable men filled Hellman's life from year to year, every year, no one
but Hammett became so much a part of her. If others, like neighbor Bill
Styron, thought their affection for each other like "a couple of old dogs sniff-
ing each other," Hammett and Hellman thought so too, pleased.[5]
Difficult, impatient, and easily irritated, Hellman took on the burden of
Hammett's care during his last years. Hammett's daughter Jo Marshall heard
Hellman's complaints but saw only Hellman's kindness when her father was
there. Jo recalls one night when Hammett tried to grill a steak, hands shaking

badly, only to let it fall into the ashes, "a terrible moment." But Hellman made a joke, continued cooking, and treated him with affection and dignity. Marshall, no great fan of Hellman's, said, "Much of what they had had together was gone—the fun, the sex, the fighting—but the love remained. I could be wrong about a lot of things with Lillian, but not about that."[6] Characteristically, Hellman turned to writing to make sense of the chaos she felt about Hammett's illness and impending death. But in this instance, she kept the written word hidden.

On a page hidden in a diary sleeve, Hellman's diary notes for the last days of Hammett's life record a maelstrom of feeling. For December 27 or 28, 1960: "I was afraid to talk as I always have been. Afraid and hating it, always afraid and hating it. . . . I am so torn with pity and love and hate and sobered by the struggle." For December 28 or 29: "Cathy Kober came to see him. He was cheered up and wanted it, as he does with women now. I have the feeling that a last sexual surge is there and I have fantasies that I used to have. There is grabbing and feeling and such, but not for me, and I have a little of the old jealousy, a little of moral crap about don't harm, don't touch, don't seduce. Foolish . . . It is sad. It is a last try." On December 31, the night of his collapse, Hellman recorded at 8:00 P.M. that Hammett said "tough" and cried one tear. "Tell me. 'No. I'm trying not to think about it.' The face grows sadder everyday."[7]

Hellman had the resources to hire others to care for him, but the buck stopped with her. He asked Hellman for nothing; he was prickly about his dignity, rigid about self-reliance. But she gave him what she could.

After the initial grief of Hammett's death, she had to act, preparing the rituals for the dead. She held Hammett's funeral at a small chapel. Over three hundred attended. Hammett's family did not attend, chiefly because the daughters could not imagine their mother—Hammett's wife—"to one side, alone, shivering in her thin California clothes, crying, and no one to comfort her."[8] They knew that Hellman would honor Hammett as he would have wished. "On a cold, icy day following the funeral, Hellman gave Hammett a soldier's burial at Arlington National Cemetery, as he had wished. Hellman, Kermit Bloomgarden, Howard Bay, his sister Reba, two cousins, and a soldier who had known him in the Aleutians saw Hammett buried, his coffin draped in a flag. When taps sounded and the color guard presented the flag to Hellman, she knew she had flouted the FBI's efforts to forbid the burial because of Hammett's politics.[9] Hammett had been a soldier in two wars, "had liked his country."[10] This effort to explain Hammett's patriotism came in her eulogy, a moving, loving piece. She touched on

Hammett's earlier life, his wife, his daughters, then recapped their life together, never trying to reconcile the overlap of wife and family with their own thirty-year relationship. She presented the value of Hammett, his ineffable manner that drew men, women, children to him: "Maybe it has to do with reserves so deep that we know we cannot touch them with charm or jokes or favors. It comes out of something more than dignity and shows on the face."[11] He might have scoffed or grinned wryly at her efforts to summarize so complex a man and relationship. But the eulogy, restrained and articulate, was one that even the hard-boiled, reclusive Hammett would have approved.

Absence and Forced Change

With Hammett dead, life changed for Hellman. His hard-won approval had provided incentive to write, and his death left her surprisingly bereft. Nevertheless, she still had moxie and sexual energy and was "determined to sit down and make some decisions about" her life, even if they were "bad ones."[12] Hellman's libido had always charged her to write, spurring wayward romantic forays and her return to Hammett. Now she wrote her last play.

The experimental *My Mother, My Father and Me*, an adaptation of Burt Blechman's novel *How Much?*, was a fiasco that alienated nearly everyone. In her mid-fifties, Hellman was too old and too tired to face the cold faces of audiences and the hot words of theatrical critics. In *My Mother, My Father and Me*, Hellman lost whatever way she had with adaptations. Her limited success with adaptations made her refuse an offer to coauthor with Morton DaCosta a script of Edna Ferber's *Saratoga Trunk*.[13] She didn't like Ferber and told DaCosta bluntly that he could not write. Something in *How Much?* tempted her, however, and in adapting it, she attempted too much. Critic Walter Kerr got it right in saying the play "attempts to mate extravagant satirical incoherence of the Absurd with homier, milder, and more plausible nonsense."[14] Dealing with a Jewish family in Manhattan, Hellman created some "outrageously funny scenes" along with some flat, incomprehensible ones. It did not gel anywhere but in her head. Given that it only played for seventeen performances, it drew more respect from critics than it seemed to deserve. Many noted its excellent first act wit, its depiction of social insanity, and its bitter truths. Leonard Bernstein sought to make amends for their troubles over *Candide* by writing a blurb used in the play's advertising: "Anyone who cares about new trends in the American theatre should not miss Miss Hellman's new play. *My Mother, My Father and Me* is funny, sad, compassionate and ruthless." Fans applauded and one named Ruth Weber wrote,

"This is a slashing fresh wind—a storm!—blown into the fetid air of our times. . . . Marvelous—you are marvelous in your wrath."[15]

But critics won the debate. Too edgy, too angry, the comedy spun in too many directions. Hellman tried to explain what went wrong: Gower Champion's foolish direction, Arthur Penn's feeble assist, star Ruth Gordon's efforts to steal the show. In fact, Hellman's script needed less experiment, more craft. Joan Mack of the Broadcasting Foundation noted that if she'd seen the play out of town without an author's name she would have said, "Listen you've gotta get Lillian Hellman here. . . . You've got to get that brilliantly clean knife that sees the score and knows it that she keeps stuck in the garter of her left leg for just such foolishness as some of this. If you want a woman who'll tell you yes or no, black or white, in or out, without hiding behind something or wavering she's the lady."[16] Hellman had experimented but did not get it quite right. Now she was tired of the theater, too tired to fight her usual hellish battles for the success of her work.

For a time, Hellman still thought of herself as a playwright. She had earned a top position in the cinematic and theatrical world and proved herself the equal of men. She wasn't about to give that up. "A man who writes plays isn't always being identified as a MAN playwright," Hellman retorted to a reporter who called her the most successful woman playwright in the nation.[17] She had jumped into a man's world and, standing just above five feet and showing an imperious profile, she commanded respect for her talent. As theater professor and critic Howard Stein explained, Hellman was familiar with the office of the theater-owning Shuberts "with its famous desk that wasn't necessarily used as a desk"—Broadway's version of a casting couch. But without Hellman's encouragement, no man dared "put his hand on her knee at rehearsal, take liberties with her as an expendable woman which those powerful men did in those days." She refused to be swatted down in the cruel, sexist world of the theater in the 1930s, 1940s, and 1950s, earning recognition by the force of her will. As Stein summed her up, "She had a vicious tongue, and instead of fighting underneath, having been put down, she never put herself in that position; she was fighting on an equal level, despite the fact that her own gender and maybe her own background did not really support that."[18] Proud, loud, and seductive by turn, she embraced her role as a great playwright in a man's world.

Hellman's dazzling theatrical reputation was hers to keep. She saw her plays produced worldwide, and she made hundreds of thousands of dollars on their production, on her production investments, on international rights and publication. Busy in the theater and behind the scenes, she kept a keen

eye on production details and an active ledger on economic transactions, to
the penny. Critic Walter Kerr called her "tough . . . there is a shrewd eye, a
stiff spine and a no-nonsense mind at work."[19]

In Givenchy or Blass designer suits and dresses, trendy hats cocked over
one eye or half veiling her face, she worked as hard as any man who rolled up
his shirt sleeves and tore off his tie to do the grunt work of "building artists
and audiences for the American Theatre."[20] In the Drama League and the
Academy of Arts and Letters she led committees and volunteered for odd jobs
few wanted, arranging meetings and interviews, shopping Manhattan real estate for new offices. More notably she served the Committee for the Artists
and Writers Revolving Fund, which nominated worthy artists for financial assistance. Refusing at first because she felt she couldn't make distinctions and
would give the money to any who applied, she was talked into it and for years
worked with a committee to nominate a diverse group for these awards, including poet Muriel Rukeyser and African American novelist Carl Ruthven
Offord. She even asked the committee to consider J. D. Salinger, though she
had trouble reaching him to verify information. Active also in nominating
members, from Kay Boyle to Bernard Malamud, she not only was visible but
had vision.[21]

She had political perspicacity. As early as the 1940s she lobbied the league
to create pension funds for dramatists, group health benefits, administrative
support. She pressured league members to include Off-Broadway playwrights
in the guild and to check into the possibility of "future outlets for drama" like
pay TV. Worried about the dearth of young, untried playwrights, she tried
various schemes, from offering prizes for original work to volunteering herself
and other playwrights to speak at colleges and universities to encourage dramatic writing.[22] In 1962 Van Wyck Brooks nominated her to fill the prestigious
place vacated by Robinson Jeffers in the Select 50 of the Academy of Arts and
Letters, which she did for life.[23]

Bringing vitality to all aspects of the dramatic world, reaping huge rewards
for her contributions, she found that after *My Mother, My Father and Me* she
could no longer write for the Broadway stage. The McCarthy era's "demoli-
tion of plays with a 'social idea' killed Hellman's themes," her power, her
electricity.[24] Given the repressive atmosphere and her political troubles, a leftist theme was out of the question. Jewish satire did not work either. She had
seen and loved Samuel Beckett's *Waiting for Godot* but knew his innovations
were not for her. The well-made play was her forte; she had seen it in *Toys in
the Attic*'s immense success, *The Autumn Garden*'s lukewarm showing, and
My Mother, My Father and Me's thud. On paper, her experiments seemed

fresh and innovative, and she longed to find a venue for an experimental theater, hence her interest in Off-Broadway, still in its infancy.[25] But Broadway
wanted straight, hard-driving Hellman with more popular themes. Hellman
had been big news on Broadway's marquees for a long time, but Arthur
Miller's advent with *All My Sons* had literally subsumed her preeminence as
the dramatic spokesperson of this newer generation. Enjoyment had leaked
out of the dramatic scene for her.

Her last failure sealed it. She told a reporter, "Opening nights are fearful
things. I generally sit in the last row and smoke furiously. It drives the firemen
crazy, but I'm too fagged out to mind anything . . . in *Watch on the Rhine* I
was so groggy I fell to the floor and bumped my head."[26] She half-joked that
"Broadway has become too much for me."[27] Edgy and tense watching a show,
Hellman laughed that Hammett had refused for years to sit with her at her
play's rehearsals. "I always made noises at plays, even my own plays. I tap my
foot and mutter." She became famous for getting out of theaters during the
show. According to columnist Joyce Haber, "George S. Kaufman once asked
her how much money she wanted in exchange for agreeing not to go to one
of his plays."[28] Her interest had lessened. "I left the theater because the fun
ran out and the raw money stuff came in," Hellman insisted, ridiculing the
"caviar audience" or "expense-account audience."[29] From 1963 till her death
in 1984 she left writing plays to others.

Hellman had always sought meaningful work and meaningful amorous relationships. Without theater as her central motivation, without Hammett's
backup to her emotional life, she determined to move forward alone. She
certainly wasn't ready to retire, and celibacy would never be an option. She
looked around for new life, romantically and intellectually.

Self-Propelled Allure

Powerful and libidinous, she experimented with men. She flirted shamelessly, sometimes in pursuit, more often for affirmation. Hellman, not so
much predatory as interested, loved men, loved the sexual rush. Her magnet-
ism dazzled men half her age. Despite Hellman's "plain" looks, men liked
her, felt the urge with her. Beauty definitely wasn't the draw, but something
clearly was. As an admirer reflected, "Men aren't always attracted to just plain
good-looking girls, but girls who have something that they can't forget. That
is what she had."[30] Men liked her husky voice, her infectious laugh, her "por-
cupinish" quality.[31] Whether drinking scotch neat out of wine glasses or
showing her profile with her cigarette prop, she presented her sexuality as a

force; she had more sense than to deny it.[32] She acted and moved like she was a sexy woman, and so she was.[33] Self-propelled allure made Hellman desirable. Old lovers still paid homage; she added zing to their lives.

But she wanted someone new. By turns seductive and dismissive with young men who courted her, she haughtily brushed aside those who disappointed her or obsessively commandeered those who challenged her. She enacted the role of the aging CEO, collecting and discarding trophies. While boy toys provided the pleasure of the moment, none would do unless there was more than sex, and romantic meaning was hard to find. But she enjoyed the high jinx, recording in her diary the dramas of women she called Madame X or Madame Gigglewitz, replaying adolescent games of call and hang up. She haughtily brushed aside those who disappointed her or obsessively commandeered those who challenged her. "She was a great amateur of love, a voracious consumer and provider, student and teacher of it . . . a powerhouse."[34] Friend Richard Poirier concurs: "When she entered the room it was in itself a great, theatrical appearance. She was an amazingly sexual woman even in the way she sat in a chair. And she would often say to men visiting her, 'take your drink dear, and come upstairs while I dress.'"[35] She hankered after men, and when she failed to entice she sometimes opened herself to friendship.

When Pulitzer Prize–winning poet Richard Wilbur's talent and youth drew her, his wife Charlee let her know that he was not to be "had." Subsequently Hellman had a long and fruitful friendship with Wilbur and Charlee. She loaned them the Vineyard house on several occasions, loaned them money. In return, both Wilburs watched out for Hellman productions in Texas, hosted her warmly, and named her as their son's godmother. Of course Hellman spoke her mind, and after twenty years of friendship still felt wounded when Wilbur called her memoirs essentially fiction, as she had depended on his literary knowledge to see her memoir method as she did.[36] But the affection and respect lasted.

Hellman's many flirtations and attempted seductions during her fifties came to light years later. Her conquests included *Saturday Evening Post* editor Stuart Rose, law professor and activist Telford Taylor, poet Archibald MacLeish, writer Philip Rahv, screenwriter Alvin Sargeant. The lively letters many exchanged with Hellman record mutual interest in the teasing, the attraction between man and woman. Marriage proposals of great wit were common on both sides, but clearly just for fun. She wrote producer Richard Roth, "I had a nice long talk with Alvin Sargeant and would still very much like to marry him, and expect you to use your influence. I am perfectly conscious that there's a few years difference in age, but then that would seem to give to him a chance for a third or even a fourth bride."[37] In another volley, Sargeant urged Hellman to stay with him: "Consider Shangri-la, why not?"[38] Neither was serious about anything but the fun of friendship. Both Hellman and the "man" usually kept it at an affectionate but light level.

Some who were rumored to have bedded her, when questioned, responded with demurrals and denials. Philip Rahv said he considered Hellman's joking proposals until he realized he'd have to sleep with her: "It would be like going to bed with Justice Frankfurter!"[39] But while their flirtation went on, he didn't seem so reluctant. Others proudly admitted the involvement. George Backer marveled that she was great in bed and then got up and cooked "one of the damndest breakfasts I've ever had in my life!"[40] Hellman in the flesh was far more persuasive than Hellman in memory, at least to some.

Hellman lived the erotic interest of the opposite sex, of her own libido and creative spirit. She played poker with Burton Bernstein's group, the only woman, reveling in the masculine ambience, the presence of intense young men. Nude swimming on the beach at Gay Head was the order of the day at a Hellman party. She ritually stripped down to nothing, wrestling out of her clothing under a towel, then boldly walked nude to the ocean. As *New York Times* editor Herbert Mitgang wrote her, "Having seen your performance on the beach, I should invite you to write a piece about strip teasing. Never towels so boldly draped."[41] Sometimes she came on too strong for the men she hoped to woo. She once set up a dinner table in her bedroom to entertain Harry Levin. The room was large, part office, part study, but Levin felt the pressure of the waiting bed. He decided to let it go and Hellman let the moment pass. He remained faithful to his wife.[42]

As a woman, Hellman took what commanding men often take: sexual opportunities to season middle age, to verify virility, to exploit power for excitement. While Hammett lived, most of Hellman's exploratory forays meant little more than friendliness of a sexual nature. Arthur W. A. Cowan, whom she immortalized in *Pentimento*, was an exception. He served as a warning to her that her excesses had consequences. In many ways Cowan was the perfect love for Hellman, or so it seemed at first. A Philadelphia lawyer turned successful entrepreneur, he was tall, handsome, buff, and rugged in that tough-guy Bogart way. He had charm too, and a tremendous energy that matched her own. He owned three Rolls-Royces and lived in one of his two houses in Philadelphia or in the Hotel Madison. He surrounded himself in men's club furnishings of leather and expensive tweed.

They began their relationship before the ailing Hammett permanently moved in with Hellman. Relatively unencumbered at the time, Hellman and

Cowan toyed with romance, had fun, and later did business together. At first Hellman thought they might have a hot affair, but she found him skittish, excessive, crazy. She could not believe his extravagant stories. What he told others and what he told her too often deviated wildly. He told his sister Sadie Raab that she proposed to him and he refused.[43] Hellman disputed that charge: "I wouldn't marry you, Arthur, I never even thought about it," to which he replied, "Like hell you wouldn't, like hell. You're lying" and stopped the car abruptly on the Pennsylvania Turnpike.[44] He chose action, and she dialogue. They played parts with each other to disrupt boredom, heighten the tension between them.

Hellman's portrait of Cowan in her memoir is a self-portrait too. She saw herself in Cowan's mirror: the two of them daring, larger than life, excessive, vain, desperate. She knew she walked the edge of profligacy with him and it frightened her. "He had become to me a man of unnecessary things and often I felt that he knew what he was, was gallant about the pain it caused him and tried to hide it from himself with new cars, new houses, new friends, new women half-forgotten at the minute they were half-loved."[45] So much of their relationship was carried out in operatic antics to heighten the hilarity that the record of their relationship is hopelessly overwritten. A friend described a scene where Cowan screamed at a waiter, "How could you serve slop like this! Get out of here! . . . The last time I was here, the chef cooked a wonderful dish of fried mockingbird's tongues."[46] The scene could be Hellman's, who made a ruckus over "goy drek" or "kike drek" in restaurants on both coasts and in New Orleans too. She saw her own tendency to be outrageous in him, and she felt tender toward him. She could confide in him. She wrote, "You are the only man in America who doesn't wear his underwear to bed who believes in the beauties of California science. . . . A psychiatrist is a sensible idea for anybody but people like us need special and brilliant people, not Beverly Hills osteopaths. However, faith is faith, and perhaps it is sinful for me to examine yours. I have some knowledge of how you feel: I have been in the worst depression since alcohol used to cause them. Mine, I think, certainly I do not know, can be traced to bad work."[47] As Cowan's moorings slipped, she desperately tried to hang on to her own.

Cowan died in 1964, leaving Hellman something of vital importance: Hammett's literary legacy. As good a business mind as Hellman had, his was better, and he had money to invest. Cowan advised her when she and Lester Osterman nearly bought the Coronet Theatre on West 45th Street. The accompanying project, designed to give playwrights a greater share of their profits, failed when the real estate deal did.[48] Too few participants were willing to take the financial and tax risks. On other occasions, Cowan's money and expertise eased the passage of their business deals. Cowan and Hellman both put up money to produce *The Heart's a Wonder*, the Nuala and Marin O'Farrell musical version of *The Playboy of the Western World*. Hellman and Cowan aborted the deal when they couldn't get absolute control of the productions even if they put up the funds.

Hellman may have had a "shyster mind" as Cowan told her, but legal, big-money matters she relegated to those in the know.[49] Cowan was the essence of such a man. He helped her break her Grandmother Sophie Newhouse's trust, an ordeal that lasted many years. She wanted to replace her Aunt Florence Newhouse's executor with her own lawyer, Paul O'Dwyer. It galled Hellman that because she had no children, funds owed to her would be passed down to distant cousins. Cowan knew the law and helped her with the matter, though he died before it was resolved. Money matters always felt intensely personal to Hellman, and her respect for Cowan came in large part to his ability to manipulate them.

The rights to Hammett's literary legacy came to Hellman because of Cowan's assistance. The IRS had attached all of Hammett's royalties, and when he died, the IRS arranged to auction off those rights. After deft maneuvers and legal haggling, Cowan and Hellman together paid $5,000 to the IRS for Hammett's literary estate, a bargain in retrospect, but valueless at the time. When Cowan died, Hellman insisted she maintained the legal rights to Cowan's half of the estate. His relatives weren't at all sure she had that legal right, but Cowan had put it in writing in a letter to Oscar Bernstein.[50] Hammett's legacy was now under her control.

Hammett's will dictated that Hellman share the copyright moneys with his children, and initially she asked Hammett's daughter Jo to share the cost of the IRS auction. But Hellman never gave Hammett's daughters what was due them financially or morally. She claimed she never received a letter from Jo saying she would assist in the costs, though Jo did indeed send one. Hellman apparently decided against sharing Hammett's literary legacy, telling herself she was better equipped to manage it. Repeatedly she directed and outmaneuvered Hammett's daughters, who signed over other rights to her. She managed these rights brilliantly, to her credit, and salved her conscience by doling out small sums to Jo and Mary. Her controlling actions showed Hellman's woeful lack of fair play and integrity where Hammett's children were concerned. She openly displayed her jealousy of his daughters, her sense of entitlement where Hammett was concerned, and her arrogant insistence that she manage Hammett's reputation. She devised a plan to honor

Hammett's memory and politics at the expense of his children. From that point on, she schemed to save for the Lillian Hellman and Dashiell Hammett Human Rights Grants, given to writers facing political oppression. While this ongoing program is noble, she exacted a stepmother's one-upmanship for years to bring it about. In bringing Cowan on board to buy Hammett's copyrights, she also took on his worst characteristics: bizarre, wayward, money focused, manipulative.

The quixotic games with Cowan grew tiresome. As she said in *Pentimento*, "I had to cut the line of me where it crossed and tangled with his."[51] And then he died in mysterious circumstances on November 11, 1964. She had enjoyed Cowan and didn't mind so much when their romance turned to friendship. But in her fifties, as lusty as ever, she wanted to fall in love again, have a man at the center of her life. She searched for a man to spur her creativity, to value her, to ignite love and passion. Although she experimented with several game, eager, brilliant men, they didn't mesh with her. Seductive, aggressive, she was a woman who pursued what she wanted.

She eagerly made men friends of professionalism and excellence: writer Norman Mailer, professor and writer Richard Poirier, director and producer Mike Nichols, MIT president Jerome Weisner. She sought some men for their intellectual brilliance, such as Nichols, Poirier, and Weisner; some for their money, such as Cowan and Max Palevsky, and some for political savvy or fame, even if it didn't jibe with her own, like Cold War liberal McGeorge Bundy. She adored good-looking men such as Warren Beatty and Richard De Combray. "Lillian! You're such a celebrity fucker!"[52] an outraged Norman Mailer shouted when Hellman interfered to stop a political fistfight in the making between Mailer and Bundy at Truman Capote's Black and White Ball. In choosing her lovers and friends, above all, Hellman picked intense men and women who made her think and feel and laugh: Sid Perelman, Maureen Stapleton, Talli and William Wyler. Laughter and a good fight were almost as good as sex—almost.

She needed to resurrect the heady excitement and potential of Hammett and, later, Melby. A life without eroticism was no life at all. Knocked off balance by Hammett's death and a stint at Harvard, where she lived alone at Leverett Hall in a veritable ivory tower, she dallied with various men. And then Hellman set her sights on Blair Clark, twelve years her junior, to fill the void. It wasn't a wise choice.

Robert Lowell had introduced Hellman to Clark and his then-wife Holly years before when he insisted they all play tennis on the Philbins' court at the Vineyard. When Clark and Hellman reconnected at Harvard, he had been divorced for a couple of years and was, as he put it, "heavily involved with a married woman who I came close to marrying."[53] Handsome and dynamic, Clark edited the *Harvard Crimson* as an undergraduate. After a stint in the army during World War II, he quickly ascended to the higher echelons of journalism: CBS foreign correspondent in Paris, anchor for CBS Radio's *The World Tonight.* By 1961, when he piqued Hellman's interest, he was vice president and general manager of CBS News. Both Hellman and Clark leaned left politically, she a national firebrand, he an active Democrat working for the campaigns of Hellman's old friend Averill Harriman and later Eugene McCarthy. Clark had what Hellman desired: looks, political connections, ambition, charm, power. He was a hotshot; she was the ultimate big man on campus.[54] Both were internationally known, charismatic, lusty, vital people. And they really really liked each other.

This "liking" became part of the problem. They became close friends, a visible couple. She sat on his lap at parties, and they necked like high schoolers. They had fun together. Her playfulness entranced him and Hellman wove elaborate fantasies of Clark's intrigues, making up hilarious false stories about his mother's love affair with him, regaling him with stories of mutual friends. For years they talked on the phone several times a day, gossiped and exchanged the intimate details of their lives. He gave her beautiful gifts of jewelry, a gold bracelet that she added to "the gold leaf Hammett pin" and Cowan's "18kt. Gold cluster pin with 18 diamonds."[55] When Hellman wanted more than jewelry, he backed off and toyed with her. He distanced her by unburdening himself to Hellman about his other women. And there were several. Later he admitted that "for a while I was being unfaithful both to Lillian and to the object of my longtime love." That set the tone for the rest of the Clark-Hellman "affair." Clark confided to Hellman the high dramas and antics associated with women threatening to leave husbands and marry him immediately, husbands threatening him, and even a woman threatening suicide if he left her.[56]

Hellman loved the drama, but her role as confidant hurt. She began to try to extricate Clark from the clutches of these other women with "ardent interventions," as Clark called them. Hellman loved a challenge, but when thwarted usually she cut bait and struck back, to use the fisherman's parlance she enjoyed. But with Clark she fell into a trap of her own making. She determined they would be lovers. Clark became her fixation. She stepped up her courting. She went to the Lowells for advice and assistance; she then urged Clark to go to her psychoanalyst, Dr. Gero, for help. Gero told him to stop fiddling with Hellman's emotions. Clark began to realize that "I caused

Lillian a lot of pain, unknowingly and probably stupidly but surely not deliberately."[57] Her diaries record the problem from her point of view. Clark "had
been interested. Fascinated? Interested professionally but never romantically
although it had been expected." Later she commented, "Would I bear with
situation a little longer—guarantee things would turn out well," and finally,
"We kissed and kissed and did everything but . . . what is wrong?"[58] Neither of
them willing to make a final break, it went on and on. He held out, knowing
Hellman could absorb him, knowing he wasn't sexually attracted to her.
Enthralled? Yes. But as one of her disgusted friends suggested, a man of any
pride at all would have left the affair since he was unwilling to do anything
about it. "Given the high school-like tone of their relationship, Clark behaved like the girl, Lillian like the boy." She was sixty and he was forty-seven.
Nearly everyone felt embarrassed.

Clark's continued liaisons made her mean and mischievous. She con-
structed a whopping lie to get even, the more wonderful for its lasting the
length of her relationship with him. Clark called it a "mystery" of "His
Excellency" that he never penetrated. His Excellency, the protagonist of
Hellman's story, was probably based on Hellman's relationship with
Yugoslavian foreign minister Srdja Prica, though she never said his name to
Clark. The story as it unfolded certainly outstripped her actual 1949 affair
with Prica.

Once upon a time, His Excellency, a Yugoslavian diplomat, wanted to
marry her but she resisted. Finally he married someone else but persisted in
returning to New York to squire Hellman about. Hellman kept Clark agog
with details he could never quite prove wrong. She and His Excellency
fought too much when together, though they were mad for each other. In the
late 1940s she had a son by him when she was in Paris and he was an ambassador; the child stayed at Pleasantville with her and Hammett before going to
live all over the world with his father, His Excellency. Clark said he wanted
to ask Hellman if Hammett had any idea about the child's "true mother."[59]

For years the story wove its way into their conversations. Every time he
had a new liaison, she excused herself to go meet His Excellency, who was
in town and sending a car to fetch her. Later she confided more intrigues
and history: the son became a world renowned physicist living in China with
a Chinese wife. This imaginary son and his imaginary Chinese wife then
had two children, making Hellman a grandmother! She saw her son and
grandchildren over the years; he became ill. She told Clark the travails of
enlisting the help of friends Ruthie Fields and Jerome Weisner to assist her
son in his last, terminal illness. Clark couldn't quite disbelieve her; "it was

all so circumstantial, so detailed." In writing it down after Hellman's death, Clark remarked, "I feel idiotic not to be able to make this tale sound more sensible and coherent." That Clark, a journalist, never challenged the story's absurdity encouraged the relish with which she told it.[60] Clark had his series of beautiful married women; Hellman had His Excellency and family.

After five or six years she got over the absurdity of the Clark-Hellman faux romance and moved on emotionally. But not before she found herself embroiled in a controversy caused by someone else's arabesque. Clark's old friend Robert Lowell, often called the last great American poet, was spinning off into another breakdown. Lowell, beset with manic depression, had a long public history of contention with his wife, critic Elizabeth Hardwick. In 1967, he went daily to Hellman's house and spun tales of woe. Lowell returned to Hardwick to repeat Hellman's "sharp comments." Hardwick, incensed, wrote the now legendary "waspish" review of Hellman's plays in the New York Review, dismissing Hellman's literary worth absolutely, saying she symbolized the failure of "left-wing popular writers of the Thirties."[61] Most theater critics agreed that Hardwick seriously misread Hellman's work, but those who had an ax to grind politically now complained that Hellman's work was mediocre. Hellman was outraged. So were respected writers and friends who wrote fierce rebuttals to Hardwick's shrill review: Richard Goodwin, Edmund Wilson, Renata Adler, and Richard Poirier. Clark wrote Hardwick a rather harsh note on Hellman's behalf, angering Hardwick enough to throw it back in Clark's face years later, calling it the worst letter she had ever received.[62]

By 1968 Hellman had distanced herself from Clark—or he from her. But he was hard to give up. In the years of Hellman's interest, he dated all manner of beautiful women, not least the woman Hellman forever after called "the Widow Kennedy." After Hellman finally broke her obsession with him, he helped establish the New York Review of Books and became associate publisher of the New York Post. His powerful connections and the challenge he represented drew her to him long after both had moved on. She recorded his calls and visits but wrote "mal" after each one. It embarrassed her to realize she had been such a sucker, playing a young girl's game with the man Mike Nichols called "tip top bread." But Clark still counted with Hellman, his person too strong to dismiss.

In her last memoir, Maybe, the character of Cameron bears more than passing resemblance to Clark. His great-great grandfather, Simon Cameron, had political influence and railroad/coal wealth that extended to Blair Clark and Clark's son Cameron. Hellman examined the Maybe of relationships— Clark's among them—in motifs of blindness, imbalance, strong feeling.

"Cameron and I liked each other, certainly, but that often makes people wait around hoping for more."[63] His importance to her crumbling sense of self can be glimpsed in the troubling end of the book, which features a telegram to Cameron: "THERE ARE MISSING PIECES EVERYPLACE AND EVERYWHERE AND THEY ARE NOT MY BUSINESS UNLESS THEY TOUCH ME. BUT WHEN THEY TOUCH ME, I DO NOT WISH THEM TO BE BLACK. MY INSTINCT REPEAT INSTINCT RE-PEAT INSTINCT REPEAT INSTINCT IS THAT YOURS ARE BLACK. LILLIAN."[64] Even if this telegram was a fiction created for *Maybe*, it illustrates the damage Clark inflicted on her—at least from her point of view. By their own accounts, each loved the other until the end of life. Hellman left him a highboy in her will; he gave it to a woman he had an "adventure with,"[65] Joan Mellen. A Hellman biographer, she portrayed Hellman as a liar. But Mellen's view is understandable, given her close relationship to Clark. Hellman's His Excellency fable had unintended consequences for her reputation.

December and May

By her mid-sixties Hellman knew that Clark would never satisfy her emotional center. She had failed with him and knew it. A man she had not considered was Peter Feibleman. She first met him when he was ten, a boy with slicked down hair brought out to greet guests at his parents' opulent party. He remembered her as a thirty-five-year-old New Orleans returnee—famous, elegant, "with a shower of sparks under the flint in her voice."[66] She had asked him how old he was, and he had replied, "just ten." She had retorted, "Ten's not so young." He had liked her refusal to treat him like a child. They saw each other occasionally when he was in his teens and "silly-handsome," and met as adults at a book party celebrating the publication of his novel *A Place Without Twilight*. Feibleman recalls, "She was wearing a black lace veil pulled up tight around her face," and the fifty-three-year-old Hellman, back rigid, turned on her firepower and wit.

The handsome young writer with the new book stood agape at another guest, Greta Garbo, and Hellman—never choosing second fiddle—finally marched to the door. The hostess commented on how young Feibleman was when Hellman had asked, "How old are you?" When Feibleman answered "twenty-eight," she said, "Twenty-eight's not so young" and swept slowly out of the room. He "was hooked again."[67]

For the next few years they met at various parties and events given by mutual friends, beginning a long friendship as New Orleans expatriots and writers.[68] Perhaps because of their age disparity or her respect for his writing or her obsession with Clark, she didn't push, didn't demand. Since Hammett's death Hellman had increasingly taken on his generosity to young writers, encouraging the talented, critiquing as editor. She had, for example, recently read and critiqued James Purdy's novels and his new play to assist him, giving generously of her time.[69] She thought the talented writer and journalist Renata Adler worthy of much encouragement and pushed her forward, too strongly at times. Now Feibleman showed much promise as a writer, with many, including Carson McCullers, encouraging him. She extended to him the same generosity.

Hellman invested much time and effort. After Feibleman produced his play *Tiger, Tiger Burning Bright* in late 1962 to terrific reviews if disappointing box office returns, Hellman invited him to stay summers at her Vineyard Haven house. She had torn down the house she shared with Hammett, opting for a new look without the lingering reminders of Hammett's illness. She kept some of Hammett's prized possessions, like a beautiful old stand-up radio, and imposed configurations of comfort and light to make the house represent a forward-looking self. Designed by her favorite set designer, Howard Bay, Hellman's new house provided a perfect setting for two writers to find an exciting exchange in their writing and in themselves. The casual beauty of Mill House, its straight angles softening the view of a rugged coast and the endless ritual pageantry of the sea, refuted fame and hype. Hellman's house reminded occupants of the need for ease but the potential for drama.

Arriving the first time, Feibleman chose a small monastic room, staying packed and ready to flee. But the bracing sea air mixed with the hot sun, and the evenings provided sunsets, cocktails, and the lush food they both cooked. Their relationship evolved as he tried to charm her without attaching much to it. But by the time Feibleman became a player in her heart's affections, she had become fed up with charm and told him so. Feibleman found that from the first, Hellman's blunt talk and hacking laugh was a relief from the voices in Hollywood and New York that courted or dismissed him with words of fake praise. Hellman made a man feel "eight feet tall" without fake adoration. She'd go for the insult that was also praise: "Lilly could find the fault and screw it in."[70] He felt he needed to prove himself since, as he said, "I had been in love with her since I was ten."[71] Hellman was the most seductive woman Feibleman ever met. "But it was her mind that was the sexiest thing in the world."[72] For these two writers, the fecundity of imagination, the sharing, exchange, and critique of writing fostered an intimacy like no other.

Each discovered in writing a profound sense of self that could not be located elsewhere. Sharing this was heady, indeed.

They became lovers by mutual consent. Oddly, they were a good match, neither bound by conventional sexual mores, both looking for a lover to double as family without the complications and restrictions of marriage. For a young man to embark on an emotional, sexual, familial relationship with a much older, very famous woman requires both confidence and erotic imagination. Hellman was, after all, twenty-five years older than he. This older woman must know her worth and be ready to combine tenacity with flexibility. They made a pact and developed their own moral code as they progressed. Certainly she had a complicated sexual history, but not as complicated as his. In the Garden District of New Orleans at the age of nine he took part in a threesome with a girlfriend of his father's from the French Quarter and his father's butler. Feibleman, raised in France and New Orleans, liked older women, and as an adult he had affairs with several—Simone Signoret, Carol Burnett, and Judy Garland among others—going through a period when he "tried to give an orgasm to every older woman he met."[73] Sometimes his lovers were men; at other times in Europe and Asia he lived out sexual fantasies. When Feibleman met Hellman, he felt "overpraised" and oversated. Hellman provided the corrective, and much else.

Battles, intrigues at home and abroad—all marked Hellman's romances in the 1960s. For a time after she and Feibleman met, Hellman clung to hope for Blair Clark's affections. Their relationship drifted as Feibleman's gained force. On one trip to Mexico she met up with John Melby with talk of love and loss, then with Feibleman where she panicked in fear of loss and jealousy[74] and also with Clark who appeared as a friend in this bedlam. She dotted her diary of this trip with snippets of feeling words, the men they refer to indistinguishable in the mess: "sorry," "disgusting," "sad." She used her usual codes of Mme X, Miss Gigglewitz, Mrs. S, Mrs. K to identify various women also involved. "Mrs. P was used again to stir MME X," and "R suggested telling Mrs. S she was a monster." Occasionally she recalled a conversation with one or the other: "I had not stood in the way—His feeling for me had stood in the way." This "juggling of oranges" as Hammett called Hellman's maintaining several relationships at once, had become too much even for Hellman. She steadied herself, and somehow agreed emotionally to the differing rules of the various games. From that point to the end of her life, Feibleman held her emotional center, with other men filling in, but not seriously.

For her part, she discovered what an interested and interesting man does to a woman.[75] Erotically and creatively, he provided interest. He excited her sense of smell, always a sure sign with Hellman. She teased him in a letter, "I sniff only those people I like very much. When I cease to sniff you, it will be my way of saying goodbye. Miss Hellman."[76] He kept her sharp, combative— ready with the laugh, with the barb. She could start an argument over anything, from his past sexual escapades to the correct way to cook mussels, then critique his defense. He would fume, accusing her of wanting to find problems, not solutions. She would caution, "Let's not have any Woolworth Freud."[77] He trusted her no-nonsense talk and her laughter; she relied on his efforts to prove himself the man she thought he was.

They became a couple, "like an old married couple, warring siblings, sentimental friends, witty accomplices."[78] Yet they also maintained a distance, asserting their own individuality and space. Feibleman learned, as had others before him, that Hellman in arousal could demand too much, take over, use her power to confine. Unlike Clark he didn't withhold, but Feibleman wisely drew practical and emotional boundaries, told her what they were, and stuck to them: they would not be monogamous; he would not live with her year round; he would live his own life as he must; they would write, call, meet, travel together, make love, live together during the summer for as long as it suited. These rules deflected Hellman's efforts to tighten their bonds, to absorb him. As he put it, "We batted back and forth like badminton birds across the States when work permitted, spent summers on the Vineyard, winters in Los Angeles and New York, and odd times traveling. In between visits there were other affairs, other people."[79] Hellman could not easily abide this enforced distance. And so there were turbulent episodes, high antics, subversive ploys. She tried everything she could to move him to a more permanent position and prevent other affairs.

Acting the seducer, the friend, the virago, she tried to get him to conform to her idea of relationship, a twisted line of convention and freeing innovation. Once she hired a detective to surveil Feibleman when she suspected a serious affair with another woman. She was right—and he was outraged. Hellman doubled the fury, striking back with her familiar defensive, "Forgive me, but . . ." Since she had originally hired the private investigator to find Ruth Field's runaway daughter Fiona, she insisted that she was simply putting the leftover time to good use. When Feibleman continued his relationship with the talented and beautiful Elaine May, Hellman complained of anonymous phone calls, undoubtedly fictional, implying they came from May. Over the top, nearly pathological at times, Hellman persevered.

What complicated the relationship further was that in some ways Hellman acted as both mother and father to Feibleman, who was estranged from his own parents. Others saw the familial aspect too, though at least one called it a relationship of mother and son, with Hellman the son.[80] At an inopportune sexual moment Hellman mused that Feibleman was "the closest thing to a child I'll ever have."[81] As Feibleman reflected, "We are validated by the plumage of those who love us and their feathers matter more than our own. Strength is a better credential for a lover than love is, but Lillian fell between parent and lover for me, so I wound up confused and irritable."[82] Hellman understood Feibleman and loved him, so she determined to maintain her tangled relationship with him: "We must, if we can, find a way to live with the love we have: for me, it must have vigor, and the face-to-face problems and pleasures of daily mess, at least part of the time."[83]

Feibleman gritted his teeth at the excesses, wondering if his "attachment to L came out of some idiot rebellion."[84] Cautiously protective of his privacy and other relationships, he resisted and stayed at the periphery, willing to love, unwilling to be subsumed. Because of this, their alliance worked, stayed honest, maintained an integrity that permitted them both to go forward. Hellman made his other relationships problematic, and his unwillingness to sever his relationship with her ruined one that had much promise with either Carol Burnett or Elaine May, according to his friends' best guesses. He stayed—his way—because "once somebody owns real estate in your gut, why you sold it to them is unimportant. The point is, you sold it."[85] Perhaps the paradox of intensity and distance suited him as it did her. Neither admitted to it. She lobbied for more, he insisted on status quo, but both of these very independent lovers gained by keeping others at bay. The arrangement provided freedom and commitment all at once.

The Art of Scheherazade

This inside-out version of Hellman and Feibleman made magic of a sort through shared writing. As she worked with him on his writing, her own approach changed. They began rituals of storytelling to amuse each other and themselves. This practice led to revelation mixed with imagination and increased their intimacy. A storyteller needs listeners, a writer needs readers. "Head back and her eyes half-closed like an ancient caster of spells, spinning yarns,"[86] Hellman kept herself and "them" alive in story- and mythmaking. She built true stories on speculation, as skewed as could be sometimes. When she learned that Arthur Miller and Marilyn Monroe had divorced, she groused, "Well, that's that—I always knew he married *her* for money."[87] Hellman liked Monroe and was furious with Miller for *After the Fall*, which portrayed in excruciating detail the Miller-Monroe marriage, she felt, at Monroe's expense. She expressed her fury by writing a pointed and rather nasty satirical story for *Show Magazine*.[88] From the ridiculous to the sublime, Hellman exercised, incensed, excoriated, and entranced her audience, but she never bored them. Her playing raconteuse to Feibleman's raconteur inevitably led to prosaic revelation, giving Hellman the erotic force to begin a new career in writing. She began to try on rhythms, words, to rework the daily stories into dramas, to reflect on and embellish everything from a trip to her hairdresser at Pierre and Freds, to the glories of the acorn, to sailing on the Kennedy yacht off Hyannisport, where she told Ted Kennedy what needed to be done in Washington.[89] She told the truth bluntly, forcefully, making each story a minivignette, spicing the anecdote, salting it exactly as she did the food she prepared.[90] She had strong opinions and adjusted her work "to the need of the moment."[91] She learned to write prose in the sun and sand of Vineyard Haven, where drinks on the patio often meant stories for the duration. She sat, head back on the lawn chair, eyes shut to the sun, musing in the reverie of story and memory—telling truths and tales.

Supplementing her storyteller's instinct, she learned the formal properties of prose as she taught it—in the writing classroom. She loved teaching and stepped up her teaching career after Hammett died. But she could not easily teach and write at the same time; she thought great teaching was "using yourself up all the time."[92] For a time, it filled the void. She had begun her teaching career as a writing adjunct in the late 1940s when she taught a weeklong course one summer at the University of Indiana–Bloomington. Ten years passed before she became a lecturer at the University of Chicago in 1958 and then a visiting lecturer at Harvard in 1961. Over the next ten years she taught writing courses at Harvard, MIT, Yale, University of California–Berkeley, and Hunter College, invited by such luminaries as Henry Kissinger and McGeorge Bundy at Harvard, Jerome Weisner at MIT, John Hersey at Yale, and Alex Szogyi at Hunter. They sought Hellman out to teach their students "writing" rather than "English" because of her writing acumen and straightforward communication. She was never one for what she called "academic puffery." That she had no undergraduate degree—having left New York University in her junior year—meant little to them since she had many honorary doctorates and great professional standing. By the time she taught at Hunter College in 1972, she was called "distinguished professor" and had published *Unfinished Woman* as the first of four best-selling memoirs. Hellman taught that writing was "the process of making use of yourself and opening things up to people," telling a story about what the writer sees.

An excellent teacher whose gravelly voice mesmerized her student audience,[93] she was, in the words of former student Ken Stuart, a "very practical, smart, shrewd, tough, cagey lady."[94] She had to be tough; Hellman's class lists read like a bull pen roster, all male with the stray female imported from Radcliffe or other nearby women's colleges. Too young even for the libidinous Hellman, the boys in her class stood aghast and in awe of the professorial Hellman. She smoked continually and dramatically, but even in the haze of the classroom, the young men noted her hair, which they considered outlandish, "very thick, very blond, and completely out of date." They worried that "her wrinkled crazed face was going to look into your face."[95]

When a hapless student fell asleep, she nailed him: "Don't do this again Mr. . . . don't fall asleep and don't come late or don't come at all."[96] When students used jargon or vague words such as "ideal" or "idealized" she snapped, "Watch that word." She told the class on one occasion, "I've got a recommendation for you. I'd like you to write this down and look at it maybe in 10 years. All young people make things simple. I'm not going to lie to you. There ain't nothing that is. It is playing into a neurosis to make out that something is simple." Hellman, ever the Grand Inquisitor herself, warned students about "putting wire fences around ideas." She did not hesitate to nip and crush when she thought one of them had strayed too far, however. When a student reading *Heart of Darkness* suggested "let's write about darkness," she demanded, "What in hell does that mean, let's write about darkness . . . Darkness about whom? How?" When another persisted and wanted to talk about "lightness," she said, "Shush. I can't stand the light theme anymore." When one entire class ("fakers, all of us") arrived without reading the week's assignment, *Robinson Crusoe*, it took her two minutes to find this out. To the students' amazement, she cried (and she never cried), telling them she "couldn't figure out what I did wrong."[97] She took her teaching as seriously as she took her writing. This made her difficult for students and even more difficult for administrators.

Hellman knew writing but feared she didn't know how to teach it. She wanted someone to tell her "what to do and how." Administrators brushed her off. Hellman would demand, "What am I supposed to do with the kiddies? What am I supposed to say to them? . . . Well, how do I say that?"[98] In teaching and in writing, Hellman took a workmanlike approach. In planning her lessons for teaching prose writing (she refused to teach playwriting), she read voraciously, assigning such works as Gertrude Stein's "Composition and Explanation," Conrad's *Heart of Darkness*, Henry James's *Portrait of a Lady*. She planned her lectures carefully, prevailing on assistant senior tutor Marvin Sadik at Harvard's Leverett House to get her a typewriter with large type so she could easily see her notes.[99] As the actress she was, she prepared herself before the performance, walking alone to class, refusing conversation, gathering herself for her presentation. Her close examinations of method and her careful planning served her. She learned to write prose by teaching it.

By all indications Hellman—charismatic, lively, committed to writing— was a rousing success in the classroom. But inevitably her inexperience, her lack of disciplinary knowledge, and students being what they are, led to disappointment. She continued to teach on piecemeal contracts, deciding she could not devote the rest of her life to teaching full-time in the classroom. Instead, she might still find time to teach if she wrote only short features for journalism.

Hellman used her connections to get interesting assignments for *Colliers*, the *New Yorker* and *Ladies' Home Journal*. For a time, she resurrected her journalistic career, such as it was. The protests in the 1960s gave her a new home in the world of political outrage, and she found herself rising out of the doldrums of 1950s repression and right-wing spite. The *Ladies' Home Journal* hired Hellman to cover the August 1963 civil rights march on Washington. The *Journal* decided to turn away from "cold political analysts, seeking instead the artist, whose insights probe the true humanity of the events. Miss Hellman brought to the march the clear eye of a trained observer, the sensitivity and skill of one of America's major dramatists, and the tempered affection for the South."[100] In the piece that resulted, "Sophronia's Grandson Goes to Washington," Hellman got it right by demonstrating the dignity of the marchers, the political necessities of a peaceful revolution for equality. In the article she recalled her childhood to show the South's implicit racism and her own rebellious nature chafing against it. Beginning the piece as she stood in the cool of the morning on the steps of the Lincoln Memorial waiting for the grandson of her childhood nurse Sophronia, she immediately merged the personal with the political.

Her homespun start gave way to a focus on three protestors from Gasden, Alabama, who described "the electric cow prodders used on them by the police." Hellman graphically exposed the cruelty of southern law enforcement, though she did not name names. Her article outraged a southern sheriff enough that he sued her for libel, demanding a retraction. Thus began a trial by letter in the *Journal*'s pages. The *Journal* retracted Hellman's accusation immediately, but Hellman refused to renege on what she had been told (indeed, her diary records even more violent details told her by the young people). She stiffly replied that "my article in all important matters, tells the truth and I wish to disassociate myself from the above retraction. . . . What is true should not be obscured by fear of lawsuits."[101]

In a surprise show of support, fellow playwright Lorraine Hansberry defended Hellman against charges of libel. Hansberry's letter to the publisher insisted that Hellman had demonstrated "raw integrity" by writing such articles. "As is her habit in her art, she has dealt with the essences which are presently transpiring in the South."[102] Apparently the libel suit went nowhere once the *Journal* issued the retraction. Hellman put her public and personal personas in the middle of events she covered. She felt inextricable from the events surrounding her life. Editors grew wary of Hellman-induced political controversy, however, and tried a different subject.

In 1964, *Journal* editors asked the religiously iconoclastic Hellman, of all writers, to visit the Holy Land during Pope Paul VI's pilgrimage there, to observe and write about "what this mysterious and sacred place seems to mean to the Christians and Jews and Arabs who inhabit it."[103] What they got, of course, was Hellman's very personal account: "I sat for a long time on the ledge of the roof thinking that I was seeing the land that held the legend of my life—all that I believe and do not believe, the first words I ever heard, and someday, the last I will hear, the morals and the ethics, the rules in all their truth or lack of truth, here, right here." The piece had drama, interest, and atmosphere, but the journey she recorded was her own, not the pope's. The *Ladies' Home Journal* curtailed Hellman's journalism career. It hadn't suited her well, either. Her mix of personal and political made editors wary and she didn't like the restrictions.

She finally made one last stab at writing for Hollywood, perhaps forgetting the restrictions and forced collaborations in writing for screen. In 1965, at Warren Beatty's suggestion, producer Sam Spiegel invited her to adapt Horton Foote's novel, *The Chase*. At first she didn't believe the project would fly, but Beatty convinced her to try it. She went ahead when Arthur Penn agreed to direct. Hellman told the *New York Times* that she was "intrigued by the prospect of dissecting a Texas town, in light of the Kennedy assassination, to reveal the undercurrents of brutality."[104] In her notes she writes thoughtfully of Texas, its importance in the handling of the Kennedy murder, a "kind of anger that its convictions do not govern the rest of America."[105] Nevertheless, she asked for complexities in the culture of Texas, its people's great generosity, and angry politics: "I would like to try for a political commentary on Texas now. We needn't invent—newspapers will do." But Spiegel fell back on clichés and gratuitous violence, and Arthur Penn did little to stop it. Spiegel exacerbated the craziness of collaboration and ego that ruled Hollywood and that Hellman hated. Given a preliminary plot and script, she worked to make it dramatic and balanced. When Spiegel hired Horton Foote to modify her script, she turned her fury inward, knowing she'd been a fool to think Hollywood had changed and that she could cope with the superficial gloss of events only Hollywood could glamorize.

Released with a dazzling cast in 1966, the movie should have sizzled: Marlon Brando, Jane Fonda, Robert Redford, Miriam Hopkins, Angie Dickinson, and Robert Duvall, among others. But right from the start there was trouble. Brando said he took the film on because Hellman's politics "lent the script a cutting-edge slant."[106] The other actors and actresses didn't like Brando's high-handed attitude and accused him of "being asleep on his feet."[107] By many accounts Brando's malaise came about because Spiegel so thrashed the script that it became unrecognizable. Penn accused Spiegel of snatching Penn's footage when he was away in New York and spiriting it to the United Kingdom where he edited it according to his own interpretations. Penn's fury did not dissipate: "I was a babe in the woods. I didn't know from fancy Hollywood fucking."[108] But Hellman did. The film's images absolutely overpowered any subtlety of theme.

She forever washed her hands of the industry: "It wasn't the picture I wrote, and I was upset by it. Its accents were totally different than what I wrote. I didn't mean that kind of violence. I meant a Texas town gone wild on a Saturday night."[109] Although the film did well in Europe, critic Pauline Kael ripped it as "a liberal sadomasochistic fantasy."[110] Stanley Kauffman promptly reviewed it for the *New Republic*, calling Hellman "the most overrated American dramatist of the century," though critic Bernard Dick noted that "the film contained the basic ingredients of Hellman's plot, little of her dialogue and little of her art."[111] She really called it quits after *The Chase*; at sixty-one, she no longer had the patience for Hollywood power plays, unless she was making them. She told one reporter that the perfect script would be writing with only the end result in view: "You would write only the first few lines of each scene, leaving the rest to be improvised . . . that's the kind of script I'd like to try someday. But never, never again these old, weary disappointments."[112] Theoretically a Hellman script such as that would be innovative, visionary. But in practice she would never be able to relinquish a script to be improvised by others. She felt that as the writer, she was also the owner.

In 1967 she sued Samuel Goldwyn Productions, Samuel Goldwyn, and CBS for $500,000 over a live TV production of *The Little Foxes*. Hellman insisted her 1940 contract gave her sole and exclusive rights. Hollywood had not changed since her work in the 1930s and 1940s, but she had grown more cantankerous. When she left she thought she would always have a say, would always be its citizen. But after *The Chase* and Goldwyn's televising her work without her earning anything, she knew it had never been her shtick. Despite the fun she had and the people she met and liked, she viewed Hollywood as cruel and empty. Yet it drew her until the end of her life—its sunshine, its celebrities, its adulation of her fame. But Hollywood, for all its glitz and glamour, made the wrong choices. The slick celluloid strips turned images into action too glibly. "Tinsel town shimmers in illusions and so do its inhabitants. It still stands as the most preposterous civilization of all time."[113] The exhibitionist, judgmental Hellman should have fit right in, but she was nearly finished with the "promised land."

The journalism, the teaching, the failed film, the experimentation with story all came together one summer morning in the mid-1960s. After a long ride on the crest of fame, she had not realized, had not even considered, that her cultural capital had slipped. This moment came when Feibleman appeared for breakfast at Mill House and found an irate Hellman with the *New York Times* crumpled in her hands, pacing and storming. This was the moment she discovered that she didn't number among the playwrights who counted: Williams, Miller, and Albee. In shock she declared she would "get back on top."[114] She realized, however, that she couldn't go back to the theater. Her forte, the well-made play, no longer interested audiences and she knew it. She faced an ugly truth. As a writer she could no longer rest on her laurels, dabbling with journalism and teaching. Feibleman felt sorry for her—old, frail, and past her prime—a pity he later realized was misdirected. On that morning she decided to do something that had been niggling at her brain. She would invent a new form of autobiography, write a memoir with a difference.[115]

Literary pedestals are made to be toppled, especially when occupied by a mouthy, opinionated, politically incorrect woman outside the established literati. Hellman's ascent brought new rewards, but the woes were many. She wrote four memoirs, each different in intent, style, and creative endeavor, which made literary history: *Unfinished Woman* (1969), *Pentimento* (1973), *Scoundrel Time* (1976), and *Maybe* (1980). Few who read these books, written over the course of a decade, can forget Hellman. She invented a new form of the memoir, a literary legacy that changed the face of autobiography/fiction studies. In these memoirs, Hellman makes meaning of her life through prose, searching for an individual truth that can never be—given the writer's personal filter. She did not so much self-mythologize—as some critics complained—as show through literature that memory creates every person's myths of life—hers and her readers'.

Hellman never hankered after the alone-in-the-garret writing life; she did want to create new forms, new ways of thinking. She depended on the dramas of life, the libido, and the rush of politics to give her the impulse to create a literature that lasted.

Early in her newfound career, Hellman found fresh energy when publishing, power and sex mixed. And as she planned and wrote *Unfinished Woman*, a man got caught up in Hellman's mix of lust and creative license. Stan Hart, an editor at the venerable Little, Brown publishing house, fell victim to an idea and to the woman behind the idea. As a very young man, he had met Hellman on the Vineyard. Now years later in the 1960s, Hart was entranced by her growing reputation, feeling the whole world knew her alliances with radical New Frontier politics and politicians—intellectuals from Blair Clark to the Kennedys. He later wrote that "she was thought of as gutsy, brilliant, witty, noble, socially desirable, and sexually liberated." Hart's idea centered on getting this famous woman to write a memoir, something she had already begun, and then getting the publishing contract. As he said, "Lillian was beyond making news: she was news."[116]

He plotted to get her publishing allegiance and wrote a letter to Robbie Lantz, her literary agent. His timing was right. Her longtime relationship with Random House had faltered. Hellman refused to sign the Random House contract, decrying as rubbish the legal stipulations requiring her to promise she would not violate anyone's privacy and would pay court costs if anyone sued.[117] Hellman and Lantz cast about for a more respectful and fitting publishing house. Lantz was keen on Little, Brown but told Hart, "In order for her to go with your company, she has to get to know you." Somehow from Lantz's business proposition, the unhappily married thirty-six-year-old Hart decided that the sixty-three-year-old Hellman, whom he had not seen for fifteen years, wanted sex with him in order to promise publication. He made this leap of logic based on rumors that she had "an extensive love life." He quite boldly admitted thinking, "If I slept with Lillian Hellman, I could get her signature on a contract." (Hellman's editor for years had been Bennett Cerf, with whom she most certainly did not have sex.)

But Hart got what he wanted; after their first dinner, Hellman signed the contract and took Hart to bed. Lantz then informed him she might break the new contract, and Hart understood that to mean he would have to go to bed with Hellman more often. Lantz joined in the intrigue and teased Hart: "If you don't love and treasure this particular author from here on in, the whole deal will yet end in murder. For all you know, I am a pretty good shot, so — never, never, never upset Lillian Hellman."[118] At the time it seemed like good fun, but Hart began to feel like a "gigolo." That this cast the highly respected Lantz as Hellman's pimp apparently did not occur to him.

Hart "tagged along," but he never really understood Hellman or her penchant for dramatic scenes. She deliberated long and hard and loudly about asking George McBundy to dinner, given his hawkish stance on the Vietnam War. When she invited him, Hart could scarcely believe she had violated her political principles as she had. She switched to silly and operatic panic when she discovered that she and Hart had engaged in noisy, exuberant sex in a hotel room next to Leonard Bernstein, who might have heard them (since they clearly heard him do the same). Predictably, Hart tired of being Hellman's trophy boy, on hand when she needed a date, a bit player for her dramas. The best he could come up with for his actions is that Hellman was "game and sexy and flirtatious and a warm hearted trooper." They could play as long as she signed contracts and he drank. But "dead sober, I could not abide her. She was too irritable, too self-centered, she was aging and ungainly. When I spoke to her, I had to look past her face over her shoulder." On their last evening together he realized "she didn't like me and I didn't like her." Hart took credit for suggesting the Hammett leitmotiv as a unifying element in her memoirs. She might have been an "adventurer, a tough cookie with allure"[119] who disgusted the man who sold himself to get her signature, but she had value; *Unfinished Woman* became a huge success.

Remaking: Unfinished Woman

In storytelling, journalism, and teaching, Hellman had unintentionally prepared herself for an innovative foray into memory and story. *Unfinished Woman*, billed a memoir, focused more on memory and story than the storyteller's autobiography. Hellman had never lost her eager voyeuristic enjoyment of human antics. She wrote of the inhabitants at the Metropole Hotel in Russia, the middle-aged American who "is disturbed by the almost nightly arrival of a big Russian girl who pushes into his room, looks around and screams," or "Miss Butter Fingers," who "stole an icon on a visit to a German-destroyed monastery near Moscow" and "returned the loot" only when threatened with a "kangaroo trial in the lobby of the hotel."[120] Anecdote, not chronology, organized the book.

Snapping turtles in a cold spring at Hardscrabble leads her to the story of show-ing a turtle, its penis extending in fear, to Dottie Parker, who quipped, "It must be pleasant to have sex appeal for turtles. Shall I leave you alone together?"[121] What Hellman chose to reveal is in itself revelatory of a woman looking for commitment, depth, irony, pure fun.

She carefully chose her vignettes to portray herself as woman and writer-in-process. She wrote of her reasons for leaving the theater, for example, "maybe it happened because I started out wanting to write novels and didn't have much interest in the theatre or movies; maybe my own nature does not fit the rushing strong tones of the theatre; maybe because I like fame, but don't like, and am no good at, its requirements; or maybe vanity of any kind other than my own seems to me at first funny and at last boring.[122] In prose, she added the personal to the drama of the theater, painting scenes, adding dialogue and rhythms to make them comic opera. In writing this first mem-oir, she made use of materials she had already written to depict a writer's life, still unfinished. Hellman insisted the book be presented as memoir, not auto-biography, since she wrote herself in as a writer surrounded by the events and people of her life that mattered.

At the end of *Unfinished Woman* she moved forward stylistically, experi-menting with a more focused portrayal of three lives that heavily influenced her own. She had written loving eulogies for Dorothy Parker and Hammett and by adding a similar eulogistic piece on Helen, her long-time maid, she paid homage to friendship, love, and a struggle between differing points of view. This ending of *Unfinished Woman* pointed to the literary possibility to come, something not strictly autobiographical but a literary try for the truth of a life not found in fact alone but in supposition and theme. Readers hoping for an inclusive autobiographical portrayal or erudite musings about her public life as screenwriter and playwright were disappointed. Some seemed shocked that she had portrayed herself as a lit-erary character, a writer's invention. Some could not distinguish between a memoir and an autobiography. In ominous rumblings of discontent, others felt cheated because she failed to show how her politics developed, how she became so famous. She did not answer the questions many wanted an-swered. Though her first memoir clearly had flaws of organization and continuity, relying too heavily on previously written texts of various kinds and styles with little attempt to unify, Hellman nevertheless exposed a dif-ferent kind of life and the crafted nature of its telling.

The reading public, seeking a glimpse of personality, not a full confes-sional, got it: "By juxtaposing odd pieces of her life she has given us a detailed portrait of a person who doesn't want to be portrayed. And she makes us understand."[123] *Unfinished Woman* won a National Book Award, hit the *New York Times* best-seller list and stayed for weeks. The University of California–Berkeley appointed her Regents Professor, she was named Distinguished Professor of Romance Languages at Hunter, and Richard Moody published the first critical biography. Drawing on her newfound acclaim, Little, Brown published her *Collected Plays*—something that would have been highly unlikely a few years before. She was back.

Political Detour

In her late fifties, at her peak, she had rejected the political limelight to become a new kind of thinker and writer, a professor and memoirist. It took Richard Nixon to stir her political passion. Nixon's rise to political power served as a "provocation"[124] to Hellman, who despised him. His election as president of the United States in 1969 raised her hackles and long buried fears: "It is not true that when the bell tolls it tolls for thee: if it were true we could not have elected . . . Richard Nixon."[125] She had been on the receiving end of Nixon's political dirty tricks and thought he lacked character. Nixon's cohorts—henchmen—had sat at the accuser's dais across from her when she appeared before the House Un-American Activities Committee. Hellman had a long memory, and her politics were always deeply personal. Robbie Lantz reflected, "She had a tremendous sense of justice in daily life. I don't mean going into courts and having lawsuits." God knows that was part of it. But "Lillian had a strong feeling about the decent thing to do . . . when she had to take a stand and she did. She was not short of guts."[126]

After lying low politically for over two decades, Hellman prepared to take another stand. She hated Nixon's "trivial little smile" and didn't trust him a bit.[127] When statesman and writer George Kennan spoke before a Princeton conference appealing to scholars and public intellectuals to give the new Nixon administration a chance, Hellman responded, "But is it a question of chance? Chance is rather too sporting a word. Perhaps it would be best to wait and applaud the administration, if and when it deserves applause."[128] In her heart of hearts she knew applause would not be forthcoming. She watched him with a sneering despair as he wooed a country with his brand of politics, sent troops to fight a war in Vietnam, lied to the country about a war in Cambodia, smeared left-wing politicians and Hellman's friends. She was no longer the frightened middle-aged woman facing HUAC. She was aging and poisoned by the political resurgence of scoundrels.[129]

Impatient with middle-of-the-road Democrats and absolutely contemptuous of Republicans and right-wing zealots, she assessed what she had and what she needed.[130] Not just "anybody's follower," she gathered a group of proven, trusted intellectuals and lawyers who had influence and either money or the ability to raise it.[131] Her experience told her that standing alone was foolhardy and that party alliances could fall apart—or worse, turn knavish in unexpected ways. She built a network.

In 1969, three years before the burglary that began the Watergate scandal, Hellman, along with producer Hannah Weinstein and MIT president Jerome Weisner, formed the Committee for Public Justice. Stephen Gillers, the attorney Hellman recruited to do the committee's day-to-day work, described the purpose of the committee as "just based on the fear that we were headed for much worse than McCarthyism . . . something that would deprive people of their liberty."[132] Weinstein was a longtime friend, and Weisner's mind entranced her. All three, Weinstein later recalled, were from a "generation that felt they could change the world."[133] Hellman aligned herself with people of brilliance and flexibility—big minds or wallets. "Lillian decided that the country was in trouble because of the ascendancy of the Nixon administration. She perceived that the American Civil Liberties Union was at a low point, and she decided that we needed . . . the quick and prominent reaction of famous people to violations of constitutional liberty."[134] Hellman argued that "the mistake we made in the McCarthy era was no one with any substance was standing by."[135] To combat political pressures in the United States, public citizens with influence needed to stand firm.

Under the premise that "this country had entered one of its recurring periods of dangerous political repression," on Bill of Rights Day, December 15, 1970, the committee took out a full-page advertisement in the *New York Times*. Hellman, Weinstein, and Weisner "set up an early-warning system against the invasions of our freedoms. . . in order to make our own investigations, form broadly based coalitions to defend rights." Asking for funds to assist the committee, the ad was signed by the executive council, big names one and all: Roger Wilkins, assistant attorney general under Lyndon Johnson; Blair Clark, CBS News executive and national campaign manager for Senator Eugene McCarthy's 1968 presidential bid; Ramsey Clark, former U.S. attorney general; Robert Coles, a young psychiatrist already known for winning the *Saturday Review*'s Anisfield-Wolf Award in Race Relations (1968) and the American Psychiatric Association's Hofheimer Award (1968); Norman Dorsen, general counsel to the American Civil Liberties Union; Burke Marshall, former assistant attorney general under both Kennedy and

Johnson, Robert Silvers, coeditor of the *New York Times Book Review*; Telford
Taylor, prosecutor before the Nuremberg trials; Harold Willens, cofounder of
Business Executives Move for Vietnam Peace; and Jerome Weisner, who was
also President John F. Kennedy's special assistant for science and technology,
producer Hannah Weinstein, and Lillian Hellman, writer. The impressive
names on the committee's roster pushed its egalitarian agenda, and they garnered the dollars that would pressure Nixon in ways not yet conceived.

Despising amateurs, disdainful of the untried, she chose allies with professionalism and proof of their mettle from the likes of Warren Beatty and
Candice Bergen to Leonard Bernstein and Warren Christopher. The "quick
and prominent reaction of famous people" could best halt threats to civil liberties.[136] Her approach had weaknesses, she knew. Gillers reflected, "From
the very first day to the last, she and the entertainment faction pitted in a
friendly way (more or less) against the lawyers."[137] But the committee needed
both approaches and together, they worked.

Gillers stood in awe of her determination and strength but dreaded her
"lacerating" criticism. Always the boss, Hellman made certain committee
members came from varied political backgrounds, thwarting any effort to
label it red or a front organization. She had too much of that in her past.
Loath to do the footwork alone, Hellman worked with writer-journalist Jean
Stein and actress-writer Felicia Bernstein (Leonard Bernstein's wife) on the
committee's earliest project. The three women, sometimes accompanied by
Robert Coles, investigated the Women's House of Detention to inspect the
treatment of prisoners. There Hellman ran the show, "no matter the presence
of wardens."[138] Coles remembered her standing next to him tapping her foot
impatiently as he interviewed prisoners about their psychology—not the
group's focus. A prisoner noticed her irritation and told Coles he had better
go or he'd get in trouble.[139] Hellman "wasn't large but she took command of
her space."[140]

These early activities served as warm-ups for the concerted national actions the committee would later direct. For a time, members made speeches,
held fund-raisers, spoke at meetings in high schools, libraries, colleges.
Hellman bided her time; if she didn't have her youthful patience for the
grunt work of politics, she had influence and backbone and gave orders with
the fervor of a party whip. Despite the notables on the committee, "Hellman
ALWAYS commandeered the meeting. Of the fifteen people responsible for
week to week management, regardless of who was speaking, Bob Silvers was
the only one with the courage to interrupt!"[141] Hellman drew the line at offending Silvers, prestigious editor of the *New York Review*.

The group vigilantly watched the political climate to preserve the Bill of Rights. Hellman found Nixon's enemies list frightening because they weren't enemies at all, just those who disagreed with his party's politics. Hellman had a long enemies list of her own, of course, and also knew firsthand she couldn't trust the government. Agents had followed her and Hammett for years, read her mail, taped her phone conversations. In her mind they had ruined Hammett, ruined another lover, John Melby, and ruined men she admired from a further distance like Paul Robeson and Martin Luther King Jr. She hated the chilling effect FBI spying had on the burgeoning new left, certain that the FBI was responsible for much of the repression of the antiwar protestors.

With plenty of pluck and real rage, Hellman and the Committee for Public Justice prepared to take on J. Edgar Hoover's FBI. In October 1971, The committee, in conjunction with the Woodrow Wilson School at Princeton, sponsored a conference to investigate the FBI. They invited Hoover to come and speak in the FBI's defense. Hoover shot back a reply saying the FBI needed no defense. He then crafted a ten-page, single-spaced explanation and "leaked" it to the New York Times; in essence, he wrote his defense of the bureau. The letter and the leak backfired on Hoover, however, as it brought public attention to the conference.

Hoover doubted the conference sponsors' "impartiality," and Ramsey Clark, using his clout as a former attorney general, retorted that the bureau suffered from "a lack of objectivity in pursuing facts and an intolerance of internal criticism."[142] Hoover again changed his mind and sent two agents to defend the bureau. The conference established long-standing FBI abuses and "put the Committee for Public Justice on the map."[143]

Successfully harassing J. Edgar Hoover, hardly small fry, prepared the committee for snagging the president. By the time Nixon's "plumbers" broke into the office of Daniel Ellsberg's psychiatrist in September 1971, the committee was actively keeping track. Hellman had "very few gray areas," Lisa Weinstein remembered. "She had an extraordinary intelligence and a kind of bravery" that informed her strong opinions.[144] Still, that gut instinct sometimes erred, which she hated to admit. Politics mattered deeply and she didn't trust the public memory for political deceit: "We can be deprived of a great deal without knowing it, without realizing it, waking up to it."[145]

Layered Portraits

Even as Hellman's politics against the Nixon White House reached a fever pitch, she did not abandon her writing. In fact, political fire and romance gave her the energy to create. Hellman began work on her next memoir. *Pentimento*, more literary than autobiographical, referred in its title to memory depicted: "Old paint on canvas, as it ages, sometimes becomes transparent. When that happens it is possible, in some pictures, to see the original lines. . . that is called *pentimento* because the painter 'repented,' changed his mind. Perhaps it would be as well to say that the old conception replaced by a later choice, is a way of seeing and then seeing again. That is all I mean about the people in this book. The paint has aged now and I wanted to see what was there for me once, what is there for me now."[146] Hellman insisted to anyone who would listen that she had not written an autobiography but "a book of portraits." This important distinction—had anyone been interested—should have saved her much criticism as to her purpose and intent. Editor Robert Manning, after advertising Hellman's "memoir" in *Atlantic Monthly*, replied to her insistent note: "The confusion about memoirs vs. portraits or profiles is inexplicable to me, but I have inserted a corrective in the forthcoming July issue."[147]

Straight autobiography would require no corrective, but Hellman had written a book of memories with more literary than autobiographical intent. Each of the seven portraits in the book focused on a different part of Hellman's life, a different aspect of the self as mirrored and reflected in another, a different kind of truth and a different kind of love. She brought the craft of writing to the fore, writing each of the seven chapters in a different style. Content and style merge, memory moves, and characters grow and recede. A very complex Hellman emerges through these portraits.

As she did in her plays, Hellman invited readers to recognize themselves in the portraits while she staked out individual territory. In "Bethe," a young Hellman discovers the mystery of man and woman, its romance, its violence, its intrigues; "Willy" recalls how she learned to lust—for money, for food, for sex—in lush Louisiana. Originally she thought her third chapter, "Julia," a rather boring story about a train ride and a simple exchange of money, but Hellman embellished it with intimations of political fear and the power of friendship.[148] She followed the plot-centered "Julia" with "Theatre," a collage of portraits of those who peopled her life in film and theater. The excesses of Hollywood and Broadway is followed by "Arthur W.A. Cowan," a portrait of a man who was as excessive and compelling to Hellman as the theater was, as she herself was at times. "Turtle" follows the craziness. An odd kind of fable, a secular homily about the meaning of life, "Turtle" depicts metaphorically the struggle for physical and metaphysical answers. Finally in "Pentimento," the last chapter, Hellman closes with scenes of grief and loss covered over with the memory's tendency to elevate and idealize. In all these portraits of others, Hellman portrays herself—obliquely, artfully.

Pentimento came out in spring 1973 to laudatory reviews as an "absorbing and probing series of portraits."[149] Hellman eagerly awaited what she considered the true test of the book—the *New York Times Book Review*. She got big play in that issue, which also featured her interview by Nora Ephron at Martha's Vineyard. But the big story for Hellman was Mark Schorer's praise, which she could not influence. He called the book "brilliantly finished" and honored Hellman for her "poised power." He astutely noted that the book was not autobiography in the strictest sense but rather "major outlines: and the pervasive presence. . . of her person."[150] Hellman wrote William Abrahams, her friend and editor: "And today, great, great news. Mark [Schorer] review. It really is wonderful for me and even my fake modesty is put aside for the minute and I bought myself an ice cream soda." Riding high on the critical acclaim of *Pentimento* and her induction into the Theatre Hall of Fame, Hellman reveled in the press and the parties given in her honor.

Unsurprisingly, amid the mélange of innovation within the book, critics began to quarrel bitterly over the ethics of autobiography: could an author purposely and admittedly distort memory and call it memoir? Could an author devote a whole section to a cousin she saw fewer than ten times and skip the myriads of friends and lovers readers wanted to know about? Could Hellman in particular get away with telling partial and shifting truths her own way? Literary critics, journalists, and historians vehemently disagreed about whether Hellman had the right to use this particular method to present herself. Many critics, taking it at face value, simply did not understand the book. Those who did saw a truth of a different kind. As with *Unfinished Woman*, women in particular glimpsed themselves and their experiences told in Hellman's story. Insisting that Hellman's unremitting focus on a woman's point of view made them "ladies books," some men belittled both its focus on a woman's point of view and the complexity of its style and content. Clearly *Pentimento* was not autobiography but something new, causing much critical angst. Thousands of readers, however, loved the book, and their readership made Hellman an American icon. *Pentimento's* remarkable success seemed like a kind of life insurance, but trouble was coming. Who would have thought that memoirs and competing views about truth could electrify a reading public?

She had worried about the book when its publication didn't go as smoothly as she wanted at Little, Brown. She was on the outs with editor Hart, and she found herself at odds with Fred Hill, director of advertising, publicity, and promotion. Hellman meddled in every detail of the process and took Hill to task for what she saw as his errors in promoting her book. Hill and Hellman had words. In fury, Hill wrote her saying that "you are trying to make a driveling eight-year-old idiot out of me." She responded that she did "not like such personal remarks and I do not wish to exchange them with you or anybody else. Therefore, I will be grateful if you will let me know by letter with whom I should deal. Let us both be regretful that we have wasted so much time on so little, caused so much mess that didn't have to be."[151] Hellman thought Hill had caused the mess by his ineptitude and his furious letter to her. However, she had provoked Hill by second-guessing every decision he made. No author gets that kind of power over a publisher.

Yet Hellman always tried to control the marketing of her work. She had running feuds with publishers of her plays and the public relations departments of theaters. Hellman kept a watchful eye on the publisher's choice of book cover, quotes on the jacket, and bookseller availability. Those involved ran afoul of her temper about their handling of her manuscripts. As early as 1939 she chastised publisher Bennett Cerf at Random House, forcing him into a defensive posture. He wrote her, "I will be delighted to talk to you about advertising on *The Little Foxes* at any time. I should like to say, in our own defense, that we did advertise *The Little Foxes*. Furthermore, we featured it at the very top of all our play announcements. . . I hope you will come into the office some day and let me show you just what has been done."[152] She never let up. Now thirty-six years later, she found herself seething over the details of publishing *Pentimento*.

Now she had clout and was ready to rumble. Executive editor Roger Donald wrote her immediately after the Hill-Hellman debacle: "Good grief! This should be a time of celebration for you. It is a damn shame that you should be distressed right now. . . . As to the Fred Hill situation: It would be absurd for me to go on at length about your importance to us, or about the affection that there is for you throughout the house." He suggested that Joe Consolino had the "smarts and the authority" to talk to her about the "whole publishing process." Donald called her problems with Fred Hill a "foul-up." Soothing Hellman had become part of Donald's job.[153]

At this point she had little inkling that critics might find fault with her facts; her writing perhaps, but not the story itself. Therefore she was surprised in 1973 when she received a vociferous complaint from a source she hadn't even considered. Dr. Jan Van Loewen had been Jean Anouilh's agent in their 1954 negotiations over Hellman's adaptation of *The Lark* for Broadway. Even then, Van Loewen and Hellman had exchanged testy letters about conditions and each other's rudeness.

In the "Theatre" chapter of *Pentimento*, Hellman wrote a vignette about meeting Dr. Van Loewen, suggesting that the "mischief" of her adapting *The Lark* came out of that meeting. Van Loewen and Hellman had disagreed about whether the play could be adapted by someone other than a poet. He didn't think Hellman qualified. When Hellman suggested he needed George Bernard Shaw, Van Loewen snapped, "Shaw was not a poet. I do not think he would have been the right adaptor, either."[154] Hellman wrote in *Pentimento* that she had written his comment on her menu. She lightly satirized the meeting with the rather stiff doctor, but her account was more amusing than critical.

From London, Van Loewen wrote that he had read *Pentimento* with "interest and pleasure," but when he read about himself he was "stunned." "The cause was not your depicting me as a bumbling automaton (agents are used to such insults) but my amazement that not only had you told a story which was almost entirely untrue but also one of which by your own admission you were rightly ashamed. Now let us set the record straight." He proceeded to detail the discrepancies: they had "tea" not "lunch" at the Ritz; the Ritz did not have menus at tea; her timing of the meeting was off as she had already written a draft; their disagreement was on changes, not the adaptation conditions. He admitted to the discussion on "poetical qualities." However, he fervently denied that contrary to her assertion in the book, he had never called her honest. He thought she was a "writer who for the sake of monetary reward undertakes to adapt another dramatist's work." He ended in a huff, saying he was a doctor of law, not medicine, which she implied in her memoir.

As stunned as he, Hellman answered the "non-subjective points of his letter." She wrote that maybe it was tea, rather than lunch, but there most certainly was a menu on the table, which she still owned; she admitted her French was not good, argued once again about the translation, said producer Kermit Bloomgarden verified all other issues, said she never said he was a doctor of medicine. In a flurry she wrote, "If you think I am inaccurate, I know that you are an inaccurate reader. I do not say this in unfriendliness: I say it only to defend myself."[155]

Indeed, documents verify Hellman's version of events almost entirely. But her tone incensed him, and he turned spiteful. He wrote to her again, "I wish that you had not answered my letter. Were you a lesser woman and had you had the grace to accept the slight rap over the knuckles which you deserved, I would have forgotten this miserable chapter of your book. But now you force me to a real spanking."[156] He let her have it, accusing her of a "shabby slur" and a "mercenary act." Presumably their correspondence ended there.

Van Loewen never lost his sense of being wronged. On June 5, 1984, he wrote editor William Abrahams "re *Pentimento* pp. 200–202." It had been "tea not dinner"; she had made a "bowdlerized" version of Anouilh's *The Lark* but without his previous knowledge or authority. Van Loewen still felt wronged and wanted him to know that the play had been "a great success but it has been an even greater one all over Europe and South America in its original form."[157] Hellman assuredly had not written *The Lark* adaptation without Anouilh's authority, and Abrahams knew it. So did Van Loewen, really. But time and bad feeling warped his memories too.

For every complaint, Hellman received hundreds of accolades. Honorary doctorates from NYU, Smith, and Yale and speaking engagements at Bryn Mawr College and the Smithsonian supplemented hoards of letters from academics, friends, and complete strangers who read the book in excitement at its innovation and for the pure pleasure of the text. Her friends celebrated with her at every opportunity, and she enjoyed her renewed acclaim against a backdrop of A-list parties that would have made Truman Capote envious. Hellman, ever the contrarian, loved people and parties as much as she desperately sought controversy and solitude. Even before *Pentimento* was released, Little, Brown gave Hellman star receptions and dinners with the publication of her books. Hellman carefully drew up the lists, recorded the RSVPs, and watched carefully to see who would celebrate with her. Her *Unfinished Woman* party had to be divided into two events—an elaborate dinner party at the Four Seasons and a later reception in the library room at the 21 Club.[158] The guest list read like a cross between a gossip column and a society register. Most were close friends: the Leonard Bernsteins, the John Herseys, the Lionel Trillings, the Edmund Wilsons, the Robert Penn Warrens, the Sidney Perelmans, Ruth Field, Richard Poirier, Hannah Weinstein, Howard Bay, Blair Clark, Arthur Kober, Edmund Wilson, Fred Gardner, and many more of Hellman's acquaintances. Spouses were welcome, a show of largess in a woman who more often than not preferred her male friends to show up without wives. Some guests had star power: Jacqueline and Ari Onassis, Studs Terkel, and Kay Graham. If anything, the 1973 *Pentimento* party dazzled even more. Held at the 21, it included her old friends but added a new collection: Warren Beatty, Mike Nichols, Jules Feiffer, Albert Hackett, Don Congdon, and literary and political lights from New York City and Martha's Vineyard. Photographers everywhere photographed Hellman with celebrities and the less well known. She loved it all, the center of glitter and glamour, toasted by friends, riding the success of another book.

Always the hostess, eager to entertain, she went to lunch daily when in New York City. She loved good food, and even good chefs eagerly awaited her yea or nay when she ate at their restaurant. She did business and pleasure at the table, smoking half cigarettes or cigars at times in a desperate attempt to quit smoking, eagerly awaiting each course. She liked restaurants near her Park Avenue apartment, which she bought in 1972 after selling her house on 82nd Street. She became part of the tony neighborhood, meeting friends by chance or design, keeping in touch. She and Marvin Sadik had met when she taught at Harvard; she cooked him venison at Leverett House, where he was senior tutor, and for years after met him at a restaurant on Madison and 72nd in Manhattan where they both liked to dine.[159] If it wasn't Sadik, it was someone else. She networked and flirted and reigned as queen at her table at various establishments that welcomed her, despite the occasional drama. She slid under the table on one occasion to evade notice from a beautiful woman she saw as a rival; on another, she and Maureen Stapleton nearly got thrown out of a fancy restaurant after Hellman backed into a waiter carrying a dessert tray, who dropped it with crashing and clatter and chocolate everywhere. The women collapsed with laughter.[160] She was glamorous, fun, and much feted.

In 1975 the Circle in the Square Theatre honored her with a night of readings from her memoirs and plays. Over five hundred attended the tribute to her and to her founding of the Committee for Public Justice. Newspapers featured a gallery of photos from the evening. So many were taken that Hellman snapped at not even getting to sip coffee without the paparazzi in attendance. But her guests invited the camera's click: Ron Galella, Jackie O, Oliver Smith, Candice Bergen with escort Mike Nichols, Maureen Stapleton, Warren Beatty. Hellman saucily went from guest to guest, flirting, joking. She asked Beatty why he didn't play a part in the theatrical proceedings, and he grinned, "I offered to play you." All aglitter, the cast moved to Gallaghers: "All stars—a den with a dramatis personae of romp-aholics, enfants terrible of yesteryear, literati, veteran performers and political pundits." Bejeweled in four strands of pearls, surrounded by admirers, she played the high life, enjoying every minute. *Ladies' Home Journal* named her Woman of the Year for 1975, following the example of New York University alumnae naming her their first Woman of the Year in 1973. It seemed to be her decade.

She gambled and partied in Barbados or traveled by train, plane, and yacht to Brugge, Paris, Egypt. Meeting up with friends as she traveled the world was a favorite pastime of hers, though inevitable glitches broke bonds on occasion. In Barbados she raised a stink over someone else a friend invited but overcame her ire to hit the casinos. Once she expected to rendezvous at the airport with Abrahams, but his plane was late and they got their signals crossed: "Lillian was so mad she said she wanted 'to get a gun and shoot you.'"[161] Knowing how difficult she could be didn't stop Max Palevsky from inviting her on yachting trips from Maine to Egypt. She could cut up, start arguments with other guests, startle them by appearing nude for swims, steal food for midnight snacks, even knowing she could order it. But she livened any trip with her wit and even her malice.[162] She, Sid Perelman, the Hacketts, and "a couple of poets" rented a house in Sarasota Springs, Florida, one February. Their efforts at communal living sizzled, not always happily. Hellman often met Peter Feibleman, in Mexico, in New Orleans, in Los Angeles. Active, involved, ever curious about the history, the food, and the dramas of other cultures, Hellman made travel part of the action. She didn't just dine out at famous restaurants. She loved to visit museums and go on tours, taking notes on the guide's information. Even late in life, struggling against glaucoma and barely able to see, she insisted on being everywhere with everyone, taking in the world.

As infirmity set in, she began to lug around a seventy-five-pound breathing machine, insisting that any health problems she had came from emphysema, something she diagnosed herself because she recognized Hammett's symptoms. Doctors did not necessarily agree, but she coerced one into giving her the oxygen. Her machine involved a cumbersome process made frightening by her insistence on lifting the mask and smoking, then placing her cigarette on top of it, although it was clearly labeled "No Smoking." Eventually she wearied of being on the go, eating "drek," being beholden to others' whims.

So the jet-setter Hellman entertained at home, mixing smart people and excellent food. She was as good a hostess as she was a celebrity. When she cooked, she insisted on perfect ingredients and had many of them shipped from point of origin; Virginia ham had to come from Virginia or Kentucky; the horseradish needed to be sharp and fresh. She grew hers over an old septic tank at Mill House and it was luxurious. She expressed herself in food, generously giving and advising, arguing over its proper function. She once called physician friend Jonathan LaPook's mother Elsa to settle a screaming row with friend Hannah Weinstein about what part of the cow "flanken" came from.[163] She began a friendship with Richard De Combray in part because he cooked and could find her coriander. Particular and with a penchant for New Orleans cooking, she could be tart about the ability of others, finding fault with the way Bill Styron served cold ham, Mike and Annabel Nichols's thick creams, and Feibleman's use of olive oil. She used food as gift, as communication; a Hellman invitation meant an evening of excellent conversation, great food, and plenty of liquor.[164]

Hellman as she aged held harsher opinions and was more demanding of attention, but guests eagerly accepted her requests to dine, and she captured invitations from everywhere. Pulitzer Prize–winning composer Ned Rorem invited Hellman to a dinner party also attended by Hellman's admired mentor Janet Flanner; the guests talked cooking and Cuisinarts among other topics. Flanner, somewhat senile, was upset and hysterical as she left because she couldn't find her address, which she had written down and put in her purse; Hellman tried to play down Flanner's desperate straits to preserve her dignity by insisting "she's just putting on."[165] Every evening was a drama, even when these famous men and women talked mostly of cooking and food processors.

When teaching in Berkeley, Hellman, her friend and editor Billy Abrahams, and his partner Peter Stansky accepted an invitation for dinner at the home of radical lawyer Bob Truehalf and his wife, Jessica Mitford. As Mitford was something of a rival and to make sure she was appropriately armed, Hellman ordered Billy to stop at a liquor store to get her hostess a gift. Even with Hellman haranguing him about the necessity of such a gift, Abrahams refused because the neighborhood was very bad. Edna O'Brien, another grand lady and wonderful writer, had also been invited to dinner. She arrived with a huge bouquet of flowers. Hellman turned to Billy and Peter and muttered, "We've lost round one." Then added, "She probably took them from the hotel vase."[166]

Hellman negotiated parties as she did theater contracts. She loved the Styrons and they did much mutual entertaining on the Vineyard. But Hellman let it be known that she would stay away from Styron parties if his friend civil rights activist Virginia Durr attended. Hellman, jealous of Durr, "could be fractious about trivial matters."[167] "Raddled and bone-thin, chain-smoking and chic," Hellman awed nearly everyone.[168]

A Rage of the Mind

Despite the pleasures of politics and celebrations, friends and parties, age began to take its toll. A fierce smoker since she was twelve, she had breathing problems. She also had an enlarged heart and progressive glaucoma. All this illness wore her down. She had a series of falls, not her usual "laundry bag" falls caused by her failure to look down, but serious, inexplicable ones: in a Paris hotel room, on Madison Avenue in New York, at the Watergate in Washington, D.C.[169] Beginning in the mid-1970s, Feibleman, Mike Nichols, Lantz, Dick Poirier, and Rita Wade—friends she had known for years—worried she had undergone changes that had damaged her judgment. Increasingly she raged out of control over all manner of slights. She saw physicians and specialists only when Feibleman forced her to.

When she finally consented to seek health care, she wanted instant remedies for her ailments and didn't get them. She reacted in fury. When a Dr. Savetsky sent her a bill that she received less than a day after her appointment and must have been mailed even before she saw him, she sent a scathing, satiric commentary. "I have to conclude that you have a machine or a privilege which does not belong to you by democratic principles and must be reported to the Postmaster General in Washington." She asked for an explanation "before I do anything rash in what is certainly the worst black comedy episode I have ever known in American Medicine."[170] A classic of the complaint genre is the letter she wrote to a pacemaker company when her pacemaker faltered on a Saturday. The emergency number she called played Muzak, followed by a recorded message telling her the office was closed. She found age and illness not only inconvenient but contemptible.

Increasingly litigious, she threatened to sue the New England Telephone Company for poor service, contemplated a lawsuit against Massachussetts for seaweed problems, successfully challenged a parking ticket in Edgartown and unsuccessfully challenged one in Tisbury, complained to Tisbury township over trash collection, and got into a big tiff with a Mr. MucKerheide over his maintenance of her Jacuzzi.[171]

She counted it a good day to fish in a boat off the Island with John Hersey, Jack Koontz, or anyone else she could coerce into taking her. She swam daily, walking down the rocky trail from her house to the shore to submerge, to let the water hold her weightless so she could return to a calm sense of self. When she came back to the house, she put on her swimsuit and her troubles.[172] But increasingly her fishing lines tangled, she could not hold her pole for large fish, and others had to watch out for her falling or stumbling. One day she swam and suddenly could not see to find her way to shore. While speaking in New Orleans at Tulane University, she lit a Kleenex on fire with her cigarette and nearly set the stage aflame until Feibleman leaped to his feet and put it out. She thought the university president acted rudely, not knowing that Feibleman had averted a catastrophe of her making.

Friends cautioned her about putting lit cigarettes down everywhere, about cooking by herself, about drinking too much. Her dependence and disability enraged her.

Her physique diminished, though her presence did not. When she re-turned from Paris after one of her falls, Feibleman had to bring a wheelchair to pick her up. Trying to distract Hellman from something he knew she hated, he saw a little boy and asked his mother how old he was. The mother said three. Hellman, not in the best of moods but still with her wit about her, said, "Four if he's a day."[173] Her wit stayed sharp as her body failed. She often had to be carried from place to place. Feibleman hired men and nurses to do the carrying when friends could not. But she so outraged nurses on two coasts that Home Nursing Companies hung up when Feibleman called. She once went through thirty nurses in a month.[174] She still insisted on going every-where, doing everything. East Coast winters ultimately forced her to Los Angeles, a city she despised. She stayed at the Wylers' when she could, as they offered room and privacy. She demanded a degree of independence, and friends became surreptitious about helping her. On one occasion, her young doctor friend Jonathan LaPook asked to fly to California with her, pre-tending to be traveling to a conference so she wouldn't refuse his escort. He then turned around and flew back to New York.

Hellman could make life interesting for those around her. But as interest-ing as she was, and as loyal as her intellectual, talented friends were, going anywhere with Hellman became a trial. It wasn't just her physical disability that made some reluctant to spend a week in Los Angeles or a weekend at the Vineyard with her. Hellman seemed to orchestrate discord. Even if things went well on the surface, everyone felt the tension as they waited for her to berate a waiter or turn hostile toward others on the beach. Once she slapped a child who had inadvertently shoved her, shocking the parents, appalling her apologetic friends. As charming and fun as she often was at parties, play-ing Scrabble with Rose Styron or Feibleman, or drinking cocktails with Jerome Weisner and author John Hersey and his wife, Barbara, as Hellman aged, her friends waited for the other shoe to drop.[175]

She hired a series of college girls to assist her at the Vineyard, the horrors of which Rosemary Mahoney recorded in A Likely Story. Why Hellman in-sisted on college girls as helpers, particularly from the excellent Wells College, to assist her in cooking, cleaning, and driving is inexplicable. She would quiz them about their education and then offer to help them sue the college for their poor showing. Her remarks were joking but nevertheless in-sulting. She liked to hire English majors, though she made it quite clear in hiring them that she would not read anything they had written, nor were they to write about her. She had housekeepers as well and might have been better off with an older, more experienced person with little intellectual interest in her. These young women had to be strong to endure. As one of them recalled, "Hellman pushed everyone to the limits of their endurance."[176] Not all of these young women were as cowed or as insensitive as Mahoney, but they recognized the experience for what it was.

The young college women served as a lifeline to Hellman, increasingly blind, infirm, and paranoid. With them she could continue her social whirl and her doctor's appointments. Linda Lightner was a young student just graduated from Wells College in upstate New York when she went to work for Hellman in the spring of 1981. She extended the summer hiring period and stayed until just before Christmas. Lightner remembers the atmosphere as inevitably tense. Hellman never kept a relaxed house. "She really had her hands into everything from how many cases of beer she had on hand to the grocer's wrong delivery." Lightner recalled "Miss Hellman standing there supervising the process of everything, repeating the necessity of finely sliced chicken for sandwiches, packing picnic baskets, gathering towels—a very hands-on personality that pushed to the extreme. Interesting, but not relaxing."[177] Hellman kept to her routines and insisted others carry out orders exactly. That could be wearing, very wearing.

Of all the stories about thankless summers with Hellman, the most horrifying concern Hellman's failure to provide adequate living quarters for the young women. Hellman told Lightner how much fun it would be for her to camp in a tent in front of the house when visitors took over one of the guest rooms that served (ever temporarily) as Lightner's sleeping quarters. Lightner had only to stay in the tent once, but Hellman's decision-making process clearly had slipped. Sometimes Hellman was kind and generous, arranging for Lightner's hair to be colored by her hairdresser, taking her on Max Palevsky's yacht on the Maine trip, and to Los Angeles to the Beverly Wilshire Hotel. As Lightner recalled, "She could be very mean, cold, and cruel. But more than any person I've ever known, she really had a lot of contradictory qualities: really noble, really petty; very focused and lucid, then obtuse—childish. All of those things were part and parcel for her. I liked her, but she could be exasperating."[178]

When *The Little Foxes* revival was held in Washington, D.C., in March 1981 for President Reagan, Hellman had an ugly fall in her Watergate hotel room but insisted on attending the president's reception. There, once again, she and Maureen Stapleton created a scene. This one concerned Stapleton's husband, Max Allentuck, and the first lady's distant past in Hollywood. As Stapleton told it, she, Elizabeth Taylor, and Hellman made up the end of the reception line, Hellman wobbly and leaning on a cane. Stapleton said, "Hello, Mr. President" and then "Hello, Nancy." Hellman came next and behaved admirably, a relief to those worried about her lingering liberal sensibilities. Then Hellman hissed to Stapleton, "You *knew* them! . . . You called her Nancy and she called you Maureen." Stapleton ignored Hellman, who grew agitated, keeping up a litany of "you know her, you know her." At the end of her patience, Stapleton turned to Hellman and "slowly, deliberately, rather audibly, said 'For God's sake, I don't know her. Max fucked her. We're practically family. That's how I know her.' Lillian Hellman laughed so hard she could barely catch her breath. She sagged on the cane and crumpled at the knees."[179] As it turned out, when Hellman fell earlier she had fractured her "pubic ramus bone," which as she told Weisner, "is not sexual in case you think it is."[180] Hellman had not lost her humor nor her zest for a good sexual drama.

Her irascible nature increasingly erupted as she lost her independence and her ability to influence opinion. Writing became a challenge, then nearly impossible. She bought typewriters with increasingly large type, and she still couldn't see. Dictating wasn't writing. She had to change the habits of a lifetime of sitting in a chair, typing, and thinking as the words appeared on the page. As she wrote to her friend Dorothy Pritchett, "It pleases me to manage to write about 50 words a day and catch a small porgy for dinner. What a silly game is sighing for what [we] one once had and how boring because it is useless."[181]

Something she wrote in *Maybe* sounds more true than fictional: "I had never had bad physical troubles and now they were happening. I had never thought about my age, complained enough but never really acknowledged troubles. They came, they went and often they stayed. Suddenly I was all grown up and always in a bad humor or worried about who had done what to me. It's almost out of control when it comes so late."[182] What she had written of her father thirty-five years before now applied to herself. The violence of her angers was worse than ever.[183]

Yet she retained her sense of humor. At one gathering a young man asked her if she thought menopause had disrupted her writing career. Her guffaw turned into coughing and snorting before she could say, breathless, that she didn't think so. Another heckler incited an unexpected Hellman response, as Peter Feibleman recalled years later: "Lillian gave a lecture in Iowa in an amphitheater at the same time as Anita Bryant spoke across town. She had made herself famous by attacking gay people: gay rights, gay lib (in those days), gay anything. So, both amphitheaters were full and there was a certain amount of speculation about whether Lillian would even refer to Bryant or Gay Rights. She didn't until a woman in the audience stood up when she asked for questions and said, 'Miss Hellman, have you ever endorsed gay lib?' Lillian said, 'No,' and the woman said, 'Why not?' and Lillian said, 'Fucking does not require my endorsement.' The whole amphitheater rose to its feet like a football stadium."[184]

Hellman had plenty of opportunities to air her opinions. Her secretary Rita Wade brought coffee to a reporter interviewing Hellman in her Park Avenue co-op just in time to hear Hellman answer his question about the difference between men and women writers: "Well, for one thing their sex organs are different." Wade dropped the coffee.[185] Hellman's abrasive directness and larger-than-life persona kept those facing her at bay, but critics assailed her from the comfortable distance of print. She herself wielded an envenomed pen.

Wounded vanity combined with arrogance on the part of reader and writer created controversy for Hellman in this last troubled decade. She had sown the seeds of discord throughout her life and now she used any means at her disposal to air grievances. Writing book reviews for the *New York Times Book Review* often gave her what she needed: a respected forum with a huge audience. The editors asked her, for example, to write a "personal chronicle and an intimate narrative of the Jewish South" for a November 11, 1973, review. *The Provincials: A Personal History of Jews in the South* by Eli Evans at first seems an odd choice for a Hellman review. She had not lived in the South for fifty years. Still, she had grown up there, was a Jew, and definitely had opinions. She wrote a biting review beginning with the first line: "Liberalism, fair of face, good heart, good manners, the most civilized of hosts at the table of the mind, is too often a bloody mess." Her irritation with the book apparently stemmed from the "Southern Jew liberalism" of Evans's narrative. Hellman wrote, "We read that Southern store-keepers—Mr. Evan's father was one of them—early on opened their stores to Negroes and even allowed them to try on clothes before investing. Well, I spring from Southern store-keepers and maybe Mr. Evans' family had noble reasons for allowing such favors to Negroes, but mine did it for money, nothing else, and so did all their friends and brother-merchants."

She based her assessment of the South on her family's experience, which she alternately called "a Banana Republic family" or the "little foxes." Her view had a strong bias, but she probably came close to the truth. "The South made for many good things—maybe the best writers of our time—but it made very few rebels or reformers, then or now, Jew or non-Jew." Her decade of work in civil rights made her contemptuous of liberal southerners of the "I have black friends" variety, particularly during the Nixon presidency, which sought to dismantle hard-won civil rights legislation. Her typewriter clacked with disdain.

Hellman wasn't the only one nursing old grievances. Opponents waited for her to slip from her newfound state of grace. As founder of the Committee for Public Justice, she had political respect for the first time in years. This acclaim infuriated those who despised her politics. Instantly they brought up, yet again, the Stalinism of her thirties and forties.

Fierce Political Combatant

She received a letter from artist Jules Heller after her negative review of *The Provincial*. He complained that the article was "not an isolated example of prejudice on your part. I recall that one or two years ago you wrote a letter to the *NY Times* branding a Soviet writer by the name of [Anatoly] Kuznetsov who had defected to England as being a coward for not remaining in Russia to fight against what he considered oppression. It is your Marxist leaning that prompted you to condemn him because had he been a Greek or Spaniard who had defected from one of those fascist countries, I am positive you would have applauded his act. It is ironical, is it not, that those fascist countries have less stringent laws against emigration than does the 'Worker's Fatherland.'"[186]

Heller struck a nerve and Hellman uncharacteristically responded, saying he had made a mistake in his memory about her letter to the *New York Times*. "I have little understanding of the rest of your letter, but that is of no importance." Hellman rightly judged Heller's misreading. She had indeed written an article critical of Kuznetsov, not because he defected from Russia but because in doing so he betrayed poet Yevgeny Yevtushenko and physicist Andrei Sakharov's plan to start an underground magazine. In essence, he had "named names." She also naively blamed Kuznetsov for not protesting Soviet censorship before leaving Russia, but that was a sidenote. The irony of her anti-Soviet stance being misinterpreted was not lost on Hellman.

Hellman acknowledged the Soviet Union's totalitarian excesses to many friends and acquaintances in both countries, and did so far earlier than her detractors realized. She, along with other notable American writers such as Edward Albee, Hannah Arendt, W. H. Auden, Saul Bellow, Norman Mailer, and Lionel Trilling, had signed a letter of protest, published in the *New*

Republic in 1966, about the Soviet imprisonment of Andrei Sinyavsky and Yuli Daniel.[187] But her signature among many did not make news. Other liaisons she also kept hushed. On trips to the Soviet Union in 1966 and 1967, her old translator Raya and Raya's husband, Lev Kopelev, had introduced her to Alexander Solzhenitsyn.

She didn't take to his solemn, distant manner. No longer thirty-nine years old, as she had been in 1944, no longer in Moscow on a mission for the U.S. president, no longer in love with John Melby, Hellman found all of Russia gray and unwelcoming. She recognized the lasting effect of Stalin's censorship of artists and intellectuals, condemning it obliquely at the Fourth Union of Writer's Congress in Moscow, toasting to "the freedom of writers." Even before her return trips to Russia, she had sent money and books undercover. In the late 1960s and early 1970s she used anyone traveling to Russia as a conduit. When the Styrons' oldest daughter went to Moscow, Hellman sent contraband money through her to Raya. She asked acquaintance Richard Bridgman to also act as a conduit, writing him about Raya's husband Kopelev: "He. . . is one of the heroes in 'The First Circle.' Solzhenitsyn and Lev were nine years in a camp together."[188] Hellman knew a great deal about Solzhenitsyn's *The First Circle* after returning from another short trip to Moscow in 1967. She agreed to assist Solzhenitsyn's publication of the book the West, even becoming his power of attorney for a brief time.[189]

Legal wrangling convinced her of the difficulty of acting as an agent for him, and Solzhenitsyn finally wrote her and told her he had arranged for a Swiss agent to take over the book's release. Relieved, she nevertheless adamantly backed his work, which was relentlessly anti-Stalin. She wrote to a friend, "The plain truth is that Solzhenitsyn has allowed people to handle him badly, and he now seems to have a lawyer in Switzerland. . . . I tell you all this in case you know anybody who is going to the Soviet Union and is trustworthy enough to carry a message to Raya, or if you feel that you can manage to couch all this in terms that will not bring them harm."[190] Hellman certainly knew the score.

In public, however, she proceeded warily. Why Hellman seemed so reluctant to refute Soviet policies publicly is a matter for speculation. Perhaps she feared that in acknowledging the horror of Stalin, she would seem to approve the Joe McCarthy agenda. So she hedged. On returning to the United States from Russia in 1967, she mildly said that she was "a writer concerned that Russian writers are in jail for what they wrote."[191] She certainly didn't advertise her assistance to Solzhenitsyn. As Nora Ephron wrote her, "When are you going to write your reflections on Solzhenitsyn . . . you always refer darkly to odd reasons why you can't do it."[192] She had written a short piece on Solzhenitsyn for the *Times* in the early 1970s but replied to a query from Alfred Kazin about why she didn't say more about her own assistance to him: "It would now be unwise: it could endanger people to whom I regularly send help, and who are of great value to him and to others."[193] To all public questions about repression in the Soviet Union she demurred, "My ears are not right for the sounds of political intrigue and more important to Russians, I don't ask questions because gossip doesn't keep my attention for long."[194] This last comment was disingenuous, an attempt to excuse her failure to recognize Stalin's repression of artists earlier.

By then she certainly knew the facts. As early as 1958 she wrote a Russian archivist who had requested information about her friend Sergei Eisenstein. His "work and his life suffered from the imposition of rules that bewildered him."[195] But Hellman never uttered loudly or forcefully enough her recognition of Stalin's horrible oppression. She kept her deepening mistrust of the Soviet system quiet; she hated admitting she was wrong. But after lying low for two decades, around 1970 she began to admit her previous mistakes. She had to concede that she had been wrong about Stalin if she was to righteously lash out at anticommunists she felt had betrayed America's left. Her concessions made little difference to those gunning for her.

In early forays against long-standing enemies, she used the power of her vitriol. She welcomed the chance to criticize those who had "shamelessly" sided with McCarthy.[196] She did it by indirection, but she wanted to go on the record after all the years of repressed, boiling anger following her McCarthy hearing.

Rebecca West was a socialist turned anticommunist turned FBI informer. She had media access and the ear of the public in much the same way Hellman did, but used it from the other side. In the 1950s West had written several articles on Stalin in the *London Evening Standard*, reprinted in the *U.S. News & World Report*. In those articles she made clear that "Communism was not a political ideology; it was a criminal conspiracy that deserved to be investigated and rooted out of Western democracies."[197] Hellman had vehemently disagreed, thinking West immoral for defining the word "witch-hunting" as communist propaganda. West haughtily proclaimed, "McCarthy had done no significant damage to American institutions or to the political climate."[198] These were fighting words, but Hellman did not have the fight left in her during the 1950s. She retreated from political confrontation to save herself and Hammett from further anguish. Opportunity knocked in the early 1970s.

Asked by the *New York Times Book Review* to write a review of Gordon N. Ray's *H. G. Wells and Rebecca West*, which was as Hellman described it, "a collection of love letters, and some that aren't so loving . . . almost all of which were written by Wells to West."[199] Hellman wrote a witty, intelligent review. She distrusted Ray's objectivity as a biographer and spent most of the long review critical of West: as a contributor to Ray's biography, as a feminist turned whining lover, as a "great complainer about servants," as a writer about whom Hellman had "reservations." At last Hellman could impugn the integrity of a so-called socialist Dame of the British Empire who had turned her back on the left in America.

This time around it wasn't theories of communism that drew Hellman's ire, but something far more personal. Hellman took the high ground and lashed out at West for personal tawdriness, not her writing or politics. She criticized West for sharing love letters. She found West guilty not of "a betrayal of what two people were together, but of what one is alone." Having just published two memoirs of her own featuring the memories of her love affair with Dashiell Hammett, it required some degree of hypocrisy for Hellman to insert the needle where West had always been most vulnerable— her love life. The high priestess of Martha's Vineyard evened the score for past slights whenever and however she could.[200]

And she thought about exacting a form of vengeance on her new enemy, Richard Nixon. In May 1973 the Senate Watergate Committee began to televise hearings to get to the bottom of the break-in and the subsequent cover-up. Hellman, as mesmerized as the rest of America by the criminal antics of a committee intent on reelecting a president, watched Watergate all summer. Hellman put it in the "fascinated-by-the-snakes department. The feeling one gets: a nest of snakes."[201] Nixon had lied to the American people and this time they knew it. Hot on Nixon's trail, the *Washington Post* reveled in Nixon's complicity in the crimes and cover-up. Much to Hellman's dismay, Nixon managed to squelch investigations into his high jinks until after his reelection in November. She began to lobby hard against him and his cohorts. She later sarcastically snapped, "Watergate made me conscious that time is no guarantee against shock."[202]

On July 13, 1973, the people found the means to end the bitter suspicion of a president's malfeasance. On that date, Alexander Butterfield, deputy assistant to the president, revealed that from 1971 Nixon had taped all conversations and telephone calls. Nixon had installed five microphones in his desk, two in wall lamps by the fireplace, still more in the cabinet room, at his hideaway in the Old Executive Office Building and at the presidential retreat at Camp David.[203] At last, Nixon could prove his enemies wrong—or right. The tapes would tell the tale, and the Watergate Committee demanded them.

A week later, Nixon flat out refused to turn over the tapes to the Senate Watergate Committee or the special prosecutor, Archibald Cox. The president stonewalled, disconnected the tapes, fired Cox, and abolished the office of the special prosecutor. He demanded resignations from the attorney general and called in political favors to avoid impeachment. For two years, men in nearly every level of government had heard the increasing clamor for justice, for either proof or vindication of their president's involvement in the Watergate cover-up. Now the time had come for the president to put up or shut up.

Nixon's lawyers vigorously fought the tapes' inclusion. Others fought just as vigorously for their release. Few trusted the heavily edited transcripts Nixon presented to the House Judiciary Committee. In July, the Supreme Court demanded sixty-four taped conversations; the House Judiciary Committee passed the first of three articles of impeachment, and Lillian Hellman, a "lioness in appearance and full of strength and argument," prepared the Committee for Public Justice to file for the tapes to be released under the Freedom of Information Act.[204] Distrustful of the slow speed of governmental processes, suspicious of political power brokers—whether ex-presidents, congressman or judges—several organizations and individuals with the chutzpah, the money, and the political courage to do so filed lawsuits to increase the pressure on Nixon. The president might have expected the other litigants. Jack Anderson and J. Anthony Lukas, as members of the press, had been out to get him as long as he could remember. Relentless Lillian Hellman must have seemed a scratchy irritant resurrected from a better past when he sat in the seat of ascending power in Congress, joining Joseph McCarthy to root out and destroy the left. A Supreme Court docket in stark black type told Nixon and his lawyers that the Committee for Public Justice, under Hellman's imperious command, had tenaciously joined the chorus of public interest groups to speak for the people at the fall of the errant king. The pressure of the courts, the lawsuits, public clamor, and legal paper, paper, paper weighing everywhere on Nixon's head brought him down. He resigned on August 8, 1974.

Hellman had learned at HUAC that "I don't like confrontations I can lose."[205] Now she had no trouble publicly venting: she wasn't worried that Nixon would institute another era of McCarthyism but feared he was "on the brink of something worse." Nixon was more "intelligent and powerful" than McCarthy. "History doesn't repeat itself; it transfigures into a new design."

She survived McCarthy's battering ax in 1952, though it cost her dearly. She did not forget the fear or the committee's injustice. She fooled herself into believing that she "didn't feel much" against the McCarthy committee accusers "who punished me,"[206] but she scorned the "sly miserable methods of McCarthy, Nixon and colleagues."[207] Scoundrel Richard Nixon got his comeuppance only in small part because of Lillian Hellman and her sharpened weapons: words, influence, networks. This time the law was on her side. Public pressure sealed his fate. Still, suing Richard Nixon took serious nerve. If she turned mean and vindictive politically in the last decade of life, she had earned her ire.

Hellman's public profile with the Committee for Public Justice and its investigation of J. Edgar Hoover, its lawsuit against Richard Nixon, as well as her own public tussles with Evans and West and private wrangling with Van Loewen, merely gave off the first whiffs of the stink that would come when she wrote *Scoundrel Time*, her memoir about her life during the McCarthy era. In this book about scoundrels, Hellman defined the McCarthy group as "a loose term for all the boys, lobbyists, Congressmen, State Department bureaucrats, CIA operators," who "chose the anti-Red scare" to make political prestige.[208] Friends urged Hellman to refrain from publishing the book. They warned her she would look self-serving, out of sync with the political climate.

Still, even with illnesses and eccentricities and failures of judgment, Hellman worked daily, managed rights to her plays, wrote reviews, short pieces of journalism, and carried out drama league business. The political furor of the 1970s and Nixon's reign gave her courage; how could she not write about the 1950s? Smarmy politicians from McCarthy to Nixon had hypocritical smirks that drove her wild.[209] She decided to go forward and write *Scoundrel Time* as a memoir, not history. "I don't want to write about my historical conclusions—it isn't my game. I tell myself that the third time out, if I stick to what I know, what happened to me, and a few others. I have a chance to write my own history of the time."[210]

Remembering Old Enemies

For over twenty years she had wanted to write about her life in the early 1950s. Getting in her jabs whenever she could, as Rebecca West's review showed, she published next to nothing about HUAC and her appearance before the Congressional Committee. While others wrote memoirs and remembrances of the politics of 1950s Washington, she did not. Countless times publishers and agents asked her to tell the story of her appearance.

New York Times editor Herbert Mitgang, for example, wrote Hellman in May 1969 asking her for "a piece about the McCarthy period." With "regards and regrets" in early August she wrote, "I now have 13 pages, mostly duplicates, of a piece on why I can't write a piece about the McCarthy period.[211] Please don't count on me because that will make me feel a burden. But for a few weeks more I'll try—first for myself."[212] She refused all offers.

In the mid-1970s, with Hellman's political stature rising because of her founding the Committee for Public Justice, public interest groups and publishers began to seek her out as a survivor of the McCarthy era. She geared up to write and speak out as she hadn't before. The Council of New York Law Associates, for instance, asked her to speak because "she was an 'idol' and an example to lawyers because she stood up to tyranny." As she talked to these high-powered lawyers, she showed the firmness of her convictions and a recovered political strength: "Her voice was her voice and she wasn't going to be compromised there . . . she was certainly not going to be silenced."[213] The nation's renewed attention to civil rights gave her the impetus to try again. If only she could write it all down. "What made it easier, I guess, was Watergate. I was so convinced in the Nixon years that the bad years were on their way again, but that these would make McCarthyism look like peanuts."[214] She wrote this time of clowns, scoundrels, and villains through her eyes, her experience. She wanted "controversy and sensation," and she had blame aplenty to spread around.[215]

Putting memory into words and ire into phrases released her from the hold the witch-hunt had on her. Nowhere in the book does she try to impose a historical reality on the period, repeatedly writing that she wasn't writing history. So she wrote of "the sly, miserable methods of McCarthy, Nixon and colleagues, as they flailed at Communists, near-Communists, and nowhere near-Communists" and called it *Scoundrel Time*.[216]

In this memoir, Hellman remembered "The Witch Hunt," "The Plague Years," "The Time of Vigilantes." She traced the early whiplash of interrogation that arrived in fall 1947, when HUAC called Hollywood notables along with writers and actors to testify about the communist "influence" in movies. In Hellman's telling, big names meant big press, and Hollywood writers were particularly vulnerable to accusations of covertly putting propaganda into movies. Hellman recalled that she and a great many others wanted to shout what she—or they—hadn't the courage to say until years later: "You are a bunch of headline seekers, using other people's lives for your own benefits. You know damn well that the people you've been calling before you never did much of anything."[217] In the book, she berated Hollywood's blacklist, which appeased the committee for a time but ruined the lives and reputations of many writers. Hellman belittled the materialism of competing for "better bathrooms," showing a vulgar bitterness in noting, "It is even possible that feces are not pleased to be received in such grand style and thus prefer to settle in the soul."[218]

Her book told how she moved from the Hollywood outrage to that in Washington, D.C., recalling her fear, scattered actions, and finally the event itself. She revisited the ordeal as she saw it, the most trying personal and political time of her life. She wrote of her bewilderment. Other agonies she had chosen; "here I didn't choose anything. That's always an awful kind of trouble—things you don't deserve and can't control."[219] She recalled her reliance on lawyer Joe Rauh, her relief that she had not buckled under the pressure, described her moment of vindication in the spotlight by reading her letter of explanation aloud, and her regret that she took the Fifth. In characteristic style she bluntly vilified the enemy, told the events from her point of view, and made no pretense of objectivity.

By the time Hellman published *Scoundrel Time*, the blacklist and the unconstitutional methods of the committee were hardly breaking news. Dalton Trumbo's 1949 self-published book *The Time of the Toad*, for example, pointedly ridiculed congressional actions. Trumbo felt these years represented a reality so hideous he couldn't stomach it, a time he felt forced each day to eat a gigantic, hideous toad. Although Trumbo attacked the villains when they were still operative, his book didn't inflame controversy the way Hellman's *Scoundrel Time* did nearly thirty years later. Perhaps Trumbo was more easily dismissed because he bore the stigma of his membership in the Hollywood Ten—the men sentenced, convicted, and jailed for contempt of Congress. Or perhaps he directed his anger unambiguously at the committee and producers who colluded. Hellman's book pointedly did not forgive any who cooperated with the committee or looked away because of what they thought was political necessity. Her book is about anger, not vindication.

Hellman's personal truth and chosen facts and distorted recall made up the content of her memoirs, and *Scoundrel Time* was no exception. Preparing an outline, she wrote a researcher, "I find that I have a strange blank after my House Un-American Activities Committee appearance in May 1952, and have evidently lost the diary of that year. (I begin to remember things again in about Spring of 1953.)" She needed reminders: "Perhaps the names of a few plays or movies that opened would help me."[220] What she remembered, she doggedly looked for: Clifford Odets's testimony, the ad Elia Kazan put in the *New York Times* to explain his position, a copy of the loyalty oath Hollywood producers demanded.[221] She questioned her own perceptions on several occasions as she dug for proof. In regard to receiving a passport, prohibited to members of communist organizations, communist-fronts, or communist-infiltrated organizations under the McCarran Act of 1950, Hellman queried her researcher, "Was I only one to get passport? What about Carl Foreman?"[222]

Hellman mounted a research project of her own, taking in the Whitaker Chambers case, Memorandum on the Hiss Case, summaries of Irving Kristol's Civil Liberties 1952: A Study in Confusion, Robert Griffith's Politics of Fear, John Cogley's Report on Blacklisting, transcripts from the hearings themselves. If she found she erred, she changed it.[223] She wrote lawyer Joseph Rauh for information and he replied with three pages worth and told her "your testimony is one of my proudest moments."[224] She did not blindly call up the period, but she did put the stamp of her personal reflections on it. As she said early in the book, "I am, of course, making my political history too simple: personal conflicts, work problems, whisky, too much money after The Children's Hour, the time of my time, Hammett, all had to do with whatever I believed."[225] This book brought the personal and the political together.

To her editor's dismay, Hellman interfered in every step of the publication process, from the cover photo to the introduction by Garry Wills. She worried that Wills's text might be a problem. Indeed, it fomented nearly as much critical hostility as the book itself because of his condescending critique of McCarthy, his scorn for anticommunist liberals, and his wholesale, uncritical honoring of Hellman. She wrote William Abrahams, her editor, about Wills's account: "Dear Billy: My chief worry about this piece . . . is that there is a certain slickness in it. . . . Maybe that fact, however, that he thinks differently than I do can be taken care of in two ways that might benefit us: 1) that he say so, and 2) that the book jacket could point it out." Such maneuvers did not help. Commentary reported that Wills's introduction disgraced Hellman's book. But if she let the Wills introduction slide, in the book itself she was more careful and clear than critics later gave her credit for. Biased? Absolutely. Political? Pure Hellman.

Scoundrel Time came out to wide and wonderful acclaim. Hellman collected the Edward MacDowell Model for outstanding contributions to literature, the Actors' Equity Association's Paul Robeson Award, the Lord and Taylor Rose Award, an honorary doctorate at Columbia University. But best of all were the reviews: Robert Coles speculated that "Kierkegaard would have loved Scoundrel Time for its fine, sardonic humor, its unsparing social observation and, not least, its skill of its narration."[226] The New York Times

Book Review lauded the book as a "beautiful work of self-definition,"[227] and another *Times* article praised it as "a meditation on Miss Hellman's self—wry, ironic, not quite apologetic but close to it."[228] Even the *New Yorker* praised Hellman for her wry humor and lack of self-righteousness.[229] For a time it seemed her friends had been wrong to caution her against writing the book.

Hellman's friends knew better than she, however, that the enemies she held in contempt had been wounded enough by Nixon's fall to come out fighting. They expected a renewed attack on an outspoken woman, a leftist Jew whose flagrant opinions left her vulnerable to ideological critique. Without question, Hellman took on the left-wing intellectuals who disappointed her in 1952. Her political identity demanded it.[230] Finding themselves defying their own principles in the name of anticommunism, they too wanted to cut Hellman down to size. *Scoundrel Time*'s publication elicited a deafening barrage of outraged wails.

The McCarthy crowd "were what they were: men who invented when necessary, maligned even when it wasn't necessary."[231] The "cheap baddies" and their followers didn't need to change their positions. They knew where they stood from the start, and they despised leftists and defenders of leftists. Their opposition to Hellman's book was a given. As might be expected, conservative political commentator and ideologue William F. Buckley Jr. was particularly virulent. A friend of Watergate burglar Howard Hunt and godfather to his children, at least according to Nixon aide Charles Colson, Buckley despised Hellman's politics and her public acclaim.[232] He denounced Hellman in a personal and demeaning way, noting the seventy-two-year-old-woman's "ugliness," calling the book "tasteless, guileful, self-enraptured."[233] In another diatribe, "Down with Hellman!" published in the *Los Angeles Times*, Buckley wrote, "The difference between Lillian Hellman and Albert Speer, the Nazi war criminal, is that Albert Speer repented his professional service in behalf of totalitarianism."

In London, Melvyn Laski wrote "Left-wing America's Martyr-in-Waiting."[234] He wondered how Hellman could be irate about McCarthyism when she only testified before the House Un-American Activities Committee for "an hour and seven minutes," and McCarthy wasn't even in the room. Like many critics, Laski accused Hellman of rewriting history and failing to give a "clear and unambiguous idea of who were the true scoundrels." His real complaint was that "Stalin and his henchmen" didn't seem to be among the scoundrels she exposed. These critics wanted Hellman to recant her leftist views after all these years, followed by a baptism and rebirth to their own political viewpoint. When *Scoundrel Time* didn't deliver, they got foul.

Making few distinctions between the McCarthy crowd and its appeasers, Hellman forgave no one. She turned the screws on any in the liberal intellectual community who did not support those under fire by HUAC. "My belief in liberalism was mostly gone. I think I have substituted for it something private called, for want of something that should be more accurate, decency."[235] The lack of liberal leadership during that period she called indecent.

She had come out swinging at many of her former friends—liberals who had been friendly witnesses and those who had supported HUAC's "inquisition" by their silence and tacit support. The anticommunist left of the 1950s should have seen it coming. In *Pentimento* Hellman admitted, "It is eccentric, I suppose, not to care much about the persecutors and to care so much about those who allowed the persecution, but it was as if I had been deprived of a child's belief in tribal safety."[236] As she put it, she had for years "shut up about the whole period." *Scoundrel Time* marked the end of silence.

Those who had "named names" had already come under fire by critics and thus stayed out of the fray, even though she made pointed references to Clifford Odets and Elia Kazan. But those unused to critique of their behavior did not suffer the affront mildly. Hellman's lawyer during the 1950s, Joseph Rauh, went on record to say that *Scoundrel Time* was not really "against the liberals" though he acknowledged her criticisms. "But why shouldn't there be? Some liberals hid during the McCarthy-HUAC period, some rationalized what they were doing, and some even cooperated. If Ms. Hellman overgeneralized from specific cases in her own experience, certainly one can understand her feeling of isolation and resentment."[237] Hellman felt that even if the left disagreed with the radicals' stance, they should have defended the rights of citizens: "Since when do you have to agree with people to defend them from injustice?"[238]

Hellman claimed the book was not about the left or the right but about herself only, though her title disputes that claim. Nevertheless, her vignettes of blame were quite general; she didn't like naming names even here. But those whose names she did mention in print felt slapped and went public. Everyone involved was as willing as Hellman to adjust history and its explanations to justify their own point of view, their own behavior. *Scoundrel Time* opened up a whole new cavern of controversy. Sidney Hook argued that Hellman "seems to have duped a generation of critics devoid of historical memory and critical common sense." Considering other articles, speeches, and books by HUAC critics, her book is not particularly condemning or rancid in its critique. But Hellman always baited people, irritated them with an assumed moral superiority. One observer wrote, "There is something about

Lillian Hellman that makes many men, and some women, want to throw whisky at her."[239]

Little, Brown's edition of *Scoundrel Time* invited controversy. Right in the center of the book an insert reads, "Lillian Hellman: An American Heroine." This made critics choke, but the publisher included it, not Hellman. By that time, of course, she had enough influence that if she wanted it out, she could have demanded it. She had previously sworn she would avoid "blowing her own trumpet . . . she couldn't do that and get away with it—nobody could."[240] She let the publisher do it, and the book's insert seems the height of self-promotion.

Hellman thought she had been fair. The book acknowledged "the confusions of honest people . . . who hearing a few bars of popular notes, made them into an opera of public disorder. . . staged and sung."[241] She admitted that many of the intellectuals who had not supported those in trouble "found in the sins of Stalin Communism—and there were plenty of sins and plenty that for a long time I mistakenly denied—the excuse to join those who should have been their hereditary enemies."[242] One phrase of confession in an accusing sentence didn't assuage her critics. They used the verified reports of Stalin's villainy to vindicate what a congressional committee had done to its own citizens. This view didn't wash with Hellman, who saw the issues as separate.

Twenty-five years after her HUAC appearance, critics saw the memoir as historical revision, an "apology for her generation's unpaid defense of Stalinism."[243] Oddly enough, while they went after her notions of truth, they found little factual deviation to eradicate her credibility. Political interpretations were something else. William Wright, a biographer who took her to task about her truthfulness in many regards, highlighted only three "errors" in *Scoundrel Time*. Wright said she lied when she said she feared jail, lied about hearing someone in the press gallery say, "Thank God somebody finally had the guts to do it,"[244] and lied when she denied being a Stalinist. Neither accusations nor denials could be proved. Truthfulness was not the issue in *Scoundrel Time*. Interpretive politics was.

Crosscurrents of charged emotions blustered in an early legal flurry over a passage in the memoir. In describing strategy sessions with her lawyer Joseph Rauh, Hellman mentioned "sharp words" they exchanged when Rauh suggested they consult his friend at the *New York Post*, writer James Weschler. She wrote, "I had never met Weschler, didn't like what he wrote; and wanted no advice from him." A bit later she wrote, "Rauh didn't like my attack on his friend Weschler, but when Weschler was later called before the Committee,

I know Joe could not have liked the fact that his friend not only was a friendly witness, but had high-class pious reasons for what he did."[245]

When Weschler read this passage, he wrote immediately to Little, Brown and demanded that the publisher remove the word "friendly" from subsequent books; if they did not, he would sue for libel. The issue was complicated. Weschler had been contentious and adversarial toward the committee, but he also "named names." Weschler had told McCarthy that he was a "responsive but not a friendly witness." Weschler expected history to respect his own designation. Hellman huffed but under pressure from her publisher finally agreed to refer to him as "cooperative," not "friendly." Neither seemed happy with the new language, but Weschler dropped the complaint. To Hellman, a "black and white person," naming names meant sharing a bed with the devil.[246] This early dustup prepared Hellman for more to come, but the next attack surprised her.

The Book and Newspaper Wars

The first blowout among friends involved Hellman's old friend Diana Trilling. In the New York "intellectual family," Trilling's husband, Lionel, was a leading thinker, a liberal anticommunist, and an esteemed professor at Columbia University. Despite the differences in their politics, Hellman was fond of Lionel and liked Diana too. And her friendship was reciprocated. A little over a year before she published *Scoundrel Time* she had written them a note, with "affection to you both," asking them to think again about spending the summer at the Vineyard so they could be together.[247]

Hellman, scratching but not drawing blood, brought up the Trillings' defense of Whittaker Chambers in her memoir. Hellman loathed Chambers, most famous for accusing Alger Hiss of passing secrets to the Soviet Union. Hellman believed in Hiss's innocence, and thus Chambers seemed a man intent on saving his own skin at the expense of others. Recent discoveries point to Hiss's guilt, but throughout the 1950s, the Hiss case divided political friends into enemy camps. It certainly did for Hellman and the Trillings, though they ignored the rift until Hellman made it public in *Scoundrel Time*. She wrote, "Nixon is a villainous liar. Lionel Trilling, a distinguished critic and teacher, an early anti-Communist, the author of a novel roughly based on the career of Whittaker Chambers, is an honest man."[248] She wondered "how Diana and Lionel Trilling, old, respected friends, could have come out of the same age and time with such different political and social views from my own."[249] And that was all she said of the

Trillings, short of some "facts are facts" pontificating about Hiss. Mild stuff for Hellman.

All hell broke loose in August 1976, when Diana Trilling accused Hellman of interfering in the Little, Brown publication of her book of essays, as yet untitled. The essay that Hellman supposedly took issue with—enough so that Little, Brown did indeed cancel Trilling's contract—was "Liberal Anti-Communism Revisited." Trilling's essay addressed Hellman's refusal to accuse the Soviet Union of its intolerance and suppression of dissent and found fault with Hellman for picking on the United States only. She targeted Hellman for her refusal to see "fellow traveling" as dangerous and called Hellman's stand before HUAC showmanship, not true courage. Hellman said she laughed at the same old arguments Trilling brought out to counter *Scoundrel Time*, but her literary editor and other supporters were irate. Hellman denied pressuring Little, Brown to cancel Trilling's contract, saying "Mrs. Trilling will, of course, testify that I immediately agreed that she must print anything, anywhere and at any time that is the truth."[250] Hellman denied having anything to do with censoring Trilling's book.

As the women's mutual fury peaked, even the respected *London Times Literary Supplement* leaped into the breach. Hellman's editor William Abrahams responded to its critique of Hellman by citing the *TLS* critic Richard Mayne and Trilling for their own revisionist history: their failure to remember that Great Britain, the United States, and the Soviet Union were allies, "fighting against the fascist powers . . . the war was fought; the alliance existed—these are historical facts, and Mrs. Trilling's failure to mention them allows her to impart a wealth of derisive innuendo to Miss Hellman's visit to Russia in wartime. . . . Made at the express request of President Roosevelt and Harry Hopkins."[251] Old political battles never die.

Given Hellman's reputation for meddling, even her best friends never believed her claims of nonintervention, suspecting that she protested "emphatically" to Arthur Thornhill, Trilling's editor.[252] But Roger Donald, editor in chief, thought the controversy was a Trilling public relations ploy since, as he wrote Hellman, "your total lack of involvement was soundly established."[253] Whatever the sequence of events, Little, Brown refused to publish Trilling's book. It was later published as *We Must March My Darlings* by Harcourt, Brace in 1977.

The resulting furor festered in Hellman. She wrote Sir Victor Pritchett, a distinguished British writer and critic, and his wife, Dorothy: "Victor's words about 'Scoundrel Time' came in a good week. I don't know if you've read about the Trilling Hellman mess but it sure has been disagreeable, with the

London Times adding to the furor that the *New York Times*, our newest gossip sheet, was so glad to put on the front page. . . . Her attack has led a pack of others now, although, of course, I am lucky it didn't happen when the book first came out."[254] In her early seventies, Hellman underestimated the damage of the public skirmish.

Increasingly beset by periods of paranoia and outrage, she could not tolerate the attacks on her that followed the publication of *Scoundrel Time*. Milton Wexler, psychologist and friend, recalled, "She knew what kind of tomfoolery, what kind of wickedness, what kind of cheapness, what kind of civility, what kind of pretensions were going on and she couldn't stand it—it enraged her . . . she'd go after it like a hound dog."[255] She fired back salvo after salvo, sure of her position, shocked at critical shortsightedness from friends and enemies. She had earlier severed ties with liberal-turned-conservative writer-editor Norman Podhoretz over his use of the term "anti-American." "What bothered her profoundly was our use of the term anti-American to characterize the point of view not only of extremist groups like the Weatherman and the Black Panthers but even of a 'liberal' publication like *The New York Review of Books*."[256] Hellman never saw criticism of America as "un-American" and swore "anti-American" meant the same thing. Podhoretz disagreed vehemently.

Podhoretz hailed from a privileged male bastion of New York intellectuals, certain of their position and the correct course of patriotism. To many of them, Hellman's aberrant positions in favor of dissent seemed blasphemous. They parted ways. Now *Scoundrel Time*, a sharp contradiction to their way of thinking, brought her back in the public eye.

Scoundrel Time reopened rifts between Podhoretz and Hellman that had never really closed, and as editor of *Commentary*, he had power to discredit her point of view, calling her view of the period "outrageous distortions and . . . far more serious lies."[257] Hellman had taken *Commentary* and *Partisan Review* to task for doing nothing to stop McCarthy's suspension of constitutional rights. Podhoretz simply could not stand Hellman's unrepentant view, her focusing on McCarthy as the enemy of the American people, not Stalin. His focus was international; her interest was in American abuse of civil rights. Immediately after *Scoundrel Time* was published, Podhoretz recruited the writer Nathan Glazer to answer the "necessary points" to rebut Hellman's view. He did so in ways one might expect of this period—political and polemical—putting as big a spin on the HUAC trials as Hellman did; Glazer belittled her HUAC appearance, accused her of "simplifying history," and disparaged her focus on HUAC rather than Stalin. This two-pronged critique was repeated by Irving Howe in *Dissent*.[258]

Hellman accused Podhoretz and his disciples of being part of "an organized anti-Communist conspiracy" led by Daniel Patrick Moynihan against her book. Podhoretz called it nonsense but admitted that "it also contained a minuscule element of truth." By this time, the truth and lies, and the right and wrong of the period were obscured in charges and countercharges. In 1983 *Harper's* writer Robert M. Kaus, sensing that the ailing Hellman did not have the strength to sue, could not resist: "Ever since she first rose to public prominence during the Salem witch trials, Lillian Hellman has been a skilled controversialist. Her decades-long affair with the dashing Communist, Joseph Stalin . . ." and on he wrote.[259]

Fifteen years after Hellman's death Podhoretz still sought to correct the record, saying those suffering the blacklist didn't have it as bad as those imprisoned by Stalin. "It was nothing short of blasphemous to compare the fate of 'dissidents in Eastern Europe' whose 'punishment' consisted of execution, torture, or long years of imprisonment under conditions of hardship scarcely imaginable to Lillian Hellman with, say, the six months Dashiell Hammett spent in jail cleaning bathrooms, let alone with the luxury in which she herself lived even when she could no longer command huge fees for writing Hollywood films."[260] Hellman never compared her losses (or Hammett's) to those dissidents. She insisted that McCarthyism was not justified by Stalin's actions in Russia. She was concerned about her country, not the Soviet Union. To Podhoretz and other conservative critics, criticizing a congressional committee for civil abuses seemed beside the point, "anti-American." Only the Cold War counted. To Hellman, any other way was immoral, and she decried the nation's failure to connect "Shakespeare's venal kings to our own."[261] Fighting for political dominion, the combatants faced off.

It maddened critics of *Scoundrel Time* that in the late 1970s, the public renewed its interest in Hellman and Hammett and the McCarthy era. Cartoonist Jules Feiffer, her good friend and Vineyard neighbor, said in an interview, "She was a troglodyte, a dinosaur and then suddenly she is this glamorous figure."[262] As usual, Hollywood took the curiosity and cashed in on it. The industry's regard for Hammett's literary works, Hellman's memoirs, and the legendary lady herself should have pleased Hellman. Not so. An aging Hellman most definitely wanted life on her own terms.

Revived Interest, Revived Acrimony

The revived interest in Hellman and Hammett did not come without cost to Hellman, who determined she would salvage their reputations. She managed to stave off Francis Ford Coppolla's fictional Hammett for a few years and allowed Ted Zinneman's *Julia* to go forward, perhaps a mistake with Cold Warriors eager to tear apart reputations. She fought valiantly with Zinneman over the depiction of both herself and Hammett, irritating Zinneman so much that he penciled an addendum to the copy of a letter he sent her: "You are a severe rectal pain, I'm sorry to say." Common sense reigned, however, and he did not include that line in the letter itself. After finally agreeing that she and Hammett did not come off too badly, Hellman said she liked the film, though she noted, "It's up to its ass in good taste." As with *Scoundrel Time*, the flamboyant public depiction of her character brought much praise and much condemnation. The "maestress," as poet Theodore Roethke once called her,[263] goaded status-quo liberals and conservatives in ways others far more famous, far further left, did not: poet Lincoln Steffens, writers Theodore Dreiser and H. G. Wells, dramatists Arthur Miller and George Bernard Shaw, painter Pablo Picasso.[264] Something about Hellman made those in other political camps lose their cool. Hellman rarely pulled back, and when controversy erupted around her, it was her lifeblood. As entrenched in her hatred as those who hated her, she felt both wounded and vindictive.

The honors and insults heaped on Hellman with the publication of *Scoundrel Time* brought her stage front; her inability to effectively counter accusations opened her to attack, and she didn't have the health or the strength to counter the onslaught. Those outraged by her interpretation of events surrounding the House Un-American Activities Committee actions incited critics to examine every word and phrase of all her memoirs, looking for error and mythmaking—anything to brand Hellman a liar. They turned to *Pentimento* in particular to find the evidence they needed to depict Hellman as a "mythomaniac grump."[265] This was a strange exercise, since Hellman admitted to mixing up times and events, to changing names and places radically. *Pentimento*, clearly a literary text, was vulnerable to attack about lies and lying, though it had been carefully vetted by lawyers for Little, Brown.

Hellman's natural disregard for dates was not the sole source of confusion, however. The chapters in *Pentimento* featured friends and relatives long dead for the most part, but her publisher's lawyers worried about lawsuits, not veracity. They required Hellman to obscure the identity of anyone who might sue for libel. A series of three letters from Haussermann, Davidson & Shattuck to David Otte of Little, Brown responded to this concern about potential legal difficulties in *Pentimento*. The law firm insisted that name changes would not necessarily be enough if events and other defining characteristics made "defamation" obvious. They demanded she make no living persons recognizable in any feature if public record could not verify it. That meant obscuring time and place. The lawyers demanded that she censor even the living minor characters. They had missed the slur on Van Loewen, either because they had seen Bloomgarden's verification or thought the story innocuous.

Hellman responded carefully to all their concerns. They wanted proof, for example, that Tallulah Bankhead used cocaine and demanded to know whether Aunt Lilly Bowman would be recognized by those willing to sue. Hellman's response to this last was characteristically tart: "Aunt Lilly Bowman is dead, although her son-in-law is still alive. But I have changed his name, as I have changed all names. But I would not guarantee that the son-in-law would not recognize her. However, I very much doubt that he can read." Hellman's sharp impatience and viper tongue sliced through her letters to lawyers.

Nothing prepared her for the claw-and-fang response to her "lies" in the memoirs. The discrepancies still cause even those who do not know her work to snarl in contempt and rage, insisting she is a liar. A "Julia" controversy erupted, with all manner of critics calling this chapter from *Pentimento* everything from a wholesale lie to a stolen story of another's life. Hellman critics—not literary critics—began snapping at the irregularities of time and place, the exaggerations, the distortions. Some critics looked for a lesbian subtext, others for political errors, some for Hellman's self-aggrandizement. Piece by piece, fact by fact, they have sifted the story for accuracy in a book founded on the artistic rendering of memories. The first line of "Julia" says: "I have changed most of the names. I don't know that it matters anymore." As her editor Abrahams asked, "Why is she put on the witness stand?"

For those seeking history, Peter Feibleman observes that "at worst *Pentimento* is mistaken, at best it is rooted in the subconscious, that uncharted place where things become other things."[266] The controversy pits reader against reader, literary scholar against political historian, all anathema to Hellman's purpose. Literary scholars now dismiss the furor as a tempest in a teapot, covering the same old literary ground, fought endlessly over the place of self in art.

Vengeance wasn't only Hellman's, apparently. The quarrels over the truth of *Scoundrel Time* and then *Pentimento* transcended scholarly and political critique and became deeply personal for those with decades-long grudges. Payback for personal and political slights incited some to pick through the memoirs to unseat the Grande Dame, to whittle away her presence. What made the headlines was the falling out of women, for reasons known only to them. Hellman had written of Martha Gellhorn and Ernest Hemingway years before in *Unfinished Woman*. In 1981, after the initial frenzy about *Scoundrel Time* and then *Pentimento*, Gellhorn, the "sacred cow of combat reporting," viciously blasted Hellman.[267] She labeled Hellman's memoirs a "selection of apocryphisms . . . astonishing that they have not been noticed and mocked before," which of course they had.[268] Hellman offended Gellhorn in *Unfinished Woman*—not least for subordinating her to her famous ex-husband Ernest. Gellhorn, in the latter years of her life, did not permit her name to be used in conjunction with her husband of five years, Ernest Hemingway. She required writers to tell the truth about her without mentioning E*—a euphemism reporters used to get past her restrictions.[269]

Gellhorn "screamed, hollered, fussed, fumed, thwarted, threatened, obstructed, and probably put a hex on [any] offending reporter" using Hemingway's name in conjunction with her own.[270] Hellman had violated that taboo. In "On Apocryphism," Gellhorn took on Stephen Spender for his reporting on Hemingway's training of Gellhorn for the rigors of war and then switched to a long attack on Hellman, calling her a "self-serving apochryphiar." Gellhorn detailed Hellman's failures of etiquette along with the smallest inconsistencies in Hellman's account of her trip to Spain during the Spanish Civil War. Hellman had written in *Unfinished Woman* that she brought the couple "two cans of sardines and two cans of pate."[271] Gellhorn's memory told her Hellman brought nothing. Gellhorn took particular exception to Hellman's recounting E* and Martha's observing the "beauty of the shelling." Gellhorn decried Hellman's self-reported panic and danger, saying there had been none.

Although Gellhorn admitted that Hellman's book "reads like a novel . . . like excellent short stories," her spiteful tongue could not forgive Hellman's mistaken memory.[272] Gellhorn knew that "art renders beautiful, and refines the shapeless raw material of life."[273] But not when she became part of the mix. Others doubted Gellhorn and Hemingway's versions of truth as much as they did Hellman's. Hemingway complained to the *New Yorker*'s Harold Ross during World War II that Gellhorn had picked up some gossip to the effect that "she and I took no part in this war because we were used to going to little wars where we could be important."[274] Why the frenzied battle over words and cans of sardines in times of public and personal crisis? At issue is each writer's historical immortality and version of truth. Conflict had replaced sexual conquest and affirmation as a means to feel alive.

Hellman haughtily declared, "I have no intention of answering her; it's not worth answering for one thing. . . . It's so much nonsense. She couldn't possibly have known [my experience]; she wasn't there for most of it."[275] Hellman's answer nevertheless appeared in print; the *New York Times* gave her the venue. Hellman got her licks in, saying Hemingway "attacked her to me as early as Spain, before he married her, my sacred word of honor."[276] Of course, Hellman's honor showed tarnish by this time; her enemies had convicted her of perjury in the court of public opinion.

Politics still draws the battle lines. Was Hellman a liar? Or did she tell a poetic truth based on memory and a writer's penchant for a good story? "Strange that the special fabric of longing she worked so hard to weave would one day be examined thread by thread, picked bare by all those nimble writers whose finest tools are a magnifying glass and a pair of tweezers, until the impact of the whole was lost to them because of it."[277]

When Hammett's daughter Josephine Marshall recently wrote *Dashiell Hammett: A Daughter Remembers*, she wisely disclaimed absolute accuracy. As different as Marshall and Hellman are, they certainly shared a sense of the frailty of memory and the quality of memoir. Marshall wrote: "What I remember—impressions that are imperfect, imprecise, biased, maybe even poorly interpreted. It is not true. But it is as true as I can make it."[278] Hellman noted that she remembered "fairly accurately" what people said, but not "where they said it or when they said it" and admitted: "Everybody's memory is tricky and mine's a little trickier than most, I guess."[279]

The excesses of her critics encouraged those who loved her to defend her. Aware of the political combustion erupting about her, friend John Hersey tried to explain her fury and the furor: "The pepper in her psyche—her touchiness her . . . out of control anger whenever she feels she has been dealt with unjustly—all have contributed in the end to her being radically political while essentially remaining outside formal politics."[280] Her political foes were convinced that she was everything from a KGB spy to a Soviet apologist.

The cauldron really boiled over in 1976–1977, when Muriel Gardner Buttinger came forth and accused Hellman of taking her life and fictionalizing it in "Julia," Hellman's depiction of a friend's martyrdom in Nazi Germany. Gardner's life, told in her book *Code Name: "Mary"*, seemed an exact parallel to Julia's. The furor gained momentum when it was discovered that a lawyer of Hellman's, Wolf Schwabacher, also was a close friend of Gardner's. This made it possible that Hellman heard of the outlines of Gardner's life through him, and then adapted it to her "memoir."[281] Hellman stoutly denied the accusations and held firm as to the "shape" of the story, admitting she had changed names and details because many people in the story still lived. Gardner swore Hellman never contacted her to resolve the issue, but Blair Clark wrote that he and Hellman had an appointment to see Gardner, which Gardner canceled when she realized Hellman was going to bring a lawyer with her.[282] Hellman, as litigious as she was confrontational, used legal means to settle disputes as her frailty diminished her capacity to fight back.

An old enemy, Mary McCarthy, brought the case against Hellman's honesty to a wider public on a memorable appearance in 1979 on the *Dick Cavett Show*. McCarthy, "a woman who wielded such a mean and gleeful scalpel," had criticized Hellman and her writing for years.[283] As early as 1946 she complained about Hellman's "oily virtuosity," a "lubricity."[284] As politics further separated them, McCarthy's venom became more poisonous. Finally, in 1964, Hellman's own sharp tongue, customarily easy on other writers, spouted: "I think Miss McCarthy is often brilliant and sometimes even sound. But, in fiction, she is a lady writer, a lady magazine writer. Of course, that doesn't mean that she isn't right about me. But if I thought she was, I'd quit."[285] Asked by Cavett to name overrated authors, McCarthy's response was quick and more political than literary: "The only one I can think of is a holdover like Lillian Hellman, who I think is tremendously overrated, a bad writer, and dishonest writer, but she really belongs to the past, to the Steinbeck past." She presumably meant the liberal, radical past of the 1930s. McCarthy, an early defender of Leon Trotsky and later an organizer of left-wing anticommunist writers during the Cold War, could not resist the temptation to brandish the sharp weapons of her political and literary judgment. She showed her own age and politics as she did so. "Our leading bitch intellectual," as Podhoretz called McCarthy, would have been on firm ground legally had she stopped there.[286] But when Cavett asked, "What is dishonest about her?" McCarthy famously said, "Everything. But I said once in some interview that every word she writes is a lie, including 'and' and 'the.'"[287]

Known as the "dark lady of American letters," Mary McCarthy preferred factual fiction to fictionalized fact, the opposite of Hellman's literary style. McCarthy's friends, ex-husbands, and scores of lovers appeared transparently disguised in her novels. Hellman left out as much as she put in and then added detail, tweaked the plots, and made stories of her memoirs. Too much of McCarthy's writing was, in biographer Frances Kiernan's phrase, nakedly confessional, too naked for Hellman who nevertheless reluctantly respected some of her nonfiction writing as witty and honest.[288] Hellman did not rank McCarthy as an amateur but did not consider her an artist either. The rigid McCarthy, liberated from a Catholic girlhood, was simply not the New Orleans Jew's kind of woman.

Nearly twenty years later, the story circulated that Hellman had been watching television (a rare occurrence since she could see next to nothing by 1980) and heard McCarthy's blatant accusation on the Cavett show. Seething and contemptuous of McCarthy, Hellman sued for slander, asking for $2.25 million. When Cavett learned Hellman was suing McCarthy, PBS, and him, he reportedly squeaked, "And me?" just as the phone rang and he heard Hellman's "whisky-and-cigarettes" baritone demanding to know why he had not defended her. He said he didn't think she was defenseless. Hellman bellowed, "That's bullshit. I'm suing the whole damn bunch of you." And she did.[289] Cavett reflected that he felt sorrier for McCarthy than "old Scaly Bird," but that in fact "everybody lost."[290]

Blind, clearly dying, this last burst of anger overrode any common sense she had. Hellman's friends begged her not to get involved, to put the insult down to McCarthy's legendary mean-spirited jealousy. Milton Wexler, a friend, analyst, and former lawyer, laid down the law before Hellman, telling her she could only lose. She didn't listen. "She said, 'I'm going to destroy that bitch. I'm going to prove that she's stupid, I'm going to prove that she doesn't know how to write, that nobody should respect her.'[291] She had a kind of war going on in her mind—this was a crusade. How could I not understand that she as a crusader had to destroy this meaningless wench?"[292]

McCarthy was "a Valkyrie maiden, riding her steed into the circle, amid thunder and lightning, and out again, bearing the body of some dead hero across her saddle."[293] She deserved Hellman's wrath, but perhaps not a lawsuit. Hellman armed herself for battle. Warren Beatty believed that "she saw herself brandishing the sword that would cut Mary McCarthy to pieces."[294] No flashy maiden warrior like the beautiful McCarthy, Hellman nevertheless focused on a battle plan with shimmering intensity. As Norman Mailer said, "If she'd been a man she'd have been a great general."[295]

Reason meant nothing. The women detested each other. A friend to both, Mailer guessed that "Lillian understood that she now had enough money so she could carry on a legal campaign that would absolutely strip Mary McCarthy of her money, before it was over. It was a punitive legal suit. And it was very ugly."[296] Hellman, notoriously thrifty, hated legal expenses and once offered to drop the lawsuit if McCarthy would write a line or two saying she had exaggerated and lied about Hellman.[297] Neither ever backed down—the trouble was worth it to both. Mailer, trying his role as "peacemaker," wrote an article for the New York Times, saying in effect that "all writers are liars, we always make up things—what Mary said was too strong—but ladies, let's not cheapen literature by going to war over this one."[298] Mailer failed to see that the two women embroiled in a literary and political war over the nature of truth and good writing would never be "ladies." "There is no rage like the rage of the self-righteous, and Lillian herself had once observed that the drying up of gonads in the most delicate of literary ladies has a tendency to make them irritable not only during the drying process, but long after the fact."[299] She would never have put herself in that category.

Admitting that "if there were literary queens, Lillian would be it," Mailer should not have been surprised at her off-with-her-head mentality. Not able to stand or see, bent and frail, still she persisted, brandishing the law. Money meant love and honor to Hellman, and she wanted to recoup the costs from those who dishonored her.[300] "Oh she was mean," Norman Mailer recalled years later, "manipulative and heroic—she was a mighty little woman."[301] Hellman knew her own nature well and called herself a loyal friend but a very bad enemy.[302] The McCarthy suit proved the latter, as she won a preliminary legal round. "Everyone still remembers what McCarthy said about Hellman . . . but few know that a judge later ruled that Hellman's suit should proceed to trial, finding that McCarthy's comments could be defamatory and the product of actual malice."[303] It pitted "free expression and public discussion—represented by McCarthy" against Hellman's "interest in her personal and professional reputation."[304] But, as a Harper's critic quipped, "If you can't call Lillian Hellman a liar on national TV, what's the First Amendment all about?"[305]

"Lillian Hellman the liar" had become dogma, with no referee checking the opponent's gloves for dirty tricks. In most fighting matches, if one fighter bleeds badly enough, the fight is called a technical knockout. Not so in literary and political squabbles.

In the last ten years of her life, Hellman fought her battles in courts of law and public opinion. She brought powerful friends together to sue President Nixon for his "villainous lies," and she won. She deeply felt this political vindication; the tapes do indeed tell the tale of governmental abuse, as she knew they would. For personal reasons of honor and memory, she publicly fought

Mary McCarthy about her own "lies." Age had weakened her voice and her pen, but not her audacious certainty, not her guts. She remained litigious to the end.

Hellman's final public act was to testify in court in support of actress Vanessa Redgrave's lawsuit alleging blacklisting by the Boston Symphony Orchestra. Because Redgrave supported the Palestine Liberation Organization, the orchestra had canceled her contract for her performance as narrator in Stravinsky's *Oedipus Rex*. She sued and asked Hellman to testify on behalf of her civil rights. (Redgrave won the breach of contract claim but not the civil rights violation claim.) As Daniel J. Kornstein observed in his "Literary/Legal Defense" of Hellman for *Fordham Law Review*, "Hellman had nothing to gain personally from doing so—just the feeling of once again doing what she thought was right although others might disapprove."[306] In her affidavit before the court, the seventy-nine-year-old writer called herself an expert witness about blacklisting. She went on, "It was not only my right, it was my duty to speak or act against what I thought was wrong or dangerous . . . lives were being ruined and few hand[s] were raised to help."[307]

LILLIAN HELLMAN DIED FIVE WEEKS LATER, ON JUNE 30, 1984, AT HER Martha's Vineyard home. Blind, half-paralyzed, unable to eat or walk, for weeks she struggled through each day. She still had the fire of political rage and the urge for romance. She maintained a social schedule as always, and had hired a strong young man to carry her from place to place on her social rounds. On the night before her death, Hellman had dinner at the home of her dear friends John and Barbara Hersey. As Barbara remembered, "A man named Gil Harrison was there. He brought her a bag of candy. I went out of the room for a moment, and John was cooking fish, and when I came back in I heard her say to Gil, 'we must meet up alone one day.'" She believed in her future. That also meant work.

Just a few days before, she had told Peter Feibleman that things were "not good." She had "writer's block. The worst case."[308] The two had just finished her last book—their book—*Eating Together: Recollections and Recipes*, a book Feibleman had suggested to give Hellman purpose and joy. She returned to her old workmanlike way to do her half, this time on a tape recorder. Anxious for the galleys, she demanded he bring them to her immediately. She was waiting for him to arrive when she died. He arrived just hours too late. Her new nurse reported that just as she began to massage her, Hellman had said, "I think you and I are going to get along just fine.' And then she died."[309]

In preparation for the day of her death, she had a few years before prepared a tray full of her heirlooms: pieces of jewelry that ranged from expensive diamond pins to pretty shoe buckles; labels signified pieces of her art and furniture. When friends visited, she insisted they pick, then chided them over their choices, which were always subject to her amendment. But knowing the reality of death and facing it are two different things, and Hellman never quite faced that reality. Denial is strong. As her old friend and literary agent Robbie Lantz mused, "The impertinence of such an intervention from the outside must have infuriated her."

Her will had indeed been a *living* will. She tweaked and dickered with it endlessly, changing codicils and bequests as the sweep of time changed her opinions. As the Surrogate's Court of New York wrote, "The testatrix was a complex person who executed a complex will. While her literary works can be characterized as creative genius, her will cannot." The literary executorship was incredibly complicated, but the will itself—this final version—was not. She left half of her $3.5 million to Peter Feibleman, the rest to the Dashiell Hammett and Lillian Hellman Funds to assist writers. She left property on the Vineyard for use by residents of Gay Head and bequeathed Mike Nichols her manuscripts and a Toulouse-Lautrec poster. No one was much surprised by who benefited, but many were surprised by her worth. She always acted as if she lived on the edge of insolvency: at her request, friend Max Palevsky had sent her "rent" money for years. She could cajole and manipulate and control, but she wasn't strong enough to rewrite her last act.

The friends of Lillian Hellman stood at her graveside in Chilmark Cemetery on July 3, 1984. They had taken this ritual journey to bury her and didn't so much mourn for her as celebrate her life. In awe at the force of her personality, they were not yet accustomed to her absence. They half-expected her to hobble over the hill in order to stage manage the entire event. If reality needed dramaturgical correction, Hellman inevitably offered it.[310] Her cast of famous, glittering friends from writer Bill Styron to theater maven Robert Brustein offered eulogies, Patricia Neal blew a kiss, and Hellman went into the earth—ashes to ashes, dust to dust.

Her death ended her politics, her romances, her writing, and the contentious noise, but not the clamor surrounding her life. In 1987, Mary

McCarthy scolded Hellman's biographer William Wright: "How can you write a book about a liar, it's like building a castle on sand." Wright, however, gamely noted that Hellman was "*still* talking."[311] Still drawing respect and applause or wrath and spit, Hellman's life still commands biographers. She created and recreated herself and her life in a virtual mine field of potentially explosive obstacles.[312] Where did she get that swagger, that resilience? Where did she get the *cajones*?[313]

EPILOGUE

Twenty-one years after Lillian Hellman's death I am haunted by her presence. In writing this biography, I sought to show Hellman's character as it remained constant or shifted over time. Life movement, traced in a woman like Hellman, offers insight into the lived experience itself. Last spring Lika Miyake, a young lawyer journeying along with me in my biographical quest, returned with me to the Harry Ransom Center for the Humanities in Austin, Texas, spending days sifting through Hellman documents. Finally, dazed and bleary eyed from research, we ended a day's work and stepped out into the twilight. Lika, who had spent the day reading letters written by the aging Hellman, turned to me and said, "Promise me I won't get like that when I get old." Startled, I said, "I can't promise you that." She retorted, "Promise me you won't get like that." I couldn't promise that either. Lika and I, two women separated by generations, professions, and profound philosophical differences, both find ourselves fascinated by Lillian Hellman. Almost unwillingly, we identify with her in ineffable ways, find ourselves contemplating more than her life—the complexity too of all our lives and all our deaths. Hellman made no promises for an easy life or an easy death, and neither can I.

I can promise, however, that Hellman and her life tell a truth of sorts. She was a woman who lived fully, to the extent of her energy and intelligence and emotional capacity. That quality repels some but draws others. I am surprised by the reactions of those who know I write about Hellman. A young Haitian American looked taken aback when she noticed Hellman's picture in my office: "But she's not pretty! She had so many lovers. She did what she wanted to. How did she do it?" Another young woman wrote from New York that her friend Shannon was reading *Unfinished Woman*, "taking it real slow, the read, because Hellman's work makes her feel safe since she is in a place of heart sick." That sense of safety may be explained by Britta, an educational psychologist who wrote that she admired Hellman because she followed "her bliss and sinned courageously." Hellman had a romantic vision of what life could be, of what love could do, and lust definitely had its part. Hellman's desire, tempered by a code perhaps known only to her, could not make her immune to public disapproval. She wasn't always right and she wasn't always nice. But she was willing to take the punishment to live and think as she saw fit—no easy feat. Hellman accepted herself and loved who she was. A poet laughingly told me that "Hellman was a pistol." That blast of rebellious heat must be what draws some of us to the woman Hellman, irrespective of her politics, even of her art.

When I began this biography, I wanted to show Hellman the woman, not the legend distorted by friends and critics alike. But she was so much of her time, so part of the events of her life span, that events threatened on every page to overtake this small woman. They did not; art and politics were personal to her, part of her. They are profoundly personal to me too. She wasn't just a writer or a political mouthpiece, but a most public intellectual who read deeply and well for the entirety of her life. Whether on Park Avenue in New York City, Sunset Boulevard in Hollywood, or "Murderer's Row" on Martha's Vineyard—the literatis' shoreline neighborhood—she spoke out but was never careless in her thinking. She listened to the best, the brightest, the most talented minds of each generation. She put herself out front on every stage offered to her. She used up all she had of her energy and her character to live the time of her life.

I am plagued by what I chose to include of the millions of details a life comprises as well as what I left out. The myriad details that together make up a life can obscure, can overtake the story, can hide the complexity rather than demonstrate it. Sometimes irrelevant facts just did not fit: her tiny feet; the silly, arrogant bell she used to ring her staff; the beautiful china of varying patterns that she used to set lovely tables where the flowers matched the linens; her love of color, particularly hot pink; her Tea Rose perfume that everyone hated but she thought of as her "signature." I admired her impersonating a maid or a housekeeper on the telephone when she didn't feel like talking, but I could not find a place for it in the biography. Thousands of details like this sit in file after file in my office, failing to make it to the page.

More disturbing are the details I didn't understand well enough to include. She named her conflicting selves Nursie and Madam and Mimsie. Surely they represent the many selves we all have—but her naming them and readily admitting to that seemed inexplicable. All those who worked for her called her "Miss Hellman," which seems so southern, so haughty and formal to me, yet for them and for her the label fit. I also have little idea of where her increasingly exhibitionist actions came from, nor why. As a woman ages, she usually doesn't begin to expose her body as she has not before. Hellman did. Similarly, though I know with absolute certainty that she was no racist, I cannot explain the outrageous language she used to refer to every ethnic group in the world. And where in a biography is it appropriate to speculate on her asthma, her broken ankle, her enlarged heart, the diminished flow of the oxygen to the brain, or the possibility of sexually transmitted diseases that caused vaginal polyps. Surely all this makes her human, and I chose to include some of it. I feared, however, that flooding the biography with this kind of detail would overwhelm her character, and her writing and her politics would begin to fade.

Lillian Hellman has not faded from memory, at least not from mine. When I told Rita Wade, her secretary of more than twenty years, that Hellman kept showing up in my dreams, she asked me how old Hellman was in those dreams. I paused and then said, "Well. She's my age." Rita laughed. As a friend of Hellman's said about her funeral, "Lillian was much more present than the dead person usually is at these things."[1] My hope is that Lillian Hellman is also present in this biography. In my anxiety, I console myself, knowing there will be other Lillian Hellman biographies, other perceptions of this woman who lived a life surrounded by foxes and scoundrels and prevailed—wholly alive.

ACKNOWLEDGMENTS

No biographer writes without guidance, advice, and hours of labor from others. Many gave me an idea, a cheerful go-ahead, listening time; the following did all that and much more. I thank them.

This book would not have happened without the help of Lika Miyake, Gloria Mazzella, Phillip Schopper, Jerilynn Powers, Peter Feibleman, Pat Hoy, Howard Stein, Elias Rodriguez, my agent Nat Sobel, my editor Ellen Garrison, and my husband Barry Martinson.

Others read drafts, loaned me books or photographs, took me to Hellman places, listened to me and talked to me, made suggestions, stayed the course: Sandra Chrystal, Stefanie Flaxman, Jacqueline O'Connor, Arthe Anthony, Marsha Staley, Pam Ball, Nancy McDonnell, Leila Hadley Luce, Richard De Combray, Rita Wade, Bob Duxbury, Michael Smith, Michael Gibby, John Domesick, Hope Mendez, Jay Martinson, Darsie Bowden, Tom Burkdall, Katie Mills, Britta VanDun, Shannon Sirc, Julie Harkleroad, Ann Huntoon, and those regulars in the Occidental Writers Network: Mary Elizabeth Perry, mb kalis, Anna Waite, Dan Fineman, Scott Harstein, and JoAn Kunselman.

I am grateful to those who granted me (or Phillip Schopper) interviews for this book:

Warren Beatty	Stephen Gillers
Art Buchwald	Kitty Hart
Don Congdon	Barbara Hersey
Bernard Dick	Kim Hunter
Peter Feibleman	Robert Lantz
Jules Feiffer	Ring Lardner, Jr.

Norman Mailer
Walter Mathau
Marsha Norman
Patricia Neal
Max Palevsky
Austin Pendleton
Richard Poirier
Daniel Pollitt

Sky Robins
Carl Rollyson
Maureen Stapleton
Rita Wade
Lisa Weinstein
Milton Wexler
William Wright

Other interviews:

Ann Blythe
Virginia B. Chileworth
Robert Coles
Don Congdon
Richard De Chambray
Carol Gelderman
David L. Goodrich
Annabel Davis-Goff
Lee Israel
Jonathan LaPook
Linda Lightner

Leila Hadley Luce
Robert Newman
Julie Rivett
Ned Rorem
Marvin Sadik
Phillip Schopper
Peter Stansky
Howard Stein
Rita Stein
Alex Sygozi
Sheril Catherine Kober Zeller

Some institutions deserve special recognition: the Sophie Newcomb College of Tulane University gave me a grant to do research in New Orleans. The National Endowment of the Humanities awarded me a summer seminar fellowship at Columbia University in New York City. Occidental College in Los Angeles awarded me time to write in two semester leaves.

Writing a life is as complicated, almost, as living one. The following libraries and archives gave me the riches of research. The librarians and archivists to a one were unfailingly hard-working and helpful.

Archives and Libraries

- The Academy of Arts and Letters, New York
- The Academy of Motion Picture Arts and Sciences, Margaret Herrick Library, Los Angeles
- CIA Files, Lillian Hellman

- Columbia University, Special Collections and Oral History Archives, New York
- FBI Files, Lillian Hellman and Dashiell Hammett
- Harry Ransom Humanities Research Center, Special Collections, Lillian Hellman and Dashiell Hammett Collection, Austin, Tex.
- The Historic New Orleans Collection, New Orleans
- Jewish Museum, New York
- The Library of Congress, Washington D.C.
- Martha's Vineyard Historical Society; Vineyard Haven Public Library, Mass.
- Mormon Genealogical Study Center, Los Angeles
- Mt. Pleasant Public Library, Pleasantville, N.Y.
- Museum of the City of New York Theatre Archives, New York
- National Archives and Records Administration, Washington, D.C.
- City of New Orleans, Official Archives, New Orleans
- New Orleans Notarial Archives, New Orleans
- New Orleans Public Library, Oral Histories Collection, New Orleans
- New York Public Library, Berg Collection, Special Collections, New York
- New York Public Library, Library for the Performing Arts at Lincoln Center, Billy Rose Theater Collection, New York
- Newberry Library Letters Collection, Chicago
- Newcomb College Center for Research on Women, New Orleans
- Occidental College Library, Special Collections, Los Angeles
- RKO Pictures, Los Angeles
- Schomberg Center for Research in Black Culture, New York
- Shubert Theatre Archives, New York
- Southeastern Architectural Archives, New Orleans
- Stanford University Green Library, Special Collections, William Abrahams Collection, Palo Alto, Calif.
- State Department Library, Washington, D.C.
- Tulane University, Amistad Research Center, New Orleans
- University of California–Los Angeles, Special Collections and Oral History Collections, Los Angeles
- University of Southern California, Special Collections, Los Angeles
- University of Washington, Letter Collections, Seattle
- Warner Brothers and Theatre Collections, Los Angeles
- Wisconsin Historical Society Theater Archives, Madison, Wis.
- Yale University, Beinecke Library and Manuscripts and Archives Collections, New Haven, Conn.

NOTES

Prologue

1. *Lilliam Hellman and Jackson R. Bryer*, Conversations with Lillian Hellman *(Jackson: University Press of Mississippi, 1986)*.
2. "Fortune's Little Funster," *New York Post*, July 1, 1939, p. 9.
3. Sidney Carroll, "The Happy Tragedist," *Esquire*, January 1942, p. 185.
4. *New York Post*, July 1, 1939, p. 9.
5. Hellman's description of Hammett in *An Unfinished Woman: A Memoir* (Boston: Little, Brown, 1999).
6. Lillian Hellman, *Pentimento* (Boston: Little, Brown, 1973).
7. Lillian Hellman, letter to Francis Ford Coppola, January 21, 1976.
8. Lillian Hellman, *Pentimento*; William Wright, *Lillian Hellman: The Image, the Woman* (New York: Simon & Schuster, 1986).
9. Lillian Hellman, letter to Katherine Lederer, April 12, 1977.
10. Peter Feibleman, interview by Phillip Schopper, August 7, 1998.
11. Lillian Hellman, letter to William Maxwell, 1971.
12. Lillian Hellman, interview by Marilyn Berger, 1979; in Hellman and Bryer, *Conversations with Lillian Hellman*, p. 265.
13. Lillian Hellman, letter to William Wenders, n.d., Harry Ransom Humanities Research Center, Special Collections, Lillian Hellman and Dashiell Hammett Collection, Austin, Tex.
14. Lillian Hellman, *An Unfinished Woman: A Memoir* (Boston: Little, Brown, 1969).
15. Lillian Hellman, letter to Otto Penzler, June 9, 1974.
16. Julie Rivett, interview by Deborah Martinson, October 13, 2001.
17. Lillian Hellman, letter to William Maxwell, 1971.
18. Lillian Hellman, letter to Tennessee Williams, May 7, 1982, Harry Ransom Humanities Research Center, Special Collections, Lillian Hellman and Dashiell Hammett Collection, Austin, Tex.

19. Lillian Hellman, letter to Louis Kronenberger, June 27, 1952.

20. Lillian Hellman, quoted in Nora Ephron, "Lillian Hellman Walking, Cooking, Writing, Talking," *New York Times Book Review*, September 23, 1973, p. 2.

21. Lillian Hellman, interview by Nora Ephron, in "Lillian Hellman Walking, Cooking, Writing, Talking."

22. Milton Wexler, interview by Deborah Martinson, May 2000.

23. Lillian Hellman, interview by Fred Gardner, 1968; Hellman and Bryer, *Conversations with Lillian Hellman*, p. 109.

24. Lillian Hellman, interview by Lewis Funke, 1968; Hellman and Bryer, *Conversations with Lillian Hellman*, p. 93.

25. "Articles of Faith: A Conversation with Lillian Hellman, *American Theatre*, May 1984.

26. Hellman, *Pentimento*, p. 184.

27. Hellman, *Pentimento*, p. 197.

28. Hellman and Bryer, *Conversations with Lillian Hellman*, p. 59.

29. Carl E. Rollyson, *Lillian Hellman: Her Legacy and Her Legend* (New York: St. Martin's, 1988).

30. Terry Teachout, "Scoundrel Time," review of *Hellman and Hammett: The Legendary Passion of Lillian Hellman and Dashiell Hammett, New York Times*, June 23, 1996.

31. John Hersey, eulogy at Lillian Hellman funeral, reported in the *New York Times*, July 4, 1984.

32. Jo Hammett, Richard Layman, and Julie Rivett, *Dashiell Hammett: A Daughter Remembers* (New York: Carroll & Graf), p. 14.

Chapter One: Unlovely Legend

1. Herbert Kretzmer, "The Mail T.V. Critic," Daily Mail, August 4, 1979.

2. Nat Sobel, interview by Deborah Martinson, August 18, 1999.

3. Kitty Hart, interview by Phillip Schopper, August 12, 1998.

4. Variously attributed to Talullah Bankhead, Mary McCarthy, and others.

5. Rosemary Mahoney and Lillian Hellman, *A Likely Story: One Summer with Lillian Hellman* (New York: Doubleday, 1998).

6. Walter Matthau, interview by Phillip Schopper, August 25, 1998; Matthau, interview by Deborah Martinson, November 1999.

7. Norman Mailer, interview by Phillip Schopper, August 7, 1998.

8. Warren Beatty, interview by Phillip Schopper, August 25, 1998.

9. Norman Mailer, interview by Phillip Schopper, August 7, 1998; interview by Deborah Martinson, November 1999.

10. Lillian Hellman, quoted in *Ms.*, October 1976; Burt Britton, ed., *Self-Portrait: Book People Picture Themselves* (New York: Random House, 1976), p. 75.

11. Peter Feibleman, interview by Phillip Schopper, August 7, 1998.

12. Richard A. Posner, *Public Intellectuals: A Study of Decline* (Cambridge: Harvard University Press, 2002).

13. Marsha Norman, interview by Phillip Schopper, August 19, 1998.

14. Peter Feibleman, interview by Phillip Schopper, August 7, 1998.

15. Richard De Combray, e-mail to author, June 16, 2002.

16. Jules Feiffer, interview by Phillip Schopper, August 7, 1998.

17. Conversation between Ansel Adams, Dorothea Lange, and Imogen Cunningham, *U.S. Camera*, August 1955.

18. Lillian Hellman, letter to Imogen Cunningham, December 26, 1973, Imogen Cunningham Papers, roll 5038, Archives of American Art, Smithsonian Institution, Washington, D.C.

19. Lillian Hellman, letter to William F. Schmick Jr., May 7, 1976, Harry Ransom Humanities Research Center, Special Collections, Lillian Hellman and Dashiell Hammett Collection, Austin, Tex.

20. *Washington Post* attachment to letter from Lillian Hellman to Blair Clark, December 12, 1979, Harry Ransom Humanities Research Center, Special Collections, Lillian Hellman and Dashiell Hammett Collection, Austin, Tex.

21. Blackglama advertisement, *Harper's Bazaar*, December 1976.

22. From Jane Trahey Associates, www.adage.com/century/campaigns.

23. Warren Beatty, interview by Phillip Schopper, August 25, 1998.

24. Rita Wade, telephone interview, July 2, 2002; Joan Mellen and Stacey D'Erasmo, "Hellman and Hammett: The Legendary Passion of Lillian Hellman and Dashiell Hammett," *The Nation* 262, no. 25, p. 414.

25. Jo Hammett, interview by Joan Mellen and Stacey D'Erasmo, in "Hellman and Hammett," p. 414.

26. John Melby, interview, in Carl E. Rollyson, *Lillian Hellman: Her Legacy and Her Legend* (New York: St. Martin's, 1988), p. 3.

27. Dashiell Hammett, letter to Lillian Hellman, August 11, 1943, Williams Miller Abrahams Papers, M1125, Special Collections, Stanford University Libraries, Stanford, Calif.

28. Dashiell Hammett, letter to Lillian Hellman, August 30, 1944, in Dashiell Hammett, Richard Layman, and Julie M. Rivett, *Selected Letters of Dashiell Hammett, 1921–1960* (Washington, D.C.: Counterpoint, 2001).

29. Dashiell Hammett, letter to Lillian Hellman, August 8, 1952, in Hammett, Layman, and Rivett, *Selected Letters*.

30. Peter Feibleman, interview by Phillip Schopper, August 7, 1998.

31. William Specht, "Playwright from Prytania St.," *Times-Picayune*, May 17, 1951.

32. Sidney Carroll, "The Happy Tragedist," *The New Yorker*, January 1942, pp. 59–183.

33. Jo Hammett, Richard Layman, and Julie M. Rivett, *Dashiell Hammett: A Daughter Remembers* (New York: Carroll & Graf, 2001), p. 81.

34. Dashiell Hammett, letter to Lillian Hellman, January 8, 1944, in Hammett, Layman, and Rivett, *Selected Letters*.

35. Walter Matthau, interview by Phillip Schopper, August 25, 1998.

36. Robert Lantz, interview by Phillip Schopper, August 13, 1998; August 18, 1998.

37. Richard De Combray, interview by Deborah Martinson, January 7, 2002.

38. Jules Feiffer, interview by Phillip Schopper, August 7, 1998.

39. Lillian Hellman, letter to Francis Ford Coppola, January 26, 1976, Harry Ransom Humanities Research Center, Special Collections, Lillian Hellman and Dashiell Hammett Collection, Austin, Tex.

40. Richard Layman, forward to Hammett, Layman, and Rivett, *Dashiell Hammett*, p. 11.

41. Ricard Paul, letter to Francis Ford Coppola, January 21, 1976, copy to Lillian Hellman, Harry Ransom Humanities Research Center, Special Collections, Lillian Hellman and Dashiell Hammett Collection, Austin, Tex. Paul was Jo Hammett Marshall's lawyer.

42. Fred Zinnemann Collection, JULIA, 38.f.491, Academy of Motion Pictures Arts and Sciences, Margaret Herrick Library, Los Angeles.

43. Fred Zinnemann, letter to Lillian Hellman, June 1977, copy, Academy of Motion Pictures Arts and Sciences, Margaret Herrick Library, Los Angeles.

44. Christopher P. Anderson, *Citizen Jane: The Turbulent Life of Jane Fonda* (New York: Holt, 1990), p. 207.

45. Max Palevsky, interview by Phillip Schopper, August 25, 1998.

46. Andersen, *Citizen Jane*, p. 206.

47. Andersen, *Citizen Jane*, p. 206.

48. Jane Fonda, interview, "A Profile of Lillian Hellman," 60 *Minutes*, March 8, 1977; Lillian Hellman and Jackson R. Bryer, *Conversations with Lillian Hellman* (Jackson: University Press of Mississippi, 1986), p. 215.

49. Jane Fonda, interview in *Newsweek*, October 10, 1977.

50. Lillian Hellman, letter to Jane Fonda, October 4, 1977, Harry Ransom Humanities Research Center, Special Collections, Lillian Hellman and Dashiell Hammett Collection, Austin, Tex.

51. Jane Fonda, letter to Lillian Hellman, n.d., Harry Ransom Humanities Research Center, Special Collections, Lillian Hellman and Dashiell Hammett Collection, Austin, Tex.

52. Lillian Hellman, letter to Jane Fonda, November 7, 1977, Harry Ransom Humanities Research Center, Special Collections, Lillian Hellman and Dashiell Hammett Collection, Austin, Tex.

53. Jane Fonda, letter to Lillian Hellman, November 12, 1977, Harry Ransom Humanities Research Center, Special Collections, Lillian Hellman and Dashiell Hammett Collection, Austin, Tex.

54. Lillian Hellman, speech before the Academy of Motion Picture Arts and Sciences Academy Awards Program, March 28, 1977.

55. Norman Podhoretz, *Ex-Friends: Falling Out with Allen Ginsberg, Lionel and Diana Trilling, Lillian Hellman, Hannah Arendt, and Norman Mailer* (New York: Free Press, 1999), p. 137.

56. William F. Buckley, *New York Post*, April 2, 1977.

57. William F. Buckley, cover, *National Review*, January 21, 1977.

58. Podhoretz, *Ex-Friends*, p. 137.

59. Austin Pendleton, interview by Phillip Schopper, August 19, 1998.

60. Austin Pendleton, interview by Phillip Schopper, August 19, 1998.

61. Maureen Stapleton, interview by Phillip Schopper, August 2, 1998.

62. Robert Lantz, interview by Phillip Schopper, August 13, 1998; August 18, 1998.

63. Peter S. Feibleman, *Lilly: Reminiscences of Lillian Hellman* (New York: Morrow, 1988), p. 115.

Chapter Two: The Curve and the Edge

1. Architectural Archives, Howard Tilton Library, Tulane University, Special Collections, Oral Histories Collection, New Orleans.

2. Bertram Wallace Korn, *The Early Jews of New Orleans* (Waltham, Mass.: American Jewish Historical Society, 1969).

3. Architectural Archives, Howard Tilton Library, Tulane University, Special Collections, Oral Histories Collection, New Orleans.

4. Lillian Hellman, *An Unfinished Woman: A Memoir* (Boston: Little, Brown, 1999), p. 10.

5. 1920 Louisiana Census.

6. Lillian Hellman, interview by John Phillips and Anne Hollander, 1964; Lillian Hellman and Jackson R. Bryer, *Conversations with Lillian Hellman* (Jackson: University Press of Mississippi, 1986), p. 71.

7. Hellman, quoted in Margaret Case Harriman, "Miss Lily of New Orleans: Lillian Hellman, in *Take Them Up Tenderly* (New York: Knopf, 1944), p. 102.

8. New Orleans Public Library Census Records, New Orleans.

9. Harriman, "Miss Lily of New Orleans," p. 57.

10. Sophie Newcomb College Archives, no. 76 of 1897, Tulane University, Special Collections, Oral Histories Collection, New Orleans.

11. Brandt V. B. Dixon, *A Brief History of H. Sophie Newcomb Memorial College* (New Orleans, 1928), p. 33.

12. Lillian Hellman in loose clipping, Harry Ransom Humanities Research Center, Special Collections, Lillian Hellman and Dashiell Hammett Collection, Austin, Tex.

13. Lillian Hellman, *Pentimento* (Boston: Little, Brown, 1973), p. 57.

14. Marsha Norman, "Articles of Faith: A Conversation with Lillian Hellman," *American Theatre*, May 1984.

15. New Orleans Notarial Archives, 195/760.

16. Sophie Newcome Archives, Architectural Archives, Tulane University, Special Collections, Oral Histories Collection, New Orleans.

17. Hellman, *Unfinished Woman*, p. 10.

18. Hellman, *Unfinished Woman*, p. 43.

19. Milton Wexler, interview by Deborah Martinson, May 2000.

20. Many pictures of the child Lillian Hellman appear in the *Times-Picayune*, April 19, 1959, pp. 29–32.

21. Hellman, *Unfinished Woman*, p. 5.

22. Hellman, *Unfinished Woman*, pp. 20, 23.

23. New Orleans Public Library, Obituary files.

24. James Gill, *Lords of Misrule: Mardi Gras and the Politics of Race in New Orleans* (Jackson: University Press of Mississippi, 1997), p. 97.

25. Kitty Hart, interview by Phillip Schopper, PBS special, August 12, 1998.

26. Leonard V. Huber, *New Orleans: A Pictorial History* (New York: Crown, 1971), p. 201.

27. New Orleans Commercial File, Historical New Orleans Collection, New Orleans.

28. Architectural Archives, Howard Tilton Library, Tulane University, Special Collections, Oral Histories Collection, New Orleans.

29. Leonard Huber, Oral History, Friends of the Cabildo Transcripts, Howard Tilton Library.

30. Hellman, *Pentimento*, p. 15.

31. Hellman, *Unfinished Woman*, p. 47.

32. Kerri McCaffety, "Stand Up for Repeal Tujague's," in *Obituary Cocktail: The Great Saloons of New Orleans* (New Orleans: Pontalba, 1998), p. 70.

33. Guillermo Nunez Falcon, *A Catalogue*, 1981, New Orleans: Howard-Tilton Memorial Library, Rosemonde E. and Emile Kuntz Collection Tulane University, Special Collections, Oral Histories Collection, New Orleans.

34. Lillian Hellman and Peter S. Feibleman, *Eating Together: Recipes and Recollections* (Boston: Little, Brown, 1984), p. 64.

35. Huber, *New Orleans*, p. 198.

36. Adele Levy, Oral History Collection, Friends of the Cabildo, Howard Tilton Library.

37. Peter Feibleman, *Lilly* (New York: Morrow, 1988), p. 73.

38. Hellman, *Pentimento*, p. 26.

39. Rosemary Mahoney and Lillian Hellman, *A Likely Story: One Summer with Lillian Hellman* (New York: Doubleday, 1998), p. 73.

40. New Orleans Public Library documents, Mrs. Bernard Koschland as Lillian Hellman's grandmother, *Times-Picayune*, July 22, 1912.

41. Hellman, *Pentimento*, pp. 6–7.

42. Hellman, *Pentimento*, p. 69.

43. 1900 Louisiana Census Index, Orleans County.

44. Hellman, *Pentimento*, pp. 43–80.

45. "A Jonah Who Swallowed the Whale," *American Magazine*, September 1933, p. 114.

46. Lillian Hellman, interview, in Burns Mandtle, *The Best Plays of 1946–47* (New York: Dodd Mead, 1947), p. 163.

47. John Hersey, interview by Peter Feibleman, August 29, 1998.

48. Hellman, *Pentimento*, p. 51.

49. Lester D. Langley and Thomas Schoonover, *The Banana Men* (Lexington: University of Kentucky Press, 1995), p. 81.

50. Hellman, *Unfinished Woman*, p. 18.

51. Hellman, *Unfinished Woman*, p. 18.

52. Hellman, *Pentimento*, p. 49.

53. Hellman, *Unfinished Woman*, p. 15.

54. Hellman, *Pentimento*, p. 23.

55. Hellman, *Pentimento*, p. 32.

56. Hellman, *Pentimento*, p. 53.

57. New Orleans Public Library; Mormon Genealogical Study Center, Los Angeles.

58. Langley and Schoonover, *Banana Men*, p. 80.

59. Langley and Schoonover, *Banana Men*, p. 80.

60. In Lillian Hellman, *Six Plays* (New York: Vintage, 1979), p. 475.

61. Marjorie Roehl, "Looking Back," *Times-Picayune-States Item*, May 26, 1985.

62. Lillian Hellman, letter to S. Zimmerman, Harry Ransom Humanities Research Center, Special Collections, Lillian Hellman and Dashiell Hammett Collection, Austin, Tex.

63. Max Palevsky, interview by Phillip Schopper, August 25, 1998.

64. Peter Feibleman, *Lilly* (New York: Morrow, 1988), 23.

65. Peter Feibleman, e-mail to Deborah Martinson, September 13, 2001.

66. Max Hellman, letter to Lillian Hellman, Harry Ransom Humanities Research Center, Special Collections, Lillian Hellman and Dashiell Hammett Collection, Austin, Tex.; New York Census, 1920.

67. Mahoney and Hellman, *Likely Story*.

68. *Baltimore Sun*, December 16, 1949.

69. Hellman, *Unfinished Woman*, pp. 7–23.

70. Theresa Bernstein, referring to Mrs. Wm Meyerwitz memories, letter, Williams Miller Abrahams Papers, M1125, Special Collections, Stanford University Libraries, Stanford, Calif.

71. Lillian Hellman, interview by Marilyn Berger, KERA Television, Hoblitzelle Theatre Arts Library, University of Texas, Austin; copy at OID Instructional Library, University of California Los Angeles, Special Collections and Oral Histories Collections.

72. *New York Post*, July 1, 1939.

73. Helen Schiff, quoted in Carl E. Rollyson, *Lillian Hellman: Her Legacy and Her Legend* (New York: St. Martin's, 1988), p. 27.

74. Hilary Mills, interview by Carl E. Rollyson, *Lillian Hellman: Her Legacy and Her Legend* (New York: St. Martin's, 1988), p. 27.

75. Harriman, "Miss Lily of New Orleans."

76. Korn, Bertram. *The Early Jews of New Orleans*. Review. New Orleans Public Library, General File, B38.

77. Parker W. Chase, *New York, the Wonder City* (1932).

78. Lisa Weinstein, interview by Phillip Schopper, August 24, 1998.

79. Lillian Hellman, "The Land That Holds the Legend of Our Lives," *Ladies' Home Journal*, April 1964. Harry Ransom Humanities Research Center, Special Collections, Lillian Hellman and Dashiell Hammett Collection, Austin, Tex.

80. Walter Matthau, interview by Phillip Schopper, August 25, 1998; Matthau, interview by Deborah Martinson, November 1999.

81. Lillian Hellman, *The Little Foxes: Six Plays by Lillian Hellman* (New York: Vintage, 1960), p. 206.

82. Harriman, "Miss Lily of New Orleans."

83. Lillian Hellman and Peter S. Feibleman, *Eating Together: Recipes and Recollections* (Boston: Little, Brown, 1984), p. 25.

84. Kingswood College Library, American Cultural History 1920–1929; Lloyd Morris, *Incredible New York: High Life and Low Life of the Last Hundred Years* (New York: Random House, 1951); "NYC 100: High Stepping to an Uptown Beat," *New York Times*, January 25, 1998.

85. Lillian Hellman, *Diaries* (1920–). Harry Ransom Humanities Research Center, Special Collections, Lillian Hellman and Dashiell Hammett Collection, Austin, Tex.

86. Harriman, "Miss Lily of New Orleans."

87. Alexander Woollcott told her she looked like the "prow head on a whaling ship," perhaps in retaliation for her leaving his class at NYU whenever he bored her, which was often. In Hellman, *Unfinished Woman*, p. 26.

88. Hellman and Feibleman, *Eating Together*, p. 25.

89. Harriman, "Miss Lily of New Orleans."

90. William Wright, interview by Frances Schiff Bolton, in William Wright, *Lillian Hellman* (New York: Simon & Schuster, 1986), p. 30.

91. Hellman, *Unfinished Woman*, pp. 34–39.

92. Alex Szogyi, interview by Phillip Schopper, August 1998; Szogyi, interview by Deborah Martinson, January 18, 2002.

93. *Junior Bazaar*, August 1946, Harry Ransom Humanities Research Center, Special Collections, Lillian Hellman and Dashiell Hammett Collection, Austin, Tex.

94. Louis Kronenberger, "A Time to Speak Words of Praise," *New York Times Book Review*, July 12, 1953; Kronenberger, *Company Manners: A Cultural Inquiry into American Life* (New York: Bobbs, 1954), p. 229.

95. Emmy Kronenberger, interview by Joan Mellen, May 18, 1994.

Chapter Three: Still Life

1. Lillian Hellman, *Diaries* (1920–), Harry Ransom Humanities Research Center, Special Collections, Lillian Hellman and Dashiell Hammett Collection, Austin, Tex.

2. Hellman, *Diaries*.

3. Lillian Hellman, *Pentimento: A Book of Portraits* (New York: New American Library, 1974), p. 61.

4. Hellman, *Diaries*.

5. Hellman, *Diaries*.

6. Hellman, *Diaries*.

7. Lillian Hellman, letter to Arthur Kober, n.d., Arthur Kober Papers, Wisconsin Historical Society, Madison, Wis.

8. Walker Gilmer, *Horace Liveright: Publisher of the Twenties* (New York: Lewis, 1970).

9. Louis Kronenberger, "Gambler in Publishing: Horace Liveright," *Atlantic Monthly*, January 1965, p. 97.

10. Kronenberger, "Gambler in Publishing," p. 99.

11. "Liveright, 49, Ex-Publisher Dies," *New York Herald-Tribune*, September 25, 1933.

12. Lillian Hellman, *An Unfinished Woman: A Memoir* (Boston: Little, Brown, 1999), p. 31.

13. Kronenberger, "Gambler in Publishing" p. 97.

14. Arthur Kober, letter, 1940, Arthur Kober Papers, Wisconsin Historical Society, Madison, Wis.

15. Hellman, *Unfinished Woman*, p. 32.

16. Louis Kronenberger, *Company Manners: A Cultural Inquiry into American Life* (New York: Bobbs, 1954).

17. Hellman, *Diaries*.

18. Hellman, *Unfinished Woman*, pp. 29–44.

19. Herman Shumlin, quoted in Gary Blake, "Herman Shumlin: The Development of a Director" (Ph.D. diss., City University of New York, 1973).

20. Sam Marx, *A Gaudy Spree: The Literary Life of Hollywood in the 1930s When the West Was Fun* (New York: Franklin Watts, 1987), p. 150.

21. Arthur Kober Diary 1921, Arthur Kober Papers, Wisconsin Historical Society, Madison, Wis.

22. Hellman, *Diaries*.

23. Margaret Case Harriman, "Miss Lily of New Orleans," *The New Yorker*, November 8, 1941.

24. Hellman, *Unfinished Woman*.

25. Blake, "Herman Shumlin," p. 11.

26. Blake, "Herman Shumlin," p. 21.

27. Richard Moody, *Lillian Hellman, Playwright* (New York: Pegasus, 1972), p. 24.

28. Moody, *Lillian Hellman*, p. 26.

29. Hellman, *Diaries*.

30. Passport no. 515370 to Arthur Kober, with Lillian Hellman included, issued March 28, 1928.

31. Moody, *Lillian Hellman*, p. 25.

32. Hellman, *Maybe*, p. 23.

33. Stella Bowen, *Drawn from Life* (London: Virago, 1984), p. 55.

34. John Bright, Hollywood Blacklist Oral History, interview by Larry Ceplair, University of California–Los Angeles, Special Collections and Oral Histories Collections.

35. Bowen, *Drawn from Life*, p. 117.

36. Ernest Hemingway, *A Moveable Feast* (New York: Scribner's, 1964).

37. Anthony Hughes, *Paris Writer's Cafes* (1995). Available at http://www.web.archive.org/web/20000208094614.

38. Lillian Hellman, letter to Helen Berlin Schneider, [1928?], Raphaelson Collection, Columbia University, Special Collections and Oral History Archives, New York City.

39. "The Lost Generation," *Historic Traveler*. Now only available at http://webarchive.org.

40. Hellman, *Maybe*, pp. 24–26.

41. Lillian Hellman, letter to Helen Berlin Schneider.

42. "A New Lillian Hellman Looks at Yesterday and Today," July 1, 1969, loose article, Harry Ransom Humanities Research Center, Special Collections, Lillian Hellman and Dashiell Hammett Collection, Austin, Tex.

43. Lillian Hellman, letter to Helen Berlin Schneider.

44. Arthur Kober, letter to Helen and Isador Schneider [1928?], Raphaelson Collection, Columbia University, Special Collections and Oral History Archives, New York City.

45. Lillian Hellman, letter to Helen Berlin Schneider.

46. Janet Flanner, quoted in Leslie Bennett, "Creative Women of the 20's Who Helped to Pave the Way," *New York Times*, n.d., clipping, Harry Ransom Humanities Research Center, Special Collections, Lillian Hellman and Dashiell Hammett Collection, Austin, Tex.

47. Arthur Kober, letter to Norman Podhoretz, 1966, Arthur Kober Papers, Wisconsin Historical Society, Madison, Wis.

48. Lillian Hellman, letter to David Cort; and David Cort, letter to Lillian Hellman, 1976. Courtesy of Pearl London in Joan Mellen, *Hellman and Hammett: The Legendary Passion of Lillian Hellman and Dashiell Hammett* (New York: HarperCollins, 1996).

49. Justice Michael Kirby, quoting Cort, in "The Expense of Spirit," Monash University, March 30, 1988. Available at http://www.hcourt.gov.au/speeches/kirbyj/kirbyj-inaugural.htm.

50. Mellen, *Hellman and Hammett*.

51. Lillian Hellman, letter to D.C. letters, courtesy of Pearl London to Joan Mellen

52. Lillian Hellman, letter to D.C. letters, courtesy of Pearl London to Joan Mellen.

53. Lillian Hellman, "Janet Flanner Tribute," draft (1978), Harry Ransom Humanities Research Center, Special Collections, Lillian Hellman and Dashiell Hammett Collection, Austin, Tex.

54. Lillian Hellman, letter to Helen Berlin Schneider.

55. Moody, *Lillian Hellman*, p. 25.

56. K. S. Angell, letter to Lillian Hellman (1927–1928), New York Public Library, Special Collection.

57. Hellman, *Unfinished Woman*, p. 44.

58. Hellman, *Unfinished Woman*, p. 54.

59. Moody, *Lillian Hellman*, p. 26.

60. Katherine Rogers, *Troublesome Helpmate: A History of Misogyny in Literature* (Seattle: University of Washington Press, 1966).

61. Arthur Miller, *Timebends* (New York: Grove, 1987), p. 236.

Chapter Four: From Still Life to Celluloid

1. *Ira Gershwin, letter to Arthur Kober, [1930], Arthur Kober Papers, Wisconsin Historical Society, Madison, Wis.*

2. Arthur Kober, "Having Terrible Time," unpublished autobiography, Arthur Kober Papers, Wisconsin Historical Society, Madison, Wis.

3. Lillian Hellman, *An Unfinished Woman: A Memoir* (Boston: Little, Brown, 1999), p. 45.

4. Kober, "Having Terrible Time."

5. Hellman, *Unfinished Woman*, p. 45.

6. Draft of untitled manuscript, La Luma paper, Harry Ransom Humanities Research Center, Special Collections, Lillian Hellman and Dashiell Hammett collection, Austin, Tex.

7. Hellman, *Unfinished Woman*, p. 52.

8. Laura Perelman's diary, quoted in Dorothy Hermann, *S.J. Perelman: A Life* (New York: Simon & Schuster, 1986).

9. Steven Alan Carr, *Hollywood and Anti-Semitism* (Cambridge: Cambridge University Press, 2001); Neal Gabler, *Empire of Their Own: How the Jews Invented Hollywood* (New York: Doubleday, 1988).

10. Bruce Torrence, *Hollywood: The First 100 Years* (Hollywood: The Hollywood Chamber of Commerce/Fiske Enterprises, 1979).

11. Kober, "Having Terrible Time."

12. Manuscript draft on Hotel Luma paper, Orizaba, Mexico, [late 1950s], Harry Ransom Humanities Research Center, Special Collections, Lillian Hellman and Dashiell Hammett Collection, Austin, Tex.

13. Lillian Hellman, letter to Christine Doudna, 1976, in Lillian Hellman and Jackson Bryer, Jackson R. 1986. *Conversations with Lillian Hellman* (Jackson: University Press of Mississippi, 1986), p. 202.

14. Hirschfield, quoted in David L. Goodrich, *The Real Nick and Nora: Frances Goodrich and Albert Hackett, Writers of Stage and Screen Classics* (Carbondale: Southern Illinois University Press, 2001), p. 115.

15. Torrence, *Hollywood*, pp. 108–110.

16. Peter S. Feibleman, *Lilly: Reminiscences of Lillian Hellman* (New York: Morrow, 1988), p. 52.

17. Hellman, *Unfinished Woman*, p. 47.

18. Hellman, *Unfinished Woman*, p. 49.

19. Carolyn Heilbrun, quoted in Leslie Bennett, "Creative Women of the 20's Who Helped to Pave the Way," *New York Times*, n.d., clipping from Harry Ransom Humanities Research Center, Special Collections, Lillian Hellman and Dashiell Hammett Collection, Austin, Tex.

20. Lillian Hellman, interview by Bill Moyers, 1974, in Hellman and Bryer, *Conversations with Lillian Hellman*, p. 150.

21. Margaret Case Harriman, "Miss Lily of New Orleans," *The New Yorker*, November 8, 1941, p. 24.

22. Arthur Kober Diaries, Arthur Kober Papers, Wisconsin Historical Society, Madison, Wis.

23. Jean Cohen Friedlander, letter to Arthur Kober, October 16, 1930, Arthur Kober Papers, Wisconsin Historical Society, Madison, Wis.

24. Sam Marx, *A Gaudy Spree: The Literary Life of Hollywood in the 1930s When the West Was Fun* (New York: Franklin Watts, 1987), p. 151.

25. Marx, *Gaudy Spree*, p. 151.

26. Marx, *Gaudy Spree*, p. 150.

27. Robert Winter, interview by Deborah Martinson, 2001.

28. Lillian Hellman, letter to Lucius Beebe, in Hellman and Bryer, *Conversations with Lillian Hellman*, p. 5.

29. Hellman, *Unfinished Woman*, p. 49.

30. Torrence, *Hollywood*.

31. Anita Loos, *A Girl Like I* (New York: Viking, 1966), p. 121.

32. Hellman, *Unfinished Woman*, p. 47.

33. www.gretagarbo.biz

34. Joan Mellen, *Hellman and Hammett: The Legendary Passion of Lillian Hellman and Dashiell Hammett* (New York: HarperCollins, 1996), p. 46.

35. Bernard F. Dick, *Hellman in Hollywood* (Rutherford, N.J.: Fairleigh Dickinson University Press, 1982), p. 20.

36. S.J. Perelman, quoted in Herrmann, *S.J. Perelman*, p. 97.

37. Jay Presson Allen, quoted in Steven Mintz, review of *Script Girls: Women Screenwriters in Hollywood*, Noteworthy H-Net Reviews, www.mediahistory.com.

38. Hellman, *Unfinished Woman*, p. 48.

39. Hellman, *Unfinished Woman*, pp. 48–49.

40. Marx, *Gaudy Spree*, p. 149.

41. Barbara Barondness, http://new.sag.org.

42. Mellen, *Hellman and Hammett*.

43. William Wright, *Lillian Hellman: The Image, the Woman* (New York: Simon & Schuster, 1986).

44. Lillian Hellman in Lillian Hellman and Peter S. Feibleman, *Eating Together: Recipes and Recollections* (Boston: Little, Brown, 1984), p. 165.

45. Diane Johnson, *Dashiell Hammett: A Life* (New York: Random House, 1983), p. 95.

46. Richard Layman and Julie Rivett, *Selected Letters of Dashiell Hammett, 1921–60* (New York: Counterpoint, 2001).

47. William Luce, *Lillian Hellman*, 1984, based on Hellman's "Autobiographical Works," script at the New York Public Library for the Performing Arts, Billy Rose Theatre Collection, p. 24.

48. Rudy Behlmer, *Memo: David O. Selznick* (New York: Viking, 1972).

49. Johnson, *Dashiell Hammett*, p. 125.

50. Hellman, *Unfinished Woman*, p. 52.

51. Dashiell Hammett, letter to Lillian Hellman, November 27, 1937, in Layman and Rivett, *Selected Letters*.

52. Dashiell Hammett, letter to Lillian Hellman, March 10, 1939, in Layman and Rivett, *Selected Letters*.

53. Johnson, *Dashiell Hammett*, p. 92.

54. Phillips and Hollander, 1964, in Hellman and Bryer, *Conversations with Lillian Hellman*, p. 68.

55. Hellman, *Unfinished Woman*, p. 53.

56. Emily Hahn, interview by Joan Mellen, 1993.

57. Hellman, *Unfinished Woman*, pp. 52–53.

58. Hedda Hopper, *The Whole Truth and Nothing But* (New York: Doubleday, 1963), p. 116.

59. Julie Rivett, interview by Deborah Martinson, October 13, 2001.

60. Dorothy Parker, review of *Glass Key*, *New Yorker*, April 15, 1931.

61. Burton Bernstein, *Drinking with Thurber: A Biography* New York: Ballantine, 1976), p. 291.

62. Arthur Kober, Diary, Arthur Kober Papers, Wisconsin Historical Society, Madison, Wis.

63. Layman and Rivett, *Selected Letters*, p. 66.

64. Layman and Rivett, *Selected Letters*, p. 75.

65. Ted Thackrey, "After a Top-speed life, N.O.'s Rebel," *Lagniappe: Times-Picayune*, June 8, 1984.

66. Arthur Kober, Diary, Wisconsin Historical Society, Madison, Wis.

67. Lillian Hellman to Arthur Kober, 1931 letters in Hellman Correspondence File, Arthur Kober Papers, Wisconsin Historical Society, Madison, Wis.

68. Layman and Rivett, *Selected Letters*, p. 75.

69. Lillian Hellman, letter to Arthur Kober, Letters to Hellman Correspondence File, Arthur Kober Papers, Wisconsin Historical Society, Madison, Wis.

70. Layman and Rivett, *Selected Letters*, p. 65.

71. Layman and Rivett, *Selected Letters*, p. 73.

72. Layman and Rivett, *Selected Letters*, p. 76.

73. Layman and Rivett, *Selected Letters*, p. 67.

74. Layman and Rivett, *Selected Letters*, p. 75.

75. Alvin Sargent, quoted in Williams Miller Abrahams Papers, M1125, Department of Special Collections, Stanford University Libraries, Stanford, Calif.

76. Albert Hackett, taped interview by Steven Marcos, in Johnson, *Dashiell Hammett*, p. 123.

77. Williams Miller Abrahams Papers, M1125, Department of Special Collections, Stanford University Libraries, Stanford, Calif.

78. Layman and Rivett, *Selected Letters*, p. 77.

79. Dashiell Hammett to Arthur Kober, April 21, 1931, in Layman and Rivett, *Selected Papers*, p. 34.

80. Patricia Riley Foster, letter to Arthur Kober, October 5, 1932, Arthur Kober Papers, Wisconsin Historical Society, Madison, Wis.

81. Dashiell Hammett, letter to Lillian Hellman, April 30, 1931, in Layman and Rivett, *Selected Letters*, p. 74.

82. Lillian Hellman, letter to Marilyn Berger, TV transcripts, University of California–Los Angeles, Special Collections and Oral Histories Collections, Los Angeles.

83. Wright, *Lillian Hellman*, p. 76.

84. David Minter, *William Faulkner: His Life and Times* (Baltimore: Johns Hopkins Press, 1980).

85. William Faulkner, quoted in Joseph L. Blotner, *William Faulkner: His Life and His Work* (New York: Random House, 1974).

86. Bernstein, *Drinking with Thurber*, p. 291.

87. Layman and Rivett, *Selected Letters*, p. 81.

88. Arthur Kober Diary, Arthur Kober Papers, Wisconsin Historical Society, Madison, Wis.

89. Dashiell Hammett to Lillian Hellman, May 5, 1932, in Layman and Rivett, *Selected Letters*, p. 80.

90. Dashiell Hammett to Lillian Hellman, May 5, 1932, in Layman and Rivett, *Selected Letters*, p. 81.

91. Johnson, *Dashiell Hammett*, p. 107.

92. Layman and Rivett, *Selected Letters*, p. 91.

93. Goodrich, *The Real Nick and Nora*, p. 79.

94. Dashiell Hammett, *Women in the Dark*, 1988; originally serialized in *Liberty* magazine, 1933, p. 25.

95. "Bethe," in Hellman, *Pentimento*.

96. Lillian Hellman, Diaries, 1960, Harry Ransom Humanities Research Center, Special Collections, Lillian Hellman and Dashiell Hammett Collection, Austin, Tex.

97. Herrmann, *S.J. Perelman*, p. 68.

98. "Dashiell Hammett: A Memoir," *New York Review of Books*, November 25, 1965.

99. Lillian Hellman, in *Playwrights at Work*, ed. George Plimpton (New York: Modern Library, 2000).

100. Lillian Hellman, 1957 interview, in Layman, *Shadowman*.

101. Layman, *Shadowman*, p. 141.

102. Layman and Rivett, *Selected Letters*, p. 83.

103. Hellman, *Unfinished Woman*, p. 236.

104. Layman, *Shadowman*, p. 146.

105. Jan Herman, *A Talent for Trouble: The Life of Hollywood's Most Acclaimed Director, William Wyler* (New York: Putnam, 1995), p. 86.

106. Herrmann, *S.J. Perelman*, p. 120.

107. Herrmann, *S.J. Perelman*, p. 94.

108. Jay Martin, *Nathanael West: The Art of His Life* (New York: Farrar, Strauss & Giroux, 1970), p. 351.

109. Laura Perelman, diary, in Herrmann, *S.J. Perelman*, pp. 88–89.

110. Herrmann, *S.J. Perelman*, p. 89.

111. Hellman and Bryer, *Conversations with Lillian Hellman*, p. 64.

112. New York Public Library, *New Yorker* Box 184, October 9, 1933.

113. "Fortune's Little Funster."

114. Lewis Funke, interview, 1968, in Hellman and Bryer, *Conversations with Lillian Hellman*, p. 97.

115. Diane Johnson, "Investigative Efforts," *LA Herald Examiner*, November 29, 1983.

116. Hammett, Layman, and Rivett, *Dashiell Hammett*, p. 171.

117. "Dashiell Hammett: A Memoir," *New York Review of Books*, November 25, 1965.

118. John Leonard, review of *Dash and Lilly*, New York Metro.com.

119. Hammett, Layman, and Rivett, *Dashiell Hammett*, p. 128.

120. Milton Wexler, interview by Deborah Martinson, May 2000.

121. Hellman, *Unfinished Woman*, p. 44.

122. Layman and Rivett, *Selected Letters*, p. 59.

123. Hammett, Layman, and Rivett, *Dashiell Hammett*, p. 94.

124. Hellman, *Pentimento*.

125. Hellman and Bryer, *Conversations with Lillian Hellman*, p. 69.

126. Lillian Hellman, quoted in *Vineyard Gazette*, December 7, 1948.

127. "Fortune's Little Funster."

128. Marilyn Berger, *Profile: Lillian Hellman* (Jackson: University Press of Mississippi, 1972).

129. Jean Potter, letter to Stephen Talbot, March 8, 1982, in Johnson, *Dashiell Hammett*, p. 322.

130. Lillian Hellman, letter to Lois Fritsch, 1953.

131. Dashiell Hammett obituary, *New York Times*, January 10, 1961.

132. Howard Benedict, interview by Joan Mellen, 1993, in Mellen, p. 476; LH to AK letter, 1934, Wisconsin Historical Society, Madison, Wis.

133. Lillian Hellman, *Four Plays: Introductions* (New York: Random House, 1942).

134. Phillip Schopper, letter to Deborah Martinson, June 8, 2001.

135. Gary Blake, "Herman Shumlin: The Development of a Director" (Ph.D. diss., City University of New York, 1973).

136. Blake, "Herman Shumlin."

137. Edward Choate, interview, in Blake, "Herman Shumlin," p. 10.

138. Eric Pace, *New York Times*, June 15, 1979.

139. Irving Drutman, "Miss Hellman and Her First Screen Venture," 1941, clipping, Harry Ransom Humanities Research Center, Special Collections, Lillian Hellman and Dashiell Hammett Collection, Austin, Tex.

140. Carl E. Rollyson, *Lillian Hellman: Her Legacy and Her Legend* (New York: St. Martin's, 1988) p. 62.

141. Drutman, "Miss Hellman."

142. Blake, "Herman Shumlin," p. 38.

143. Blake, "Herman Shumlin," p. 18.

144. Feibleman, *Lilly*, p. 89.

145. Layman and Rivett, *Selected Letters*, p. 88.

146. Rollyson, *Lillian Hellman*, p. 65.

147. Phillip Schopper, interview by Deborah Martinson, December 7, 2003.

148. Phillip Schopper, interview by Deborah Martinson, December 7, 2003.

149. Mellen, *Hellman and Hammett*, p. 94.

150. Howard Teichmann, quoted in Eric Pace, *New York Times*, June 15, 1979.

151. Drutman, "Miss Hellman."

152. Tony Randall's diary, in Blake, "Herman Shumlin," p. 106.

153. Blake, "Herman Shumlin," p. 42.

154. Hellman and Bryer, *Conversations with Lillian Hellman*, p. 9.

155. Blake, "Herman Shumlin," p. 39.

156. Eugenia Rawls, interview, in Blake, "Herman Shumlin," p. 42.

157. *Hollywood Reporter*, November 1934.

158. Arthur Kober Papers; Blake, "Herman Shumlin," p. 41.

159. John Chapman, *New York Daily News*, December 23, 1934.

160. Van Hoogstraten, *Lost Broadway Theatres* (Princeton, N.J.: Princeton Architectural Press, 1991), p. 109.

161. Phillip Schopper, interview by Deborah Martinson, December 7, 2003.

162. Blake, "Herman Shumlin."

163. Blake, "Herman Shumlin," p. 42.

164. Blake, "Herman Shumlin," p. 61.

165. Herman Shumlin, quoted in Alan Keller, *New York World Telegram*, April 25, 1941.

166. John Chapman, *New York Daily News*, December 23, 1934.

167. *The Children's Hour* file, Lillian Hellman Collection, clipping, Harry Ransom Humanities Research Center, Special Collections, Lillian Hellman and Dashiell Hammett Collection, Austin, Tex.

168. Brooks Atkinson, *New York Times*, December 2, 1934.

169. Walter Winchell, *New York Daily Mirror*, November 21, 1934.

170. Robert Benchley, *New Yorker*, December 1, 1934.

171. "'Children's Hour' Attracts Large Audience to Shubert 1936," clipping, Newark, Harry Ransom Humanities Research Center, Special Collections, Lillian Hellman and Dashiell Hammett Collection, Austin, Tex.

172. *The Children's Hour* file, Lillian Hellman Collection, clipping, Harry Ransom Humanities Research Center, Special Collections, Lillian Hellman and Dashiell Hammett Collection, Austin, Tex.

173. *New York Times,* December 16, 1936.

174. *Variety,* February 5, 1936.

175. Clipping, Harry Ransom Humanities Research Center, Special Collections, Lillian Hellman and Dashiell Hammett Collection, Austin, Tex.

176. *New York Times,* May 8, 1935.

177. Clipping, November 26, 1934, Harry Ransom Humanities Research Center, Special Collections, Lillian Hellman and Dashiell Hammett Collection, Austin, Tex.

178. Johnson, *Dashiell Hammett,* pp. 118–120.

179. *New York Times,* September 23, 1973.

180. Lillian Hellman, *Maybe: A Story* (Boston: Little, Brown, 1980), p. 54.

181. Herman Shumlin, letter to Lillian Hellman, December 27, 1934, Herman Shumlin Collections, Wisconsin Historical Society, Madison, Wis.

182. Johnson, *Dashiell Hammett,* p. 118.

183. Pauline Kael, *For Keeps: 30 Years at the Movies* (New York: Dutton, 1994) p. 252.

184. Dorothy Parker, quoted in David Galligan, *Dramalogue* magazine, n.d., clipping file, New York Public Library.

185. Lillian Hellman, letter to Fred Gardner, 1968, in Hellman and Bryer, *Conversations with Lillian Hellman,* p. 111.

186. Lillian Hellman, letter to John Phillips and Anne Hollander, 1964, in Ally Acker and Judith Crist, *Reel Women: Pioneers of the Cinema, 1896 to the Present* (New York: Continuum, 1991), p. 131.

187. Lillian Hellman to Lucius Beebe, 1936, in Hellman and Bryer, *Conversations with Lillian Hellman,* p. 5.

188. Herman, *Talent for Trouble,* p 235.

189. Gilbert Harrison, letter to Lillian Hellman, Library of Congress, Gilbert Harrison Papers, September 26, 1966.

190. Lillian Hellman, letter to John Phillips and Anne Hollander.

191. Lillian Hellman, letters to Gilbert Harrison, Library of Congress, Gilbert Harrison Papers, October 2, 1966.

192. Marion Meade, *Dorothy Parker* (New York: Penguin, 1989), p. 246.

193. Hellman, *Unfinished Woman,* p. 188.

194. Lillian Hellman to Arthur, Maggie, and Catherine Kober, Arthur Kober Papers, Wisconsin Historical Society, Madison, Wis.

195. Lillian Hellman, letter to Arthur Kober, Arthur Kober Papers, Wisconsin Historical Society, Madison, Wis.

196. Marx, *Gaudy Spree,* p. 163.

197. Maurice Zolotov, *Billy Wilder in Hollywood* (New York: Limelight, 1987).

198. Paul Jerrico, interview by Larry Ceplair, 1991, "Hollywood Blacklist," University of California–Los Angeles, Special Collections and Oral Histories Collections, Los Angeles.

199. Arthur Mayer, quoted in Andrew Scott Berg, *Goldwyn: A Biography* (New York: Alfred Knopf: 1989), p. 91.

200. Hellman, *Pentimento*, pp. 136–137.

201. Dashiell Hammett, quoted in Margaret Harriman, Profiles, *New Yorker*, November 8, 1941, p. 34.

202. Dick, *Hellman in Hollywood*, p. 28.

203. Berg, *Goldwyn*, p. 107.

204. Carr, *Hollywood and Anti-Semitism*, pp. 127–130.

205. Carr, *Hollywood and Anti-Semitism*, pp. 127–130.

206. Dead End file, PCA correspondence, Academy of Motion Pictures Arts and Sciences, Margaret Herrick Library, Los Angeles.

207. Berg, *Goldwyn*, p. 266.

208. Berg, *Goldwyn*, p. 265.

209. William Wyler Southern Methodist University Oral History Project, no. 175, Academy of Motion Pictures Arts and Sciences, Margaret Herrick Library, Los Angeles.

210. Graham Greene, "These Three," "The Cinema," Stage and Screen, *The Spectator*, May 1, 1936.

211. Berg, *Goldwyn*, p. 271.

212. Berg, *Goldwyn*, p. 267.

213. Sylvia Sidney, quoted in Herman, *Talent for Trouble*, p. 169.

214. Berg, *Goldwyn*, p. 270.

215. Axel Madsen, *William Wyler* (New York: Crowell, 1973), p. 133.

216. Lillian Hellman, letter to Arthur Kober, [1936], Arthur Kober Papers, Wisconsin Historical Society, Madison, Wis.

217. Graustark Treatment, Lillian Hellman files, Academy of Motion Pictures Arts and Sciences, Margaret Herrick Library, Los Angeles.

218. H. N. Swanson, letter to Lillian Hellman, February 7, 1948, Harry Ransom Humanities Research Center, Special Collections, Lillian Hellman and Dashiell Hammett Collection, Austin, Tex.

219. Berg, *Goldwyn*, p. 500.

220. Paris interviews, "Women Writers at Work," *Paris Reviews Interviews* 1949, p. 280.

221. First Fan Letter, 1934, Arthur Kober Papers, Wisconsin Historical Society, Madison, Wis.

222. *New York Post*, November 23, 1934.

223. Hillary Mills, interview, in Rollyson, *Lillian Hellman*.

224. Hillary Mills in Mellen, *Hellman and Hammett*, p. 92.

225. Margolick, *Vanity Fair*, January 1999, pp. 116–132.

226. Roy Hoopes, in *Vanity Fair*, January 1999, p. 121.

227. Lillian Hellman, "Flipping for a Diamond," *New York Review of Books*, September 20, 1973.

228. Layman and Rivett, *Selected Letters*, p. 60.

229. Layman and Rivett, *Selected Letters*, p. 60.

230. Clipping, *New York Herald Tribune*, Harry Ransom Humanities Research Center, Special Collections, Lillian Hellman and Dashiell Hammett Collection, Austin, Tex.

231. Hellman, *Pentimento*, p. 141.

232. Lillian Hellman, letter to Arthur Kober, [1936], Arthur Kober Papers, Wisconsin Historical Society, Madison, Wis.

233. Richard E. Sherwood, *There Shall Be No Night* (New York: Scribner's, 1940).

234. Lillian Hellman, letter to Arthur Kober, [1936], Arthur Kober Papers, Wisconsin Historical Society, Madison, Wis.

235. Arthur Kober, letter to Lillian Hellman, n.d., Arthur Kober Papers, Wisconsin Historical Society, Madison, Wis.

236. Lillian Hellman, interview by Lusius Beebe, in Hellman and Bryer, *Conversations with Lillian Hellman*, p. 3.

237. Harry Ransom Humanities Research Center, Special Collections, Lillian Hellman and Dashiell Hammett Collection, Austin, Tex.

238. Lillian Hellman, interview by Lusius Beebe, in Hellman and Bryer, *Conversations with Lillian Hellman*, p. 5.

239. Lillian Hellman, *Days to Come: The Collected Plays* (Boston: Little, Brown, 1936).

240. Hellman, *Unfinished Woman*.

241. Hellman, "Flipping for a Diamond."

242. Hellman and Bryer, *Conversations with Lillian Hellman*, p. 590.

243. Clipping, December 16, 1936, Harry Ransom Humanities Research Center, Special Collections, Lillian Hellman and Dashiell Hammett Collection, Austin, Tex.

244. Richard Maney *Fanfare: The Confessions of a Press Agent* (New York: Harper, 1957), p. 254.

245. Hellman, "Flipping for a Diamond."

246. Maney, *Fanfare*, p. 334.

247. Frank S. Nugent, review, in Joe Morella, Edward Z. Epstein, and John Griggs, *The Films of World War II* (Secaucus, N.J.: Citadel).

248. Arthur Kober, letter to Lillian Hellman, 1936, Arthur Kober Papers, Wisconsin Historical Society, Madison, Wis.

249. Library of Congress Information Bulletin, Washington D.C., October 7, 1963.

250. Editorial on Dead End, *New York Post*, [1937?], Academy of Motion Pictures Arts and Sciences, Margaret Herrick Library, Los Angeles.

251. Script, Academy of Motion Pictures Arts and Sciences, Core Collection, Margaret Herrick Library, Los Angeles.

252. A. M. Sperber and Eric Lax, *Bogart* (London: Weidenfeld & Nicolson, 1997), p. 84.

253. Script, Academy of Motion Pictures Arts and Sciences, Core Collection, Margaret Herrick Library, Los Angeles.

254. B. B. Breene, letter to Samuel Goldwyn, 1936, Motion Pictures & Distributors of America, Inc., Hays office, Academy of Motion Pictures Arts and Sciences, Core Collection, Margaret Herrick Library, Los Angeles.

255. Herman, *Talent for Trouble*, p. 169.

256. Herman, *Talent for Trouble*, p. 169.

257. Sam Jaffe, interview by Barbara Hall, Oral History no. 109, 1992, Academy of Motion Pictures Arts and Sciences, Core Collection, Margaret Herrick Library, Los Angeles.

258. Hellman, *Pentimento*, p. 135.

259. Herman, *Talent for Trouble*, p. 143.

260. Berg, *Goldwyn*, pp. 299–300.

261. Hellman, *Pentimento*, pp. 137–139.

262. Berg, *Goldwyn*, p. 299.

263. Berg, *Goldwyn*, p. 304.

264. Berg, *Goldwyn*, p. 309.

265. Gabler, *Empire of Their Own*, p. 316.

266. Albert Hackett and Frances Hackett, interview by Mark Rowland, in Patrick McGilligan, *Backstory: Interviews with Screenwriters of Hollywood's Golden Age* (Berkeley: University of California Press, 1986), p. 204.

267. McGilligan, *Backstory*, p. 197.

268. Peter Feibleman, interview by Deborah Martinson, November 1998.

269. Sean Mitchell, "Lip Service," *LA Times Magazine*, March 25, 2001.

270. Ring Lardner Jr., interview by Phillip Schopper, September 17, 1998.

271. Maurice Rapf, quoted in Schwartz, *Hollywood Writers' Wars*.

272. Ring Lardner Jr., interview by Phillip Schopper, September 17, 1998.

273. Lillian Hellman, interview by Marilyn Berger, NTSC Video from KERA-TV in Dallas/Fort Worth, University of California–Los Angeles, Special Collections and Oral Histories Collections, Los Angeles.

274. Quoted in Sean Mitchell, Written By: Hereinafter Referred to as the Author, June-July 2000, www.wga.WrittenBy.

275. Joel W. Finler, *The Hollywood Story* (London: Wallflower, 1988), p. 153.

276. John Bright, "Hollywood Blacklist," University of California Los Angeles, Special Collections and Oral Histories Collections, Los Angeles.

277. Bright, "Hollywood Blacklist."

278. Bright, "Hollywood Blacklist."

279. Frances Goodwin, quoted in Schwartz, *Hollywood Writers' Wars*, p. 124.

280. Arthur Kober Diary, June 17, 1937, Arthur Kober Papers, Wisconsin Historical Society, Madison, Wis.

281. Lillian Hellman, interview by Marilyn Berger, KERA Television, Hoblitzelle Theatre Arts Library, University of Texas, Austin, copy at University of California–Los Angeles, Special Collections and Oral Histories Collections, Los Angeles.

282. Alvin Sargeant, interview, in Mellen, *Hellman and Hammett*, p. 124.

283. Marilyn Berger, quoted in Hellman and Bryer, *Conversations with Lillian Hellman*, p. 268.

284. Hellman, *Unfinished Woman*, p 62.

285. Lillian Hellman, quoted in N.Y. *Sun*, clipping, August 17, 1937.

286. Hellman, *Unfinished Woman*, pp. 67–68.

287. Lillian Hellman, letter to Alvin Sargeant, Harry Ransom Humanities Research Center, Special Collections, Lillian Hellman and Dashiell Hammett Collection, Austin, Tex.

288. John Taylor Williams, letter to Lillian Hellman, March 7, 1973.

289. Draft, Harry Ransom Humanities Research Center, Special Collections, Lillian Hellman and Dashiell Hammett Collection, Austin, Tex.

290. Hellman, *Unfinished Woman*, p. 78.

291. Peter Feibleman, e-mail to Deborah Martinson, July 2004.

292. All three letters to Lillian Hellman are at Harry Ransom Humanities Research Center, Special Collections, Lillian Hellman and Dashiell Hammett Collection, Austin, Tex.

293. Peter Feibleman, interview by Deborah Martinson, 2000; Lillian Hellman, interview by Marilyn Berger, 1979, in *Conversations*, pp. 232–273.

294. Ring Lardner Jr., interview by Phillip Schopper, September 17, 1998.

295. Hellman, *Unfinished Woman*, p. 69.

296. Arnold Rampersand, *The Life of Langston Hughes* (New York: Oxford University Press, 1986), p. 348.

297. Hellman, *Unfinished Woman*, p. 99.

298. Hellman, *Unfinished Woman*, p. 76.

299. Langston Hughes, *I Wonder As I Wander: An Autobiographical Journey* (New York: Hill & Wang, 1993), p. 363.

300. Peter N. Carroll, *Odyssey: Abraham Lincoln Brigade Newsletter*.

301. FBI files, Lillian Hellman.

302. Hellman, *Unfinished Woman*, p. 89.

303. Hellman, *Unfinished Woman*, p. 101.

304. Lillian Hellman to Herman Shumlin, June 26, 1941, Herman Shumlin Collection, Wisconsin Historical Society, Madison, Wis.

305. George Orwell, *Looking Back on the Spanish War*, 1943.

306. Archie Brown, ILWU Local 10, 1938, *Dispatcher*, January 2002.

307. Harvey Schwartz, quoted in ILWU Local 10, *Dispatcher*, January 2002.

308. September 9, 1937, Harry Ransom Humanities Research Center, Special Collections, Lillian Hellman and Dashiell Hammett Collection, Austin, Tex.

309. Hammett, Layman, and Rivett, *Dashiell Hammett*.

310. Hammett, Layman, and Rivett, *Dashiell Hammett*, p. 98.

311. Albert Hackett, in Goodrich, *Real Nick and Nora*, p. 9.

312. Joyce Haber, "Lillian Hellman Takes Look at Today's Theater." *Los Angeles Times*, November 2, 1969.

313. Bernard College address, May 1975, Harry Ransom Humanities Research Center, Special Collections, Lillian Hellman and Dashiell Hammett Collection, Austin, Tex.

314. Nate Witt, quoted in Schwartz, *Hollywood Writers' Wars*, p. 116.

315. Zannick, quoted by Milton Sperling in Schwartz, *Hollywood Writers' Wars*, p. 60.

316. Westbrook Pegler, "As Pegler Sees It," September 7, 1951.

317. FBI files, Lillian Hellman; HRC correspondence, Spanish Refugees Collection, Columbia University, Special Collections and Oral History Archives, New York.

318. Neal Gabler, *Winchell: Gossip, Power and the Culture of Celebrity* (New Yorl: Knopf, 1994), p. 227.

319. Richard Maltby, *Hollywood Cinema* (Malden, Mass: Blackwell, 1995), p. 281.

320. Maria Brooks, *Carrying It On*, ILWU Local 10, *Dispatcher*, January 2002.

321. John Melby, testimony at State Department Loyalty Board, 1952, in Robert Newman, *The Cold War Romance of Lillian Hellman and John Melby* (Chapel Hill: University of North Carolina Press, 1989), p. 9.

322. Ring Lardner Jr., interview by Phillip Schopper, September 17, 1998.

323. Draft, April 28, 1952, Library of Congress, Manuscript Division, Joseph Rauh Collection.

324. Irving Howe and Lewis A. Coser, *The American Communist Party: A Critical History 1919–1957* (Boston: Beacon, 1957), pp. 385–386.

325. Newman, *Cold War Romance*, p. 10.

326. FBI files, Lillian Hellman, 1937, 1938.

327. Walter Duranty, quoted in Newman, *Cold War Romance*, p. 10.

328. Oral History with Larry Ceplair, University of California–Los Angeles, Special Collections and Oral Histories Collections, Los Angeles.

329. Sheril Catherine Kober Zeller, interview by Deborah Martinson, October 26, 2004.

330. Phil Nel, About the Newspaper PM. www.cofc.edu/~nelp/

331. Edward Zwick, "Life in Art: A Study of Lillian Hellman and *Watch on the Rhine*," WA *Papers* 73, no. 5, p. 40.

332. Lillian Hellman, draft of HUAC statement, Library of Congress, Manuscript Divsion, Joseph Rauh Collection, April 28, 1952.

333. Zwick, "Life in Art," p. 44.

334. Zwick, "Life in Art," p. 40.

335. Sophie Smith Collection, Smith College.

336. Lillian Hellman, letter to Millen Brand, Brand Collection, Columbia University Archives, January 11, 1940.

337. Herbert Lehman, letter to Lillian Hellman, Herbert H. Lehman Collection, New York Public Library, Columbia University, Special Collections and Oral History Archives, New York.

338. Peter Feibleman, e-mail to Deborah Martinson, July 2004.

Chapter Five: Fame and Foxes

1. *Lillian Hellman, quoted in Clarke Robinson, "Silhouettes of Celebrities,"* World Digest, *January 1942, 78–83. First published in* Christian Science Monitor, *December 5, 1941.*

2. Lillian Hellman, *Pentimento* (Boston: Little, Brown, 1973), p. 142.

3. "The Slyest Little Fox; Lillian Hellman, Still Provocative," *Washington Post*, Show sec., June 11, 2002.

4. *Washington Post*, June 11, 2002.

5. Charles David Haller, "The Concept of Moral Failure in the Eight Original Plays of Lillian Hellman" (Ph.D. diss., Tulane University, 1967), p. 8.

6. *Jambalaya* interview, 1977, New Orleans Public Library.

7. www.curtainup.com

8. Harry Ransom Humanities Research Center, Special Collections, Lillian Hellman and Dashiell Hammett Collection, Austin, Tex.

9. Peter Feibleman, interview by Deborah Martinson, November 1998.

10. Tallulah Bankhead, *Tallulah: My Autobiography* (New York: Harper, 1952), p. 237.

11. *New York Times*, January 2, 2002.

12. Lillian Hellman, interview by Jan Albert, 1975, in *Conversations*, p. 169.

13. Dashiell Hammett, quoted in Cantwell, *Vogue*, October 1983.

14. Lillian Hellman and Herman Finkelstein Collection, Library of Congress, 1939, *The Little Foxes* (New York: Random House), draft, Harry Ransom Humanities Research Center, Special Collections, Lillian Hellman and Dashiell Hammett Collection, Austin, Tex.

15. Richard Layman and Julie Rivett, *Selected Letters of Dashiell Hammett, 1921–60* (New York: Counterpoint, 2001), p. 334.

16. Marilyn Berger, *Profile: Lillian Hellman* (Jackson: University Press of Mississippi, 1972), p. 24.

17. Lillian Hellman and Jackson R. Bryer, *Conversations with Lillian Hellman* (Jackson: University Press of Mississippi, 1986).

18. David Galligan, "Peter Feibleman Remembers 'Eating' with Lillian Hellman," clipping, Harry Ransom Humanities Research Center, Special Collections, Lillian Hellman and Dashiell Hammett Collection, Austin, Tex.

19. Gary Blake, "Herman Shumlin: The Development of a Director" (Ph.D. diss., City University of New York, 1973).

20. Ruth Leon, *Applause: New York's Guide to the Performing Arts* (New York: Applause, 1991), p. 78.

21. *Boston Herald*, March 7, 2001.

22. Herman Shumlin, interview by Walker, in Blake, "Herman Shumlin," p. 57.

23. Blake, "Herman Shumlin," p. 57.

24. Lillian Hellman, "Theatre Features," *Esquire*, August 1973, 67.

25. John H. Walker, "Mr. Herman Shumlin Is Speaking!" *New York Herald-Tribune*, May 7, 1939.

26. *Sunday News*, February 3, 1974.

27. Bankhead, *Tallulah*, p. 257.

28. John Symon, www.talkinbroadway.com.

29. Tennessee Williams, *Cry of the Heart: An Intimate Memoir of Tennessee Williams* (New York: New American Library, 1985), p. 243.

30. Dorothy Parker, quoted in Hellman, *Pentimento*, p. 147.

31. Margaret Case Harriman, "Miss Lily of New Orleans," *New Yorker*, November 8, 1941, p. 28.

32. Annabel Goff-Davis, interview by Deborah Martinson, January 17, 2002.

33. Lee Israel, note to William Abrahams, [July 1], Williams Miller Abrahams Papers, M1125, Department of Special Collections, Stanford University Libraries, Stanford, Calif.

34. *New York Times*, October 22, 1967.

35. Hellman, *Pentimento*, p. 151.

36. Gerald Green, "In the Desert with Joseph Wood Krutch," *Columbia Magazine*, 2000, p. 48.

37. Hellman, *Pentimento*, p. 152.

38. Milton Wexler, interview by Deborah Martinson, May 2000.

39. Lillian Hellman, *The Little Foxes* notebooks, Harry Ransom Humanities Research Center, Special Collections, Lillian Hellman and Dashiell Hammett Collection, Austin, Tex.

40. *New York Post*, March 11, 1939.

41. *Daily Eagle*, February 16, 1939.

42. Blake, "Herman Shumlin," p. 72.

43. *Time*, February 27, 1939; Brooks Atkinson, *New York Times*, February 16, 1939; Robert Benchley, *New Yorker*, February 25, 1939, p. 25.

44. Lillian Hellman, letter, April 22, 1972, in Blake, "Herman Shumlin."

45. Sidney Carroll, "The Happy Tragedist," *New Yorker*, January 1942, pp. 59–183.

46. Lillian Hellman to Arthur Kober, Arthur Kober Papers, Wisconsin Historical Society, Madison, Wis.

47. Peter Feibleman, interview by Deborah Martinson, December 16, 1997.

48. Carroll, "Happy Tragedist," p. 182.

49. Andrew Scott Berg, *Goldwyn: A Biography* (New York: Knopf, 1989), p. 355.

50. Berg, *Goldwyn*, p. 356.

51. Jan Herman, *A Talent for Trouble: The Life of Hollywood's Most Acclaimed Director, William Wyler* (New York: Putnam, 1995), p. 223.

52. Berg, *Goldwyn*, p. 355.

53. Berg, *Goldwyn*, p. 356.

54. Bernard Dick, interview by Deborah Martinson, 2002.

55. Lillian Hellman, letter to Arthur Kober, July 23, 1941, Arthur Kober Papers, Wisconsin Historical Society, Madison, Wis.

56. Niven Busch, interview, in *Backstory: Interviews with Screenwriters of Hollywood's Golden Age*, ed. Pat McGilligan (Berkeley: University of California Press, 1988), p. 100.

57. Herman, *Talent for Trouble*, pp. 217–224.

58. Herman, *Talent for Trouble*, p. 226.

59. Berg, *Goldwyn*, p. 358.

60. Academy of Motion Pictures Arts and Sciences, Margaret Herrick Library, Los Angeles.

61. William Wyler, Oral History no. 1422, Columbia University, Special Collections and Oral History Archives, New York.

62. Lillian Hellman, letter to Catherine Wyler, Documentary Film: Directed by William Wyler, transcripts.

63. Howard Barnes, review, *New York Herald-Tribune*, August 22, 1941.

64. Berg, *Goldwyn*, p. 500.

65. Jo Hammett, Richard Layman, and Julie Rivett, *Dashiell Hammett: A Daughter Remembers* (New York: Carroll & Graf, 2001), p. 83.

66. Carroll, "Happy Tragedist," pp. 59–183.

67. Ward Morehouse, *Baltimore Sun*, March 11, 1939.

68. Ellery Queen, *Napolean's Razor*, Guest Armchair Detectives, Shumlin Archives, no. 10, July 9, 1939, Wisconsin Historical Society, Madison, Wis.

69. Arthur Kober Papers, n.d., Wisconsin Historical Society, Madison, Wis.

70. Lillian Hellman, "Flipping for a Diamond," *New York Review of Books*, September 20, 1973.

71. Berger, *Profile*, p. 242.

72. Diane Johnson, "Obsession," *Vanity Fair*, January 1985, p. 118.

73. Johnson, "Obsession," p. 118.

74. Joyce Haber, "Lillian Hellman Takes a Look at Today's Theater," *Los Angeles Times*, Calender, November 2, 1969.

75. Berger, *Profile*, p. 243.

76. Joan Mellen, *Hellman and Hammett: The Legendary Passion of Lillian Hellman and Dashiell Hammett* (New York: HarperCollins, 1996), p. 142.

77. Layman and Rivett, *Selected Letters*, p. 378.

78. Mellen, *Hellman and Hammett*, p. 142.

79. Lillian Hellman, letter to Arthur Kober, August 24, 1948, Arthur Kober Papers, Wisconsin Historical Society, Madison, Wis.

80. Marsha Norman, *New York Times*, Theater sec., August 26, 1984.

81. Hammett, Layman, and Rivett, *Dashiell Hammett*, p. 110.

82. Hammett, Layman, and Rivett, *Dashiell Hammett*, p. 85.

83. James Feron, "Pleasantville," *New York Times*, April 5, 1987.

84. *New York Herald Tribune*, June 7, 1939.

85. www.wordsmith.org

86. Layman and Rivett, *Selected Letters*, p. 63.

87. Virginia Chilworth, interview by Deborah Martinson, 2003.

88. Letter Fizdale and Gold, Harry Ransom Humanities Research Center, Special Collections, Lillian Hellman and Dashiell Hammett Collection, Austin, Tex.

89. Letter Fizdale and Gold, Harry Ransom Humanities Research Center, Special Collections, Lillian Hellman and Dashiell Hammett Collection, Austin, Tex.

90. Harry Gilroy, *New York Times*, February 25, 1951.

91. Annabel Goff-Davis, interview by Deborah Martinson, January 17, 2002.

92. Letter to Fizdale and Gold, Harry Ransom Humanities Research Center, Special Collections, Lillian Hellman and Dashiell Hammett Collection, Austin, Tex.

93. *New York Post*, March 6, 1951.

94. Hammett, Layman, and Rivett, *Dashiell Hammett*, p. 113.

95. Lillian Hellman and Peter S. Feibleman, *Eating Together: Recipes and Recollections* (Boston: Little, Brown, 1984).

96. Clipping, June 26, 1946, Harry Ransom Humanities Research Center, Special Collections, Lillian Hellman and Dashiell Hammett Collection, Austin, Tex.

97. Lillian Hellman to Arthur Kober, Arthur Kober Papers, Wisconsin Historical Society, Madison, Wis.

98. FBI file, Lillian Hellman.

99. Arthur Kober, letter, n.d., Arthur Kober Papers, Wisconsin Historical Society, Madison, Wis.

100. *Vineyard Gazette*, January 7, 1948.

101. Lillian Hellman to Arthur Kober, September 25, 1941, Arthur Kober Papers, Wisconsin Historical Society, Madison, Wis.

102. Lillian Hellman to Arthur Kober, September 25, 1941, Arthur Kober Papers, Wisconsin Historical Society, Madison, Wis.

103. Letter to Fitzdale and Gold, Harry Ransom Humanities Research Center, Special Collections, Lillian Hellman and Dashiell Hammett Collection, Austin, Tex.

104. *New York Herald Tribune*, June 7, 1939.

105. Henry E. Sigerist, *Autobiographical Writings* (Montreal: McGill University Press, 1966).

106. Lillian Hellman, letter to Maggie Kober, 1950, Arthur Kober Papers, Wisconsin Historical Society, Madison, Wis.

107. Maggie Kober, letter to Arthur Kober, n.d., Arthur Kober Papers, Wisconsin Historical Society, Madison, Wis.

108. Lillian Hellman, letter to Maggie Kober, May 23, 1950, Arthur Kober Papers, Wisconsin Historical Society, Madison, Wis.

109. Lillian Hellman, letter to John Melby, May 1946, Harry Ransom Humanities Research Center, Special Collections, Lillian Hellman and Dashiell Hammett Collection, Austin, Tex.

110. Lisa Weinstein, interview by Phillip Schopper, August 16, 1998.

111. Lillian Hellman, letter to Dorothy Pritchitt, March 13, 1979, Harry Ransom Humanities Research Center, Special Collections, Lillian Hellman and Dashiell Hammett Collection, Austin, Tex.

112. Johnson, "Obsession," p. 79.

113. Robert Coles, interview by Deborah Martinson, November 5, 2003.

114. Hellman reports the story in *Unfinished Woman*, p. 235. Critics questioned its truth, but a letter from Hellman to Toto Bass, July 24, 1946, confirms it; Hamilton Bass Collection, Tulane University, Special Collections, Oral Histories Collection, New Orleans.

115. Arthur Kober to Cathy Kober, June 25, 1945, Arthur Kober Papers, Wisconsin Historical Society, Madison, Wis.

116. Layman and Rivett, *Selected Letters*, p. 168.

117. Hammett, Layman, and Rivett, *Dashiell Hammett*, p. 111.

118. Mellen, *Hellman and Hammett*.

119. Hammett, Layman, and Rivett, *Dashiell Hammett*, p. 111.

120. Richard Moody, *Lillian Hellman, Playwright* (New York: Pegasus, 1972), p. 158.

121. Lusius Beebe, "Stage Asides," *New Yorker*, May 1941.

122. Leonard Lyons, Lyons Den, July 1941.

123. Memos in the Bancroft Library, University of California–Berkeley; Carl E. Rollyson, *Lillian Hellman: Her Legacy and Her Legend* (New York: St. Martin's, 1988), pp. 121–122.

124. Nancy Lynn Schwartz, *The Hollywood Writers' Wars* (New York: Knopf, 1982), p. 173.

125. Lillian Hellman, *Scoundrel Time* (Boston: Little, Brown, 1976), p. 67.

126. Sean Mitchell, "Lip Service," *LA Times Magazine*, March 25, 2001.

127. Lillian Hellman, quoted in David L. Goodrich, *The Real Nick and Nora: Frances Goodrich and Albert Hackett, Writers of Stage and Screen Classics* (Carbondale: Southern Illinois University Press), p. 102.

128. Goodrich, *The Real Nick and Nora*, p. 101.

129. McGilligan, *Backstory*, p. 5.

130. Donald Ogden Stewart, letter to Lillian Hellman, n.d., Harry Ransom Humanities Research Center, Special Collections, Lillian Hellman and Dashiell Hammett Collection, Austin, Tex.

131. Philip Dunne, *Take Two: A Life in Movies and Politics* (New York: McGraw-Hill, 1980), p. 129

132. Academy of Motion Pictures Arts and Sciences, Margaret Herrick Library Special Collections, Los Angeles.

133. Draft, April 28, 1952, Manuscript Division, Joseph Rauh Collection, Library of Congress.

134. Schwartz, *Hollywood Writers' Wars*, p. 83.

135. Frank Nugent, "Blockade," *New York Times*, September 16, 1938.

136. Lillian Hellman, quoted in *New York Telegram*, December 11, 1935.

137. Maurice Zolotov, *Billy Wilder in Hollywood* (New York: Limelight, 1987), p. 77.

138. John Bright, "Hollywood Blacklist," OID Instructional Library, University of California-Los Angeles, Special Collections and Oral Histories Collections, Los Angeles

139. Dashiell Hammett, letter to Mary Hammett, September 11, 1936, in Layman and Rivett, *Selected Letters*.

140. Bernard Gordon, *Hollywood Exile: or How I Learned to Love the Blacklist* (Austin: University of Texas Press, 1999).

141. Judith Crist, introduction, *The Films of World War II* (Secaucus, N.J.: Citade, 1973), p. 6.

142. Bernard F. Dick, *Hellman in Hollywood* (Rutherford N.J.: Fairleigh Dickinson University Press, 1982), p. 83; Harry Ransom Humanities Research Center, Special Collections, Lillian Hellman and Dashiell Hammett Collection, Austin, Tex.

143. Lillian Hellman, "The Time of the Foxes," *New York Times*, October 22, 1967.

144. Albert Camus, quoted in Allen Guttmann, *The Wound in the Heart: American Involvement in Spain* (New York: Macmillan, 1962).

145. Beebe, "Stage Asides."

146. Robert Van Gelder, "Of Lillian Hellman: Being a Conversation with the Author of Watch on the Rhine," 1941; Hellman and Bryer, *Conversations with Lillian Hellman*, p. 11.

147. *Esquire*, August 1973, p. 68.

148. Lillian Hellman, *The Collected Plays* (Boston: Little, Brown, 1972), p. 213.

149. Moody, *Lillian Hellman*, p. 117.

150. *Washington Post*, April 2, 1941.

151. Carroll, "Happy Tragedist," p. 185.

152. Caption accompanies a photo found at Harry Ransom Humanities Research Center, Special Collections, Lillian Hellman and Dashiell Hammett Collection, Austin, Tex.

153. Williams, *Cry of the Heart*, p. 173.

154. Katherine Lederer, *Lillian Hellman* (Boston: Twayne, 1979), p. 51.

155. Van Gelder, "Of Lillian Hellman," in Hellman and Bryer, *Conversations with Lillian Hellman*, p. 11.

156. Lederer, *Lillian Hellman*, p. 51.

157. Beebe, "Stage Asides."

158. Moody, *Lillian Hellman*, p. 133.

159. A. Goldstein, *Post-Dispatch*, April 5, 1941.

160. Lillian Hellman, *An Unfinished Woman: A Memoir* (Boston: Little, Brown, 1999).

161. Unfinished Woman File, Lillian Hellman Folder, p. 12 n. 27, Williams Miller Abrahams Papers, M1125, Department of Special Collections, Stanford University Libraries, Stanford, Calif.

162. *New Masses*, April 15, 1941.

163. Ralph Warner, "*Watch on the Rhine*: Poignant Drama of Anti-Fascist Struggle," *Daily Worker*, April 4, 1941, p. 7.

164. Schwartz, *Hollywood Writers' Wars*, p. 173.

165. "Message Without Hysteria: Watch on the Rhine Presents Subtle Indictment of Nazis," *Newsweek*, April 14, 1941, p. 70.

166. Bernard F. Dick, opinion, *The Record*, December 7, 1998.

167. Lillian Hellman, *Watch on the Rhine: The Collected Plays* (Boston: Little, Brown, 1971), p. 276.

168. Hellman, "Theatre Pictures," p. 67.

169. FBI files, Lillian Hellman.

170. Joe Morella, Edward Z. Epstein, John Griggs, *The Films of World War II* (Secaucus, N.J.: Citadel, 1973).

171. Lillian Hellman, letter to Arthur Kober, 1941, Arthur Kober Papers, Wisconsin Historical Society, Madison, Wis.

172. Morella, Epstein, Griggs, *Films of World War II*, p. 12.

173. Berg, *Goldwyn*, p. 367.

174. Morella, Epstein, Griggs, *Films of World War II*, p. 7.

175. Louis Kronenberger, "Watch on the Rhine Is Called One of Our Few Good Plays," *Theatre*, clipping, n.d., Harry Ransom Humanities Research Center, Special Collections, Lillian Hellman and Dashiell Hammett Collection, Austin, Tex.

176. Dick, *Hellman in Hollywood*, p. 88.

177. "Red Critic Assails Hellman Drama," *LA Times*, November 13, 1944.

178. Dick, *Hellman in Hollywood*.

179. Dashiell Hammett, telegram to Hal Wallis, April 13, 1942, in Layman and Rivett, *Selected Letters*, p. 176.

180. Dick, *Hellman in Hollywood*, p. 82.

181. Sam Goldwin, letter to Herman Shumlin, February 1943, Herman Shumlin Collection, Wisconsin Historical Society, Madison, Wis.

182. Dick, *Hellman in Hollywood*, p. 96.

183. George Haight, letter to Herman Shumlin, May 3, 1938, Herman Shumlin Collection, Wisconsin Historical Society, Madison, Wis.

184. S. Marcus, letter to Miriam Howell, September 25, 1941, Herman Shumlin Collection, Wisconsin State Historical Society, Madison, Wis.

185. Herman Shumlin, letter to Nathan Spingold, June 20, 1940, Herman Shumlin Collection, Wisconsin State Historical Society, Madison, Wis.

186. George Haight, letter to Herman Shumlin, February 12, 1943, Herman Shumlin Collection, Wisconsin State Historical Society, Madison, Wis.

187. Lillian Hellman, letter to Catherine Kober, Arthur Kober Papers, Wisconsin Historical Society, Madison, Wis.

188. Albert Hackett, interview by Mark Rowland, in McGilligan, *Backstory*, p. 98.

189. Lillian Hellman, letter to Joe Breen, Hal Wallis Special Collection, Margaret Herrick Library, Los Angeles.

190. Rudy Behlmer, *Memo: David O. Selznick* (New York: Viking, 1972), p. 457.

191. Sylvia Thompson, "Martini Time in the Garden of Allah," *LA Times Magazine*, November 5, 2000, pp. 38–40.

192. Lillian Hellman, letter to Arthur Kober, 1945, Arthur Kober Papers, Wisconsin Historical Society, Madison, Wis.

193. American Soviet Medical Society, Soyuzmultfilm production, distributed by Brandon Films; advertisement, *New York Times*, November 11, 1944.

194. Berg, *Goldwyn*, p. 367.

195. Lillian Hellman, letter to Catherine Kober, n.d., Arthur Kober Papers, Wisconsin Historical Society, Madison, Wis.

196. Lillian Hellman, letter to Hal Wallis, Hal Wallis letter to Lillian Hellman, Wallis Collection, Margaret Herrick Library, July 1942.

197. Script, Lillian Hellman, *The Negro Soldier*, University of California–Los Angeles, Special Collections and Oral Histories Collections, Los Angeles.

198. Hellman, *Unfinished Woman*, pp. 105–106.

199. Lillian Hellman, letter to Arthur Kober, n.d., Arthur Kober Papers, Wisconsin Historical Society, Madison, Wis.

200. Lillian Hellman, letter to Arthur Kober, n.d., Arthur Kober Papers, Wisconsin Historical Society, Madison, Wis.

201. Irving Drutman, "Miss Hellman and Her First Screen Venture," 1941, clipping, Harry Ransom Humanities Research Center, Special Collections, Lillian Hellman and Dashiell Hammett Collection, Austin, Tex.

202. Lillian Hellman, letter to Arthur Kober, n.d., Arthur Kober Papers, Wisconsin Historical Society, Madison, Wis.; notebook, Harry Ransom Humanities Research Center, Special Collections, Lillian Hellman and Dashiell Hammett Collection, Austin, Tex.

203. Drutman, "Miss Hellman."

204. Lillian Hellman, *The North Star* (New York: Viking, 1943).

205. Lillian Hellman, letter to Arthur Kober (Artola, Megola, and Catherine), n.d., Arthur Kober Papers, Wisconsin Historical Society, Madison, Wis.

206. Lillian Hellman, quoted in *New York Times*, December 19, 1943.

207. Berg, *Goldwyn*, p. 375.

208. Berg, *Goldwyn*, p. 375; Peter S. Feibleman, *Lilly: Reminiscences of Lillian Hellman* (New York: Morrow, 1988), pp. 204–205.

209. *Daily Mirror*, November 5, 1943.

210. "A Second Look," *Cineaste* 22, no. 1 (1996): 45–48.

211. Dashiell Hammett, letter to Lillian Hellman, January 1944, Williams Miller Abrahams Papers, M1125, Department of Special Collections, Stanford University Libraries, Stanford, Calif.

212. Harry Ransom Humanities Research Center, Special Collections, Lillian Hellman and Dashiell Hammett Collection, Austin, Tex.

213. Samuel Goldwyn clipping file, Margaret Herrick Library, Los Angeles; *New York Times*, October 24, 1943.

214. Berg, *Goldwyn*, p. 378.

215. Mary McCarthy, "A Filmy Version of the War," *Town and Country*, April 1944.

216. "Second Look," p. 45.

217. Theodore Strauss, "Lillian Hellman: A Lady of Principle," *New York Times*, August 29, 1943.

218. Academy of Motion Pictures Arts and Sciences, Margaret Herrick Library, Wallis Collection, Los Angeles.

219. Lillian Hellman, letter to Catherine Kober, n.d., Arthur Kober Papers, Wisconsin Historical Society, Madison, Wis.

220. Lillian Hellman, letter to Catherine Kober, n.d., AArthur Kober Papers, Wisconsin Historical Society, Madison, Wis.

221. Carroll, "Happy Tragedist," p. 189.

222. FBI Files, Lillian Hellman, 133–138.

223. Diane Johnson, *Dashiell Hammett: A Life* (New York: Random House, 1983), pp. 170–171.

224. Layman and Rivett, *Selected Letters*, August 1952, p. 587.

225. Layman and Rivett, *Selected Letters*, September 28, 1942, p. 185.

226. Layman and Rivett, *Selected Letters*, September 28, 1942, p. 185.

227. Lillian Hellman, interview by Diane Johnson, in *Dashiell Hammett*, p. 171.

228. Dashiell Hammett, letter to Lillian Hellman, December 30, 1943, in Layman and Rivett, *Selected Letters*, p. 260.

229. *Washington Post*, July 31, 1943.

230. Hellman, *Unfinished Woman*, p. 203.

231. John Chapman, *New York Daily News*, June 13, 1944.

232. Interview by Helen Ormsbee, *New York Herald Tribune*, April 9, 1944.

233. Dashiell Hammett, letter to Lillian Hellman, February 3, 1944, in Layman and Rivett, *Selected Letters*, p. 277.

234. Layman and Rivett, *Selected Letters*, March 13–15, 1944.

235. Layman and Rivett, *Selected Letters*, pp. 289–290.

236. Moody, *Lillian Hellman*, p. 142.

237. Howard Bay, interview by Carl Rollyson, in *Lillian Hellman*.

238. Layman and Rivett, *Selected Letters*, p. 283.

239. Warner, *Daily Worker*, April 17, 1944.

240. Playbill, Fulton Theatre, October 29, 1944.

241. Burton Rascoe, *New York World-Telegram*, April 22, 1944.

242. Barnes, *New York Herald Tribune*, April 23, 1944.

243. Warner, Daily Worker, April 28, 1944.

244. Warner, *Daily Worker*, April 17, 1944.

245. Layman and Rivett, *Selected Letters*, April 17, 1944, p. 316.

246. Hellman, *Unfinished Woman*, p. 107.

247. FBI files, Lillian Hellman.

248. Lillian Hellman, letter to Arthur Kober, [1943], Arthur Kober Papers, Wisconsin Historical Society, Madison, Wis.

249. John Melby, interview by Robert P. Newman, in *The Cold War Romance of Lillian Hellman and John Melby* (Chapel Hill: University of North Carolina Press, 1989), p. 16.

250. Newman, *Cold War Romance*, p. 14.

251. Lillian Hellman, *Diaries* (1944). Harry Ransom Humanities Research Center, Special Collections, Lillian Hellman and Dashiell Hammett Collection, Austin, Tex.

252. Harold Ross to Lillian Hellman, 1940, *New Yorker* Correspondence, 1940s, New York Public Library, September 18, 1944.

253. FBI files, Lillian Hellman.

254. Lillian Hellman, letter to Arthur and Maggie Kober, October 1944, Arthur Kober Papers, Wisconsin Historical Society, Madison, Wis.

255. Hellman, *Unfinished Woman*, p. 108.

256. Lillian Hellman, *Diaries* (1920–). Harry Ransom Humanities Research Center, Special Collections, Lillian Hellman and Dashiell Hammett Collection, Austin, Tex.

257. Lillian Hellman, *Diaries* (1944). Harry Ransom Humanities Research Center, Special Collections, Lillian Hellman and Dashiell Hammett Collection, Austin, Tex.

258. Lillian Hellman, *Unfinished Woman*, p. 108.

259. Joan Mellen, "Confessions of an Ex-Biographer," *Biography and Source Studies* 3 (1997): 151–163.

260. Lillian Hellman, "Meet Some Front Line Russians," *Colliers*, March 31, 1945, p. 68.

261. Newman, *Cold War Romance*, p. 39.

262. John Melby, letter to Lillian Hellman, February 24, 1945, in Newman, *Cold War Romance*, p. 51.

263. Sergei Eisenstein, letter to Lillian Hellman, June 1, 1944, Harry Ransom Humanities Research Center, Special Collections, Lillian Hellman and Dashiell Hammett Collection, Austin, Tex.

264. Hellman, *Unfinished Woman*, p. 112.

265. Raya Orlova, *Memoirs* (New York: Random House, 1983), p. 116.

266. Orlova, *Memoirs*, p. 118.

267. Lillian Hellman, *Diaries* (1944). Harry Ransom Humanities Research Center, Special Collections, Lillian Hellman and Dashiell Hammett Collection, Austin, Tex.

268. Hellman, *Unfinished Woman*, p. 119.

269. Orlova, *Memoirs*, p. 117.

270. Melby hearings, June 1, 1952, pp. A14–15, in Newman, *Cold War Romance*, p. 39.

271. Copy of document, Harry Ransom Humanities Research Center, Special Collections, Lillian Hellman and Dashiell Hammett Collection, Austin, Tex.

272. Lillian Hellman, *Diaries* (1944). Harry Ransom Humanities Research Center, Special Collections, Lillian Hellman and Dashiell Hammett Collection, Austin, Tex.

273. Lillian Hellman, *Diaries* (1944). Harry Ransom Humanities Research Center, Special Collections, Lillian Hellman and Dashiell Hammett Collection, Austin, Tex.

274. Newman, *Cold War Romance*, p. 40.

275. U.S. Department of State, *Foreign Relations of the United States: The Soviet Union*, vol. 4, telegram correspondence, May–August 1944.

276. Lillian Hellman, *Diaries* (1920–). Harry Ransom Humanities Research Center, Special Collections, Lillian Hellman and Dashiell Hammett Collection, Austin, Tex.

277. Lillian Hellman, *New York Daily News*, February 2, 1945.

278. "Reports on Trip Through Russia," *New York Herald Tribune*, May 1, 1945.

279. Lillian Hellman, *Diaries* (1920-). Harry Ransom Humanities Research Center, Special Collections, Lillian Hellman and Dashiell Hammett Collection, Austin, Tex.

280. Orlova, *Memoirs*, p. 117.

281. Orlova, *Memoirs*, p. 117.

282. Newman, *Cold War Romance*, p. 25.

283. John Melby, reflections, in Newman, *Cold War Romance*, p. 33.

284. Newman, *Cold War Romance*, p. 34.

285. John Melby, letter to Lillian Hellman, December 27, in Newman, *Cold War Romance*, p. 36.

286. Lillian Hellman to John Melby, December 24, 1945, Harry Ransom Humanities Research Center, Special Collections, Lillian Hellman and Dashiell Hammett Collection, Austin, Tex.

287. Lillian Hellman, *Diaries* (1950). Harry Ransom Humanities Research Center, Special Collections, Lillian Hellman and Dashiell Hammett Collection, Austin, Tex.

288. Newman, *Cold War Romance*, p. 38.

289. Lillian Hellman, letter to John Melby from Baku, Harry Ransom Humanities Research Center, Special Collections, Lillian Hellman and Dashiell Hammett Collection, Austin, Tex.

290. Newman, *Cold War Romance*, p. 38.

291. John Melby, letter to Lillian Hellman, quoted in Newman, *Cold War Romance*, p. 50.

292. Lillian Hellman, *Diaries* (1920–). Harry Ransom Humanities Research Center, Special Collections, Lillian Hellman and Dashiell Hammett Collection, Austin, Tex.

293. Lillian Hellman, *Diaries* (1920–). Harry Ransom Humanities Research Center, Special Collections, Lillian Hellman and Dashiell Hammett Collection, Austin, Tex.

294. Orlova, *Memoirs*, p. 117.

295. Lillian Hellman to Shipley, July 13, 1951, in Newman, *Cold War Romance*, p. 39.

296. www.insults.net

297. FBI files, Lillian Hellman, March 1945.

298. FBI files, Lillian Hellman, *New York Times* clipping.

299. Newman, *Cold War Romance*, p. 54.

300. Quoted in Newman, *Cold War Romance*, p. 54.

301. Harold Ross, letter to Lillian Hellman, September 18, 1944, *New Yorker* Archives, New York Public Library, Special Collections.

302. Harold Ross, letter to Lillian Hellman, April 2, 1945,*New Yorker* Archives, New York Public Library, Special Collections.

303. Lillian Hellman to John Melby, April 17, 1945, Harry Ransom Humanities Research Center, Special Collections, Lillian Hellman and Dashiell Hammett Collection, Austin, Tex.

304. Correspondence, 1944–1945, Harry Ransom Humanities Research Center, Special Collections, Lillian Hellman and Dashiell Hammett Collection, Austin, Tex.

305. *Colliers* manuscript, p. 11, Harry Ransom Humanities Research Center, Special Collections, Lillian Hellman and Dashiell Hammett Collection, Austin, Tex.

306. Westbrook Pegler, "Fair Enough," *Washington Times Herald*, April 24, 1945.

307. Lillian Hellman, letter to John Melby, April 17, 1945, Harry Ransom Humanities Research Center, Special Collections, Lillian Hellman and Dashiell Hammett Collection, Austin, Tex.

308. Lillian Helman to John Melby, Sunday, [1945?], Harry Ransom Humanities Research Center, Special Collections, Lillian Hellman and Dashiell Hammett Collection, Austin, Tex.

309. Lillian Hellman to John Melby, [1945?], Harry Ransom Humanities Research Center, Special Collections, Lillian Hellman and Dashiell Hammett Collection, Austin, Tex.

310. Only thirty-four of Hellman's letters to Melby survived the Red Scare investigations. When it became clear that both Hellman and Melby were being investigated, she insisted they exchange the letters they had written each other. She subsequently destroyed her letters. John preserved his. The few Hellman letters survived because a temporary secretarial agency, ordered to destroy them, did not.

311. John Melby, letter to Lillian Hellman, February 13, 1945.

312. John Melby, letter to Lillian Hellman, in Newman, *Cold War Romance*, p. 63.

313. John Melby, letter to Lillian Hellman, in Newman, *Cold War Romance*, p. 63.

314. Lillian Hellman, letter to John Melby, May 1946, Harry Ransom Humanities Research Center, Special Collections, Lillian Hellman and Dashiell Hammett Collection, Austin, Tex.

315. Lillian Hellman, letter to John Melby, December 30, 1946, Harry Ransom Humanities Research Center, Special Collections, Lillian Hellman and Dashiell Hammett Collection, Austin, Tex.

316. John Melby, in Newman, *Cold War Romance*, p. 107.

317. Newman, *Cold War Romance*, p. 95.

318. Dashiell Hammett, letter to Lillian Hellman, May 2, 1945.

319. Lillian Hellman, letter to Hal Wallis, Academy of Motion Pictures Arts and Sciences, Margaret Herrick Library, Wallis Collection, Los Angeles.

320. Harry Ransom Humanities Research Center, Special Collections, Lillian Hellman and Dashiell Hammett Collection, Austin, Tex.

321. Layman and Rivett, *Selected Letters*, p. 366.

322. Norman Mailer, interview by Phillip Schopper, August 7, 1998.

323. Layman and Rivett, *Selected Letters*, p. 197.

324. Arthur Kober, letter, [1948], Arthur Kober Papers, Wisconsin Historical Society, Madison, Wis.

325. Arthur Kober Papers, Wisconsin Historical Society, Madison, Wis.

326. Kermit Bloomgarden letters, June 13, 1951, Bloomgarden Collection, Wisconsin Historical Society, Madison, Wis.

327. Paramount Contract Files, Academy of Motion Pictures Arts and Sciences, Margaret Herrick Library, Los Angeles.

328. *Hollywood Reporter*, May 10, 1946.

329. Joseph Breen, letters to Hal Wallis, November 12, 1945–August 25, 1946, Academy of Motion Pictures Arts and Sciences, Margaret Herrick Library, Wallis Collection, Los Angeles.

330. Moody, *Lillian Hellman*, p. 181.

331. Christine Conrad, "Unfinished Memoirs of Kermit Bloomgarden," Billy Rose Theatre Collection, New York Public Library.

332. Virginia Chilworth, interview by Deborah Martinson, 2003.

333. *New York Times*, August 25, 1942.

334. Kermit Bloomgarden, quoted in clipping, September 26, 1946, Billy Rose Theatre Collection, New York Public Library.

335. Virginia Chilworth, interview by Deborah Martinson, January 18, 2002.

336. John Chapman, *New York Daily News*, November 21, 1946.

337. Moody, *Lillian Hellman*, p. 181.

338. Robert Lantz, interview by Phillip Schopper, August 18–19, 1998.

339. Patricia Neal with Richard DeNeut, *As I Am: An Autobiography* (New York: Simon & Schuster, 1988), p. 82.

340. Neal, *As I Am*, p. 74.

341. Neal, *As I Am*, p. 75.

342. Billy Wilder, *Billy Wilder: Interviews* (Jackson: University Press of Mississippi, 2001).

343. Bernard F. Dukore, *American Dramatists, 1918–1945* (Publishing Group West, 1984), p. 144.

344. Robert Coleman, *New York Daily Mirror*, November 21, 1946.

345. Louis Kronenberger, *PM*, November 22, 1946, Harry Ransom Humanities Research Center, Special Collections, Lillian Hellman and Dashiell Hammett Collection, Austin, Tex.

346. Brooks Atkinson, *New York Times*, November 21, 1946.

347. Kermit Bloomgarden, interview by Emuoy Lewis, *Sunday Record*, May 11, 1975.

348. Moody, *Lillian Hellman*, p. 179.

349. Lillian Hellman, letter to Hannah and Jenny Hellman, April 7, 1948, Harry Ransom Humanities Research Center, Special Collections, Lillian Hellman and Dashiell Hammett Collection, Austin, Tex.

350. Hannah Hellman, letter to Edith Keanes, July 1, 1949, Harry Ransom Humanities Research Center, Special Collections, Lillian Hellman and Dashiell Hammett Collection, Austin, Tex.

351. Letter, April 7, 1948, Harry Ransom Humanities Research Center, Special Collections, Lillian Hellman and Dashiell Hammett Collection, Austin, Tex.

352. Caption, *New York Times* photo, July 1945.

353. Ann Clark, quoted in Mysterypages.com/hammett8 from *Hitchcock's Mystery Magazine*, 2000.

354. Johnson, *Dashiell Hammett*, p. 212.

355. Dashiell Hammett, letter to Nancy Bragdon, September 4, 1946, p. 473, in Layman and Rivett, *Selected Letters*, September 4, 1946.

356. Neal, *As I Am*, p. 75.

357. Johnson, *Dashiell Hammett*, p. 211.

358. Virginia Chilworth, interview by Deborah Martinson, 2003.

359. Neal, *As I Am*, p. 78.

360. Hammett, Layman, and Rivett, *Dashiell Hammett*.

361. Hammett, Layman, and Rivett, *Dashiell Hammett*, pp. 104–108.

362. Hammett, Layman, and Rivett, *Dashiell Hammett*, p. 129.

363. Mellen, *Hellman and Hammett*, pp. 256–257.

364. Lillian Hellman, letter to John Melby, Harry Ransom Humanities Research Center, Special Collections, Lillian Hellman and Dashiell Hammett Collection, Austin, Tex.

365. Lillian Hellman, letter to John Melby, April 1946, Harry Ransom Humanities Research Center, Special Collections, Lillian Hellman and Dashiell Hammett Collection, Austin, Tex.

366. Norman Mailer, interview by Phillip Schopper, August 7, 1998.

367. Mellen, *Hellman and Hammett*, p. 258.

368. Norman Mailer, interview by Phillip Schopper, August 7, 1998.

369. Hellman, *Scoundrel Time*, p. 64.

370. Harry Ransom Humanities Research Center, Special Collections, Lillian Hellman and Dashiell Hammett Collection, Austin, Tex.

371. Swanson, Cablegram letter to Lillian Hellman, February 1948, Harry Ransom Humanities Research Center, Special Collections, Lillian Hellman and Dashiell Hammett Collection, Austin, Tex.

372. Lillian Hellman, interview by Phillips and Hollander, 1965, in Hellman and Bryer, *Conversations with Lillian Hellman*, pp. 67–68.

373. Hedda Hopper and James Brough, *The Whole Truth and Nothing But* (Garden City, N.Y.: Doubleday, 1963), p. 273.

374. House of Representatives, Committee on Un-American Activities, 80th Cong., 1st sess., October 1947, in Hearings regarding the Communist Infiltration of the Motion Picture Industry (Washington, D.C.: Government Printing Office, 1947), p. 136.

375. Larry Ceplair, "SAG and The Motion Picture Blacklist, from 50 Years: SAG Remembers the Blacklist," special edition of *National Screen Actor*, January 1998, www.sag.org/blacklist.

376. Ceplair, "SAG."

377. Phillips and Hollander in Hellman and Bryer, *Conversations with Lillian Hellman*, p. 67.

378. Frank Pierson, "Hollywood Plays to the Pimply," *LA Times*, May 26, 2003.

379. Hellman, *Scoundrel Time*, pp. 76–78.

380. Norman Mailer, interview by Phillip Schopper, August 7, 1998.

381. Hopper, and Brough, *Whole Truth*, pp. 272–274.

382. Edward Dmytryk, *Odd Man Out: A Memoir of the Hollywood Ten* (Carbondale: Southern Illinois University Press, 1995).

383. Lillian Hellman, "The Judas Goats," *Screenwriter*, December 3, 1947, Harry Ransom Humanities Research Center, Special Collections, Lillian Hellman and Dashiell Hammett Collection, Austin, Tex.

384. Paul Jerrico, Oral History, p. 121, University of California–Los Angeles, Special Collections and Oral Histories Collections, Los Angeles.

385. Hellman, "Judas Goats."

386. George F. Custen, *Twentieth Century's Fox: Darryl F. Zanuck and the Culture of Hollywood* (New York: Basic, 1997), p. 229.

387. Hellman, "Judas Goats."

388. Lillian Hellman, in Berg, *Goldwyn*, p. 436.

389. Berg, *Goldwyn*, p. 436.

390. *Variety*, October 1947, available at www.film.com/reviews/encyclopedia.

391. "Hollywood Blacklist," in *Encyclopedia of the American Left* (Urbana: University of Illinois Press, 1992).

392. Joseph Breen, letter to Samuel Goldwyn, January 22, 1941, Academy of Motion Pictures Arts and Sciences, Margaret Herrick Library, MPAA Collection, Los Angeles.

393. Lillian Hellman, interview by Berg, *Goldwyn*, p. 290.

394. Lillian Hellman, interview by Irving Drutman, in "Hellman: A Stranger in the Theater?" *New York Times*, February 27, 1962.

395. Schwartz, *Hollywood Writers' Wars*, p. 254.

396. Paul Jerrico, interview by Larry Ceplair, 1991, University of California Los Angeles, Special Collections and Oral Histories Collections, Los Angeles.

397. Jerrico, interview.

398. Jerrico, interview.

399. Lillian Hellman, in *Women for Wallace Speech*, pamphlet, Harry Ransom Humanities Research Center, Special Collections, Lillian Hellman and Dashiell Hammett Collection, Austin, Tex.

400. Schwartz, *Hollywood Writers' Wars*, p. 205.

401. Victor Navasky, *Naming Names: Degradation Ceremonies* (New York: Viking, 1980), pp. 314–329.

402. Berg, *Goldwyn*, p. 435.

403. www.film.com/reviews/encyclopedia/1950

404. Jerrico, interview.

405. Lillian Hellman, letter to Fred Gardner, in Hellman and Bryer, *Conversations with Lillian Hellman*, p. 117.

406. Berg, *Goldwyn*, p. 438.

407. Berg, *Goldwyn*, p. 437.

408. Lisle Rose, *The Cold War Comes to Main Street: America in 1950* (Lawrence: University Press of Kansas, 1999).

409. www.danzfamily.com/texts/hollywood/communists

410. Schwartz, *Hollywood Writers' Wars*, pp. 272–275.

411. Bright, "Hollywood Blacklist."

412. Sam Jaffe, Academy of Motion Pictures Arts and Sciences, Oral History Collection.

413. FBI files, name of informant blacked out.

414. Lillian Hellman, letter to Fred Gardner, 1968; Dan Rather, "A Profile of Lillian Hellman," March 3, 1977, in Hellman and Bryer, *Conversations with Lillian Hellman*, p. 212.

415. Kim Hunter, interview by Deborah Martinson, August 22, 2000.

416. Alan Grogan, letter to Lillian Hellman, June 5, 1952, Harry Ransom Humanities Research Center, Special Collections, Lillian Hellman and Dashiell Hammett Collection, Austin, Tex.

417. Hellman, *Scoundrel Time*, p. 47.

418. Navasky, *Naming Names*, pp. 391–392.

419. Peter Feibleman, quoted in David Galligan, *Dramalogue* magazine, n.d., Clipping File, New York Public Library.

420. Dorothy Herrmann, *S.J. Perelman: A Life* (New York: Simon & Schuster, 1986), p. 97.

421. Peter Feibleman, quoted in Galligan.

422. Dick, *Hellman in Hollywood*, p. 19.

423. Arthur Orrmont, director Author Aid Associates, Williams Miller Abrahams Papers, M1125, Department of Special Collections, Stanford University Libraries, Stanford, Calif.

424. Dashiell Hammett, public letter, October 28, 1947, in Layman and Rivett, *Selected Letters*, p. 494.

425. Thomas Irwin Emerson Papers, Manuscript and Archives Division, Sterling Memorial Library, Yale University.

426. *New York Post*, Lyon's Den, September 22, 1948.

427. Arthur Schlesinger Jr., *LA Times*, May 12, 2000.

428. Norman Mailer, interview by Phillip Schopper, August 7, 1998.

429. Norman Mailer, interview by Phillip Schopper, August 7, 1998.

430. An Address by Lillian Hellman to the Women of America, February 10, 1948, Harry Ransom Humanities Research Center, Special Collections, Lillian Hellman and Dashiell Hammett Collection, Austin, Tex.

431. Hellman, *Scoundrel Time*, p. 120.

432. Thomas I. Emerson, interview by Dr. Harlen Phillips, 1957, Columbia University, Oral History Collection.

433. Sheril Catherine Kober Zeller, interview by Deborah Martinson, October 26, 2004.

434. Norman Mailer, interview by Phillip Schopper, August 7, 1998.

435. John Melby, letter to Lillian Hellman, May 20, 1947, in Newman, *Cold War Romance*, p. 112.

436. John Melby, letter to Lillian Hellman, September 11, 1947, in Newman, *Cold War Romance*, p. 114.

437. Randall "Pete" Smith, quoted in Rollyson, *Lillian Hellman*, p. 267.

438. Quoted in Rollyson, *Lillian Hellman*, p. 269.

439. Randall "Pete" Smith, quoted in Rollyson, *Lillian Hellman*, p. 269.

440. Randall "Pete" Smith, quoted in Rollyson, *Lillian Hellman*, p. 270.

441. Dashiell Hammett, letter to Lillian Hellman, February 14, 1950.

442. Randall "Pete" Smith, quoted in Rollyson, *Lillian Hellman*, p. 270.

443. Lillian Hellman, series of six articles, *New York Star*, November 4–10, 1948.

444. Mellen, *Hellman and Hammett*, p. 262.

445. Lillian Hellman, *Diaries* (1920–). Harry Ransom Humanities Research Center, Special Collections, Lillian Hellman and Dashiell Hammett Collection, Austin, Tex.

446. Lillian Hellman, *Diaries* (1920–). Harry Ransom Humanities Research Center, Special Collections, Lillian Hellman and Dashiell Hammett Collection, Austin, Tex.

447. Lillian Hellman, *Diaries* (1920–). Harry Ransom Humanities Research Center, Special Collections, Lillian Hellman and Dashiell Hammett Collection, Austin, Tex.

448. Lillian Hellman, "Tito's Personal Regime Isn't Socialism, Czechs Say," *New York Post*, November 5, 1948.

449. Lillian Hellman, headline in *New York Star*, November 8, 1948.

450. Jonathan Citt, "A Conversation with Studs Turkel," *Rolling Stone*, August 2, 2001.

451. Hammett, Layman, and Rivett, *Dashiell Hammett*, p. 131.

452. Hellman, *Unfinished Woman*.

453. Lillian Hellman, letter to Maggie Kober, 1948, Arthur Kober Papers, Wisconsin Historical Society, Madison, Wis.

454. Lillian Hellman, introduction to *The Big Knockover: Stories by Dashiell Hammett* (New York: Random House, 1966–), ix.

455. Murray Schumach, *New York Times*, November 23, 1949.

456. Lillian Hellman, letter to Malcom Cowley, n.d., Newberry Library Letters Collection, Chicago.

457. Bernard Rubin, *Daily Worker*, November 9, 1949.

458. Murray Schumach, "Miss Hellman Discusses Directors," *New York Times*, October 23, 1949.

459. Schumach, "Miss Hellman."

460. *Commonweal*, review of *Monserrat*, November 18, 1949.

461. *New York Herald Tribune*, November 5, 1949.

462. John Mason Brown, *Saturday Review of Literature*, November 19, 1949.

463. "The Theater: New Play in Manhattan," *Time*, November 14, 1949, p. 46.

464. John Chapman, *New York Daily News*, October 31, 1949.

465. Bernard Rubin, *Daily Worker*, November 9, 1949.

Chapter Six: Politics and Power

1. Thomas I. Emerson, interview by Harlan Phillips, 1957, Special Collections and Oral History Archives, Columbia University, New York.

2. Cedric Belfrage, *The American Inquisition: 1945–1960: A Profile of the McCarthy Era* (New York: Thunder's Mouth, 1989), p. 98.

3. Dashiell Hammett, letter to Jo Hammett Marshall, April 25, 1949, in Richard Layman and Julie Rivett, *Selected Letters of Dashiell Hammett, 1921–60* (New York: Counterpoint, 2001), p. 514.

4. D. Angus Cameron, interview recorded by Louis Shaeffer, 1977, vol. 3, Oral History, Special Collections and Oral History Archives, Columbia University, New York.

5. Dramatists League Collection, Harry Ransom Humanities Research Center, Special Collections, Lillian Hellman and Dashiell Hammett Collection, Austin, Tex.

6. Lillian Hellman, letter to John Melby, June 1945, Harry Ransom Humanities Research Center, Special Collections, Lillian Hellman and Dashiell Hammett Collection, Austin, Tex.

7. Dashiell Hammett, letter to Mary Hammett, August 29, 1949, in Layman and Rivett, *Selected Letters of Dashiell Hammett*, p. 520.

8. Dashiell Hammett, letter to Lillian Hellman, January 31, 1950, in Layman and Rivett, *Selected Letters of Dashiell Hammett*, p. 534.

9. Dashiell Hammett, letter to Mary Hammett, July 30, 1950, in Layman and Rivett, *Selected Letters of Dashiell Hammett*, p. 542.

10. Jo Hammett, Richard Layman, and Julie M. Rivett, *Dashiell Hammett: A Daughter Remembers* (New York: Carroll & Graf, 2001), p. 143.

11. Lillian Hellman, *Diaries* (1920–). Harry Ransom Humanities Research Center, Special Collections, Lillian Hellman and Dashiell Hammett Collection, Austin, Tex.

12. Hellman, *Diaries*.

13. Dashiell Hammett, quoted in Hellman, *Diaries*.

14. Harry Gilroy, *New York Post*, February 25, 1951.

15. Harry Gilroy, *New York Times*, February 25, 1951.

16. Marvin Felheim, *Modern Drama*, September 19, 1960, p. 192.

17. Arthur Kober, letter to Lillian Hellman, 1950, AG critique, Arthur Kober Papers, Wisconsin Historical Society, Madison, Wis.

18. Arthur Kober, letter to Lillian Hellman, 1950, AG critique, Arthur Kober Papers, Wisconsin Historical Society, Madison, Wis.

19. Lillian Hellman, *Autumn Garden*, in *Collected Plays* (Boston: Little, Brown, 1957), p. 568.

20. Murray Schumach, *New York Times*, November 23, 1949.

21. Harold Clurman, *Collected Works* (New York: Applause, 2000), pp. 980–981.

22. Clurman, *Collected Works*, pp. 980–981.

23. Lillian Hellman, *An Unfinished Woman: A Memoir* (Boston: Little, Brown, 1969), p. 268.

24. Louis Scheaffer, "Curtain Times," *Brooklyn Bugle*, March 8, 1951.

25. Brooks Atkinson, *New York Times*, March 8, 1951.

26. *World Telegram Sun*, March 8, 1951.

27. *New York Journal American*, March 19, 1951.

28. Sidney Carroll, "The Happy Tragedist," *New Yorker*, January 1942.

29. Lillian Hellman, letter to Stanley Isaacs, September 28, 1951, Harry Ransom Humanities Research Center, Special Collections, Lillian Hellman and Dashiell Hammett Collection, Austin, Tex.

30. Lillian Hellman, *Pentimento* (Boston: Little, Brown, 1973), p. 164.

31. Sheril Catherine Kober Zeller, interview by Deborah Martinson, September 2004.

32. Copy of FBI deposition and summary findings, Lillian Hellman Collection, Harry Ransom Humanities Research Center, Special Collections, Lillian Hellman and Dashiell Hammett Collection, Austin, Tex.

33. FBI files, Lillian Hellman.

34. FBI files, Lillian Hellman.

35. Danton Walker, "Broadway," *New York News*, December 10, 1945.

36. J. Edgar Hoover to SACs, September 2 and December 6, 1939; J. Edgar Hoover, letter to Quin Tamm, November 9, 1939, in Curt Gentry, *J. Edgar Hoover: The Man and the Secrets* (New York: Norton, 1991), p. 213.

37. FBI files, Lillian Hellman, October 20, 1943.

38. Francis Biddle, letter to Assistant Attorney General Cox and J. Edgar Hoover, July 16, 1943; quoted in Gentry, *J. Edgar Hoover*, p. 244.

39. Lillian Hellman, letter to Lucile Turner, July 22, 1940, Harry Ransom Humanities Research Center, Special Collections, Lillian Hellman and Dashiell Hammett Collection, Austin, Tex.

40. FBI files; Marshall Field, letter to Herman Shumlin, June 21, 1941, Herman Shumlin Collection, Wisconsin Historical Society, Madison, Wis.

41. FBI clip; Milton Meltzer, "Hollywood Does Right by 'The Little Foxes,'" August 24, 1941.

42. FBI memo, Lillian Hellman.

43. Lillian Hellman et al. to Sam and Bella Spewack, 1939, Spewack Collection, Columbia University, New York.

44. *Daily Worker*, November 18, 1946; FBI files, Lillian Hellman.

45. FBI files, Lillian Hellman.

46. *Time*, May 23, 1949.

47. Lillian Hellman, letter to Richard Morford, March 16, 1950, Joseph Rauh Collection, Collections of the Manuscript Division, Library of Congress, Washington, D.C.

48. Harlan Phillips, interview, December 21, 1954, Thomas Irwin Emerson Papers, Special Collections and Oral History Archives, Columbia University, New York.

49. Dashiell Hammett, letter to Mary Hammett, March 26, 1947, in Layman and Rivett, *Selected Letters of Dashiell Hammett*, p. 484.

50. Dashiell Hammett, letter to Maggie Kober, April 16, 1951, in Layman and Rivett, *Selected Letters of Dashiell Hammett*, p. 558.

51. Robert P. Newman, *The Cold War Romance of Lillian Hellman and John Melby* (Chapel Hill: University of North Carolina Press, 1989), p. 144.

52. Newman, *Cold War Romance*, p. 144.

53. FBI files, Lillian Hellman.

54. Harlan Phillips, interview, December 21, 1954, Thomas Irwin Emerson Papers, Special Collections and Oral History Archives, Columbia University, New York; verified FBI files.

55. FBI files, Lillian Hellman.

56. Herbert Mitgang, *Dangerous Dossiers: Exposing the Secret War Against America's Greatest Authors* (New York: Fine, 1988), www.english.upenn.edu.

57. Diane Johnson, *Dashiell Hammett: A Life* (New York: Random House, 1983), p. 140.

58. Dashiell Hammett, letter to Jo Marshall, April 18, 1949, in Layman and Rivett, *Selected Letters of Dashiell Hammett*, p. 512.

59. Hammett, Layman, and Rivett, *Dashiell Hammett*, p. 147.

60. Hammett, Layman, and Rivett, *Dashiell Hammett*, p. 147.

61. Victor Rabinowtiz, 1992, vol. 1 of 4, coedited by Lenore Bradeson Hogan, October 1978, Special Collections and Oral History Archives, Columbia University, New York.

62. Layman and Rivett, *Selected Letters of Dashiell Hammett*, p. 562.

63. FBI files, Lillian Hellman.

64. Lillian Hellman, letter to Sophie Lange, n.d., in Diane Johnson, *Dashiell Hammett: A Life* (New York: Random House, 1983), pp. 144–147; Harry Ransom

Humanities Research Center, Special Collections, Lillian Hellman and Dashiell Hammett Collection, Austin, Tex.

65. Treasury Department, quoted in Johnson, *Dashiell Hammett*, p. 248.

66. Lillian Hellman, letter to Dashiell Hammett; Dashiell Hammett, letter to Lillian Hellman, quoted in Johnson, *Dashiell Hammett*, p. 295.

67. Hammett, Layman, and Rivett, *Dashiell Hammett*, p. 151.

68. Hammett, Layman, and Rivett, *Dashiell Hammett*, p. 151.

69. Lillian Hellman, passport file, courtesy of the State Department, Washington, D.C.

70. Hellman, passport file, courtesy of the State Department, Washington, D.C.

71. Hammett, Layman, and Rivett, *Dashiell Hammett*, p. 151.

72. Lillian Hellman, letter to Sophie Lange, 1951, Harry Ransom Humanities Research Center, Special Collections, Lillian Hellman and Dashiell Hammett Collection, Austin, Tex.

73. Lillian Hellman, letter to Sophie Lange Layman, in Layman and Rivett, *Selected Letters of Dashiell Hammett*, p. 484; Harry Ransom Humanities Research Center, Special Collections, Lillian Hellman and Dashiell Hammett Collection, Austin, Tex.

74. Dashiell Hammett, letter to Jo Hammett Marshall, October 28, 1951, in Layman and Rivett, *Selected Letters of Dashiell Hammett*, p. 564.

75. Hammett, Layman, and Rivett, *Dashiell Hammett*, p. 151.

76. Lillian Hellman, letter to Sophie Lange, 1951, Harry Ransom Humanities Research Center, Special Collections, Lillian Hellman and Dashiell Hammett Collection, Austin, Tex.

77. Lillian Hellman, letter to Sophie Lange, 1951 Correspondence, Harry Ransom Humanities Research Center, Special Collections, Lillian Hellman and Dashiell Hammett Collection, Austin, Tex.

78. Victor S. Navasky, *Naming Names* (New York: Penguin, 1981), p. 75.

79. FBI files, Lillian Hellman.

80. Ring Lardner, interview by Phillip Schopper, September 17, 1998.

81. Newman, *Cold War Romance*, p. 165/

82. Lillian Hellman, Melby hearings, quoted in Newman, *Cold War Romance*, p. 242.

83. Dashiell Hammett, letter to Lillian Hellman, August 8, 1951, in Layman and Rivett, *Selected Letters of Dashiell Hammett*, p. 569.

84. Layman and Rivett, *Selected Letters of Dashiell Hammett*, p. 577.

85. Hardscrabble documents, Harry Ransom Humanities Research Center, Special Collections, Lillian Hellman and Dashiell Hammett Collection, Austin, Tex.

86. Lillian Hellman, letter to Sophie Lange, September 10, 1951, Harry Ransom Humanities Research Center, Special Collections, Lillian Hellman and Dashiell Hammett Collection, Austin, Tex.

87. Layman and Rivett, *Selected Letters of Dashiell Hammett*, p. 577.

88. Dashiell Hammett, letter to Jo Hammett Marshall, April 10, 1952.

89. Hellman, *Scoundrel Time*, p. 114.

90. In 1999, even with all the changes in the farm spaces, Lika Miyake and I observed a small herd of deer wandering in the space Hellman describes in *Scoundrel Time*.

91. Hellman, *Scoundrel Time*, p. 114.

92. Lillian Hellman, letter to Stephen Greene, n.d., Stephen Greene Papers, Archives of American Art.

93. Hellman, *Scoundrel Time*, p. 83.

94. Hellman, *Scoundrel Time*, p. 49.

95. Hellman, *Scoundrel Time*, p. 50.

96. Milly S. Barranger, "Women on Trial," *Journal of American Drama and Theatre*, Fall 2003, p. 15.

97. "*Enemies of the State*: Newly Disclosed Transcripts Indicate Once Again That Sen. Mccarthy Was Among Those Overly Zealous Officials Who Subvert Democracy," *LA Times*, May 6, 2003.

98. Daniel Pollitt, interview by Phillip Schopper, July 22, 1998.

99. Joseph Rauh, quoted in Griffen Fariello, *The Red Scare* (New York: Avon, 1995), p. 338.

100. Joseph Rauh, letter to Lillian Hellman, April 30, 1952, Joseph Rauh Collection, Collections of the Manuscript Division, Library of Congress, Washington, D.C.

101. Joseph Rauh, letter to Lillian Hellman, April 30, 1952, Joseph Rauh Collection, Collections of the Manuscript Division, Library of Congress, Washington, D.C.

102. Hellman, *Scoundrel Time*, pp. 54–55.

103. Joseph Rauh to Lillian Hellman, Joseph Rauh Collection, Collections of the Manuscript Division, Library of Congress, Washington, D.C.

104. All above letters and documents from Joseph Rauh to Lillian Hellman, Joseph Rauh Collection, Collections of the Manuscript Division, Library of Congress, Washington, D.C.

105. Daniel Pollitt, interview by Phillip Schopper, July 22, 1998.

106. Joseph Rauh, quoted in Fariello, *Red Scare*, p. 339.

107. Dashiell Hammett, letter to Jo Hammett Marshall, April 16, 1952.

108. Hellman, *Scoundrel Time*, p. 63.

109. Eric Bentley, *Thirty Years of Treason* (1971; New York: Thunder's Mouth, 2000), p. 485.

110. Bentley, *Thirty Years*, p. 46.

111. Elia Kazan, *Elia Kazan: A Life* (New York: Doubleday, 1989).

112. Holliday, quoted in Barranger, "Women on Trial," p. 18.

113. Daniel Pollitt, interview by Phillip Schopper, July 22, 1998.

114. Lillian Hellman, testimony, Communist Infiltration of the Hollywood Motion Picture Industry, pt. 8, United States House of Representatives, Committee on Un-American Activities, May 21, 1952, transcript, Harry Ransom Humanities Research Center, Special Collections, Lillian Hellman and Dashiell Hammett Collection, Austin, Tex.

115. Daniel Pollitt, interview by Phillip Schopper, July 22, 1998.

116. Lillian Hellman, testimony, Communist Infiltration of the Hollywood Motion Picture Industry, pt. 8, United States House of Representatives, Committee on Un-American Activities, May 21, 1952, transcript, Harry Ransom Humanities Research Center, Special Collections, Lillian Hellman and Dashiell Hammett Collection, Austin, Tex.

117. Communist Infiltration of the Hollywood Motion Picture Industry, pt. 8, United States House of Representatives, Committee on Un-American Activities, May 21, 1952,

transcript, Harry Ransom Humanities Research Center, Special Collections, Lillian Hellman and Dashiell Hammett Collection, Austin, Tex.

118. *Time*, June 2, 1952, p. 74.

119. Daniel Pollitt, interview by Phillip Schopper, July 22, 1998.

120. Brooks Atkinson, quoted in Barranger, "Women on Trial," p. 7.

121. John Earl Haynes, "Hellman and the Hollywood Inquisition," *Film History* 10, no. 3 (1988): 409.

122. Lillian Hellman, interview by Marilyn Berger, 1979, in Lillian Hellman and Jackson R. Bryer, *Conversations with Lillian Hellman* (Jackson: University Press of Mississippi, 1986), p. 249.

123. Victor Navasky, *Naming Names: Degradation Ceremonies* (New York: Viking Penguin, 1980), p. 314.

124. Abraham Polonsky, USC Jenny Hozer Monument, Blacklist, 1999.

125. Garmel, *Indianapolis News*, September 29, 1973.

126. Letters to Lillian Hellman after HUAC appearance, Harry Ransom Humanities Research Center, Special Collections, Lillian Hellman and Dashiell Hammett Collection, Austin, Tex.

127. Lillian Hellman, letter to John Melby, May 1952, Harry Ransom Humanities Research Center, Special Collections, Lillian Hellman and Dashiell Hammett Collection, Austin, Tex.

128. Sarah Rollits, letter to Lillian Hellman, HUAC file, Harry Ransom Humanities Research Center, Special Collections, Lillian Hellman and Dashiell Hammett Collection, Austin, Tex.

129. Murray Kempton, *New York Post*, May 26, 1952.

130. Lillian Hellman, letter to John Melby, May 1952, Harry Ransom Humanities Research Center, Special Collections, Lillian Hellman and Dashiell Hammett Collection, Austin, Tex.

131. Newman, *Cold War Romance*, p. 181.

132. Joseph Rauh, letter to Herbert Levy, December 20, 1952, Joseph Rauh Collection, Collections of the Manuscript Division, Library of Congress, Washington, D.C.

133. Herbert Monte Levy to Joseph Rauh, January 7, 1953, Joseph Rauh Collection, Collections of the Manuscript Division, Library of Congress, Washington, D.C.

134. Newman, *Cold War Romance*, p. 181.

135. John Melby, testimony before State Department Loyalty Security Board, Washington, D.C., in Newman, *Cold War Romance*, p. 186.

136. John Melby, interview, in Newman,*Cold War Romance*.

137. John Melby, interview, in Newman, *Cold War Romance*, p. 38.

138. John Melby, transcripts, State Department Loyalty Security Board, Washington, D.C., in Newman, *Cold War Romance*, pp. 192–267.

139. John Melby, transcripts, State Department Loyalty Security Board, Washington, D.C., in Newman, *Cold War Romance*, pp. 192–267.

140. Lillian Hellman, testimony before Loyalty Security Board, Washington, D.C., February 2, 1953 in Newman, *Cold War Romance*, p. 235.

141. Lillian Hellman, testimony before Loyalty Security Board, Washington, D.C., February 5, 1953, in Newman, *Cold War Romance*, p. 245.

142. John Melby, diary, in Newman, *Cold War Romance*, p. 38.

143. Lillian Hellman, letter to John Melby, May 1952, Harry Ransom Humanities Research Center, Special Collections, Lillian Hellman and Dashiell Hammett Collection, Austin, Tex.

144. Kim Hunter, interview by Deborah Martinson, August 22, 2000.

145. Patricia Neal with Richard DeNeut, *As I Am: An Autobiography* (New York: Simon & Schuster, 1988), p. 156.

146. Kim Hunter, interview by Deborah Martinson, August 22, 2000.

147. Lisa Weinstein, interview by Phillip Schopper, August 16, 1998.

148. Arthur Miller, *Timebends* (New York: Grove, 1987), p. 346.

149. Eric Pace, *New York Times*, November 16, 1979.

150. Joan Mellen, *Hellman and Hammett: The Legendary Passion of Lillian Hellman and Dashiell Hammett* (New York: HarperCollins, 1996), p. 312 n. 523.

151. Lillian Hellman, letter to Paul Robeson, September 29, 1941, in Martin Bauml Duberman, *Paul Robeson: A Biography* (New York: Ballantine, 1989), p. 654.

152. Duberman, *Paul Robeson*, p. 409.

153. Dashiell Hammett, letter to Lillian Hellman, August 21, 1952, in Layman and Rivett, *Selected Letters of Dashiell Hammett*, p. 587.

154. Dashiell Hammett, quoted in Layman and Rivett, *Selected Letters of Dashiell Hammett*, p. 578.

155. Dashiell Hammett, quoted in in Duberman, *Paul Robeson*, p. 430.

156. Johnson, *Dashiell Hammett*, p. 258.

157. Lillian Hellman, letter to Ruth Shipley, February 5, 1953, Lillian Hellman passport files, courtesy of the State Department, Washington, D.C.

158. Lillian Hellman, interview by Marilyn Berger, in Hellman and Bryer, *Conversations with Lillian Hellman*, p. 258.

159. Lillian Hellman, letter Lois Fritsch, 1953, Lillian Hellman Collection, Harry Ransom Humanities Research Center, Special Collections, Lillian Hellman and Dashiell Hammett Collection, Austin, Tex.

160. Stephen Greene, quoted in Carl E. Rollyson, *Lillian Hellman: Her Legacy and Her Legend* (New York: St. Martin's, 1988), p. 349.

161. Lillian Hellman, letter to Lois Fritsch, 1953, Lillian Hellman Collection, Harry Ransom Humanities Research Center, Special Collections, Lillian Hellman and Dashiell Hammett Collection, Austin, Tex.

162. Lillian Hellman, letter to Lois Fritsch, 1953, Lillian Hellman Collection, Harry Ransom Humanities Research Center, Special Collections, Lillian Hellman and Dashiell Hammett Collection, Austin, Tex.

163. Dashiell Hammett, *Tulip*, quoted in Layman and Rivett, *Selected Letters of Dashiell Hammett*, p. 578.

164. All foregoing quotes from Lillian Hellman and Lois Fritsch correspondence, 1953, Harry Ransom Humanities Research Center, Special Collections, Lillian Hellman and Dashiell Hammett Collection, Austin, Tex.

165. *Newsweek*, November 28, 1955.

166. *Theatre Arts*, January 30, 1956.

167. William Wright, *Lillian Hellman: The Image, the Woman* (New York: Ballantine, 1988), p. 266.

168. Lillian Hellman and Jean Anouilh, *The Lark* (New York: Random House, 1956), p. 70.

169. Louis Botto, *At This Theatre* (New York: Dodd Mead, 1984), p. 52.

170. Richard Maney, "The Night of the Long Knives," in *Fanfare* (New York: Harper, 1957), p. 253.

171. Hammett, Layman, and Rivett, *Dashiell Hammett*, p. 90.

172. Leonard Bernstein, letter to Helen Coates, November 14, 1951, Bernstein Collection, Library of Congress, Washington, D.C., http://memory.loc.gov/cgi.

173. Howard Kissel, *Daily News*, April 30, 1997.

174. Brooks Peters, "Making Your Garden Growl: Brooks Peters Tells the Tale of *Candide* Collaborators Lillian Hellman and Leonard Bernstein, a Marriage Not Made in Heaven," *Opera News* 65, no. 1 (2000): 38.

175. Peters, "Making Your Garden Growl," p. 38.

176. Clive Barnes, *New York Post*, April 30, 1997.

177. Ben Brantley, *New York Times*, April 30, 1997.

178. Tyrone Guthrie, *A Life in the Theatre* (New York: McGraw-Hill, 1959), p. 250.

179. Barbara Cook, quoted in Peters, "Making Your Garden Growl."

180. Peters, "Making Your Garden Growl," p. 38.

181. Charlee Wilbur, letter to Lillian Hellman, December 1956, Harry Ransom Humanities Research Center, Special Collections, Lillian Hellman and Dashiell Hammett Collection, Austin, Tex.

182. Harry Raymond, *The Worker*, FBI files, Lillian Hellman.

183. *Candide* draft, Lillian Hellman Collection, Harry Ransom Humanities Research Center, Special Collections, Lillian Hellman and Dashiell Hammett Collection, Austin, Tex.

184. Lillian Hellman, letter to Leonard Bernstein, "The History of the Record," n.d., Harry Ransom Humanities Research Center, Special Collections, Lillian Hellman and Dashiell Hammett Collection, Austin, Tex.

185. Lillian Hellman, letter to Leonard Bernstein, November 25, 1971, Harry Ransom Humanities Research Center, Special Collections, Lillian Hellman and Dashiell Hammett Collection, Austin, Tex.

186. Hammett, Layman, and Rivett, *Dashiell Hammett*, p. 111.

187. Marion Meade, *Dorothy Parker: What Fresh Hell Is This?* (New York: Penguin, 1988), pp. 369–370.

188. Lillian Hellman, interview by Christine Doudna, 1976, in Hellman and Bryer, *Conversations with Lillian Hellman*, p. 202.

189. Patricia Neal, interview by Phillip Schopper, August 7, 1998.

190. Meade, *Dorothy Parker*, p. 249.

191. Meade, *Dorothy Parker*, p. 248.

192. Garson Kanin, quoted in David L. Goodrich, *The Real Nick and Nora* (Carbondale: Southern Illinois University Press, 2001), p. 206.

193. Frances Goodrich journal, quoted in Goodrich, *Real Nick and Nora*, p. 210.

194. Lawrence Graver, *An Obsession with Anne Frank: Meyer Levin and the Diary* (Berkeley: University of California Press, 1995).

195. Dashiell Hammett, letter Jo Hammett Marshall, October 14, 1955, in Layman and Rivett, *Selected Letters of Dashiell Hammett*, p. 614.

196. Goodrich, *Real Nick and Nora*, p. 237.

197. Many articles and books have been written on this controversy. See Graver, *Obsession with Anne Frank*; Ralph Melnick, *The Stolen Legacy of Anne Frank: Meyer Levin, Lillian Hellman, and the Staging of the Diary* (New Haven: Yale University Press, 1997); Goodrich, *Real Nick and Nora*.

198. Anne Frank file, Kermit Bloomgarden Collection, Wisconsin Historical Society, Madison, Wis.

199. Victor W. Navasky, quoted in Graver, *Obsession with Anne Frank*, p. 212.

200. Peter Feibleman, interview by Deborah Martinson, August 2000.

201. David Selznick, letter to Henry Weinstein, February 14, 1961, in David O. Selznick, *Memo from David O. Selznick* (New York: Viking, 1972).

202. Lillian Hellman, letter to William Wyler, August 9, 1960, Harry Ransom Humanities Research Center, Special Collections, Lillian Hellman and Dashiell Hammett Collection, Austin, Tex.

203. Lillian Hellman, letter to William Wyler, August 9, 1960, Harry Ransom Humanities Research Center, Special Collections, Lillian Hellman and Dashiell Hammett Collection, Austin, Tex.

204. *Time*, quoted on cover of the second American edition of O'Connor, *A Good Man Is Hard to Find*.

205. Bernard F. Dick, *Hellman in Hollywood* (Rutherford: Fairleigh Dickinson University Press, 1982), p. 49.

206. Hellman, *Pentimento*, p. 170.

207. Lillian Hellman, *Toys in the Attic*, in *Collected Plays* (Boston: Little, Brown, 1971), p. 732.

208. Harold Clurman, "Theatre," *Nation*, March 19, 1960.

209. Kermit Bloomgarden, letter to Lillian Hellman, August 28, 1959, Harry Ransom Humanities Research Center, Special Collections, Lillian Hellman and Dashiell Hammett Collection, Austin, Tex.

210. Stapleton, interview by Phillip Schopper; Stapleton, telephone interview by Deborah Martinson.

211. Stapleton, interview by Phillip Schopper; Stapleton, telephone interview by Deborah Martinson.

212. Frank Aston, "Toys in the Attic Takes Apart Lives of Five," *New York World-Telegram and Sun*, February 26, 1960.

213. Clurman, "Theatre."

214. Brooks Atkinson, *New York Times*, February 26, 1960.

215. *Time*, March 3, 1960.

216. Hellman, *Pentimento*, p. 171.

217. Hellman, *Pentimento*, p. 170.

218. Robert Giroux, interview by Joan Mellen, in *Hellman and Hammett*, p. 334.

219. Marsha Norman, interview by Phillip Schopper, August 19, 1998.

Chapter Seven: Death and Ressurection

1. Jo Hammett, Richard Layman, and Julie Rivett, Dashiell Hammett: A Daughter Remembers *(New York: Carroll & Graf, 2001), pp. 163–164.*

2. Lillian Hellman, An Unfinished Woman: A Memoir (Boston: Little, Brown, 1999), pp. 223–244.

3. Dashiell Hammett to Lillian Hellman, November 25, 1943.

4. Dashiell Hammett, letter to Lillian Hellman, in Diane Johnson, *Dashiell Hammett: A Life* (New York: Random House, 1983), pp. 259–260.

5. William Styron, interview by Joan Mellen, in *Hellman and Hammett: The Legendary Passion of Lillian Hellman and Dashiell Hammett* (New York: HarperCollins, 1996), p. 317.

6. Hammett, Layman, and Rivett, *Dashiell Hammett*, p. 166.

7. Lillian Hellman, *Diaries* (1920–). Harry Ransom Humanities Research Center, Special Collections, Lillian Hellman and Dashiell Hammett Collection, Austin, Tex.

8. Hammett, Layman, and Rivett, *Dashiell Hammett*, p. 169.

9. FBI files, Dashiell Hammett, memo, January 17, 1961.

10. Hellman, *Unfinished Woman*, p. 239.

11. Hellman, *Unfinished Woman*, p. 236.

12. Lillian Hellman, letter to Charlee Wilbur, May 23, 1961, Harry Ransom Humanities Research Center, Special Collections, Lillian Hellman and Dashiell Hammett Collection, Austin, Tex.

13. Bernard Dick, e-mail to Deborah Martinson, March 14, 2001.

14. *New York Theatre Critics' Reviews*, 1963, 24:302.

15. Ruth Weber, letter to Lillian Hellman, n.d., Harry Ransom Humanities Research Center, Special Collections, Lillian Hellman and Dashiell Hammett Collection, Austin, Tex.

16. Joan Mack, letter to Lillian Hellman, n.d., Harry Ransom Humanities Research Center, Special Collections, Lillian Hellman and Dashiell Hammett Collection, Austin, Tex.

17. Betty Walker, *Chicago Daily Tribune*, Woman's World sec., October 15, 1947.

18. Howard Stein, interview by Deborah Martinson, August 22, 2000.

19. Walter Kerr, letter to Charles David Haller, August 18, 1962.

20. http://www.dramaleague.org

21. Rebuttal to "Hell on a Short Fuse," *New Yorker*, June 21, 1993.

22. Hellman Collection Drama League records, Harry Ransom Humanities Research Center, Special Collections, Lillian Hellman and Dashiell Hammett Collection, Austin, Tex.

23. Hellman Collection, Academy of Arts and Letters Archives, New York.

24. Howard Stein, interview by Deborah Martinson, August 22, 2000.

25. The Off-Broadway League had been founded in 1959.

26. *New York Post Magazine*, November 12, 1946.

27. Joyce Haber, "Lillian Hellman Takes a Look at Today's Theater," *LA Times*, Calendar, November 2, 1969.

28. Haber, "Lillian Hellman."

29. Peck Seymour, *New York Times*, April 1973, Harry Ransom Humanities Research Center, Special Collections, Lillian Hellman and Dashiell Hammett Collection, Austin, Tex.

30. Alex Szogyi, letter to Deborah Martinson, May 2003.

31. Peter Adam, letter to Lillian Hellman, June 9, 1979, Harry Ransom Humanities Research Center, Special Collections, Lillian Hellman and Dashiell Hammett Collection, Austin, Tex.

32. Marvin Sadik, interview by Deborah Martinson, January 2004.

33. Leila Hadley, interview by Deborah Martinson, November 11, 2003.

34. Richard Stern, professor of English, University of Chicago, July 2, 1984, William Miller Abrahams Papers, M1125, Dept. of Special Collections, Stanford University Libraries, Stanford University.

35. Richard Poirier, interview by Phillip Schopper, August 18, 1998.

36. Lillian Hellman, letter to Richard Wilbur, May 23, 1975, Amherst.

37. Lillian Hellman, letter to Richard Roth, May 20, 1976, Harry Ransom Humanities Research Center, Special Collections, Lillian Hellman and Dashiell Hammett Collection, Austin, Tex.

38. Alvin Sargeant letter to Lillian Hellman, November 27, 1978.

39. Philip Rahv, quoted in Mellen, *Hellman and Hammett*, p. 323.

40. A. Robert Wobin and Judith Firth Sanger, interviews by Joan Mellen, in *Hellman and Hammett*, p. 197.

41. Herbert Mitgang, letter to Lillian Hellman, August 23, 1970.

42. Mellen, *Hellman and Hammett*, p. 321.

43. Sadie Raab, interview by Joan Mellen, September 17, 1993, in Mellen, *Hellman and Hammett*, p. 322.

44. Lillian Hellman, *Pentimento* (Boston: Little, Brown, 1973), p. 195.

45. Hellman, *Pentimento*, p. 213.

46. Thomas McBride, interview by Carl Rollyson, *Lillian Hellman: Her Legacy and Her Legend* (New York: St. Martin's, 1988), p. 475.

47. Lillian Hellman, letter to Arthur Cowan, n.d., Harry Ransom Humanities Research Center, Special Collections, Lillian Hellman and Dashiell Hammett Collection, Austin, Tex.

48. *New York Times*, May 14, 1959.

49. Hellman, *Pentimento*, p. 207.

50. Arthur Cowan, letter to Oscar Bernstein, n.d., Harry Ransom Humanities Research Center, Special Collections, Lillian Hellman and Dashiell Hammett Collection, Austin, Tex.

51. Hellman, *Pentimento*, p. 213.

52. Norman Mailer, interview by Phillip Schopper, August 16, 1998.

53. Blair Clark, written narrative, William Miller Abrahams Papers, M1125, Department of Special Collections, Stanford University Libraries, Stanford, Calif.

54. Ned Rorem, interview by Deborah Martinson, October 2004.

55. Lillian Hellman, unattributed quote in Mellen, *Hellman and Hammett*, p. 371.

56. Blair Clark, written narrative.

57. Blair Clark, written narrative.

58. Lillian Hellman, *Diaries* (1962–1964). Harry Ransom Humanities Research Center, Special Collections, Lillian Hellman and Dashiell Hammett Collection, Austin, Tex.

59. Clark, written narrative.

60. Clark, written narrative.

61. Elizabeth Hardwick, "The Little Foxes Revived," *New York Review of Books*, December 21, 1967.

62. Clark, written narrative.

63. Lillian Hellman, *Maybe: A Story* (Boston: Little, Brown and Company, 1980), p. 85.

64. Hellman, *Maybe*, p. 101.

65. Rita Wade, interview by Deborah Martinson, January 2004; Mellen, *Hellman and Hammett*, p. 376.

66. Peter S. Feibleman, *Lilly: Reminiscences of Lillian Hellman* (New York: Morrow, 1988), p. 32.

67. Feibleman, *Lilly*, pp. 50–51; Feibleman, interview by Deborah Martinson, August 1999.

68. Feibleman, *Lilly*, p. 51.

69. Lillian Hellman, letter to James Purdy, James Purdy Collection, Beinecke Library, Yale University, Beinecke Library and Manuscripts and Archives Collections, New Haven.

70. Peter Feibleman, interview by Deborah Martinson, December 1997.

71. Peter Feibleman, interview by Deborah Martinson, December 1997.

72. Peter Feibleman, interview by Deborah Martinson, December 1997.

73. Peter Feibleman, interview by Deborah Martinson, December 1997.

74. Lillian Hellman, *Diaries* (1920–). Harry Ransom Humanities Research Center, Special Collections, Lillian Hellman and Dashiell Hammett Collection, Austin, Tex.

75. Lillian Hellman, letter to Peter Feibleman, in Feibleman, *Lilly*, p. 53.

76. Lillian Hellman, letter to Peter Feibleman, in Feibleman, *Lilly*, p. 113.

77. Peter Feibleman, interview by Deborah Martinson, December 1997.

78. Carly Simon, quoted in "Shanghai Lilly," *Vanity Fair*, June 1993.

79. Feibleman, *Lilly*, p. 131.

80. Ned Rorem, interview by Deborah Martinson, October 27, 2004.

81. Peter Feibleman, interview by Phillip Schopper, July 27, 1998.

82. Feibleman, *Lilly*, p. 231.

83. Lillian Hellman, letter to Peter Feibleman, in Feibleman, *Lilly*, p. 129.

84. Feibleman, *Lilly*, p. 200.

85. Feibleman, *Lilly*, p. 299.

86. Peter Feibleman, interview by Phillip Schopper, July 27, 1998.

87. Feibleman, *Lilly*, p. 55.

88. Lillian Hellman, "Lillian Hellman Asks a Little Respect for Her Agony," *Show*, May 1964, pp. 12–13.

89. Max Palevsky, interview by Deborah Martinson, May 1, 2000.

90. Alex Szogy, interview by Phillip Schopper, July 22, 1998.

91. Robert Lantz, interview by Phillip Schopper, September 17, 1998.

92. Lillian Hellman, transcripts of teaching at Yale University, 1966–1967, Harry Ransom Humanities Research Center, Special Collections, Lillian Hellman and Dashiell Hammett Collection, Austin, Tex.

93. Alex Sygozi, interview by Deborah Martinson, January 18, 2002.

94. Ken Stuart, interview by Rollyson, *Lillian Hellman*, pp. 396–397.

95. Stuart, interview by Rollyson, *Lillian Hellman*, pp. 396–397.

96. Lillian Hellman, transcripts of teaching at Yale University, 1966–1967, Harry Ransom Humanities Research Center, Special Collections, Lillian Hellman and Dashiell Hammett Collection, Austin, Tex.

97. Stuart, interview by Rollyson, *Lillian Hellman*, pp. 396–397.

98. Professor Walter Jackson Bate, chairman of Harvard English Department, 1961; Alex Szogyi, interview by Deborah Martinson, January 18, 2002.

99. Marvin Sadik, interview by Deborah Martinson, January 15, 2004.

100. *Ladies Home Journal*, letters, Harry Ransom Humanities Research Center, Special Collections, Lillian Hellman and Dashiell Hammett Collection, Austin, Tex.

101. Lillian Hellman, letter to Curtis Publishing Company, February 28, 1964.

102. Lorraine Hansberry Archives, Croton-on-Hudson, New York.

103. *Ladies Home Journal*, April 1964.

104. Peter Bart, *New York Times*, June 20, 1965.

105. Lillian Hellman, partial manuscript and notes, *The Chase*, Harry Ransom Humanities Research Center, Special Collections, Lillian Hellman and Dashiell Hammett Collection, Austin, Tex.

106. Marlon Brando, quoted in Peter Manso, *Brando* (New York: Hyperion, 1994).

107. Lillian Hellman, notes, short writing, *The Chase*, Harry Ransom Humanities Research Center, Special Collections, Lillian Hellman and Dashiell Hammett Collection, Austin, Tex.

108. Manso, *Brando*, p. 595.

109. Lillian Hellman, interview by Irving Drutman, *New York Times*, February 27, 1966.

110. Pauline Kael, *New Yorker*, February 2, 1966.

111. Bernard Dick, interview by Deborah Martinson, July 5, 1999.

112. Irving Drutman, *New York Times*, February 27, 1966.

113. Lillian Hellman, interview by Lucius Beebe, 1936, in Lillian Hellman and Jackson R. Bryer, *Conversations with Lillian Hellman* (Jackson: University Press of Mississippi, 1986), p. 5.

114. Peter Feibleman, interview by Phillip Schopper, July 27, 1998.

115. Feibleman, *Lilly*, p. 34.

116. Stan Hart, "Lillian Hellman and Others," *Sewanee Review*, Summer 1999.

117. Random House 1966 correspondence, Harry Ransom Humanities Research Center, Special Collections, Lillian Hellman and Dashiell Hammett Collection, Austin, Tex.

118. Robert Lantz, letter to Stan Hart, Little, Brown correspondence, William Miller Abrahams Papers, Special Collections, Stanford University Libraries, Stanford, Calif.

119. Hart, "Lillian Hellman and Others."

120. Hellman, *Unfinished Woman*, p. 121.

121. Hellman, *Unfinished Woman*, p. 192.

122. Hellman, *Unfinished Woman*, p. 63.

123. Christopher Lehmann-Haupt, "The Incomplete Lillian Hellman," *New York Times*, June 1969.

124. Richard Poirier, interview by Phillip Schopper, September 17, 1998.

125. Lillian Hellman, *Scoundrel Time* (Boston: Little, Brown, 1976), p. 159.

126. Robert Lantz, interview by Peter Feibleman.

127. Peter Feibleman, interview by Phillip Schopper, July 27, 1998.

128. FBI file, Lillian Hellman.

129. Sheril Catherine Kober Zeller, interview by Deborah Martinson, October 26, 2004.

130. Warren Beatty, interview by Phillip Schopper, August 16, 1998.

131. Richard Poirier, interview by Phillip Schopper, September 17, 1998.

132. Stephen Gillers, interview by Phillip Schopper, September 17, 1998.

133. Lisa Weinstein, interview by Phillip Schopper, August 16, 1998.

134. Stephen Gillers, interview by Phillip Schopper, September 17, 1998.

135. Lillian Hellman, press conference, November 12, 1977; New Orleans Public Library, audiovisual department, tapes, transcriptions by Deborah Martinson.

136. Stephen Gillers, interview by Phillip Schopper, September 17, 1998.

137. Stephen Gillers, interview by Phillip Schopper, September 17, 1998.

138. Stephen Gillers, interview by Phillip Schopper, September 17, 1998.

139. Robert Coles, interview by Deborah Martinson, November 5, 2003.

140. Stephen Gillers, interview by Phillip Schopper, September 17, 1998.

141. Stephen Gillers, interview by Phillip Schopper, September 17, 1998.

142. Ramsey Clark, quoted in *New York Times*, October 16, 1971.

143. Lillian Hellman press conference, November 12, 1977; tapes New Orleans Public Library: Transcriptions DM.

144. Lisa Weinstein, interview by Phillip Schopper, August 16, 1998.

145. Lillian Hellman, interview by Marilyn Berger, 1979, in Hellman and Bryer, *Conversations with Lillian Hellman*, p. 256.

146. Lillian Hellman, frontispiece, *Pentimento*.

147. Robert Manning, letter to Lillian Hellman, June 4, 1973, Harry Ransom Humanities Research Center, Special Collections, Lillian Hellman and Dashiell Hammett Collection, Austin, Tex.

148. Peter Feibleman, interview by Phillip Schopper, July 27, 1998.

149. *Publishers Weekly*, July 6, 1973, p. 106.

150. Mark Schorer, *New York Times Book Review*, September 23, 1973.

151. Lillian Hellman, letter to Fred Hill, William Miller Abrahams Papers, M1125, Department of Special Collections, Stanford University Libraries, Stanford, Calif.

152. Bennett Cerf, letter to Lillian Hellman, October 11, 1939, Columbia University, Special Collections and Oral History Archives, New York.

153. Roger Donald, letter to Lillian Hellman, William Miller Abrahams Papers, M1125, Department of Special Collections, Stanford University Libraries, Stanford, Calif.

154. Hellman, *Pentimento*, p. 166.

155. Lillian Hellman, letter to Jan Van Loewen, January 1974, Harry Ransom Humanities Research Center, Special Collections, Lillian Hellman and Dashiell Hammett Collection, Austin, Tex.

156. Jan Van Loewen, letter to Lillian Hellman, January 18, 1974, Harry Ransom Humanities Research Center, Special Collections, Lillian Hellman and Dashiell Hammett Collection, Austin, Tex.

157. Jan Van Loewen, letter to Lillian Hellman, January 18, 1974, William Miller Abraham Papers, M1125, Department of Special Collections, Stanford University Libraries, Stanford, Calif.

158. Little, Brown memo, May 19, 1969, Williams Miller Abrahams Papers, M1125, Department of Special Collections, Stanford University Libraries, Stanford, Calif.

159. Marvin Sadik, interview by Deborah Martinson, January 2004.

160. Marvin Sadik, interview by Deborah Martinson, November 12, 2003.

161. Peter Stansky, interview by Deborah Martinson, May 30, 2001.

162. Max Palevsky, interview by Deborah Martinson, May 1, 2000.

163. Jonathan LaPook, interview by Deborah Martinson, January 16, 2002.

164. Annabel Goff-Davis, interview by Deborah Martinson, January 17, 2002.

165. Ned Rorem, interview by Deborah Martinson, October 2004; *The Nantucket Diary of Ned Rorem, 1973–1985* (San Francisco: North Point, 1987), p. 160.

166. Peter Stansky, interview by Deborah Martinson, May 30, 2001.

167. James L.W. West III, *William Styron: A Life* (New York: Random House, 1998), pp. 421–433.

168. Liz Cowley, "Lillian's World," *Daily Mail,* n.d., clipping, Harry Ransom Humanities Research Center, Special Collections, Lillian Hellman and Dashiell Hammett Collection, Austin, Tex.

169. Peter Feibleman, interview by Deborah Martinson, December 1997.

170. Lillian Hellman, letter to L Savetsky, M.D., March 25, 1982, Harry Ransom Humanities Research Center, Special Collections, Lillian Hellman and Dashiell Hammett Collection, Austin, Tex.

171. Martha's Vineyard files, Harry Ransom Humanities Research Center, Special Collections, Lillian Hellman and Dashiell Hammett Collection, Austin, Tex.

172. Rita Wade, interview by Phillip Schopper, August 19, 1998.

173. Peter Feibleman, interview by Deborah Martinson, November 1997.

174. Rita Wade, interview by Phillip Schopper, August 19, 1998.

175. Max Palevsky, interview by Deborah Martinson, May 1, 2000; Annabell Goff-Davis, January 2002; Peter Feibleman, December 1997; Art Buchwald, interview by Phillip Schopper, August 1998.

176. Linda Lightner, interview by Deborah Martinson, January 2002.

177. Linda Lightner, interview by Deborah Martinson, January 2002.

178. Linda Lightner, interview by Deborah Martinson, January 2002.

179. Maureen Stapleton and Jane Scovell, *A Hell of a Life* (New York: Simon & Schuster, 1995).

180. Lillian Hellman, letter to Jerome Weisner, June 30, 1981, Harry Ransom Humanities Research Center, Special Collections, Lillian Hellman and Dashiell Hammett Collection, Austin, Tex.

181. Lillian Hellman, letter to Dorothy Parker, June 11, 1979, Harry Ransom Humanities Research Center, Special Collections, Lillian Hellman and Dashiell Hammett Collection, Austin, Tex.

182. Lillian Hellman, *Maybe: A Story*, second draft, Harry Ransom Humanities Research Center, Special Collections, Lillian Hellman and Dashiell Hammett Collection, Austin, Tex.

183. Lillian Hellman, letter to Jenny and Hannah Hellman, June 7, 1948, Harry Ransom Humanities Research Center, Special Collections, Lillian Hellman and Dashiell Hammett Collection, Austin, Tex.

184. Peter Feibleman, interview by Phillip Schopper, July 27, 1998.

185. Rita Wade, interview by Deborah Martinson, October 16, 2002.

186. Jules Heller, letter to Lillian Hellman, December 20, 1973, Harry Ransom Humanities Research Center, Special Collections, Lillian Hellman and Dashiell Hammett Collection, Austin, Tex.

187. Lillian Hellman, letter of protest, *New Republic*, January 1, 1966.

188. Lillian Hellman, letter to Richard Bridgeman, April 11, 1974, Williams Miller Abrahams Papers, M1125, Department of Special Collections, Stanford University Libraries, Stanford, Calif.

189. OB [unknown lawyer], letter to Lillian Hellman, November 8, 1966, Harry Ransom Humanities Research Center, Special Collections, Lillian Hellman and Dashiell Hammett Collection, Austin, Tex.

190. Lillian Hellman, letter to Margaret T. Babby, March 11, 1971.

191. Lillian Hellman, interview by Helen Dudar, *New York Post*, June 3, 1967.

192. Nora Ephron, letter to Lillian Hellman, n.d., *Esquire* letterhead, Harry Ransom Humanities Research Center, Special Collections, Lillian Hellman and Dashiell Hammett Collection, Austin, Tex.

193. Lillian Hellman, letter to Alfred Kazin, postcard, January 1974, New York Public Library, Berg Collection, New York.

194. Lillian Hellman, interview, *New York Times*, August 23, 1969.

195. Lillian Hellman, letter to Zemskov of the Eisenstein Literary Archives in Moscow, March 19, 1958.

196. Christine Doudna, *Rolling Stone*, February 24, 1997, p. 54.

197. Carl Rollyson, *New Criterion*, February 1998.

198. Rollyson, *New Criterion*, February 1998.

199. Lillian Hellman, "Lillian Hellman Reviews Gordon N. Ray's *H. G. Wells and Rebecca West*," *New York Times Book Review*, 1974.

200. West, *William Styron*, pp. 421–422.

201. *New York Post*, photo by Frank Leonardo accompanying Jerry Talmer, "Seen Again," May 1973.

202. *New York Magazine*, September 10, 1973.

203. Mike Feinsilber, *Houston Chronicle Interactive*, June 7, 1997, www.chron.com/content/interactive/special/watergate/tapes.html.

204. Robert Lantz, interview by Phillip Schopper, August 19, 1998.

205. Bill Moyers, transcript of Lillian Hellman interview. Eliz Karnes of CBS sent transcripts to William Miller Abrahams Papers, M1125, Department of Special Collections, Stanford University Libraries, Stanford, Calif.

206. Hellman, *Scoundrel Time*, p. 35.

207. Hellman, *Scoundrel Time*, p. 82.

208. Hellman, *Scoundrel Time*, pp. 36–37.

209. Peter Feibleman, interview by Phillip Schopper, June 1999.

210. Hellman, *Scoundrel Time*, p. 39.

211. Lillian Hellman, letter to Herbert Mitgang, August 5, 1969, Herbert Mitgang Letters, Berg Collection, New York Public Library, New York.

212. Herbert Mitgang Letters, August 5, 1969, Berg Collection, New York Public Library, New York.

213. Council of New York Law Associates, Associates of the Bar of the City of New York, May 26, 1976; Gillers, interview by Phillip Schopper, September 18, 1998.

214. *Woman's Wear Daily*, May 5, 1976.

215. Richard Poirier, interview by Phillip Schopper, August 18, 1998.

216. Hellman, *Scoundrel Time*, p. 82.

217. Hellman, *Scoundrel Time*, p. 52.

218. Hellman, *Scoundrel Time*, p. 67.

219. Howard Kissel, "Lillian Hellman: Survival and the McCarthy Era," *Women's Wear Daily*, May 5, 1976, p. 28.

220. *Scoundrel Time* notes; instructions to assistant, Harry Ransom Humanities Research Center, Special Collections, Lillian Hellman and Dashiell Hammett Collection, Austin, Tex.

221. *Scoundrel Time* notes; instructions to assistant, Harry Ransom Humanities Research Center, Special Collections, Lillian Hellman and Dashiell Hammett Collection, Austin, Tex.

222. *Scoundrel Time* notes; assistant's instructions, Harry Ransom Humanities Research Center, Special Collections, Lillian Hellman and Dashiell Hammett Collection, Austin, Tex.

223. *Partisan Review* statement, Harry Ransom Humanities Research Center, Special Collections, Lillian Hellman and Dashiell Hammett Collection, Austin, Tex.

224. Joseph Rauh, letter to Lillian Hellman, June 27, 1975, Rauh Collection, Library of Congress, Washington, D.C.

225. Hellman, *Scoundrel Time*, p. 45.

226. *Washington Post*, May 9, 1976, p. 5.

227. Maureen Howard, *New York Times Book Review*, April 25, 19TK.

228. Christopher Lehmann-Haupt, *New York Times*, April 15, 19TK.

229. *New Yorker*, April 26, 1976.

230. Richard Poirier, interview by Phillip Schopper, August 18, 1998.

231. Hellman, *Scoundrel Time*, p. 5.

232. Stanley Kutler, *Abuse of Power: The New Nixon Tapes* (New York: Free Press, 1997), p. 98.

233. "Scoundrel Time: And Who Is the Ugliest of Them All?" *National Review*, January 21, 1977, pp. 101–106.

234. Clipping, no source, Harry Ransom Humanities Research Center, Special Collections, Lillian Hellman and Dashiell Hammett Collection, Austin, Tex.

235. Hellman, *Scoundrel Time*, p. 109.

236. Hellman, *Pentimento*, p. 185.

237. Typescript, n.d., William Miller Abrahams Papers, M1125, Department of Special Collections, Stanford University Libraries, Stanford, Calif.

238. Hellman, *Scoundrel Time*, p. 81.

239. *Scoundrel Time* clippings, unidentified source, Harry Ransom Humanities Research Center, Special Collections, Lillian Hellman and Dashiell Hammett Collection, Austin, Tex.

240. Peter Fiebleman, interview by Phillip Schopper, July 27, 1998.

241. Hellman, *Scoundrel Time*, p. 36.

242. Hellman, *Scoundrel Time*, p. 38.

243. William F. Buckley, "Down with Lillian Hellman," April 10, 1977; *Scoundrel Time* clippings, Harry Ransom Humanities Research Center, Special Collections, Lillian Hellman and Dashiell Hammett Collection, Austin, Tex.

244. Hellman, *Scoundrel Time*, p. 106.

245. Hellman, *Scoundrel Time*, p. 59.

246. Victor Navasky, *Naming Names: Degradation Ceremonies* (New York: Viking, 1980), pp. 46–47.

247. Lillian Hellman, letter to Lionel and Diana Trilling, April 18, 1974, Trilling Collection, New York Public Library, New York.

248. Hellman, *Scoundrel Time*, p. 81.

249. Hellman, *Scoundrel Time*, p. 81.

250. Lillian Hellman, quoted in Judy Klemsrud, "Lillian Hellman Denies Having Played a Role in Little Brown's Rejection of Trilling Book," *New York Times*, September 29, 1976.

251. William Abrahams, letter to *Times Literary Supplement*, December 15, 1976.

252. Richard Poirier, interview by Phillip Schopper, August 18, 1998.

253. Roger Donald, letter to Lillian Hellman, October 12, 1976, Williams Miller Abrahams Papers, M1125, Department of Special Collections, Stanford University Libraries, Stanford, Calif.

254. Lillian Hellman, letter to Dorothy Pritchett, n.d., Harry Ransom Humanities Research Center, Special Collections, Lillian Hellman and Dashiell Hammett Collection, Austin, Tex.

255. Milton Wexler, interview by Deborah Martinson, May 3, 2000.

256. Norman Podhoretz, *Ex-Friends: Falling Out With Allen Ginsberg, Lionel & Diana Trilling, Lillian Hellman, Hannah Arendt, and Norman Mailer* (New York: Free Press, 1999), p. 128.

257. Podhoretz, *Ex-Friends*, pp. 103–138.

258. *Dissent*, Fall 1976, pp. 378–382; *Commentary*, June 19, 1976, pp. 36–39.

259. Robert Kaus, "The Plaintiff's Hour," *Harper's* 266 (1983): 14.

260. Podhoretz, *Ex-Friends*, p. 131.

261. Barnard College address, 1975.

262. Jules Feiffer, interview by Phillip Schopper, July 27, 1998.

263. Theodore Roethke, letter to Lillian Hellman, December 1957, in Ralph J. Mills, *Selected Letters of Theordore Roethke* (Seattle: University of Washington Press, 1968).

264. "Communist Illusion and Scourge," *Modern Age*, Fall 2001, p. 353.

265. Kenward Elmslie, *Blast from the Past* (Austin: Skanky Possum, 2000).

266. Feibleman, *Lilly*, p. 149.

267. Peter Kirth, letter to *Salon*, March 17, 1998.

268. Martha Gellhorn, *Paris Review*, Spring 1981, pp. 280–301.

269. Peter Kirth, letter to *Salon*, March 17, 1998.

270. Peter Kirth, letter to *Salon*, March 17, 1998.

271. Hellman, *Unfinished Woman*, p. 101.

272. Martha Gellhorn, "Close Encounters of the Apocryphal Kind." Mark W. Estrin, *Critical Essays on Lillian Hellman* (Boston: Hall, 1989), p. 176.

273. Martha Gellhorn, letter to Leonard Bernstein, n.d., available at www.leonardbernstein.com/studio/element.asp?FeatID=8AssetID=1.

274. Ernest Hemingway, letter to Harold Ross, November 28, 1942, *New Yorker* Archives, Special Collections, New York Public Library, New York.

275. Lillian Hellman, interview, *New York Times*, July 29, 1980, C18.

276. Lillian Hellman, interview, *New York Times*, July 29, 1980.

277. Peter Feibleman, interview by Phillip Schopper, July 27, 1998.

278. Hammett, Layman, and Rivett, *Dashiell Hammett*, p. 15.

279. Lillian Hellman, *Rolling Stone*, February 23, 1977.

280. John Hersey in Mark W. Estrin, *Critical Essays on Lillian Hellman* (Boston: Hall, 1989).

281. Melissa Burdick Harmon, "Secrets and Lies: The Life of Lillian Hellman," *Biography*, June 1999.

282. Blair Clark, William Miller Abrahams Papers, M1125, Department of Special Collections, Stanford University Libraries, Stanford, Calif.

283. Pam Rosenthal, "Seeing Mary Plain: A Life of Mary McCarthy by Frances Kiernan," *Salon*, March 8, 2000, http://archive.salon.com/books/review/2000/03/08/kiernan/print.html.

284. *Partisan Review*, November-December TK.

285. Lillian Hellman, interview by John Phillips and Anne Hollander, 1964, in Hellman and Bryer, *Conversations with Lillian Hellman*, pp. 60–61.

286. Podhoretz, *Ex-Friends*, p. 102.

287. Dick Cavett clip in Nora Ephron, *Imaginary Friends*, 2002.

288. Frances Kiernan, *Seeing Mary Plain: A Life of Mary McCarthy* (New York: Norton, 2000).

289. Dick Cavett, "Lillian, Mary, and Me," *New Yorker*, December 16, 2002.

290. Cavett, "Lillian, Mary, and Me."

291. Milton Wexler, interview by Deborah Martinson, May 2000.

292. Milton Wexler, interview by Deborah Martinson, May 2000.

293. William Barrett, quoted in Paul Monk, *Mary McCarthy: A Truly Sexy Intellectual*, available at www.austhink.org/monk.

294. Warren Beatty, interview by Phillip Schopper, August 25, 1998.

295. Norman Mailer, interview by Phillip Schopper, July 28, 1998.

296. Norman Mailer, interview by Phillip Schopper, July 28, 1998.

297. Peter Feibleman, interview by Phillip Schopper, July 27, 1998.

298. Norman Mailer, interview by Phillip Schopper, July 28, 1998.

299. Feibleman, *Lilly*, p. 340.

300. Johnson, "Obsession," May 1985.

301. Norman Mailer, interview by Phillip Schopper, July 28, 1998.

302. Rita Wade, interview by Phillip Schopper, July, 1998.

303. Daniel J. Kornstein, *Fordham Law Review* 713.

304. Kornstein, *Fordham Law Review* 711.

305. Robert Kaus, "The Plaintiff's Hour," *Harper's* 266 (1983): 14.

306. Kornstein, *Fordham Law Review* 719.

307. Kornstein, *Fordham Law Review* 722 n. 259.

308. Feibleman, *Lilly*, p. 332.

309. Feibleman, *Lilly*, p. 333.

310. Robert Lantz, interview by Phillip Schopper, August 13, 1998.

311. William Wright, *Hollywood Reporter*, 1987.

312. Milly W. Barranger, "Lilian Hellman: Standing in the Minefields," *New Orleans Review* 15 (1988): 1.

313. Ernest Hemingway, quoted in Hellman, *Unfinished Woman*, p. 88.

REFERENCES

Acker, Ally. *Reel Women: Pioneers of the Cinema, 1896 to the Present.* Foreword by Judith Crist. New York: Continuum, 1991.

Adler, Jacob H. *Lillian Hellman.* Austin: Steck-Vaughn, 1969.

Allen, Brooke, Paul Theroux, and V. S. Naipaul. "Sorcerers' Apprentices: Rosemary Mahoney's 'One Summer with Lillian Hellman.'" *Hudson Review* 52, no. 1 (1999): 150.

Andersen, Christopher P. *Citizen Jane: The Turbulent Life of Jane Fonda.* New York: Holt, 1990.

Anouilh, Jean. *The Lark.* New York: Random House, 1956.

Anouilh, Jean, and Lillian Hellman. *The Lark.* New York: Dramatists Play Service, 1957.

Atkinson, Brooks. *The Lively Years.* New York: Association, 1973.

Atkinson, Brooks. *New York Times,* November 21, 1946.

Austenfeld, Thomas C. *American Women Writers and the Nazis: Ethics and Politics in Boyle, Porter, Stafford, and Hellman.* Charlottesville: University Press of Virginia, 2001.

Bald, Wambly. *It's Just Like Having Another Baby. New York Post,* November 12, 1946.

Bankhead, Tallulah. *Tallulah: My Autobiography.* New York: Harper, 1952.

Barranger, Milly S. "Lillian Hellman: Standing in the Minefields." *New Orleans Review* 15 (1988): 1.

Beebe, Lucius. "Stage Asides." *New Yorker,* May 1941.

Behlmer, Rudy. *Memo: David O. Selznick.* New York: Viking, 1972.

Bentley, Eric. *Thirty Years of Treason.* New York: Viking, 1971.

Berg, Andrew Scott. *Goldwyn: A Biography.* New York: Knopf, 1989.

Berger, Marilyn. *Profile: Lillian Hellman.* Jackson: University Press of Mississippi, 1972.

Bernstein, Burton. *Drinking with Thurber: A Biography.* New York: Ballantine, 1976.

Bernstein, Leonard, et al. 2003. *Candide Broadway Cast Recording.* Deluxe expanded ed. Vol. 1. New York: Columbia Broadway Masterworks.

Bills, Steven H. *Lillian Hellman: An Annotated Bibliography.* New York: Garland, 1979.

Blake, Gary. "Herman Shumlin: The Development of a Director." Ph.D. diss., City University of New York, 1973.

Booker, Margaret. *Lillian Hellman and August Wilson: Dramatizing a New American Identity.* New York: Peter Lang, 2003.

Botto, Louis. *At This Theatre.* New York: Dodd Mead, 1984.

Brantley, Will. *Feminine Sense in Southern Memoir: Smith, Glasgow, Welty, Hellman, Porter, and Hurston.* Jackson: University Press of Mississippi, 1993.

Bright, John. "Hollywood Blacklist." OID Instructional Library, University of California–Los Angeles, Special Collections and Oral Histories Collections, Los Angeles.

Britton, Burt, and Saul Bellow. *Self-Portrait: Book People Picture Themselves.* New York: Random House, 1976.

Broggiotti, Mary. "Most Sincerely, Lillian Hellman." *New York Post,* July 31, 1943.

Brooks, Maria. 1938. *Carrying It On.* ILWU Local 10. In *Dispatcher,* January 2002.

Buckley, William F. "Down with Lillian Hellman," April 10, 1977. *Scoundrel Time* clippings, Harry Ransom Humanities Research Center, Special Collections, Lillian Hellman and Dashiell Hammett Collection, Austin, Tex.

———. *New York Post,* April 2, 1977.

Cantwell, Mary. 1998. "Comparative: Lillian Hellman, J. D. Salinger." *Vogue,* October 1998, p. 214.

Carroll, Sidney. "The Happy Tragedist." *New Yorker,* January 1942, pp. 59–183.

Castle, Terry, and Rosemary Mahoney. "A Likely Story: One Summer with Lillian Hellman." *London Review of Books* 21, no. 8 (1999): 3.

Cavett, Dick. "Lillian, Mary, and Me." *New Yorker,* December 16, 2002.

Chapman, John. *New York Daily News,* November 21, 1946.

"*Children's Hour* Attracts Large Audience to Shubert 1936." Clipping, Harry Ransom Humanities Research Center, Special Collections, Lillian Hellman and Dashiell Hammett Collection, Austin, Tex.

Clurman, Harold. *Collected Works.* New York: Applause, 2000.

The Children's Hour File, Lillian Hellman Collection, Harry Ransom Humanities Research Center, Special Collections, Lillian Hellman and Dashiell Hammett Collection, Austin, Tex.

Coleman, Robert. *New York Daily Mirror,* November 21, 1946.

Conrad, Christine. Unfinished Memoirs of Kermit Bloomgarden. New York Public Library for the Performing Arts, Billy Rose Theatre Collection.

Corrigan, Robert W. *The Modern Theatre.* New York: Macmillan, 1964.

Cowley, Liz. "Lillian's World," *Daily Mail,* n.d. Harry Ransom Humanities Research Center, Special Collections, Lillian Hellman and Dashiell Hammett Collection, Austin, Tex.

Custen, George F. 1997. *Twentieth Century's Fox: Darryl F. Zanuck and the Culture of Hollywood.* New York: Basic, 1997.

"Dashiell Hammett: A Memoir." *New York Review of Books,* November 25, 1965.

"Dashiell Hammett and Lillian Hellman: In Dark Days, They Stuck to Their Convictions—and Each Other." *People*, February 12, 1996, p. 149.

D'Erasmo, Stacey. "Loving Lillian." *Nation*, June 24, 1996, p. 25.

Dick, Bernard F. *Hellman in Hollywood*. Rutherford N.J.: Fairleigh Dickinson University Press, 1982.

_____. "Newman: The Cold War Romance of Lillian Hellman and John Melby." *Journal of American History* 77, no. 1 (1990): 354–354.

_____. *Radical Innocence: A Critical Study of the Hollywood Ten*. Lexington: University of Kentucky Press, 1989.

Dmytryk, Edward. *Odd Man Out: A Memoir of the Hollywood Ten*. Carbondale: Southern Illinois University Press, 1995.

Duberman, Martin Bauml. *Paul Robeson: A Biography*. New York: Ballantine, 1989.

Dunne, Philip. *Take Two: A Life in Movies and Politics*. New York: McGraw-Hill, 1980.

Drutman, Irving. "Miss Hellman and Her First Screen Venture." 1941. Clipping, Harry Ransom Humanities Research Center, Special Collections, Lillian Hellman and Dashiell Hammett Collection, Austin, Tex.

_____. *New York Times*, February 27, 1966.

Estrin, Mark W. *Critical Essays on Lillian Hellman*. Boston: Hall, 1989.

_____. *Lillian Hellman, Plays, Films, Memoirs: A Reference Guide*. Boston: Hall, 1980.

Falk, Doris V. *Lillian Hellman*. New York: Ungar, 1978.

Fariello, Griffen. *The Red Scare*. New York: Avon, 1995.

Feibleman, Peter S. *Lilly: Reminiscences of Lillian Hellman*. New York: Morrow, 1988.

Feron, James. "Pleasantville." *New York Times*, April 5, 1987.

Fleche, Anne. "The Lesbian Rule: Lillian Hellman and the Measures of Realism." *Modern Drama* 39, no. 1 (1996): 16.

"Fortune's Little Funster." 1939. Clipping, William Miller Abrahams Papers, M1125, Department of Special Collections, Stanford University Libraries, Stanford, Calif.

Gabler, Neal. *Empire of Their Own*. New York: Crown, 1988.

Galligan, David. *Dramalogue*, n.d., Clipping File, New York Public Library for the Performing Arts, Billy Rose Theatre Collection.

Gellhorn, Martha. "On Apocryphism." *Paris Review*, Spring 1981. Reprinted as "Close Encounters of the Apocryphal Kind." In Mark Estrain, ed., *Critical Essays on Lillian Hellman*. Boston: Hall, 1986, p. 176.

Gentry, Curt. *J. Edgar Hoover: The Man and the Secrets*. New York: Norton, 1991.

Gill, James. *Lords of Misrule: Mardi Gras and the Politics of Race in New Orleans*. Jackson: University Press of Mississippi, 1997.

Goodrich, David L. *The Real Nick and Nora: Frances Goodrich and Albert Hackett, Writers of Stage and Screen Classics*. Carbondale: Southern Illinois University Press, 2001.

Gould, Jean. *Modern American Playwrights*. New York: Dodd, Mead, 1966.

Graver, Lawrence. *An Obsession with Anne Frank: Meyer Levin and the Diary.* Berkeley: University of California Press, 1995.

Griffin, Alice, and Geraldine Thorsten. *Understanding Lillian Hellman.* Columbia: University of South Carolina Press, 1999.

Guthrie, Tyrone. *A Life in the Theatre.* New York: McGraw-Hill, 1959.

Haber, Joyce. "Lillian Hellman Takes Look at Today's Theater." *Los Angeles Times,* Calendar, November 2, 1969, p. 15.

Haller, Charles David. "The Concept of Moral Failure in the Eight Original Plays of Lillian Hellman." Ph.D. diss., Tulane University, 1967.

Halline, Allan G. *Six Modern American Plays.* New York: Modern Library, 1951.

Hammett, Dashiell, Richard Layman, and Julie M. Rivett. *Selected Letters of Dashiell Hammett, 1921–1960.* Washington, D.C.: Counterpoint, 2001.

Hammett, Jo, Richard Layman, and Julie M. Rivett. *Dashiell Hammett: A Daughter Remembers.* New York: Carroll & Graf, 2001.

Hardwick, Elizabeth. "The Little Foxes Revived." *New York Review of Books,* December 21, 1967.

Harmon, Melissa Burdick. "Secrets and Lies: The Life of Lillian Hellman." *Biography,* June 1999.

Harriman, Margaret Case. "Miss Lily of New Orleans." *New Yorker,* November 8, 1941, p. 57.

Hart, Stan. "Essays: Lillian Hellman and Others." *Sewanee Review* 107, no. 3 (1999): 402.

Hellman, Lillian. Address to Barnard College, 1975. Draft in the Lillian Hellman Collection, Harry Ransom Humanities Center, University of Texas, Austin.

_____. *The Autumn Garden: A Play in Three Acts.* Boston: Little, Brown, 1951.

_____. *The Collected Plays.* Boston: Little, Brown, 1972.

_____. *Days to Come: The Collected Plays.* Boston: Little, Brown, 1936. Original play typescript.

_____. *Diaries* (1920–). Harry Ransom Humanities Research Center, Special Collections, Lillian Hellman and Dashiell Hammett Collection, Austin, Tex.

_____. "Flipping for a Diamond." *New York Review of Books,* September 20, 1973.

_____. *Four Plays: Introductions.* New York: Random House, 1942.

_____. *The Little Foxes.* New York: Random House, 1939.

_____. *Maybe: A Story.* Boston: Little, Brown, 1980.

_____. *The North Star.* New York: Viking, 1943.

_____. *Pentimento: A Book of Portraits.* Boston: Back Bay, 2000.

_____. *An Unfinished Woman: A Memoir.* Boston: Little, Brown, 1999.

_____. *Scoundrel Time.* Boston: Little, Brown, 1976.

_____. "The Time of the Foxes." *New York Times,* October 22, 1967.

_____. *An Unfinished Woman: A Memoir.* Boston: Little, Brown, 1969.

_____. *Watch on the Rhine: A Play in Three Acts.* New York: Random House, 1941.

Hellman, Lillian, and Jackson R. Bryer. *Conversations with Lillian Hellman.* Jackson: University Press of Mississippi, 1986.

Hellman, Lillian, and Peter S. Feibleman. *Eating Together: Recipes and Recollections.* Boston: Little, Brown, 1984.

Hellman, Lillian, and Manfred Triesch. *The Lillian Hellman Collection at the University of Texas.* Austin: Humanities Research Center, University of Texas, 1968.

Herman, Jan. *A Talent for Trouble: The Life of Hollywood's Most Acclaimed Director, William Wyler.* New York: Putnam, 1995.

Herrmann, Dorothy. *S. J. Perelman: A Life.* New York: Simon & Schuster, 1986.

Hopper, Hedda, and James Brough. *The Whole Truth and Nothing But.* Garden City, N.Y.: Doubleday, 1963.

Horn, Barbara L. *Lillian Hellman: A Research and Production Sourcebook.* Vol. 15. Westport, Conn.: Greenwood, 1998.

Hughes, Langston. *I Wonder as I Wander: An Autobiographical Journey.* New York: Hill & Wang, 1964.

Human Rights Watch Free Expression Project. *Persecuted, Banned, Censored, and Jailed Writers Receive Grants: 30 Writers from 17 Countries Recognized by Lillian Hellman/Dashiell Hammett Funds.* New York: Human Rights Watch Free Expression Project, 1994.

Jerrico, Paul. Interview by Larry Ceplair, 1991. University of California–Los Angeles, Special Collections and Oral Histories Collections.

Johnson, Diane. *Dashiell Hammett: A Life.* New York: Random House, 1983.

———. "Obsession." *Vanity Fair,* January 1985.

Kael, Pauline. *For Keeps.* New York: Dutton, 1994.

Kiernan, Frances. *Seeing Mary Plain: A Life of Mary McCarthy.* New York: Norton, 2000.

Kutler, Stanley. *Abuse of Power: The New Nixon Tapes.* New York: Free Press, 1997.

Layman, Richard. *Shadowman: The Life of Dashiell Hammett.* New York: Harcourt Brace Jovanovich, 1981.

Layman, Richard, and Julie M. Rivett. *Selected Letters of Dashiell Hammett, 1921–1960.* New York: Counterpoint, 2001.

Leach, Laurie F. "Lying, Writing, and Confrontation: Mary McCarthy and Lillian Hellman." *LIT: Literature Interpretation Theory* 15, no. 1 (2004): 5–28.

Lederer, Katherine. *Lillian Hellman.* Boston: Twayne, 1979.

Lehmann-Haupt, Christopher. "The Incomplete Lillian Hellman." *New York Times,* June 1969.

Leon, Ruth. 1991. *Applause: New York's Guide to the Performing Arts.* New York: Applause, 1991.

Lillian Hellman: A drawing by Edward Sorel. Literary Lives. *Atlantic Monthly,* December 2003.

Loos, Anita. *A Girl Like I.* New York: Viking, 1966.

Luce, William, and Lillian Hellman. *Lillian: A One-Woman Play Based on the Autobiographical Works of Lillian Hellman.* New York: Dramatists Play Service, 1986.

Madsen, Axel. *William Wyler: The Authorized Biography.* New York: Crowell, 1973.

Mahoney, Rosemary, and Lillian Hellman. *A Likely Story: One Summer with Lillian Hellman.* New York: Doubleday, 1998.

Maltby, Richard. *Hollywood Cinema.* Malden, Mass: Blackwell, 1995.

Maney, Richard. *Fanfare: The Confessions of a Press Agent*. New York: Harper, 1957.

_____. "The Night of the Long Knives." In *Fanfare: The Confessions of a Press Agent*. New York: Harper, 1957.

Manso, Peter. *Brando: The Biography*. New York: Hyperion, 1994.

Marx, Sam. *A Gaudy Spree: The Literary Life of Hollywood in the 1930s When the West Was Fun*. New York: Franklin Watts, 1987.

McCarthy, Mary. "A Filmy Version of the War." *Town and Country*, April 1944.

McGilligan, Patrick. *Backstory: Interviews with Screenwriters of Hollywood's Golden Age*. Berkeley: University of California Press, 1986.

Meade, Marion. *Dorothy Parker: What Fresh Hell Is This?* New York: Penguin, 1989.

Melby, John F. *The Mandate of Heaven: Record of a Civil War, China 1945–1949*. Toronto: University of Toronto Press, 1968.

Mellen, Joan. *Hellman and Hammett: The Legendary Passion of Lillian Hellman and Dashiell Hammett*. New York: HarperCollins, 1996.

Melnick, Ralph. *The Stolen Legacy of Anne Frank: Meyer Levin, Lillian Hellman, and the Staging of the Diary*. New Haven: Yale University Press, 1997.

Miller, Arthur. *Timebends*. New York: Grove, 1989.

Mitchell, Sean. "Lip Service." *LA Times Magazine*, March 25, 2001.

_____. Written By: Hereinafter Referred to as the Author. June–July 2000. www.wga.WrittenBy.

Monk, Paul. Mary McCarthy: A Truly Sexy Intellectual. www.austhink.org.

Moody, Richard. *Lillian Hellman, Playwright*. New York: Pegasus, 1972.

Morehouse, Ward. *Baltimore Sun*. March 11, 1939.

Morella, Joe, Edward Z. Epstein, and John Griggs. *The Films of World War II*. Introduction by Judith Crist. New Jersey: Citadel, 1973.

Navasky, Victor. *Naming Names: Degradation Ceremonies*. New York: Viking, 1980.

Neal, Patricia, with Richard DeNeut. *As I Am: An Autobiography*. New York: Simon & Schuster, 1988.

"New Hellman Play," September 26, 1946. Clipping, Kermit Bloomgarden File, Billy Rose Collection, New York Public Library.

Newman, Robert P. *The Cold War Romance of Lillian Hellman and John Melby*. Chapel Hill: University of North Carolina Press, 1989.

Norman, Marsha. *New York Times*, theater sec., August 26, 1984.

Orlova, Raya. *Memoirs*. New York: Random House, 1983.

"Pentimento Notebook." *Women's Wear Daily*. Harry Ransom Humanities Research Center, Special Collections, Lillian Hellman and Dashiell Hammett Collection, Austin, Tex.

Peters, Brooks. "Making Your Garden Growl: Brooks Peters Tells the Tale of *Candide* Collaborators Lillian Hellman and Leonard Bernstein, a Marriage Not Made in Heaven." *Opera News* 65, no. 1 (2000): 38.

Pierson, Frank. "Hollywood Plays to the Pimply." *LA Times*, May 26, 2003.

Plimpton, George. *Women Writers at Work: The Paris Review Interviews*. New York: Penguin, 1989.

Podhoretz, Norman. *Ex-Friends: Falling Out with Allen Ginsberg, Lionel and Diana Trilling, Lillian Hellman, Hannah Arendt, and Norman Mailer.* New York: Free Press, 1999.

Posner, Richard A. *Public Intellectuals: A Study of Decline.* Cambridge, Mass.: Harvard University Press, 2001.

Queen, Ellery. *Napoleon's Razor.* Guest Armchair Detectives. Madison, Wis.: Shumlin Archives, Wisconsin Historical Society, 1939.

Rampersand, Arnold. *The Life of Langston Hughes.* New York: Oxford University Press, 1986.

Rather, Dan. "A Profile of Lillian Hellman," March 3, 1977. In Lillian Hellman and Jackson R Bryer. *Conversations with Lillian Hellman.* Jackson: University Press of Mississippi, 1986.

Raymond, Harry. "Voltaire's 'Candide" to Be Done as Musical." *Daily Worker,* February 15, 1954, p. 7. Clipping in Lillian Hellman FBI file.

Review of *Montserrat. Commonweal,* November 18, 1949.

Riordan, Mary M. *Lillian Hellman: A Bibliography, 1926–1978.* Metuchen, N.J.: Scarecrow, 1980.

Rollyson, Carl E. *Lillian Hellman: Her Legacy and Her Legend* New York: St. Martin's, 1988.

Rose, Lisle Abbott. *The Cold War Comes to Main Street: America in 1950.* Lawrence: University Press of Kansas, 1999.

Rosenthal, Pam. *Salon,* March 8, 2000.

Scheaffer, Louis. "Curtain Times." *Brooklyn Bugle,* March 8, 1951.

Schwartz, Harvey. ILWU Local 10. In *The Dispatcher,* January 2002, 1938.

Schwartz, Nancy Lynn. *The Hollywood Writers' Wars.* New York: Knopf, 1982.

"Scoundrel Time: And Who Is the Ugliest of Them All?" *National Review,* January 1977, pp. 101–106.

"A Second Look." *Cineaste,* 1996, p. 45.

Sherwood, Richard E. *There Shall Be No Night.* New York: Scribner's, 1940.

Showalter, Elaine, Lea Baechler, and A. W. Litz, eds. *Modern American Women Writers.* New York: Scribner's, 1991.

Sigerist, Henry E. *Autobiographical Writings.* Montréal: McGill University Press, 1966.

"The Slyest Little Fox; Lillian Hellman, Still Provocative." *Washington Post,* show sec., June 11, 2002.

Sperber, A. M., and Eric Lax. *Bogart.* New York: Morrow, 1997.

Stapleton, Maureen, and Jane Scovell. 1995. *A Hell of a Life.* New York: Simon & Schuster, 1995.

Strauss, Theodore. "Lillian Hellman: A Lady of Principle." *New York Times,* August 29, 1943.

Thackrey, Ted. "After a Top-Speed Life, N.O.'s Rebel." *Times-Picayune,* June 8, 1984.

Thompson, Sylvia. "Martini Time in the Garden of Allah." *LA Times Magazine,* November 5, 2000, pp. 38–40.

Torrence, Bruce. *Hollywood: The First 100 Years.* Hollywood, Calif.: Hollywood Chamber of Commerce, 1979.

U.S. Camera. 1938.

Weiner, Justus R. "Lillian Hellman: The Fiction of Autobiography." *Gender Issues* 21, no. 1 (2003): 78–84.

West, James L.W., III. *William Styron: A Life.* New York: Random House, 1998.

Wilder, Billy. *Billy Wilder: Interviews.* Jackson: University Press of Mississippi, 2001.

Williams, Tennessee. *Cry of the Heart: An Intimate Memoir of Tennessee Williams.* New York: New American Library, 1985.

Wright, William. *Lillian Hellman: The Image, the Woman.* New York: Ballantine, 1988.

Zanuck, Darryl F., and Rudy Behlmer. *Memo from Darryl F. Zanuck: The Golden Years at Twentieth Century-Fox.* New York: Grove, 1993.

Zinnemann, Fred et al. *Julia.* Vol. 1. Videocassette. Beverly Hills: Fox Video, 1993.

Zolotov, Maurice. *Billy Wilder in Hollywood.* New York: Limelight, 1987.

INDEX

Printed in the United States
by Baker & Taylor Publisher Services